The State of Asian Cities 2010/11

World Habitat Day
Shanghai, 4 October 2010

United Nations Human Settlements Programme (UN-HABITAT)
Regional Office for Asia and the Pacific
ACROS Fukuoka Building, 8th Floor
1-1-1 Tenjin, Chuo-ku, Fukuoka 810-0001, Japan
Tel: +81-92 724-7121 / 23
Fax: +81-92 724-7124
E-mail: habitat.fukuoka@unhabitat.org
Website: www.unhabitat.org, www.fukuoka.unhabitat.org

DISCLAIMER

HS Number: HS/162/10 E
ISBN Number: (Volume) 978-92-1-132274-3

Cover image:
Shanghai, China. With Pudong's skyscrapers in the background, early risers come to the Bund for their morning exercises.
©Qilai Shen/Panos Pictures

Design and Layout by MJS
Nairobi | Kenya

Acknowledgements

This first-ever *State of Asian Cities Report 2010/11* (the Report) reviews and documents the trends in inclusive and sustainable urban development throughout the Asia-Pacific region. The preparation of the Report has drawn on the latest data, good practices and examples, the rich knowledge of a broad range of specialists, and peer reviews by experts.

The Report was prepared jointly by the United Nations Human Settlements Programme (UN-HABITAT) and the United Nations Economic and Social Commission for Asia and the Pacific (ESCAP). From UN-HABITAT, it was prepared under the direction of Daniel Biau, Director of the Regional and Technical Cooperation Division (RTCD) and Toshi Noda, Director of the Regional Office for Asia and the Pacific (ROAP) of the United Nations Human Settlement Programme (UN-HABITAT). From ESCAP, it was prepared under the direction of Yap Kioe Sheng, Chief, Poverty Reduction Section. The conceptualization and coordination of the Report was undertaken by Bharat Dahiya, Human Settlements Officer of the UN-HABITAT ROAP and by Adnan Aliani, Chief, Sustainable Urban Development Unit of ESCAP. Technical advice was provided by Natalja Wehmer and Karin Andersson; Surendra Shrestha, Director, Strategic Resource Mobilization/Special Initiatives, Dechen Tsering, Deputy Regional Director for Asia and the Pacific, and Hanna Uusimaa, Focal Point and Junior Professional Officer, UN Environment Programme (UNEP); and Mayor Kim Bum Il, President, Krishna Prasad Jaishi, Co-President, Jatin V Modi, Co-President, and Peter Woods, Secretary General of the United Cities and Local Governments – Asia-Pacific Regional Section (UCLG-ASPAC).

Chapter 1, The State of Asian Cities: Overview and Key Findings, was written by Bharat Dahiya. Dinesh Mehta, assisted by Sangeetha Raghuram and Kinjal Pillai, wrote Chapter 2 – Urbanizing Asia, Chapter 3 – The Economic Role of Asian Cities, and Chapter 4 – Poverty and Inequality in Asian Cities. Brian Roberts and Xuemei Bai drafted Chapter 5 – Urban Environment and Climate Change. Aprodicio Laquian was the author of Chapter 6 – Urban Governance, Management and Finance. The Statistical Annex features the latest urban data available from the UN *World Urbanization Prospects 2009*; latest slum related data from the *State of the World's Cities 2010/11* and the water and sanitation data from the *2010 Update of the Joint Monitoring Programme for Water Supply and Sanitation*.

The following also contributed to the Report with reviews of earlier drafts and/or boxed items: Karin Andersson, Victor Ban, Desra Hilda Defriana, Rudolf Hauter, Sachiyo Hoshino, Sharadbala Joshi, Abhay Kantak, Alain Kanyinda, Jacob Kurian, Lajana Manandhar, Jos Maseland, Jan Meeuwissen, Thierry Naudin, Pushpa Pathak, Angela Pinzon, Lalith Lankatilleke, Chris Radford, Lowie Rosales, Mariko Sato, Tunnie Srisakulchairak, Anna Stabrawa, Bernadia Tjandradewi, Danai Thaitakoo, Natalja Wehmer, Belinda Yuen and Jinhua Zhang.

The earlier drafts of the Report were reviewed by the following groups of experts:
- *Expert Group Meeting* held at the UCLG Asia-Pacific Regional Congress, Pattaya, Thailand on 14 July 2008: Charlie Bae, Israel Cruzado, Koen DeWandler, Sushil Gyewali, Hae-Doo Lee, Nimit, Hansa Patel and Chamniern Vorratnchaiphan.
- *Habitat Seminar* held at the World Urban Forum – 4, Nanjing, China on 3 November 2008: Mayor Hilmy Mohammed, Wahyu Mulyana, Prafulla Man Pradhan, Wicaksono Sarosa and Bang Anh Tuan.
- *Expert Group Meeting* held at Chiang Mai, Thailand on 1-3 June 2009: Daniel Biau, Shabbir Cheema, Atsushi Deguchi, Koen DeWandler, Rudolf Hauter, Abhay Kantak, Jos Maseland, Toshi Noda, Sneha Palnitkar, Ranjith Perera, Marivel Sacendoncillo, Wicaksono Sarosa, Donovan Storey, Bernadia Tjandradewi, David Villeneuve, Haryo Winarso and Belinda Yuen.

Thierry Naudin undertook the editing. Additional editorial support was provided by Peter Marcotullio and Robert Sullivan.

UN-HABITAT and ESCAP thank the CEPT University, Ahmedabad, and CITYNET for their support.

Administrative support was provided by Sayaka Azuma De Castro and Rujiraporn Polchai.

UN-HABITAT is grateful for the financial support provided by the Government of Norway.

Contents

▲
Sakura cherry blossoms in Fukuoka, Japan. ©**Tristan Scholze/Shutterstock**

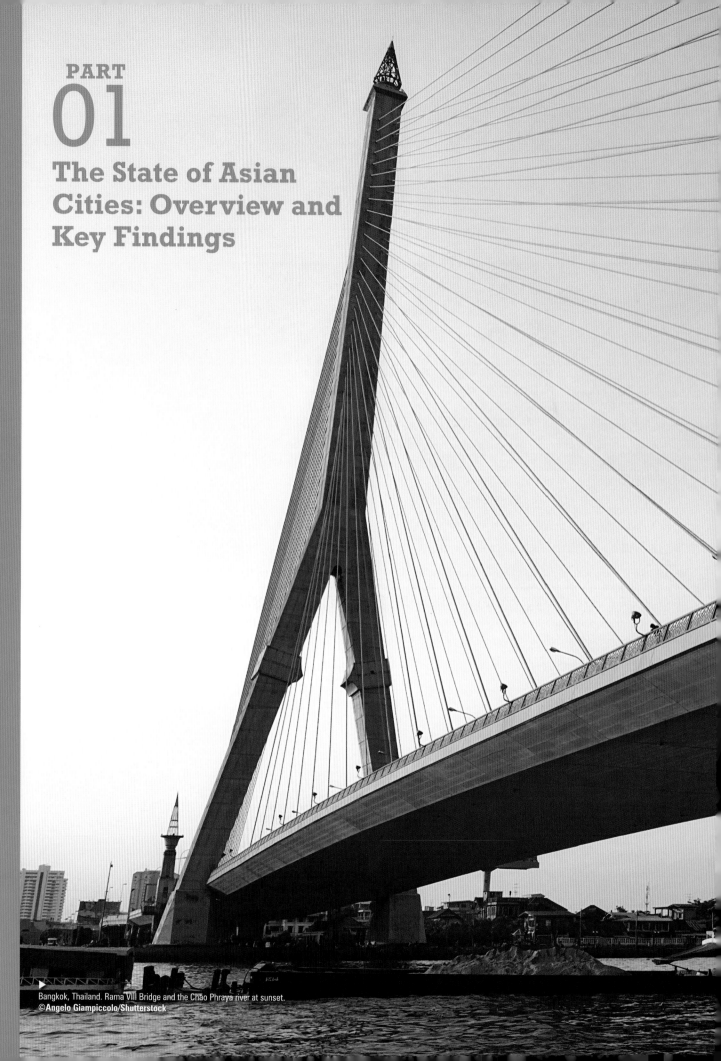

The State of Asian Cities: Overview and Key Findings

Bangkok, Thailand. Rama VIII Bridge and the Chao Phraya river at sunset.
©Angelo Giampiccolo/Shutterstock

1.1 Introduction

Asia is the largest region in the world with 30 per cent of the land mass and 60 per cent of the population. Given its vast geographical expanse, Asia and the Pacific is perhaps also the most diverse region in terms of economy, society, culture, environment and human settlements. Geographically, the 58 countries in the region have been grouped in five subregions: East and North-East Asia, South-East Asia, South and South-West Asia, North and Central Asia, and the Pacific. The vast spread of the Asia-Pacific region features high-, middle- and low-income economies, as well as a wealth of diverse societies and cultures. The region's environment also presents a varied picture with tropical and temperate climates, and some of the world's most arid and water-rich biomes, not to mention the highest mountains (the Himalayas) and the gigantic river valleys and deltas (those of the Brahmaputra, Ganges, Indus, Irrawaddy, Mekong, Red, Yangtze and Yellow rivers). Finally, with regard to human settlements, the region is host to highly urbanised countries such as Australia, New Zealand and Japan and others much less urbanised such as Nepal, Papua New Guinea and Sri Lanka (see Figure 1.1).

For all the rapid demographic expansion of Asian cities, with an urbanisation rate of 41.7 per cent in 2009 the region ranked as the second least-urbanised in the world after Africa's 39.6 per cent, although half the world's urban population now lives in Asian-Pacific cities. In 2009, Asia was home to 1.72 billion people. While the world became predominantly urban in 2008, Asia is not expected to reach the 50 per cent mark before 2026. The number of mega-cities (those with populations of 10 million or more) is increasing and half (11 out of 21) are now in the Asia-Pacific region. Moreover, mega urban regions, urban corridors and city-regions reflect the emerging links between city growth and new patterns of economic activity.

The Asia-Pacific region has been urbanising rapidly. The phenomenon has both provided urban economies with the human resources they needed and been stimulated by cities' growing prosperity. This is reflected in the fact that the proportion of Asia's urban population increased from 31.5 per cent in 1990 to 41.7 per cent in 2009, the highest percentage increase (10.2 per cent) among all regions in the world (the second highest being the 9 per cent increase in Latin America and Caribbean during the same period).

The Asian-Pacific economy is the most dynamic in the world. Growth has been spectacular, especially over the past two decades, enabling the region to contribute as much as 30 per cent of global economic output in 2008. Urban areas have acted as the engines of growth and prosperity in most countries whether they are characterized by relatively high incomes (such as China, the Republic of Korea, Singapore or French Polynesia), middle incomes (like Azerbaijan, India, Iran, Kiribati, Mongolia, Pakistan, Timor-Leste or Turkmenistan) or low incomes (such as Bangladesh, Cambodia, Kyrgyzstan,

the Lao People's Democratic Republic or Viet Nam). Although this economic momentum has stalled on two occasions – during the Asian financial crisis of 1997-98 and the global economic crisis of 2008-09 – the region has shown remarkable resilience and has bounced back, largely thanks to governments' stimulating policies and domestic demand.

Cities in the Asia-Pacific region are highly productive and creative: the 42 per cent of the population living in urban areas contribute 80 per cent of the region's gross domestic product. As they became more integrated into the world economy, Asian cities made the most of comparative advantage, international specialisation and 'economies of agglomeration'. In the process they managed the transition from low-productivity agriculture to higher-productivity industry and services. Indeed, urbanisation in the region has been shown to enhance productivity and increase gross domestic product per head, which doubled from US $1,795 per head in 1990 to US $2,718 per head in 2008. Building on the demographic expansion and multi-cultural richness that add to creativity, Asian cities are diversifying away from being the factory of the world to international financial centres and 'knowledge economies'.

The Asia-Pacific region is leading the reduction of overall poverty in the world. Between 1990 and 2005, extreme poverty was reduced worldwide from 43 to 26 percent, largely reflecting a 50 per cent decline (from 49 per cent to 25 per cent of the population) in Asia and the Pacific. The region achieved this on the back of export-led economic growth and expanding domestic demand. For all this success, though, progress on urban poverty reduction remains slow and as a result urban inequality is on the rise. This calls on national governments and local authorities to develop and implement well-focused strategies and programmes to alleviate urban poverty.

Asia is also at the forefront with regard to the 'slum target' set out under the Millennium Development Goals (MDGs), i.e., "By 2020, to have achieved a significant improvement in the lives of at least 100 million slum-dwellers". Asia has made "successful efforts to reach the slum target, with governments in the region improving the lives of an estimated 172 million slum-dwellers between the year 2000 and 2010". However, these successful efforts must continue as the region is still home 505.5 million slum-dwellers.

All these remarkable achievements are not without problems, though. In their quest for economic growth, Asian cities have not paid sufficient attention to urban environment and climate change issues. The state of the urban environment in the Asia-Pacific region is very much a tale of two types of city. On the one hand, cities in more developed countries – Australia, Brunei Darussalam, Japan, New Zealand, the Republic of Korea and Singapore – are clean, well-managed, prosperous and safe places to live. On the other hand, fast expanding cities in newly industrialized and rapidly developing countries, which together concentrate large proportions of the region's urban populations, experience serious environmental, poverty and development problems. The imminent effects of

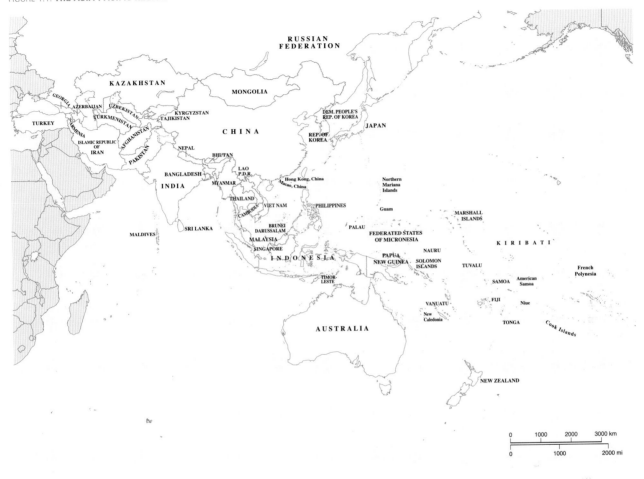

Source: www.un.org/Depts/Cartographic/map/profile/escap.pdf

climate change add to the problems Asian-Pacific cities are facing today. Asian-Pacific countries must focus on improving the environment in their cities and hinterlands. Asian-Pacific cities must prepare for the consequences of climate change, and keep in mind that the poor stand to be most affected. Working towards 'green growth', Asian-Pacific economies should also make efforts to improve the eco-efficiency of their economic model if, as the UN Economic Commission for Asia and the Pacific recently noted, they are to meet "the most important challenge to sustainable development in this region: reducing the pressure on the natural resource base while continuing to meet human needs".

Urban governance, management and finance have featured on the urban policy agenda in the Asia-Pacific region for over two decades now. With the worldwide economic crisis that began in 2008, however, these issues have taken on a more visible and acute dimension. In recent years, many Asian-Pacific cities have sought to improve governance in a bid to achieve sustained economic and social development. Involving civil society groups, grassroots and non-governmental organizations in decisionmaking has enabled local authorities

to expand the scope of urban governance and experiment with concepts such as participatory budgeting. Participatory decisionmaking approaches are needed for the management of urban infrastructure and services. Through decentralisation schemes, Asian governments have supported the devolution of authority to local authorities. However, many smaller urban settlements are finding it difficult to achieve development goals due to inadequate financial, human, institutional and legal resources or frameworks, as well as poor political leadership. Clearly, national governments must improve the governance of smaller cities and towns, which are growing fast and account for major shares of urban population. Mega urban regional development is an emerging, complex challenge for national governments and local authorities. In terms of city-to-city exchange of lessons learnt and good practices, the regional and national networks of local authorities provide new avenues to improve urban governance in the Asia-Pacific region.

In the remainder of this Chapter, the following five sections (1.2 to 1.6) summarise the key findings of this first *State of Asian Cities Report*. Section 1.7 outlines the structure of the Report.

▲
A planned area on the outskirts of Hanoi, Viet Nam. ©**UN-HABITAT/Nguy Ha**

1.2 Urbanising Asia

1.2.1 Demographic trends and patterns

Asia is urbanising rapidly but the region's population is still predominantly rural. In 2009, Asia was the second least-urbanised region of the world with 41.7 per cent of the population living in urban areas, or slightly more than Africa's 39.6 per cent. However, compared with 1990 (31.5 per cent), current rates reflect Asia's brisk urbanisation rate: indeed, over the last two decades, the increase in its urban population equalled the combined populations of the USA and the European Union. No other continent has experienced such an increase in absolute numbers in such a short span of time.

Urbanisation rates vary widely across subregions. North and Central Asia and the Pacific stand out as the most urbanised areas. In the Pacific, this is largely due to Australia and New Zealand, where more than 85 per cent (2009) of the population lives in urban areas. However, among the Pacific island-states, only a few feature large proportions of urban populations while in many others these are very low (under 25 per cent). In North and Central Asia, urban areas are hosts to over 50 per cent of the population in most countries, with the exception of Kyrgyzstan and Tajikistan, where the proportion remains under 35 per cent. This subregion is the only one in Asia-Pacific where the urban population has not increased over the last two decades, demonstrating patterns more akin to those observed in Europe. East and North-East Asia has urbanised rapidly over the last two decades and is estimated to have crossed the 50 per cent mark in 2010. South-East Asia's urban growth has closely tracked that of Asia as a whole. South and South-West Asia remain the least urbanised subregion, with more than 60 per cent of the population living in rural areas. In the more heavily populated countries of the subregion, like India and Bangladesh, urbanisation rates remain very close to 30 per cent.

While the world population became predominantly urban in 2008, this 'tipping point' will not occur in Asia before 2026. Just as it took 15 years for its urbanisation rate to increase by 10 per cent, Asia is not expected to move from the current 41.7 per cent to 50 per cent before early 2026, still on the back of urban-led economic growth.

This evolution means that over the next decade, two-thirds of the demographic expansion in the world's cities will take place in Asia, which is already host to 50 per cent of the global urban population. Indeed, by 2020, of the 4.2 billion urban population of the world, 2.2 billion will be in Asia. In other words, it is estimated that between 2009 and 2020, a total 450 million people will be added to Asian cities, or 60 per cent of the growth in the world's urban population.

Governments should encourage balanced urban growth, steering private capital expenditure towards cities of different sizes. Most Asian countries are in the early stages of urbanisation. These countries have an opportunity to prepare for prospective urban expansion, learning from the experience of more urbanised countries. If Asian-Pacific countries put themselves in a position to plan and manage balanced urban growth through necessary infrastructure investments, they can alleviate the negative aspects associated with urbanisation, such as congestion, pollution and slums. It is equally important that for urban policies to succeed, they are mainstreamed in national development plans. Urban and regional infrastructure should be given a higher priority in national development strategies.

The 'Youth Bulge'. The Asian-Pacific population is young and the region has benefitted from this 'youth bulge'. In 1960, 284 million Asians were aged 15 to 24; by 2007, they were 737 million. Over the past 40 years, the proportion of Asia's population in the 15-24 age bracket increased – from 17 per cent in 1960 to 21 per cent in 1985, before beginning to decline (18 per cent in 2007). A further decline, to 14 per cent, is projected by 2040. Approximately one third of East Asia's increase in gross domestic product between 1965 and 1990 can be attributed to the 'youth bulge'. Although many young people across the region are now better prepared than ever before to enter the workforce, many remain unable to secure gainful employment, and are underemployed or in informal sector employment.

For the Asian economies to continue to benefit from positive demographic trends (the 'demographic dividend') related to youth, they must provide more opportunities in order to harness the potential of the younger population.

Ageing populations. Many countries in Asia are facing dramatic demographic changes. Some are to expect declines in working populations and concomitant increases in the numbers of aged dependants sometime between 2015 and 2020. However, the process of population ageing is occurring much more rapidly in Asia than it did in Western countries, and in some parts of the region it is also occurring at a much earlier stage of economic development. All across Asia, the numbers of people aged 65 or more are expected to rise significantly. In the year 2000, the average age in Asia was 29 years, but it will rise to 40 years by 2050. That same year an estimated 6 per cent of the region's total population were aged 65 or more, 30 per cent were under 15, and 64 per cent were in the working-age group of 15 to 64 years. It is estimated that by 2050, the proportion under 15 will drop to 19 per cent, and the proportion of those aged 65 or more will rise to 18 per cent.

The ageing phenomenon and reduced fertility rates will affect most Asian countries within one or two generations. Education and urbanisation policies should be better coordinated to address this problem. Faced with an unprecedented pace of ageing of their populations, Asian cities must prepare to cater to the special needs of the elderly, including: (a) housing (as more Asians increasingly prefer nuclear as opposed to extended families); (b) medical facilities (and attendant financing); (c) changes in building regulations; and (d) changes to urban planning standards.

1.2.2 Mega-cities, mega urban regions and urban corridors

The number of mega-cities (those with populations of 10 million or more) is increasing around the world and half of the world's mega-cities (11 out of 21) are now found in Asia. Seven of the 10 most populous cities are in Asia, including Tokyo, Delhi, Mumbai, Shanghai, Kolkata, Dhaka, Karachi, Manila, Osaka-Kobe, Beijing and Istanbul. Many of these mega-cities have grown on the back of concentrations of urban-based manufacturing industries. Over time, however, the top segments of the services sector have come to concentrate in these cities, too, in order to benefit from agglomeration economies. Many mega-cities are also the seats of power, either political power as national capitals or as major economic or financial centres. People, infrastructure and capital are concentrated in mega-cities, and so is the political and social power that reinforces mega-cities' role as the engines of national development. Public investment in infrastructure fuels urban agglomeration economies. The services sector is particularly prone to agglomeration and typically prefers central locations.

Mega-cities account for only 11 per cent of Asia's urban population, but like their counterparts around the world they are dominant forces in both the regional and global economies, on top of significant other contributions to their respective countries. They are knowledge centres, often concentrating the best national educational and research institutions, as well as cultural centres, allowing a variety of cultures to coexist and thrive.

Many urban agglomerations in Asia are evolving into mega urban regions and urban corridors, which are very large urban areas the size of fully-fledged regions and are often referred to as Extended Metropolitan Regions (EMR). Many such mega urban regions have emerged in Asia. For example, the Tokyo-Yokohama-Nagoya-Osaka-Kobe-Kyoto 'bullet train' urban corridor act as the backbone of Japan's economic power, while the Beijing-Tianjin-Tangshan-Qinhuangdao transportation corridor in North-East China is a huge mega-urban region characterized by almost unbroken urban, built-up areas.

Mega urban regions and urban corridors are part of the restructuring of urban territorial space that comes with globalisation. While the concentration of economic activities in these large regional urban areas stands out as one of the positive outcomes of agglomeration economies, the sheer size of these areas can generate diseconomies of scale. Mega-cities at the core of mega urban regions are often beset with high real estate prices, traffic congestion and poor environmental quality. These 'negative externalities' drive firms and households away from core city locations to the periphery for cheaper land and better environmental quality.

Full advantage should be taken of the agglomeration effect and economies of scale provided by mega urban regions, which are already the engines of growth in many countries.

1.2.3 Small- and medium-sized cities and towns

Today, 60 per cent of Asia's urban population lives in urban areas with populations under one million. Moreover, in the region, urban settlements of less than 500,000 people have maintained their share of around 50 per cent of urban populations in the recent decades. Small- and medium-sized towns typically perform a variety of roles, as follows:

- They serve as local 'economic growth centres', i.e., markets for rural products and urban services.
- They act as 'bridges' between rural areas and large urban centres. In a rapidly growing economy, where major activities are concentrated in large urban centres, small- and medium-sized cities play an important role, providing indirect links between the rural and the global economy through connections to large conurbations. This is especially true of those small cities located in mega urban regions.
- Many small towns also serve as administrative headquarters for district or sub-district administration.
- Small- and medium-sized cities often serve as temporary 'stepping-stones' for rural migrants on their way to further destinations. In many countries, these consecutive urban-to-urban migration streams are as significant as rural-to-urban flows.

Small- and medium-sized cities act as economic growth centres, but most lack adequate infrastructure and services. Despite their significant role as links between rural and urban economies, small- and medium-sized cities feature poor infrastructure – unpaved roads, inadequate water supply and sanitation, poor telephone and Internet connectivity, and erratic power supply. Most Asian countries have deployed policies to strengthen the role of small- and medium-sized towns, but it is generally agreed that they have not quite delivered. One frequent reason was that such programmes were designed at the national level and failed to recognize the factors specific to each urban centre.

However, there is a silver lining for small- and medium sized cities, as the trend toward decentralisation seems to have worked well for them. In many Asian countries, smaller cities have begun to benefit from incipient political and administrative decentralisation, under which national governments are devolving some of their powers, including revenue-raising, to local authorities.

Since small- and medium-sized cities in the Asia-Pacific region will continue to host around 50 per cent of urban populations in the next two decades, policymakers should focus on their needs regarding infrastructure and basic urban services, and increase urban governance capacities.

1.2.4 Urban densities and the pace of urbanisation

Asian cities are characterised by high population densities and decreasing annual growth rates, averaging 2.2 per cent in 2010 (against 3.8 per cent in the 1980s). Average urban densities range from 10,000 to 20,000 per sq. km, which is almost double the rates in Latin America, triple those in Europe, and 10 times those found in US cities. Asian cities have featured high population densities for centuries. Today, demographic densities vary significantly within built-up areas. Asian cities owe their high densities to several factors:

- Density is affected by the modes of transport available to commuters. In high-density cities, the commuting population typically resorts to public transport rather than to personal vehicles, and the situation is the reverse in low-density cities. In high-density cities like Mumbai, Singapore, Tokyo and Hong Kong, China, public transport systems work well and carry millions of commuters daily.
- High density is a market-driven response to land demand and results in the efficient use of space. In well-managed cities, local floor/area ratio (also known as the 'floor space index' – a measure that determines land use intensity) values are closely linked to local demand for floor space. Floor/area ratio values are high in areas of high demand where land prices are high, and low in areas where demand for land is lower.
- High population densities also result from the rapid expansion of cities. Lack of serviced land and inadequate infrastructure often lead to higher concentrations of people in and around city centres. This goes to show that the (in)ability of Asian cities to invest in urban infrastructure and services in response to population growth has a direct bearing on densities.
- Government actions, through planning regulations (e.g., floor/area ratios) and investments in infrastructure also have significant effects on densities and prices. When local planning laws restrict floor/area ratios to control densities, this creates shortages in supply of built space and leads to higher property prices.

In Asia as a whole, urban population growth rates have been declining since 1990: from an average 2.8 per cent between 1990 and 1995 to 2.4 per cent between 2000 and 2005. In contrast, the Pacific subregion experienced a minor increase from 1.4 per cent during 1995-2000 to 1.5 per cent during 2000-2005.

At present, when the impacts of climate change on cities are increasingly considered as imminent, high population density is often seen as a cure for 'suburban sprawl' as it makes cities more compact and therefore, more efficient from the perspectives of infrastructures as well as climate change mitigation. National governments and local authorities must recognize that demand for land stands to grow as Asian cities expand; consequently, planning laws must facilitate rather than constrain urban growth while maintaining or promoting high population densities. Local authorities should see the forthcoming slowdown in urban demographic growth rates as an opportunity better to manage cities while maintaining the high densities and limited ecological footprints that characterize Asian conurbations.

1.3 The Economic Role of Asian Cities

1.3.1 Asian cities are resilient engines of economic growth

Asian cities are economically resilient, as demonstrated by their performance in times of crisis. Economic growth in Asia-Pacific has been robust over the past two decades, except for the short 1997-98 regional financial crunch and the effects of the 2008-09 global economic crisis from which the region is now recovering. The recent economic crisis, which caused world economic growth to slow down from 2.6 per cent in 2007 to 1.0 per cent in 2008, undermined the strength of export-orientated Asia-Pacific economies, where growth fell from a robust 4.7 to 2.7 per cent. Although the effects of the global economic crisis have been uneven across Asian-Pacific subregions (see below), domestic demand and timely fiscal responses (e.g. higher public spending) have enabled the Asian and Pacific economies to sustain economic growth. The pace was relatively robust where domestic demand accounted for large shares of economic growth, such as in India, the Philippines, Viet Nam and Indonesia.

The subregions of Asia and the Pacific feature variations in economic growth vis-à-vis *their urbanisation levels.* The Pacific and North-Central Asian subregions feature higher than average urbanisation levels; in all other subregions, the proportions of urban populations and urban shares of gross domestic product are similar.

- *East and North-East Asia* is the largest subregional economy in the Asia-Pacific region. The 47 per cent of the population residing in urban areas contributes 86 per cent of its gross domestic product. The economy grew an overall 5.3 per cent in 2007, with a decline to 3.4 per cent in 2008. The subregion includes the two largest, trillion-dollar economies in the whole Asia-Pacific region – China and Japan – and contributes 63 per cent of its total production of goods and services.
- *South-East Asia's* economy grew 6.3 per cent in 2007 and 4.6 per cent in 2008. This performance came as the tail-end of the rebound from the 2.5 per cent annual average of the 1996-2000 period, which reflected the 1997-98 Asian financial crisis. Economic recovery has gone hand in hand with rapid urbanisation in most countries. Urban areas contribute 79 per cent of the subregion's combined output and account for 46 per cent of its population.
- *The South and South-West Asian* economy grew a brisk 7.4 per cent in 2007, slowing down to 5.3 per cent in 2008. Cities in this subregion, currently the least urbanised in Asia, are expected to experience faster demographic and economic expansion as they increase their relative shares in national economies. On the whole, urban areas today account for 33 per cent of the total population and 76 per cent to the subregion's combined output. The subregional giant is India, contributing 68 per cent of total production, with a 7.3 per cent growth rate in 2008.
- *North and Central Asia* featured a 5.7 per cent economic growth in 2008, and thus remained the continent's fastest growing subregion (though down from 8.4 per cent in 2007). After the turmoil that followed the disintegration of the Soviet Union in 1990, high commodity prices, especially oil, natural gas, metals as well as cotton and cereals have boosted the subregion's economies. These trends have little to do with cities, which typically focus on manufacturing and services. This is why, although the share of urban areas in the region's population is quite significant (85 per cent), their demographic growth remains slow.
- *The Pacific subregion's* economic performance remained moderate to sluggish these past few years. The global economic crisis and its impact on major trading partners caused the average growth rate to decline from 3.8 per cent in 2007 to 0.9 per cent in 2008. The effect was most acute in Nauru, where the economy contracted by 12.1 per cent in 2008, due to lower consumer demand and slackening of capital expenditure by the private sector.

The productivity of Asian cities being uneven, governments of the Least Advanced Countries should learn from more advanced and emerging economies how to make their cities more competitive.

Urban-led economic growth in the Asia-Pacific region has resulted in changes in employment patterns associated with the demographic expansion of cities. The proportion of service sector employment in the region increased from 25.8 per cent in 1991 to 36.4 per cent in 2007, concomitantly with a decline in the share of agriculture (from 52.9 to 39.1 per cent). Changes in manufacturing have occurred at a slower pace in the Asia-Pacific region, with a slight overall decline in the 1990s (from 20.5 per cent in 1991 to 19.7 per cent in 2000).

Although Asian economic growth is rapid, job quality is a cause for mounting concern. Job quality is measured as the proportion of employment that involves own-account workers (self-employed) or contributing family workers (capturing aspects like wages and benefits, standard and non-standard forms of employment, working time, work-life balance and working conditions). In 2007, in the Asia-Pacific region as a whole, these workers accounted for 58.8 per cent of employment; their shares in total employment were the highest in South-East Asia (74.4 per cent) and South and South-West Asia (60.1 per cent). Overall, the quality of jobs being created in Asia and the Pacific remains poor.

The employment elasticity of growth has decreased in the Asia-Pacific region. For example, in the 1980s in China, every additional 3 per cent in total output would lead to a 1 per cent increase in employment, but by the 1990s such an increase required an additional 8 per cent in total output. This unfavourable pattern holds for most countries and cities in Asia. Another distinctive feature is that for all the rapid growth in the formal economy, the informal sector has remained stable or increased marginally in size. Globalisation has brought competition in the labour market as well, and wages in the formal economy have risen. As a result, employers tend to hire fewer workers and look to improve productivity.

In the manufacturing sector, automation has reduced labour-capital ratios.

Many Asian governments provide incentives to attract foreign investors; however, unless the policy mix is right, capital-intensive investment may not create new jobs (resulting in "jobless growth") and can even lead to downsizing or retrenchment (i.e., job losses). Those investors looking for cheap rather than skilled and productive labour tend to favour informality. Moreover, supply-side support as provided by the government to enhance competitiveness in global markets (through incentives or subsidies for export promotion, technology upgrading, tax holidays, etc.) is typically biased in favour of larger industrial enterprises. These policies may not only prevent smaller enterprises from developing their own potential or gaining access to global markets, they may also crowd informal operators and workers altogether out of a given market segment.

Asian cities must build the institutional capacity and strategic vision that will enable them to manage economic growth in a more inclusive sort of way.

1.3.2 The main drivers of Asia's urban economies

Cities in the Asia-Pacific region are well positioned to capitalise on the opportunities provided by their own demographic expansion as well as the forces behind globalization. Five inter-related factors act as key drivers of urban economies in the Asia-Pacific region:

- *Export-led growth:* Exports are a significant source of economic growth and employment for many Asian-Pacific countries, and a factor of integration in world markets. Between 1990 and 2007, the countries in the region saw a significant increase in the contribution of exports to gross domestic product. The average ratio of exports to total output in 11 countries (Bangladesh, Cambodia, China, India, Indonesia, Nepal, the Philippines, Republic of Korea, Sri Lanka, Thailand and Viet Nam) nearly doubled from 25.1 per cent in 1990 to 47.4 per cent in 2007.
- *Urban infrastructure and services:* Cities with proper infrastructure facilitate higher productivity and the resulting higher returns attract foreign direct investment. Within Asia-Pacific region, urban infrastructures display wide variations in terms of quality. In this regard, East and North-East Asia provides the best the region has to offer and therefore has attracted larger amounts of foreign direct investment than any other subregion. Cities with Special Economic Zones, which are promoted by national and local governments alike, fare much better for infrastructure and service provision, as exemplified by Shenzhen in China.
- *Foreign direct investment and competition among cities:* Foreign direct and domestic investment is typically attracted to major cities with good transportation and communications systems, and resource-rich regions with raw material supplies. The effect of competition among

cities has been the concentration and specialization of industrial development in geographic space, as cities increasingly find their own special niche in the world market. In Asia, this is demonstrated in Shanghai, Singapore, Tokyo and Hong Kong, China, which dominate regional finance and transport logistics. Other cities, like Bangkok, dominate the auto industry, while Bangalore and Taipei are global centres of information technology research and development.

- *Cities' connectivity to markets:* Economic development depends critically on connections between production centres and markets. Asian-Pacific policy-makers rightly see infrastructure as an essential growth factor. The two fastest-growing economies in the region, China and Viet Nam, are currently investing around 10 per cent of total output in infrastructure, and even at that rate they are struggling to keep pace with demand for electricity, telephones and major transport networks. Plans for economic development in the Greater Mekong area – the Lao People's Democratic Republic, Cambodia, Thailand, Viet Nam, Myanmar and China – are centred on greater integration of transport and energy markets. In India, investment in infrastructure is a top priority among policymakers.
- *Business practices:* Cities that provide better business environments attract more domestic and foreign direct investment, and in turn profit from economic growth. Some commonly used parameters to assess good business practices include ease of starting a business, registering property, getting credit and enforcing contracts. Based on these parameters, China's coastal cities offer the friendliest business environments. It is up to low-income cities to follow suit through enhanced efficiency and modern technologies, while maintaining low costs for business.

In several cities across the Asia-Pacific region, economic growth has been restricted by bottlenecks arising from institutional frameworks, human resources and infrastructure. Regulatory red tape, taxation and corruption combine to stifle potential business and can significantly cancel out other strengths a city may possess.

National governments in the Asia-Pacific region will do well to provide improved urban infrastructure and services, better connectivity to markets and business-friendly environments to attract domestic and foreign direct investment in order to facilitate urban-led economic growth. Cities must pay attention to the way infrastructure programmes fit within broader development strategies and political circumstances, how those strategies are formulated and how they bring about tangible outcomes. Fiscal and regulatory incentives should be reviewed and expanded to attract more domestic and foreign investment in Asian cities.

1.3.3 Urbanisation and the informal economy in Asia

Synergies between the formal and informal sectors account for the socio-economic dynamism of Asian cities. Asian cities feature very well-developed formal sectors in manufacturing and services that resemble those in Western countries, while simultaneously hosting large informal economies that underpin the success of the formal economy in fast-changing circumstances. The linkages between informal workers and formal businesses can be both direct and indirect. The informal economy includes the full range of "non-standard" wage employment conditions which flexible specialization has given rise to, such as sweatshop production, home-workers, contract workers, temporary or part-time work, and unregistered workers. Seen from this perspective, the informal economy includes many disguised wage employees who may not have direct links with a formal sector enterprise, but who are clearly dependent on the formal sector for the inputs, equipment, work location and sale of the final products they make.

The informal sector is a part of the urbanisation dynamics in Asia. As urbanisation continues, informal economies keep expanding in Asian cities, providing basic livelihoods to new urban residents. A significant informal economy has been a characteristic of the early phases of the urbanisation of almost all economies around the world, and therefore has often been seen as a prerequisite in the transition from developing to more developed economies. For instance, Sri Lanka combines low rates of urbanisation (14.3 per cent in 2010) and a relatively small urban informal sector. In others, like India, a low rate of urbanisation (30.0 per cent in 2010) sits side by side with high proportions of informal workers in urban areas. On the other hand, Thailand, with high incomes per head and relatively low urbanisation (34.0 per cent in 2010) also features high shares of informal workers in urban areas.

Although the linkages between the formal and informal sectors in Asian cities do contribute to the economic dynamism of the region, a few issues call for policy attention, as follows:

- *Data on the contribution of the informal sector to growth:* While it is widely accepted that the informal sector is an integral part of any urban and national economy, much of the information available relates to employment data, rather than the contribution of the sector to the economy as a whole, and its influence on urban growth.
- *Factors behind the existence of informal sector enterprises:* The proliferation of informal enterprises in cities often comes as a by-product of three types of administrative inadequacy: (i) excessive government and local authority control, (ii) the long drawn-out procedures for permits and licences, and (iii) the inefficiency and petty corruption involved in doing business.
- *The globalization of Asian cities* has also led to new and flexible forms of production relations, especially in the service sector – such as those found in call centres or in the hiring of retail sector staff. Employment in these new urban enterprises would often be classified as informal because they do not come under the purview of any regulatory framework.
- *Gender issues.* For most of the last two decades, women's participation rates in the Asia-Pacific region have been consistently high, i.e., above 65 per cent, in East and North-East Asia, while remaining under 35 per cent in South and South-West areas. With rapid economic growth in the region, more women are joining the labour force than before. However, much of the increase in female participation in the labour force is in the informal economy. Greater insecurity and lower earning capacities in the informal sector make women workers more vulnerable. Even in the formal sector, the female labour force tends to be much more occupationally segregated than is the case for male counterparts. The chances of exploitation are also greater for women regardless of work conditions, including domestic help, the informal sector illegal or quasi-legal circumstances (sex work), as well as more formal work conditions like factory floors. Social networks offer some protection in these situations. Despite their increased participation in production, women remain concentrated in the more 'invisible' areas of informal work, such as domestic labour, piece-rate homework, and assistance in small family enterprises, which offer low or irregular remuneration (where any) and little if any access to social security or protection.
- *Labour issues:* The coexistence of the 'modern' or formal sector with the 'traditional' or informal sector has become a more acute and distinctive feature of labour markets in many Asian cities and, to a significant extent, a factor in their global manufacturing competitiveness. In most Asian cities, the informal economy has been burgeoning (providing resilience in times of crisis), but for most informal workers and small businesses work remains insecure despite gruelling, overextended working days.

The informal sector should be supported rather than harassed, and play a more positive role in employment generation. The critical policy issue here is not whether informal wage workers or informal production units have direct ties with the formal economy – clearly, they do – but whether those ties are benign, exploitative or mutually beneficial. Public policies must enhance the positive linkages between the formal and informal sectors of the economy, ensuring that work conditions are decent for all, including women.

1.3.4 Asia – beyond the 'factory of the world'

Asian cities are diversifying away from serving as the factories of the world to turn into innovative service providers.

The Asia-Pacific region enjoys the unique status of 'factory of the world'. Having developed an independent, integrated regional value chain of supply, production and sales, Asia has turned into the world's manufacturing centre. As part of this process and since the 1980s, the region has created a number of manufacturing bases through the integration of global capital and the region's cheap labour. However, in recent years, manufacturing has undergone a major reshuffling within

Asia. The process has involved the geographic dissemination of production with assembly operations migrating to lower-wage economies, while more developed Asian countries are specializing in high-value-added components and capital goods.

Asian cities as 'knowledge economies'. Today, Asia no longer is just a source of cheap manufacturing goods and services. The transformations in global markets as well as production and innovation systems are providing new opportunities for Asian firms that seek to improve their innovative capabilities. The process of outsourcing, which initially sought to exploit the labour wage arbitrage, is increasingly focusing on the need to access and tap fresh talent. This pursuit is the primary driver of next-generation outsourcing. It was generally believed that innovation, in contrast to other stages of the value chain, was not transferable. It typically remained tied to specific locations, namely, the home countries of multinational companies. However, the integration of developing countries into the global economy, and attendant foreign direct investment flows, have acted as the catalysts for a major change. Indeed, the earlier forms of outsourcing have started to shift to some less-developed Asian countries, while the newer forms take over in those more developed where they appear to be more diversified, higher-end and higher value-added in terms of production and service delivery. Particularly significant is the fact that this new wave of outsourcing increasingly includes some of the research and development (R&D) functions of major Western companies. This comes as an effective recognition of Asian cities' growing potential for innovation on a global scale, on top of worldwide production and distribution networks. In 1997, 59 per cent of US corporate research and development sites were located within the USA with only 8 per cent outsourced to China or India. By 2006, the combined share of these two countries had more than doubled to 18 per cent while the US share had declined to 52 per cent.

Asian cities as financial centres. Financial services are an attractive business sector for cities. They cater to the needs of foreign and domestic investors, both direct and indirect. They are also a major economic asset on a national, regional and global scale, as they represent a dynamic, high-growth sector. Financial services are highly mobile, but more than other sectors are also directly influenced by policy (banking and financial regulation) and planning (including the property market). In addition to Tokyo, Singapore and Hong Kong, China, a few Asian cities have made efforts to turn into international financial centres. Shanghai has already emerged as one, on the back of extensive institutional and regulatory change and innovation. India's business capital, Mumbai, is aspiring to become an international financial centre, but must overcome major hurdles if it is to meet a number of essential requirements in terms of cost-effective and high-quality physical and regulatory infrastructure.

Human capital and Asian cities. Whether Asian cities aspire to serve as manufacturing centres, knowledge hubs or financial centres, they must focus on developing human capital in order to meet fast-growing needs for skilled labour. Education is highly valued in Asian society, and therefore a number of countries have established many quality educational institutions, with nationwide programmes to improve literacy and education. However, the following challenges remain:

- There is a mismatch between the type of jobs being created by cities-led economic growth and the education and skills of new labour market entrants. Export-orientated sectors, which have been growing in the region, require specific skills which general higher education in Asian cities does not provide. The proliferation of general-purpose education in schools and colleges often makes graduates 'unemployable' for jobs that require specific qualifications. As a result, it is for employers to provide on-the-job retraining for the technical and business skills they need. Computer literacy and a command of the English language are turning into major assets in Asia's rapidly growing cities.

- As for employers, they will typically focus on the number of years of schooling and graduate degrees. However, UNESCO reports that recent research based on test scores in mathematics and language skills indicates that the quality of education has a stronger impact on economic growth than total years at school.

- Economic needs often supersede educational goals among urban poor families, as they have to choose between paying for basic needs and services or funding the education of the next generation. As a result, the urban poor remain trapped in the well-known vicious cycle of poverty where lower incomes lead to lower education, which in turn result in low-paid jobs and attendant lower incomes.

For Asian cities to serve as manufacturing centres, knowledge hubs or financial centres, they must meet three policy and operational imperatives: (i) whether jobs are formal or informal, new labour market entrants must develop technical and vocational skills. Therefore, it is for national governments and local authorities to provide adequate education. (ii) For Asian cities to become, and function as, knowledge hubs, they must develop quality education systems that can promote problem-solving and critical-thinking abilities, in addition to information technology skills. (iii) With regard to the urban poor, and on top of basic education, national governments and local authorities must provide the technical and vocational skills that will enable the young generation to join the skilled workforce the region requires for its future prosperity. It is for political leaders and senior policymakers in the Asia-Pacific region to evolve a vision for long-term development based on holistic approaches that merge spatial policy with macro-economic, industrial, agricultural, energy, environmental and labour policies.

▲
Slum area in Bandung, West Java Province, Indonesia. ©**Veronica Wijaya**

1.4 Poverty and Inequality in Asian Cities

1.4.1 Poverty and Inequality

The Asia-Pacific region is leading the reduction of overall poverty in the world. According to recent estimates, extreme poverty was reduced worldwide from 43 per cent in 1990 to 26 per cent of the population in 2005. This achievement was largely due to a significant reduction in Asia and the Pacific, where overall extreme poverty was nearly halved from 49 to 25 per cent over the same period. This remarkable progress in the region has been largely due to East and North-East as well as South-East Asia. However, urban poverty is a different issue.

Economic growth has not benefited all urban dwellers in the region equally. Urban poverty in Asia is declining more slowly than its rural counterpart. In East Asia and between 1993 and 2002, for example, rural poverty declined from 407 to 223 million, a difference of 184 million; in terms of percentage, this decline was from 35 to 20 per cent, a change of 15 percentage points. During the same period, *urban* poverty in the subregion declined from 28.7 to 16.3 million, or 4 percentage points from 6 to 2 per cent.

Urban poverty in Asia is significant and increasing. In South Asia, for example, the number of urban poor increased from 107 to 125 million between 1993 and 2002, an increase of 18 million. The factors behind the increase in urban poverty and its slower decline compared with rural poverty are three-fold:

- *The pattern of urban development:* Urban development in Asia has largely been driven by concentrations of local, national and, increasingly foreign profit-seeking enterprises. This process effectively excluded the poor, as the channels through which they might have benefited from this wealth creation were simply lacking in Asian cities.
- *The problem of poverty baselines:* In practice, poverty measurement methods are identical, although the baselines are theoretically different between urban and rural areas. In urban areas, the income required for essential goods for a family of four is relatively higher than that for a similar rural household. The added deprivation in urban areas is not just due to inadequate income but also to other factors such as inadequate housing and lack of access to services. The urban poor also face challenges due to their extra-legal status, which makes them vulnerable to unlawful intrusions and natural hazards as well.
- *Policy focus:* In many Asian countries, given the predominant rural population, national policy-makers have often considered poverty as a rural, not an urban problem. Hence, policies for poverty alleviation have focused more on rural poverty than its urban counterpart. (The fact that rural poverty has declined more than urban poverty underlines this fact.)

Urban inequality is rising in the Asia-Pacific region. Inequality is not so steep in Asia-Pacific cities as in their African or Latin American counterparts. However, urban inequality is on the rise in the Asia-Pacific region. In Asia's three largest countries between 1990 and 2005, inequality has increased in urban areas: in China from 26 to 35 per cent, in India from 34 to 38 percent, and in Indonesia from 35 to 40 per cent. Rising inequality in Asia reflects governments focus on economic growth rather than reducing inequality (such as through redistribution).

Policymakers in Asia-Pacific must address mounting urban poverty. Given the increasing incidence of urban poverty in the region, and the fact that it is a more complex problem compared to rural poverty, Asia-Pacific countries should address urban poverty in a systematic manner. National governments and local authorities must make concerted efforts to reduce urban inequality in the region.

1.4.2 Meeting the Millennium slum target in Asia

Slums in Asian cities reflect a deep-seated phenomenon of structural poverty. They come as an emanation of social, political, and institutional disparities and deprivations that is exacerbated by the pressures of sustained urban growth. Slums effectively segregate urban areas into the "rich" and the "poor" city – what UN-HABITAT refers to as the 'urban divide' resulting from economic, social, political and cultural exclusion. Slums are also the most glaring physical manifestation of the inconsistency between the demand for labour in Asia's urban areas and inadequate supply of the affordable housing and infrastructure the workforce needs for the safe, decent living conditions they are entitled to expect.

Since the year 2000, the lives of 172 million slum-dwellers in Asia have been improved through various policies and programmes. As reported by UN-HABITAT a few months ago, "Asia was at the forefront of successful efforts to reach the Millennium slum target between the year 2000 and 2010, with governments in the region improving the lives of an estimated 172 million slum-dwellers; these represent 75 per cent of the total number of urban residents in the world who no longer suffer from inadequate housing. The greatest advances in this region were recorded in Southern and Eastern Asia, where 145 million people moved out of the "slum-dweller" category (73 million and 72 million, respectively); this represented a 24 per cent decrease in the total urban population living in slums in the two subregions. Countries in South-Eastern Asia have also made significant progress with improved conditions for 33 million slum residents, or a 22 per cent decrease."

How was the Millennium slum target achieved? UN-HABITAT policy analysis shows that public authorities took the responsibility for slum reduction squarely on their shoulders, backing commitments with bold policy reforms, and preventing future slum growth with equitable planning and economic policies. More specifically, their success was based on five specific, complementary approaches: (i) awareness and advocacy, (ii) long-term political commitment, (iii) policy reforms and institutional strengthening, (iv) proper implementation and monitoring, and (v) scaling up successful local projects.

The Asia-Pacific region still has over half of the world's slum population, and huge sub-regional disparities remain. Estimates for 2010 show that the Asia-Pacific region is host to a slum population of 505.5 million. The numbers of slum-dwellers in Asian-Pacific subregions are as follows: 190.7 million (35.0 per cent) in South Asia; 189.6 million (or 28.2 per cent of the urban population) in East Asia; 88.9 million (31.0 per cent) in South-Eastern Asia; 35.7 million (24.6 per cent) in Western Asia; and 0.6 million (24.1 per cent) in Oceania/Pacific.

Asian governments should continue to spend on slum upgrading and low-cost housing. Local authorities and national governments should upscale pilot projects into citywide and national programmes respectively. With the fast expansion of Asian cities, decision-makers and urban planners should deploy proactive policies and plans for slum prevention.

1.4.3 Land and housing

Poor access, where any, to decent, secure, affordable land is the major factor behind Asia's abundance of slums. In many Asian cities, much larger numbers of people are without any form of secure tenure than with secure land titles. The poor are priced out of formal land markets, on top of which the opportunities for them to squat unused public land are declining. With rapid economic growth, many private landowners and government agencies continue to develop vacant urban land and evict slum-dwellers for commercial development or urban infrastructure projects. Evicting slum households might be an effective way of clearing land for other uses, but almost all evictions, directly or indirectly, result in increased poverty.

For the poor, the best option will always be secure tenure on the site they are occupying. This enables them to stay in the same place without dislocation or disruption to their livelihoods and social support systems. An alternative is to make tenure collective through long-term, non-individual leases, or granting land titles to community cooperatives. However, collective tenure can work only where the community is well organized. Collective tenure rights can act as powerful buffers against market forces, binding communities together and giving them good reason to remain that way. A collective community structure can act as a significant survival mechanism.

Governments should review urban land policies with a view to making residential land more accessible and affordable to low- and middle-income households. Local authorities should avoid unlawful evictions which destroy the social fabric of poor neighbourhoods. Slum eradication, where necessary, should be combined with fair relocation and compensation schemes.

In many Asian countries, shelter does find a prominent place in national policy, but the public resources devoted to housing remain well short of requirements. In the poorer Asian countries, too many households need homes, and governments have too few resources to build even a fraction of the numbers that are required.

Asian countries have attempted to address the housing problem through five main institutional models:

- *Public housing:* Singapore, the Republic of Korea, and Hong Kong, China, have implemented public housing projects as part of government housing policies and their vigorous pursuit of slum-free cities. In Singapore, for example, such efforts have resulted in a private/public housing ratio of about 20 to 80.

- *Public-private partnerships in housing:* Several Asian cities have established partnerships with private developers to stimulate affordable housing construction for the poor. In most cases, commercial development rights on plots were granted to private sector enterprises who, as a *quid pro quo,* would build affordable housing on a specified percentage of the total land under development. Examples include the *Ashraya Nidhi* ('shelter fund') programme in Madhya Pradesh, India; the revitalization of the rivers Fu and Nan in Chengdu, Sichuan Province, China; and Indonesia's housing policies whereby private developers build a minimum of three middle-class houses and six basic or very basic ones for every high-cost house.

- *Private sector housing delivery:* Many Asian governments have "enabled" the private sector to provide housing for the low-earning segments of the population. However, formal private sector housing tends to favour the rich while disregarding the poor, although Asian cities are hosts to more poor (insolvent) than rich households. This problem is partly caused by the relatively finite and therefore 'inelastic' supply of serviced land, which the real-estate developers find themselves hard put to meet demand, causing an overall rise in property prices.

- *Rental housing:* The overall share of rentals in Asian cities is estimated at 30 per cent of the housing market. Although a significant proportion of urban dwellers are tenants, the number of governments giving effective support to rental housing development is small. When privately owned, the bulk of rental housing accommodates low-income households through informal, flexible lease arrangements, which entail lower rents but weaker security of tenure and probably lower-quality public amenities. Some cities, like Bangkok, have seen innovative rental housing where low-income communities have evolved practical arrangements with landowners to enable them to live in areas reasonably close to their place of work.

- *The 'people's process' of housing and slum improvement:* Asia has pioneered the people-led process of housing provision as spearheaded by dedicated civil society groups. These are strong in the region and have gained ground in many cities as a result of efforts by organisations like Slum Dwellers International or the Asian Coalition for Human Rights, among others, with technical support provided by UN agencies such as UN-HABITAT and the UN Economic and Social Commission for Asia and the Pacific. They promote community-led housing development in Cambodia, India, Indonesia, Mongolia, Nepal, Pakistan, the Philippines, Sri Lanka and Thailand. Asia also is testament to the fact that while the private sector is able to meet the housing requirements of the rich, the 'people sector' has been able to cater to the poor (see Chapter 4).

The 'people's process' of housing and slum improvement should be encouraged by all tiers of government through training, financial incentives and legal recognition. National governments and local authorities should develop and implement housing policies and programmes in partnership with civil society groups, which have demonstrated their capacity to address the problem of housing for the urban poor in a number of innovative ways.

1.4.4 Access to basic urban services

A key feature of inclusive and harmonious cities is access to basic urban services. With high urban densities, access to safe and reliable water supply and sanitation services is critical for health, business, social status, dignity and basic security for women and children. Efficient provision of solid waste management, health, energy and transport services is essential for well-being of rich and poor alike.

Most Asian cities are on their way to achieving the target set under the Millennium Development Goals (MDGs) for access to water. Asian-Pacific subregions seem to have done better for water supply than sub-Saharan Africa, but have fallen behind Latin America and Northern Africa. According to the latest available data, East and North-East Asia has forged ahead, serving 98 per cent of the population. This subregion is closely followed by Western Asia with 96 per cent coverage, South Asia with 95 per cent, and South-Eastern Asia with 92 per cent. Between 1990 and 2008, access to water supply has improved in most Asian-Pacific cities, but the share of the urban populations with access to safe drinking water has declined by 3 to 12 per cent in Bangladesh, Indonesia, Myanmar and Nepal.

Though most subregions and countries in the Asia-Pacific region are likely to achieve the Millennium Development Goal for water supply, they are left to grapple with the fact that 4 to 8 per cent of the population remain persistently deprived of access in most subregions, except East and North-East Asia. This suggests that even after an overall improvement in service coverage, a 'last mile' effort is necessary to ensure *universal* access to basic urban services.

Although Asian cities have made considerable progress in providing access to improved sanitation, many are likely to miss the Millennium sanitation target. Between 1990 and 2008, access to improved sanitation has become more widespread in the urban areas of most Asian-Pacific subregions. According to the latest available (2008) data, 94 per cent of urban populations had access to improved sanitation (defined as improved facilities) in Western Asia, followed by 81 per cent in Oceania, 79 per cent in South-East Asia, 61 per cent in East Asia, and 57 per cent in South Asia.

Lack of access to safe sanitation in Asian cities is remedied through increased reliance on shared as opposed to individual household facilities. With the inclusion of 'shared facilities', the proportion of urban populations with access to improved sanitation is higher: 100 per cent in Western Asia, 91 per cent in East Asia, 89 per cent in South-East Asia, 77 per cent in South Asia, with no change in Oceania (81 per cent). However, the Millennium targets do not formally take in 'shared facilities'. The Joint Monitoring Programme for Water Supply and Sanitation raises serious concerns about two aspects: actual accessibility throughout the day, and security of users especially at night.

In countries where access to urban water supply has declined, governments should take the steps required to ensure that safe water is supplied to all urban residents. Governments should assess the state of sanitation in cities, establish national targets to ensure improved sanitation for all, and monitor progress on a regular basis.

Solid waste management. Due to different consumption and conditioning/packaging patterns, the urban poor in Asia generate less waste (including solid) than their counterparts in higher income countries. Besides consuming fewer non-food items, they tend to collect, re-use, recover and recycle materials, since 20 to 30 per cent of their waste is recyclable. In this way the urban poor already play an important role in solid waste management. Non-governmental organizations have improved solid waste collection and the attendant job creations with a variety of projects, such as Waste Concern in Dhaka, Bangladesh.

Health. The poor living in informal settlements and slums constitute the single largest group of vulnerable populations in Asian cities today. Compelling evidence links various communicable and non-communicable diseases, injuries and psychosocial disorders to the risk factors inherent to unhealthy living conditions, such as faulty buildings, defective water supplies, substandard sanitation, poor fuel quality and ventilation, lack of refuse storage and collection, or improper food and storage preparation, as well as poor/unsafe locations, such as near traffic hubs, dumpsites or polluting industrial sites. The health impacts of such unhealthy living conditions are clear: for instance, infant mortality rates in Ahmedabad (Gujarat, India) are twice as high in slums as the national rural average. Slum children under five suffer more and die more often from diarrhoea and acute respiratory infections than those in rural areas. Poor health in turn results in reduced incomes as the urban poor are forced to spend disproportionate amounts on health care.

Energy. An estimated one billion people in Asian-Pacific countries have no access to electricity. Disparities in access to power grids are wide across the region – from 99 per cent of the population in China to 56 per cent in India and 20 per cent in Cambodia. A variety of reasons – irregular land tenure, shared spaces, ill-defined responsibilities for payment, and low consumption – can account for the deficiencies of energy utilities with regard to poor urban communities. These also tend to pay high prices both for relatively poor kerosene-based lighting and for low-quality biomass cooking fuels. To address this issue, some Asian cities have made innovative efforts that could be replicated and up-scaled (see Chapter 4).

Urban Transport. The poor need easy, affordable access to their places of low-paid work or employment. This is because they cannot afford motorised vehicles and road conditions that make walking or bicycling unsafe. Although Asian cities need good public transport, they fare worse than their American and European counterparts. Inadequate planning, where any, has caused a decline in walking and non-motorised vehicles, Asia's two traditional modes. All of this negatively affects the urban poor, who spend significant shares of household incomes on (mini)bus fares, in addition to the waste of time.

Asian cities must urgently provide adequate solid waste management, health, energy and transport services to the low-income segments of their populations. Local authorities and private sector enterprises should support the initiatives and efforts deployed by civil society groups and local communities to improve solid waste management at the local level. Governments must provide improved health services if conditions are to improve for slum-dwellers in urban areas. Cities must make adequate provision of energy services to slum-dwellers in order to improve their quality of life. Decision-makers and urban planners must integrate institutional and spatial provisions for non-motorised and public transport in view of the transportation needs of the urban poor.

Malé, Maldives. ©**Mohamed Shareef/Shutterstock**

1.5 The Urban Environment and Climate Change

1.5.1 Asia's urban development and the environment

"In Asia and the Pacific, overall, there has been a coincidence of rapidly expanding economies, poverty and substantial future consumption pressures, as well as a natural resource base that is more limited than any other in per capita terms. Thus, a focus on meeting human needs and improving well-being with the lowest possible ecological cost is more relevant in Asia and the Pacific than in any other global region," the UN Economic and Social Commission for Asia and the Pacific recently noted. *In their quest for economic growth, Asian cities have not paid sufficient attention to environmental and climate change issues.*

The state of the urban environment in the Asia-Pacific region is very much a tale of two types of city. On the one hand, conurbations in more developed countries – Australia, Brunei Darussalam, Japan, New Zealand, the Republic of Korea and Singapore – are clean, well-managed, prosperous and safe places to live. On the other hand, expanding cities in newly industrialized and rapidly developing countries, which together concentrate large proportions of Asia's urban populations, experience serious environmental, urban management, poverty and development problems. Therefore, to a majority of urban Asians, life is difficult: earning a living

is fraught with risks, and the quality of life is poor. The imminent effects of climate change add to the problems Asian cities face today.

Although the state of the environment in Asian cities inspires widespread pessimism, the situation is not entirely devoid of promising signs. Governments and expanding urban middle classes are increasingly aware that environmental degradation results from an unsustainable approach to urban and economic development. The challenge is to maintain economic development while substantially reducing environmental damage. Making cities more sustainable in the future is one of the greatest challenges facing governments, civil society and the business sector in Asia. Few solutions have been found, but many promising initiatives offer opportunities for replication across the region.

1.5.2 The Defining features of Asia's urban environmental challenges

The following features characterise the urban environmental challenges faced by the Asia-Pacific region:

The dynamics between economic development and urban environmental issues: The pace of economic development in Asian countries is much faster than in the industrialised world. Challenges related to poverty, environmental pollution and consumption – which are thought to be related to different stages of development and have been faced by the industrialized countries over a longer period of time – are confronting Asian cities within a short time span. This phenomenon is unprecedented, and Asian and Pacific cities are only starting now to deal with the complex urban environmental issues associated with it.

The environmental incidence of globalization on Asian cities: Thanks to enormous amounts of foreign direct investment, Asia has become the 'factory of the world' with mass relocation of labour-intensive, less technology-dependent and environmentally hazardous industries. In many cases, national governments and urban authorities in Asia have provided very attractive tax and other incentives to secure foreign direct investment projects, with the jobs, exports and the build-up in foreign exchange reserves that come with them. For many Asian countries, this has brought greater economic prosperity and development, though often at a heavy cost to the environment.

Mega-demand for land and natural resources: Demographic growth and peri-urban developments led by industrialization are leading to massive suburban expansion. On average, Asia's combined urban population grows by over 45 million a year, resulting every day in the conversion of more than 10 sq km of (mainly productive) rural land to urban uses. More than 20,000 new housing units are needed every day to meet basic needs for shelter, creating a huge demand for construction materials and an additional six million ('mega') litres of potable water. Much of this water draws down on existing aquifers, many of which are becoming depleted or contaminated.

The ecological footprints of Asian cities: In most Asian cities today, the average ecological footprint is in excess of five hectares per head, indicating that current consumption patterns are unsustainable. The 'ecological footprint' is an average measure of the amount of land required to sustain one individual. Planet Earth can offer a nominal 1.7 global hectares per head ('ghph') of habitable land to support the needs of the human race. Although the footprints of Asian cities tend to be smaller than those in developed countries, they are on an upward trend, a phenomenon that is not without consequences for the global environment.

High vulnerability to climate-change factors: The unique geography (highest mountain systems, extensive coastlines and large river floodplains and deltas) and climate (monsoon, tropical cyclones and typhoons) combine with high population densities and lack of planning to make Asian-Pacific cities highly vulnerable to the effects of climate change on top of natural disasters. From this perspective, urban centres in the Pacific islands are even more at risk than those in Asia.

The growth of Asian cities is not environmentally sustainable. Infrastructure development and growth patterns may lock Asian cities into unsustainable consumption and production models for years to come.

So far, faced with poverty and unemployment, Asian governments have given high priority to economic growth and development through industrialisation. Many have accepted that environmental issues are associated with this approach, but consider that these can be addressed once the nation reaches a certain level of development, by which time it is believed that *more public funds can be allocated to environmental management and improvements. Fresh and innovative approches to urban development and environmental improvement are required. Massive investment in basic services is needed to improve the sustainability of Asian cities.*

1.5.3 Environmental conditions in Asian cities

Air quality. Air pollution in Asian cities originates mainly from two sources: (i) stationary sources, which include power plants, industrial activities, and residential and commercial buildings; and (ii) mobile sources, mainly motor vehicles, which in turn can be attributed to poor maintenance, poor fuel quality and inadequate traffic management.

Air pollution in Asia causes as many as 519,000 premature deaths every year. Urban dwellers are exposed to micro-particle (particles of 10 micrometres or less – 'PM$_{10}$') inhalation as well as to sulphur and nitrous dioxide emissions.

Information on air quality is of variable quality, and altogether missing for many cities. No comprehensive survey can be found that provides a comprehensive picture of the current status of, and changes in, urban air quality across Asia. At best, a range of studies provide measures of change in air quality in specific cities. Some studies on specific cities show that air quality is improving in Bangkok, Colombo, Dhaka, Ho Chi Minh City and Pune; this research also shows that air quality is declining in Jakarta, Phnom Penh and Ulaanbaatar due to increasing rates of vehicle ownership, high manufacturing concentrations in inner city areas, poor vehicle maintenance and (in Ulaanbaatar) use of low-quality coal and wood in cooking/heating stoves.

Some Asian cities have managed to improve air quality. Delhi and Dhaka, for instance, have phased out two-stroke engines and introduced cleaner fuels and other emission reduction measures to improve air quality. In Ho Chi Minh City, Jakarta and Pune, efforts involve improvements in traffic management, public transport and policing.

Asian cities must improve air quality in order to reduce premature deaths caused by air pollution and to maintain competiveness.

Water management. Asia is host to some of the world's most arid and water-rich biomes, and water management is an increasingly important issue in both types of area. Apart from drought and flooding, threats to water resources result from many factors, including inadequate fresh water and sanitation infrastructures, river pollution and groundwater overuse.

Water supply. Since 1990, Asia has made significant progress with regard to access to safe drinking water (as noted earlier). At the same time, water resource management cannot be overlooked. According to UNESCO, a country can be considered to be 'water-scarce' if total withdrawals are greater than 40 per cent of annual water resources. According to an Asian Development Bank survey of 18 Asian cities, most were drawing down more than 60 per cent of annual replenishment volumes earlier in this decade, and in Chengdu and Shanghai (China) the rate was greater than 80 per cent. Another challenge for many urban authorities in Asia is the maintenance and/or replacement of the older segments of water-supply systems, many of which are plagued by serious amounts of leakage. In Kathmandu, for example, the distribution system loses 35-40 per cent of clean water through leakage; in Karachi the proportion is 30 per cent and in Chennai, 25 to 30 per cent. Moreover, the poor end up paying more for water supplies than their richer neighbours in Asian cities.

Sanitation and wastewater. Along with access to improved sanitation, wastewater treatment is a major issue in water management in the Asia-Pacific region. This is because only a few Asian cities have the capacity or resources to deploy large-scale wastewater treatment facilities. Dense housing development and narrow roads combine with land ownership and compensation issues to act as major constraints on any deployment of large-scale treatment systems in Asian cities. Consequently, communal septic tanks, small-bore sewerage and local treatment facilities, together with wastewater treatment plants on industrial estates, appear as the most viable and cost-effective alternative ways of improving urban sanitation and reducing industrial water pollution in Asia's newly developed urban and peri-urban areas.

All Asian cities will need to make greater efforts to improve water management if they are to avoid further contamination of supplies and meet increasing demand, including for improved sanitation. Enhanced public awareness of water conservation is also essential if the costs of treatment and the incidence of water-related and sanitation-related diseases and infection are to be reduced. Greater equity in water charges is also required to avoid a situation where the poor are paying many times more for water (such as purchased from street vendors) than those better off enough to afford home connections.

Solid waste management. Many Asian cities face serious problems with regard to solid waste management despite significant government efforts to improve services and facilities. In the developing countries of the Asia-Pacific region, solid waste management is often inadequate, as is sanitary and industrial waste disposal due to technical and financial constraints. All countries in the region have environmental legislation and policies in place to manage solid waste collection and disposal, but in the lesser-developed countries enforcement is often poor, or local communities are unaware or dismissive of the regulations. In many cities, polluters go unpunished.

Waste collection services are very deficient in many Asian cities, but are improving. In China, 60 per cent of urban solid waste is collected, compared with 70 per cent in the Philippines. However, open dumping is the dominant solid waste disposal method in most Asian cities. This is the case with more than 60 per cent of the waste in Bangkok, for instance. Inadequate collection and disposal of solid waste in urban Asia is a source of health hazards and environmental degradation.

Solid waste can be used as a resource, as demonstrated in several Asian cities. As a response to this problem, civil society groups and local communities have established community-based organizations and implemented self-help schemes that have improved solid waste management in many Asian cities, such as 'Civic Exnoras' in India.

Asian cities must make concerted efforts to improve solid waste management including the technical, institutional and financial aspects. Enforcement of rules and regulations is essential to manage solid waste and the negative environmental impacts caused by industrial waste disposal. At the same time, local authorities must support and/or build linkages with any initiatives or schemes launched by civil society or local communities for improved solid waste management.

Poor urban environment and health. Large numbers of people are in poor health in Asian cities, due mainly to malnutrition, poverty, cramped living conditions, polluted air and contaminated water. Many lack access to adequate medical facilities and other health services. The emergence of viral diseases such as severe acute respiratory syndrome (SARS) and avian flu in the past decade posed serious threats to Asia's urban populations and economies. The risk of a major pandemic in Asia remains very high: the frequent combination of high population densities and unsanitary conditions is particularly conducive to the breeding, mutation and spread of disease. *Since cities are by now well-connected to the rest of the world, they are potentially exposed to communicable diseases originating in other parts of the world.*

Urban biospheres. The changes caused by rapid urban expansion in Asia pose a number of serious threats to urban biospheres, including: (i) loss of vegetation (flora), and hence (ii) loss of biodiversity (both flora and fauna); (iii) changes in micro-climates; (iv) loss of fertile arable land (a major issue in China and India in connection with future food security); (v) soil degradation, and related (vi) groundwater pollution (on which many low-income urban dwellers depend for water supplies).

Efforts by agencies like UNESCO are under way for the creation or maintenance of urban biosphere reserves. In Asia, one of the best examples of urban biosphere restoration is the Can Gio mangrove forest east of Ho Chi Minh City, an area that was almost destroyed by defoliant spray and clearing during the unification war. High degrees of biodiversity have been restored to the mangrove forest, which today is host to more than 200 species of fauna and another 52 of native flora.

Through appropriate urban and environmental planning and deployment of systematic programmes, national governments and local authorities must ensure that cities and city-regions preserve urban biospheres in order to prevent the irreversible negative impacts of urban growth.

1.5.4 The challenge of climate change

The Asia-Pacific region stands to be most affected by climate change. Its exposure and sensitivity to climate change is bound to have significantly adverse physical, economic and social consequences. Cities in Asia are the most exposed to the effects of climate change: due to size, geographic location or elevation, they are especially vulnerable to frequent extreme weather events such as droughts, floods, cyclones and heat wave.

Estimates vary as to the total contribution of the world's cities to greenhouse gas emissions. However, it is clear that the energy demands of urban areas – including Asia's rapidly growing cities – are major contributors to greenhouse gases. This contribution could be as low as 40 percent, but others suggest that as much as 78 per cent of worldwide greenhouse gas emissions from fossil fuels can be attributed to urban areas. Specific estimates for the Asia-Pacific region have yet to be calculated. More accurate estimates have been made for energy use, of which a combined 66 per cent can be ascribed to the cities of the world.

As most of Asia's future demographic growth is to occur in cities, these are where the problem of climate change must be addressed most urgently.

The causes of climate change and the challenge of mitigation

Climate change will affect energy use and costs, transportation systems and building designs.

Energy, economic growth and the environment. The consumption of energy has grown along with, and has fuelled, economic growth in Asia and the Pacific, especially over the past two decades. Moreover, despite volatile oil prices, total consumption of primary energy continues to increase in most Asian-Pacific countries. In 2006, over 80 per cent of the region's total primary energy supply was made of fossil fuels, including coal, with the remainder split between nuclear power, hydropower and traditional fuels (biomass) such as wood and animal dung. Less than 0.25 per cent came from geothermal or other new and renewable energy sources. As one might expect, fossil and traditional fuels dominated where access to electricity was poor. Since 1990, the region's total energy consumption has increased significantly on the back of substantial increases in electric generation capacity in order to support rapid economic development.

The immediate fallout of the rapid urbanisation and economic growth in Asia is increased energy demand for transportation. This particular sector contributes an estimated one-third of greenhouse gas emissions worldwide. Although technological change and the implementation of tighter emission norms have produced a decline in greenhouse gas emissions per car, these have kept growing overall on the back of increasing urban car numbers across the region. According to the International Energy Agency, the number of motor vehicles in Asia will increase by more than four times in the next 20 years. Asia's share of global energy consumption is expected to increase nearly threefold from the current 6.5 per cent to 19 per cent by 2030.

Buildings and climate change. According to the International Energy Agency, buildings account for as much as 40 per cent of total end-use of energy and about 24 per cent of greenhouse gas emissions in the world. In countries like China, Japan and the Republic of Korea, buildings – especially high-rise – tend to be made of materials with high embodied energy (i.e., the materials were energy-intensive to manufacture). On top of this, building design has little regard for the local environment.

Mitigation responses in urban Asia. Asian countries can already begin mitigating the longer-term impacts of climate change in a variety of ways. This is of particular importance to the larger polluting countries like China, India, Japan and the Republic of Korea. These and other countries are beginning to reduce greenhouse gas emissions by switching to cleaner fuels and alternative sources as far as electric power generation is concerned; they have also taken to reduce industrial, domestic and public transport demand for fossil fuels, but the pace of change is not fast enough.

In the transportation sector, the conversion of private (cars, motorized tricycles) and public vehicles (public transport) to natural gas in several Asian cities has brought significant reductions in greenhouse gas emissions. Delhi, for instance, converted public transport and para-transit vehicles from diesel or petrol engines to compressed natural gas and introduced low-sulphur fuel, which demonstrated that major change could occur on a large scale, as long as appropriate policies were deployed.

With regard to buildings, according to the International Energy Agency, energy-efficiency standards in buildings across the world would reduce energy use by about 11 per cent by 2030 compared with a business-as-usual scenario. In China, the city of Rizhao has demonstrated that overall energy demand and greenhouse gas emissions can be reduced through sustainable building design and energy use.

The energy efficiency of transport systems should be assessed and monitored with a view to reducing fossil energy inputs while facilitating people's urban mobility. Energy-efficient building designs should be promoted to reduce greenhouse gas emissions.

The effects of climate change and the challenge of adaptation

The effects of climate change on cities. The impacts of climate change on Asian and Pacific cities will be significant. They will affect not only the human, but also the physical, economic and social environments.

Increases in natural disasters. Asian cities are among the most vulnerable in the world to natural disasters, with many informal settlements located in fragile environmental areas on shorelines and major river basins. Climate change will increase the risk of storm and flood damage in many cities in the region. Some authors have found that Bangkok, Dhaka, Guangzhou, Hai Phong, Ho Chi Minh City, Jakarta, Kolkata, Mumbai, Shanghai and Yangon – all located under the tropics – are the world's most exposed cities to increased flooding due to climate change. Many Asian cities lie on coastal plains, which are bound to suffer more frequent flooding from tidal surges and storm damage. Exposure to extreme weather events – heat waves, tropical cyclones, prolonged dry spells, intense rainfall, tornadoes, thunderstorms, landslides or avalanches – is already high in the Asia-Pacific region. In the 20th century, Asia accounted for 91 per cent of all deaths and 49 per cent of all damage due to natural disasters.

Rising sea levels. Climate change will have a significant impact on the future development of Asia's coastal cities. An estimated 54 per cent of Asia's urban population lives in low-lying coastal zones. Particularly vulnerable are deltas and low coastal plains where many large cities are located, such as in Bangladesh. Island-states, such as Maldives and Tuvalu, are particularly exposed. According to some authors, more than 238 million people currently live in cities located in Asia's Low Elevation Coastal Zone (i.e., less than 10 metres above sea level) which as a result of climate change is exposed to rising sea levels and storm surges. Six of the 10 major port cities most at risk (in terms of exposed population) of flooding and inundation are in Asia. Adapting to climate change is a challenge for poorer Asian countries such as Bangladesh, as well as the smaller Pacific and Indian Ocean island states, due to very limited resources and options.

Due to the effects of climate change, urban and rural areas will face the challenges of water supplies, food security and 'eco-refugees'. Climate change will result in significant changes in weather and rainfall patterns, which will cause profound but highly variable direct and indirect effects on cities. Many of the effects expected in rural areas will also be felt by cities and towns. Loss of agricultural land due to inundation and other climate-related events (such as drought) will affect food security in villages and cities alike. The implications for food security will be significant as desertification makes further progress in countries such as China and India. Water supply for rural and urban areas will be affected by changes in rainfall patterns.

In urban areas, the poor are most vulnerable to climate change. For lack of proper land plots or housing, the urban poor live in environmentally vulnerable sites such as low-lying areas, along the banks of rivers or lakes, steep slopes or in the proximity of waste dump-sites. These areas are likely to become more vulnerable due to the effects of climate change such as increased rainfall and inundation, stronger cyclones, typhoons and storms or sea level rise. Moreover, the poor are more likely to be affected due to water supply and food shortages, as well as health epidemics.

The challenge of 'eco-refugees'. Many people living in thousands of cities and towns across the Asia-Pacific region face increasing uncertainty about their future, with millions potentially exposed to upheaval and relocation as 'eco-refugees' (known as 'climate change refugees'). The relocation of eco-refugees will pose a significant challenge, requiring new urban settlements that will further reduce the amounts of land available for food production.

Asian cities have only just started to take adaptation measures in response to climate change. In most countries, more investments in urban infrastructure are in order. Managing massive relocation will be challenging, and requires careful planning which should begin now, *rather than later when natural disasters brought on by climate change become more intense.*

Financing climate change policies. Although difficult to predict, the economic costs of unmitigated climate change in Asia are likely to be very high. In Asia as elsewhere in the world, a major question when addressing the issue of climate change is, who will bear the costs?

Adaptation will be expensive and will require significant national and international borrowing and the raising of revenue through a variety of user-pay means. Most costs will have to be borne by urban dwellers, since cities contribute most to greenhouse gas emissions. Reducing these will call for a variety of strategies. Some – such as the introduction of cleaner fuels and engine conversions for public transport, which is already occurring in many South Asian cities – will become widespread across the region. Because of the diversity in climatic, geographic and economic conditions, however, individual cities will also need specific strategies to suit their own circumstances.

As far as the financial dimension of climate change adaptation/mitigation is concerned, some Asian countries have adopted, or are considering schemes involving emissions trading, carbon taxes and the Clean Development Mechanism (CDM), a legacy of the Kyoto Protocol that is very much in favour with developing countries. The Clean Development Mechanism is particularly efficient because reductions take place where they can be made most cheaply, and it also offers developing countries an incentive to address their environmental problems. Asian countries currently account for more that 75 per cent of the total certified emission reduction credits issued by the UN Framework Convention on Climate Change (UNFCCC) through the mechanism, with China and India among the more extensive issuers, accounting for more than 70 per cent together with the Republic of Korea.

National governments and local authorities should start assessing the financing needs and developing (innovative) financial solutions in order to meet the imminent challenges of climate change mitigation and adaptation.

Asian and Pacific cities are facing serious environmental problems which, if not addressed, will have serious local, regional and worldwide consequences. If Asia's urban development is to become more sustainable, governments and communities must give priority to better urban planning and management of development, improvements to environmental management, and better environmental governance and compliance.

1.6 Urban Governance, Management and Finance in Asia

Urban governance, management and finance had been on the policy agenda in Asia for over two decades when, with the worldwide economic crisis that began in 2008, these issues took on a more visible and acute dimension. In recent years, many Asian cities have sought to improve governance in a bid to achieve sustained economic and social development in the face of serious problems such as such as slum and squatter settlements, traffic gridlock, inadequate water supply, poor sanitation, unreliable energy systems and serious environmental pollution. The gated communities of the rich and the ghettoized enclaves of the poor come as dramatic illustrations of an 'urban divide' often characterized as 'a tale of two cities.' Inner cities deteriorate as development moves to outlying areas and results in automobile-induced urban sprawl. Pervasive graft and corruption mar the implementation of many projects. All these problems dent the capacity of urban areas to act as development hubs and highlight a vital need for improved governance.

1.6.1 Urban governance and operational structures

Urban authorities in Asia have traditionally relied on operational structures and processes such as city and regional plans, zoning codes, regulations and standards, financing schemes, proper personnel management and the use of performance evaluation and audit methods for the sake of cost-effectiveness and accountability. However, *experience has shown that, on their own, the technocratic approaches traditionally used by urban authorities in Asia have had limited effectiveness* for two main reasons: (i) the informal sector makes a significant contribution to local economies, and (ii) urban authorities are chronically short of capital and operating funds. In recent years, urban authorities have greatly benefited from the participation of citizens, business, community and other civil society groups that have become actively involved in the governance process. *Accordingly, the past two decades have seen a broadening of the scope of governance in Asia with a shift away from the 'business' of government to the 'process' of governance which involves various stakeholders.*

Recent constitutional and statutory changes in a number of Asian countries reflect the recognition of the vital role of civil society participation in urban governance, as non-governmental and grassroots organisations demand greater involvement in local affairs. For instance, the 73rd and 74th amendments to the Constitution of India have specified the roles to be played in governance by grassroots or community-based organizations, women's groups, the urban poor and various emanations of civil society. In Pakistan, the law reorganizing urban authorities grants a formal role to non-elected members of the public: 'Citizen Community Boards' are empowered to spend one fourth of budgets on community needs. In Thailand, the Constitution Act of 1997 prescribes the establishment of local personnel committees with representatives not only from government agencies, but also "qualified persons" from local populations.

Basic stakeholders in urban governance. Eight types of governance stakeholders are considered crucial to economic, social and environmental sustainability in urban areas; local authorities, civic institutions, interest groups (including the business sector and labour/trade unions), the academic community, national government, non-governmental organizations, individual citizens and local communities. These stakeholders contribute to urban governance in the following ways:

- Individual citizens, interest groups and communities, together with civic institutions, the academic community and non-governmental organisations, provide for the accurate identification of peoples' needs and requirements through interest aggregation and expression, a process that can guide public authorities when devising policies and programmes, facilitate monitoring and evaluation as well as promote transparency and accountability. Civil society can act as a two-way channel, including for feedback about the nature and performance of public policies and the need for any changes.

- Local and central governments are guided by grassroots participation in the formulation, implementation and evaluation of those policies and programmes designed to achieve common societal goals.

- Good urban governance enhances direct or indirect involvement of communities and various sectors of society in government affairs, which contributes to democratic decision-making.

- Active involvement of individuals, communities, interest groups, civic institutions and non-government organisations in urban governance facilitates the collection and allocation of resources in a fair, equitable and inclusive manner.

- Good urban governance comes hand in hand with agreed, appropriate ethical standards of behaviour and performance for holders of public office.

Effective, broad-based governance enhances cities' contributions to national economic, social and environmental development. Therefore, national governments and local authorities should expand institutional frameworks in order systematically to involve the various stakeholders in urban governance.

1.6.2 The principles of urban governance

In most Asian-Pacific cities, the population can participate in the performance of public functions such as elections, the budgetary process and reviews of public actions. Experience also shows that the process of urban governance requires more than formal adherence to government procedures. The emphasis on governance as a 'process' calls for active involvement from various stakeholders, including business and the public. The following four principles of urban governance are increasingly put to good use in Asian and Pacific cities:

Participation and representation. In most Asian-Pacific cities urban populations participate in ballots to elect local representatives, i.e., councillors and mayors. While local elections generally secure fair degrees of public participation, the fact that the lowest tiers of municipal authority generally lack resources to pursue public programmes acts as a major hindrance. With ever more complex urban conditions and pervasive globalization, grassroots and special-interest groups as well as non-governmental organizations have demanded greater participation in local affairs. Beside local elections, the most direct form of participation includes referendums, petitions and attendance at committee meetings. In China, for instance, direct participation has taken the form of community consultation and dialogue with local officials. In the Republic of Korea, urban communities have come up with frequent demands for audits of, and investigations in, government programmes. In Thailand, the government has set up a "court of governance" which citizens can turn to in order to resolve conflicts with public authorities. Participatory policymaking has been introduced in a number of Asian-Pacific cities, for instance in India and Pakistan, as mentioned above. Some Asian-Pacific governments have deployed 'accommodating' policies that include marginalized groups in governance; for example, most low-cost housing programmes for the urban poor in Asian cities now include clear provisions for self-help, mutual aid and co-financing, as well as tapping the capacities of the urban poor themselves in a bid to augment limited government resources through so-called 'enabling' strategies.

Participatory budgeting. Participatory budgeting leads to improvements in infrastructure, services and accountability, but various elements in Asian urban governance are standing in the way. Participatory budgeting, whereby ordinary residents decide local resource allocations among competing items, has been quite late in coming to the Asia-Pacific region but it is gaining in popularity. In Pune, India, municipal authorities enabled participatory budgeting to involve residents at the ward level. Pilot projects on participatory budgeting implemented by the Asian Development Bank in Indonesia and Pakistan showed that: (i) municipal technical staff tended to dominate the budgetary process; (ii) community leaders and local politicians tended to be the main participants; (iii) as a result, projects tended to benefit mainly to specific groups, and (iv) the interests of the poor and marginalized groups were upheld only when vocal civil society and other non-governmental organizations championed their own causes. These lessons are useful for the promotion of participatory budgeting in Asian cities.

The mechanisms for accountability and transparency. Two of the most serious governance problems in Asian cities are how to enhance the transparency of public decision-making and how government officials can be made more accountable for their actions. Although legislation formally enhances transparency and accountability, corruption remains a serious issue in many Asian countries. The following measures and practices have put Asian urban authorities in a better position to tackle corruption: (i) turning corruption (specifically with regard to bribery, embezzlement, theft, fraud, extortion or abuse of authority) into a criminal offence, as in Hong Kong, China, and Singapore; (ii) adoption of a Code of Ethics to guide daily routines, as in the case of 'City Managers' Association Gujarat'; (iii) a strong and vocal press has not only enhanced transparency but also restrained corruption; and (iv) civil society activism has also forced local authorities to become more transparent and accountable.

New technologies and e-governance. Recent advances in information and communication technologies (ICTs) in Asia have had significant effects on urban governance. Many local authorities have by now introduced computers and the Internet in governance systems. Application of new technologies to governance ranges from improved transport management to accounting systems, payment of municipal charges, property assessment, tax collection, police operations, on-line response to public enquiries, grievances or complaints, electronic libraries, as well as information collection and dissemination campaigns (as in India and Malaysia). The new technologies have also enhanced efficiency with a shift away from manual paperwork, enabling a significant degree of services consolidation, for instance, the One-Stop Processing Centre for foreign companies looking to invest in projects in Suzhou, China. At the moment, three issues stand in the way of more widespread application of information and communication technologies to e-governance: (i) *equity*, as there is a wide gap among citizens (and geographical areas) in terms of access to electronic communication (the 'digital divide'); (ii) *interoperability* among the vast variety of information and communications systems available in the region; and (iii) *security* as applied to dealings with public authorities (related to the problems of computer hacking, identity theft, etc.).

Local authorities must strive to implement the above-mentioned principles if the practice of urban governance is to improve in Asian and Pacific cities. An increasing number of examples is available within the region for other cities to learn from and adapt to local circumstances.

1.6.3 Types of urban governance systems

Asian-Pacific urban governance systems involve autonomous municipal corporations, metropolitan bodies and central government. Also involved are smaller local government units like districts, regencies, prefectures, cantonments and neighbourhood councils, but these are usually in a state of functional or other subordination under constitutional provisions or legislation. Municipal authorities are typically governed by charters that specify their objectives, territorial scope, structure and functionalities. Metropolitan entities can be set up by municipal bodies in a bid to create region-wide federations, or alternatively they can be imposed by higher tiers of government. Central government is usually in charge of the areas where national capital cities are located (e.g., the Kuala Lumpur federal territory in Malaysia and the Bangkok Municipal Authority in Thailand).

The governance of towns and smaller cities. In almost all towns and smaller cities in the Asia-Pacific region, governance structures include a policymaking body such as a town or city council and an executive arm like a mayor. For all the efforts at decentralization and local autonomy, most municipal officials are, in fact, vested with only limited authority and power, and any effectiveness they may have is a function of linkages with national legislative or executive bodies, including government departments. *Many smaller urban settlements are finding it difficult to achieve development goals due to inadequate financial, human, institutional and legal resources or frameworks, as well as poor political leadership, but national governments tend to ignore their predicament.*

City cluster development. City cluster development promotes the potential of cities and towns within a single urban region through strategic links with a combination of urban infrastructure and services as well as innovative financing schemes. Drawing the lessons of cluster-based economic and industrial development as a way of enhancing the competitiveness of certain areas where resources are concentrated, the Asian Development Bank has adopted the approach as an integral part of a long-term strategy designed to reduce poverty through "inclusive development and growth promoting activities." Well-formulated and well-executed city cluster development schemes can bring a number of benefits, including the following:

- Deployment of integrated urban infrastructure and services over whole city-regions, rather than confined to individual towns and cities.

- Availability of financial and other resources to develop urban clusters, with common taxation standards and operations, improved credit ratings and more equitable tax burdens among cities and towns in any given cluster.

- Better opportunities for attracting private sector participation in area-wide development projects, especially those focused on urban infrastructure and services.

- Improved capacity to deal with urban problems like environmental pollution, health, flooding and others that ignore political boundaries.

- Inclusive development that integrates both urban and rural areas in a region.

The methodology can give rise to planned development of clusters of towns and small cities or urban authorities located close to a large city within a metropolitan region. The development of the Bangkok-centred region shows how the cluster process can help plan mega-city expansion.

Clustered development and smaller city-regions. Smaller city-regions generally lack urban infrastructure and services. Because urbanized nodes are typically separated from each other by rural areas, building and managing integrated infrastructure and services is expensive. In these conditions, the clustered development approach can enhance integrated development of urban and rural areas through well-planned, comprehensive provision of urban infrastructure and services. The method can also be used to strengthen economic links among urban clusters. China, India and Japan have used the city cluster approach for the planning and development of urban nodes and their rural hinterlands.

Since the highest rates of urban growth in Asia are found in smaller cities and towns, these must be empowered to manage their own development. Urban governance initiatives should be directed to smaller settlements, in the process stimulating development in adjoining rural areas. Well-formulated, well-executed city cluster development schemes can bring a number of benefits, including much-needed employment and integrated infrastructure and services.

The governance of metropolitan and mega urban regions. In recent years, most Asian governments have been focused on mega-cities and mega urban regions. These sprawling city-regions are usually governed by a plurality of bodies, and on top of this also suffer from administrative fragmentation among central and provincial/state departments and agencies. Lack of cooperation or coordination among urban authorities and central and provincial/state bodies poses major challenges to metropolitan planning and governance. In general, Asian governments currently resort to three types of approaches for the governance of metropolitan areas and city-regions:

(i) *Autonomous urban authorities*, where cities, towns and municipalities within a city-region are distinct from each other both functionally and territorially. Every local authority is in charge of its own planning, policymaking, regulations and programme/project execution.

(ii) *Mixed systems of regional governance*, where authority and power are vested in formal structures such as central government departments, regional authorities, metropolitan bodies, special-purpose authorities, cities, towns and villages. Each of these government bodies is responsible for functions such as policy-setting, financing, planning and implementation of programmes and projects. Specific functions can be carried out by separate agencies operating at different levels. These functions can also be shared by a number of government bodies.

(iii) *Unified metropolitan government*, where city-regions come under a single governing body which plans, manages, finances, supports and maintains services in an area-wide territory. Any local authorities within the city-region are subordinated to the unified government. This approach has been used mainly in national capitals where the central government's authority is dominant (e.g., Seoul).

Historical and cultural factors have influenced the evolution of each type of governance system. Each type also comes with specific benefits and shortcomings.

Mixed systems of government are predominant in Asia and are well-placed to bring about more comprehensive planning, mobilize appropriate financial resources, improve management efficiency, and involve the private sector.

1.6.4 Mega urban regional development

The emergence of mega urban regions in Asia has posed serious challenges to both urban planning and governance. According to UN-HABITAT, "Mega-regions, urban corridors and city-regions reflect the emerging links between city growth and new patterns of economic activity. These regional systems are creating a new urban hierarchy and the scope, range and complexity of issues involved require innovative coordination mechanisms for urban management and governance". Traditional approaches to planning in the region have focused on the physical dimension, i.e., building and maintaining infrastructure and services. However, this focus on 'hardware' is sorely inadequate when it comes to managing the growth of mega urban regions whose development is closely linked to the economic and social forces of globalization. Governing frameworks in mega urban regions are extremely fragmented: vertical division among various tiers of government (national, regional, metropolitan, city, district and neighbourhood) mixes with the functional fragmentation of government departments (public works, transportation and communications, environmental control) and territorial fragmentation (metropolitan area, chartered cities, municipalities, villages). An important challenge posed by mega urban regions is the need to manage and govern the multiple political jurisdictions at work in expanded built-up areas.

Mega urban regions in Asia-Pacific need new urban planning and governance structures. The scope, range and complexity of issues faced by these regional urban systems require innovative coordination mechanisms for urban management and governance. The World Bank has identified the three main issues that these configurations face, namely:

- Coordination, "conceiving the development of cities in parallel with the development of regions and subregions, rather than isolated nodes in economic space", a process that calls on metropolitan, regional and even national planners to work together;

- Broader plans for regional planning/development, "requiring dispersion of specific urban functions (i.e., solid waste treatment, airports, skills and training centres) within a continuous region, rather than crowding them in a large city"; and

- Coping with horizontal fiscal disparities, and more specifically "designing mechanisms to transfer fiscal resources among urban governments in a region."

1.6.5 Decentralization and government functions

In their decentralising drive, Asian governments have resorted to three types of policies: *deconcentration, administrative delegation* and *political devolution* of authority and power.

- *Deconcentration* shifts administrative responsibilities for urban affairs from central government ministries and departments to regional and local bodies, establishing field offices and transferring some decision-making to field staff.
- *Delegation* involves shifting management authority from the central government to local authorities, semi-autonomous or parastatal bodies, state enterprises,

regional planning or area development agencies, as well as multi- or single-purpose public authorities.

- *Devolution* is a form of decentralization that involves the transfer of authority and power from central to local government units with the aim of enabling the latter to provide services and infrastructure, raise local revenue, and to formulate, adopt and carry out policies and programmes. Recent decentralization in India and the Philippines is a good example.

If urban governance is to be effective and sustainable, devolution of authority and power to urban authorities is needed, along with adequate financial, revenue-raising and human capacities. Decentralization requires central government support to avoid excessive regional disparities within countries.

1.6.6 Financing urban development

Urban authorities in Asia would need to spend close to US $10 trillion over 10 years if they were to meet all their requirements in terms of infrastructures and institutional frameworks.

In almost all Asian cities, the lack of financial, human and technological resources poses a serious challenge to good governance. It has been said that many Asian countries have "rich cities, but [economically] poor city governments." One possible reason for this is that most urban authorities in the region are not using to the full their powers to raise revenue from local sources. As a result, they are heavily dependent on tax revenue allocations, grants-in-aid and other forms of financial assistance from central and provincial/state government. Furthermore, the power of urban authorities to borrow from domestic and foreign sources to finance infrastructure and other capital-intensive projects is often legally constrained by central government. Institutional and private sector investors as well as foreign venture capitalists are often reluctant to extend credit for local urban projects without national government ('sovereign') guarantees. The following outlines the various sources of finance for urban development in Asian and Pacific region, and the related issues:

Intergovernmental transfers. Although recent decentralization drives have given urban governments more authority and power to raise revenue and decide on expenditures (such as in Thailand), they have traditionally been heavily dependent on central government fund transfers. When determining the allocation of authority between central and urban or local authorities, governments face two problems: *vertical imbalance,* where the bulk of resources go to central government, creating a serious "fiscal gap" at the local level; and *horizontal imbalance,* where inequality occurs across various local government units with different developmental resources and capacities.

Local revenue sources. In Asia, local authorities have the power to collect revenue within their jurisdictions. However, the tax base is rather limited for those revenues which local authorities can keep. In fact, the bulk of local revenues are collected by central governments under the form of personal or corporate income taxes, import duties, value-added (VAT) and excise taxes, user charges and income from government enterprises.

Property-based taxes. These are considered to be the most appropriate sources of local revenue, and one that is typically used to fund urban development and services. Still, evidence shows that in Asia, property tax proceeds account for less than 20 per cent of local authority revenues. As some of those authorities have found, streamlining collection and property assessment systems (such as the unit-area method in India), combined with information technology (and geographic information systems (GIS) in particular), has dramatically improved property tax collection.

Domestic and foreign borrowings. With their fairly large capital amounts, long durations and revenue-generating capacity, large urban infrastructure projects lend themselves well to domestic or foreign borrowings (including syndicated bank loans and bond issues). China and India have issued bonds to finance urban infrastructure. In most Asian countries, though, the problem with domestic or foreign market borrowings has to do with lack of access: either because it is formally restricted (especially in the case of foreign borrowings), or because local banking or financial markets are not large enough, or because borrowers are not considered suitable for one reason or another. This is where regional development banks and their financial expertise can play a significant intermediary role. The Asian Development Bank, for one, has started issuing local currency loans that enable cities and other local authorities or bodies to avoid foreign exchange risk on interest and principal payments, making project costs more predictable.

The private sector and urban infrastructure finance. Private sector participation (PSP) is playing an increasingly significant role in urban Asia as a source of both revenue and management expertise. The benefits of private sector participation include access to capital in order to finance significant infrastructure projects, together with the ability to use the advanced technologies offered by modern firms and to secure funding from regional or global financial institutions that are familiar with the PSP format. China has taken advantage of these features in a large number of projects, so much so that by 2005, it was estimated that more than 40 per cent of the country's total output, 60 per cent of economic growth and 75 per cent of new employment were contributed by the private sector.

Privatization of urban infrastructure and services. In many Asian cities, the private sector currently carries out the financing, operation and management of urban infrastructures such as transport, electricity, gas supply, telecommunications, and solid waste collection and disposal. All government does is to set policies and procedures for private companies to go by. The main argument in favour of privatization is that private companies tend to be more efficient than public bodies when it comes to managing business-like operations like public utilities. The crucial issue facing urban authorities in Asia is how to determine the benefits and drawbacks of privatization schemes. Important questions raised by privatization include: (i) Are such schemes really more efficient and cost-effective than publicly-run utilities? (ii) Do such schemes actually tap into private sector capital and expertise? (iii) How does privatization affect the lives of the urban poor? (iv) Are privatization schemes conducive to political interference, anomalies, graft or corruption?

Land as a resource for development. In Asian cities, urban land is a frequently neglected resource. Tapping land as a resource is a distinct advantage in socialist countries like China and Viet Nam where land is owned by government. In these countries, land is usually not sold outright but leased for periods of 50 to 70 years. Land use fees fund urban infrastructure and services, with the attendant drawback that such investment tends to encourage short-term developments. Elsewhere in Asia, where land is privately owned, using it as a resource to support development is a more complex endeavour. In these countries (for instance, Bangladesh, India, the Philippines and the Republic of Korea), the government must purchase private land at fair market value if it is to be used for public purposes, though the process can entail expensive and long drawn-out litigation.

1.6.7 Performance in service delivery management

Water supply and sanitation. Traditionally in urban Asia, water providers tended to be more interested in expanding networks than in proper management. As a result, under the Millennium Development Goals, sustainable access to drinking water and basic sanitation has improved between 1990 and 2008. However in recent years, good water managers have highlighted demand regulation and management as a solution to water problems. Demand regulation and management includes rational allocation of water among competing users based on a system of priorities, using quotas as a method of water allocation, and appropriate pricing. In the past few years, some utilities have proved particularly successful against various socio-economic and political backgrounds, such as Hai Phong, Jamshedpur (India), Manila, Phnom Penh and Singapore. Their experience can provide a basis for performance improvement by others. Experience has shown that community involvement in sanitation can help improve the provision of and access to these services.

Successful experiences in utility management should be replicated in order to improve water supply and sanitation services in Asian-Pacific cities.

Solid waste collection and disposal. One of the major challenges faced by Asian-Pacific cities is the collection and disposal of solid waste. Most urban authorities have set up specialist departments to deal with this issue, but their efforts are often complemented by community-based alternatives where voluntary grassroots groups fill the gaps in waste collection. This type of scheme is found in Bangalore (garbage collection and composting), Dhaka (marketing of backyard-produced compost), Chennai (collection, sorting, recycling and composting), and Delhi and Hanoi (garbage collection and recycling). However, in many instances, private solid waste collection and disposal companies and local government units have not been supportive, often viewing civil society groups as overly critical and, at times, confrontational competitors. As a result, these environment-concerned efforts have rarely been integrated into municipal solid waste management systems.

Local authorities should build and facilitate partnerships with civil society initiatives and community-based alternatives in order to improve solid waste collection and disposal services.

1.6.8 Cooperation networks

The recognition of good governance as a vital development instrument has given rise to national, regional and global cooperative networks that enable various types of participants to exchange ideas, best practice and lessons learned, sharing them with municipal officials, administrators and researchers. United Cities and Local Government (UCLG) is a worldwide association of local government organizations dating back to 1913. The UCLG Asia-Pacific Regional Section supports "strong and effective democratic local self-government throughout the region/world through promotion of unity and cooperation among members" and facilitates information exchange among local authorities in the region. CITYNET, a regional network of local authorities, supports the strengthening of institutional planning and management capabilities at the local and grassroots levels through technical cooperation among local authorities as well as governmental and non-governmental bodies.

In almost all Asian countries, associations of local governments and local government officials are there to support good governance. For all their hard work, four main factors tend to dampen their effectiveness, namely: (i) most local officials belong to political parties and partisan groups and this tends to make sustained and truly collaborative actions difficult; (ii) elective local officials may be in office only for short periods, which stands in the way of continuity in policies and programmes; (iii) many of the associations lack the financial and technical capacities required for effective good governance programmes; and (iv) given the wide variety of local governance systems in Asia, lessons learned in one jurisdiction might not be replicable in others.

Local government associations should promote city-to-city ('C2C') cooperation in order to support sharing and exchange of lessons learnt and good practices in the areas of sustainable urban development and good urban governance.

1.7 The Structure of the Report

This first-ever *State of Asian Cities Report 2010/11* (the Report) is divided into five chapters. Throughout the Report, an effort has been made to discuss the inclusive and sustainable urban development issues, based on the latest information available and documenting good practices and examples in boxed items. The Report uses the demographic data from the *World Urbanization Prospects 2009*, the latest available from the United Nations.

Chapter 2, *Urbanising Asia*, reviews urban demographic trends and patterns in Asia-Pacific and its five subregions; this includes the 'youth bulge' and population ageing; the factors behind emerging mega-cities, mega urban regions and urban corridors; the demographic growth and roles of small- and medium-sized cities and towns, and their development challenges; and urban densities and the pace urbanisation in Asian and Pacific region.

Chapter 3, *the Economic Role of Asian Cities*, focuses on the role of Asian cities as engines of economic growth: the trends prevailing in the five subregions; the main drivers of their urban economies; and the issues related to urbanisation and the informal economy. The Chapter shows how Asia is gradually diversifying away from the role of the 'factory of the world' to embrace the global 'knowledge economy' and develop international financial centres, with the challenges the region faces in this process. The Chapter concludes with a review of the role of Asian cities in local development.

Chapter 4, *Poverty and Inequality in Asian Cities*, lists the region's achievements with regard to extreme poverty and examines the challenges of deprivation and inequality. The Chapter commends Asia for improving the lives of 172 million slum-dwellers over the past decade, well beyond the relevant Millennium Development Goal. The Chapter goes on to discuss the critical issues of land and housing as well as access to basic urban services.

Chapter 5, *the Urban Environment and Climate Change*, looks into the challenges of economic growth and environmental sustainability, which are particularly acute in Asian-Pacific cities. The defining features of the environmental challenges are discussed, followed by a review of current conditions. With regard to cities and climate change, the Report examines the issues of mitigation and adaptation, and highlights some good practice. By way of conclusion, the Chapter outlines the ways in which urban planning and management could be improved to tackle environmental and climate change issues.

Chapter 6, *Urban Governance, Management and Finance*, first discusses urban governance and operational structures, and proceeds with a review of the principles of urban governance and their practice in Asian and Pacific region. The types of urban governance systems operating in Asia today are examined next, followed by a review of mega urban regional development and its challenges, and decentralization efforts in Asia. The various institutional frameworks for financing of urban development are reviewed in detail, followed by a discussion of performance in service delivery management. Finally, the Chapter highlights the role of regional and national cooperation networks of local authorities (especially city-to-city) and the challenges they face.

A *Statistical Annex* features the latest urban data available from the UN *World Urbanization Prospects 2009*. Data of slums and related issues are reproduced from the *State of the World's Cities 2010/11* and the *2010 Update of the Joint Monitoring Programme for Water Supply and Sanitation*.

PART
02
Urbanizing Asia

Quick Facts

1. Asia is urbanising rapidly but the region's population is still predominantly rural. However, the urbanization rates vary widely, from 33% in South and South-West Asia and 63 per cent in North and Central Asia to 70 per cent in the Pacific in 2010.

2. While the world population became predominantly urban in 2008, this 'tipping point' will not occur in Asia before 2026.

3. Nearly half the world's urban population now lives in Asian cities which, during the next decade, will absorb two-thirds of the growth in the world's urban population.

4. The number of mega-cities (those with populations of 10 million or more) is increasing around the world and half of the world's mega-cities (11 out of 21) are now found in Asia. Seven of the 10 most populous cities are in Asia.

5. Many urban agglomerations in Asia are evolving into mega urban regions and urban corridors.

6. Sixty per cent of Asia's urban population lives in urban areas with populations under one million.

7. Small- and medium-sized cities act as economic growth centres, but most lack adequate infrastructure and services.

8. Asian cities are characterised by high population densities and decreasing annual growth rates, averaging 2.2 per cent in 2010 (against 3.8 per cent in the 1980s).

Policy Points

1. Governments should encourage balanced urban growth, steering private capital expenditure towards cities of different sizes.

2. Urban and regional infrastructure should be given a higher priority in national development strategies.

3. The ageing phenomenon and reduced fertility rates will affect most Asian countries within one or two generations. Education and urbanisation policies should be better coordinated to address this problem.

4. Full advantage should be taken of the agglomeration effect and economies of scale provided by mega urban regions, which are already the engines of growth in many countries.

5. Since small- and medium-sized cities in the Asia-Pacific region will continue to host around 50 per cent of urban populations in the next two decades, policymakers should focus on their needs regarding infrastructure and basic urban services, and increase urban governance capacities.

6. Local authorities should see the forthcoming slowdown in urban demographic growth rates as an opportunity better to manage cities while maintaining the high densities and limited ecological footprints that characterize Asian conurbations.

Chengdu, China. ©Mark Henley/Panos Pictures

2.1
Urbanization trends

Old Dehli, India. Nearly half the world's urban population now lives in Asian cities. ©**Jeremy Richards/Shutterstock**

The process of urbanization in developing countries has captured media attention. This is partly because the year 2008 marked a watershed in world history – the point where more than half the world's population lived in places designated as urban (UN-HABITAT, 2008). With rapid economic growth in many countries, Asia is on a similar path, though with a significant lag. The region is expected to take some 15 years for the urban segment of its overall population to increase from 41.7 per cent in 2009 to 50 per cent at the beginning of 2026.

Asia is the largest of all major regions with 30 per cent of the global land mass and 60 per cent of world's population. With an urbanization rate of 41.7 per cent in 2009, Asia ranked as the second least-urbanized major region of the world after Africa's 39.6 per cent. Asian cities are home to 1.7 billion people, nearly half the urban population of the world. This proportion is expected to increase slightly by 2020, when Asian cities will be host to 2.2 billion of the world's 4.2 billion urban population. Between 2009 and 2020, a total 450 million people will be added to Asian cities, or 60 per cent of the growth in the world's urban population.

Asia's urban population has grown from 31.5 per cent of the total in 1990 to a projected 42.2 per cent in 2010. Due to the region's large size and diversity, urbanization patterns are geographically uneven. It is particularly important to point out that overall trends are dominated by two demographic giants, China and India. These two nations together account for 2.5 billion people and therefore include more than 37 per cent of the world's total population. Moreover, six of the world's most heavily populated countries are found in Asia: China, India, Indonesia, Pakistan, Bangladesh and Japan. Together, these account for 45 per cent of the global population and 77 per cent of all Asians (Biau, 2007).

Why has urbanization been, on the whole, a much slower process in Asia than in most of the rest of the world? Five distinct factors are at work here. First, there are varying definitions of what is 'urban' (see Box 2.1). Second, most countries define a place as 'urban' based on administrative criteria. Thus urbanization and urban population growth rates may be under-reported. On the other hand, there are also cases where municipal boundaries include rural populations. Fourth, where population growth occurs in the urban periphery, which may be beyond municipal or city boundaries, this may not be

BOX 2.1: THE DEFINITION OF 'URBAN' IN ASIA

'Urban' population refers to the *de facto* population living in areas classified as 'urban' according to the criteria used by each area or country. Far from any common, Asian-wide definition of what is 'urban', the variety of criteria is bewildering. For example, of the 26 countries and territories in Asia surveyed by the UN Economic and Social Commission for Asia and the Pacific (ESCAP), 15 define urban areas based on administrative criteria and another four based on population size and/or density; two countries categorize as 'urban' those areas where certain economic functions or infrastructures and services are available, and in the remaining five countries in the sample, 'urban' refers to a combination of administrative boundaries, population size and density (ESCAP, 2008a:17).

Below is a select list of definitions used to classify a settlement as 'urban' in the Asia-Pacific region.

Cambodia: Towns as notified by the government.

China: 'City' only refers to the city proper, as designated by the State Council. In the case of cities with district status, the city proper refers to the whole administrative area of the district if the population density is 1,500 per square kilometre or higher, or the seat of the district government, and other areas or streets under the administration of the district if the population density is less than 1,500 per sq km In the case of cities without district status, the city proper refers to the seat of the city government and other areas or streets under the administration of the city. As for city districts with population densities below 1,500 per sq km and cities without district status, if the urban construction of the district or city government seat has extended to some part of the neighbouring designated town(s) or township(s), the city proper does include the whole administrative area of the town(s) or township(s).

India: 'Urban' refers to towns (places with a municipal corporation, municipal area committee, town committee, notified area committee or cantonment board). Also considered 'urban' are places with populations of 5,000 or more, a density of no less than 1,000 per sq. m. (or 400 per sq km) with pronounced urban characteristics and at least 75 per cent of the adult male population employed in pursuits other than agriculture.

Indonesia: Places with urban characteristics.

Islamic Republic of Iran: Every district with a municipality.

Japan: A city (*'shi'*) is host to 50,000 or more, with 60 per cent or more of the houses located in the main built-up areas and 60 per cent or more of the population (including dependants) engaged in manufacturing, trade or other urban type of business. Alternatively, a *shi* with urban facilities and conditions as defined by a prefectural order is considered as urban.

Republic of Korea: Any amount of population living in designated cities.

Malaysia: Formally designated areas with populations of 10,000 or more.

Maldives: Malé, the capital.

Mongolia: The capital and district centres.

Pakistan: Places with a municipal corporation, town committee or cantonment.

Sri Lanka: All municipal and urban council areas.

Thailand: Municipal areas.

Viet Nam: Urban districts or quarters and towns. All other local administrative units (*'communes'*) belong to rural areas.

Source: United Nations, 2005 (footnotes to Table 6)

---

reflected in official urban statistics. Finally, many large Asian countries like China, India, Pakistan and Bangladesh are still predominantly rural, with about one-third of their population living in urban areas. In the largest countries such as China and India, economic growth is a more recent phenomenon and has a significant influence on the region's urban population growth. China is expected to become 50 per cent urban sometime between 2010 and 2020, while India will have to wait for another three decades or so.

Although Asia's overall urbanization rate is admittedly low, the next two decades are to see unprecedented urban demographic growth. Urbanization in Asia typically comes with the economic transition from low-productivity agriculture to higher-productivity industry and services. Cities have stood at the forefront of the rapid economic growth prevailing in many Asian countries; this is because they have been able to attract manufacturing and services, the concentration of which enhances productivity and growth. These so-called 'agglomeration economies' in Asian cities have facilitated integration into regional and global markets. For all their relatively low rates of demographic growth, the region's cities have made significant economic contributions

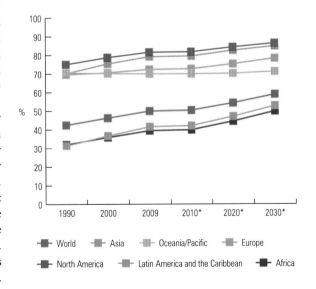

CHART 2.1: **GLOBAL URBANIZATION RATES, 1990-2030**

Legend: World, Asia, Oceania/Pacific, Europe, North America, Latin America and the Caribbean, Africa

* Projections
Source: United Nations (2010)

URBANIZING ASIA

31

TABLE 2.1: **URBAN SHARE IN TOTAL POPULATION, 1990-2030***

REGION	1990	2000	2009	2010*	2020*	2030*
World	42.6	46.4	50.1	50.5	54.4	59.0
Asia	31.5	36.8	41.7	42.2	47.2	52.9
Oceania/Pacific	70.7	70.4	70.2	70.2	70.4	71.4
Europe	69.8	70.8	72.5	72.8	75.4	78.4
North America	75.4	79.1	81.9	82.1	84.6	86.7
Latin America and the Caribbean	70.3	75.5	79.3	79.6	82.6	84.9
Africa	32.1	36.0	39.6	40.0	44.6	50.0

* Projections.
Source: United Nations (2010)

to national output (see Chapter 3 for details). For instance in Viet Nam, 30 per cent of the population live in urban areas (2010) but contribute 70 per cent of gross domestic product (GDP). In China, 120 cities contribute as much as 75 per cent of the country's economic production. In the Republic of Korea, the capital area of Seoul produces about half of the country's wealth, while in the Philippines the contribution of Metropolitan Manila and its surrounding areas is about 60 per cent (World Bank, 2007a).

In many Asian countries, economic growth is reflected in rapid urban expansion. In the Asia-Pacific region as a whole, the urban population grew an average 2.8 per cent a year between 1990 and 2010, or higher than an overall (rural plus urban) 2.4 per cent pace. Moreover, this urban population is expected to increase by two-thirds over the next two decades (i.e., between 2010 and 2030), implying that 53 per cent of the world's urban population growth will occur in Asia – an annual addition of 840 million, or a daily increase of 115,000 (United Nations, 2010) see Table 2.1. Managing this transformation will pose enormous challenges to local and national governments.

The diversity of urbanization patterns in Asia

In the past, urbanization patterns in Asia were a function of trade and colonization, with the region already a major contributor to world trade. Settlements developed with trade along the land-based Silk Road and maritime routes within Asia and all the way to the West. Many of these urban settlements later also became seats of political power. Colonization spawned urban processing and trade centres specializing in raw materials and agricultural products. Many settlements developed as harbour towns or administrative centres.

More recently, economic growth on the back of manufacturing and services sector expansion has led to accelerated urbanization in Asia (see Chart 2.2). Both demographic and economic patterns have remained diverse across the region, although up until the 1960s economic growth was concentrated in a few highly urbanized countries, with most others remaining largely rural. Subsequent accelerated growth in the 1980s and 1990s changed Asia's demographic features[1] and four distinct patterns have emerged in the region, as follows:

(i) Well-developed countries combine high rates of urbanization (exceeding 60 per cent) and low urban growth rates, like Japan (see Box 2.2) and the Republic of Korea.

(ii) Other countries, like Malaysia and the Philippines, feature urbanization rates (40 to 60 per cent) and urban growth rates (two to four per cent) that are both moderate to high.

(iii) Some other countries combine low rates of urbanization (under 40 per cent) and fast-growing urban populations, as is typical of China and India.

(iv) Another pattern of urbanization matches low with slow-growing urban populations, as is the case in Myanmar, Nepal (see Box 2.3) and the Lao People's Democratic Republic.

▲
Yangon City, Myanmar. Myanmar features a low urban growth rate.
©**UN-HABITAT/ Veronica Wijaya**

BOX 2.2: JAPAN: ASIA'S MOST URBANIZED COUNTRY

Japan has a long urban history and currently combines a high degree of urbanization with slow demographic growth. Urbanization and economic development have occurred in tandem, and this bears an important lesson for other Asian countries: high urbanization rates do not necessarily come with high economic, social or environmental costs, provided that the urbanization process is properly managed. In Japan's case, this process today is largely due to natural increases rather than to rural migration; although the urban population keeps increasing,

the pace is uneven with a trough in the year 2000, probably reflecting the country's sluggish economic performance at the time.

A number of defining features set Japanese cities apart from their counterparts elsewhere in Asia. First, although the major modern cities have not necessarily proved successful when it came to managing their own expansion, on the whole they can be commended for bringing about stable, well-balanced communities. Much of this success is attributable to high national incomes and a social structure characterised by a narrow gap between

rich and poor. This equity-orientated, egalitarian approach is a unique feature of Japanese cities. Starting with the post-war dissolution of the 'zaibatsu' (family-run conglomerates), a series of equality-orientated policies – including the local tax system and income redistribution through social security schemes, with Keynesian approaches to economic development and public sector management – proved quite successful.

Second, Japanese cities cater well to the basic needs of everyday life such as health care, peace and security. Average life expectancy in the country is 81.9 years, with the infant mortality rate at a very low 0.3 per cent – both of these figures being among the very best in Asia. Thanks to a low crime rate, Japan is also known as one of the safest countries in the world.

Third, Japanese cities promote harmony with the environment. Although they have had their share of problems due to rapid economic growth, they have overcome many of them. For instance, most of the cities that had flourished during the country's economic boom had to face major environmental challenges such as extensive air and water pollution by manufacturing industries. Municipal authorities have responded with a series of well-adapted environmental policies while also deploying more energy-efficient urban configurations.

TABLE 2.2: URBANIZATION IN JAPAN

Year	Total Population (1,000s)	Urban Population (1,000s)	Urban Population (%)	Average Annual Urban Growth Rate (%)
1990	123 191	77 726	63.1	0.82 (1985-1990)
1995	125 442	81 079	64.6	0.48 (1990-1995)
2000	126 706	82 633	65.2	0.18 (1995-2000)
2005	127 449	84 068	66.0	0.23 (2000-2005)
2010*	126 995	84 875	66.8	0.26 (2005-2010)
2015*	125 791	85 527	68.0	0.34 (2010-2015)
2020*	123 664	85 848	69.4	0.42 (2015-2020)

*Projections
Source: United Nations (2010)

Tokyo, Japan. ©Neale Cousland/Shutterstock

CHART 2.2: **ASIA'S URBANIZATION TRENDS, 1970-2030***

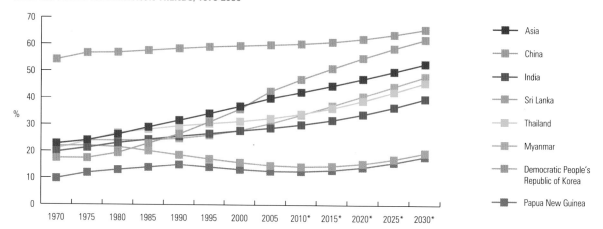

Legend:
- Asia
- China
- India
- Sri Lanka
- Thailand
- Myanmar
- Democratic People's Republic of Korea
- Papua New Guinea

*Projections
Source: United Nations (2010)

BOX 2.3: **NEPAL: ONE OF ASIA'S LEAST URBANIZED COUNTRIES**

Nepal is a small country of 29 million people with a 147,000 sq km surface area. Its elongated territory stretches 500 km east-west and 290 km north-south. From a morphological point of view, Nepal lies in a transitional mountain area between the fertile Ganges plain in India and the arid Tibetan plateau. It ranks among the poorest countries in the world with an annual income per head equivalent of US $290, matched by low human development indicators. A large share of the population has little access to basic social services. Nepal is divided into three regions: Mountains, Hills and Terai (lowland plains). With the country's development centred on the capital, Kathmandu, the valley has experienced rapid urbanization. It is host to five of the country's 58 municipalities and to some 30 per cent of the total urban population. These towns act as economic hubs, attracting huge inflows of migrants. The environmental changes taking place in the Kathmandu Valley are a threat to sustainability. Air pollution and, more specifically the concentration of particulate matter, exceeds national and international standards by a wide margin.

The table shows that urban demographic growth peaked in the late 1990s, suggesting a slowdown in the numbers of rural people moving to towns and cities in search of better conditions. Human development has made progress in Nepal in recent years. Poverty has been reduced over the past decade. During that period, social and human development indicators – life expectancy, infant and maternal mortality rates, adult literacy and primary school enrolment – have all improved. Still, Nepal faces immense challenges on the way to stronger growth and sustainable urban development, in view of a tough topography, poor basic infrastructures and the weakness in institutions and governance.

Source: Basyal & Khanal (2001)

▲
Kathmandu Valley is the most urbanized region in Nepal. ©**Shutterstock**

TABLE 2.3: **URBANIZATION IN NEPAL**

Census Year	Urban Population (Million)	Urban Population (%)	Average Annual Urban Growth Rate (%)
1990	1.7	8.9	3.63 (1985-1990)
1995	2.4	10.9	4.15 (1990-1995)
2000	3.3	13.4	4.19 (1995-2000)
2005	4.3	15.9	3.40 (2000-2005)
2010*	5.6	18.6	3.14 (2005-2010)
2015*	7.0	21.6	2.95 (2010-2015)
2020*	8.7	24.8	2.76 (2015-2020)

*Projections
Source: United Nations (2010)

Christchurch, New Zealand. Urbanization rates vary considerably across the Asia-Pacific region. ©Tupungato/Shutterstock

Sub-regional variations in Asia and the Pacific

North and Central Asia and the Pacific stand out as the most urbanized areas in the whole region (see Chart 2.3 and Table 2.4). In the Pacific, this is largely due to Australia and New Zealand, where more than 85 per cent (2009) of the population live in urban areas. However, among the Pacific island-states, only a few feature large proportions of urban populations while in many others these are very low (under 25 per cent) (ESCAP, 2008a). In North and Central Asia, urban areas are host to over 50 per cent of the population in most countries, with the exception of Kyrgyzstan and Tajikistan, where the proportion remains under 35 per cent. This subregion is the only one in Asia-Pacific where the urban population has not increased over the last two decades, demonstrating patterns more akin to those observed in Europe. In contrast, the East and North-East Asia has urbanized rapidly over the last two decades and is estimated to have crossed the 50 per cent mark in 2010. South-East Asia's urban growth has closely tracked that of Asia as a whole. South and South-West Asia remain the least urbanized, with under 40 per cent of the population living in urban areas. In the more heavily populated countries of the subregion, like India and Bangladesh, urbanization rates remain very close to 30 per cent.

CHART 2.3: **PERCENTAGE OF URBAN POPULATIONS IN THE ASIA-PACIFIC REGION**

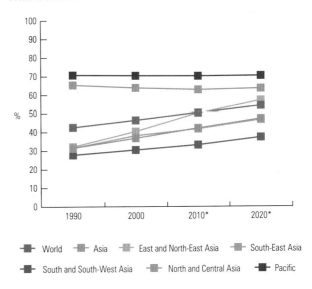

*Projections
Note: The trend-lines for South-East Asia and Asia as a whole track each other very closely.
Source: United Nations (2010)

REGION	Urban Population (1,000s)				Percentage Urban (%)			
	1990	2000	2010*	2020*	1990	2000	2010*	2020*
World	**2 254 592**	**2 837 431**	**3 486 326**	**4 176 234**	**42.6**	**46.4**	**50.5**	**54.4**
Asia	**1 002 731**	**1 360 900**	**1 757 314**	**2 168 798**	**31.5**	**36.8**	**42.2**	**47.2**
East and North-East Asia	430 533	594 676	784 688	940 684	32.2	40.4	50.2	57.3
South-East Asia	138 996	197 360	246 701	305 412	31.6	38.2	41.8	46.7
South and South-West Asia	351 062	467 323	598 207	765 125	27.9	30.6	33.3	37.4
North and Central Asia	140 475	139 358	137 184	140 435	65.4	63.9	62.9	63.6
Pacific	18 872	21 899	25 059	28 175	70.7	70.4	70.2	70.4

*Projections
Source: United Nations (2010)

CHART 2.4: **URBANIZATION IN EAST AND NORTH-EAST ASIA**

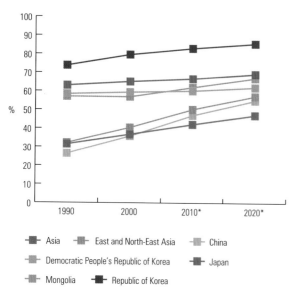

- ■ Asia
- ■ East and North-East Asia
- ■ China
- ■ Democratic People's Republic of Korea
- ■ Japan
- ■ Mongolia
- ■ Republic of Korea

*Projections
Source: United Nations (2010)

2.1.1 Urbanization patterns in Asia-Pacific subregions

East and North-East Asia

East and North-East Asia is rapidly urbanizing. Countries like Japan, Republic of Korea, Democratic People's Republic of Korea and Mongolia are the most urbanized (nearly 68 per cent on average).

The overall degree of urbanization is surprisingly high in Mongolia, despite slow economic growth. Two main factors lie behind the underlying rural migration: (i) rapid conversion from a centrally planned to a market economy, with the attendant dismantling of the agricultural/rural collective and the social services systems, and (ii) a combination of harsh winters and summer droughts in the late 1990s. Mongolia's small urban population is dominated by one city, the capital Ulaanbaatar, which is host to nearly one-third of the country's population. In 2009, the capital was host to 949,000 inhabitants, dwarfing Darkhan the second largest (80,000). In some of the small provincial towns, known as '*aimag*' (country subdivision) centres, populations are shrinking due to migration to Ulaanbaatar.

In the Republic of Korea, too, urban primacy stands out as a defining feature. The Seoul metropolitan area accounts for nearly 25 per cent of the national population, although other urban centres, and especially the port cities of Busan and Ulsan on the south-eastern coast, have grown rapidly over the past two decades.

In China, only 26 per cent of the population was urban in 1990, but recent trends testify to a brisk rate of expansion to a projected 47 per cent in 2010. Such a vast country is bound to feature significant variations across its length and breadth. While the urbanization rate is above 50 per cent in Guangdong province (with Shenzhen and Guangzhou growing rapidly) and Liaoning province (with large cities like Shenyang and Dalian), in the more remote provinces of Yunnan and Tibet less than 20 per cent of the population reside in urban areas. Cities such as Jinan and Qingdao in Shandong province, and Nanjing in Jiangsu province, have experienced rapid demographic growth, but the pace of urbanization remains sluggish in Guizhou and Qinghai provinces. China's rate of urbanization has averaged an annual 3.3 per cent over the last two decades, but is expected to slow down by about 50 per cent over the next 10 years (see Table 2.5).

Thanks to China, East and North-East Asia's population was expected to become more urban than rural in 2010. In contrast to China, though, other countries in the subregion feature low to moderate population growth rates, and urbanization has stabilised as a result. In urban Japan, the net reproduction rate is under one per cent, i.e., each generation of mothers no longer has enough daughters to replace themselves in the population. In the Republic of Korea, the urbanization rate has remained high on the back of the rapid expansion of 'city regions' like Seoul and Busan. Clearly, the

TABLE 2.5: **URBANIZATION IN EAST AND NORTH-EAST ASIA, 1990-2020***

COUNTRY	Urban Population (1,000s)				Percentage Urban (%)			
	1990	2000	2010*	2020*	1990	2000	2010*	2020*
Asia	**1 002 731**	**1 360 900**	**1 757 314**	**2 168 798**	**31.5**	**36.8**	**42.2**	**47.2**
East and North-East Asia	**430 533**	**594 676**	**784 688**	**940 684**	**32.2**	**40.4**	**50.2**	**57.3**
China	301 995	453 029	635 839	786 761	26.4	35.8	47.0	55.0
Democratic People's Republic of Korea	11 760	13 581	14 446	15 413	58.4	59.4	60.2	62.1
Japan	77 726	82 633	84 875	85 848	63.1	65.2	66.8	69.4
Mongolia	1 264	1 358	1 675	2010	57.0	56.9	62.0	67.0
Republic of Korea	31 740	36 967	40 235	42 362	73.8	79.6	83.0	85.6

*Projections
Source: United Nations (2010)

▲
The Republic of Korea has urbanized rapidly over the past two decades. ©JinYoung Lee/Shutterstock

Country	Urban Population (1,000s)				Percentage Urban (%)			
	1990	2000	2010*	2020*	1990	2000	2010*	2020*
Asia	**1 002 731**	**1 360 900**	**1 757 314**	**2 168 798**	**31.5**	**36.8**	**42.2**	**47.2**
South-East Asia	**138 996**	**197 360**	**246 701**	**305 412**	**31.6**	**38.2**	**41.8**	**46.7**
Brunei Darussalam	169	237	308	379	65.8	71.1	75.7	79.3
Cambodia	1 221	2 157	3 027	4 214	12.6	16.9	20.1	23.8
Indonesia	54 252	86 219	102 960	122 257	30.6	42.0	44.3	48.1
Lao PDR	649	1 187	2 136	3 381	15.4	22.0	33.2	44.2
Malaysia	9 014	14 424	20 146	25 128	49.8	62.0	72.2	78.5
Myanmar	10 092	12 956	16 990	22 570	24.7	27.8	33.6	40.7
Philippines	30 333	37 283	45 781	57 657	48.6	48.0	48.9	52.6
Singapore	3 016	4 018	4 837	5 219	100.0	100.0	100.0	100.0
Thailand	16 675	19 417	23 142	27 800	29.4	31.1	34.0	38.9
Timor-Leste	154	198	329	538	20.8	24.3	28.1	33.2
Viet Nam	13 418	19 263	27 046	36 269	20.3	24.5	30.4	37.0

*Projections
Source: United Nations (2010)

CHART 2.5: **URBANIZATION IN SOUTH-EAST ASIA – TRENDS, 1990-2020***

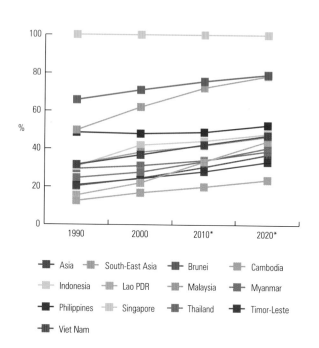

- ■ Asia
- ■ South-East Asia
- ■ Brunei
- ■ Cambodia
- ■ Indonesia
- ■ Lao PDR
- ■ Malaysia
- ■ Myanmar
- ■ Philippines
- ■ Singapore
- ■ Thailand
- ■ Timor-Leste
- ■ Viet Nam

*Projections
Note: The trend-lines for South-East Asia and Asia as a whole track each other very closely.
Source: United Nations (2010)

high urbanization rates prevailing in East and North-East Asia relative to the rest of Asia is largely due to differences in economic development. Japan, the Republic of Korea and China are the economic powerhouses of the global economy, contributing to over one-third of the world's output.

South-East Asia

South-East Asia is the most diverse subregion in the whole Asia-Pacific area: countries like Indonesia, Malaysia and the Philippines feature relatively high urbanization rates, but urban populations remain relatively small in many others like Cambodia, the Lao People's Democratic Republic, Myanmar, Thailand and Viet Nam.

In Cambodia and the Lao People's Democratic Republic, the pace of urban population growth is brisk, but urbanization rates remain low. In both countries, high urban demographic growth is primarily due to large-scale rural-to-urban migration. In Cambodia, after the 1991 Paris Peace Agreement that put an end to three decades of civil unrest and war, the capital Phnom Penh experienced rapid demographic growth. At the same time, several intermediate-sized cities, such as Sihanoukville (with port, manufacturing and tourism activities), Battambang (with a significant agri-business sector), and Siem Reap (which benefits from tourism at Angkor Wat) are also growing as economically viable settlements.

In a large country like Indonesia the urban population grew at a brisk 4.7 per cent annual pace during 1995-2000, which was nearly twice the rate for the whole of Asia (2.9 per cent) during the same period. This pace of urban growth slowed down to 1.7 per cent between 2005 and 2010. In this

▲
The Bangkok Metropolitan Region is host to almost one half of the urban population of Thailand. ©**Alistair Michael Thomas/Shutterstock**

country the bulk of urban demographic growth takes place on the island of Java, which is currently 65 per cent urban. Within this large island, expansion has been concentrated in the 'Jabodetabek' (Jakarta-Bogor-Depok-Tangerang-Bekasi) metropolitan area, which has a population of 17 million. Five other cities are hosts to over a million on Java Island. It must be noted that a substantial part of the rise in urbanization in Indonesia has been due to reclassification of areas from 'rural' to 'urban'. The number of rural '*desa*' (villages) classified as 'urban' almost doubled between 1980 and 1990, from around 3,500 to approximately 6,700. There also has been an increase in the lateral extent of cities, along main transport routes radiating out from major urban areas (Hugo, 2003).

The Philippines is highly urbanized and over 50 per cent of its population are expected to be living in urban areas by 2015. The Extended Metropolitan Manila area is home to more than 12 million and accounts for over one-third of the country's urban population, the growth of which has been slowing down – from a very rapid 5 per cent annual rate between 1960 and 1995, to some 3 per cent since then. Still, in view of the country's relatively slow economic development over the last three decades, this pace of urbanization is rather brisk. This is partly due to the change in the national definition of urban areas. After decentralization, large tracts of rural areas were included into municipal boundaries. This may have led to an overestimation of the urban population during the 1990s.

In contrast to the Philippines, Thailand has undergone rapid economic expansion but its urbanization rate is surprisingly low, being comparable to those of the Lao People's Democratic Republic and Myanmar. This is largely due to the fact that demographic expansion and economic

development in Thailand are concentrated in and around the capital Bangkok. The Bangkok Metropolitan Region (BMR) is host to almost half of the urban population; when the Eastern Seaboard (the area adjoining the metropolitan region) is included, the combined area would account for nearly 80 per cent of the country's urban population. Other factors that contribute to this trend include under-counting of urban populations in nominally rural areas, as well as large numbers of rurally registered migrants in urban areas.

South and South-West Asia

This is one of the least urbanized subregions in Asia and the Pacific. In the two larger countries – India and Bangladesh – seven out of every 10 people still live in rural areas. In 1950, India (17 per cent) was more urbanized than China (12 per cent), but by 2009 China was 46 per cent urban while the proportion in India lagged behind at just under 30 per cent. High concentrations of urban populations can be found in some countries. Dhaka in Bangladesh and Karachi in Pakistan dominate the economic and urban demographic landscapes of their respective countries – one out of three urban dwellers in Bangladesh lives in the capital Dhaka and one in five urban dwellers in Pakistan lives in Karachi, the country's economic capital. In smaller countries like Nepal and Sri Lanka, only one in every five lives in urban areas. These urbanization patterns are comparable to those of many countries in Africa. In recent years, however, many countries in South and South-West Asia have experienced high economic growth. As a consequence, urbanization has been rapid, a pace that is expected to be sustained in future.

India is expected to add 226 million people to its urban areas in the next two decades, with its urbanization rate

Country	Urban Population (1,000s)				Percentage Urban (%)			
	1990	2000	2010*	2020*	1990	2000	2010*	2020*
Asia	**1 002 731**	**1 360 900**	**1 757 314**	**2 168 798**	**31.5**	**36.8**	**42.2**	**47.2**
South and South-West Asia	**351 062**	**467 323**	**598 207**	**765 125**	**27.9**	**30.6**	**33.3**	**37.4**
Afghanistan	2 277	4 148	6 581	10 450	18.1	20.2	22.6	26.4
Bangladesh	22 908	33 208	46 149	62 886	19.8	23.6	28.1	33.9
Bhutan	90	143	246	348	16.4	25.4	34.7	42.4
India	220 260	288 430	364 459	463 328	25.5	27.7	30.0	33.9
Iran (Islamic Republic of)	31 958	42 952	53 120	63 596	56.3	64.2	70.7	75.9
Maldives	56	75	126	186	25.8	27.7	40.1	51.5
Nepal	1 692	3 281	5 559	8 739	8.8	13.4	18.6	24.8
Pakistan	35 400	49 088	66 318	90 199	30.6	33.1	35.9	39.9
Sri Lanka	3 217	2 971	2 921	3 360	18.6	15.8	14.3	15.5
Turkey	33 204	43 027	52 728	62 033	59.2	64.7	69.6	74

*Projections
Source: United Nations (2010)

reaching 39.7 per cent by 2030. Within India, the states of Maharashtra, Gujarat and Tamil Nadu are relatively more industrialised and experience more rapid urban expansion. Their populations are expected to become 50 per cent urban by 2025. However, in those few larger states like Uttar Pradesh, Bihar, Orissa and Assam, where agriculture remains predominant, the proportion of urban to total population remains below 20 per cent.

In Pakistan, Sindh is the most urbanized province with 49 per cent of the population living in towns and cities. The North-West Frontier Province (now formally known as Khyber Pakhtunkhwa) is the least urbanized (17 per cent). Approximately three-quarters of Sindh's total urban population reside in three urban centres: Karachi, Hyderabad and Sukkur (Shirazi, 2006).

Afghanistan has been experiencing rapid growth in its urban population. However, the bulk of this growth has been due to the ongoing political conflict, with rural migrants moving *en masse* to the relative safety of the capital (see Box 2.4). From 6.6 million in 2010, it is expected to reach 10.4 million by 2020. The Islamic Republic of Iran is another country that has experienced rapid urban demographic expansion since the 1980s, to become the most urbanized nation in South and South-West Asia. In the adjacent provinces of Tehran and Qom, as many as 85 per cent of the population live in urban areas. The capital city of Tehran accounts for over 14 per cent (2010) of the country's total urban population; other major cities and smaller urban centres are spread all over the country. Iran's economic growth has been rapid in recent years, mainly due to oil resources. Rapid urban demographic expansion is expected to continue, and by 2020 just under 76 per cent of all Iranians will live in urban areas.

Sri Lanka's urban population seems to be relatively low. In part, this is due to the definition of 'urban', which in this country only refers to the areas included in cities' administrative boundaries. If Sri Lanka were to apply the concept of 'urban agglomeration' to its dense settlements, as is the case with India and other Asian countries, its urbanization rate might be as high as 48 per cent (Indrasiri, 2005).

The Pacific subregion

The Pacific subregion has been traditionally divided in three distinct geographical areas: Melanesia, Micronesia and Polynesia. It is made up of a diverse set of thinly populated islands, stretching from New Guinea to the tiny atolls of Micronesia (Federated States) and Polynesia. Melanesia is

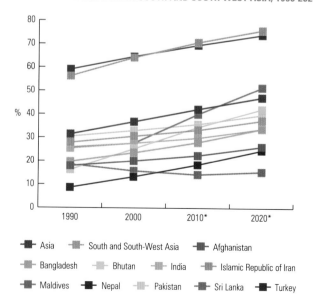

CHART 2.6: **URBANIZATION IN SOUTH AND SOUTH-WEST ASIA, 1990-2020***

*Projections
Source: United Nations (2010)

▲
Ancient city of Yazd, Iran. ©**Vladimir Melnik/Shutterstock**

the largest area, extending from Indonesia to Fiji, with Papua New Guinea the most populated island. With the rapid growth recently experienced in the capital towns of these island nations, the overall urbanization rate is relatively high at 35 per cent (Connell & Lea, 2002).

Overall, eight of the 22 Pacific countries are now predominantly urban, and by 2020 more than half the population in a majority of these countries will live in towns. Throughout the Pacific, high demographic growth has led to migration from smaller outer islands to larger ones and from rural areas to towns, especially national capitals (World Bank, 2000). Storey (2005:8) captures the overall urbanization trends in this subregion as follows:

"Throughout the Pacific there is a clear trend towards urbanization with very high growth rates in Kiribati and peri-urban areas in Fiji and around Port Vila (Vanuatu). One of the difficulties is that often this growth is not recorded in 'urban' statistics. Typically official urban growth rates are double those of the national rate of population growth and peri-urban areas are higher still. Though Fiji's urbanization rates are comparatively modest, there has been a substantial shift to cities since 2000 as a result of the expiry of land leases for Indo-Fijians and issues of security following the 2000 coup. This has resulted in a rapid growth in informal settlements, especially evident in Suva and Lautoka".

North and Central Asia

In the North and Central Asian subregion, the overall demographic growth rate is very low. This is also reflected in urban population growth rates, which range from quasi-stagnant to less than one per cent. In countries such as Armenia and the Russian Federation, urban populations are shrinking. As for urbanization rates, they range between Russia's 73.2 per cent and Tajikistan's 26.3 per cent. Cities in former Soviet countries and the Central Asian Republics are coping with a unique set of challenges inherited from

TABLE 2.8: **URBANIZATION IN THE PACIFIC SUBREGION, 1990-2020***

Country	Urban Population (1,000s)				Percentage Urban (%)			
	1990	2000	2010*	2020*	1990	2000	2010*	2020*
Asia	**1 002 731**	**1 360 900**	**1 757 314**	**2 168 798**	**31.5**	**36.8**	**42.2**	**47.2**
Pacific	**19 037**	**21 932**	**25 167**	**28 406**	**70.7**	**70.4**	**70.2**	**70.4**
Australia	14 596	16 710	19 169	21 459	85.4	87.2	89.1	90.6
New Zealand	2 869	3 314	3 710	4 058	84.7	85.7	86.8	86.9
Melanesia	**1 093**	**1 329**	**1 614**	**2 110**	**19.9**	**19.0**	**18.4**	**19.9**
Fiji	301	384	443	501	41.6	47.9	51.9	56.4
New Caledonia	102	127	146	169	59.5	59.2	57.4	58.5
Papua New Guinea	619	711	863	1 194	15.0	13.2	12.5	14.1
Solomon Islands	43	65	99	152	13.7	15.7	18.5	23.0
Vanuatu	28	41	63	95	18.7	21.7	25.6	31.0
Micronesia	**261**	**326**	**390**	**454**	**62.6**	**65.6**	**68.1**	**70.4**
Guam	122	144	168	188	90.8	93.1	93.2	93.5
Kiribati	25	36	44	54	35.0	43.0	44.0	46.5
Marshall Islands	31	36	45	56	65.0	68.4	71.8	75.3
Micronesia (Federated States)	25	24	25	29	25.8	22.3	22.7	25.1
Nauru	9	10	10	11	100.0	100.0	100.0	100.0
Northern Mariana Islands	39	62	81	96	89.7	90.2	91.3	92.4
Palau	10	13	17	20	69.6	70.0	83.4	89.6
Polynesia	**218**	**253**	**285**	**325**	**40.1**	**41.2**	**42.4**	**44.7**
American Samoa	38	51	64	76	80.9	88.8	93.0	94.8
Cook Islands	10	11	15	17	57.7	65.2	75.3	81.4
French Polynesia	109	124	140	160	55.9	52.4	51.4	52.7
Niue	1	1	1	1	30.9	33.1	37.5	43.0
Samoa	34	39	36	38	21.2	22.0	20.2	20.5
Tonga	21	23	24	28	22.9	23.0	23.4	25.6
Tuvalu	4	4	5	6	40.7	46.0	50.4	55.6

*Projections
Source: United Nations (2010)

CHART 2.7: **URBANIZATION IN THE PACIFIC SUBREGION, 1990-2020***

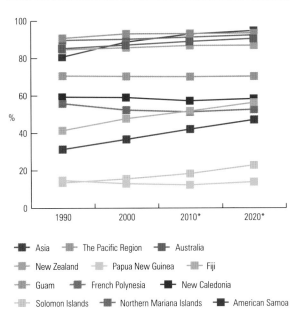

- Asia
- The Pacific Region
- Australia
- New Zealand
- Papua New Guinea
- Fiji
- Guam
- French Polynesia
- New Caledonia
- Solomon Islands
- Northern Mariana Islands
- American Samoa

*Projections
Source: United Nations (2010)

the demographic growth of historic towns like Samarkand (Uzbekistan). Similarly, the population of Kazakhstan's urban areas has increased 500 per cent over the past eight years. Even though Kyrgyzstan is one of the least urbanized Central Asian country, moderate migration to cities like Bishkek, Osh and Tokmok is now taking place. Migration nowadays takes on more rural-to-urban patterns, causing areas like Bishkek, the Chui Region and Almaty to become ever more crowded.

Economic growth in the North and Central Asia region has been robust in the past decade, largely on the back of rising fossil fuel prices. Continued worldwide demand for oil may sustain a high rate of income growth in the next decade and beyond. Urbanization rates in the oil-rich central Asian countries are also very high. In contrast, non-fossil-fuel-producing and less diversified economies, such as Kyrgyzstan and Tajikistan feature low urbanization rates more akin to South Asia's.

2.1.2 The demographic 'youth bulge'

The population of the Asia-Pacific region is young. A temporary increase in the proportion of young people (age group 15-24) in a population is known as a 'youth bulge.' The phenomenon typically results from a demographic transition that began some 15 years earlier. A youth bulge occurs within a population when large numbers of individuals are born during a short but intense period of increasingly high fertility. Thereafter fertility rates decline rapidly. As a result, a large number of individuals of similar age move through life together, creating a 'bulge' in the nation's population structure, as graphically reflected in age pyramids. In Japan, the youth bulge occurred during the 1960s; in Singapore and Hong Kong, China, the phenomenon started during the 1970s and peaked by 1980. In contrast, countries like

their centrally planned systems. Urban populations are now shifting away from the planned settlement patterns that prevailed during the Soviet era.

There are a few large cities in the Central Asian Republics. Tashkent (Uzbekistan) is the largest with over two million registered residents. In Uzbekistan and Kazakhstan, urban demographic growth rates exceed the sub-regional average. Testifying to this expansion is the emergence of new towns in Uzbekistan like Almalyk and Navoi, as well as

TABLE 2.9: **URBANIZATION IN NORTH AND CENTRAL ASIA, 1990-2020***

Country	Urban Population (1,000s)				Percentage Urban (%)			
	1990	2000	2010*	2020*	1990	2000	2010*	2020*
Asia	**1 002 731**	**1 360 900**	**1 757 314**	**2 168 798**	**31.5**	**36.8**	**42.2**	**47.2**
North and Central Asia	**140 475**	**139 358**	**137 184**	**140 435**	**65.4**	**63.9**	**62.9**	**63.6**
Armenia	2 390	1 989	1 984	2 087	67.4	64.7	64.2	65.7
Azerbaijan	3 876	4 158	4 639	5 332	53.7	51.2	51.9	54.2
Georgia	3 005	2 498	2 225	2 177	55.0	52.6	52.7	54.7
Kazakhstan	9 301	8 417	9 217	10 417	56.3	56.3	58.5	62.3
Kyrgyzstan	1 660	1 744	1 918	2 202	37.8	35.2	34.5	35.7
Russian Federation	108 670	107 582	102 702	100 892	73.4	73.3	73.2	74.5
Tajikistan	1 679	1 635	1 862	2 364	31.7	26.5	26.3	28.0
Turkmenistan	1 653	2 062	2 562	3 175	45.1	45.8	49.5	54.6
Uzbekistan	8 241	9 273	10 075	11 789	40.2	37.4	36.2	37.8

*Projections
Source: United Nations (2010)

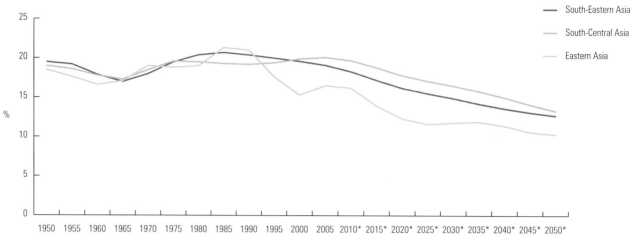

—— South-Eastern Asia

—— South-Central Asia

—— Eastern Asia

*Projections
Source: United Nations (2009)

Nepal and Pakistan are only now beginning to experience declines in overall fertility; with this relatively late, incipient demographic transition, the number of young people will not peak until around 2040 (East West Center, 2006). In some countries in South-East and South and Central Asia, as in most of East Asia, the period of rapid expansion in the youth population is already over.

In 1960, 284 million Asians were aged 15 to 24; by 2007, they were 737 million. Over the past 40 years, the proportion of Asia's population in the 15 to 24-year age bracket increased, and then declined – from 17 per cent in 1960 to 21 per cent in 1985 and 18 per cent in 2007. A further decline, to 14 per cent, is projected by 2040.

Countries in Asia have benefited from the youth bulge (i.e., the acceleration in economic growth due to a rising share of working age people in a population). Between 1965 and 1990, approximately one third of East Asia's GDP increase can be attributed to this phenomenon[2]. The extent to which Asian economies will continue to benefit from this demographic trend will depend on how they develop and harness the potential of the younger population. One challenge is that although many young people across Asia are now better prepared than ever before to enter the workforce, many are unable to secure employment.

In the Asia-Pacific region, nearly 11 per cent of people aged 15 to 24 are without a job and looking for one. In South-East Asia and the Pacific, youth are five times as likely as older workers to be unemployed; in South and East Asia, this multiple is 'only' three. In their recent national demographic surveys, Kiribati, Samoa and Vanuatu all reported relatively low rates of youth unemployment, but high rates of youth engaged in unpaid family activities. In contrast, the Marshall Islands and Micronesia (Federated States) reported high rates of youth unemployment, i.e., over 60 per cent and 35 per cent respectively. In the latter, the rate was reported as 50 per cent in Chuuk, the largest federated state (Abott &

▲
Statue of a student in Ulaanbaatar, Mongolia. ©**UN-HABITAT/Bharat Dahiya**

Pollard, 2004). The rates of youth unemployment conceal underemployment and poverty among working youth. Young women find it especially difficult to secure decent work and are more likely to be employed in the informal economy, where they are typically underpaid relative to men. They also perform disproportionate shares of unpaid domestic work (United Nations, 2007b).

Urbanization and globalization have transformed the values and culture of youth in Asia. The openness of Asian economies and the exposure of youth to foreign goods, services and information have encouraged the development of an international youth culture. Rapidly developing communication technologies have enabled many young people from countries large and small to access information that may otherwise have been unavailable. Rapid economic growth and higher incomes have enabled Asian youth to adopt Western consumption patterns and lifestyles. Asian youth more readily challenge traditional authority structures and experience both the disorientation and anomie caused by the day-to-day experience of clashes between traditional and modern norms and values (Yap, 2004).

2.1.3 An ageing population

Many countries in Asia are facing dramatic demographic changes. Some are to expect declines in working populations and concomitant increases in the numbers of aged dependants sometime between 2015 and 2020. All across Asia, the numbers of people aged 65 or more are expected to grow significantly. In the year 2000, the average age in Asia was 29. An estimated 6 per cent of the region's total population were aged 65 or more, 30 per cent were under 15, and 64 per cent were in the working-age group of 15 to 64 years (United Nations, 2001a). It is estimated that by 2050, the proportion under 15 will drop to 19 per cent, and the proportion of those aged 65 or more will rise to 18 per cent. By that time, the average age in Asia will be 40 (United Nations, 2009).

Macroeconomic theory suggests that those economies with large shares of ageing populations are likely to grow more slowly than those with relatively fewer elderly people, largely due to attendant reductions in labour force and output. To some extent, this can be anticipated and mitigated by increases in labour productivity. However, the process of population ageing is occurring much more rapidly in Asia than it did in Western countries, and in some parts of Asia it is bound to occur at a much earlier stage of economic development. Facing an unprecedented pace of population ageing, Asian cities must prepare to cater to the needs of the elderly which will include: (a) housing for the elderly, as more Asians increasingly prefer nuclear as opposed to extended families; (b) medical facilities (and attendant financing) for the elderly; (c) changes in building regulations that take into account the needs of the elderly; and, (d) appropriate changes in urban planning standards. This large-scale demographic shift will also have implications for the economic growth of cities, as the urban labour force will increasingly become older (Heller, 2006; East West Center, 2008).

Japan's population is to undergo a protracted period of rapid ageing over the next several decades. Average life expectancy in the country climbed sharply after World War II, and today is the highest in the world. In 2007, life expectancy at birth was 86.0 years for women and 79.2 years for men. Japan's senior population (65 years and over) was approximately 27.5 million, or 21.5 per cent of the total population, and reaching record highs both in terms of absolute numbers and percentage (Government of Japan, 2007). According to UN estimates, in 2010, there will be 34 elderly dependants for every 100 people working in Japan. By 2050, the ratio will rise to 74 retired dependants for every 100 working people. Unless birthrates rise, Japan's total population is to shrink by one half of its current size by 2100. In an ageing society, medical and pension costs increase but the number of workers who pay for the welfare support system decreases. The declining working-age population will arguably affect the country's productivity, economic growth and global competitiveness.

Another country in Asia that is ageing rapidly is China. Unique among developing countries, the phenomenon is extremely fast (United Nations, 2009) and very similar to patterns in more developed Japan, Singapore, the Republic of Korea and Hong Kong, China. The difference is that in China this is happening at a time when the country is still relatively poor. The 'old before rich' phenomenon in China is partly due to the stringent 'one couple, one child' policy that has proved highly effective in stabilising population growth (this policy is now being reconsidered).[3] Over the next few decades, the ratio of elderly dependants to people of working age is to rise steeply, from 10 per cent in 2005 to 40 per cent by 2050. The pace of ageing in China's cities has been much faster than in rural areas, reflecting both sustained lower fertility and higher longevity in urban compared with rural areas. With rapid growth in the urban population expected over the next two decades, Chinese cites are bound to face many critical policy issues regarding care for an ageing society (United Nations, 2008b; England, 2005).

2.2
The factors behind urban growth

Jakarta, Indonesia. Jakarta has experienced significant migration over the past decades.
©Veronica Wijaya

Rural-to-urban migration is often viewed as the main factor behind urban demographic growth. Many countries that have experienced rapid urbanization have attempted to reduce rural-urban flows. There is not a single precedent, however, of a country that has succeeded to do that over the long term. Past experience notwithstanding, the major factor behind urban growth in most countries nowadays is the natural increase in the urban population. Another factor is reclassification of areas from 'rural' to 'urban', or expansion of urban boundaries to include the rural periphery and/or to absorb settlements in the urban periphery – a process often referred to as *in situ* urbanization (United Nations, 2001b).

In many countries in South Asia where urban populations are in a minority, natural increase accounted for over half of urban demographic growth during the 1980s. For example, in India estimates suggest that the contribution of net rural-urban migration remained relatively constant at 18 to 20 per cent of total urban growth from the 1960s to the 1980s (Pathak & Mehta, 1995a, 1995b). Reclassification and expansion of urban boundaries was another major factor of urban growth in India. Similarly in Nepal, most of urban growth was due to natural increase and reclassification (United Nations, 2001b).

In East Asia, where urbanization rates are higher than in the southern part of the region, rural-to-urban migration is often the most visible factor behind the ongoing rapid urban demographic growth. This is the case in China, although reclassification is another significant factor, accounting for over 70 per cent of urban growth in the 1980s and about 80 per cent in the 1990s (United Nations, 2001b:31). Reclassification in China occurred alongside two major administrative changes: in 1984, the criteria for township status were relaxed and in 1986, urban areas were encouraged to incorporate adjoining counties. This resulted in significant reclassification of rural into urban areas over the course of the 1980s.

Estimates for Indonesia indicate a steady decline in the contribution of natural increase to urban demographic growth, from nearly 70 per cent in the 1960s to 32 per cent in the 1990s (United Nations, 2008b). The share of migration/reclassification in urban growth rose over this period, from 32 per cent in the 1960s to 59 per cent in the 1980s (United Nations, 2001b). Jakarta and its periphery in West Java experienced significant migration in this period. Urban migration, especially to the national capital Jakarta, started in the 1950s due to civil unrest in other parts of the country. Even after the unrest subsided, streams of people moving to urban centres continued through the 1990s, primarily because of rapid industrialization in and around Jakarta and other major cities (Sarosa, 2006).

TABLE 2.10: **CONTRIBUTION OF MIGRATION/RECLASSIFICATION TO URBAN GROWTH IN EAST ASIA, 1970-2030* (%)**

Country	1970s	1980s	1990s	2000s	2010s*	2020s*
East Asia	**45**	**58**	**64**	**68**	**72**	**76**
Cambodia	33	24	40	53	57	59
China	45	65	72	76	80	86
Indonesia	53	62	67	66	63	61
Malaysia	45	44	44	41	35	34
Philippines	35	46	48	43	38	37
Republic of Korea	65	65	54	48	61	85
Thailand	41	40	34	47	67	75
Viet Nam	29	28	44	57	65	72

*Projections
Source: World Bank (2007a:64).

More recent estimates of the factors behind urban demographic growth are available from the World Bank (2007a). These estimates are based on a number of assumptions about natural growth rates in select East Asian countries. The residual growth is then attributed to migration and reclassification of rural into urban areas. The findings based on this model suggest that migration and reclassification together account for an increasing share of urban population growth in East Asia, from 45 per cent in the 1970s to a projected 76 per cent in the 2020s (see Table 2.10)[4]. Exceptions to this pattern are Malaysia and the Philippines, where urban demographic growth will be due solely to natural increases.

2.2.1 Internal migration

According to economic theory, individuals migrate from low-wage to high-wage areas seeking to maximize their earnings. Migration is a strategy adopted by rural populations to improve family livelihoods and benefit from better services in urban areas. Migration also enables rural households to ensure against a number of risks and, in the absence of well-functioning credit markets, to fund investment in rural housing and economic activities. Rural migrants with education and skills are often more likely to do well in urban areas. Rural-urban migration is only one component of internal migration, though. Other forms include rural-rural, urban-urban and urban-rural migration. Many migrants to urban areas come from other towns or cities. Furthermore, not all rural-urban migrants are poor; many come to the city because they are educated and cannot find suitable jobs elsewhere. Rural-urban migration is generally beneficial for migrants, including access to better opportunities and remittances for relatives back home.

Rural-urban migration benefits cities as well, as it provides a steady supply of labour for a range of economic activities. Migration opens opportunities for women, giving them access to jobs outside the home, thereby contributing to their empowerment. Maintaining rural-urban links through remittances enables rural households to improve incomes and sustain local development.

Many rapidly expanding Asian economies have seen increases in the rate of internal migration over the past two decades, because of increased opportunities in urban areas. Of these movements, circular migration – where trips vary from daily commutes to those lasting several months and where urban migrants retain strong links to rural areas – appears to be emerging as a dominant trend for poorer groups. This is partly because rural migrants are unable to find permanent jobs in cities. Circular migration is a coping mechanism, enabling them to keep families in rural areas and migrate to the city during lean agriculture periods.

While most Asian countries do not impose any barriers to internal population movements, some have adopted mechanisms to regulate migration to urban areas. Reducing or even reversing the flow of rural-urban migrants has been the most common policy goal pursued by governments bent on changing the spatial distribution of the population. Most governments have sought to control rural-urban flows through a combination of rural employment creation programmes, anti-slum drives and restricted entry to urban areas. While some have relaxed restrictions recently, others continue to design policies and programmes that discourage people from moving.

For example, in China internal migration is predominantly temporary and from rural to urban areas. In 2006, the National Bureau of Statistics estimated at 132 million the number of rural-to-urban migrants in the country. Another phenomenon is a continuous outflow of labourers from agricultural areas to industrializing regions in China. A majority of these are circular migrants (known as the "floating population") (ODI, 2006). Migration affects and is also affected by the *hukou* [household registration], which is essentially a migration regulatory system in force over the past half century (Chan, 2008). The *hukou* system, directly and indirectly, remains a major barrier preventing China's rural population from settling in the city.[5]

In Viet Nam, people have traditionally migrated from north to south and from rural to urban areas. Still, migrants need residency permits to work in cities. Temporary permits are now granted to ensure a steady supply of labour. Surveys

Dhaka, Bangladesh. Circular migration appears to be emerging as the dominant trend for poorer groups. ©**Manoocher Deghati/IRIN**

have shown that after the economic reforms of the late 1980s, temporary migration to urban areas and rapidly industrialising zones became a major form of spatial mobility. Every year, Ho Chi Minh City receives around 700,000 new registered temporary migrants; these include so-called 'KT3' migrants with temporary registration for a period of six months and more; and 'KT4' migrants with temporary registration for a period of under six months (ODI, 2006).

In Cambodia, rural migration has emerged in response to the pressures of a rapidly growing labour force in search of livelihoods. Increasing numbers of migrants are also (informally) moving to neighbouring Thailand. Currently, the top destination for rural migrants is Phnom Penh, which alone receives about one third of all inter-provincial migrants in Cambodia. Alternative destinations include Kandal, Banteay Meanchey and Koh Kong (which together account for another 30 per cent of total migrants). Phnom Penh and Kandal are the main urban destinations, while the two rural

provinces of Koh Kong and Banteay Meanchey feature large average farm sizes and low population densities. Therefore, Cambodians move to locations where they find potential for employment (Acharya, 2003).

As an indirect way of controlling the movement of people out of rural areas, India has recently introduced the National Rural Employment Guarantee Act (NREGA). The policy promises 100 days of wage labour for one adult member in every rural household who volunteers for unskilled work. The NREGA ranks among the most powerful initiatives ever undertaken for the transformation of rural livelihoods in India. The unprecedented commitment of financial resources is matched only by its imaginative structure, which promises a radically fresh programme of rural development. The NREGA effectively enshrines the right to work in Indian law. This development-orientated initiative focuses on critical public investments and durable assets, short of which the growth processes will not gather momentum as required in

▲
Roadside settlements in Karachi, Pakistan. ©**Asianet-Pakistan/Shutterstock**

the most backward regions of rural India. The emphasis on water conservation as well as drought and flood-proofing is also critical, underscoring water security as the pre-requisite and foundation for rural transformation. The legislation does not allow any middlemen or contractors to interfere in the implementation of this policy, and transparency and accountability are highly emphasized (Ambasta *et al.*, 2008).

For all the restrictions on migration flows and rural development programmes such as NREGA, however, rural populations continue to move to cities. By comparison with rural areas, cities *seem* to offer better choices for employment, access to better social services, such as health and education, and higher social status. However, many migrants remain in the urban informal sector for long periods of time. Their informal status excludes them from the wider benefits of economic growth in cities. Across Asia, large numbers of temporary migrants and others intending to stay permanently, but who have moved without formally

acquiring a house or a job, are regarded as illegal. In some countries, however, migrants without formal housing and jobs do obtain legal registration and can even vote. The informal sector is discussed further in Chapter 3.

2.2.2 International migration[6]

Along with international flows of capital, information and technology, international migration is one of the major forces of change in the world. Many emigrants move to urban areas abroad. The number of international migrants in Asia nearly doubled between 1960 and 2005, growing from an estimated 28 million in 1960 to more than 53 million in 2005. In the Pacific area, the number increased from two to five million over the same period. In 2005 and relative to the total population, international migrants represented 15 per cent of the population of the Pacific subregion. In contrast, they accounted for less than 2 per cent of the total population in Asia. The Asia-Pacific region currently hosts over 30 per cent of the world's estimated 191 million international migrants (ESCAP, 2008b).

In the region, flows of people across borders, especially to neighbouring countries, have been prevalent for a long time. As in the case of internal migration, people move across borders in search of better economic opportunities or safety, although such movements face more restrictions than domestic migration, through national migration policies. However, movement of people across countries in the region has become easier, especially within the Association of Southeast Asian Nations (ASEAN) and other sub-regional economic groupings. Cross-border emigration in Asia is propelled by various 'push' and 'pull' factors, including persistent inter-country disparities in development, stronger regional economic integration and divergent demographic dynamics. Changes in labour markets combine with technical progress and economic inter-linkages to create new demand for both skilled and less skilled migrant workers. Cross-border emigration is also influenced by government policies, existing migration networks and private agencies that recruit migrant workers. The 'push' factors behind cross-border emigration include, *inter alia*, protracted natural disasters, wars and internal conflicts. For example, war and drought have triggered cross-border emigration from Afghanistan into Pakistan and Iran, as has internal conflict from Myanmar into Thailand (ESCAP, 2008b).

The Asia-Pacific region is a major source of permanent emigration to Australia, Canada, Europe, New Zealand and the United States. Several labour-surplus countries in Asia are actively involved in promoting labour emigration. However, the limited role of governments in the process of recruitment has led to widespread commercialization of migrant labour flows. Asian countries like China, India and the Philippines rank among the top 10 sources of immigrants to those more developed countries. Several others in the region report large-scale outflows in the form of contractual labour. Over the past few decades, the Philippines has remained at the top of the list of major source countries of migrant workers (UNHCR, 2006).

Between 1990 and 2005, annual labour emigration from Bangladesh more than doubled from 103,000 to 252,000, soaring beyond 800,000 in 2007, with the Middle East and Malaysia as the main destinations. From 1992 to 2002, labour migration from India to the Middle East averaged about 355,000 per year. In 2006, some 712,000 Indonesians left to work abroad. Between 2000 and 2006, an average 204,000 labour migrants left Sri Lanka every year, the majority to destinations in the Middle East. While these figures are high, they remain estimates and the actual numbers of migrant workers from the region are likely to be greater, since unknown numbers do not register with national authorities.

Human trafficking is a pernicious form of irregular migration that involves elements of deception, coercion, exploitation, abuse and violence. The economic vulnerability of the victims is often compounded by physical and psychological abuse, exposure to life-threatening conditions including sexually transmitted diseases and HIV/AIDS, as well as abuse at the hands of authorities. Human trafficking has been a growing category of transnational crime and a major issue of concern for many governments in the Asia-Pacific region. Initiatives have been taken by the South Asian Association for Regional Cooperation (SAARC) and the Association of South East Asian Nations (ASEAN) to combat human trafficking in their respective regions (ESCAP, 2008b).

Some countries like Thailand and Malaysia are both receivers and senders of international labour. For instance, Thailand exports labour to places such as Singapore and Taiwan, Province of China, and imports labour from Cambodia and Myanmar. The main reason for importing labour is the continuing need for a cheap workforce, in order to be able to produce goods and services in countries where economic development has already reached, or is on the threshold of reaching, industrialized status. Another reason is the depletion in the number of people amenable to agricultural and manual work in many receiving countries, which creates opportunities for foreign low-skilled workers. Exporting labour occurs where unemployment is growing and through expansion of local business abroad. The complex system of recruitment and deployment of migrant workers is in itself an industry that supports the economic growth of the region.[7]

In the mid-1990s, 400,000 people from the Pacific subregion lived abroad. While not very significant relative to the sub-regional population as a whole (six million), the figure matters to the small countries and territories across that area, including Polynesia and Micronesia (Federated States). For instance, emigrants account for 75 per cent of the Polynesian population. As many as 30 to 40 per cent of the population of Samoa and Tonga are estimated to be living abroad. Most are in New Zealand (170,000), where between 1992 and 1997 the three Pacific island countries of Samoa, Fiji and Tonga were among the top 10 countries of origin for immigrants (Connel, 2003).

A major benefit of international emigration is the flow of remittances to the home countries. In 2007 in the Asia-Pacific region, migrant remittances totalled US $121 billion (World Bank, 2008a). This is equivalent to nearly two-thirds of all foreign direct investment in developing countries. In India, China, Pakistan, Bangladesh and the Philippines, remittances are a major source of foreign currency holdings. At the household level, remittances improve economic security on top of providing income for investment, savings and entrepreneurial activities. Emigrant remittances have boosted the urban real estate market, as housing and property are safe and profitable forms of investment. For example, in the state of Kerala, India, and in many cities in the Philippines, the urban real estate market is driven largely by remittances from migrants in the Middle East. Although the average value of remittances per emigrant is small, the cumulative impact on land and house prices is quite tangible.

Forced migration due to conflicts and natural disasters

Forced migration is a general term that refers to the movements of refugees and internally displaced people (those displaced by conflicts, by natural or environmental disasters and by development projects). Since the year 2000, the world has witnessed over 35 major conflicts and some 2,500 disasters. Over two billion people have been affected, and millions have been forced to migrate. Many displaced persons move towards cities in the hope of finding shelter and basic support. It happens often that displaced persons do not return back to their homes for fear of insecurity. As a result, destination cities experience demographic bulges (UNHCR, 2006).

Many Asian countries have seen sudden increases of migrants in their urban areas, mainly in the capital cities, as a result of conflict. For example, and as a result of forced migration, the population of Kabul has more than doubled in the last 15 years from 1.6 million in 1995 to an estimated 3.7 million in 2010 (see box 2.4).

Natural disasters have already caused considerable displacement in recent years in Asia. The impact of a disaster is not determined entirely by the magnitude of the event itself, but also by communities' ability to respond. In many instances, the poor are the hardest hit. The late 2004 Asian tsunami affected 14 countries after an earthquake off Indonesia. The tsunami accounted for 37 per cent of all recorded fatalities from natural disasters since the year 2000. The 2005 earthquake in the mountains of Pakistan garnered significant media attention because of the scope of the disaster. Almost 75,000 people died and 3.5 million were left homeless at the onset of winter. Cities near disaster-affected areas are usually the destination for many of the displaced persons (UNHCR, 2006). The number of forced migrants to cities in connection with global environmental and climate change ('eco-refugees') is likely to increase in the future (see Chapter 5 for more details).

Asian cities lack the capacity to deal with forced migrants. Forced migration leads to sudden rises in local populations, putting inordinate pressure on already inadequate urban services and infrastructure. Furthermore, in the short run, with more low-skilled workers available in the local labour market, wages decline, especially in the construction sector. Sudden large inflows of forced migrants also pose security risks in cities. For example, internal conflict has become the predominant threat to the security and stability of many of the small island nations in the Pacific, and particularly Melanesia. Since the late 1980s, social conflicts of varying nature and intensity have occurred in Papua New Guinea, Fiji, Vanuatu and the Solomon Islands. In the latter, ethnic conflict has led to deterioration in law and order and a flight of foreign investment from the capital and tourist hub Honiara. Whereas in rural areas a majority of the population lives on customary land and therefore retains access to food, the consequences of social and economic breakdown are most apparent in urban centres. Rapid population growth, poor infrastructure and inadequate labour markets have led to a crisis in urban governance (Talbot & Ronnie, 2007).

BOX 2.4: THE CHALLENGE OF RECONSTRUCTION AND DEVELOPMENT IN KABUL

▲
Kabul, Afghanistan. ©Manoocher Deghati/IRIN

As the internal strife of the previous decades abated somewhat, since 2002 3.5 million Afghan refugees have returned from neighbouring countries, of which one million to the Kabul area. In addition, many internally displaced persons (IDPs) have also moved to the capital. As a result, Kabul's population grew by as high as 17 per cent per year between 1999 and 2002, before slowing down to about 5 per cent for the past few years, making the city one of the fastest growing in the world for its size class. The current population of Kabul is an estimated 3.7 million (2010), or 56.7 per cent of the country's total urban population.

As the capital and the largest city in the country, Kabul has a critical role to play in economic development and poverty reduction. At the same time, however, the challenges are daunting. For instance, basic services remain scarce due to massive wartime destruction, poor investment in infrastructure and rapid population growth. As a result, more than 50 per cent of the drains are not functional, with wastewater often over-flowing on the roads; only 10 per cent of households have the benefit of piped water supply, less than 5 per cent of households are connected to the sewerage network, and only about 50 per cent of solid waste is collected and transported to dumpsites. The extent of the damage to the city's infrastructure, combined with a rapid increase in the population due to refugees and internally displaced people over the past five years, places an additional burden on central and local government, increasing the scale of reconstruction and development needed in the city.

Source: Pushpa Pathak, Senior Urban Adviser to Kabul Municipality

2.3
Urban corridors, mega-cities and mega urban regions

Kobe, Japan. ©**J. Aa/Shutterstock**

Mega-cities

Mega-cities in developing countries have long been the focus of media attention. In popular writings on cities of the developing world, the largest receive the most attention. It may be a natural thing, when considering Asian conurbations, that those the size of Tokyo, Mumbai, Bangkok or Shanghai come readily to mind. The reasons are obvious and related to economic and social conditions. In 2005, the world's 30 most productive cities generated 16 per cent of global output. The top 40 mega urban regions, which make up about 18 per cent of the world's population, produce 66 per cent of goods and services and 86 per cent of patented innovations (UN-HABITAT, 2010a; World Bank, 2008b; Montgomery *et al.,* 2004; da Silva, 2008).

In 1975, Tokyo stood out as the only mega-city in Asia. By the year 2000, the region housed 9 of the world's largest urban agglomerations and by 2020, the number of such mega-cities might increase to 15 (see Table 2.11 and Chart 2.9). Mega-cities share common features like very large populations (from 10 million in Istanbul to 36 million in Tokyo, as in the year 2009), extensive geographic sprawl, and economic and social dominance over regions or even countries (see Box 2.5). Two Asian mega-cities (Tokyo and Osaka-Kobe) are located in a technologically advanced country where they play significant global roles. Tokyo is the largest city in the world (see Box 2.6) and will remain so for the next three decades. Cities in rapidly growing Asian economies – Delhi, Mumbai (formerly Bombay), Shanghai and Kolkata (formerly Calcutta) – are

on the list of the top five Asian mega-cities (2009). Those in China (Shanghai, Beijing and Tianjin) have grown after decades of governmental attempts to limit their size. Initially, this took the form of outright controls on internal migration; but after liberalization, Chinese economic modernization policies effectively opened up many cities to the outside world, particularly those on the eastern seaboard. In South Asia, internal migration and natural increases contribute to high rates of population growth in Delhi, Mumbai, Kolkata, Dhaka (see Box 2.7) and Karachi. Two Asian mega-cities are national capitals (Jakarta Raya and Metro Manila) and primate cities. They are the seats of national political power and significantly larger than other cities in the national urban hierarchy. The governance of mega urban regions is discussed in Chapter 6.

Some studies suggest that the United Nations underestimates the populations of mega-cities. For example, the UN estimates the population of Seoul at 9.8 million (2009), which is consistent with municipal boundaries. Others, however, have estimated the city's population at between 17 to 23 million, depending on the way the urban agglomeration is defined. Likewise, the UN figure for Manila's population is 11.4 million (2009), based on official boundaries and include Manila city together with 16 other municipalities. If the surrounding suburban expansion is included, however, the city's population reaches 19 million. On the other hand, both Shanghai and Beijing rank as 'Special Municipalities' with the status of provinces, and include rural counties within their borders. In these cases, UN population numbers refer to these special municipalities, and therefore overestimate their populations (Richard *et al.,* 2006).

BOX 2.5: ASIA'S NEW URBAN CONFIGURATIONS

Kuala Lumpur, Malaysia. ©**Ronen/Shutterstock**

As the world becomes more urban, new residents will continue to be distributed across cities of all sizes and much along the current prevalent pattern. In many instances, though, cities are merging together to create urban settlements on a scale never seen before. These new configurations take the form of mega-regions, urban corridors and city-regions. *Mega-regions* are natural economic units that result from the growth, convergence and spatial spread of geographically linked metropolitan areas and other agglomerations. They are polycentric urban clusters surrounded by low-density hinterlands, and they grow considerably faster than the overall population of the nations where they are located. *Urban corridors*, on the other hand, are characterized by linear systems of urban spaces linked through transportation networks. Other dynamic and strategic cities are extending beyond their administrative boundaries and integrating their hinterlands to become full-blown *city-regions*. These are emerging in various parts of the world, turning into spatial units that are territorially and functionally bound by economic, political, socio-cultural, and ecological systems. All of these new urban configurations—cities in clusters, corridors and regions—are becoming the new engines of both global and regional economies.

Mega-regions today are accumulating even larger populations than any mega- or meta-city (defined by UN-HABITAT as a city with a population over 20 million), and their economic output is enormous. The population of China's Hong Kong-Shenzhen-Guangdong mega-region, for example, is about 120 million, and it is estimated that Japan's Tokyo-Nagoya-Osaka-Kyoto-Kobe mega-region is likely to be host to 60 million by 2015. Although more widespread in North America and Europe, mega-regions are happening in Asia and other parts of the world as cities converge apace, with the typical huge demographic concentrations, large markets, significant economic capacities, substantial innovative activities and high skills that come with them. Recent research shows that the world's 40 largest mega-regions cover only a tiny fraction of the habitable surface of our planet, and are home to fewer than 18 per cent of the world's population, even as they account for 66 per cent of global economic activity and about 85 per cent of technological and scientific innovation.

Urban corridors, in contrast, present a new type of spatial organization with specific economic and transportation objectives. In urban corridors, a number of city centres of various sizes are connected along transportation routes in linear development axes that are often linked to a number of mega-cities. New developments in fringe areas experience the fastest growth rates and the most rapid urban transformation. An example is the industrial corridor developing in India between Mumbai and Delhi, which will stretch more than 1,500 kilometres from Jawaharlal Nehru Port (in Navi Mumbai) to Dadri and Tughlakabad (in Delhi). Another good example is the manufacturing and service industry corridor in Malaysia's Kuala Lumpur, clustered within the Klang Valley conurbation that stretches all the way to the port city by the same name. The best illustration of a mature urban corridor is the 1,500 kilometre-long belt stretching from Beijing to Tokyo via Pyongyang and Seoul, which connects no less than 77 cities with populations of 200,000 or more. Over 97 million people live in this urban corridor, which, in fact, links four separate megalopolises in four countries, merging them into one as it were.

Urban corridors are changing the functionality of cities and even towns both large and small, in the process stimulating business, real estate development and land values along their ribbon-like development areas. They are also improving inter-connectivity and creating new forms of interdependence among cities, leading to regional economic development growth. In some cases, however, urban corridors can result in severe urban primacy and unbalanced regional development, as they strengthen ties to existing economic centres rather than allowing for more diffused spatial development.

City-regions come on yet another, even larger scale as major cities extend beyond formal administrative boundaries to engulf smaller ones, including towns. In the process, they also absorb semi-urban and rural hinterlands, and in some cases merge with other intermediate cities, creating large conurbations that eventually form city-regions. Many such city-regions have grown enormously over the last 20 to 30 years, owing to the effects of agglomeration economies and comparative advantages. The extended Bangkok Region in Thailand, for example, is expected to expand another 200 kilometres from its current centre by 2020, growing far beyond its current population of over 17 million. Some of these city-regions are actually larger in both surface area and population than entire countries like Belgium, the Czech Republic or the Netherlands.

Mega-regions, urban corridors and city-regions are creating a new urban hierarchy. The scope, range and complexity of issues faced by these regional urban systems require innovative coordination mechanisms for urban management and governance. The World Bank* has identified the three main issues that these configurations face, namely:

- *Coordination,* "conceiving the development of cities in parallel with the development of regions and subregions, rather than isolated nodes in economic space", a process that calls on metropolitan, regional and even national planners to work together;
- *Broader plans for regional planning/ development,* "requiring dispersion of specific urban functions (i.e., solid waste treatment, airports, skills and training centres) within a continuous region, rather than crowding them in a large city"; and
- *Coping with horizontal fiscal disparities,* and more specifically "designing mechanisms to transfer fiscal resources among urban governments in a region."

* Indermit & Homi. An East Asian Renaissance: Ideas for Economic Growth. Washington, D.C.: World Bank, 2007

Source: UN-HABITAT (2010a)

1975			2000			2009			2020*		
Ranking	City	Pop. (mil.)	Ranking	City	Pop. (mil.)	Ranking	City	Pop. (mil.)	Ranking	City	Pop. (mil.)
1	Tokyo	26.6	1	Tokyo	34.4	1	Tokyo	36.5	1	Tokyo	37.1
			2	Mumbai	16.1	2	Delhi	21.7	2	Delhi	26.3
			3	Delhi	15.7	3	Mumbai	19.7	3	Mumbai	23.7
			4	Shanghai	13.2	4	Shanghai	16.3	4	Shanghai	19.1
			5	Kolkata	13.1	5	Kolkata	15.3	5	Dhaka	18.7
			6	Osaka-Kobe	11.2	6	Dhaka	14.2	6	Kolkata	18.4
			7	Dhaka	10.3	7	Karachi	12.8	7	Karachi	16.7
			8	Karachi	10.0	8	Manila	11.4	8	Manila	13.7
			9	Manila	9.9	9	Osaka-Kobe	11.3	9	Beijing	14.3
						10	Beijing	12.2	10	Istanbul	11.7
						11	Istanbul	10.4	11	Osaka Kobe	11.4
									12	Jakarta	10.3
									13	Shenzhen	10.6
									14	Chongqing	10.5
									15	Guangzhou	10.4

*Projections
Source: United Nations (2010)

Mega-cities account for only 11 per cent of Asia's urban population (see Table 2.13), but like all those around the world they act as dominant forces in the regional and global economies on top of significant contributions to their respective countries. They are also knowledge centres, often concentrating the best national educational and research institutions, as well as cultural centres, allowing a variety of cultures to coexist and thrive.

Many of these mega-cities have grown on the back of concentrations of manufacturing industries. Over time, the top segments of the services sector have come to concentrate in these cities, too, in order to benefit from agglomeration economies. Many mega-cities are also the seats of power, either as national capitals or as major economic or financial centres. People, infrastructure and capital are concentrated in mega-cities, and so is the political and social power that reinforces their role as powerful engines of national development. Media concentrations in mega-cities enable these to influence sub-national and national policies. Public investment in infrastructure is substantial and this, in turn, fuels urban agglomeration economies. The services sector is particularly prone to agglomeration and typically prefers central city locations.

The spin-offs from the concentrations of manufacturing and services in mega-cities are enormous and further attract people and capital. This continued expansion defeats efforts to move business away from the core of these cities. As the populations and surface areas of Asian mega-cities kept expanding, inadequate infrastructure in the peripheries caused densification of the core, since people prefer to remain in the inner city where infrastructure is relatively better. The compact form of Asian mega-cities results from these high densities and has also promoted mixed uses. While this may make streets more congested and chaotic, the flip side of urban

density is enhanced efficiency through reduced commuting between residence and work places.

The economies of mega-cities are often as large as those of some countries and, as is the case in Asia, their pace of growth can outstrip the national average. The problem is that the benefits of high economic growth are not necessarily shared by all residents. Indeed, Asian mega-cities display such stark inequalities in residents' conditions that they seem to be split between a rich and a poor city, with large proportions of the

CHART 2.9: **THE TOP 10 ASIAN MEGA-CITIES**

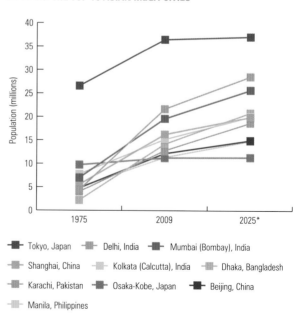

- ■— Tokyo, Japan
- ■— Delhi, India
- ■— Mumbai (Bombay), India
- ■— Shanghai, China
- ■— Kolkata (Calcutta), India
- ■— Dhaka, Bangladesh
- ■— Karachi, Pakistan
- ■— Osaka-Kobe, Japan
- ■— Beijing, China
- ■— Manila, Philippines

*Projections
Source: United Nations (2010)

BOX 2.6: TOKYO, THE WORLD'S LARGEST MEGA-CITY

The greater Tokyo region, including the prefectures of Chiba, Kanagawa and Saitama, is the most heavily populated metropolitan region in the world with over 35 million. The Tokyo Metropolitan Region consists of 23 wards, 26 cities, five towns and eight villages. It is home to 26 per cent of Japan's total population. The Japanese capital is one of the world's three leading financial centres along with New York and London. Tokyo's metropolitan economy is the largest in the world, with a total gross domestic product equivalent to US $1,191 billion in 2005. Tokyo also serves as a hub for Japan's transportation, publishing and broadcasting industries.

The history of the city of Tokyo stretches back some 400 years. Originally named Edo, the city started to flourish after Tokugawa Ieyasu established his shogunate there in 1603. As the centre of politics and culture in Japan, Edo grew into a huge city with a population of over a million during the 18th century. The Edo Period lasted for nearly 260 years until the Meiji Restoration in 1868, when the Tokugawa shogunate ended and imperial rule was restored. The Emperor moved to Edo, which was renamed Tokyo.

Like many other cities in Japan, Tokyo is prone to earthquakes and flooding. In September 1923, the city was devastated by the Great Kanto Earthquake. During the rebuilding process, suburban districts were developed with rail connections to the city centre. In 1941, the dual administrative system of Tokyo-*fu* (prefecture) and Tokyo-*shi* (city) was abolished and a metropolitan structure was established with a governor as head of the city administration. Tokyo expanded dramatically after World War II. By the 1980s, the city had become a major centre for global business, finance, technology, information and culture.

Being home to a relatively wealthy and homogenous population, the city is composed of narrow building plots and closely packed commercial districts such as Shibuya, Shinjuku, Ginza or the new Roppongi Hills development. The Greater Tokyo area is a consistently dense and multi-centred urban region that is well-served by an integrated system of trains, underground and buses used by nearly 80 per cent of daily commuters. For all its scale and complexity, Tokyo provides a highly efficient urban model and is now seeking to make greater use of its assets based on denser development clusters near the centre, and regenerating the under-used waterfront along Tokyo Bay.

Rapid developments in the Tokyo region have led to a slew of urban problems such as environmental degradation, traffic congestion and deficient disaster preparedness. From 1986 onwards, land and stock prices spiralled upwards, a phenomenon known as a 'bubble'. While development spread to the suburbs, urban infrastructure such as drainage and the road network did not catch up with the rapid increase in housing construction. Restricting demographic growth to the outskirts has become difficult; associated problems such as excessive demographic concentrations, heavy congestion of railways and roads, and the deterioration of the urban environment in residential areas, remain major challenges.

Source: Inputs from UN-HABITAT Regional office for Asia and the Pacific; and http://www.metro.tokyo.jp/ENGLISH

---

poor living in slum and squatter settlements. Chapter 4 focuses on poverty and inequality in Asian cities.

A consequence of the large size of mega-cities is that they are also plagued by a variety of problems. One of the more common of these has to do with highly competitive land markets that drive the poor, as well as long-established businesses, away to the periphery, resulting in longer commuting distances. This phenomenon calls for efficient, high-speed transit systems, which many Asian mega-cities lack. As a consequence, all roads to the city centre are congested during the morning and evening peak commuting hours. Congestion leads to long delays, air and noise pollution. These types of nuisance have cascading effects on the costs of transport and on health, not to mention those, of a longer-term nature, on the environment. High concentrations of activities in mega-cities also put infrastructures and services under severe strain.

However, multiple business and other connections with the rest of the world are not the sole privilege of mega-cities. Some medium-sized cities also play significant roles in global trade through product specialization. For example, in Pakistan, Sialkot produces sports and medical goods, and Faisalabad specialises in apparel, like Bandung in Indonesia. In India, Jaipur produces gems, as does Kanchanaburi in Thailand. These urban centres compete in the global market and command major shares of trade in these specialty items. The problems they face are similar to those of mega-cities, albeit on an admittedly smaller scale.

'Mega' urban regions and urban corridors

These are very large urban areas the size of fully-fledged regions and are often referred to as Extended Metropolitan Regions (EMR). Many such mega-urban regions have emerged in Asia. For example, the "bullet train" corridor making up the Tokyo-Yokohama-Nagoya-Osaka-Kobe-Kyoto backbone of Japan's development, and the Beijing-Tianjin-Tangshan-Qinhuangdao transportation corridor in Northeast China, are huge mega-urban regions characterized by almost unbroken urban, built-up areas. The Manila-centred mega-urban region in the Philippines nearly spreads over the whole island of Luzon. In Indonesia, the so-called 'Jabodetabek' (Jakarta-Bogor-Debok-Tangerang-Bekasi) area stretches all the way to the medium-sized city of Bandung. In southern China, the population of the urban cluster made up of Shanghai, Nanjing, Suzhou, Changzhou, Zhenjiang, Nantong, Yangzhou, and Wuxi is estimated at more than 73 million, while the Guangzhou-Shenzhen-Hong Kong-Macao-Zhuhai region in the Pearl River Delta is host to 150 million.

These mega urban regions are important for national economies. They make major contributions to national output and are homes to large proportions of a country's population. For example, Tokyo's extended metropolitan region is host to 40 million, or almost one-third of Japan's total population, and almost one in two South Koreans live in Seoul. In Taiwan, Province of China, 37 per cent of the population reside in Taipei. It often happens that in mega urban regions,

Mega Urban Region	Population 1990 (1,000s)	Population 2000 (1,000s)	Average Annual Increase (%)
Bangkok (BMR)	5 882	6 320	0.72
Rest of BMR	2 707	3 760	3.30
BMR	8 590	10 080	1.60
Thailand	54 549	60 607	1.05
Jakarta	8 259	8 385	0.16
'Botabek'[1]	8 876	12 749	3.70
'Jabotabek'[2]	17 135	21 134	2.10
Indonesia	179 379	202 000	1.20
Metropolitan Manila	7 945	10 491	2.90
Manila outer zone	6 481	9 458	3.90
Manila EMR[3]	14 426	19 949	3.30
Philippines	60 703	72 345	1.80

[1] Short for the conurbation including Bogor, Tangerang and Bekasi
[2] Short for the conurbation including Jakarta, Bogor, Tangerang and Bekasi
[3] Short for Extended metropolitan region
Source: Jones (2001)

demographic growth at the core is much slower than in the periphery. Many rural settlements and small or medium-sized towns on the periphery of mega urban regions are growing rapidly (see Table 2.12). In the Bangkok Metropolitan Region, between 1990 and the year 2000, the core population grew at less than one per cent per year, compared with 3.3 per cent in the peripheral area. A similar pattern prevailed in Jakarta during the same period. In Manila, however, the population in both the core and the periphery grew at similar rates during that same decade.

Mega urban regions and urban corridors are part of the restructuring of urban territorial space that comes with globalization. While the concentration of economic activities in these large urban areas stands out as one of the positive outcomes of agglomeration economies, the sheer size of these areas also generate diseconomies of scale. For instance, the mega-cities at the core of mega urban regions are beset with high real estate prices, traffic congestion and poor environmental quality. These negative externalities drive firms and households away from core city locations to the periphery with cheaper land and better environmental quality. Such developments usually occur along transportation corridors, which link the small and medium-size cities along the corridor and help form the mega urban region. These connections relieve pressure on land and services in the core city, promote growth in the rural hinterland, and enable small and medium-sized towns in the mega urban regions to partake in the economic growth process.

BOX 2.7: **DHAKA: MANAGING GROWTH IN A POOR MEGA-CITY**

Dhaka is one of the fastest expanding mega-cities in the world, with its population growing an average 5.6 per cent per year. The population is currently estimated at 14.6 million (2010) and is projected to grow to 18.7 million in 2020. The capital of Bangladesh receives an estimated 300,000 to 400,000 new migrants every year. The Centre for Urban Studies at Dhaka University estimates that around 140,000 'eco-refugees' (i.e., affected by floods) move to the city every year. Most come from rural areas in search of opportunities for new livelihoods. The migrants' contribution to Dhaka's economic growth is significant, as they provide much-needed labour for manufacturing, services and other sectors. However, this migration also adds tremendous strain on an already crowded city, with only limited scope for any expansion of habitable land due to Dhaka's peculiar topography (being located on the lower reaches of the Ganges Delta).

The attractions of Dhaka to migrants come as no surprise – it is a dynamic city and has attracted substantial industrial investments, particularly in the readymade apparel industry, with the attendant demand for workers and services. However, the city is increasingly characterized by large slums, poor housing, traffic congestion, water shortages, and poor urban governance, which results in mounting law and order problems. The poor mainly live in slums scattered throughout the city, of which nearly 80 per cent are located on privately-owned land that is devoid of basic services. In the poorest quintile of Dhaka's population, only 9 per cent of households are connected to the sewerage network, and only 27 per cent obtain water through piped supply (compared with 83 per cent of the wealthiest quintile). Spatial mapping shows that only 43 of the 1,925 identified slums have a public toilet within 100 metres. Many slum settlements are

within 50 metres of the river and are exposed to frequent flooding.

Urban management in Dhaka is a major challenge. As many as 40 different agencies are involved, with little coordination or planning. As a result, major gaps characterize services and infrastructure. The poorer segments of the population are particularly affected as they lack the resources to find alternative ways of meeting their basic needs. Dhaka has not been able to keep up with the needs of a rapidly growing population. The environment has deteriorated at a sustained pace. The city is prone to frequent flooding, especially during the rainy season. Traffic congestion causes serious air pollution. A large slum population and poor quality housing have combined with water shortages, poor sanitation and inadequate drainage to lower the quality of life in Dhaka to a significant degree for the average resident.

Sources: World Bank (2007b), UNEP (2005)

2.4
Small and medium-sized cities

▲
Port Vila, Vanuatu. Small and medium-sized cities in the Pacific pose unique development challenges. ©**Brian Philips**

Urbanization in Asia is broad-based rather than concentrated in just a few cities. The urban population is distributed over a range of city sizes. Nearly half the urban population of Asia lives in small and medium-sized cities of less than 500,000.[8] The distribution of settlements in many Asian countries conforms to the 'rank-size rule'.[9] Cities of all sizes are often well distributed over the geographic expanse. There are, however, some exceptions to this rule. Some countries (e.g. Afghanistan, Cambodia, Mongolia and Thailand) exhibit clear signs of urban primacy, with Kabul, Phnom Penh, Ulaanbaatar and Bangkok accounting for over 50 per cent of the urban population of their respective countries.

In Asia, urban settlements with fewer than 500,000 inhabitants have maintained that 'primate' share of around 50 per cent in recent decades, and are expected to keep it over the next two decades (see Chart 2.10). Countries for which more details are available suggest that small and medium-sized towns account for significant proportions of the urban population. For example, in India, around 50 per cent of the 285 million urban dwellers live in towns with populations under 100,000. The demographic growth rates of many of these small towns are not very different from those of large cities. In China's mega urban regions along the coast, small towns with populations under 100,000 have expanded rapidly, too, in a sharp contrast with the declining demographic growth rates in small towns in the hinterland.

Small and medium-sized towns typically perform a variety of roles. They serve as local 'growth centres', i.e., markets for rural products and urban services. In a rapidly growing economy, where major activities are concentrated in large urban centres, small and medium-sized cities play an important role, providing indirect links between the rural and the global economy through connections to large cities. This is especially true of those small cities located in the mega urban regions, which have grown far more rapidly than those of the same size in rural areas. Many small towns also serve as administrative headquarters for district or sub-district administration.

Small and medium-sized cities often serve as temporary 'stepping-stones' for rural migrants on their way to further destinations. In many countries, these subsequent urban-to-urban migration streams are as significant as rural-to-urban flows. The bulk of urban-to-urban migration is from small and medium-sized cities to larger ones. In mega urban regions, this may also involve migration from large to small or medium-sized cities in the periphery.

Despite their significant role as links between rural and urban economies, small and medium-sized cities feature poor infrastructure – unpaved roads, inadequate water supply and sanitation, poor telephone and Internet connectivity and erratic power supply. Hewett and Montgomery (2001) show that smaller cities are less well served than larger ones. Far from negligible as they can be on occasion, these intra-urban differences are not as large as urban-rural differences in access to services. India's smaller towns, and particularly those with populations under 50,000, typically feature low incomes per head and high incidence of poverty. This incidence is inversely proportional to the size class of cities, i.e., the smaller a town, the poorer it will be. The percentage of households that are deprived of access to basic amenities, such as drinking water, toilets and electricity, is also inversely proportional to the size of urban centres in India (Kundu & Bhatia, 2002). Smaller cities also typically benefit from fewer human, financial and technical resources. These deficiencies constrain economic growth in small towns, which as a result often remain as service centres for the rural hinterland.

Most Asian countries have deployed policies to strengthen the role of small and medium-sized towns, but it is generally agreed that these schemes have not worked well. One frequent reason was that such programmes were designed at national level, and therefore failed to recognize the factors specific to each urban centre. Moreover, in many countries, government control over agricultural prices did not provide adequate stimulus for agro-processing in small towns. Another factor was that industrialization policies were not often targeted at small enterprises (Satterthwaite & Tacoli, 2003).

What seems to have worked in favour of small and medium-sized town development, though, is the trend toward decentralization in Asian countries. In many of these, smaller cities have begun to benefit from incipient political and administrative decentralization, under which national governments are devolving some of their powers, including revenue-raising, to local authorities. The smaller of these have found that devolution opened up fresh opportunities to become financially stronger and exercise the powers devolved on them (see Box 2.8). Better resourced, more adept and

CHART 2.10: **THE DISTRIBUTION OF SETTLEMENTS IN ASIA**

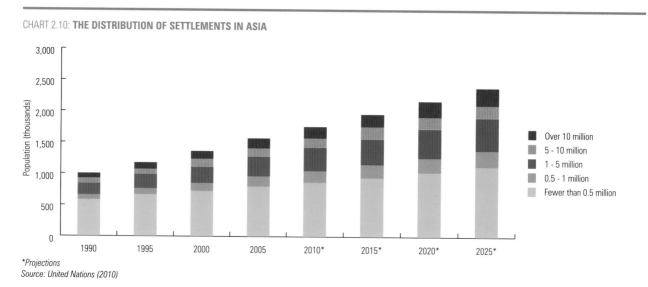

*Projections
Source: United Nations (2010)

TABLE 2.13: **POPULATION DISTRIBUTION IN ASIA, 2010***

Size Class of Cities	Population		
	Number of Agglomerations	Combined Population (1,000s)	Urban Population (%)
10 million or more	11	184 642	11
5 to 10 million	20	145 062	8
1 to 5 million	191	372 490	21
500 000 to 1 million	275	190 525	11
Fewer than 500 000	-	864 595	49
Total urban	-	1 757 314	-
Total rural	-	2 409 427	-
Total	-	4 166 741	-

* Projections
Source: United Nations (2010)

accountable local authorities in smaller urban centres are able to compete with larger cities for new investment, and help retain added value from local productions that hold the best promise for more decentralized urban systems. However, due to their poor management capacities, local authorities have not been able fully to benefit from the opportunities afforded by decentralization (Tacoli, 2003).

In many Asian countries, efforts are underway to support infrastructure development in small and medium-sized towns. India, for instance, launched an Urban Infrastructure Development Scheme for Small and Medium Towns in late 2005. Beyond improved infrastructures, the objective is to "help create durable public assets and quality-orientated services in cities and towns, and promote planned integrated development" (GoI, MoUD, 2009:3).

In China, small town development policies have resulted in a massive effort to build small cities across the country, in a bid to absorb excess rural populations that were surplus to requirements on farms. This 'rural urbanization' policy is encapsulated in the slogan, "Leave the land, but not the countryside; enter the factory, not the city". The aim is to channel agricultural labourers into new towns and small cities that are close to the countryside. Small market towns and townships are upgraded into incorporated towns, and major towns are being developed into small cities (Gale & Dai, 2002).

BOX 2.8: DECENTRALIZATION: BEST PRACTICE FROM TARAKAN, INDONESIA:

Decentralization and democratization have helped small towns in Indonesia and the case of Tarakan proves the point. This is a 251-sq. km island-city in East Kalimantan with a population of 160,000. Historically, Tarakan served as a trading centre and a stopover or transit point for travellers in the East Kalimantan–Sulawesi–Sabah area. During Dutch occupation, the town was an oil exploration centre and as such attracted many migrants. However, the oil sector now contributes only around 6 per cent (US $7.7 million) of Tarakan's total annual production of goods and services (equivalent to US $120 million). After decentralization became effective in 2001 and under the strong leadership of its mayor, Tarakan underwent significant changes, especially in the areas of good governance, urban management, financing, and cost recovery as well as environmental sustainability. These innovations and changes have led to a development-orientated approach in which economic growth is balanced with environmental protection and social advancement. The initiative behind innovative changes in Tarakan is mostly local with the mayor taking a dominant role, and with minimum external support from national government or aid from donor agencies.

Source: Sarosa (2006)

▲ Feng Huang Cheng (Phoenix Town), Hunan Province, China. **©Henry Tsui/Shutterstock**

2.5
Density and the pace of urbanization

▲
Mumbai is the densest city in the Asia-Pacific region. ©**Sapsiwai/Shutterstock**

2.5.1 Urban densities in Asia-Pacific

Unlike their counterparts in other regions, Asian cities are very dense from a demographic point of view. Average urban densities range from 10,000 to 20,000 per sq. km, which is almost double the rates in Latin America, triple those in Europe, and 10 times those found in US cities. This comparison across continents clearly suggests that although many Asians do not live in cities, those who do are crowded into relatively small areas (World Bank, 2007a).

Of the top 20 densest cities in the world, 16 are in Asia (see Chart 2.11), the other four are Bogotá, Kinshasa, Lagos and Lima. A good way of gauging the demographic density of Asian cities is to compare them with others in the world – London, Moscow and Tokyo have approximately the same density, but Mumbai is six times denser. Densities in New York and Paris are lower by half than those found in Bangkok. Shanghai accommodates six million people within a seven km. radius, but Seoul hosts just as many within a 10 km radius and Paris within a 14 km radius. Still, the geographic expanse of a city is not the only factor affecting demographic density: also at play are complex interactions among land markets, transportation systems, local culture and government decisions.

At the moment, the inner cities of Asia's urban areas are undergoing major spatial transformations, the origins of which are of a cultural nature.

"The production of *globally orientated spaces* in the inner city cores can be seen in the massive and continuing construction of office and hotel space mostly by transnational corporations… The production of *consumption spaces* can be observed by the immense conversion of living space into commercial space in the city cores…[which] are increasingly developing into a place of consumption, with modern supermarkets, fancy restaurants, and posh coffee and retail shops…in the urban periphery, large shopping complexes have been established" (Douglass & Huang, 2007:22).[10]

Asian cities have been dense for centuries. Beijing's *hutongs*, Hanoi's Old Quarter (the '36 streets'), Delhi's *Katras* and Ahmedabad's *Pols* provide glimpses of how dense these cities already were in medieval times. In modern Asian cities, demographic densities vary significantly within built-up areas, with high concentrations in some locations. The pattern of densities within the built-up area is an important factor in land use efficiency (Bertaud, 2007). In general, a city's land use is considered more efficient when the pattern of densities reduces daily commuting distance, with employment concentrated in or around the centre or in a few specific areas. Higher densities towards the centre and lower densities in the periphery is the pattern prevailing in most cities of the world.

Density in cities is affected by the modes of transport available to commuters. In high-density cities, the commuting

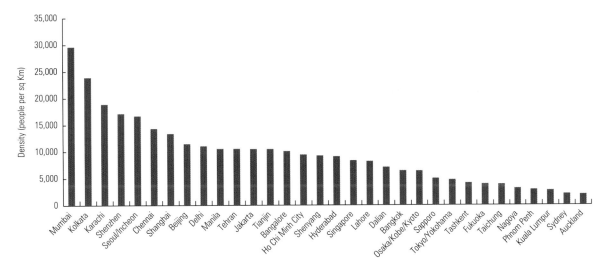

Source: http://www.citymayors.com/statistics/largest-cities-density-125.html[11]

population typically resorts to the proper public transport services available rather than to personal vehicles, and the situation is the reverse in low-density cities. High-density cities are not suitable for high rates of private car use, as road capacity per person is low. Moreover, private automobiles take up large amounts of space when in motion and for parking, and these two types of congestion can become very serious in dense cities even when only a small proportion of the resident population own cars. Still, in some high-density cities like Tokyo, Singapore, Mumbai and Hong Kong, China, public transport systems work well and carry millions of commuters daily. These tend to be the exception, though, as many Asian cities lack well-functioning public transport systems and commuters have little alternative but personal vehicles. This creates major traffic congestion and results in longer commuting times. Such cities must plan for lower densities in central areas; they must also spend more on public transport (Bertaud, 2007), as some Asian cities have done in recent years: Delhi and Bangkok now have underground railway and skytrain networks, and both Manila and Kuala Lumpur have introduced light rail transit (LRT) systems.

Walking or cycling is an efficient mode of individual transport, and one that is compatible with high densities, including the narrow streets of the old quarters of Asian cities. In Viet Nam, the contrast between two dense cities is very visible. The capital Hanoi has retained its character, with traditional old residential buildings and shops in the central area. While bicycles remain a major mode of transport, motorcycles and electric bikes are becoming the preferred form, and cars are the exception. One of the defining features of Ho Chi Minh City, on the other hand, is a more modern make-up, including wide boulevards and increasing numbers of automobiles. The commercial core of the city is crowded and as in so many Asian cities, it has become increasingly difficult to travel there by foot or bicycle. Chapter 4 (on poverty and inequality in

Asian cities) further discusses urban transport.

Land markets in high-density cities reflect the growing demand for land in central urban areas. Scarce supply drives up land prices in prime locations. The business districts in Mumbai, Shanghai and Hong Kong, China, command higher property values than those in London, New York or Tokyo. Of the world's top 10 expensive cities in terms of property prices, four are in Asia – Tokyo, Singapore, Mumbai and Hong Kong, China, with Mumbai being the only one in 10 located in a developing economy. Residential apartment prices in Hong Kong, China, range from US $10,490 to US $14,780 per sq. m., compared with US $7,600 to US $11,870 in Tokyo, up to US $11,500 to US $13,340 in Singapore and US $8,600 to US $10,300 in Mumbai. By comparison, Chinese cities are significantly cheaper by global standards. Prices of flats in Shanghai range between US $2,870 and US $3,540 per sq. m. while those in Beijing are priced at US $2,100 to US $2,330 per sq. m. In South-East Asia, the price of a 120 sq. m. condominium in Jakarta is around US $1,073 per sq. m., i.e., cheaper than in Kuala Lumpur (US $1,400), Manila (US $1,969) or Bangkok (US $2,819).[12]

As a market response to land demand, high density results in more efficient use of space. It acts as a cure for urban sprawl as it makes cities more compact and hence more efficient from the perspective of infrastructure investment. Government actions, through planning regulations and investments in infrastructure, can also have a significant impact on densities and prices. Density is measured with the floor-area ratio (FAR), i.e., the ratio between the total built-up space and the plot area, which assesses the intensity of land use. For instance in New York City, the floor-area ratio varies from 15 in the Wall Street district to 0.4 in suburbs. In some Asian cities like Bangkok and Shanghai, the maximum authorised floor-area ratio is 10, i.e., total built-up space can be up to 10 times the plot area. In market economies, local floor-area ratios are

Region	1990-1995	1995-2000	2000-2005	2005-2010*	2010-2015*	2015-2020*	2020-2025*	2025-2030*
World	2.4	2.2	2.2	1.9	1.8	1.8	1.7	1.5
Asia	**3.2**	**2.9**	**2.8**	**2.3**	**2.2**	**2.0**	**1.9**	**1.7**
Oceania/Pacific	**1.5**	**1.4**	**1.5**	**1.3**	**1.2**	**1.2**	**1.2**	**1.1**
Europe	0.3	0.1	0.3	0.4	0.4	0.3	0.3	0.2
North America	1.7	1.7	1.4	1.3	1.2	1.1	1.0	0.9
Latin America and the Caribbean	2.5	2.2	1.9	1.6	1.4	1.2	1.0	0.9
Africa	3.8	3.4	3.4	3.4	3.3	3.1	3.0	2.8

*Projections
Source: United Nations (2007a)

▲
Residential apartments in Hong Kong, China, range from US $10,490 to US $14,780 per sq. m. ©Oksana.perkins/Shutterstock

closely linked to local demand for floor space: high demand means high ratios. When local planning laws restrict floor-area ratios in order to control densities, the resulting shortages in the supply of built-up space lead to higher property prices. While there is no ideal floor area ratio, urban planning in Asia must recognize that demand for land is bound to grow in rapidly expanding cities, a phenomenon which planning laws must facilitate rather than constrain.

2.5.2 Pace of urbanization in Asia-Pacific

The high density of Asian cities is also often seen as a result of their own rapid expansion. Together with lack of serviced land, inadequate infrastructure in the periphery leads to higher concentrations of people in and around city centres. Cities' ability to invest in infrastructure in response to expanding populations has a direct bearing on densities.

Although the growth in the Asia-Pacific region's urban population is faster than in Latin America and the Caribbean and the world average, it is slower than in Africa. In the region as a whole, urban population growth is projected to slow down from an annual 3.2 per cent rate during 1990-1995 to 2.8 per cent between 2010 and 2015 (see Table 2.14). Within the Asia-Pacific region, this slowdown is clearly visible since the early 1990s (see Chart 2.12).

The pace of urbanization is dependent on many factors, and simple projections based on past trends may not be correct. For example, Kolkata, Seoul and Chennai (formerly Madras) had fewer residents in the year 2000 than was forecast by the United Nations in 1985. In many Asian countries, the prospective 'tipping point' of 50 per cent urban populations has been pushed back due to the above-mentioned slowdown in urban demographic expansion. For instance, India's 2001 census showed that urban population numbers were much lower than predicted earlier. On a worldwide scale, the growth rate of the urban population is expected to slow down over the next few decades.

Asia's 20 fastest-growing cities are listed in Table 2.15. All had populations above 500,000 in 2005, and as many as 15

CHART 2.12: **URBAN GROWTH RATES IN ASIA-PACIFIC, 1990-2005 (%)**

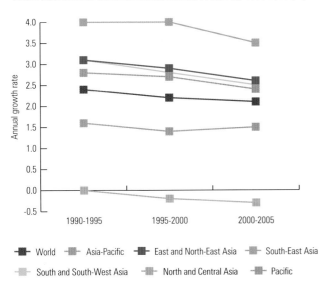

- ■ World
- ■ Asia-Pacific
- ■ East and North-East Asia
- ■ South-East Asia
- ■ South and South-West Asia
- ■ North and Central Asia
- ■ Pacific

Source: ESCAP (2010)

were located in China. All but one on the list have grown rapidly on the back of economic expansion. The exception is Kabul, where demographic growth is largely due to migration of internally displaced people. Many Chinese cities on the list are in the rapidly growing Pearl River Delta region. Others on the list are near major mega-cities, e.g., Ghaziabad (near Delhi) and Goyang (near Seoul). Surat, western India, is a major national centre for diamond polishing and textiles. If these cities continue to grow at the same rates as in the last decade, some stand to double their populations in less than 10 years.

These prospects raise a critical question, which has to do with the capacity of Asian cities to accommodate such demographic growth. Many cities in China have plans for major capital investment in infrastructures and therefore seem to be in a better position to cater to the needs of business and people. In contrast, a city like Kabul (see Box 2.4) struggles to cope with a rapidly expanding population that does not come associated with economic development.

TABLE 2.15: **ASIA'S FASTEST GROWING CITIES, 1995-2005**

Rank	Country	City	Urban Population 1995 (1,000s)	Urban Population 2005 (1,000s)	Urban Population Growth Rate (% /Year)	Population Doubling Time (Years)
1	China	Shenzhen	2 304	7 233	11.44	6.4
2	China	Suzhou, Anhui	623	1 849	10.88	6.7
3	China	Shangqiu	574	1 650	10.56	6.9
4	China	Xinyang	571	1 450	9.32	7.8
5	China	Nanyang, Henan	753	1 830	8.88	8.1
6	China	Xiamen	1 124	2 371	7.46	9.6
7	China	Wenzhou	1 056	2 212	7.39	9.7
8	China	Luzhou	706	1 447	7.18	10.0
9	China	Nanchong	1 029	2 046	6.87	10.4
10	China	Fuyang	376	726	6.58	10.9
11	China	Zhuhai	518	963	6.20	11.5
12	Afghanistan	Kabul	1 616	2 994	6.17	11.6
13	China	Quanzhou	745	1 377	6.14	11.6
14	India	Ghaziabad	675	1 237	6.06	11.8
15	Malaysia	Klang	466	849	6.00	11.9
16	India	Surat	1 984	3 558	5.84	12.2
17	Republic of Korea	Goyang	493	859	5.55	12.8
18	China	Shaoxing	426	731	5.40	13.2
19	China	Dongguan, Guangdong	2 559	4 320	5.24	13.6
20	China	Yantai	1 188	1 991	5.16	13.8

Source: United Nations (2007a)

2.6
Urbanization in Asia: Diagnosis & policies

Asia is home to nearly two-thirds of the world population, and to the world's three most heavily populated nations. Many Asian countries have benefited from the 'demographic dividend' in the form of cheaper labour as well as the large pool of qualified technicians required for rapid economic growth.

The basic diagnosis based on the foregoing analysis is that urbanization in Asia is inevitable. According to the latest available figures from the United Nations, by early 2026 half of Asia's population will live in urban areas. This is inevitable because urbanization comes hand in hand with economic development. Historically, the relationship between urbanization and economic development is seen as an 'S' shaped curve. Low levels of development typically go hand in hand with low urbanization rates and moderate urban demographic growth. The more sustained development phase of a country is characterised by rapid urban population growth (largely through migration and reclassification). In more mature economies, urban demographic growth tapers off and urbanization stabilizes at high rates. This is the path that countries in other regions of the world have trodden, and this is the path the Asia and the Pacific region is to follow in turn.

Various Asian countries find themselves on different trajectories of economic development and demonstrate different urbanization patterns. Many are still classified as 'low income' and consequently, are less urbanized than others. Thus while on the whole, the Asia-Pacific region is less urbanized as compared with others, many countries there are gradually catching up and are expected to cross the tipping point of '50 per cent urban' in the next two decades.

What, then, makes the Asian urbanization process different from other continents? Asian cities are in a constant state of flux and a major difference lies in the scale of the demographic expansion. Over the last two decades (1990 to 2010), Asia's urban demographic expansion amounted to the combined populations of the USA and the European Union. No other continent has experienced any increase this size and in such a short time span.

A second defining feature of urban Asia is high densities – indeed, the highest in the world, ranging between 10,000 to 20,000 residents per sq km This is due not just to modern skyscrapers and high-rise residential buildings, but also to the myriads of small, low-rise, high-density buildings that are typical of the traditional layout of older areas. As one might expect, high densities come with average spaces per head – both open and residential – that are among the lowest in the world.

The third defining feature of Asian cities comes under the form of mixed land-use development. More specifically, residential areas sit next to commercial activities, just as traditional buildings stand alongside modern skyscrapers, and formal and informal activities take place in the same space.

This diagnosis clearly suggests that the scale of Asia's urban population growth calls for significant increases in infrastructure investment. Short of this, the growth and prosperity of Asian cities could be seriously jeopardised. Given the continent's large population and rapid economic growth, it is imperative to ensure that urban development in Asia is 'green' and low-carbon. Chapter 5 discusses the urban environment further.

In the past, adequate investment in urban infrastructure has been lacking as policy-makers did not view urbanization as a process that was compatible with economic development. More specifically, the notion prevailed that urbanization *per se* did not contribute to development, and instead came only in response to poor economic and living conditions in rural areas. Public policy was regarded as biased towards cities which, in turn, increased the attraction of rural people to urban areas. The dominant policy paradigm was to prevent urbanization and encourage potential migrants to remain in rural areas. In many countries this was evident in restrictive policies regarding rural to urban movements of people, combined with a lack of funding for urban infrastructure development. A survey by the United Nations (2008:12) reports that:

"Faced with the numerous opportunities and challenges associated with urbanization, many Governments have consistently considered their population's spatial distribution as a concern. In 2007, 85 per cent of Governments expressed concern about their pattern of population distribution, a percentage comparable to that recorded in the 1970s... Among developing countries, 56 per cent wished to make a major change in the spatial distribution of their populations, whereas 32 per cent desired a minor change. Among developed countries, 37 per cent desired a major change and 39 per cent a minor change. Dissatisfaction regarding patterns of population distribution was highest in Africa (74 per cent of its countries desired a major change) and Asia (51 per cent desired a major change). In Latin America and the Caribbean, Oceania and Europe, about 40 per cent of Governments considered that major changes in spatial distribution were desirable."

For example, in Papua New Guinea, opposition to urbanization has continued from both urban authorities and influential leaders. In the mid-1990s, the prime minister of Morobe province sought to expel all illegal settlers from the coastal capital city Lae. Similar policies in other centres in Papua New Guinea have continued throughout the decade. In Vanuatu, too, slum settlements have been seen as blighted places from which people had to be removed. Pervasive opposition to urbanization is not specific to the Pacific island countries, though. Policymakers in many other countries have held similar notions.

The turning point in many Asian countries came during the 1990s with a shift of focus in national policies that clearly linked urbanization and economic growth. This came with a recognition that economic growth required links between national and global economies and that this could be achieved through urban development. Subsequently, many Asian countries have implicitly promoted urbanization, though political rhetoric may have stated otherwise.

In Viet Nam, the *Doi Moi* process[13] which the government endorsed in 1987 effectively ended a period of urban neglect. The policy changes that accompanied *Doi Moi* made cities more acceptable and attractive as centres for formal and informal business and opportunity. Controls on official migration continued but were less strictly enforced over time. It became politically and socially acceptable to move to a town or city, although government policies to this day still seek to balance development and capital investment between urban and rural provinces.

In China since the 1990s, controls on population movements have become weaker, and recently many rural people have been able to migrate to cities. Nearly 100 million rural Chinese did so over the course of the 1990s. China also took to granting city or town status to many settlements, with

the attendant prestige and other benefits. Although freedom of movement remains restricted somehow in China, the need to urbanize is widely accepted by now. In anticipation of rapid urban expansion, major investments in urban infrastructure are taking place. For example, throughout the 1980s, Shanghai spent five to eight per cent of its GDP on urban infrastructure and redevelopment. Beijing and Tianjin now spend more than 10 per cent of their respective GDPs on roads, water and sewerage networks, housing construction and transportation (Yusuf & Saich, 2008).

Many Asian countries have benefited from the 'demographic dividend' and have achieved rapid economic growth. Far from being considered a drawback, demographic size is now seen as providing major benefits such as cheaper labour, large pools of skilled technical staff and more generally the ability to tap the enormous potential of the Asian population. The positive benefits deriving from urbanization include a diverse and strong economy, together with the potential for poverty reduction. Thanks to economies of scale, demographic concentrations in urban areas greatly reduce the unit costs of good quality services, healthcare, education and cultural activities (Satterthwaite, 2002).

Most Asian countries are still in the early stages of urbanization. This gives them an opportunity to prepare for urban expansion. If they are able to plan and pave the way for such expansion with proper infrastructures, they will find themselves in a better position to alleviate the negative aspects of urbanization, such as congestion, pollution and slums. For this to happen, urban policies must become part and parcel of national development policies.

ENDNOTES

1 The only exception to this region-wide pattern was the Philippines. Most of the country's urbanization occurred between 1980 and the year 2000 but real GDP per head changed little over the period. It is unlikely that a single factor can fully explain this phenomenon, but the highly concentrated nature of the country's urbanization, coupled with the haphazard fashion in which it has been occurring (and possibly a fragmented geography, too), may offer some clues, as mentioned in World Bank (2007a - East Asia and Pacific update).

2 According to Bloom, Canning & Jamison (2004), declining mortality and fertility rates in Asia between 1960 and the year 2000 led to a rise in the ratio of working-age people (15–64) to the dependent population (0–14 and 65 plus), from about 1.3 to over 2, resulting in substantial increases in worker productivity and GDP per head.

3 Shanghai's Municipal Population and Family Planning Commission has launched a public information campaign to highlight exemptions to the country's otherwise uniform one-child policy. For instances, those couples whose members were both only children are now allowed a second child (BBC News, 2009).

4 It is not possible to split the 'migration' and 'reclassification' components of these estimates.

5 *Hukou* is the household registration system in China under which some changes of permanent residence are subject to approval from one or more authorities. Movement within urban or rural areas is free. However, permits are required for changes from rural to urban areas or from a smaller to a larger city. The "floating population" *(liudong renkou)* is a unique concept in China that is tied to the *hukou* system. Individuals who are not living at their *hukou* location are considered "floating". This concept is based on the notion that the *hukou* location is where one belongs and that migration is not considered official and permanent until the migrant's *hukou* location is also changed (Chan, 2008; Fan, 2008).

6 This section is based on ESCAP (2008b and 2008c).

7 The source of this information is Osaka (1996). This situation appears to have held even in recent years.

8 *World Urbanization Prospects 2007* does not provide information on settlements with populations below 500,000. For the purpose of this section, the small and medium towns are referred to as towns below 500,000, although for some countries in Asia this may not be an adequate assumption.

9 The rank-size rule, or Zipf's law, refers to the distribution of cities by size within a system. Cities are listed in descending order of population and given a rank, with the city of highest population as rank one, and the next city as rank two etc. The Zipf's law states that the size of the city ranked second is roughly half of the one ranked first, and the size of the one ranked third is roughly half that of the one ranked second, etc. (see Soo, 2004).

10 Waibel, M. (2006) "The production of urban space in Viet Nam's metropolis in the course of transition". *Trialog* 89(2): 43-48, as quoted in Douglass and Huang (2007).

11 The boundaries of the cities in the chart may not match those in the UN *World Urbanization Prospects*, resulting in discrepancies in density figures.

12 The figures are based on the average price of a 120 sq. m, good-condition, high-end apartment in the city centre, i.e., where most foreigners are likely to buy. Data were collected during 2008. The US dollar exchange rate is as at January 27, 2009 *(Global Property Guide, 2009).*

13 The *Doi Moi* process was an economic reform and poverty eradication programme which the Government of Viet Nam launched in 1986. The comprehensive scheme enabled the country's transition from central planning to a market-orientated economy.

Abott, David, & Steve Pollard. *Hardship and Poverty* in the Pacific: *A summary*. Manila: Asian Development Bank, 2004

Acharya, Sarthi. "Labour migration in the transitional economies of south-east Asia". *Working paper on migration and urbanization*. Emerging Social Issues Division, UN Economic Commission for Asia and the Pacific, December 2003

Ambasta, Pramathesh, P S Vijay Shankar, & Mihir Shah. "Two Years of NREGA: The Road Ahead". *Economic & Political Weekly,* Vol 43, No. 8, February 23, 2008 41-50

Basyal, Gopi Krishna, & Narendra Raj Khanal. *Process and characteristics of urbanization in Nepal.* Kathmandu: Research Centre for Nepal and Asian Studies, 2001

BBC News. *Shanghai urges 'two-child policy'.* July 24, 2009. http://news.bbc.co.uk/2/hi/asia-pacific/8166413.stm (accessed 21 September 2009)

Bertaud, Alain. *Urbanization in China: land use efficiency issues.* 2007. http://alain-bertaud.com/AB_Files/AB_China_land_use_report_6.pdf (accessed 18 July 2009)

Biau, Daniel. "Chinese Cities, Indian Cities – A Telling Contrast". *Economic and Political Weekly,* Vol 42 No. 33, August 18-24, 2007: 69-72

Bloom, David E., David Canning, & Dean T. Jamison. "Health, Wealth and Welfare". *Finance and Development,* March, 2004: 41, 10-15

Chan, Kam Wing. "Internal Labour Migration in China: Trends, Geographical Distribution And Policies". Seminar paper, *United Nations Expert Group Meeting On Population Distribution, Urbanization, Internal Migration And Development-*

UN/POP/EGM-URB/2008/05. New York: UN Population Division, Department of Economic and Social Affairs, January 3, 2008

Connel, John. "Migration in Pacific Island countries and territories". In *Migration Patterns and Policies in the Asian and Pacific Region, Asian Population Studies Series No 160-ESCAP ST/ESCAP/2277,* by John Connel. Bangkok: ESCAP, 2003: 35-65

Connell, John, & John P. Lea. *Urbanization in the Island Pacific: towards sustainable development,.* London: Routledge, 2002

da Silva, Fernando Nunes. *Urbanism and Transports.* September 2008. https://dspace.ist.utl.pt/bitstream/2295/214538/1/FNS_Cidades_redes_Set08.pdf (accessed 10 April 2009)

Douglass, Mike, & Liling Huang. "Globalizing The City In Southeast Asia: Utopia On The Urban Edge – The Case Of Phu My Hung, Saigon". *International Journal of Asia-Pacific Studies 3* November 2007: 1-41

East West Center. "Asia's ageing population". *The Future of Population in Asia.* Honolulu, Hawaii: East West Center Research Programme-population and health, 2008

— "Asia's Changing Youth Population". 2006. http://www.eastwestcenter.org/fileadmin/stored/misc/FuturePop06Youth.pdf (accessed 18 July 2009)

England, Robert Stowe. Ageing China: The Demographic Challenge. Westport, CT: Praeger Publishers, 2005

Economic and Social Commission for Asia and the Paicific (ESCAP). *Statistical Yearbook for Asia and the Pacific 2010.* Bangkok: UNESCAP, 2010

—. *Statistical Yearbook for Asia and the Pacific 2008.* Bangkok: UNESCAP, 2008a

—. "Key Trends and Challenges on International Migration and Development in Asia and the Pacific". *United Nations Expert Group Meeting on International Migration and Development in Asia and the Pacific-UN/POP/EGM-MIG/2008.* Bangkok: Population Division, Department of Economic and Social Affairs, United Nations, September 18, 2008b

—. *Situation Report on International Migration in East and South-East Asia.* Bangkok: UNESCAP, 2008c

Fan, C. Cindy. "Migration, Hukou, and the City". In *China Urbanizes: Consequences, Strategies, and Policies,* edited by Shahid Yusuf and Anthony Saich, 65-90. Washington, D.C.: World Bank, 2008

Gale, Fred, & Hongguo Dai. "Small Town Development in China: A 21st century Challenge". *Rural America,* 17 Spring 2002: 12-19

Global Property Guide. *Global Property Guide.* 2009. http://www.globalpropertyguide.com/Asia (accessed 10 February 2009)

Government of India, Ministry of Urban Development (GoI, MoUD). *Urban Infrastructure Development Scheme for Small and Medium Towns: an Overview.* 2009. http://urbanindia.nic.in/programme/ud/uidssmt_pdf/overview.pdf (accessed 19 April 2010)

Government of Japan. *White Paper on Ageing Society-Summary 2007.* 2007. http://www8.cao.go.jp/kourei/english/annualreport/2007/2007.pdf (accessed 19 June 2009)

Heller, Peter. "Is Asia prepared for an Ageing Population?" *Working Paper, WP/06/272.* Washington D.C.: Fiscal Affairs Department, International Monetary Fund (IMF), December 2006

Hewett, Paul C., & Mark R. Montgomery. "Poverty and public services in developing-country cities". *Policy Research Division Working Paper no. 154.* New York: Population Council, 2001

Hugo, Graeme. "Urbanization in Asia: An Overview". *Conference on African Migration in Comparative Perspective, Johannesburg, South Africa.* June 4-7, 2003. http://pum.princeton.edu/pumconference/papers/2-Hugo.pdf (accessed 19 June 2009)

Indrasiri, L.H. "Urbanization and Urban Redefinition – Sri Lanka 2005". *Urban Development Authority, Sri Lanka.* 2005. http://www.uda.lk/reports/Urbanization and Urban Redefinition 2005.pdf (accessed 24 September 2009)

Jones, Gavin. "Studying Extended Metropolitan Regions in South East Asia". *The XXIV General Conference of the IUSSP.* Salvador, August 18-24, 2001

Kano, Hiromasa. "Urbanization in Post Revolution Iran". *The Developing Economies,* December 1996: 34 (4): 424-46

Kundu, Amitabh, & Sutinder Bhatia. "Industrial growth in small and medium towns and their vertical integration: the case of Gobindgarh, Punjab, India". *MOST Discussion Paper, No. 57.* Paris: UNESCO, 2002

Montgomery, Mark, Richard Stren, Barney Cohen, & Holly E. Reed. *Cities Transformed.* London: Earthscan, 2004

ODI. "Internal migration, poverty and development in Asia". *Briefing Paper 11.* London: Overseas Development Institute, 2006

Osaka, Hurights. "Migrant Workers and Human Rights". *Asia Pacific News-Vol.4.* June 1996. http://www.hurights.or.jp/asia-pacific/no_04/02migrantwand.htm (accessed 24 September 2009)

Pathak, Pushpa, & Dinesh Mehta. "Trends, Patterns and implications of rural-to-urban migration in India". *Asia Population Studies Series No 138.* New York: United Nations, 1995a

—. "Recent Trends in Urbanization and Rural-Urban Migration in India : Some Explanations and Projections". *Urban India,* 15 1995b 1-17

Richard.L, Forstall, Richard P. Greene, & James B. Pick. *Which Are The Largest? Why Published Populations For Major World Urban Areas Vary So Greatly.* 2006. http://www.eukn.org/ netherlands/themes/Urban_Policy/ Urban_environment/Land_use/ Urbanisation/Why-published-populations-for-major-world-urban-areas-vary-so-greatly_1035.html (accessed 26 June 2009)

Sarosa, Wicaksono. "Indonesia". In *Urbanization and Sustainability in Asia: Case Studies of Good Practice,* by Brian Roberts and Trevor Kanaley, edited by Brian Roberts and Trevor Kanaley. Manila: Asian Development Bank, 2006: 155-187

Satterthwaite, David. *The Ten and a Half Myths that may Distort the Urban Policies of Governments and International Agencies.* 2002. http://www.eukn.org/netherlands/ themes/Urban_Policy/ten-and-a-half-myths_3399.html (accessed 2 June 2010)

Satterthwaite, David, & Cecilia Tacoli. "The urban part of rural development: the role of small and intermediate urban centres in rural and regional development and poverty reduction". *Working Paper Series on Rural-Urban Interactions and Livelihood Strategies: Working Paper 9.* London: International Institute for Environment and Development, 2003

Shirazi, Safdar Ali. *Patterns of Urbanization in Pakistan: A Demographic Appraisal.*

2006. http://paa2006. princeton.edu/download. aspx?submissionId=61209 (accessed September 24, 2009)

Soo, Kwok Tang. "Zipf's Law for Cities: A Cross Country Investigation". *CEP Discussion Paper No 641.* London School of Economics, 2004

Storey, Donovan. *Urbanization in Pacific, State, Society and Governance in Melanesia Project.* 2005. http://www.unescap.org/ EPOC/documents/R3.12_Study_2. pdf (accessed 7 January 2009)

Tacoli, Cecilia. "The links between urban and rural development". *Environment and Urbanization,* 15, April 2003 3-12

Talbot, Jon, & Buddley Ronnie. "Postcolonial town planning in Commonwealth nations: A case study of the Solomon Islands - an agenda for change". *The Round Table,* 96 2007 319 - 329

UNEP. *Dhaka City State of Environment Report 2005.* United Nations Environment Programme, 2005

UN-HABITAT. *State of the World's Cities 2010/11 – Bridging the Urban Divide.* Nairobi: UN-HABITAT, 2010a; London: Earthscan 2010

UNHCR. "Chapter 1: Current dynamics of displacement". In *The State of the World's Refugees 2006 - Human displacement in the new millennium,* by UNHCR. Geneva: UNHCR, 2006: 9-29

United Nations. *World Urbanization Prospects: The 2009 revision. CD-ROM Edition - Data in digital form* (POP/DB/WUP/ Rev.2009). New York: Population Division, Department of Economic and Social Affairs, United Nations, 2010

— *World Population Prospects: The 2008 revision.* New York: Population

Division, Department of Economic and Social Affairs, United Nations, 2009

— "Executive Summary". *World Urbanization Prospects:* The 2007 Revision. New York: Population Division, Department of Economic and Social Affairs, February 26, 2008

— *World Urbanization Prospects:* The 2007 Revision. New York: Department of Economic and Social Affairs, United Nations, 2007a. http://esa.un.org/unup (accessed 20 July 2009)

— *World Youth Report 2007-Young People's Transition to Adulthood:Progress and Challenges.* New York: Department of Economic and Social Affairs, United Nations, 2007b

— *World Population Prospects:* The 2006 Revision. New York: Population Division of the Department of Economic and Social Affairs of the United Nations Secretariat, 2006

— "Definition of Urban". *Demographic Yearbook 2005,* Table 6 New York: United Nations Statistics Division. 2005. http://unstats.un.org/unsd/ demographic/sconcerns/densurb/ Defintion_of%20Urban.pdf (accessed 19 July 2009)

— *World Population Prospects.* New York: Population Division, Department of Economic and Social Affairs, United Nations, 2001a

— "The Components of Urban Growth in Developing Countries". ESA/P/WP. 169. Population Division, Department of Economic and Social Affairs, September 2001b

World Bank. *"Migration and Remittances Factbook 2008".* Washington DC, World Bank, 2008a

—. *New Thinking Sees Cities as Key to Improving National Growth Potential, Says World Bank-News*

Release No. 402/2008/EAP. June 25, 2008b. http://go.worldbank.org/ QJR4F6AYJ0 (accessed 20 July 2009)

— "East Asia and Pacific Update-10 years after the crisis". *Special focus: Sustainable development in East Asia's urban fringe.* World Bank, 2007a http:// siteresources.worldbank.org/ INTEAPHALFYEARLYUPDATE/ esources/550192-1175629375615/ EAP-Update-April2007-fullreport.pdf (accessed 21 July 2009)

— "Dhaka:Improving Living Conditions of Urban Poor". *Bangladesh Development Series Paper No.17.* Dhaka: World Bank, 2007b

— "Effects of Population Growth and Urbanization in the Pacific Islands". *In Cities, seas and storms-Managing change in Pacific Island economies-Vol 2-Managing Pacific Towns,* by World Bank, 1-15. Washington, DC: World Bank, 2000 http://siteresources.worldbank.org/ INTPACIFICISLANDS/Resources/ Chapter+1.pdf (accessed 21 July 2009)

Yap, Kioe Sheng. "Youth and urban conflict in Southeast Asian cities". In *Youth, Poverty, and Conflict in Southeast Asian Cities-Comparative Urban Studies Project,* by Lisa M. Hanley, Blair A. Ruble & Joseph S. Tulchin. Washington, DC: Woodrow Wilson International Center for Scholars, 2004: 37-54

Yusuf, Shahid & Saich, Anthony. eds *"China Urbanizes: Consequences, Strategies, and Policies"* pp 65-90. Washington, D.C.: World Bank, 2008

PART
03

The Economic Role
of Asian Cities

Quick Facts

1. Asian cities are highly productive – the 40 per cent of the population living in urban areas contribute 80 per cent of the region's gross domestic product.

2. Asian cities are economically resilient, as demonstrated by their response to the global economic crises.

3. The cities in Asia-Pacific region are well positioned to capitalise on the opportunities provided by their own demographic expansion as well as the forces behind globalization.

4. Synergies between the formal and informal sectors account for the socio-economic dynamism of Asian cities.

5. Asian cities are diversifying away from their role as the factories of the world to one of innovative service providers.

6. Asian cities are drivers of rural development by bringing investments into rural regions and providing markets to agricultural products.

Policy Points

1. Asia's least advanced countries should learn from more developed and emerging economies in the region in order to make their cities more productive and competitive.

2. Fiscal and regulatory incentives should be reviewed and expanded to attract more domestic and foreign investment in Asian cities.

3. The informal sector should be supported rather than harassed and play a more positive role in employment generation and housing production.

4. Asian cities must build the institutional capacity and strategic vision that will enable them to manage economic growth in a more inclusive sort of way.

5. Cities must pay attention to the way infrastructure programmes fit with broader development strategies and political circumstances, how those strategies are formulated and how they bring about tangible outcomes.

6. It is for political leaders and senior policymakers in the Asia-Pacific region to evolve a vision for long-term development based on holistic approaches that merge spatial policy with macro-economic, industrial, agricultural, energy, environmental and labour policies.

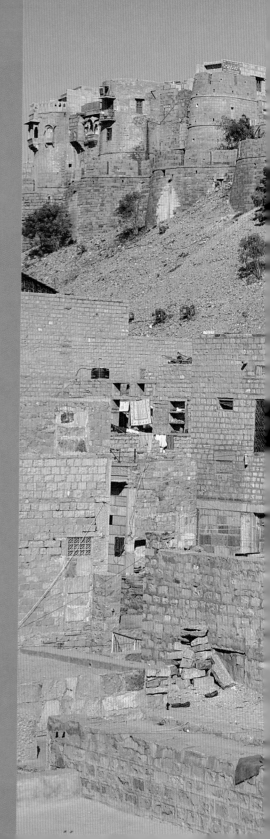

Jaisalmer 'the Golden City', India.
©Dirk Ott/Shutterstock

3.1
Cities as engines of economic growth

▲
Guangzhou, China. ©**Agophoto/Shutterstock**

Cities have become the major drivers of national economies in the Asia-Pacific as in other regions. Being highly productive, they make significant contributions to national economies. On the whole, just over 40 per cent of the Asian-Pacific population contributes 80 per cent of the region's gross domestic product (GDP) (see Chart 3.1).

3.1.1 Asian economic growth is led by cities

Over the past few decades and in many Asian countries, urban economies have grown rapidly, thanks to the superior productivity resulting from location-specific factors. Economies of agglomeration, representing the efficiency benefits of business concentrations in urban areas, are known to induce growth. Urbanization enhances productivity and increases gross domestic product per head. In other words, the contributions of urban areas to national wealth keep increasing in Asia, and are turning into major determinants of economic strength.

Economic growth in Asia-Pacific region has been robust over the past two decades, except for the short 1997-98 financial crunch and the effects of the global economic crisis from which the region is now recovering. The region's combined production nearly doubled between 1990 and

CHART 3.1: **SHARE OF URBAN AREAS IN GDP, ASIA AND THE PACIFIC, 1990-2008**

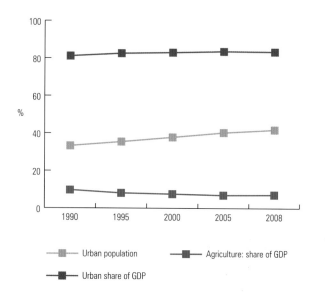

Source: Computed from ESCAP (2010b)
Note: Data for urban share of GDP is not readily available. Estimates are derived from the share of non-agricultural sectors in GDP as provided by ESCAP Statistical Yearbook 2010. It is assumed that 90 per cent of non-agricultural production is generated in urban areas.

Region	1990-1995	1995-2000	2000-2005
Asia and the Pacific	1.4	2.6	4.4
Africa	-1.2	1.8	2.3
Europe	0.3	2.8	1.9
Latin America and the Caribbean	1.6	1.5	1.4
North America	1.1	3.0	1.4
Rest of the world	2.0	1.4	2.1
World	0.7	2.2	2.3

Source: ESCAP (2010b:104)

CHART 3.2: **GDP PER WORLD REGION, 1990-2008 (IN 1990 US $ BILLION)**

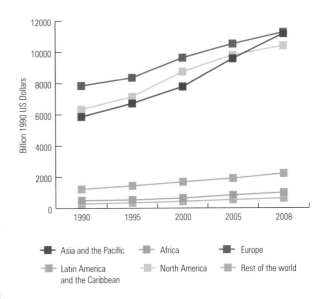

Source: Computed from ESCAP (2010b)

2008 (see Chart 3.2), in the process turning into a significant contributor to world economic output (30 per cent in 2008).

Table 3.1 shows that GDP growth per head in the Asia-Pacific region has been increasing without interruption since 1990, and between 2000 and 2005, the region experienced the world's highest growth rate per head – an annual 4.4 per cent average rate, nearly double the average rates for the world as a whole and for Africa, the second best-performing region (see Chart 3.3).

3.1.2 The global economic crisis and Asian economies

The recent economic crisis has caused world economic growth to slow down from 2.6 per cent in 2007 to 1.0 per cent in 2008 (see Chart 3.3). Although the impact was most felt in North America (especially the USA) where it started, the crisis has undermined the strength of export-orientated Asia-Pacific economies, where growth fell from a robust 4.7 per cent in 2007 to 2.7 per cent in 2008.

The effects of the global economic crisis have been uneven across Asian-Pacific subregions. However, domestic demand and timely fiscal responses (e.g. fiscal stimulus policies) have helped the Asian and Pacific economies to sustain economic growth. The pace was relatively robust where domestic demand accounts for large shares of GDP growth, such as in India, the Philippines, Viet Nam and Indonesia (ESCAP, 2010a). Fiscal stimulus mainly took the form of infrastructure spending, cash transfers and tax cuts. In China, Japan, Malaysia and Viet Nam fiscal stimulus helped these countries to overcome the crisis and sustain economic growth. Along with other expansionary policies, these have helped Asian and Pacific economies to reverse their declines by the second half of 2009. The annual Economic and Social Survey of Asia and the Pacific 2010 noted "[a] notable recovery is expected in 2010. For the developing economies of the region, GDP is expected to grow by 7.0% in 2010, following an estimated

growth of 4.0% of the previous year" (ESCAP, 2010a:41). The same Survey also forecast (as of mid-April 2010) real (i.e., adjusted for inflation) GDP growth rates of 4.0 per cent for East and North-East Asia, 5.1 per cent for South-East Asia, 6.1 per cent for West and South-West Asia, 3.7 per cent for North and Central Asia, and 2.3 per cent for the Pacific subregion (ESCAP, 2010a:42-43).

3.1.3 Foreign financial inflows

Foreign direct investment

Asia is a major destination for foreign direct investment (FDI). Capital expenditure by multi-national or foreign companies has made a significant contribution to Asia's rising importance in global production networks. Low labour costs and the attractions of large consumer markets made Asian urban areas the favoured destination for foreign direct investment over the 2000-2007 period. Asia as a whole received 40 per cent of the cumulative FDI going to developing countries during that period. Foreign direct investment has risen rapidly in Central Asia since 2005 (and in Europe as well – see Chart 3.4).

Those enterprises associated with foreign direct investment are typically located in and around major cities. In some countries like China, such investment takes place in special economic zones that offer many advantages and tax concessions. Foreign direct investment in industrial enterprises has led to further concentrations of populations and businesses in and around major cities. The mega urban regions described in Chapter 2 are among the spatial by-products of foreign direct investment in the manufacturing sector.

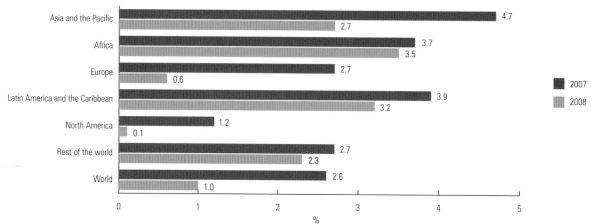

Source: Generated with data from ESCAP (2008, 2010b)

Foreign indirect (portfolio) investment

Asia also attracts a high share of global foreign indirect ('portfolio') investment. Of the total estimated US $145.1 billion of portfolio equity investments that were made in developing countries in 2007, about US $84 billion (58 per cent) went into Asia-Pacific stock markets, particularly East and South Asia. These inflows contributed to rapid economic growth and infrastructure investment through private capital (see Table 3.2).

3.1.4 National & sub-regional economic growth

On the whole, 42 per cent of Asia's population live in urban areas and they contribute around 80 per cent of the region's total output of goods and services. As can be seen in Chart 3.5, only the Pacific and North-Central Asian subregions feature higher than average urbanization levels; in all other subregions, the proportions of urban populations and urban shares of gross domestic product are similar.

East and North-East Asia

Asia's brisk pace of economic growth is linked to rapid urbanization in the East and North-East subregion, where 47 per cent of the population now reside in urban areas. The share of urban areas in GDP is as high as 86 per cent. East and North-East Asia as a whole grew an average 5.3 per cent in 2007, which declined to 3.4 per cent in 2008 (ESCAP, 2008, 2010b). The subregion includes the two largest, trillion-dollar economies in the whole Asia-Pacific region – China and Japan – and contributes 63 per cent of its total production of goods and services. With a GDP amounting to a projected US $4.9 trillion in 2010, China is the second largest economy in the world in both nominal and Purchasing Power Parity (PPP) terms (World Bank, 2009a). In 2007, China experienced the highest economic growth rate (11.4 per cent) in the entire Asia-Pacific region (ESCAP 2008), which slowed down to 9.0 per cent in 2008 (ESCAP, 2010b) and 8.5 per cent in 2009, before re-accelerating to 11.1 per

cent in the first half of 2010 (tradingeconomics.com, 2010). However, these figures being only nationwide averages, some cities in China have experienced higher growth rates. China has attracted more foreign direct investment than any other country in Asia. The country has performed much better than the East and North-East Asia subregion as a whole, where the average annual growth rate was about 60 per cent lower at 3.4 per cent during 2008 reflecting the sluggish performance of the Japanese economy, which grew only 0.4 per cent but contributes 54 per cent to the subregion's total output. Another robust performer is Mongolia, whose economy grew 9.9 per cent in 2007 and 8.9 per cent in 2008, buoyed by a robust mining sector, which contributes one third of the country's total output (ESCAP, 2008, 2010b).

South-East Asia

South-East Asia grew 6.3 per cent in 2007 and 4.6 per cent in 2008. This performance came as the tail end of the rebound from the 2.5 per cent annual average of the 1996-2000 period, which reflected the 1997-98 Asian financial crisis. Prior to that, cities had made a robust contribution to South-East Asia's 7.6 per cent annual average growth rate of the 1990-95 period. Economic recovery has gone hand in hand with rapid urbanization in most countries. Urban areas contribute 79 per cent of the subregion's combined output and account for 46 per cent of its population. In 2008, the Lao PDR recorded the highest economic growth rate (7.5 per cent) in the subregion on the back of high commodity (tin) prices, although it was lower compared with 2007 (8.0 per cent). In 2008, economic growth remained relatively strong in Cambodia (6.0 per cent, compared with 10.2 per cent in 2007) and Viet Nam (6.2 per cent, compared with 8.3 per cent in 2007), driven by domestic consumption and booming private investment (see Box 3.1). As for Indonesia, the main factors behind its performance (6.0 per cent growth in 2008) shifted from external demand during the first half to investment and domestic consumer demand in the second half. Similarly, Malaysia's economy grew 4.5 per cent in 2008,

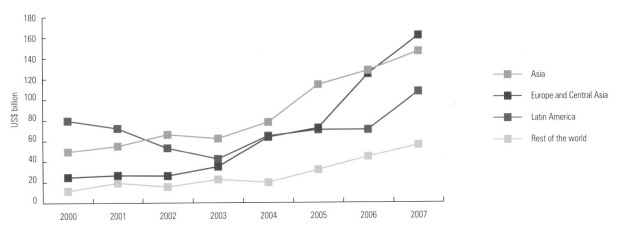

Source: World Bank (2008a:46)[1]

with domestic demand offsetting slower export growth. In the same year, the Philippines grew 4.6 per cent, down from 7.3 per cent in 2007, which reflected higher public capital expenditure and private consumption (ESCAP, 2008, 2010b; World Bank, 2008a).

South and South-West Asia

The South and South-West Asian economy grew a brisk 7.4 per cent in 2007, slowing down to 5.3 per cent in 2008. Cities in this subregion, currently the least urbanised in Asia, are expected to experience faster demographic and economic expansion as they increase their relative shares in national economies. On the whole, urban areas today account for 33 per cent to the total population and 76 per cent to the subregion's combined output. The sub-regional giant is India, contributing 68 per cent of total production, with an annual growth rate of 7.3 per cent in 2008. Between the years 2000 and 2007, India doubled its share of foreign direct investment within the Asia-Pacific region (from 2 to an estimated 4 per cent). Urban centres in India contribute nearly two-thirds of the country's output of goods and services. As for Pakistan, its economy grew 6 per cent in 2007 and 2008. In Bangladesh, the economy grew 6.2 per cent in 2008; however, poor infrastructure, especially unreliable power supply, remains a significant constraint, costing the country as much as 2 per cent in GDP growth every year (World Bank, 2008a; ESCAP, 2008). South and South-West Asia as a whole has experienced consistent growth and was not significantly affected by the 1997-98 Asian financial crisis.

North and Central Asia

In 2008, with a 5.7 per cent annual average rate, North and Central Asia remained the continent's fastest growing subregion (down from 8.4 per cent in 2007). After the turmoil that followed the disintegration of the Soviet Union in 1990, high commodity prices, especially oil, natural gas, metals as well as cotton and cereals have boosted the subregion's economies. These trends have little to do with

CHART 3.5: **SHARE OF URBAN AREAS IN GDP, ASIA AND THE PACIFIC, 2008**

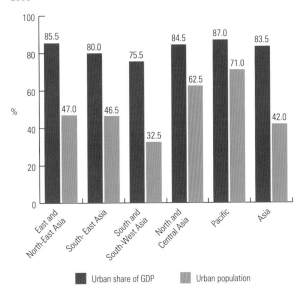

Source: Computed from ESCAP (2010b)

urban economies, which typically focus on manufacturing and services. This is why, although the share of urban areas in the region's population is quite significant (85 per cent), their demographic growth remains slow. Thanks to an abundance of minerals, both public and private capital expenditure have soared in a few countries, which have subsequently experienced rapid growth. For example, Azerbaijan's annual average growth was the highest in the subregion – as much as 10.8 per cent in 2008 (though down from 25.1 per cent in 2007).

The Pacific

This subregion's economic performance remained moderate to sluggish these past few years. The global financial crisis and its impact on major trading partners caused the average an-

TABLE 3.2: **EQUITY INFLOWS BY MAJOR WORLD REGION, 2000-2007 (US $ BILLION)**

Region	2000	2001	2002	2003	2004	2005	2006	2007e
East Asia	6.6	1.8	3.8	12.5	19.3	26.1	54.8	48.6
Europe	0.7	-0.4	0.1	-0.7	5.1	7.9	11.1	20.7
Latin America and the Caribbean	-0.6	2.5	1.4	3.3	-0.6	12.5	11.4	28.1
Middle East and North Africa	0.2	0.0	-0.6	0.2	0.9	2.6	2.0	2.1
South Asia	2.4	2.7	1.0	8.0	9.0	12.4	10.4	35.4
Sub-Saharan Africa	4.2	-0.9	-0.4	0.7	6.7	7.4	15.1	10.2
Total	**13.5**	**5.7**	**5.3**	**24.0**	**40.4**	**68.9**	**104.8**	**145.1**

2007e: Estimates for 2007
Source: World Bank (2008a:46)

nual growth rate to decline from 3.8 per cent in 2007 to 0.9 per cent in 2008. The effect was most acute in Nauru, where the economy contracted by 12.1 per cent in 2008, due to lower consumer demand and slackening of capital expenditure by the private sector (ESCAP, 2010b). Tonga and Fiji grew 1.2 per cent each in 2008; this came as an improvement over 2007 when their economies contracted 3.5 and 3.9 per cent respectively as Tonga was struggling with civil disorder and Fiji with a military coup. On the other hand, Papua New Guinea and the Solomon Islands benefited from the commodity boom in early 2008 and grew 7.6 and 6.0 per cent respectively. Samoa owed its own 4.7 per cent growth in 2007 to agricultural and industrial expansion, which was followed by a 3.4 per cent contraction in the following year (ESCAP, 2008, 2010b).

3.1.5 Employment growth in Asia

Around two-thirds of the world's working population are employed in the Asia-Pacific region, although that proportion has been falling over the past two decades. In 2008, China (with 752 million workers), India (452 million), and Indonesia (103 million) accounted for 43 per cent of world employment, and 68 per cent in the Asia-Pacific region. While employment numbers have been increasing – from 1.8 billion in 2005 to 1.9 billion in 2008 – they have done so at a slower pace: from 1.5 per cent in 2006 to 1.3 per cent in 2008 (ESCAP 2008, 2010b). In 2006, countries with employment growth above 5 per cent included Bhutan (7.2 per cent), the Maldives (6.1 per cent), Timor-Leste (5.9 per cent) and Pakistan (5.4 per cent); however, by 2008 the highest growth rate was only of 4.5 per cent, and was recorded in Singapore.

▲
Thimphu, Bhutan. **©Oksana.perkins/Shutterstock**

This picture of employment success in the Asia-Pacific region must be qualified. The quality of employment is reflected in the respective proportions of formal-sector jobs (which are generally considered as 'high quality') than of own-account (self-employed) workers or contributing family workers; these in 2007 accounted for 58.8 per cent of total employment in the Asia-Pacific region. A sub-regional breakdown shows that the share of these jobs in total employment was highest in South-East Asia (74.4 per cent) and South and South-West Asia (60.1 per cent). Overall, the quality of jobs being created in Asia and the Pacific remains poor (ESCAP, 2008).

In most countries, economic development results in higher proportions of workers in the services sector. In Asia and the Pacific, this share has been growing continuously since the 1990s: from 25.8 per cent of total employment in 1991 to 36.4 per cent by 2007. The highest proportion is found in the Pacific subregion, where in 2007 the tertiary sector provided 63.3 per cent of all jobs, followed by North and Central Asia, where this proportion was 56.4 per cent. However, East and North-East Asia is where the most rapid growth in services has taken place: from 22.9 to 37.1 per cent of total employment between 1991 and 2007. Being inherent to urbanization, the growth in services has been accompanied nearly every-where by a declining share of agriculture in total employment, which over the same period fell from 53.7 to 41.1 per cent in the region as a whole. In this respect, the most dramatic decline, from 60.2 to 43.1 per cent of total employment (a difference of 17.1 percentage points), occurred in South-East Asia, and was largely due to massive inflows of rural people moving into an expanding services sector in urban areas. During the same period, the share of agriculture declined from 52.9 to 39.1 per cent (a difference of 13.8 percentage points) in East and North-East Asia, followed by South and South-West Asia (from 59.2 to 47.1 per cent, a difference of 12.1 percentage points).

Changes in manufacturing have occurred at a slower pace in the Asia-Pacific region, with a slight overall decline in the 1990s (from 20.5 per cent in 1991 to 19.7 per cent in 2000). However, the trend in manufacturing in Asia as a whole has been looking up again, with the sector providing 22.6 per cent of total jobs in 2007 (ESCAP, 2010b).

In Asia and the Pacific, unemployment has remained stable at low rates from 1990 to 2007, averaging between 4 and 5 per cent of the active population, with surprisingly little variation between males and females. However, this overall picture conceals significant variations across subregions. For

Delhi, India. Many employers in the textile industry eschew minimum wages. ©**Paul Prescott/Shutterstock**

instance, in North and Central Asia the unemployment rate has been almost double the regional average, largely on the back of structural adjustment in the transition to market-based economies (ESCAP, 2008).

As Asian economies have been growing at a brisk pace, though, employment elasticity has become more unfavourable. For example, in the 1980s in China, every additional 3 per cent in total output would lead to a 1 per cent increase in employment, which by the 1990s took 8 per cent GDP growth. This unfavourable pattern holds for most countries and cities in Asia. Another distinctive feature is that for all the rapid growth in the formal economy, the informal sector has remained stable or increased marginally in size. Globalization has brought competition in the labour market as well, and wages in the formal economy have risen. As a result, employers tend to hire fewer workers and look to improve productivity. In the manufacturing sector, automation has reduced the labour-capital ratio. As Asia's urban economies gradually move closer to global markets, many 'old' enterprises have closed down and most of the redundant workers have ended up in the informal economy.

Many Asian governments provide incentives to attract foreign investors; however, unless the policy mix is right, capital-intensive investment may not create new jobs (resulting in "jobless growth") and can even lead to downsizing or retrenchment (i.e., job losses). Those investors looking for cheap rather than skilled and productive labour tend to favour informality. For instance, the apparel industry works with contractors who pay workers by the piece and in most cases eschew minimum wages. Moreover, supply-side support as provided by the government to enhance competitiveness in global markets (through incentives or subsidies for export promotion, technology upgrading, tax holidays, etc.) is typically biased in favour of larger industrial enterprises. These policies may not only prevent smaller enterprises from developing their own potential or gaining access to global markets: they may also crowd informal operators and workers altogether out of a given market segment. For instance, in Sri Lanka, export promotion policies in favour of the coir (coconut fibre) industry have led to a shift in the supply of coconut husks to mechanized units owned by males with access to credit, and away from the manual units typically owned by females with little access to credit (ILO, 2002a).

3.2
The main drivers of Asia's urban economies

▲
The port in Hong Kong, China - the third largest in Asia. ©**Leungchopan/Shutterstock**

Cities have become the economic engines not just of Asia but also, and increasingly, the world. Looking to the future, they are well positioned to capitalise on the opportunities provided by their own demographic expansion as well as the forces behind globalization.

3.2.1 Export-led growth: Taking advantage of globalization

Trade liberalisation is a major factor behind the global economy, thanks to the gradual elimination or lowering of national trade barriers. An open economy can offer consumers a wider variety of goods at lower prices, as well as strong incentives for domestic industries to remain competitive as the geographical reach of their markets keeps expanding. Exports have become a significant source of economic growth for many Asian countries, stimulating domestic job creation. More generally, trade enhances national competitiveness, steering the workforce into those industries where their skills, and their country, have a competitive advantage. Greater openness can also stimulate foreign investment, which in turn can boost local employment while bringing along new and more productive technologies (IMF, 2009).

Cities in East and South-East Asia have been particularly keen to capitalize on the opportunities the global economy has been making available for some time. In the late 1980s, many cities across Asia were struggling with poor economic performance under protectionist policies, and by the early 1990s the continent was still one of the most adverse to trade in the whole world. Subsequently, many countries proceeded to dismantle barriers to international trade and to take advantage of the benefits of reciprocal tariff and other concessions, in the process making the most of improved access to the global economy. As a result, a significant share of Western manufacturing has relocated to the region on the spur of lower production costs. Cities, and especially those along or close to seaboards, flourished during this period.

This was when many countries in the Asia-Pacific region came to realise that exports to the rest of the world opened up the opportunities for economic progress which their respective narrow or as yet under-developed domestic markets had so far been unable to afford or sustain. An added, significant benefit was that in the process, these economies were forced to adjust, if only gradually, to the norms and standards prevailing in more developed countries, helping them to secure market shares and adapt supply to changes in demand. As the export-orientated manufacturing sector expanded, so did domestic markets, especially as these found it easy to integrate with increasingly homogenised regional and global markets in manufactured goods. As a result, the share of emerging Asia in world trade flows rose to 34 per cent in 2006, up sharply from

21 per cent in 1990. Regional specialisation is a significant factor (see Section 3.4 below), as reflected in the fact that the rise in trade within emerging Asia accounted for roughly 40 per cent of the total increase in world trade over the period.

Between 1990 and 2007, the region experienced significant increases in the contribution of exports to production of goods and services. The average ratio of exports to total output in 11 selected countries (see Chart 3.6) was 25.1 per cent in 1990. By 2007, the proportion had increased to 47.4 per cent.

3.2.2 Infrastructure and services

Growth is higher in cities since these are more productive than rural areas, due to infrastructure and services, proximity to markets, economies of scale and concentrations of cheap labour. It is essential for cities to maintain their productive edge. Besides serving people, infrastructure enhances the efficiency of cities. For example, the manufacturers surveyed in the World Bank's most recent *Investment Climate Assessment* noted that power shortages cost them around 12 per cent in lost sales every year (World Bank, 2008b).

Cities with proper infrastructure facilitate higher productivity, and the resulting higher returns attract foreign direct investment. Within Asia, urban infrastructures display wide variations in terms of quality. In this regard, East and North-East Asia provides the best the region has to offer and therefore has attracted larger amounts of foreign direct investment than any other subregion. However, it must be noted that the quality of that infrastructure still falls short of the standards prevailing in OECD countries.

If they are to make any progress, Asia's urban local governments must deploy land use policies that are geared to rationalization of logistics, infrastructure and ports. This could include priority earmarking of land resources for future road or rail development, together with land banks, and also ensuring that land is available for those ancillary and other services that require access to ports, airports, etc. Businesses tend to cluster together because it is to their mutual advantage.

The resulting positive productivity externalities include a stimulus to innovation, information exchange, access to inputs and specialized skills – the so-called 'agglomeration economies'. These become more important as production moves up the value-added chain. Infrastructure development plays a significant role in Asia's high-growth story.

3.2.3 FDI and competition among cities

Sassen (1991) has shown how 'global city' economies are hosts to broad, complex ranges of specialized service industries that enable transnational corporations to coordinate production, capital expenditure and finance on a world scale. The worldwide geographical dispersion of production is intrinsically linked to an increasing centralization of key command and control capacities within the agglomeration economies of global cities. These trends are becoming more and more visible in many cities located in developing countries (Sassen, 2002).

Urban and regional economies are now shaping the development of national economies. Cities are complementary to one another in the sense that they are involved in mutual trading of specialized products. But they also compete strongly with one another, as each city is anxious to secure its own position in the global economy. Each has a direct interest in securing new investment, in widening external markets for its products, and in attracting visitors from outside. The competitive benefits of globalization are jointly appropriated as externalities by all firms and residents within a city (Scott, 2006).

Integration of cities in global production systems has been made possible through the deregulation of national economies, together with allocation of greater powers to urban authorities when it comes to attracting domestic and foreign investments. Today, cities compete against each other to attract investment – be it domestic or foreign. Cities have been able to attract large shares of world trade, finance, communication and information, in the process turning

CHART 3.6: **CONTRIBUTION OF EXPORTS TO GDP, 1990 AND 2007 (%)**

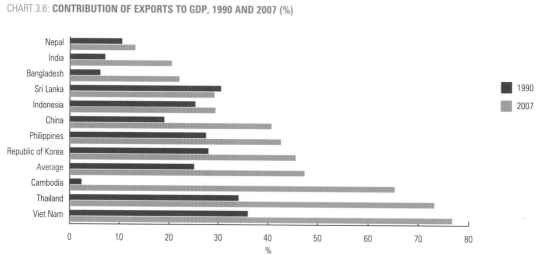

Source: Asian Development Bank (2008a)

into major engines for modern economies. Resource-rich regions that can supply raw materials also attract productive investment. Competition among cities has resulted in the geographical concentration and specialization of industrial development, as cities come to find their own special niches in the regional and world markets.

In Asia, a good illustration of this phenomenon can be found in Singapore, Shanghai, Tokyo and Hong Kong, China, four cities that dominate regional finance and transport logistics, just like Bangkok does with the automobile industry, while Bangalore and Taipei are global centres for information technology research and development. The growing specialization of cities is leading to the emergence of powerful industrial clusters, which often involve very broad-ranging agglomerations of interdependent industries and supplier networks.

Regardless of variations across countries, the policies adopted in Asia have effectively boosted the export competitiveness of cities. There is no one-size-fits-all standard solution. Instead, policies and strategies have been continuously adjusted to the vagaries of business cycles and market requirements. The emergence of Thailand as a hub for automobile exports from South-East Asia, instead of Malaysia, Indonesia or the Philippines, is an outcome of the deliberate policies adopted by distinct national governments (see Box 3.2).

Cities must remain competitive if they are to avoid long-term emigration, stagnant capital expenditure, declines in income per head and rising unemployment. This is why they need a flexible strategic vision (UN-HABITAT, 2010) that allows them continually to adjust to changing circumstances, promote competitiveness, ensure a diversified range of interdependent ventures, and link the academic and manufacturing spheres. So far, high-quality infrastructure, public gardens and improved residential areas have contributed to the economic success of Asian cities, attracting foreign and domestic investors as well as highly qualified professionals and tourists.

3.2.4 Cities' connectivity to markets

Economic development depends critically on connections between production centres and markets. Progress can be monitored using data on cargo and passenger movements. Between 2005 and 2006, the number of containers handled by the world's ports increased by 12 per cent, half of which in the Asia-Pacific region. In 2006, of the world's top 25 container ports in terms of throughput, 17 were located in Asia. The countries handling the most traffic were China, Singapore, Japan and the Republic of Korea (ESCAP, 2008). China has made substantial investments in container ports, several of which now handle many million TEUs (20-foot equivalent container units) annually. Table 3.3 shows that among Asia's 10 busiest container ports in 2008, six were located in China.

Major investments in transport infrastructure have also facilitated connections between cities, hinterlands and external markets. Examples include the Republic of Korea's Seoul-Busan highway built in the 1960s, Malaysia's road network built in the 1970s and 1980s, China's rail network and more recent expressway development, as well as Viet Nam's Hanoi-Ho Chi Minh City and Hanoi-Hai Phong highways, all of which have contributed to enlarge and integrate domestic markets. Further investment in links to global markets can facilitate the development of urban economies of scale and enhance specialized production of goods and services. Even with the diminishing returns that come with it, "the creation of infrastructure networks could contribute to the rate of innovation and technological advance in the economy, and thereby lift the long-term growth rate." (Straub *et al.*, 2008:4).

Asian policy-makers rightly see infrastructure as an essential growth factor. The two fastest-growing economies in the region, China and Viet Nam, are currently investing around 10 per cent of GDP in infrastructure, and even at that rate they are struggling to keep pace with demand for electricity, telephones and major transport networks. Plans for growth in the Greater Mekong area – the Cambodia, China, Lao People's Democratic Republic, Myanmar, Thailand and Viet Nam – are centred on greater integration of transport and

▲
Singapore's financial district. Singapore is Asia's number one city in terms of GDP.
©Junjie/Shutterstock

BOX 3.6: **THE BANGALORE REVOLUTION**

▲
Bangalore, India. ©**Ajay Bhaskar/Shutterstock**

Geographically, most of today's 'world cities' are located on or near coasts. This location has enhanced their ability to trade with other parts of the world. However, under the new economic dispensation as defined by information technologies (IT), the concept of 'remoteness' has been altered. Today, if linked to the Worldwide Web, no city is remotely located, being only one click away from a connection. Over the past several years, Bangalore, a city located right in the middle of southern India, has been put on the global map by its achievements in the information technology sector. According to Software Technology Parks of India, Bangalore's information technology exports have risen from about US $1 billion in 2001 to more than US $10 billion in 2006. The city has also benefited from the employment spin-offs of the information technology industry: according to India's National Association of Software Services Companies (NASSCOM), one IT job results in four indirect jobs (Gokarn *et al.*, 2007). This is the success of Bangalore, which has triggered a software revolution in Indian cities.

The IT industry tends to flourish where technology professionals are available. Bangalore-based Infosys Limited, India's second largest IT firm, concentrates most of its staff, or nearly so, in a single location. Interestingly, these professionals are not located in Bangalore but some 750km up north in Pune (south-east of Mumbai). From an international perspective, the rapid rise of Bangalore has forced major software companies to consider alternative locations outside the developed world.

Cities in India are now competing against each other in order to attract major software companies. Apart from Pune, cities like Bhubaneswar, Chennai, Gurgaon, Hyderabad and Jaipur are all following Bangalore's example of excellence in the software business.

Source: Prepared with information from Gokarn et al. (2007)

This pattern is further reflected in the geographic dispersion of production, with assembly operations migrating to lower-wage economies while more developed Asian countries specialize in high-value-added components and capital goods. The resulting increase in vertical intra-industry trade, as furthered by foreign direct investment, has created a sophisticated production network in emerging Asia; this in turn facilitates the 'catch-up' process for developing Asian countries through technology transfers. India is making its mark, too, with a focus on trade in specialist services (e.g., software, call centres) rather than hardware (IMF, 2008).

Asia's growing share in world trade has resulted largely from increased regional trade integration. While trade flows in the rest of the world roughly tripled between 1990 and 2006, inter-regional trade involving emerging Asia rose by a multiple of five, and intra-regional trade within emerging Asia by a multiple of eight (IMF, 2008).

3.4.2 The next major innovations are to come from Asia's 'knowledge economies'

Specialisation is an evolving process. Asia no longer serves just a source of cheap manufacturing goods and services. The transformations in global markets, production and innovation systems are providing fresh opportunities for those Asian firms bent on improving their innovative potential. The process of outsourcing that was initially designed to exploit the labour wage arbitrage is slowly giving way to access to high-class skills as the primary driver of next-generation outsourcing.

It was generally believed that in contrast to other stages along the value chain, there was a strong aspect of inertia to innovation: it would typically remain tied to specific locations that were the home countries of multinational companies. However, the integration of developing countries into the global economy, combined with foreign direct investment flows, has brought about a major change. This change is visible in those locations that were the early recipients of global outsourcing: as this phenomenon now tends to favour other Asian nations, the early beneficiaries are becoming more diversified and moving to higher-end, higher value-added processes of production and service delivery. Moreover, as outsourcing is taking on a larger share of global research and development (R&D), Asian cities build local capabilities for innovation. World-scale companies increasingly rely on knowledge sourcing from Asia to manage global production, distribution and innovation networks. The network flagships relocate research and development to countries where knowledge workers come cheaper. In 1997, 59 per cent of US corporate R&D sites were located within the USA, while only 8 per cent had been outsourced to China or India. By 2006, these two countries had increased their shares to 18 per cent, while the US share had declined to 52 per cent (Ernst, 2008a).

Asian cities now offer the benefits of proximity to higher-end specialized supply networks for components, manufacturing and knowledge-intensive business services. Global firms are expanding and upgrading their research and development centres in Asia. Intel currently has seven R&D laboratories in

BOX 3.2: THAILAND'S EMERGENCE AS A HUB FOR AUTO EXPORTS

Thailand's automobile cluster emerged during the 1990s and grew rapidly after the Asian financial crisis of the late 1990s to become one of the country's leading export sectors. The 'automobile belt' is concentrated around Bangkok, the adjoining province of Samut Prakan and the Eastern Seaboard. Between 1997 and 2004, automobile production increased by an average 81.2 per cent per year. By 2005, Thailand was the largest hub for automobile production in South-East Asia, exporting about 540,000 cars per year and generating over US $5 billion in export revenues. Thailand is also currently the second largest exporter of pickup trucks in the world and offers more customized model variations than anywhere in the world.

Thailand owes this success to favourable economic and policy environments in the late 1980s and early 1990s. To begin with, demand for motor vehicles in the region is nowhere higher than in Thailand. From 1989-96, an average 405,800 motor vehicles were sold every year in the country, accounting for as much as 42 per cent of total sales in the four largest South-East Asian countries (the other three being Indonesia (27 per cent), Malaysia (21 per cent) and the Philippines (10 per cent).

Another major factor behind Thailand's automobile success was none other than the policy environment, which was relatively more liberal and stable than in the other three major countries in the subregion. The first and foremost advantage of production in Thailand was the absence of an explicit goal to promote a national car – a major difference with Malaysia – or of nationalizing local parts firms, as was the case with Indonesia and the Philippines. Furthermore, the degree of policy uncertainty, i.e., the frequency of policy shifts and reversals, was relatively higher in Indonesia and the Philippines than in Thailand. Furthermore, Thailand was the first country in South-East Asia to embark on unilateral liberalization of the automobile industry, which gave it 'first mover' advantage. Thailand could even afford to stimulate import competition with a dramatic reduction in tariffs, although this still left the country's domestic automobile industry better protected than other sectors. Moreover, in 1997 in Bangkok, the government relaxed the Foreign Business Act to allow greater foreign ownership in Thai enterprises, in response to the need to recapitalize the export-orientated sector. Together with the depreciation in the national currency (which made foreign capital expenditure cheaper and exports more competitive), these policies promptly sparked further inflows of investment by foreign-based assemblers and auto-parts manufacturers. These various factors have combined further to entrench Thailand's automobile 'cluster' and increase the country's value-added exports. As a result, the value of imported parts per 1,000 cars dropped from US $8.1 million (in real terms) during the late 1980s to around US $1.2 million during 2004-05.

Source: Kohpaiboon (2008) and Zsin Woon et al. (2007)

China

The attractions of Chinese cities are well documented in the *Doing Business* series. The criteria include ease of starting a business, registering property, obtaining credit and enforcing contracts. Findings suggest that China's coastal cities offer the friendliest environments for business in the country, with Guangzhou ranked as the best overall, followed by Nanjing, Shanghai, Hangzhou, Jinan, Fuzhou, Tianjin and Beijing. On the other hand, cities in the western and central Chinese hinterland provide the most challenging business environments.

Under China's nationwide regulations, it takes 14 distinct procedures to set up a business. Some cities like Hangzhou, Nanjing and Fuzhou have opened one-stop administrative centres for some of the procedures. The most efficient city is Guangzhou, where it takes 28 days to complete the process to start a limited liability company. In contrast, in Yinchuan and Taiyuan would-be entrepreneurs must spend an average 55 days, or nearly a month longer (World Bank, 2008b).

Chinese cities actively promote business. For instance, as many as 53 different reforms have been introduced at the local level to accelerate the property registration process (land titles, ownership of buildings, etc.). In this particular respect, the city of Chongqing stands out as the top reformer, having managed to streamline existing procedures into four stages only, instead of 12 as in other Chinese cities. Still, even the country's best performers leave room for improvement when compared with those in the rest of the world. For example, starting a business in Hangzhou still takes 12 procedures, 30 days and 5.7 per cent of annual income per head, against Hong Kong, China's five procedures, 11 days and 3.1 per cent of annual income per head for the same process (World Bank, 2008b).

Prior to reforms in Zhengzhou, completing a building survey used to take almost five months, compared with only one to two weeks now. In this respect, the 'one stop shop' service has been adopted in cities like Shanghai, Guangzhou and Fuzhou, where distinct windows within a single centre take applicants through the successive administrative steps. Chongqing, Guangzhou, Shanghai, Tianjin and Xiamen have also merged the former land and building certificates into a single format, improving efficiency and reducing costs, including when compared with the national average (World Bank, 2008b).

India

Although Mumbai stands out as India's undisputed financial centre, the city does not rank high in terms of business-friendly environment. The process of starting a business in Mumbai is fairly smooth, but the city lags behind others in India on several crucial counts, such as the time required to have a contract enforced, to process construction permit applications and to transfer property titles, as well as starting costs, and the cumulative tax burden on businesses. Hyderabad, on the other hand, sits at the top of the rankings for business-friendly cities in the country. Bhubaneswar and Jaipur also stand as examples of lower-income cities that have made efforts to offer more business-friendly environments through better efficiency and modern technologies, while keeping low the costs of doing business.

BOX 3.3: SHANGHAI, AN URBAN REVIVAL

Shanghai, China. ©**Mateo Pearson/Shutterstock**

China's most populated city (over 16 million) Shanghai is also one of the largest in the world, and its hosting of the 2010 World Expo (with 'Better City, Better Life' as its theme) came as an apt symbol of its recent revival. Originally established as a fishing and textiles town, Shanghai grew in national importance during the 19th century due to the favourable location of its port (midway along the coast, at the mouth of

the river Yangtze). It was among the few cities opened to foreign trade by the 1842 Treaty of Nanking. Shanghai subsequently continued to play an important role in China's social and economic development. The city flourished as a trade centre between East and West, and by the 1930s had become an international banking and business centre.

The 1990 economic reforms triggered an intensive

effort to improve infrastructures across the city. In 2005, Shanghai became the world's largest cargo port. Today, the city on its own contributes 8 per cent towards China's total industrial output, 17 per cent of the country's port cargo handling volume, 25 per cent of its total exports and 13 per cent of financial revenues.

On top of port facilities, Shanghai has expanded its role in finance, banking, and as a location for corporate headquarters. These developments are fuelling demand for a highly educated, forward-looking workforce.

Between 1992 and 2007, Shanghai's economy grew at double-digit rates every single year. In 2007, the city's nominal GDP grew 13.3 per cent to reach US $176 billion. Up until the end of 2008, combined foreign direct investment amounted to over US $73 billion, which supported as many as 31,440 distinct projects. Shanghai is also making its presence felt as a business centre of choice among international investors. As far as foreign indirect investment is concerned, Shanghai's emergence is also becoming conspicuous in the financial world. Foreign banks hold 14 per cent of the financial assets domiciled in Shanghai. As China gradually liberalizes its financial sector, Shanghai's foreign exchange market may come to rival those in Singapore and Hong Kong, China.

Source: Abhay Kantak, CRISIL Infrastructure Advisory Services, India, based on various sources.

The time it takes to start a business in India is shortest in Noida and Mumbai (30 days) and lengthiest in Kochi (41 days). The differences in start-up costs among cities can be pronounced. In Patna, Kolkata and Bhubaneswar, would-be entrepreneurs need to spend less than 40 per cent of income per head[2] to launch a business. For those in Bangalore and Mumbai, the cost is almost double due to local government fees and taxes. Registration for value-added tax costs the equivalent of 12 per cent of income per head in Mumbai, but is free of charge in Jaipur and Ahmedabad. Similarly, it costs entrepreneurs 15 per cent of income per head to register under the Shops and Establishments Act in Bangalore, a service that comes free of charge in Chennai (World Bank, 2009b).

When it comes to registering property in Indian cities, Ahmedabad, Bangalore and Chennai are where the number of procedures is the smallest – 15, compared with 37 distinct steps in Mumbai. Property registration will take 80 days or so in Hyderabad, but as many as 258 in Kolkata. Variations are due mainly to the time it takes to obtain pre-construction clearances, zoning and building permits, as well as connections to power grids. The procedures required to register property are similar across the 17 Indian cities surveyed by the World Bank (2009b). However, the time and costs required to complete these procedures vary substantially across cities. In

Gurgaon, it would take an entrepreneur 26 days and 7.7 per cent of the value to transfer property, while in Guwahati the same process would last three times longer and cost 15.4 per cent of the property value. Cost differences have to do mostly with stamp-duty rates, as set by individual states, which account for an average 69 per cent of all the costs incurred. Stamp duty can be as high as 12.5 per cent of the property value in Kochi, and as low as 3 per cent in New Delhi (World Bank, 2009b).

The Philippines

In the Philippines, business regulations and enforcement vary widely across cities. While all local authorities come under one and the same legal and institutional framework, they also enjoy some degree of leeway when it comes to interpretation and implementation. Some cities like Taguig and Marikina (both in the Metropolitan Manila area) have used their authority to streamline procedures and reduce regulatory costs for business. Local requirements account for 12 of the 23 procedures to start a business in Davao, but only four (out of a total of 15) in Marikina and Taguig. The time it takes to start a business ranges from 27 days in Taguig to 52 in Manila. The delays to obtain a permanent connection to the power grid also vary widely across cities: from only five days

TABLE 3.4: **ASIA'S TOP 20 CITIES FOR GROSS DOMESTIC PRODUCT**

Ranking	City/Urban Area	Country	GDP (US $ bn)	GDP Per Head (US $)
1	Singapore	Singapore	161	37,597
2	Hong Kong	China	244	35,159
3	Tokyo	Japan	1,191	33,835
4	Osaka/Kobe	Japan	341	30,177
5	Seoul	Republic of Korea	218	22,602
6	Bangkok	Thailand	89	13,499
7	Shanghai	China	139	9,586
8	Beijing	China	99	9,238
9	Ho Chi Minh City	Viet Nam	40	7,935
10	Jakarta	Indonesia	98	7,424
11	Bangalore	India	48	7,080
12	Hanoi	Viet Nam	30	7,073
13	Mumbai	India	126	6,923
14	Pune	India	32	6,829
15	Bandung	Indonesia	28	6,685
16	Kolkata	India	94	6,573
17	Wuhan	China	40	6,542
18	Ahmedabad	India	34	6,364
19	Hyderabad	India	40	6,359
20	Chengdu	China	22	6,342

Source: www.citymayors.com/statistics, and for Singapore data: www.singstat.gov.sg/stats/themes/economy

in Tanauan, to about three months in Metropolitan Manila. Differences in costs and delays reflect those in local practice and administrative efficiency from one city to another. Registering property takes 21 days in Mandaluyong, but as many as six weeks in Mandaue.

3.2.6 Productivity and competitiveness

High productivity of factors is essential to any city's competitiveness. Some Asian cities produce more goods and services than some smaller countries in the whole region. Their total outputs per head can be much higher than nationwide averages. For example, Ho Chi Minh City's output per head is nearly eight times as high as that of Viet Nam as a whole; in Bangalore, the multiple is nearly sevenfold. In Bangkok, Jakarta and Shanghai, output per head is three times as high as the nationwide average.

Cities where gross domestic product per head is the highest are also those with the best infrastructure, a significant factor in productivity (see Table 3.4). Asian cities like Singapore, Shanghai and Hong Kong, China, have built world-class urban infrastructure, allowing them to compete with other major cities in the world. Singapore has positioned itself as a business hub for the whole Asia-Pacific region. Other cities in Asia, such as Mumbai, aspire to turn themselves into international financial centres but lack of quality infrastructure is the major stumbling block, for all the sophistication of the city as a financial marketplace. If Mumbai remedies its perennial lack

of proper physical infrastructure, it is likely to attract more capital from some of the well-established financial centres of the world (GoI, Ministry of Finance, 2007).

Singapore and Hong Kong, China, are both global financial centres and major transhipment ports. Both are vying to create a niche for themselves as the 'business centre of choice' in Asia. Hong Kong, China, is ranked number one and Singapore number three in the MasterCard *Worldwide Centers of Commerce Index* (MWCCI) (MasterCard Worldwide, 2008). For all their well-entrenched economic power, though, these two centres are not without regional rivals. Shanghai's expansion comes as a direct threat to Hong Kong, China. Most of Hong Kong's gross domestic output is linked to the vagaries of global trade and financial markets, both of which are susceptible to severe volatility during swings in the business cycle. Singapore faces similar challenges on account of comparable economic structures.

Shanghai and to a lesser extent Beijing and Jakarta, are emerging as financial powerhouses, too. Shanghai's market capitalization is second only to Tokyo's and is growing at a faster rate. However, according to the MasterCard report, Tokyo still inspires more investor confidence due to strong financial and regulation systems. As for Beijing, it is home to the world's second largest number of headquarters of 'global 500' companies. In Indonesia, Jakarta is beginning to show signs of growing financial influence in the region. Its market capitalization is now larger than Bangkok's and the potential for rapid expansion seems to be significant (PwC, 2008).

▲
Istanbul, Turkey. ©**Sailorr/Shutterstock**

3.2.7 Measuring competitiveness

The Global Urban Competitiveness Project (GUCP) assesses individual cities and as such can exercise a degree of influence over urban policy deliberations.[3] Urban competitiveness is defined by the Project as a city's ability to create more wealth in a faster and better way than others. The Project routinely assesses the competitiveness of 500 cities around the world based on nine parameters, as follows: (i) gross domestic product; (ii) gross domestic product per head; (iii) GDP per unit area (also known as 'GDP density'); (iv) labour productivity; (v) number of multi-national enterprises located in the city; (vi) number of patent applications; (vii) price advantage; (viii) economic growth rate; and (ix) employment rate. The Project has ranked three Asian cities – Tokyo, Singapore and Seoul – among the top 20 most competitive in the world. In China, Hong Kong, Shanghai, Shenzhen and Beijing ranked 26th, 41st, 64th, and 66th respectively. The majority of cities in the list were in North America and Europe. However, the report recognized that Asian cities were becoming increasingly competitive, and many, especially in China, rank among the top 10 with the fastest economic growth in the world (GUCP, 2008).

PricewaterhouseCoopers has come up with similar findings. According to their forecasts, several Asian cities are set to improve their global rankings by 2020. For example, Shanghai is seen moving from 32nd in 2005 to 16th in 2020. Other Asian cities expected to climb higher include Mumbai (37th to 24th), Istanbul (34th to 27th), Beijing (44th to 29th) and Manila (42nd to 30th). Lower down the list, notable "climbers" include Jakarta (46th to 33rd), Delhi (51st to 34th), Guangzhou (60th to 36th), Kolkata (49th to 38th) and Bangkok (55th to 46th) (PwC, 2007).

3.2.8 The bottlenecks constraining growth

In several cities across the Asia-Pacific region, economic growth has been restricted by bottlenecks arising from institutional frameworks, human resources and infrastructure. Regulatory red tape, taxation and corruption combine to stifle potential business and can significantly cancel out other strengths a city may possess. Singapore and Hong Kong, China, demonstrate how planning policies can encourage business through low corporate tax rates and uncomplicated, flexible employment environments, while also maintaining a tough stance on corruption (PwC, 2008).

Hong Kong, China, has been made more business-friendly through a broad range of programmes. In 2006, the government, working with the private sector, established a dedicated cross-sector consultation team to improve authorisation procedures. The team identified redundant procedures as well as channels for improved communication and coordination, while suggesting regulatory 'easy fixes' that might improve efficiency. In 2007-08 in Singapore, the time for dealing with construction permit applications was reduced significantly, as the agencies in charge cut internal deadlines by half. To save more time, the Building and Construction Authority's new data management system makes processing smarter and more user-friendly. Today in Singapore, builders regularly receive updates on the status of permit applications by e-mail and text-messaging systems.

In Dhaka, Bangladesh, the relevant authority introduced a one-stop shop for building permits in August 2007. Almost a year later, inconsistent fire safety regulations would still force builders to visit each agency in charge of approvals. By law, only buildings with more than 10 floors require fire safety clearance. The fire department insists that the cut-off should be six floors, as in previous regulations. The upshot is that builders can spend up to six months shuttling between agencies, trying to make sense of inconsistent rules (World Bank, 2008c).

3.3
Urbanization and the informal economy in Asia

▲
Luang Prabang, Lao People's Democratic Republic. ©**William Casey/Shutterstock**

3.3.1 The formal and informal economies in Asia

Synergies between the formal and informal economic sectors are a defining feature of Asian cities. With rapid economic growth, gains in the formal lead to growth in the informal sector. The informal sector refers to those sections of the economy that do not abide by the rules and regulations applicable to organized economic activities. Urbanization is another factor behind the growth of informal economies in Asian cities – indeed, the informal sector is part of the dynamics of the urbanization process. A significant informal economy has been a characteristic of the early phases of the urbanization of almost all economies around the world, and therefore has often been seen as a prerequisite in the transition from developing to more developed economies.

Some countries, like Sri Lanka, combine low rates of urbanization and a relatively small urban informal sector; in others like India, a similar low rate sits side by side with high proportions of informal workers in urban areas. These high proportions are also found in Thailand, although the country features a relatively high income per head, as does Taiwan, Province of China though with a lower share of informal workers in urban areas than Thailand.

Because of its inherently 'informal' nature, the 'grey' or 'underground' economy largely eludes standard statistical methods, and reliable data remain patchy in many ways (see Chart 3.7). While it is widely accepted that the informal sector is an integral part of urban and national economies, much of the available information relates to employment data, rather than to its share in national production of goods and services, or its influence on urban growth. The informal economy is vast and heterogeneous, but a common feature that binds informal sector workers is exclusion – from social security, from trade unions, from GDP and other statistical surveys, as well as from the productive resources typically available to larger enterprises (ILO, 2006a). According to the International Labour Organization (ILO), the conditions of those employed in the informal economy are best defined in terms of *decent work deficits*. These deficits can include poor-quality, unproductive and un-remunerative jobs that are not recognized or protected by law, absence of rights at work, inadequate social protection, and lack of representation and voice. Decent work deficits are most pronounced in the informal economy, especially at the bottom end among women and younger workers (ILO, 2002a).

Informal economy workers are exposed to significant degrees of risk on a daily basis, with lack of security making

BOX 3.4: WHEN CIVIL SOCIETY TACKLES EMPLOYMENT DEFICITS: GOOD PRACTICE FROM AHMEDABAD

▲
Umeed house-visits for enrolment and publicising on-site night show. ©**Saath**

The substantial role the informal sector plays in India's economy, and the country's labour deficit, transpire from a number of official statistics. Economic growth has slightly slowed down but remains sustained (7.3 per cent in 2008, 9 per cent in 2007 and 8.5 per cent in 2006). The labour force (total: 516.4 million) grows some seven million every year. India's problem is that against this 2.5 per cent rate, employment is growing by only 2.3 per cent. For instance, manufacturing sector growth is too slow, at an annual 7 per cent, to absorb much of the shortfall. The 7.2 per cent official unemployment rate conceals a situation where the formal sector contributes only 10 per cent of jobs, compared with 60 per cent self-employed and 30 per cent casual workers. Overall, 70 per cent of the labour force in all sectors is either illiterate or educated below primary level[1]. Since some of the employment in the agricultural sector is of a seasonal nature, many families migrate to urban, especially metropolitan areas, where they live in informal settlements with poor access to basic infrastructure or health, and education services. This is the type of background against which in 1989 in Ahmedabad, a non-governmental organization known as *Saath* adopted an integrated approach to help slum-dwellers out of this cycle of poverty. Its 'Integrated Slum

Development Programme' started at the micro-level focusing on children and youth (i.e., those 15-35 years of age according - Government of India definition). Poverty and slums deprive youth of opportunities through poor access to basic services, sub-standard education, and inadequate social skills for transactions with the formal sector. The initial phase of the scheme proved to be such a success that by 1994-95 slum residents asked for the programme to include income-generation activities (see saath. org for more details), which *Saath* did on a small scale. Since then, though, two livelihood programmes have undergone sustained expansion. Known as *Umeed* and *Urmila*, they provide youth and other slum residents the skills they need for employment in the varied and growing market for services in the business and domestic sectors.

The *Umeed* Programme

In 2005 and in partnership with the Ahmedabad Municipal Corporation, Saath launched a livelihood programme for youth called *Ek Mouka Udaan* (meaning 'an opportunity to fly', as with a fledgling bird's first flight out of the nest). The scheme enhances young people's money-earning capacities and identifies suitable jobs for their placement. It includes classroom training, guest

lectures, exposure visits, on-the-job training, and a detailed evaluation of the student's progress. In September 2005, the first *Umeed* Training Centre was established in Behrampura area of Ahmedabad, where more than 1,200 youth were trained, and subsequently found employment in the formal sector.

As news of the success of the programme spread, in February 2007 the state government decided to promote the scheme through the Gujarat Urban Development Mission (GUDM) which became known as *Umeed* ('hope', 'aspiration' in Gujarati).

For admission to the job placement-based programme, candidates must (i) be of 18-35 years of age; (ii) have dropped-out of school or college (less than 14 years of formal education); (iii) be from a vulnerable family living either in a slum or in a rural area, and (iv) pay a fee of Rs. 500 (US $11). The rationale behind the fee is to ensure that only candidates who are serious about enhancing their skills and the training will participate. The total cost per student is about Rs.4,500 (US $98), and the remaining Rs.4,000 (US $87) is funded partly by the government and partly by an international foundation[2]. In those few cases where the would-be trainee cannot afford to make a single payment for the fee, s/he is allowed to do so in two instalments. In

Source: Sharadbala Joshi, researcher and volunteer, Saath

Classroom training. ©**Manoj Pillai/Creatives Against Poverty**

those very rare cases where candidates cannot pay the fees, Saath resorts to charity fundraising Websites or individual donations.

Saath's innovative marketing with roadshows has proved to be effective. *Umeed* graduates, faculty and members of the core team go out to communities to talk to youth and convince parents about the benefits of the programme, and in the process enrol young people. Road shows include the following:

i.   Door-to-door marketing, involving 30 youth, faculty and other Saath team members.

ii. Tents in public places such as temples, markets, the local *Umeed* (training) Centre etc, with the option for on-the-spot registration. This aspect also involves diffusion of pamphlets and information in the vicinity to direct people to the tent.

iii. Mobile advertising: *Umeed* hires auto-rickshaws, whose drivers are mostly slum residents, with audio systems to spread the word across settlements and public places.

iv. On-site night shows reach out to those many slum residents who are away at work during the day. Up to 150 people at a time gather in easily accessed locations to watch films on the *Umeed* programme and its benefits. The events and venues are advertised locally throughout the day. Screenings are followed by a discussion to enable people to seek more information and clarify any doubts.

The assurance of job placement is the main attraction for young people to join the programme. Placement is ensured in partnership with the Saath Livelihood Resource Centre (a specialist body). *Umeed* trainers play a major role, being familiar with graduates and having worked in the sector they specialize in at *Umeed*. On top of this, many employers run their own in-house training programmes for all entry-level employees during the probation period, enabling *Umeed* graduates to refine their familiarity with the relevant sector, such as retail, sales, marketing, business process outsourcing, etc. So far, *Saath* has tied up with over 100 companies in Gujarat, providing them with entry-level staff. Most employers find that compared with individually recruited employees, *Umeed* students are more committed, efficient and punctual, as well as more respectful towards clients. In addition, no task is menial for them (source: interviews with various human resources managers who have hired Umeed graduates).

Umeed's achievements over the past four years are as follows:

a) 53 *Umeed* Centres have been set up operating across Gujarat and Rajasthan;

b) As at 31 March 2010, a total 29,110 young people had enrolled, of which 23,841 (82 per cent) had completed training and 17,273 (59.3 per cent) had been placed.

c) *Umeed* students earn between Rs. 3,000-6,000 (US \$65-\$131) per month after job placement, compared with the national minimum wage of Rs. 1700 (US \$37) per month in February 2004 or Rs 2500 (US \$55) per month November 2009 onwards.

Saath's pilot models for employment and entrepreneurship show great potential for scaling-up through social enterprises. The idea is to evolve sustainable "social entrepreneurship" business models in large urban centres that are not dependent on donor or government funding. This comes in response to empirical evidence that the aspirations and purchasing power of the "bottom of the pyramid markets" are far beyond the narrow perspectives and bureaucratic processes of subsidized welfare programmes, and can be activated at grassroots level by civil society.

Notes:

1. www.indiaonestop.com/unemployment.htm
2. Memorandum of Understanding (MoU) between *Saath* Charitable Trust with Gujarat Urban Development Mission

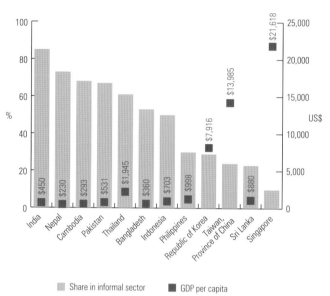

■ Share in informal sector ■ GDP per capita

Source: Asian Development Bank (2005)

Repairing ships in Dhaka, Bangladesh. Informal economy workers are exposed to significant degrees of risk on a daily basis. ©**Manoocher Deghati/IRIN**

them – and small entrepreneurs – highly vulnerable. They are not recognised under law and therefore largely stay out of legal or social protection frameworks. Informal workers are unable to enforce contracts or enjoy the security of property rights. They are excluded from, or have limited access to, public infrastructure and other social amenities. They are left to rely as best they can on informal, often exploitative institutional arrangements, whether for information, markets, credit, training or social security. It falls to innovative initiatives from civil society to give them the training and access to opportunities they so badly need (see Box 3.4).

The linkages between informal workers and formal businesses can be both direct and indirect. The informal economy includes the full range of "non-standard" wage employment conditions which flexible specialization has given rise to, such as sweatshop production, home-workers, contract workers, temporary or part-time work, and unregistered workers. Seen from this perspective, the informal economy includes many disguised wage employees who may not have direct links with a formal sector enterprise, but who are clearly dependent on the formal sector for the inputs, equipment, work location and sale of the final products they make.

Dualism – the coexistence of the modern or formal sector with the traditional or informal sector – has become a more acute and distinctive feature of labour markets in many Asian cities and, to a significant extent, a factor in their competitiveness on the world market for manufactured goods. Their well-developed formal manufacturing and services sectors are largely on par with those in industrialized countries, but their large informal economies underpin the success of the formal one. In most Asian cities, the informal economy has been burgeoning, while continuing to offer most workers and small businesses insecure work conditions as well as gruelling, overextended working days. The important policy issue here is not whether informal wage workers or informal production units have direct ties with the formal economy – clearly, they do – but whether those ties are benign, exploitative or mutually beneficial. The policy concern is to enhance the positive linkages and to ensure that there is decent work all along the continuum (ILO, 2006b; Asian Development Bank, 2005).

The proliferation of informal enterprises in cities often comes as a by-product of three types of administrative inadequacy: (i) excessive government and local authority control, (ii) the long drawn-out procedures for permits and licences, and (iii) the inefficiency and petty corruption involved in doing business. Moreover, the global economic connections of Asian cities have resulted in new and flexible forms of production relations, especially in the services sector, such as call centres. Employment in these new urban enterprises will often be classified as informal because they do not come under the purview of any regulatory framework. Therefore, adjustments to rules and regulations could help turn informal into formal employment. Research into retail stores in large Indian cities has found that labour regulations remain a problem, and that more flexible laws could significantly increase employment in

3.2
The main drivers of Asia's urban economies

▲
The port in Hong Kong, China - the third largest in Asia. ©**Leungchopan/Shutterstock**

Cities have become the economic engines not just of Asia but also, and increasingly, the world. Looking to the future, they are well positioned to capitalise on the opportunities provided by their own demographic expansion as well as the forces behind globalization.

3.2.1 Export-led growth: Taking advantage of globalization

Trade liberalisation is a major factor behind the global economy, thanks to the gradual elimination or lowering of national trade barriers. An open economy can offer consumers a wider variety of goods at lower prices, as well as strong incentives for domestic industries to remain competitive as the geographical reach of their markets keeps expanding. Exports have become a significant source of economic growth for many Asian countries, stimulating domestic job creation. More generally, trade enhances national competitiveness, steering the workforce into those industries where their skills, and their country, have a competitive advantage. Greater openness can also stimulate foreign investment, which in turn can boost local employment while bringing along new and more productive technologies (IMF, 2009).

Cities in East and South-East Asia have been particularly keen to capitalize on the opportunities the global economy

has been making available for some time. In the late 1980s, many cities across Asia were struggling with poor economic performance under protectionist policies, and by the early 1990s the continent was still one of the most adverse to trade in the whole world. Subsequently, many countries proceeded to dismantle barriers to international trade and to take advantage of the benefits of reciprocal tariff and other concessions, in the process making the most of improved access to the global economy. As a result, a significant share of Western manufacturing has relocated to the region on the spur of lower production costs. Cities, and especially those along or close to seaboards, flourished during this period.

This was when many countries in the Asia-Pacific region came to realise that exports to the rest of the world opened up the opportunities for economic progress which their respective narrow or as yet under-developed domestic markets had so far been unable to afford or sustain. An added, significant benefit was that in the process, these economies were forced to adjust, if only gradually, to the norms and standards prevailing in more developed countries, helping them to secure market shares and adapt supply to changes in demand. As the export-orientated manufacturing sector expanded, so did domestic markets, especially as these found it easy to integrate with increasingly homogenised regional and global markets in manufactured goods. As a result, the share of emerging Asia in world trade flows rose to 34 per cent in 2006, up sharply from activities, such participation is also considered as evidence of the feminization of poverty (BRIDGE, 2001). Greater insecurity and lower earning capacity in the informal sector make women workers more vulnerable. Even in the formal sector, the female labour force tends to be more occupationally segregated than is the case for their male counterparts. The chances of exploitation are also greater for women, not only under the form of homework, but more generally in the informal sector, or in illegal or quasi-legal conditions (sex work), but also in more formal work conditions such as factories. Social networks offer some protection in these situations.

For all their higher degrees of economic participation, women remain concentrated in "invisible" areas of informal work, such as domestic labour, piece-rate homework, and assistance in small family enterprises, which offer low, irregular remuneration where any, and little if any access to social security or job protection. As for female-headed households, they do not share in the broader benefits of economic growth

and are more likely to be in poverty than those headed by males. However, data from Asian cities is mixed. In a sample surveyed by the Asian Development Bank (2001), only a few cities – Colombo, Kathmandu, Suva (Fiji), and Naga (the Philippines) – feature higher incidences of poverty among female-headed households.

The International Labour Organisation has noted "Programmes focusing on upgrading informal settlements, including slum upgrading schemes in growing urban centres and basic infrastructure provision for rural areas, are often seen simultaneously to upgrade living and working conditions for informal economy workers." The organisation further identified the potential to "facilitate local employment creation especially for disadvantaged youth and women and encourage labour-intensive methods to deliver goods and services. However, this potential is not always exploited due to weak governance and capacity of local institutions and unsatisfactory devolution of authority and resources" (as quoted in Chant & Pedwell, 2008:27).

▲
Roadside vegetable vendor in Yangon, Myanmar. ©LiteChoices/Shutterstock

3.4
Asia: Beyond the 'factory of the world'

▲
Shenzhen, China. The production line of the biggest CCTV surveillance camera producer in China. ©**Bartlomiej Magierowski/Shutterstock**

3.4.1 Asia as the world's manufacturing centre

Asia has for some time now been known as 'the factory of the world'. Major world-scale manufacturers of computers, electronic products, telecom devices, other consumer goods and industrial products have located their manufacturing centres on the continent. In other words, Asia has turned into the world's manufacturing centre as part of the ongoing integrated development of the value chain of supply, production and sales.

This substantial role in the world's manufacturing operations puts Asia in a favourable competitive position. It has not taken long for Asian economies to make the most of regional and international markets. Since the 1980s, the combination of international capital and Asia's cheap labour has spawned a number of manufacturing bases in the region.

At the same time, however, manufacturing has undergone a major reshuffling within Asia. Traditional manufacturing enterprises in Japan, the Republic of Korea, Taiwan, Province of China and Hong Kong, China, are being transferred to other locations. Mainland China has been one of the main ben-

eficiaries of this process. On top of manufacturing bases in the country, major foreign companies have brought their own development and research teams. These transnational groups have chosen to source inputs from Asia, especially China which combines relatively low-costs and high quality. Guangzhou, Qingdao, Shanghai and Shenzhen are the favoured investment locations. China's growing economy has attracted many foreign companies to the Pearl River Delta (between Guangzhou, Hong Kong, China and Macao, China).

China's rise as a manufacturing powerhouse is such that it has not dwarfed other centres in the region. For instance, her rapidly developing electronic sector did not cause a decline in the same industries in Taiwan, Province of China or in the Republic of Korea. On the contrary, her electronic boom increased the need for China to import components from other Asian countries. In this sense, the country's manufacturing ascendancy is a win-win situation for both China and the rest of Asia. China's huge trade surplus vis-à-vis the USA is offset by her deficit in components and parts with other Asian countries, which testifies to the pattern of specialisation within the region.

BOX 3.6: **THE BANGALORE REVOLUTION**

▲
Bangalore, India. ©**Ajay Bhaskar/Shutterstock**

Geographically, most of today's 'world cities' are located on or near coasts. This location has enhanced their ability to trade with other parts of the world. However, under the new economic dispensation as defined by information technologies (IT), the concept of 'remoteness' has been altered. Today, if linked to the Worldwide Web, no city is remotely located, being only one click away from a connection. Over the past several years, Bangalore, a city located right in the middle of southern India, has been put on the global map by its achievements in the information technology sector. According to Software Technology Parks of India, Bangalore's information technology exports have risen from about US $1 billion in 2001 to more than US $10 billion in 2006. The city has also benefited from the employment spin-offs of the information technology industry: according to India's National Association of Software Services Companies (NASSCOM), one IT job results in four indirect jobs (Gokarn *et al.*, 2007). This is the success of Bangalore, which has triggered a software revolution in Indian cities.

The IT industry tends to flourish where technology professionals are available. Bangalore-based Infosys Limited, India's second largest IT firm, concentrates most of its staff, or nearly so, in a single location. Interestingly, these professionals are not located in Bangalore but some 750km up north in Pune (south-east of Mumbai). From an international perspective, the rapid rise of Bangalore has forced major software companies to consider alternative locations outside the developed world.

Cities in India are now competing against each other in order to attract major software companies. Apart from Pune, cities like Bhubaneswar, Chennai, Gurgaon, Hyderabad and Jaipur are all following Bangalore's example of excellence in the software business.

Source: Prepared with information from Gokarn et al. (2007)

This pattern is further reflected in the geographic dispersion of production, with assembly operations migrating to lower-wage economies while more developed Asian countries specialize in high-value-added components and capital goods. The resulting increase in vertical intra-industry trade, as furthered by foreign direct investment, has created a sophisticated production network in emerging Asia; this in turn facilitates the 'catch-up' process for developing Asian countries through technology transfers. India is making its mark, too, with a focus on trade in specialist services (e.g., software, call centres) rather than hardware (IMF, 2008).

Asia's growing share in world trade has resulted largely from increased regional trade integration. While trade flows in the rest of the world roughly tripled between 1990 and 2006, inter-regional trade involving emerging Asia rose by a multiple of five, and intra-regional trade within emerging Asia by a multiple of eight (IMF, 2008).

3.4.2 The next major innovations are to come from Asia's 'knowledge economies'

Specialisation is an evolving process. Asia no longer serves just a source of cheap manufacturing goods and services. The transformations in global markets, production and innovation systems are providing fresh opportunities for those Asian firms bent on improving their innovative potential. The process of outsourcing that was initially designed to exploit the labour wage arbitrage is slowly giving way to access to high-class skills as the primary driver of next-generation outsourcing.

It was generally believed that in contrast to other stages along the value chain, there was a strong aspect of inertia to innovation: it would typically remain tied to specific locations that were the home countries of multinational companies. However, the integration of developing countries into the global economy, combined with foreign direct investment flows, has brought about a major change. This change is visible in those locations that were the early recipients of global outsourcing: as this phenomenon now tends to favour other Asian nations, the early beneficiaries are becoming more diversified and moving to higher-end, higher value-added processes of production and service delivery. Moreover, as outsourcing is taking on a larger share of global research and development (R&D), Asian cities build local capabilities for innovation. World-scale companies increasingly rely on knowledge sourcing from Asia to manage global production, distribution and innovation networks. The network flagships relocate research and development to countries where knowledge workers come cheaper. In 1997, 59 per cent of US corporate R&D sites were located within the USA, while only 8 per cent had been outsourced to China or India. By 2006, these two countries had increased their shares to 18 per cent, while the US share had declined to 52 per cent (Ernst, 2008a).

Asian cities now offer the benefits of proximity to higher-end specialized supply networks for components, manufacturing and knowledge-intensive business services. Global firms are expanding and upgrading their research and development centres in Asia. Intel currently has seven R&D laboratories in

TABLE 3.5: **ASIA'S TOP-RANKING FINANCIAL CENTRES**

City	World Ranking	Rating
Hong Kong, China	3	729
Singapore	4	719
Shenzhen	5	695
Tokyo	7	674
Shanghai	10	655
Beijing	22	613
Taipei	24	609
Seoul	35	576
Osaka	38	565
Kuala Lumpur	45	557
Mumbai	53	542
Bangkok	60	532
Jakarta	62	511

Source: City of London (2009)

▲
Seoul, Republic of Korea, is one of Asia's top-ranking financial centres.
©JinYoung Lee/Shutterstock

Asia (outside of Japan) and is planning more, with additional staff, in the near future. In Bangalore, India, Intel's largest such centre outside the USA conducts leading-edge research. In Shanghai, Intel has expanded its research and development team to focus on potential new applications for China and other emerging markets. Texas Instruments' Bangalore centre, set up in 1985, now has the global mandate for developing a broad portfolio of leading-edge chips (Ernst, 2008b).

While India has achieved limited success as a worldwide exporter of manufactured goods, Bangalore (see Box 3.6) and Hyderabad have firmly established themselves as export-orientated production centres for software and information services. Microsoft established its first Asian research centre in Beijing in 1998 and is currently spending 60 per cent of its research and development budget in Asia, amounting to almost US $4 billion. The quality of work in Microsoft's development centres in Asia rank among the best in the world. In the words of Bill Gates, "...not only is Asia benefiting from the uses of new technology, [but] Asia will increasingly be the source of advances in technology" (PTI, 2007).

Many cities in East Asia are aspiring to become creative hubs for the whole region. Local innovative capacities are conditioned by nationwide frameworks, and dynamic cities leverage specific location advantages by attracting and retaining talent (Wu, 2005). However, if they are to become creative knowledge hubs, Asian cities must spend more on institutions specializing in education, research and development.

It is the proliferation of innovation that defines leaders in the emerging global knowledge economy. Asian cities have entered this arena, challenging the leaders. But they are still lagging way behind and need to do more if they want to become leaders in their own right.

3.4.3 Asian cities as capital hubs

As suggested earlier in connection with Shanghai, Singapore and Hong Kong, China, and Asia has become a force to reckon with in the global financial market. Exports of productive capital are far from negligible. With US $150 billion in outward FDI flows in 2007, the continent has provided significant amounts of funding to other developing countries, both within and outside the region. Increasing numbers of *developed* countries are also attracting direct investment from Asia. India accounted for 16 per cent of all new foreign investment into London between 2003 and 2007, according to UK direct investment agency "Think London" (Think London, 2006). Similarly, China has surpassed the World Bank as the largest lender to Africa.

This goes to show that the direction of capital flows is no longer one way. Asian countries are using their fresh economic achievements to build a resource base for their own future growth. Asian companies are also buying global brands to compete on an equal footing with their counterparts around the world. Major world-scale firms such as Arcelor (Europe's, and one of the world's top steelmaker) and Corus Steel, or iconic automobile company brand names such as Jaguar and Land Rover, have been taken over by Indian companies.

Mumbai, India, is aspiring to become an internation financial center. ©**Mark Henley/Panos Pictures**

A Chinese firm, Lenovo, has acquired IBM's laptop, computers and peripherals range of products.

Financial services are an attractive sector for cities for two reasons: (i) this type of business has demonstrated its importance as a high-growth economic sector over the past quarter of a century, and (ii) these services are highly mobile. They also are under direct influence of policy and planning. For this reason, the competitiveness of financial centres is of great relevance to government officials and regulators. However, globalization creates new competitive pressures for established financial centres. An ever-more integrated global economy means that easily replicable, "commoditized" jobs will tend to shift to the lowest-cost locations in emerging markets. "[The] global urban landscape . . . [is] dominated by a small number of cities that are distinguished by their higher order functions of control and coordination of global economic flows. These cities are pivotally arranged in a hierarchical network of trade, investment, financial and even government transactions, and are responsible for creating value up and down the global economic chain" (Poon, 2003:136-137 as quoted in Jarvis (2009).

The City of London Corporation's *Global Financial Centres Index* assesses the competitiveness of 46 marketplaces worldwide. Regular updates pinpoint any changes in financial centre competitiveness based on a number of factors which combine into a single 'rating' for every centre. The higher the rating, the higher the ranking (City of London, 2009). The list shows that most of the larger, recent rises in ratings were achieved by Asian centres such as Shanghai, Beijing and Seoul. Shenzhen

was included in the rankings for the first time in 2009 and shot straight to fifth rank worldwide (see Table 3.5). Incidentally, the City of London report found that many Asian economies were faring better than major Western counterparts.

Shanghai's emergence as an international financial centre results from a combination of shrewd planning and economic ambition. The city was insulated from intra-national competition and provided with all the resources it needed to develop its physical infrastructure. China's national authorities have deployed a range of regulatory, institutional and liberalization measures to underpin domestic financial intermediation and financial sector development. Shanghai owes its rapid emergence as a financial centre to the introduction of change and innovation at all levels of the institutional-regulatory spectrum (Jarvis, 2009).

India's financial capital, Mumbai, is aspiring to become an international financial centre. Its competitive advantages include a high density of formal and informal financial firms (some of which are highly qualified) and supportive social infrastructures (education, healthcare and the work culture). As for time zones, Mumbai sits almost mid-point between Tokyo, Singapore and Hong Kong, China, to the east, and Frankfurt, Paris and London to the west. However, Mumbai must overcome major hurdles if it is to provide the required cost-effective, high-quality physical and regulatory infrastructure. Improvements must also include telecommunication networks, urban land-use regulations and tenancy laws.

3.4.4 Human capital and economic growth

Basic human capital and Asian cities

High-quality educational services are a necessary though not sufficient condition for economic growth. Education cannot, on its own, bring about economic transformation. It is for cities to provide adequate support and infrastructure on top of promoting economic growth. Education facilitates economic transformation through higher worker productivity. It also acts as a catalyst for entrepreneurs to develop or adopt new technologies, or to introduce new types of business. Education also helps the process of globalization by opening up the frontiers of knowledge. As education is highly valued in Asian society, the countries in the region have established many quality educational institutions. However, since demand for better and higher education increases with economic development, Asian systems are struggling to keep pace (Permani, 2009).

As in other regions, cities in Asia generally feature higher enrolment ratios than rural areas. However, economic needs often supersede educational goals among poorer urban families, as they face a tough choice between paying for basic services or for children's education (UN-HABITAT, 2010). In India's and Nepal's larger cities, enrolment ratios are higher than 90 per cent, while small cities lag behind by almost 10 per cent. In Viet Nam, enrolment ratios are almost equally high in urban and rural areas (see Chart 3.8) (UN-HABITAT, 2008).

As far as development of basic human capital is concerned, Asia has a long way to go. The continent is host to two-thirds (or 513 million) of the world's illiterate population. In South Asia, one in three adults is illiterate, but in urban areas the ratio improves to one in five. The good news is that currently, more Asians are in school than ever before. In some countries, such as the Republic of Korea, Japan and Myanmar, net enrolment ratios stand higher than 98 per cent. In other countries, where education services are lagging, enrolment ratios are significantly lower (Timor-Leste: 63

per cent; Pakistan: 66 per cent; Nepal: 76 per cent; Bhutan: 79 per cent). However, in this region, while nine out of 10 children of primary-school age are enrolled, the proportion falls to only six out of 10 in secondary education (ESCAP, 2008). In Indonesia, almost all children attend six years of schooling, with 80 per cent of even the poorest completing primary school, but subsequent enrolment numbers drop dramatically, especially among the poor.

Between 1999 and 2006, more Asians have matriculated to universities located in small towns and the average gross enrolment ratio (GER) rose from 12 to 20 per cent during the period. Among the subregions, the highest gross enrolment ratios are to be found in North and Central Asia (54 per cent), followed by the Pacific (52 per cent) and East and North-East Asia (26 per cent). In South-East Asia, the ratio was 21 per cent in 2006, while South and South-West Asia ranked last in the whole region with 12 per cent. Gross enrolment ratios under 10 per cent are found in low-growth economies including Bangladesh, Bhutan, Cambodia, the Lao People's Democratic Republic, Pakistan and Uzbekistan (ESCAP, 2008).

In its World Development Report (2007), the World Bank called on Asian governments to focus on education *quality* as well as quantity. So far, education policies on the continent have indeed focused on increasing primary school enrolment numbers. The World Bank specifically insisted on the need for improved quality of basic education services and skills acquisition. In Nepal, for instance, close to 60 per cent of children who dropped out after grade three cannot read a simple sentence. In India, remedial programmes for poorly performing pupils have had positive results, with local young women teaching basic literacy and numeracy skills. Overall in Asia, a decline in poverty has been accompanied by rising inequalities. Against this background, it is imperative for education policies to target poor and disadvantaged children, otherwise socioeconomic inequality may worsen (UNESCO, 2007; UN-HABITAT, 2010).

CHART 3.8: **NET ENROLMENT RATIOS IN PRIMARY EDUCATION**

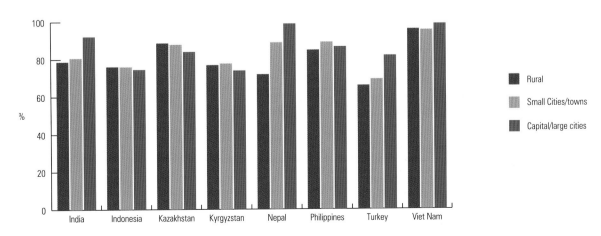

Source: UN-HABITAT (2008)

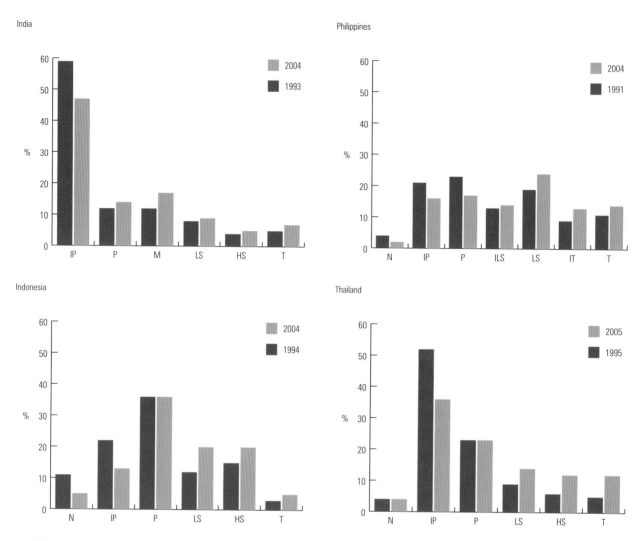

Key - N: None; IP: Incomplete Primary; P: Primary; M: Middle; ILS: Incomplete Lower Secondary; LS: Lower Secondary; HS: Higher Secondary; IT: Incomplete Tertiary (higher education); T: Tertiary.
Source: Asian Development Bank (2007)

Vocational education and Asian cities

In Asian cities, more education has raised expectations which, if unfulfilled, can lead to economic and social instability. Given the scale of economic growth and urbanization in the Asia-Pacific region, most countries will not be able to generate enough jobs to accommodate increased supplies of better educated labour. Most new labour market entrants may have to work in sectors where educational qualifications do not matter. On the other hand, general-purpose education in schools and colleges often makes graduates "unemployable" for jobs that require specific skills, and they need on-the-job retraining from employers.

Clearly, the development of technical and vocational skills is of vital importance for the future prosperity of the Asia-Pacific region. Skills enable individuals to enhance productivity and income, and therefore are of special interest to those working in the informal economy. Except for the newly industrialized economies, virtually all countries in the region will find themselves unable to generate enough formal jobs to accommodate all those entering the labour market. Most new labour market entrants in South and South-West Asia and in the Pacific will have no alternative but to work in the informal sector. The same applies to large numbers entering the labour force in China, Indonesia and Viet Nam. Knowledge and technical skills are essential for workers in the informal sector, too, as higher productivity and incomes help them break out of poverty (Asian Development Bank, 2008b; UNESCO, 2007).

In China, an estimated 140 million rural workers – most with limited education and few vocational skills – have migrated to urban areas in search of jobs and income opportunities. The flow of unskilled workers from rural to urban areas is expected to continue at a rate of at least 10 million a year for the foreseeable future. At the same time, many industries in China

Asian cities nowadays aspire to be not just the factories but also the knowledge hubs of the world. For this to happen, an adequately prepared human resource base is necessary to drive and support growth. A knowledge-economy needs a more skilled labour force. This can be achieved only through quality education systems that promote problem-solving and critical-thinking skills. In general, the focus of employers is on the number of years of schooling and graduate degrees. Corroborating the World Bank's recommendations (2007), recent research based on test scores in mathematics and language skills indicates that quality in education has a stronger impact on economic growth than the total years of schooling (UNESCO, 2007).

Cities that become knowledge hubs bring many benefits to the relevant economy. In India, for instance, growth in the information technology (IT) and IT-enabled services ('IT-ITES') sector has a substantial multiplier effect on employment and output via direct and indirect backward linkages and induced consumption spending. A significant part of this additional job creation derives from IT-ITES spending in the construction, transportation, apparel, retail, security, hospitality and entertainment sectors. The additional employment opportunities are not restricted to educated or skilled professionals, though. Surveys show that nearly three-fourths of the workforce employed by major providers of services to IT-ITES (catering, housekeeping, transport, security) have only secondary or higher secondary education (Gokarn *et al.,* 2007).

Research by the Asian Development Bank shows that India, Indonesia, the Philippines and Thailand are producing educated workers faster than they are creating jobs (see Chart 3.9). In general, economic growth is leading to rising education levels across the board, including in some sectors and types of jobs that do not pay a premium for education. The economy-wide wage returns to basic education (i.e., the percentage increase in wages associated with completing an extra year of schooling) have fallen in these countries at almost every level of the primary and secondary school system. In contrast, and regardless of a growing supply of college-educated workers, the returns to tertiary education are rising. While the output of the "knowledge economy" increases rapidly (particularly in India), the employment shares of these non-traditional services are growing slowly, if at all, and from a low base. Thus, the bulk of newly educated workers continue to find employment in traditional services, construction and manufacturing. Such workers are increasingly becoming unemployed as well, although more of them have achieved high education levels (Asian Development Bank, 2007).

The Chinese government is taking steps, including incentives, to provide college graduates with jobs in rural areas, using their skills to connect these to the markets and networks that drive the whole country's economy. Beyond support to rural development, the strategy also addresses the country's grim employment situation which the recent economic slow-down has only made worse (Lawrence, 2008).

▲
Cambodia has a gross enrolment ratio of under 10%. ©**Philip Date/Shutterstock**

face severe production constraints due to shortages of skilled workers. Other developing countries in Asia are faced with shortages of workers with adequate vocational and technical skills, and more specifically with qualifications in such critical areas like information and communication technologies and accounting (Asian Development Bank, 2008b).

Export-orientated sectors such as electronics and textiles/apparel have been growing rapidly in Asian cities. These sectors require specific skills which general higher education does not provide. In the electronics and apparel industries, many firms have to provide on-the-job training to young women entering the labour market. Computer literacy and a proper command of English are becoming major assets in rapidly growing Asian cities. In Mumbai, the earnings of those who attended English-speaking schools are much higher than those that did not. Between 1980 and the year 2000, the "English premium" – the earnings of students educated in English-speaking schools – increased from 15 to 24 per cent for men and from nearly zero to 27 per cent for women (World Bank, 2007).

3.5
Asian cities and local development

An informal settlement in Mazar-e-Sharif City, Afghanistan. ©UN-HABITAT/Wataru Kawasaki

Asia's spectacular economic growth over the past two decades has brought substantial overall improvements in incomes per head, but they have been highly uneven across and within countries. The Republic of Korea, Taiwan, Province of China, Singapore and Hong Kong, China, have achieved living standards that are more or less on par with those in the developed world, but much of South Asia has remained poor. Economic growth does not benefit all cities equally, either. Growth is largely concentrated in a few coastal cities that have grown rapidly over the past decades, while others – mostly cities in the hinterland – have languished.

The World Development Report (World Bank, 2009c:xx) argues that some locations are doing well because they have promoted transformations along the three main dimensions of geography: (i) higher densities; (ii) shorter distances between residence and work-place; and (iii) reduced spatial segmentation as countries thin out their economic borders and enter the world markets to take advantage of scale and specialization.

Lagging areas have one thing in common: they are economically distant from more successful locations. Apart from that, the economic geography is not the same across areas. In some countries, such as China, lagging areas are sparsely populated. The latest World Bank *World Development Report* (World Bank, 2009c:xxii) suggested that it does not make a lot of sense to spread expensive infrastructure in these areas or to give firms incentives to move there, but others disagree. For instance, Maringanti *et al.* (2009:45) argue that the World Bank sees unbalanced growth as a consequence of "benign forces of agglomeration, migration, and specialization, while

overlooking the political processes that ...unfairly redistributes costs to the poor and marginalised groups."

The notion that economic benefits trickle down across both income categories and geographic space all by themselves, as claimed by neo-classical economics, is not always, if at all (UN-HABITAT, 2010) verified and, where it is, does not occur at the same pace in all countries or across all regions. Rising spatial inequalities often lead to political instability and violence, and they can be prevented through proper development of lagging regions, even if the immediate economic costs are higher – this is the price to pay for more balanced economic development, with the necessary labour and capital inflows. Many countries in Asia have devised special development schemes for lagging areas, and provide more incentives to enterprises that are located there. The experience so far suggests that for these schemes to have any significant effect on lagging areas, huge investments in infrastructure are inevitable (see Box 3.7).

When labour and capital are allowed to move freely across a given geographic expanse, there will be a natural tendency for concentration. As economies shift from low to higher incomes over time, production will tend to aggregate in specific areas. Producers of goods and services will favour some types of location – cities, coastal areas and well-connected countries – over others. In China, the coastal provinces – mainly in the three areas known as the Bohai Basin (North-East China), the Pearl and Yangtze River Deltas – represent less than a fifth of the country's surface area but accounted for more than half of gross domestic product in 2005 (World Bank, 2009c). Fears are that China is fast becoming a polarized country

BOX 3.7: BALANCING URBAN AND RURAL DEVELOPMENT: CHINA'S CHONGQING METROPOLITAN REGION

▲
Chongqing on the Yangtze River. ©**Jing Aiping/Shutterstock**

The Chongqing Municipality development plan demonstrates how the right balances between urban and rural areas, and between a metropolitan area and small towns, can be achieved. Chongqing in 1997 became China's fourth centrally administered municipality after Beijing, Shanghai and Tianjin. Now formally known as a "municipality," Chongqing has become the largest urban region in China with a population of 31 million spread over a land area of 82,000 square kilometres. The region includes 40 county-level administrative divisions. Of these, nine districts form the core of the Chongqing metropolitan region with 5.5 million people. The remaining area is largely rural, accounting for 75 per cent of the municipal population. In the year 2000, the Chongqing metropolitan region's production of goods and services was equivalent to US $43.7 billion, way below Shanghai's US $271 billion and Guangzhou's US $182 billion.

In a bid to become a communication hub and a gateway to the western region under the development plan, Chongqing is establishing itself as a modern production base as well as a business and trade centre and a knowledge hub. The basic pattern, known as "One Circle and Two Wings",

radiates around the "One-Hour Economic Circle" which takes in the 23 counties and districts that can be reached within one hour by bus from the central urban area; the ' two wings' refer to the elongated territories stretching out to the northeast and south-east. The plan is to develop an "economic circle" as a core urban region, with the two 'wings' reaping spillover effects, and the region as a whole becoming an engine of growth in the upper Yangtze River valley. The one-hour drive circle is designed to attract services and manufacturing.

As far as rural areas are concerned, a "New Socialist Countryside" *(jianshe shehui zhuyi xin nongcun)* is part of the plan. The rationale is to narrow the gap between urban and rural areas that reforms and liberalization policies had opened up since the late 1970s. More specifically, the aim is to enhance agricultural productivity and upgrade grain production capabilities. This is to take place against a background of improved infrastructures, healthcare and education (nine-year compulsory school), including water conservation facilities, road construction, use of clean fuels and rural power grids.

The Chinese government's US $20 billion plan for the Chongqing municipal region is one of the most ambitious of all those aimed at balancing rural and urban development. The attendant massive infrastructure development has already begun to transform local state-owned enterprises and attract fresh capital into the manufacturing and services sectors.

Source: OECD (2007)

along two dimensions – rural-urban and coastal-inland areas. Although the urban-rural gap is much the wider, it has remained relatively constant since the early reforms of the late 1970s. In contrast, coastal-inland polarization has increased dramatically.

Kanbur & Venables (2005a) suggest that while natural endowments and agglomeration economies do lead to spatial concentration of activities, government intervention under the form of infrastructure and openness to international trade further exacerbates this phenomenon. The two authors suggest a two-pronged approach to rising spatial inequalities. To them, the first step is to remove barriers to the de-concentration of economic activity. These barriers can be of a political or institutional nature, such as the need for firms to locate near political and administrative centres. Therefore, economic and social infrastructure must be so devised as to facilitate de-concentration, in the process putting the hinterlands and poorer regions in a better position to benefit

from integration into the global economy. The second step in this de-concentration strategy is to facilitate, or at least not to impede, the migration of individuals and households to areas of high or rising well-being. In the authors' opinion, this two sided approach stands the best chance of gaining the most from the efficiencies of agglomeration and openness, without running into the potential for destabilization that derives from rising spatial inequality (Kanbur & Venables, 2005b). Chapter 2 discusses migration and remittances.

With free mobility of people, it is also important to ensure that existing institutional mechanisms provide adequate job security to migrants. Similarly required are proper school and healthcare facilities for migrants and adequate supplies of affordable housing options. When market forces are given a free rein, they do not always work in favour of the poor and marginalised. Governments and civil society organizations must ensure that the benefits of growth accrue to all segments of society (UN-HABITAT, 2010).

3.6
Diagnosis and future challenges

▲
Tokyo, Japan. ©**Amy Nichole Harris/Shutterstock**

The economic challenge Asian cities are facing in this early 21st century is to manage the trade-off between the positive and the negative externalities attached to urban areas, and to do so in coordination with inclusive, national or regional strategies that promote the geographical spread of the benefits of urbanization and economic growth. If they are to meet this challenge, cities across the region must build the institutional capacity and strategic vision that will enable them to manage economic growth in a more inclusive sort of way (UN-HABITAT, 2010). In particular, cities must pay attention to the way infrastructure programmes fit with broader development strategies and political circumstances, how those strategies are formulated and how they bring about tangible outcomes. It is for political leaders and senior policymakers in the Asia-Pacific region to evolve a vision for long-term development based on holistic approaches that merge spatial policy with macro-economic, industrial, agricultural, energy, environmental and labour policies. This vision must combine the diversity of domestic needs into a region-wide strategy that is based on inclusiveness and anticipates on inevitable future economic shocks and crises.

As cities have become more and more integrated in the global economy, urban employment patterns have undergone a structural shift. In the early phase of urbanization, economic growth was led by the manufacturing sector, which absorbed large portions of the labour force and had a large, most welcome multiplier effect. With manufacturing no longer the dominant economic activity in many Asian cities, the service sector, both formal and informal, has become the mainstay of urban economies. Along with this came explicit policies of urban de-industrialization. As a result, 'old' manufacturing enterprises had to restructure in order to pursue more decentralized production and relocate out of cities. The consequence of this process for the urban poor is that livelihood opportunities in the formal manufacturing sector have diminished over time. Many of the urban "blue-collar" jobs that were available to migrants in the 1950s and 1960s are now relocating to peripheral areas (e.g. the Eastern Seaboard in Bangkok, the lower Pearl River region in China, outside Kuala Lumpur, and in Chennai Metropolitan Region – often 50 to 100 km away from the main city).

The core city is now a preferred location for the new economic sectors offering formal, qualified jobs. The services sector also generates jobs for the poor at the lower end (e.g., cleaning, security or catering services), including the informal sector. The rise of the formal service sector has brought about fresh capital expenditure in infrastructure, construction, retail, financial services and the hospitality business. Along with highly paid employment opportunities, these businesses have also spawned large informal sectors where wages are low and unregulated.

The informal economy is usually seen as a problem by policymakers even though it generates many million dollars in revenues. Large urban informal sectors have provided employment to the millions who are unable to secure formal jobs. Informal-sector incomes may not be enough for the urban poor to pull themselves out of economic deprivation, but at least they provide basic subsistence. Informal markets also give the urban poor access to various housing options which suit their incomes although admittedly they are far from ideal: rooms in slums or squats shared by families, or rented beds in dormitories in cheap houses to suit (usually male) daily wage migrant workers. Still, the urban poor living under such difficult circumstances make a substantial contribution to the economy, and one which must be better recognized (UN-HABITAT, 2010). The challenge is all the more complex as huge needs for proper housing (see Chapter 4) and infrastructure must be met in a sustainable way in a region that is particularly vulnerable to natural disasters and the effects of climate change (see Chapter 5).

The resilience of Asian economies

Asian cities were badly affected by the 1997-98 regional financial crisis. In Indonesia, poverty rose from 11.3 per cent of the population in 1996 to 16.7 per cent in 1998, as an additional 10 to 12 million people were thrown into economic deprivation. In Malaysia, poverty spread from 8.2 per cent of the population in 1997 to 11.2 per cent in 1998. In the Philippines, as many as 17 per cent of the families in

the country reported job losses, a phenomenon that also hit 5 per cent of migrant workers in the region. In Thailand, the poverty head count grew from 11.4 per cent in 1996 to almost 13 percent in 1998, as an additional 1.1 million people fell below the poverty line. However, these countries recovered quickly. A decade later, cities in the region do not show any lingering stigma and are an integral part of the international economic momentum. There are lessons to be learnt from the way in which Asian cities dealt with the 1997-98 financial troubles, and they can have some relevance to the global economic crisis that started in 2008.

At the same time, there can be no denying that the global economic crisis that has affected the developed world, especially the USA, has undermined the strength of export-orientated Asian economies. However, the sheer scale of domestic markets in the region makes Asian cities more resilient to crises, as structural shifts in production and distribution patterns are to make regional growth less export-orientated and more domestic-led.

Apart from the circumstantial (fiscal stimulus) policies of the past few years, Asian countries are looking systematically to boost domestic consumption through innovative financing schemes. At present, in most Asian economies household debt is less than 50 per cent of GDP; in China and India it is under 15 per cent, and in many other countries consumer credit is next to non-existent. Many domestic and foreign institutions in Asian cities are now setting up consumer-credit institutions. This is promising, and all the more so as even before the crisis, emerging Asia's consumer spending contributed significantly to the growth in global demand.

Being continental Asia's largest economies, China and India stand to make significant contributions to future global economic growth. Projections suggest these two countries will continue to make their presence felt in the worldwide urban sphere. Of the 66 fastest growing urban economies in the world, one third are in China and India (Hawksworth *et al.*, 2007). This momentum will compel other cities in the Asia-Pacific region to readjust their own economic specialisation. On the whole, complementary strategies can be expected further to enhance the role of Asian cities in a more dynamic global economy.

ENDNOTES

[1] The subregions in this chart are as specified by the source.

[2] Gross national income per head in 2007 is used by the World Bank in this study and amounts to US$ 950 at a rate of US $1.00 = INR43.97 (Indian rupees).

[3] The Global Urban Competitiveness Project was founded in April 2005 by experts and scholars from around the world including the USA, the UK, Canada, Mexico, the Republic of Korea and Japan in. The Project conducts global policy research and training programmes for urban authorities.

ADB - Asian Development Bank. *Key Indicators 2008 - Special chapter: Comparing Poverty across countries: The role of Purchasing Power Parities*. Manila: Asian Development Bank, 2008a

—. *Education and Skills – Strategies for accelerated development in Asia and the Pacific*. Manila: Asian Development Bank, 2008b

—. *Asian Development Outlook 2007*. Manila: Asian Development Bank, 2007

—. "Key Indicators 2005 - Labor markets in Asia: Promoting full, productive and decent employment. "Annual Statistical Data Book, Manila: Asian Development Bank, 2005

—. "Urban Indicators for Managing Cities: Cities Data Book." Edited by Matthew S. Westfall and Victoria A. de Villa. Manila: Asian Development Bank, 2001. Soft Copy available at http://www.adb.org/Documents/Books/Cities_Data_Book/default.asp

Airports Council International. *Media Release-Airport traffic: flat growth in 2008*. July 27, 2009. http://www.airports.org/aci/aci/file/Press%20Releases/2009/PR_WATR2008_270709.pdf (accessed 4 October 2009)

Amin, A.T.M. Nurul. "The Informal Sector in Asia from the Decent Work Perspective." *Employment Paper 2002-4*. Geneva: International Labour Organization, 2002

Asia Times. "The changing face of Ho Chi Minh City." *Asia Times.* May 13, 2005. http://www.atimes.com/atimes/Southeast_Asia/GE13Ae04.html (accessed 13 July 2009)

Bhowmik, Sharit.K. "Street Vendors in Asia-A Review." *Economic and Political Weekly*, 40 May 28-June 4, 2005 56-64

BRIDGE. "Feminization of poverty." *Briefing paper.* Sussex: Swedish International Development Cooperation Agency (SIDA), Institute of Development Studies, April 2001

Chant, S., and C. Pedwell. "Women, gender and the informal economy: An assessment of ILO research and suggested ways forward." Geneva: International Labour Office, 2008

City of London. *The Global Financial Centres Index-6.* September 2009. http://www.zyen.com/PDF/GFCI6.pdf (accessed 7 January 2009)

Ernst, Dieter. "The new geography of innovation and U.S. comparative competitiveness." *Western Economic Association International 83rd conference.* Honolulu: East-West Center, July 2, 2008a

—. "Innovation Off-shoring and Asia's 'Upgradation Through Innovation' Strategies." *East-West Center Working Papers: Economics Series No.95.* Honolulu: East West Center, February 2008b

ESCAP. – *Economic and Social Survey of Asia and the Pacific 2010: Sustaining Recovery and Dynamism for Inclusive Development.* Bangkok: ESCAP, United Nations, 2010a

—. *Statistical Yearbook for Asia and the Pacific 2009.* Bangkok: ESCAP, United Nations, 2010b

—. *Statistical Yearbook for Asia and the Pacific 2008.* Bangkok: ESCAP, United Nations, 2008

GoI – Government of India, Ministry of Finance (GoI, Ministry of Finance). *Report of the High Powered Expert Committee on Making Mumbai an International Financial Centre.* New Delhi: Government of India, 2007

Gokarn, Subir, Dharmakirti Joshi, Vidya Mahambare, Pooja Mirchandani, Manoj Mohta, and Kumar Subramaniam. "The Rising Tide - Output and Employment Linkages of IT-ITES." Mumbai: NASSCOM, CRISIL, February 2007

GUCP. *Global Urban Competitiveness Report 2008.* Global Urban Competitiveness Project, 2008 http://www.gucp.org/admin/WebEdit/UploadFile/Global%20Urban%20Competitiveness%20Report.doc (accessed 1 July 2009)

Hawksworth, John, Thomas Hoehn, Meirion Gyles (2007). "Which are the largest city economies in the world and how might this change by 2020?" PriceWaterhouseCoopers UK Economic Outlook, March 2007. Available at http://www.ukmediacentre.pwc.com/Media-Library/UK-Economic-Outlook-March-2007-35f.aspx

Hugo, Graeme. "Urbanization in Asia: An Overview." Johannesburg: Conference on African Migration in Comparative Perspective, June 4-7, 2003

ILO – International Labour Organisation. "Informal Economy, Poverty and Employment: An Integrated Approach." *RAS/03/51M/UKM.* Hanoi: ILO sub-regional office for East Asia, 2006a

—. "Realising Decent Work in Asia." *14th Asian Regional Meeting.* Busan: International Labour Organization, August-September 2006b

—. "Decent work and the informal economy." Paper, International Labour Conference 90th Session, Report VI, Geneva: International Labour Organization, 2002a

—. *Good Practice Study in Shanghai on Employment Services for the Informal Economy.* Geneva: International Labour Office, 2002b

IMF – International Monetary Fund. 2009. http://www.imf.org/external/np/exr/ib/2008/053008.htm (accessed 1 July 2009)

—. *Globalization: A Brief Overview.* May 2008. http://www.imf.org/external/np/exr/ib/2008/053008.htm (accessed 1 July 2009)

Jarvis, D. S. L. *Race for the Money: International Financial Centers in Asia.* June 3, 2009. http://ssrn.com/abstract=1413524 (accessed 1 July 2009)

Kanbur, Ravi, and Anthony J. Venables. *Spatial Inequality and development.* New York: Oxford University Press, 2005a

—. "Policy Brief No 3." *UNU-WIDER project on 'Spatial Disparities in Human Development'.* Helsinki:

World Institute for Development Economics Research (WIDER), United National University, 2005b

Kohpaiboon, Archanun. "Thai Automotive Industry: Multinational Enterprises and Global Integration." *Discussion Paper No. 0004.* Bangkok: Faculty of Economics, Thammasat University, February 25, 2008

Lawrence, Dune. "Chinese graduates recruited for rural work." *New York Times.* December 16, 2008. http://www.nytimes.com/2008/12/16/world/asia/16iht-letter.1.18714156.html?scp=1&sq=Chinese%20graduates%20recruited%20for%20rural%20work&st=cse (accessed 29 September 2009)

Lee, Joanna, and Mee-kam Ng. "Planning for the World City." *In The First Decade: The Hong Kong SAR in Retrospective and Introspective Perspectives,* by Yue-man Yeung, 297-319. Hong Kong, China: The Chinese University Press, 2007

Maringanti, Anant, Eric Sheppard, and Jun Zhang. "Where is the Geography? World Bank's WDR 2009." *Economic and Political Weekly,* 44 July 18, 2009 45-51

MasterCard Worldwide. "Worldwide Centers of Commerce Index 2008." 2008 http://www.mastercard.com/us/company/en/insights/pdfs/2008/MCWW_WCoC-Report_2008.pdf (accessed 1 July 2009)

OECD – Organisation for Economic Cooperation and Development. *Chongqing Municipality's Development Strategy: Some Reflections From the International Experience of The Territorial Development Policy Committee of The OECD.* 2007. http://www.oecd.org/dataoecd/14/13/40061625.pdf (accessed 10 May 2009)

Permani, Risti. "The Role of Education in Economic Growth in East Asia: A Survey." *Asian-Pacific Economic Literature,* 23 May 2009 1-20. http://ssrn.com/

abstract=1396897 (accessed 29 July 2009)

Poon, Jessie P.H. "Hierarchical tendencies of capital markets among international financial centers," *Growth and Change,* 34 2003 135-36

PTI – Press Trust of India. *The next success will come from Asia: Gates.* New Delhi: April 23, 2007. http://www.expressindia.com/news/fullstory.php?newsid=85312 (accessed 1 July 2009)

PwC – Pricewaterhouse Cooper. *Cities of Opportunity-Asia Pacific.* Sydney: Pricewaterhouse Coopers and Sydney Chamber of Commerce, 2008

—. *PricewaterhouseCoopers UK Economic Outlook.* PricewaterhouseCoopers, 2009 http://www.pwc.co.uk/pdf/ukeo_nov09.pdf (accessed 7 January 2009)

Sassen, Saskia. Global Networks, *Linked Cities.* New York: Routledge, 2002

—. *The Global City: New York, London, Tokyo.* Princeton: Princeton University Press, 1991

Scott, Allen J. "Creative cities: Conceptual issues and policy questions." *Journal of Urban Affairs* 28 2006 1-17

Straub, Stéphane, Charles Vellutini, and Michael Warlters. "Infrastructure and Economic Growth in East Asia." *Policy Research Working Paper 4589.* Washington DC: The World Bank, East Asia and Pacific Sustainable Department Policy Unit, April 2008.

The China Post. *Kaohsiung slips as one of world's top 10 container ports.* May 6, 2009. http://www.chinapost.com.tw/business/asia/b-taiwan/2009/05/06/207123/Kaohsiung-slips.htm (accessed 4 October 2009)

Think London. "52 billion: The Value of Foreign Direct Investment to London." *London Focus.* London: Think London, October 2006. http://www.thinklondon.com/

dynamic/downloads/Think_London_reports/London_Focus/secure_D4_london_focus_52billion.pdf (accessed 29 July 2009) tradingeconomics.com. China GDP Growth Rate. 15 July 2010. www.tradingeconomics.com/Economics/GDP-Growth.aspx (accessed 9 August 2010)

UNESCO – UN Education, Science and Culture Organisation. "Education for all by 2015 - Will we make it?" *EFA-Global Monitoring Report Summary.* 2007. http://unesdoc.unesco.org/images/0015/001548/154820e.pdf (accessed 29 July 2009)

UN-HABITAT. *State of the World's Cities 2008/2009 - Harmonious Cities.* Nairobi: UN-HABITAT, 2008

— State of the World's Cities 2010/2011 – Bridging the Urban Divide. Nairobi: UN-HABITAT, 2010

World Bank. "World Development Indicators." Washington DC: World Bank, April 24, 2009a

—. *Doing Business in India 2009.* Washington DC: World Bank, 2009b

—. *World Development Report 2009 - Reshaping Economic Geography.* Washington DC: World Bank, 2009c

—. *Global development finance-The role of international banking.* Washington DC: World Bank, 2008a

—. *World Bank Supports Bangladesh to Increase Reliable Energy.* October 30, 2008b. http://www.worldbank.org.bd/WBSITE/EXTERNAL/COUNTRIES/SOUTHASIAEXT/BANGLADESHEXTN/0,,contentMDK:21959013~menuPK:295779~pagePK:2865066~piPK:2865079~theSitePK:295760,00.html (accessed 29 September 2009)

—. *Doing Business in the Philippines 2008.* Washington DC: World Bank, 2008d

—. *World Development Report 2007: Development and the Next Generation.* Washington DC: The International Bank for Reconstruction and Development and World Bank, 2007

—. *Promoting global environment priorities in the urban transport sector.* Washington DC: World Bank, 2006

World Tourism Organization. "International Conference on Metropolitan Tourism. Shanghai: November 17-18, 2006." Madrid: WTO, 2008 http://pub.world-tourism.org:81/WebRoot/Store/Shops/Infoshop/4845/3F10/E83D/50CF/BD34/C0A8/0164/88FA/080520_metropolitan_tourism_shanghai_excerpt.pdf (accessed 28 September 2009)

Wu, Weiping. "Dynamic cities and Creative Clusters." *World Bank Policy Research Working Paper 3509.* Washington DC: World Bank, February 2005

Yeung, Yue-man. "Planning Hong Kong for 1997 and Beyond." *In Globalization and Networked Societies: Urban-Regional Change in Pacific Asia,* by Yue-man Yeung, 213-30. Honolulu: University of Hawaii Press, 2000

—. *The First Decade: The Hong Kong SAR in Retrospective and Introspective Perspectives.* Hong Kong, China: The Chinese University Press, 2007

Zsin Woon, Teoh, Santitarn Sathirathai, David Lam, Lai Chung Han, and Kriengsak Chareonwongsak. "Thailand Automotive Cluster." *Microeconomics of Competitiveness 2007-Final Paper.* 2007 http://www.isc.hbs.edu/pdf/Student_Projects/Thailand_AutomotiveCluster_2007.pdf (accessed 1 July 2009)

PART
04
Poverty and inequality in Asian cities

Quick Facts

1. The Asia-Pacific region is leading the reduction of overall poverty in the world.

2. Economic growth has not benefited all urban dwellers in the region equally. Urban income poverty in Asia is declining more slowly than its rural counterpart. Urban inequality is rising in the Asia-Pacific region.

3. Since the year 2000, the lives of 172 million slum-dwellers in Asia have been improved through various policies and programmes.

4. The Asia-Pacific region remains host to over half of the world's slum population, and huge sub-regional disparities remain.

5. Most Asian cities are on their way to achieving the target set under the Millennium Development Goals (MDGs) for access to water.

6. Although Asian cities have made considerable progress in providing access to improved sanitation, many are likely to miss the Millennium sanitation target.

Policy Points

1. Asia-Pacific countries must address urban poverty with adequate policies. National governments and local authorities need to make concerted efforts to reduce urban inequality in the region.

2. Asian governments should continue to invest in slum upgrading and low-cost housing, and to upscale pilot projects into national programmes.

3. Governments should review urban land policies to make residential land more accessible and affordable to low and middle-income households.

4. Local authorities should avoid unlawful evictions which destroy the social fabric of poor neighbourhoods. Slum eradication, where necessary, should be combined with fair relocation and compensation schemes.

5. People's process of housing and slum improvement should be encouraged by all levels of government through training, financial incentives and legal recognition.

6. In countries where access to urban water supply has declined, governments should take necessary steps to ensure that safe water supply reaches all residents.

7. Governments should assess the state of sanitation in cities, set national targets to ensure improved sanitation for all, and monitor progress on a regular basis.

▶

Kabul, Afghanistan.
©Bruno Pagnanelli/Shutterstock

4.1
Poverty

▲

Colombo, Sri Lanka. Housing conditions have a direct bearing on any individual's ability to enjoy the benefits of urban life. **©Robin Hammond/Panos Pictures**

The Asian economy has grown rapidly during the past 10 years with gross domestic product growing by over 6 per cent an annual average basis in several countries. Asian cities, which are the powerhouses of the region's economy, are becoming increasingly confident, capable and self-reliant. However, for all this good economic performance and efforts to foster social development, poverty remains a major problem in the region. Over 900 million of the world's poor still live in Asia. Economic growth has not brought significant poverty reduction in all subregions, as it is not just the overall pace of growth which determines the extent of poverty reduction but also the *pattern* of such growth. Until recently and as noted in Chapter 3, this growth has been largely export-led and backed by high rates of foreign and domestic investment. For the purposes of poverty reduction, resources must be directed to the areas where the poor live, to the sectors where they work, to the factors of production they possess and to the products they consume (ESCAP, 2008a).

Income is the most commonly used measure of poverty. Different methods are used by different countries to determine national poverty lines. For example, in some countries income poverty is measured as the minimum income required for basic food consumption. Other countries include consumption of basic services (water, electricity, sanitation and health care) in addition to food. As a result, it becomes difficult to make international comparisons based on varying national poverty lines. This is why an international benchmark of "one dollar a day" per individual, and as measured in purchasing power parity (PPP, i.e., the same purchasing power that the US dollar had in the United States at a given point in time) prices, has been used as a poverty benchmark (now updated to US $1.25 a day). This definition has also been accepted as the baseline for the Millennium Development Goals. While US $1.25 a day is widely accepted as a worldwide measure of poverty, it raises some serious issues. One criticism is that PPP estimates are generated from average consumption levels, i.e., average baskets of goods that do not necessarily coincide with those more typical of the urban poor. For example, given

▲
Lao PDR. The economic and social dimensions of poverty are inter-related. ©**Muellek Josef/Shutterstock**

that food makes up a much larger share of total expenditures for the poor (often 15 to 20 per cent higher compared with the general population), food prices should be given greater weightings in the purchasing power parities used in the measurement of poverty benchmarks.

Poverty is also defined through the social exclusion approach, which refers to the phenomenon whereby individuals or groups are unable fully to participate in political processes. Since excluded groups or individuals might not be deprived materially, this concept is much broader than that of income poverty (Asian Development Bank, 2004a). An alternative definition of poverty as expounded by Townsend (1979) is 'relative poverty'; this refers to a lack of the resources required to participate in the activities and to enjoy the living standards that are customary or widely accepted in the society in which poverty is being measured. This concept of poverty is used by the European Union.

Moreover, by-now widely recognized non-monetary approaches to poverty measurement have been developed, such as the 'capabilities' approach. In *Development as Freedom*, Amartya Sen defines poverty as the deprivation of the basic capabilities that provide an individual with the freedom to choose the life s/he has reason to value. These capabilities include good health, education, social networks, control over economic resources, and influence on the decisions that affect one's life (Sen, 1999).

In functional terms, poverty can be essentially described as lack of income, of access to basic services, and of empowerment. These economic, social and political dimensions of poverty or inequality are inter-related and a deprivation in one dimension could make the poor vulnerable in others (e.g., lack of access to safe water has repercussions on health, as well as on girls' opportunities for education with the associated effects on the next generation (UN-HABITAT, 2010). Along with the three basic (economic, social and political) deprivations come issues like food security, access to employment opportunities, as well as personal, professional and tenure (i.e., land and shelter) security. For all the general acceptance that these dimensions add new understanding to the concept of poverty, their measurement can be problematic.

▲
A young boy studies in a shop selling recycled oil cans in Kabul, Afghanistan. ©Manoocher Deghati/IRIN

The international poverty line has now been updated to US $1.25 a day. This revised benchmark captures extreme poverty as defined by the national poverty lines of the 15 poorest countries in the world. Another threshold, US $2.00 a day, can be considered as 'moderate poverty' and represents the median poverty line of all developing countries (Chen & Ravallion, 2008; Asian Development Bank, 2008a; Bauer *et al.*, 2008).[1]

According to recent estimates, extreme poverty was reduced worldwide from 43 per cent in 1990 to 26 per cent of the population in 2005. This achievement was largely due to a significant reduction in Asia and the Pacific, where extreme poverty decreased from 49 to 25 per cent over the same period (see Chart 4.1). This remarkable progress in poverty reduction in this region has been largely due to East and North-East as well as South-East Asia (see Chart 4.2). On the whole, between 1990 and 2005, 20 out of the 24 countries in the Asia-Pacific region for which data are available managed to reduce the proportion of their populations living on less than

CHART 4.1: **POVERTY IN THE DEVELOPING WORLD ON $1.25 A DAY AND UNDER**

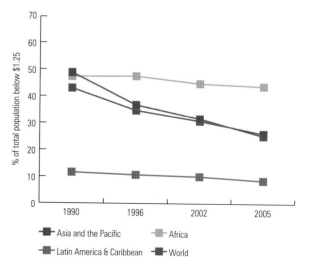

Source: Based on data from ESCAP (2010)

US $1.25 a day. Poverty has been reduced everywhere, except in North and Central Asia. In South and South-West Asia, the decline in poverty has not been as significant as in East Asia.

In East and North-East Asia, a dramatic drop in poverty trends took place in China (from 60 per cent of the population in 1990 to 16 per cent in 2005), on the back of rapid economic growth (see Chart 4.3). In Mongolia, the only other country in the subregion for which data is available, poverty actually *increased* during the same period. This has been attributed to the fact that the Mongolian economy is largely dependent on the mining sector, which provides few employment opportunities (ESCAP, 2008a).

In South-East Asia, the largest reductions in poverty were achieved in Indonesia, with a decline from 54 to 21 per cent of the population between 1990 and 2005. Urbanization has played a major role here, as labour was reallocated from low-productivity, low-paid jobs in rural areas to better-paid employment in the urban, formal economy. In Viet Nam between 1992 and 2006, the poverty rate fell from 64 to 21 per cent of the population. This favourable trend is attributed to an egalitarian redistribution of land, rapid growth in the urban economy due to liberalization, and rising demand for labour (ESCAP, 2008b; Islam, 2002; World Bank, 2008).

In South and South-West Asia, too, poverty declined over the past decade or two. In the whole subregion, the fall was from 47 per cent of the population in 1990 to 35 per cent in 2005. However, this favourable trend largely reflected the robust performance of Pakistan, where the poverty rate fell from 65 per cent in 1990 to 23 per cent in 2004 – an outstanding achievement relative to other countries in the subregion (ESCAP, 2008b).

In North and Central Asia, cross-currents resulted in little overall change in poverty rates. A few countries experienced worsening poverty, such as Uzbekistan (from 32 per cent

in 1998 to 46 per cent in 2003). In Kyrgyzstan, an increase during the late 1990s was subsequently reversed, and by 2004 the poverty rate had declined to 22 per cent.

4.2.1 Poverty in urban areas

Even though economic growth has reduced absolute poverty in several countries, the Asia-Pacific region has experienced a geographic shift in the location of poor populations: *poverty has been urbanizing*. What is remarkable is that the absolute numbers of poor people in rural areas have declined across the world, whereas the absolute numbers of poor urban dwellers have increased (see Table 4.1). Overall, poverty has declined much more slowly in urban than in rural areas. In many Asian countries, though, the rural-to-urban poverty gap remains narrow. From a more general point of view, some authors have found that 25 per cent of the world's poor live in urban areas and this proportion has kept rising over time. More specifically, the growth in urban populations has helped reduce absolute poverty overall, as it went hand in hand with economic growth, but this did little for urban poverty. Over the 1993-2002 period, the number of people on 'one dollar a day' or less fell by 150 million in rural areas but rose by 50 million in cities.[2] "The poor have been urbanizing even more rapidly than the population as a whole" (Ravallion *et al.*, 2007:1).

Why is *urban* poverty in Asian countries so significant and on the increase, despite relatively sustained economic growth? Part of the reason can be found in the pattern of development in Asian cities. Urban development has largely been driven by concentrations of local, national and, increasingly, foreign profit-seeking enterprises. This process effectively excluded the poor, as the channels through which they might have benefited from this wealth creation were simply lacking in Asian cities. In other words, there was no automatic process

CHART 4.2: **POVERTY IN ASIA**

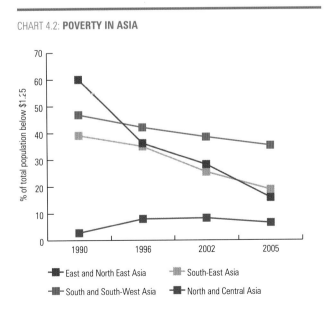

Source: Based on data from ESCAP (2008b)

CHART 4.3: **POPULATION LIVING ON LESS THAN US $1.25 A DAY IN ASIA AND THE PACIFIC**

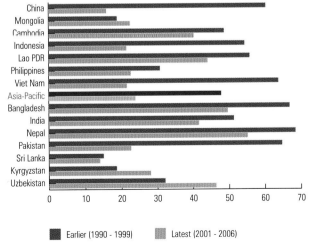

Source: Based on data from ESCAP (2008b)

▲
Karachi, Pakistan. Newly-erected shacks under the Liyairi Expressway. ©**Asianet-Pakistan/Shutterstock**

TABLE 4.1: **URBAN AND RURAL POVERTY RATES - AT/UNDER US "$ 1 A DAY"* (1993 PPP)**

	Number of Poor (Million)			Headcount Index*(%)			Urban Share of the Poor	Urban Share of Population
	Urban	Rural	Total	Urban	Rural	Total	(%)	(%)
1993								
East Asia-Pacific	28.71	407.17	435.88	5.55	35.47	26.17	6.59	31.09
China	10.98	331.38	342.36	3.33	39.05	29.05	3.21	29.77
South Asia	107.48	383.30	490.78	35.30	43.55	41.43	21.90	25.70
India	94.28	324.55	418.83	40.06	48.88	46.57	22.51	26.17
Total World	235.58	1 036.41	1 271.99	13.50	36.58	27.78	18.52	38.12
2002								
East Asia-Pacific	16.27	223.23	239.50	2.28	19.83	13.03	6.79	38.79
China	4.00	175.01	179.01	0.80	22.44	13.98	2.24	37.68
South Asia	125.40	394.34	519.74	32.21	39.05	37.15	24.13	27.83
India	106.64	316.42	423.06	36.20	41.96	40.34	25.21	28.09
Total World	282.52	882.77	1 165.29	12.78	29.32	22.31	24.24	42.34

* Refers to the proportion of the population with consumption per head below the poverty line.
Source: Ravallion et al. (2007)

whereby wealth concentrations (under the form of fresh capital expenditure or high-income residents in cities) contributed toward the costs of any infrastructure or services that might have been needed (Satterthwaite, 2004, 2005). As suggested by UN-HABITAT (2010), wealth creation hardly ever has an automatic 'trickle down' effect on the poorer segments of urban populations.

The baselines used to set poverty lines in cities are theoretically different from those for rural areas, although in practice the measurements of poverty are the same. For example, in urban areas the income required for essential goods for a family of four is relatively higher than that for a similar rural household. The added deprivation in urban areas is due not just to inadequate income but also to other factors such as poor housing conditions and lack of access to services. The urban poor also face challenges due to their extra-legal status, which makes them vulnerable to unlawful intrusions and natural hazards as well. Satterthwaite (2002) has listed eight aspects of urban poverty which suggest a range of possible policy responses. These include inadequacies in (i) shelter, (ii) provision of public infrastructure, (iii) income, (iv) asset base, (v) provision of social services and (vi) protection of rights through law enforcement, together with (vii) lack of a safety net to ensure access to shelter and (viii) powerless political systems. Since poverty lines are only rarely adjusted in order more accurately to reflect variations in the costs of non-food essentials within nations (such as the real costs of housing, transportation and services), the scale and depth of poverty is understated in places where these costs are particularly high (mainly cities). In the absence of adequate data, questionable assumptions and 'rules of thumb' are often used to set poverty lines which usually under-estimate the scale of urban poverty (Satterthwaite, 2004).

As a consequence of the phenomenal economic growth of Asian countries, much of which is attributable to cities, the urban population in the region is growing, but so is urban poverty. People move to cities (urbanization) but remain poor (the urbanization of poverty). This comes as a denial of the 'urban advantage', i.e., the blanket assumption that cities have more to offer (in terms of opportunities, etc.) than rural areas. In many Asian countries, given the predominant rural population, national policymakers have often considered poverty as a rural, not an urban problem. The rural poor, especially landless labourers, are extremely vulnerable not only to the seasonal nature of agriculture but also to the lack of diversified employment opportunities and access to infrastructure and services. Declining rural poverty suggests that Asian government efforts to address rural poverty issues have had some effect. However, declines in urban poverty have been less significant, except in China, Indonesia and Viet Nam (see Table 4.2) (ESCAP, 2007a; UN-HABITAT, 2010).

Estimates based on national poverty lines suggest that the proportion of urban poor in East and North-East Asia is very low (see Table 4.1). Ravallion & Chen (2004) estimated that in the 20-year period after 1981, the proportion of the Chinese population living below the international poverty line fell from 53 per cent to 8 per cent. By 2004, only 2 per

BOX 4.1: **NATIONAL POVERTY LINES – URBAN AND RURAL**

Most national poverty benchmarks are based on a "minimum acceptable standard of living" in a given country. The definition of this minimum standard" differs widely across nations. In developing countries, the focus is on survival and, as a result, poverty lines are often based on those food items required to achieve a minimum caloric daily intake. On the other hand, richer countries set higher benchmarks that include a range of non-food items. For example, in China and India, the national poverty line is around US $0.60 at PPP prices, compared with over US $2.50 in Malaysia and Thailand. Several countries do not calculate separate poverty lines for urban and rural areas.

CHART 4.4: **NATIONAL POVERTY LINES IN ASIA-PACIFIC: RICHER COUNTRIES TEND TO HAVE HIGHER POVERTY LINES**

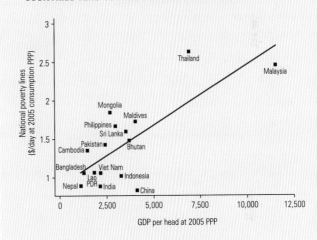

GDP = Gross Domestic Product, PPP = Purchasing Power Parity
Lao PDR = Lao People's Democratic Republic

Source: Bauer et al. (2008)

cent of the country's population were living on or below China's own national poverty line (see Table 4.2). However, it has been suggested that urban poverty in China has been underestimated because of unrealistically low poverty lines. Moreover, some 100 million temporary migrants live and work in urban areas but are classified as rural. Even if their incomes are above the poverty line, these people are deprived of access to education, housing, health care and employment (GHK & IIED, 2004) (see Box 4.1).

South-East Asia as a whole has managed to reduce absolute poverty (see Chart 4.2); however, severe rural poverty remains an unmet challenge. In Cambodia, Viet Nam and the Philippines, more than 30 per cent of the rural population live in poverty.

In South and South-West Asia, Pakistan has achieved substantial reductions in absolute poverty. The past few years' sustained economic growth created employment opportunities which helped to reduce poverty. Increased remittances from expatriates have resulted in higher consumption and greater employment opportunities, too, on the back of stronger capital expenditure in the construction industry and by small and medium enterprises or other businesses. Further poverty reduction seems to have been derived from significantly increased public sector spending on pro-poor sectors, especially education, health and infrastructure (rural electrification, roads and improved irrigation). For all these improvements and efforts, though, rural poverty rates in Pakistan are now almost double those in urban areas (see Table 4.2). This is because skewed access to assets (land) and power challenges the capacity of the rural poor to emerge from their state of economic deprivation, as does an inability to mitigate income fluctuations (Asian Development Bank, 2008b).

In India, the proportion of the population living on or below the national poverty line fell from 36 to 28 per cent between 1994 and 2005 (see Table 4.2). Given the country's large population, this means that many millions have escaped poverty. In 2004, the urban poverty rate was 26 per cent, compared with 28 per cent for the rural population. However, according to the Expert Group of the Planning Commission (Government of India, 2007), in absolute terms the number of economically poor urban dwellers did increase, while the number of rural poor decreased. Urban growth in India does seem to reduce economic deprivation, though, as poverty is found to be negatively correlated with the level of urbanization. This is because the shift away from the primary to the secondary and tertiary sectors has delivered significant gains to India's poor. Poverty also varies inversely with the size of the settlements – the incidence of poverty is lower in large than in smaller cities and towns (Hashim, 2009; Rustagi *et al.*, 2009; ESCAP, 2008b).

TABLE 4.2: **SHARE OF POPULATION ON OR UNDER NATIONAL POVERTY LINES, RURAL AND URBAN AREAS**

Country	Earlier				Latest			
	Survey Year	Rural (%)	Urban (%)	National (%)	Survey Year	Rural (%)	Urban (%)	National (%)
East and North-East Asia								
China	1998	..	..	4.6	2004	..	..	2.0
Mongolia	1998	32.6	39.4	35.6	2002	43.4	30.3	36.1
South-East Asia								
Cambodia	1994	..	..	47.0	2004	38.0	18.0	35.0
Indonesia	1996	19.8	13.6	17.6	2005	..	..	16.0
Lao PDR	1997-1998	41.0	26.9	38.6	2002-2003	..	..	33.0
Philippines	1994	45.4	18.6	32.1	1997	36.9	11.9	25.1
Viet Nam	1998	45.5	9.2	37.4	2002	35.6	6.6	28.0
South and South-West Asia								
Afghanistan	..	..	..	..	2007	45.0	27.0	42.0
Bangladesh	1995-1996	55.2	29.4	51.0	2000	53.0	36.6	49.8
India	1993-1994	37.3	32.4	36.0	2004-2005	28.3	25.7	27.5
Nepal	1995-1996	43.3	21.6	41.8	2003-2004	34.6	9.6	30.9
Pakistan	1993	33.4	17.2	28.6	2004-2005	28.1	14.9	23.9
Sri Lanka	1995–1996	27.0	15.0	25.0	2002	7.9	24.7	22.7
Turkey	1994	..	..	28.3	2002	34.5	22.0	27.0
North and Central Asia								
Armenia	1998-1999	50.8	58.3	55.1	2001	48.7	51.9	50.9
Azerbaijan	1995	..	..	68.1	2001	42.0	55.0	49.6
Georgia	2002	55.4	48.5	52.1	2003	52.7	56.2	54.5
Kyrgyzstan	2003	57.5	35.7	49.9	2005	50.8	29.8	43.1
Uzbekistan	2000–2001	33.6	27.8	31.5	2003	29.8	22.6	27.2

Sources: World Bank (2008); Rustagi et al. (2009); Pakistan Ministry of Finance (2006)

Yangon, Myanmar. ©**Piers Benatar/Panos Pictures**

4.3
Inequality

▲
Hong Kong, China. Asia's growth has had some impact on poverty reduction, but the benefits are not shared equitably. ©**Mark Henley/Panos Pictures**

While Asia's economic expansion is celebrated as an example of successful globalization, it has not been equally distributed among the populations. As mentioned above, Asia's growth has had some impact on poverty reduction, but the benefits are not shared equitably. Inequality is an important factor, since increases in inequality dampen the poverty-reducing effect of any given amount of economic growth.

Poverty is related to inequality and economic growth in different ways. The pace of poverty reduction depends on the rate of average income growth, the initial degree of inequality and subsequent changes in that degree. In particular, poverty reduction is fastest in countries where income growth is combined with falling inequality (UN-HABITAT, 2010). While overall income poverty in Asia may be falling, evidence suggests that economic growth may have exacerbated inequalities.

The distribution of income has implications for poverty reduction and, beyond that, for macro-economic outcomes. For a given growth rate in income per head, rising inequality typically means less poverty reduction. If the increase in inequality is large relative to growth, poverty could even rise. An Asian Development Bank (ADB) report shows that poverty reduction in Asian countries would have been more significant if inequalities had been less pronounced (Asian Development Bank, 2007a).

CHART 4.5: **INCOME/CONSUMPTION INEQUALITY - AVERAGE URBAN GINI COEFFICIENTS BY REGION (SELECTED COUNTRIES)**

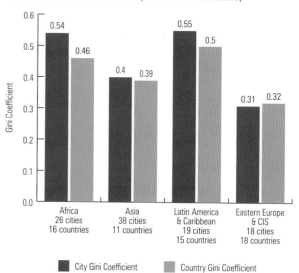

Africa
26 cities
16 countries

Asia
38 cities
11 countries

Latin America
& Caribbean
19 cities
15 countries

Eastern Europe
& CIS
18 cities
18 countries

■ City Gini Coefficient   ■ Country Gini Coefficient

Source: UN-HABITAT (2008a:63), UN-HABITAT, Global Urban Observatory, 2008.
Data from UN-ECLAC, UN-ESCAP, UNU and other sources, using various data years.
Notes: Gini data is a mix of income and consumption. Africa: income: 15 cities and 8 countries; consumption: 11 cities and 8 countries; Asia: income: 36 cities and 6 countries; consumption: 2 cities and 5 countries; LAC: income; Eastern Europe and CIS: income.

Inequality is often perceived as an intermediate outcome of the economic development process. Under the so-called 'Kuznets hypothesis', inequality rises in the early phase of development, peaks in the middle phase and then declines as the process matures, like an inverted U-shaped curve. It is often argued that income disparities are a necessary condition for capital accumulation and economic growth. The World Bank's 2009 *World Development Report* also suggests that as economies grow, production becomes more concentrated and imbalances occur. These shortcomings are considered to be inherent to the development process, and are expected to decline as countries and cities develop further.

The relationship between inequality and economic growth seems to work as follows: the higher the degree of inequality, the smaller the reduction growth can make in poverty, and higher degrees of inequality cause growth to slow down. Cornia & Court (2001) call this the "efficient inequality range" in which Noda (2009) assumes Asian countries currently find themselves.

Still, Asian cities exhibit lower degrees of inequality by comparison with the rest of the world, especially Latin America and Africa; this is corroborated by the fact that Asian countries as a whole have recorded lower degrees of inequality in comparison with these two regions (see Chart 4.5). However, high degrees of inequality have been observed in Asia when it comes to health and education, which are essential for well-being; the same applies with access to infrastructure and asset ownership (Asian Development Bank, 2007a).

Income inequality is conventionally measured through Gini coefficients and the attendant Gini index (i.e., the Gini index multiplied by 100). Gini coefficients are now available for a large number of countries, though less frequently for individual cities (UN-HABITAT, 2010). The coefficient

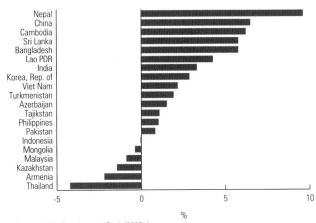

CHART 4.6: **CHANGES IN GINI COEFFICIENT FOR EXPENDITURE/INCOME DISTRIBUTIONS, 1990S–2000S (PERCENTAGE POINTS)**

Source: Asian Development Bank (2007a)

measures the distribution of either household income or consumption expenditure as a ratio of 0 to 1, where 0 indicates perfect equality (a proportional distribution of income/consumption), and 1 indicates perfect inequality (where one individual holds all of the income and no one else has any). In between, the coefficients denote the following degrees of inequality: below 0.299: low inequality; 0.3 to 0.399: relatively low; 0.4 to 0.449: relatively high; 0.45 to 0.499: high; 0.5 to 0.599: very high; and 0.6 and upwards: extremely high inequality. It must be kept in mind that inequality as measured by Gini coefficients is only relative: there can be very low inequality in the poorer (e.g., some sub-Saharan countries) as well as in the richer countries (e.g., Northern Europe), largely depending on the availability, or otherwise, of income redistribution systems (UN-HABITAT, 2010).

CHART 4.7: **NATIONAL GINI COEFFICIENTS, SELECTED ASIAN-PACIFIC COUNTRIES, VARIOUS YEARS (200–2004)**

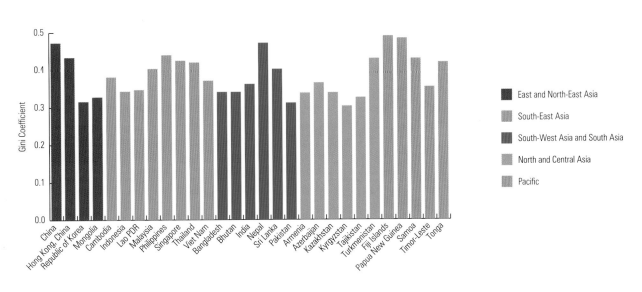

Source: Asian Development Bank (2007a)

Country	Gini Coefficient (Year)	HDI (2004)
East and North-East Asia		
China	0.473 (2004)	0.768
Hong Kong, China	0.434 (1996)	0.927
Republic of Korea	0.316 (2004)	0.912
Mongolia	0.328 (2002)	0.691
South-East Asia		
Cambodia	0.381 (2004)	0.583
Indonesia	0.343 (2002)	0.711
Lao PDR	0.347 (2002)	0.553
Malaysia	0.403 (2004)	0.805
Philippines	0.440 (2003)	0.763
Singapore	0.425 (1998)	0.916
Thailand	0.420 (2002)	0.784
Viet Nam	0.371 (2004)	0.709
South-West and South Asia		
Bangladesh	0.341 (2005)	0.530
Bhutan	0.341 (2000)	0.538
India	0.362 (2004)	0.611
Nepal	0.472 (2004)	0.527
Sri Lanka	0.402 (2002)	0.755
Pakistan	0.312 (2004)	0.539
North and Central Asia		
Armenia	0.338 (2003)	0.768
Azerbaijan	0.365 (2001)	0.736
Kazakhstan	0.339 (2003)	0.774
Kyrgyzstan	0.303 (2003)	0.705
Tajikistan	0.326 (2003)	0.652
Turkmenistan	0.430 (2003)	0.724
Pacific		
Fiji Islands	0.490 (1990)	0.758
Papua New Guinea	0.484 (1996)	0.523
Samoa	0.430 (2002)	0.778
Timor-Leste	0.354 (2001)	0.512
Tonga	0.420 (2001)	0.815

Source: Asian Development Bank (2007a)

4.3.1 Inequality at the national level

Research by the Asian Development Bank found that as measured by Gini coefficients over almost 10 years from the 1990s, inequality had increased in many Asian countries (see Chart 4.6).

Chart 4.7 shows that economic inequality is more severe in China than anywhere else in East and North-East Asia. In South and South-West Asia, Pakistan features a lower degree of inequality than Nepal.

Table 4.3 compares national Gini coefficients with the Human Development Index (HDI). The HDI is a more comprehensive measure of poverty than income alone (UN-HABITAT, 2010). The table demonstrates that some of Asia's wealthier countries also feature high degrees of inequality. For example, Singapore combines a high HDI (0.916) with a Gini coefficient similar to Thailand's, a country with a much lower HDI; in other words, Singapore features a high degree of inequality with much less overall poverty. This suggests that the link between inequality and poverty reduction can become looser in the later stages of a country's development, depending largely on the extent of redistribution (in contrast to Singapore, Northern Europe's highly redistributive socio-economic systems combine an absence of poverty with a very limited degree of inequality). In the earlier stages of development and possibly even as a country's integration into the global economy is in progress, inequality can be so entrenched as to challenge poverty reduction; however, in the later stages of development, and as can be expected, inequality is measured from a higher baseline which is no longer linked to absolute poverty (Asian Development Bank, 2008c).

In the Pacific Island countries (and particularly Papua New Guinea), both poverty and inequality are much more pronounced than in East and South Asia. The reason is that those countries have not been able to sustain economic growth and are highly dependent on subsistence agriculture (Yari, 2004).

4.3.2 Urban inequality

Chart 4.5 shows that on the whole, the Asia-Pacific region features lower urban inequality than Latin America and Africa, as noted above. In Asia's three largest countries, inequality has increased in both rural and urban areas (see Table 4.4). In India, the poverty gap ratio[3] (i.e., the mean distance separating the population from the poverty line) has not reduced significantly, but urban inequality has increased (as measured by the Gini index). In Indonesia, a significant decline in the poverty gap ratio has gone hand in hand with a marginal increase in inequality in both urban and rural areas. In China's urban areas, the poverty gap ratio appears to have been eliminated, but inequality has risen – i.e., people have become more unequal than poor, suggesting that economic expansion benefits the better-off more than other segments of society. As a result, and unlike India and Indonesia, in China the degrees of inequality are now broadly similar in urban and rural areas.

In Viet Nam, estimates are that as much as 96 per cent of the rise in inequality across the country has occurred *between* rural and urban areas, with the remaining 4 per cent due to an increase *within* rural or urban areas. In fact, during 1993-1998, it was estimated that inequality within rural areas had decreased slightly, while it had increased in urban areas (Huong, 2004).

Still, data shows that income inequalities in Asian cities stand relatively low compared with those in other developing regions except Eastern Europe and the Commonwealth of Independent States (CIS) (see Chart 4.5). However, "the

Country		Poverty Gap Ratio		Gini Index	
		Rural	Urban	Rural	Urban
China	1990	27	5	31	26
	2005	6	0	36	35
India	1993	14	11	29	34
	2004	11	10	30	38
Indonesia	1990	16	15	26	35
	2005	5	4	30	40

Source: ESCAP (2010:123)

economic urban divide is widening", warns UN-HABITAT (2010:69). Moreover, significant discrepancies in income distribution across cities, even within the same country, demonstrate that national aggregates are not necessarily reflected at the local level. Beijing can boast the lowest Gini coefficient in the world (not just China or Asia) while Hong Kong, China, and Ho Chi Minh City feature some of the highest in the region (see Chart 4.8). In Chinese cities, inequalities have been increasing since the 1980s, coinciding with the early stage of urban economic reforms. On the other hand, inequalities have been reduced in Sri Lanka after having reached extremes in the 1990s (UN-HABITAT, 2008a).

Recent evidence confirms that in those cities plagued with high inequality and poverty, and as intuition would suggest, economic growth does not benefit all segments of society and actually *increases* poverty. Moreover, particularly high degrees of inequality may hinder future growth and development prospects. Several hypotheses have sought to explain the relationship between inequality, poverty and economic growth. One suggestion is that credit market imperfections determine the way these elements interact: where there are no such imperfections, redistributing capital from capital-rich enterprises or individuals to capital-poor enterprises and credit-constrained individuals increases economic efficiency, investment and growth. The second hypothesis claims that too much inequality in a redistributive democracy leads to more redistribution and less capital accumulation. Alternatively, too much inequality may lead to social tension as expressed through collectively organized or individually-led violent 'redistribution' (Bourguignon, 2004).

Since there is no automatic link between economic growth and reductions in equality, rising inequality in Asia can also be attributed to policies. The fact is that in Asia, policies have focused largely on growth, with major initiatives directed towards liberalization, macro-economic stability, promotion of private investment, infrastructure and skill development. At the same time, there has been a conspicuous lack of serious attention to the reduction of inequality at the city level.

CHART 4.8: **INTRA-URBAN INEQUALITIES (GINI COEFFICIENTS)**

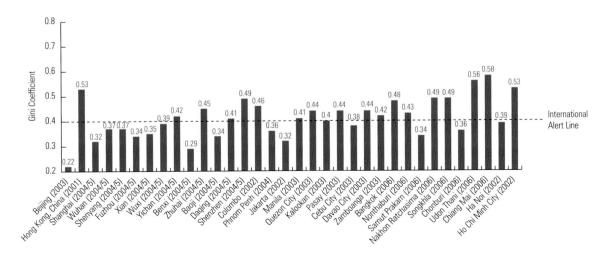

Source: UN-HABITAT (2008a:75)

4.4
Access to land and housing

▲
Jakarta, Indonesia. 505.5 million slum-dwellers still live in Asia. ©**Mark Henley/Panos Pictures**

Poor access to land and housing stands out as a major aspect of urban poverty. The high incidence of poverty in the Asia-Pacific region poses a daunting challenge to those urban planners attempting to deliver proper housing to millions of urban poor. The Asian Development Bank advocates the use of the 'US $2.00 a day' benchmark to include housing-related expenditures in the poverty line.[4] With 1.8 billion people (or 54 per cent of Asia's population in 2005) living below US $2.00 a day, the range of affordable housing the market makes available to them is limited.

4.4.1   Housing and the poor in Asian cities

As defined by the UN Human Rights Council (2007), "*the human right to adequate housing is the right of every woman, man, youth and child to gain and sustain a safe and secure home and community in which to live in peace and dignity.*" The right to adequate housing has seven components, one of them being secure tenure which, again is linked to the right to land.

Housing conditions have a direct bearing on any individual's ability to enjoy the benefits of urban life. This is particularly true for slum-dwellers, whose predicament denies them

those benefits, since shelter deprivation (i.e. living in slums) leads to many incapacities (on top of lack of basic infrastructures): lack of representation, lack of economic freedom, lack of security, lack of transparency, and lack of social opportunities (Sen, 1999; UN-HABITAT, 2010).

Although urban slum residents contribute significantly to the local economy, they are not mainstreamed into the urban socioeconomic environment. The slums in Asian cities reflect a more deep-seated phenomenon of structural poverty: they come as an emanation of social, political and institutional disparities and deprivations that are exacerbated by the pressures of sustained urban growth. Slums effectively segregate urban areas into the "rich" and the "poor" city – the 'urban divide' resulting from economic, social, political and cultural exclusion (UN-HABITAT, 2010). Instead of reaping the benefits of the 'urban advantage' as they expected, slum-dwellers pay an urban *penalty* through denial of legal status in the city and deprivation of a range of urban services. They constantly experience the risk of eviction, lack voice and are insufficiently protected. Most slum-dwellers are excluded from the main attributes of urban life – political voice, decent housing, safety and the rule of law, education and health – which remain a

BOX 4.2: FROM AN EXCLUSIVE TO AN INCLUSIVE CITY

New terms, such as "world class cities", "investment-friendly infrastructure" or "foreign direct investment" (FDI) have entered the development vocabulary. As more politicians and official planners in Asian cities use these terms, the whole approach to planning has undergone a change. Apart from 'beautification', local authorities nowadays are keen to make cities look more "global" for the sake of visitors and investors. This entails (i) building flyovers and elevated expressways, as opposed to much-needed traffic management and planning; (ii) building high-rise apartments as opposed to upgrading informal settlements; (iii) building shopping malls as opposed to traditional markets (which are gradually eliminated); (iv) removing the poor from city centres to the periphery in order to improve the city's image and attract foreign direct investment, instead of eradicating poverty; and (v) catering to tourism rather than supporting local commerce.

The nature of the investments currently being made in many Asian cities, and the mindset behind them, are exacerbating the existing urban divide in five major ways: (i) stimulating land hoarding; (ii) eviction of hawkers and informal businesses; (iii) pushing informal settlements far away from the city centre and, therefore, from social facilities; (iv) excluding (through gentrification) the poorer communities from public spaces as well as recreation and entertainment areas; and (v) the resulting piecemeal encroachments of cities onto ecologically sensitive or productive agricultural land. Turning their backs on the 1980s, the master and/or strategic plans currently deployed in too many Asian cities do not give priority to the socio-economic issues arising out of these five trends.

The rich-poor urban divide can only widen as a result of these policies which have also amplified external shocks for the poor: structural adjustment has curtailed social sector subsidisation against a background of rising inflation and higher utility charges. If the present trend continues, then the rich-poor divide, evictions, informal settlements and exclusion will increase, with the poor living in slums surrounded by rich "ghettoes" behind armed guards and security systems. As a result,

governance issues will increasingly have to do with law and order rather than justice or equity. This can only make fragmentation worse. The only thing that will hold a city together is an aggressively upwardly mobile middle class.

An inclusive and environmentally-friendly urban environment can be deployed if some principles are adhered to: (i) planning should preserve the ecology of the areas where urban centres are located; (ii) land use should be determined on the basis of social and environmental considerations, rather than effective or potential land values; (iii) planning should give priority to the needs of the majority of the population, which in the case of Asia is none other than low- and lower-middle income communities, including street vendors, informal businesses, pedestrians and commuters; and (iv) planning must preserve and promote the tangible and intangible cultural heritage of the communities that live in the city. Zoning bylaws should be developed on the basis of these principles in order to make them pedestrian- and street-friendly on top of favouring mixed (i.e., residential and commercial) land use.

Source: Adapted from Hasan (2007)

---

monopoly of a privileged minority. As a result, their quality of life is often worse than that of the rural poor.

In Asia as in other parts of the world, slums are the cruellest form the 'urban divide' can take. They are the most glaring physical manifestation of the inconsistency between the demand for labour in Asia's urban areas and inadequate supply of the affordable housing and infrastructure the workforce needs for the safe, decent living conditions they are entitled to expect.

Slum housing is typically provided by the informal housing market. Transactions in this segment of the informal economy border legality and make slum-dwellers more vulnerable. For lack of any alternative, the poor end up in those settlements where the constant threat of eviction enables housing providers and municipal authorities alike to exploit and marginalize them further. Their informal status maintains them in "the locus of deprivation" for a long time. City beautification or clean-up programmes all-too often result in forced eviction of the poor and subsequent demolition of ramshackle dwellings (UN-HABITAT, 2010; Kothari & Chaudhry, 2010). This is ignoring that instead of being a problem, slums can be a solution the poor have found for themselves (see Box 4.2).

4.4.2 Slums in Asia

In order to measure progress on the Millennium Development Goal related to slums, UN-HABITAT has adopted a functional definition of slums based on the household as the basic unit of analysis and five measurable shelter deprivation indicators:

"A slum household consists of one or a group of individuals living under the same roof in an urban area, lacking one or more of the following five amenities: (1) durable housing (a permanent structure providing protection from extreme climatic conditions); (2) sufficient living area (no more than three people sharing a room); (3) access to improved water (water that is sufficient, affordable and can be obtained without extreme effort); (4) access to improved sanitation facilities (a private toilet, or a public one shared with a reasonable number of people); and (5) secure tenure (*de facto* or *de jure* secure tenure status and protection against forced eviction). Since information on secure tenure is not available for most countries included in the UN-HABITAT database, however, only the first four indicators are used to define slum households, and then to estimate the proportion of the urban population living in slums" (UN-HABITAT, 2010:33).

FIGURE 4.1: **PERCENTAGE CHANGE IN SLUM PROPORTIONS IN SELECTED COUNTRIES IN ASIA BETWEEN 1990 AND 2010 (ESTIMATE)**

Slum proportions of selected countries in Asia (1990)

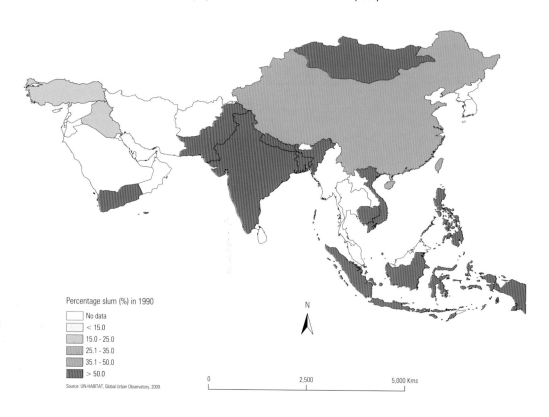

Percentage slum (%) in 1990

- No data
- < 15.0
- 15.0 - 25.0
- 25.1 - 35.0
- 35.1 - 50.0
- > 50.0

Source: UN-HABITAT, Global Urban Observatory, 2009.

N

0   2,500   5,000 Kms

Slum proportions of selected countries in Asia (2000)

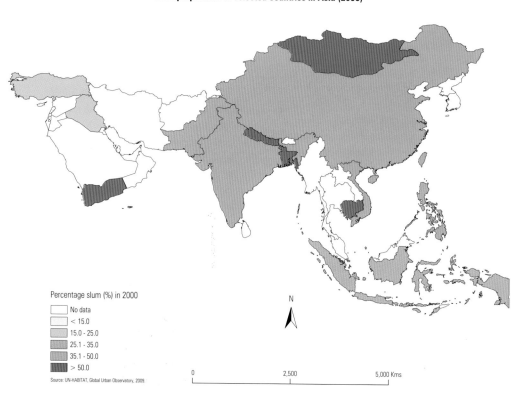

Percentage slum (%) in 2000

- No data
- < 15.0
- 15.0 - 25.0
- 25.1 - 35.0
- 35.1 - 50.0
- > 50.0

Source: UN-HABITAT, Global Urban Observatory, 2009.

N

0   2,500   5,000 Kms

Slum proportions of selected countries in Asia (2005)

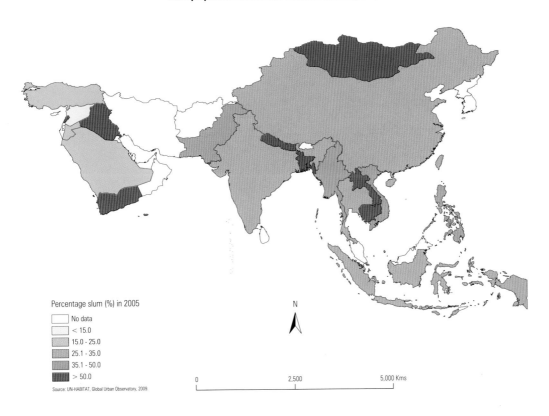

Percentage slum (%) in 2005

- No data
- < 15.0
- 15.0 - 25.0
- 25.1 - 35.0
- 35.1 - 50.0
- > 50.0

N

0   2,500   5,000 Kms

Source: UN-HABITAT, Global Urban Observatory, 2009.

Slum proportions of selected countries in Asia (2010)

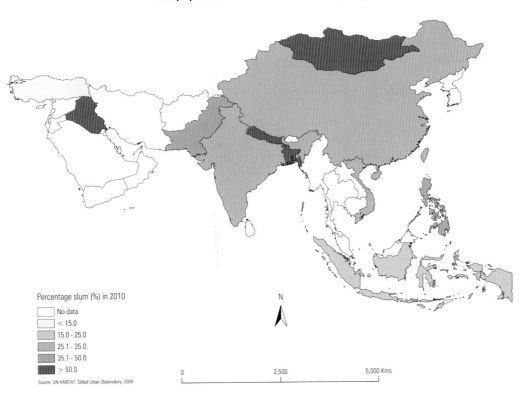

Percentage slum (%) in 2010

- No data
- < 15.0
- 15.0 - 25.0
- 25.1 - 35.0
- 35.1 - 50.0
- > 50.0

N

0   2,500   5,000 Kms

Source: UN-HABITAT, Global Urban Observatory, 2009.

A slum house in Kathmandu, Nepal. ©De Visu/Shutterstock

TABLE 4.5: **SLUM POPULATION IN ASIA AND THE PACIFIC SUBREGIONS, 2010 (PROJECTIONS)**

Region	Urban Population (1,000s)	Slum Population (1,000s)	Urban Population Living In Slums (%)
Eastern Asia	671 795	189 621	28.2
Southern Asia	545 766	190 748	35.0
South Eastern Asia	286 579	88 912	31.0
Western Asia	145 164	35 713	24.6
Oceania/Pacific	2 306	556	24.1
Asia-Pacific (Total)	**1 651 610**	**505 550**	**30.6**

Source: UN-HABITAT (2010:179)

These criteria are very different from those used by various countries in the region. This is the reason that UN-HABITAT slum data is at a significant variance from, and often much higher than, national estimates.

Slums in Asian cities are not homogeneous. The typical visual depiction of a slum house is that of a family staying in a one-room mud-and-tin shack without any water and sanitation facilities. Across the region, slums are known under a variety of names: *chawls, shanties, adugbo atiyo* and *katchi abadis*, for example. Gradations of slums are widespread, each with a different name attached. For instance, in India, a *chawl* (a densely packed block of one-room 'apartments' with shared toilets and bathrooms) is quite different from what in Pakistan is known as a *katchi abadi* (a shack made of non-durable materials, often located in a crowded settlement within or on the outskirts of a city).

UN-HABITAT statistics show that 505.5 million slum-dwellers, or over half of the world's slum population, live

CHART 4.9: **DISTRIBUTION OF URBAN POPULATION BY DEGREE OF SHELTER DEPRIVATION, 2005**

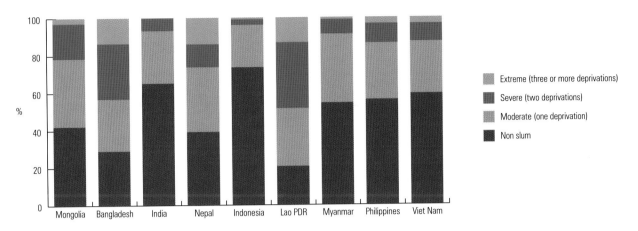

Legend:
- Extreme (three or more deprivations)
- Severe (two deprivations)
- Moderate (one deprivation)
- Non slum

Source: UN-HABITAT (2010:180)

in the Asia-Pacific region. The number is high in East Asia (mainly China) and South Asia (mainly India). Across the various subregions, the proportion of urban residents living in slums varies between 24 and 35 per cent (see Table 4.5).

Chart 4.9 shows that in many Asian countries, the high proportions of informal settlement dwellers in urban populations are due to any one or more of the five recognised deprivations that qualify those settlements as slums. It is, therefore, possible that in many inner city tenements, new low-income houses built by public entities have been counted by UN-HABITAT as slums based on the agency's definition of overcrowding, although these houses are not regarded as slums under national definitions.

In very few countries only (e.g. Bangladesh, Lao People's Democratic Republic and Nepal) slums feature three or more shelter deficiencies, i.e., belong in the 'extreme' deprivation

CHART 4.10: **DISTRIBUTION OF MODERATELY DEPRIVED SLUM-DWELLERS (ONE DEPRIVATION) BY TYPE OF DEPRIVATION, 2005**

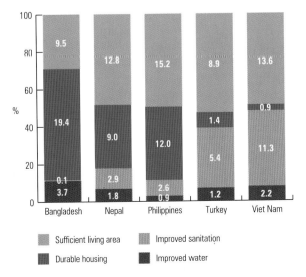

Legend:
- Sufficient living area
- Durable housing
- Improved sanitation
- Improved water

Source: UN-HABITAT (2008a:101)

category. With a majority of slums deficient in one of the five parameters, it is possible that a shift in one of the deprivations (e.g. tenure, water, sanitation), lifts the settlement out of the 'slum' category (UN-HABITAT, 2010). This phenomenon has probably had a role in some of the major shifts in the slum proportions in Asian countries between 1990 and 2005.

Estimates for a few Asian countries show that most slum-dwellers lack sufficient living areas. In Bangladesh and the Philippines, significant proportions of slum-dwellers lack durable housing (see Chart 4.10).

The estimates in Table 4.6 show that in many Asian countries, high proportions of the urban population live in slums. In four of these, slum prevalence was over two thirds: Bangladesh (71 per cent in 2007), Cambodia (79 per cent in 2005) and Lao PDR (79 per cent in 2005). In other countries such as Mongolia and Nepal, more than 50 per cent of urban dwellers live in slums[5] (see Figure 4.1).

Slum population estimates for a few Asian countries are available for 1990, 2000, 2001, 2005 and 2007[6] (see Table 4.6). Between 2001 and 2005, the only major definitional change has occurred in the measurement of sanitation access where pit latrines are now counted as another form of access. However, this change of definition has affected only those countries where pit latrines are widespread. In urban Asia, where settlements feature high densities, the population dependent on pit latrines is small, and therefore this change of definition is unlikely to have any major effect on slum estimates.

The Millennium slum target: Asia at the forefront

As highlighted by UN-HABITAT (2010:33), "Asia was at the forefront of successful efforts to reach the Millennium slum target between the year 2000 and 2010, with governments in the region improving the lives of an estimated 172 million slum-dwellers; these represent 75 per cent of the total number of urban residents in the world who no longer suffer from inadequate housing. The greatest advances in this region were recorded in Southern and Eastern Asia, where 145 million people moved out of the "slum-dweller" category (73 million

TABLE 4.6: **ASIA'S SLUM POPULATIONS: 1990-2007**

Country	Slum Population (1,000s)[a]					% Urban Living in Slums[a]				
	1990	**1995**	**2000**	**2005**	**2007**	**1990**	**1995**	**2000**	**2005**	**2007**
East and North-East Asia										
China	137 272	153 985	169 600	174 587	173 988	43.6	40.5	37.3	32.9	31.0
Republic of Korea	11 728[b]	-	14 385[c]	-	-	37.0[b]	-	37.0[c]	-	-
Mongolia	866	905	907	847	867	68.5	66.7	64.9	57.9	57.9
South-East Asia										
Brunei Darussalam	3[b]	-	5[c]	-	-	2.0[b]	-	2.0[c]	-	-
Cambodia	964	1 273	1 705	2 172	2 385	-	-	-	78.9	-
Indonesia	28 407	29 912	30 620	28 574	26 852	50.8	42.6	34.4	26.3	23.0
Lao PDR	422[b]	-	705[c]	1 230	-	66.0[b]	-	66.0[c]	79.3	-
Malaysia	177[b]	-	262[c]	-	-	2.0[b]	-	2.0[c]	-	-
Myanmar	3 105[b]	-	3 596[c]	6 703	-	31.1[b]	-	26.4[c]	45.6	-
Philippines	16 224	18 817	21 080	23 175	23 891	54.3	50.8	47.2	43.7	42.3
Timor-Leste	1[b]	-	7[c]	-	-	2.0[b]	-	12.0[c]	-	-
Thailand	-	-	-	5 291	-	-	-	-	26.0	-
Viet Nam	8 109	8 897	9 366	9 274	9 137	60.5	54.6	48.8	41.3	38.3
South, South-West and West Asia										
Afghanistan	2 458[b]	-	4 945[c]	4 629[d]	-	98.5[b]	-	98.5[c]	88.6[e]	-
Bangladesh	19 552	23 206	25 574	27 860	29 871	87.3	84.7	77.8	70.8	70.8
Bhutan	61[b]	-	70[c]	-	-	70.0[b]	-	44.1[c]	-	-
India	120 746	122 376	120 117	113 223	109 501	54.9	48.2	41.5	34.8	32.1
Iran (Islamic Republic of)	17 094[b]	-	20 406[c]	14 581[d]	-	51.9[b]	-	44.2[c]	30.5[e]	-
Nepal	1 194	1 589	2 099	2 591	2 798	70.6	67.3	64.0	60.7	59.4
Pakistan	17 620	20 271	23 304	26 189	27 508	51.0	49.8	48.7	47.5	47.0
Sri Lanka	899[b]	-	597[c]	345[d]	-	24.8[b]	-	13.6[c]	12.0[e]	-
Turkey	7 947	8 055	7 911	7 610	7 202	23.4	20.7	17.9	15.5	14.1

[a] Except for [b, c, d] and [e] (as below), computed from country household data based on the four slum criteria (water, sanitation, (durable) housing and (sufficient) living area)
[b] Data from UN-HABITAT (2006:189)
[c] Data for year 2001 from UN-HABITAT (2006:189)
[d] Data from UN-HABITAT (2008a:248)
[e] Computed using [d] above and United Nations (2010)

Source: UN-HABITAT (2010:178)[7]

and 72 million, respectively); this represented a 24 per cent decrease in the total urban population living in slums in the two subregions. Countries in South-Eastern Asia have also made significant progress with improved conditions for 33 million slum residents, or a 22 per cent decrease."

These achievements resulted from the determined, concerted efforts some Asian governments have made to improve living conditions for slum-dwellers (see Box 4.3). At city level, interventions for slum upgrading come two forms: (i) policy- and strategy-making – as in the cases of Dili, Timor-Leste and Ulaanbaatar, Mongolia (see Box 4.4) (UN-HABITAT, 2007b), and (ii) physical improvements – as in the case of Indonesia and the Philippines (see Box 4.9). However, Table 4.6 suggests a more nuanced picture which illustrates the cross-currents at play in slum demographics in Asia as in other developing regions.

Table 4.6 shows that in South and South-West Asia, the slum population declined (in absolute numbers) in only three or four countries between 1990 and 2007, with India and Turkey at the forefront. On the other hand, the numbers of slum-dwellers increased in Bangladesh and Pakistan over the same period, as they did in China. In South-East Asia, Indonesia is the only country where the slum population decreased (in absolute numbers) between 1990 and 2007.

The trend in *relative* numbers looks more encouraging, though. As shown in Table 4.6, the percentages of urban populations living in slums have declined in all Asian subregions and countries. Between 1990 and the year 2007, the declines ranged between 4.0 per cent (Pakistan) and 27.8 per cent (Indonesia). Two factors can account for this favourable trend in the relative numbers of slum-dwellers in Asia: (i) as shown in Chapter 2 (Table 2.1), the overall pace

BOX 4.3: HOW SOME ASIAN COUNTRIES BEAT THE MILLENNIUM SLUM TARGET

Over the past 10 years or so, one-third of developing countries have managed to reduce the absolute and relative numbers of slum-dwellers among their populations, according to current literature and UN-HABITAT research. In the process, they anticipated on the target set in the Millennium Declaration, improving the conditions of an estimated 227 million slum-dwellers (instead of the required 100 million) by 2010 (or 10 years earlier than the agreed deadline) (UN-HABITAT, 2010).

How did they do it? UN-HABITAT policy analysis shows that public authorities took the responsibility for slum reduction squarely on their shoulders, backing commitments with bold policy reforms, and preventing future slum growth with equitable planning and economic policies. More specifically, their success was based on five specific, complementary approaches: (i) awareness and advocacy, (ii) long-term political commitment, (iii) policy reforms and institutional strengthening, (iv)

proper implementation and monitoring, and (v) scaling up successful local projects.

As far as awareness and advocacy are concerned, Indonesia and Viet Nam have demonstrated the important role of proper monitoring systems and indicators to collect information and analyse trends. Advocacy also involves disseminating messages on improved conditions for slum-dwellers, as exemplified by some cities in India. The latter country also stands out, alongside China and Turkey for long-term political commitment to slum reduction.

India and Indonesia rank among those countries that have shown the way for policy reform and institutional strengthening. This involves a wide range of well-coordinated policies, including land, housing and infrastructures in order to integrate larger numbers of urban poor into cities' legal and social fabrics. Like Iran, the Philippines and Turkey, Indonesia has also looked beyond the housing sector and

fought slums as part of broader-ranging poverty reduction strategies, with policies shifting from entitlement to co-participation.

Transparent and pro-poor policies must be backed up by adequate human and technical resources, as demonstrated by Indonesia and the Republic of Korea. Most importantly, as happened in China, Viet Nam and Sri Lanka, slum policy implementation must involve close coordination between central, regional and municipal authorities and the private sector. Cambodia and Thailand set themselves clear targets and benchmarks, and Indonesia resorted to results-based monitoring.

Replication and scaling-up of successful, local one-off or pilot slum-upgrading projects have served a number of countries well, including Sri Lanka and Indonesia. Upscaling can involve the private sector and civil society, as in Turkey. In China, huge public subsidies have gone into housing projects for the poorest.

Source: UN-HABITAT, 2010

---

of urbanisation in Asia (measured as the share of urban in total populations) slowed down noticeably between the year 2000 and 2010 (2010 data are projections); and (ii) some countries (including China, India, Turkey and Viet Nam (UN-HABITAT, 2010) took the challenge of slums head-on and seem to have achieved tangible results as early as 2007 (see Box 4.3).

All in all, these divergent relative and absolute numbers leave the trend in Asia very much in line with slum demographics in the rest of the developing world. As UN-HABITAT (2010:30) summarised the global situation: "Proportions are declining but numbers are growing" – and all the more so as urbanisation in Asia is projected to re-accelerate between 2010 and 2030 (see Table 2.1 in Chapter 2). Practically, this means that for all the recent favourable numbers, there can be no let-up in Asia's efforts to tackle slums; if anything, success in a few countries demonstrates that determined, well-devised policies *do* achieve tangible results (see Box 4.5), and should be widely disseminated wherever relevant.

At this point, it must be stressed that if between the year 2000 and 2010 the lives of an estimated 172 million Asian slum-dwellers have improved (UN-HABITAT, 2010), they owe it to two other contributing factors. One is "the emergence of organizations formed by the urban poor that increase their influence on city-government and, where political circumstances permit, form powerful and effective partnerships with local governments to reduce the cost and increase the sup-

ply of housing and infrastructure and to make legal housing more affordable" (Satterthwaite, 2005:13). The other factor has been hinted at earlier; it has to do with UN-HABITAT's standard definition of slums, the practical import of which is that it can take an improvement on any one deprivation, e.g. access to water or access to sanitation, for a settlement to switch from 'slum' to 'non-slum', as is the case with many settlements around the world. And since, as noted earlier, UN-HABITAT's definition of slums is more stringent than those used by national governments, far from purely nominal this switchover reflects tangible realities. All it takes policymakers and urban planners to bring it about is to shift slums "from blind spot to spotlight" (UN-HABITAT, 2010:46).

Slums and poverty are closely related and mutually reinforcing, but the relationship is not always so straightforward. All slum-dwellers are not poor, and the non-poor live in slums only for lack of proper housing. As per the US $1.25-a-day poverty benchmark, over 200 million people in the Asia-Pacific region have escaped extreme poverty between 1990 and 2005. This implies that even though the proportion of slum-dwellers is declining, it is not doing so as fast as poverty itself, because the bulk of the housing stock in Asian cities remains unaffordable.

On the whole, living conditions are better in urban than in rural areas. This is attributed to the availability of better services and better health care facilities, both from the public and private sectors. However, figures do not reflect the day-

	Urban Poor NFHS* 2	Urban Poor	Urban Non-Poor	Overall Urban	Overall Rural	All India
Environmental Conditions	**2000**			**2005-2006**		
Households with access to piped water supply at home (%)	13.2	18.5	62.2	50.7	11.8	24.5
Households with access to public tap/hand pump for drinking water (%)	72.4	72.4	30.7	41.6	69.3	42.0
Household using a sanitary facility for the disposal of excreta (flush/pit toilet) (%)	40.5	47.2	95.9	83.2	26.0	44.7
Median number of household members per sleeping room	3.5	4.0	3.0	3.3	4.0	3.5
Infectious Diseases						
Prevalence of medically treated TB (per 100,000)	535	461	258	307	469	418
Prevalence of HIV among adult population (age 15-49) (%)	.	0.47	0.31	0.35	0.25	0.28

*National Family Health Survey
Source: Urban Health Resource Centre (2008)

to-day realities that face the urban poor. Where data on intra-urban differentials in health indicators is available, for instance, all it suggests is a worsening of health outcomes for the urban poor.

Available statistics for India (see Table 4.7), both national and intra-urban, show that the urban poor are worse off than average urban residents on many health-related indicators, including the prevalence of tuberculosis and AIDS, and access to health services. India's urban poor do seem to enjoy slightly better access to water and sanitation than their rural counterparts, but for both the urban and the rural poor access is much scarcer than the average for whole urban areas.

Similar research in Bangladesh has found that among the urban non-poor, who live in modern houses with all facilities, infant and child mortality is considerably lower than in rural areas, while the urban poor experience higher infant and under-five mortality rates than rural households. Poor and non-poor childhood mortality differentials are higher in urban than in rural areas. In poor urban areas, the child survival ratio is worse than average among (especially recent) migrants. The results in Bangladesh support the findings of many previous studies showing that in developing countries, housing conditions such as construction materials, access to safe drinking water and hygienic toilet facilities are the most critical determinants of child survival in urban areas (Islam and Azad, 2008).

The quality and location of shelter can make slum-dwellers vulnerable. Slum housing is often constructed of flimsy scrounged materials, such as plastic sheets, cardboard or scrap metal, or the cheapest construction materials. These structures are easily destroyed by storms, or floods since these are frequent in the locations (river banks, etc.) where many informal settlements are located. A survey of families in Manila's squatter settlements found houses made of scrap wood and makeshift materials, and consisting of one room occupied by more than one family. The majority of residents used the river or open pits to defecate. Riverbank dwellers in Manila face yearly flooding and some are flooded year-round.

Most houses surveyed were on government-owned land and earmarked for demolition (Fry *et al.*, 2002).

As for Viet Nam, the quality issues of housing in Hanoi have been described as follows by Satterthwaite (2005:16):

"In Hanoi, much of the poor quality housing is a legacy of housing stock built with government funds under central planning that was allotted to workers and public employees of plants, enterprises and government agencies. These housing blocks are generally still managed by the plant or agency that employs the residents and little attention has been given to maintenance and repair, in part because rents paid by households are low... Responsibility for the maintenance of these housing blocks is being shifted to municipal or district housing administration agencies but the process is incomplete. In addition, many households have not paid rent for years."

4.4.3 Land accessibility and affordability

In urban areas, land comes under pressure from demographic growth and economic development. Higher demand raises market prices and the process is further intensified by global economic integration. As Asian cities grow in size, population and prosperity, demand for land brings unforeseen pressures on an already scarce resource. The inaccessibility of decent, secure, affordable land is the major factor behind Asia's abundance of slums. It is also a contributing factor to urban poverty (ESCAP & UN-HABITAT, 2008a; Global Land Tool Network, 2008).

In many Asian cities, much larger numbers of people live without any form of secure tenure than with formal land titles. The poor are priced out of the land market and the opportunities for them to squat unused public land are declining. With rapid economic growth, many private landowners and government agencies continue to develop vacant urban land and evict slum-dwellers for commercial development or urban infrastructure projects. Evicting slum households

BOX 4.4: WHEN POLICYMAKING REACHES OUT TO INFORMAL SETTLEMENTS: THE CASE OF ULAANBAATAR

▲ Ger area in Ulaanbaatar, Mongolia. ©**Bharat Dahiya**

Massive rural migration lies behind the rapid demographic expansion of the Mongolian capital Ulaanbaatar in recent years. The migration was caused by a combination of three distinct factors: low incomes in the countryside, the *'dzuds'* (extremely cold winter disasters) of 1999-2001, and a Supreme Court decision in 2003 upholding "freedom of movement" within the country.

As a result, the capital's population had risen to 1.1 million* by the end of 2008, and since then the 2009-10 *dzud* has triggered further rural migration. The migrants have settled in the *ger*-areas outside the conventional built-up city which largely lie beyond the reach of infrastructure and services. As many as two thirds of Ulaanbaatar's population live in *'gers'*, i.e., traditional felt tents, and 45 per cent of them are poor. Some 10 per cent of the households in the capital are female-headed (average household size: 4.5 individuals). Being deprived of infrastructure and services, the ger areas present unique development challenges. Basic services in these low-density, unplanned settlements cost more than in formal built-up areas. Water is hand-carried from kiosks and residents use pit latrines and coal-and-wood-fired stoves for cooking and heating (a major source of air pollution); some have (informally) connected to nearby electric power lines. The areas are devoid of proper access lanes and solid waste collection is minimal.

For all these deficiencies, though, security of tenure and informal buildings are recognised, especially for those residents who register with the local authority and obtain individual land

privatisation certificates. Every household is allowed to own up to 700 sq m. of land, which are delineated with wooden fences *('khashaa')*. What the *ger* areas needed was recognition at the policymaking level in terms of planning, upgrading and development against a background of runaway, haphazard expansion.

This is why Cities Alliance and UN-HABITAT have been providing financial and technical support to the Municipality of Ulaanbaatar under the *Citywide Pro-poor Ger-area Upgrading Strategy and Investment Plan ('GUSIP')*. After a detailed assessment, including an inventory of community organisations, the Project has identified three types of ger areas which face different sets of urban development challenges (Dahiya & Shagdarsuren, 2007):

(i) *Central ger* areas have potentially easy access to water, roads and waste collection services. More modern buildings are slowly replacing traditional *gers*;

(ii) *Middle ger* areas where residents depend on kiosks and tankers for water. Access is difficult for lack of roads and drainage, and some areas are prone to flooding.

(iii) *Peri-urban ger* areas are characterized by haphazard, accelerated expansion and are farthest from basic urban services and infrastructure.

In all three types of *ger* areas, residents use pit latrines, posing a serious threat to Ulaanbaatar's water supply of which groundwater provides more than 90 per cent.

The three types of ger areas have by now been

formally recognised by the Municipality and the Ulaanbaatar Regional Council in their urban development programmes. The assessment was carried out through a structured, consultative process in which three *ger* area-specific working groups involved sector-specific agencies of the Municipality of Ulaanbaatar, the Ministry of Construction and Urban Development, the private sector, civil society organisations, *'duureg'* (district) and *'khoroo'* (sub-district) authorities, *ger*-area communities and the Mongolian Association of Urban Centres. In the next, strategy development stage, Cities Alliance and UN-HABITAT helped the Municipality of Ulaanbaatar to formulate development visions for each of the three types of *ger* areas.

The *Citywide Pro-poor Ger-area Upgrading Strategy* was developed through a four-step process, which included: (i) information inventory and sharing; (ii) information collection, review and analysis; (iii) setting the strategy's scope and framework, and (iv) consultative preparation. A citywide consultation was organised in June 2007; the strategy was approved by the Ulaanbaatar Citizens' Representative Council in July 2007 and its recommendations have been implemented through various development programmes and projects.

* Statistics Department of the Municipality of Ulaanbaatar. The figures include the registered population only, and therefore do not take in (recent) rural migrants who had not yet registered.

Source: Bharat Dahiya, UN-HABITAT

BOX 4.5: BRIDGING THE URBAN DIVIDE – UN-HABITAT'S RECOMMENDATIONS

To bridge the urban divide and make progress towards an inclusive city, UN-HABITAT recommends a rights-based approach that recognizes and simultaneously promotes the economic, social, political and cultural dimensions of inclusion. If they are to make those universally recognized rights more effective, cities must act as follows:

i) Assess the past and measure progress: a realistic, participatory assessment of a city's specific development path and shortcomings provides the sound basis required to map out the next four steps.

ii) Build more effective, stronger institutions: tackling the four dimensions of exclusion simultaneously is a complex endeavour requiring well-coordinated policies and adequate institutional frameworks to implement them. This new set-up can take the form of new institutions, or new channels between those already there.

iii) Establish new linkages and alliances between the three tiers of government – national, regional and municipal; this will secure proper resource mobilization, coordination and deployment, including public-private partnerships.

iv) Evolve a participatory, sustained vision to promote inclusiveness, starting with a general strategic plan, with broad-ranging consultation with, and subsequent dissemination among, all stakeholders and the population.

v) Ensure a more equitable distribution of opportunities. In this respect, UN-HABITAT recommends five 'levers of inclusiveness', as follows: (a) improve quality of life, especially for the urban poor; (b) invest in human capital formation; (c) foster sustained economic opportunities; (d) enhance political inclusion; and (e) promote cultural inclusion.

Source: UN-HABITAT (2010)

might be an effective way of clearing land for other uses, but almost all evictions result in increased poverty (ESCAP & UN-HABITAT, 2008a; UN-HABITAT, 2010).

Low-income households need to live close to income-earning opportunities in commercial and industrial centres in order to reduce the monies and time spent commuting to work. However, proper land in central locations is generally in high demand and therefore expensive. As a result, low-income households who need to be closer to the city centre are forced to occupy land which is not in demand because it is inappropriate or hazardous (such as land prone to flooding or landslides, or along railway lines, canal banks and roadsides, etc.) and is located on the periphery – which means that these plots are not serviced at all. Not only are these areas far from the city centre where the poor have their livelihoods, but their typical physical features are such that they force those who settle there to occupy as little space as possible, resulting in very high densities and unhealthy overcrowding (ESCAP & UN-HABITAT, 2008b).

For instance, in Beijing, it is common for low-income households to reside as many as two hours away from workplaces. Short of better land-use management that delivers more options for lower-income households, these will increasingly be pushed to those urban peripheries which middle and upper-income groups do not want for themselves, at least in the short term. However, as cities grow, those peripheral locations may become increasingly attractive to better-off residents or commercial developers, and once again, low-income informal settlements will be pushed away to the new outer bounds of the city periphery (Satterthwaite, 2005; UN-HABITAT, 2010).

In Phnom Penh, an absence of land use planning has combined with the sluggish performance of an unmitigated free-market economy to exacerbate the shortage of housing for the poor and the lower middle classes. As a result, squatter and low-income settlements have spread all over the Cambodian capital's seven districts. The country's housing policies and programmes during the 1960s, early 1970s and 1990s overlooked the expectations of the low-income segments of the population. As the land/property market expanded on the back of combined demand from domestic or foreign business, tourism and high-income housing, the poor have been driven further out to the periphery. All prime locations are purchased by the private sector and either developed or retained untouched for the sake of speculation. The bulk of these plots are government-owned, but are sold off under pressure from a powerful nexus of politicians, bureaucrats and local and foreign developers. This leaves low-income populations with little if any alternative central locations, especially given the pressure in favour of their eviction from increasingly sought-after plots (Satterthwaite, 2005; Crosby, 2004).

In many other Asian cities, a similar, powerful nexus of developers, politicians and bureaucrats is at work, too. Admittedly, these categories have everything to gain from land development, and they will oppose any land policy that might favour low-income groups. This is why those cities where much of the land is under public ownership do not make any difference with those where the private sector is predominant. In Karachi, for instance, this nexus acquires not only vacant land, but even land that has formally been set aside for recreational and amenity purposes. It can also happen that as they expand, slums come to encroach onto land that had been earmarked for infrastructure. In addition, government land and properties are often sold well below market values through political patronage for public-private partnership projects (Satterthwaite, 2005).

In Hanoi, elaborate and ineffective land-use controls have increased the costs of housing projects, as the procedures involved are very time-consuming. Private developers are admittedly encouraged by the government to provide for low-income groups in abidance with stipulated ratios or land regulations. However, the lower profits deriving from new low-income housing have discouraged many private developers from fulfilling their legal obligations (Lam, 2005).

On a more positive note, land proclamations in the Philippines have provided assurances to squatters of public land that they would not be evicted and that local social services would be improved. Between the year 2000 and 2002, more than 645,000 families in 33 informal settlements have benefited from these government exemptions. However, the policy does not apply to those squatting private land, who are the majority of informal settlers; still, this positive, pragmatic response has provided a modicum of secure tenure which, in turn, has encouraged many poor Filipino households to improve their homes and neighbourhoods (UN-HABITAT, 2004a).

Several Asian cities have tried out innovative methods to help the urban poor acquire serviced land within reasonable distance from income-earning opportunities. In Phnom Penh, urban poor organizations have been involved in city-wide surveys that have identified both the scale and location of low-income communities and any vacant land where they might be housed. In Karachi, thanks to detailed mapping of all informal settlements, the location and quality of existing infrastructures have been identified; the exercise highlighted the scale of community investments in infrastructure while providing the basis for improvements (including linking community-designed and implemented sewers and drains to city-provided trunks) (Satterthwaite, 2005).

4.4.4 Land tenure

Enhanced land rights serve as a basis for secure shelter and access to services. Land tenure can also act as a source of financial security, turning land into a transferable asset which can be sold, rented out, mortgaged, loaned or bequeathed. Tenure security creates incentives for land users to invest labour and other resources in the quality of dwellings or the value of land and property (Global Land Tool Network, 2008).

In most Asian cities, land tenure and property rights can be of a formal (freehold, leasehold, public or private rental), customary or religious nature; they can also include various types of unauthorised/informal tenure or settlement. Tenure entails varying degrees of legality, depending on the relevant legislative framework. Some tenure rights come with time limitations or with restrictions on land uses, sales, transfers or inheritance. Many governments preserve their rights of eminent domain, enabling them legally to take away an individual's or a community's right to stay in case the plot is needed for some public purpose. Moreover, in many cities more than one legal system is in force, with statutory, customary and religious tenure systems coexisting and overlapping (ESCAP & UN-HABITAT, 2008a; Global Land Tool Network, 2008).

For the poor, the best option will always be secure tenure on the site they are occupying. This enables them to stay in the same place without dislocation of, or disruption to, their livelihoods and social support systems. An alternative is to make tenure collective through long-term non-individual leases or granting land titles to community cooperatives. Collective tenure can work only where the community is well organized. Collective tenure rights can act as powerful buffers against market forces, binding communities together and giving them good reason to remain that way. A collective community structure can act as an important survival mechanism. Kathmandu's Kirtipur Housing Project shows how collective tenure has made it possible to turn a squatter settlement into a community housing project (see Box 4.6) (ESCAP & UN-HABITAT, 2008a).

Once the poor hold legal rights to the land they occupy, they can use those rights (i) to obtain access to public services, (ii) to secure bank loans, (iii) to start small home-based businesses, and (iv) to legitimize their status in the city. However, as soon as tenure in a slum is made more secure, through regularization, formalized user rights or land title issuance to residents, these formerly insecure and unattractive diminutive plots enter the urban land market virtually overnight and become marketable commodities. Real estate developers queue up to offer large sums of money to buy the poor out. This has been observed in Mumbai, where some resettled slum-dwellers have sold off their plots and gone back to slums (ESCAP & UN-HABITAT, 2008c).

4.4.5 Forced evictions

As defined by the Centre on Human Rights and Evictions (COHRE), security of tenure is the freedom from fear of forced eviction (COHRE, 2009). A 2007 report by UN-HABITAT's Advisory Group on Forced Evictions noted that millions live in constant fear of eviction, and that thousands are forcibly evicted in disregard of the law, leaving them homeless and subject to deeper poverty, discrimination and social exclusion (UN-HABITAT, 2007a).

Forced eviction is defined as the permanent or temporary removal, and against their will, of individuals, families and/ or communities from the homes and/or land they occupy, without the provision of, and access to, appropriate forms of legal or other protection. Such evictions can always be ascribed to specific decisions, legislation or government policies, or to government failure to halt forced evictions by third parties (UN-HABITAT, 2007a; ESCAP & UN-HABITAT, 2008c; UN-HABITAT, 2010). According to the UN-HABITAT dedicated Advisory Group, nearly half of all forced evictions in the world occur in Asia's four most populated countries (see Table 4.8).

The main reasons for evictions include increasing pressure on land due to rapid urbanization, large infrastructure or 'beautification' projects, as well as 'global mega events' (sport, exhibitions, major international conferences, etc.) which may not benefit the poor at all (UN-HABITAT, 2010; Kothari & Chaudhry, 2010). Eviction generates rather than alleviates poverty, and therefore is to be considered as counterproductive in terms of human development. Poor communities – the main targets for eviction in Asian cities – are also those least prepared to weather the consequences of eviction, which leaves them in an even poorer state than before (ESCAP & UN-HABITAT, 2008c).

Apart from development projects, construction of roads can also lead to relocation of poor urban residents. In China, for example, between 1988 and 1993, over 120,000 people were resettled against their will due to road projects financed

BOX 4.6: HOW TO REHABILITATE A SQUAT: NEPAL'S KIRTIPUR HOUSING PROJECT

▲
Row housing in Kirtipur. ©**Vishal Shrestha/Lumanti**

In Nepal's capital Kathmandu, the Vishnumati Link Road project involved the construction of a road running along the Vishnumati River, where a number of communities have been living in informal settlements for almost 50 years. Notices were posted warning residents in five affected communities to move, as their houses would be demolished to make way for the new road. After numerous meetings between the residents, a non-governmental organisation known as *Lumanti* ('memory', in the local Newari dialect), donors and the government, the road construction was postponed. The Kathmandu Metropolitan City Office formally agreed to provide secure housing for all affected families, as well as rental compensation until new housing was delivered.

In 2003, a municipal Urban Community Support Fund was created by the Kathmandu metropolitan authority, *Lumanti* and some donor organizations like the Asian Coalition for Housing Rights, Slum Dwellers International and Acton Aid Nepal. The Fund grants loans to groupings on affordable terms and the monies are on-lent to urban poor households, enabling them to improve socio-economic conditions, housing and physical facilities. The Fund's first project involved the resettlement to a new site in Kirtipur of the squatter families affected by the Vishnumati Link Road project. Under its 'Housing the Poor in Asian Cities' scheme, the UN Economic and Social Commission for Asia and the Pacific has helped *Lumanti* develop a low-cost, low-maintenance wastewater treatment system for the resettlement scheme together with the Asian Coalition for Housing Rights, Slum Dwellers International and Acton Aid Nepal. Similarly, the UN-HABITAT Water for Asian Cities Programme in Nepal had provided support for rainwater harvesting, and the Nepalese Department for Urban Development and Construction helped with paved open spaces.

The location for the new housing project was decided after lengthy discussions with the families regarding their needs and their visions for a new community. Affordability was a major factor, since the families must make monthly repayments to the Support Fund. The housing design was chosen by the community from several alternatives. Through the entire planning process, the low-income households demonstrated their capacity to develop viable solutions and to fight for housing rights and security of tenure; this involved organizing themselves, saving money, designing houses, developing management skills, and remaining firmly committed to building better lives for themselves and the community.

The Urban Community Support Fund made it possible for the evicted families to buy the new housing units with low-interest (five per cent) 15-year loans. On top of steering the project, the Kirtipur Housing Management Committee monitors repayments to the Support Fund. Since the housing project is a long-term venture, the Committee also makes sure that it continues to serve the community over time. Households are not allowed to sell off their houses without approval from the Committee, which makes sure that any new buyer also comes from a poor community, slum or squatter settlement. The collective nature of all aspects of the project – land tenure, house building, savings and management – generates a strong sense of community.

This project was Kathmandu's first as far as rehabilitation is concerned. Beyond providing alternative shelter to affected families, it also sets a precedent as an environment-friendly community. Another, important goal of this project is to eradicate the psychological stigma of being a squatter. Instead of just looking to relocate squatters as such, the project was designed as an opportunity for beneficiaries to become fully free, empowered citizens with the right to make major decisions regarding their lives, property and employment.

Source: www.lumanti.org/kirtipur-housing-project

TABLE 4.8: **REPORTED FORCED EVICTIONS IN MAJOR ASIAN COUNTRIES, 2001-2005 (NUMBERS OF VICTIMS)**

Year	Indonesia	China	Bangladesh	India	Total Reported Evictions - World
2001	49 205	341 754	63 750	450	498 883
2002	3 000	439 754	..	950	756 747
2003	5 184	686 779	..	150 850	993 121
2004	39 184	467 058	21 552	20 715	617 872
2005	4 425	187 064	9 355	363 795	2 090 772

Source: UN-HABITAT (2007a)

BOX 4.7: BEATING EVICTION IN A GLOBAL CITY: PEOPLE-MANAGED RESETTLEMENT IN MUMBAI

"It is hard to avoid some population displacement in any city where the government seeks to improve the provision of infrastructure and services for their populations and enterprises. In crowded central city areas, almost any improvement in provision for water, sanitation, drainage, roads, rail-ways, ports, airports and facilities for businesses needs land on which people currently have their homes. Within an increasingly competitive global economy, a successful city needs to attract new enterprises, and this also requires redevelopment and changes in land use." (Patel *et al.*, 2002:159). Between 1990 and the year 2000, Mumbai demonstrated that 60,000 people could be relocated without coercion to make way for a development project - in this instance, an improvement programme for the commuter rail system. The resettlement programme benefited from strong support from community organizations. The scheme was unusual on three counts: (i) contrary to what usually happens

with infrastructure development, those who moved were not further impoverished through resettlement; (ii) the actual move was voluntary and needed neither police nor municipal enforcers to execute; and (iii) the resettled people were involved in the design, planning and implementation of the resettlement programme as well as in the management of their new places of abode. The community has also been involved in the whole process, including the baseline survey of the households to be moved, the design of their new accommodation, and managing the relocation process, including the allocation of units.

The resettlement was facilitated by an alliance of the National Slum Dwellers Federation, a women's group called *Mahila Milan* ('women together') and the Society for the Promotion of Area Resources Centres (SPARC). The process was not easy. The alliance had to cope with an unexpected eviction when the railway company

pulled down 2,000 huts along the railway line. This was against the declared policy of the state government and the covenant of a World Bank loan to the Mumbai Urban Transport Project. The civil society alliance responded by mobilizing thousands of members who shut down the city's railway system – a move that eventually secured the emergency resettlement on which it had been insisting.

The major lessons from this experience of resettlement are the importance of community organization and the effectiveness of community engagement in the development of resettlement and relocation plans. Another important factor to keep in mind was the flexibility shown by key state and local government institutions and officials. A fourth factor was a clear policy on resettlement and rehabilitation. On the whole, it was a combination of the World Bank's policy, sympathetic government agencies and pressure from organized slum-dwellers that made the resettlement effective.

Source: Adapted from Patel et al. (2002)

BOX 4.8: SLUM UPGRADING PIONEERS IN ASIAN CITIES

Indonesia's *Kampung* Improvement Programme

The innovative *Kampung* Improvement Programme (KIP), launched in 1969 in Indonesia, was the first urban slum upgrading project in the developing world. The rationale was to provide basic urban services, such as roads and footpaths, water, drainage and sanitation, as well as health and education facilities. The programme soon became a model for the transformation of slums from illegal settlements into a regularized component of the urban fabric. Through official recognition of improved *kampungs* ('villages' or 'hamlets', in Malay) as formal settlements, municipal authorities effectively brought security of tenure to, and improved the lives of, 1.2 million slum-dwellers in Jakarta between 1969 and 1974.

In 1974, the World Bank decided to support the programme with soft loans in order to accelerate implementation and upscaling. In 1979, the Indonesian government endorsed KIP as national policy. By the time World Bank support came to an end in 1982, the programme had improved the day-to-day living conditions of close to five million urban poor. Permanent monitoring and assessment, based on trial-and-error, as well as input from the communities, were the major factors behind the success of the programme. The KIP has gone through various stages of

growth over the past 30 years, turning from a physical improvement approach to community-based development. In the early years, the scheme received adequate support from the government, international agencies and the people. More recently, and although rapid urban extension remains a major challenge for KIP, support from the government and the community has been waning and no international agency funding is available to keep the programme going at its initial pace. As a result, the first slum improvement programme in the developing world has not been able to keep pace with the current growth of slums in Indonesian cities.

Manila's *Tondo* Urban Development Project

The largest slum in Manila and another of the largest in Asia with over 180,000 residents, Tondo Foreshore is one more example of early slum upgrading efforts in the region. In the late 1970s and after having tried several small-scale resettlement plans, the Manila municipality, with World Bank support, launched an *in situ* upgrading scheme for infrastructure and services as a less disruptive and low-cost solution to the problem. As a result and over the subsequent 10 years, the slum community transformed itself into an upwardly mobile neighbourhood. In this sense, the Tondo project corroborated the assumption

that if given security of tenure and basic urban services, families will build their own housing, the quality of which, in that particular case, surpassed even the most optimistic predictions. Indeed, Tondo residents participated in upgrading efforts and became property owners with a stake in stability.

This extensive community participation was one of the most positive features of the project. It was indeed less disruptive to the community than resettlement would have been, but it entailed formidable complexities and delays. The project was anticipated to last four years, but it actually took nine. It was expected to be less costly than resettlement, but a large increase in costs occurred due to the delays associated with the massive size, complexity, and experimental nature of the scheme. The weakest element in the project was the recovery of costs which, by the end, had risen threefold. Moreover, the anticipated cross-subsidies from land sales for commercial/industrial purposes largely failed to materialise.

Unlike the Kampung Improvement Programme, community involvement in design and implementation was limited in Manila's Tondo project. Still, the lessons from what worked and what did not paved the way for major slum upgrading programmes all over Asia.

Source: http://web.mit.edu/urbanupgrading/upgrading/case-examples/ce-IO-jak.html, http://web.mit.edu/urbanupgrading/upgrading/case-examples/ce-PH-ton.html

Public housing in Singapore. ©**Mike Tan C. T./Shutterstock**

Singapore's public housing stands out amid the general "doom and gloom" stories of slums and inadequate housing in many developing countries. Under its public housing programme, the city-State provided for 80 per cent of the population, most of whom (90 per cent) are now homeowners. This was a significant achievement, even in comparison with the Western experience of mass social housing. The success of the programme is demonstrated in the 80 per cent satisfaction rate of those living in public housing.

In the early 1960s, Singapore was facing two fundamental challenges: (i) the population was fast outgrowing decent housing supplies, and (ii) housing as provided by the private sector was not affordable to low-income families. Housing surveys indicated that public housing would be required at the rate of 11,000 new units a year for those unable to afford private housing. The challenge was taken up by the newly elected government which had won the 1965 election on a manifesto where employment and housing featured prominently.

What makes Singapore experience special is that the government considered economic growth and social development as being of equal and symbiotic importance. Two statutory agencies – the Economic Development Board and the Housing and Development Board (HDB) – were set up in 1960 with financial, legal and institutional powers to enhance the supply of jobs and housing, respectively. This complementary relationship between employment and housing has (so political-legitimacy analyses have argued) played a key role in Singapore's enduring political stability.

The two basic functions of the HDB were to "provide housing of sound construction and good design for the lower income groups at rents which they can afford" (Housing and Development Board, 1962:3); and "to encourage a property-owning democracy in Singapore and to enable Singapore citizens in the lower middle income group to own their own homes" (Housing and Development Board, 1964:2). As it strengthened owner-occupier tenure through new, mass public housing specifically designed for subsequent sale, the government, acting through the Housing and Development Board, effectively assumed the role of facilitator and social engineer.

Although the public housing programme began on an exclusively rental basis, the new and innovative policy of home ownership for low-income categories, on 99-year leases, was launched in 1964 (Housing and Development Board, 1964:9). Under the public eligibility and allocation framework, which continues to this day, an income ceiling serves as a cut-off point to help low-income families gain access to the programme; applicants whose total household income exceed the eligibility ceiling do not qualify for public housing.

For all public housing beneficiaries, housing credit was made more affordable through government support for down-payments and mortgage loan interest rates. Prominent among these was a scheme enabling buyers to withdraw a portion of their savings in the Central Provident Fund (a pay-as-you-work social security scheme) for down-payments (20 per cent of purchase price) and mortgage-related payments. The remaining 80 per cent of the purchase price could be paid in instalments through a Housing and Development Board-assisted mortgage loan, with privileged interest rates set below the prime rate. Thanks to the Central Provident Fund, it became possible to own a flat on a 99-year lease without suffering a reduction in monthly disposable income.

Source: Contributed by Belinda Yuen

A poor family is evicted from a slum in Gopalgonj Town, Bangladesh, July 2009. ©UPPR/UNDP/UN-HABITAT

by the World Bank. The Bank's Urban Development Project in 'Jabotabek' (the greater Jakarta metropolitan region, see Chapter 2) led to the forced resettlement of some 50,000 people. In Mumbai, construction of five new roads has caused the forcible relocation of 6,000 families. In every case, the majority of those forcibly relocated were low-income slum-dwellers (Hook, 2006; Tiwari, 1999).

The Universal Declaration of Human Rights (Art. 25) states that *"Everyone has the right to a standard of living adequate for the health and well-being, of himself and of his household, including food, clothing and housing."* (United Nations, n.d). In this context, forced evictions are considered as violations of human rights (UN-HABITAT, 2010; Kothari & Chaudhry, 2010).

Under the 1996 Habitat Agenda, governments recognize the importance of *"protecting all people from, and providing legal protection and redress for, forced evictions that are contrary to the law, taking human rights into consideration, (and) when evictions are unavoidable, ensuring, as appropriate, that alternative suitable solutions are provided"* (Habitat Agenda, para. 40 (n)) (UN-HABITAT, 2003a). Based on this, many governments now provide alternative accommodation or options to those forcibly evicted. However, the process often requires facilitation by non-government organizations to ensure some smooth resolution. For example in Mumbai, the Society for the Promotion of Area Resource Centres (SPARC), a local non-governmental organization, facilitated the relocation of slum-dwellers who had been evicted in connection with a transportation project (see Box 4.8).

Resettlement schemes can be conflict-ridden, too. In January 2003, the Bangkok Metropolitan Administration served the residents of Pom Mahakan, a 300-strong community in the city centre, with a notice to vacate their homes in order to make way for an urban park. Despite large-scale protests, in August 2003 an administrative tribunal ruled that the eviction was legal and could proceed. After several failed attempts to evict the community, the Bangkok Metropolitan Administration agreed in December 2005 to preserve the community and develop the area as a historical site, as suggested by the community (UN-HABITAT, 2007a).

Some Asian countries have adopted anti-eviction laws, including the Philippines and India. For example, in Mumbai, all slum-dwellers who had occupied land prior to 1995 enjoy *de facto* tenure on the plots. Such anti-eviction laws regulate relations between landowner and occupier and guarantee the rights of both. However, they often fall short of the required degree of protection because the poor may have to struggle to mobilize expensive and inaccessible legal services to defend their rights. While anti-eviction laws could be a step towards more secure types of tenure, identifying who has occupancy rights on what land remains a major difficulty (UN-HABITAT, 2004b).

Almost all evictions are preventable and one of the best ways to achieve this is through provision of secure tenure and on-site upgrading. In the late 1960s and early 1970s, international agencies sought to pioneer slum upgrading in Asia. In Indonesia, Jakarta's Kampung Improvement Programme, launched in 1969, was probably the first slum upgrading project in Asia, followed by the Philippines' Tondo Urban Development Project in Manila (see Box 4.8). These examples demonstrate the enormous potential of secure tenure when it comes to generating better-quality housing and living environments for the urban poor (ESCAP & UN-HABITAT, 2008c).

▲
Seoul, Korea. ©JinYoung Lee/Shutterstock

4.4.6 Housing delivery systems

In many Asian countries, shelter does find a prominent place in national policy, but the public resources devoted to housing remain well short of requirements. In the poorer Asian countries, too many households need homes and governments have too few resources to build even a fraction of the numbers of homes required.

Public housing

Some Asian governments have tackled the housing problem head-on and have achieved remarkable results. In the Republic of Korea, Singapore and Hong Kong, China, public projects have been the hallmark of government housing policies and their vigorous pursuit of slum-free cities.

In the Republic of Korea since the mid-1970s, the government not just actively promoted but also provided new hous-

ing in order to counter the upward pressure on prices caused by short supply. This led to the development of apartments within tenement blocks, which now account for 53 per cent of the housing stock in the country (51 per cent in Seoul). Since then, the Korea National Housing Corporation has continued to improve living standards through new housing and urban renewal. By 2005, the Corporation had built 1.65 million units, focusing on mass housing for the homeless and low-income households. The scheme is funded through government grants and the National Housing Fund (RICS, 2008).

In Singapore, the private/public housing ratio is about 20 to 80. Most of the public housing flats built by the Housing and Development Board have been sold to local citizens (at subsidized prices) and permanent residents on 99-year leases (see Box 4.9). In Hong Kong, China, the Housing Authority increased its own stock by 18,000 units between 1991 and 2001 (Yu, 2004; UN-HABITAT, 2005).

Many countries have experimented with public housing, though only on a minor scale because of limited financial resources. Public rental housing has not been allocated to the poor, and if it had would not necessarily have been affordable. In some cases, these public properties have eventually been privatized as governments pursued more market-orientated policies (UN-HABITAT, 2005).

A mechanism known as Incremental Housing Development follows the same principles as those used in squatter settlements, recognizing that people are fully capable of building and developing their own houses when given the opportunity. This is achieved through "sites and services" projects, where serviced plots are sold to the poor at affordable rates. Having thus gained security of tenure on their plots, households are free to build whatever they want and can afford, on the assumption that the settlement can only improve over time as resources permit. This approach has been most widely adopted in Hyderabad (Sindh Province, Pakistan), where it is known as *Khuda-ki-Basti* ('God's own settlement' in Urdu) and has been implemented with some success by the Hyderabad Development ment Authority (PADECO, 2007).

Public-private partnerships in housing

Over the past few years, several Asian cities have established partnerships with private developers to stimulate affordable housing construction for the poor. In most cases, commercial development rights on plots were granted to private sector enterprises who, as a *quid pro quo*, would build affordable housing on a specified percentage of the total land developed.

In the year 2000, India's Madhya Pradesh state launched an innovative programme known as *Ashraya Nidhi* ('shelter fund') to give the low-income segments of the population access to residential plots or houses. In residential settlements, private developers are required to allocate 15 per cent of the total developed area for low-income households. Alternatively, a developer can build houses in 25 per cent of the developed area. The developers who do not want to opt for either of the above two formats must pay the *Ashraya Nidhi* a 'shelter fee' for the total area of the settlement at specified rates (ASCI-Centre for Good Governance, 2006).

In Chengdu (Sichuan Province, China), comprehensive revitalization of the rivers Fu and Nan has entailed the removal and subsequent on-the-spot relocation of those living in the riverside slums. Once the land was vacated, the municipal authority built decent, affordable housing for the slum-dwellers on 660 ha and opened bids for commercial development of another 860 ha. The commercial side of the plan enabled the municipality to raise an additional US $200 million for the project. The relocation of all households was completed in 18 months without a single case of forced eviction (Wang, 2001).

In Indonesia and since the 1970s, housing policies have focused on providing low-cost shelter for low-income households through a compulsory "1:3:6" rule, under which for every high-cost house, developers must build a minimum of three middle-class houses and six basic or very basic houses. On top of this, state-owned mortgage banks granted subsidised loans for low-cost housing. For all these efforts, medium- and high-cost houses, which represent only 10 per cent of housing units, have dominated the market in terms of sales value. Since private sector lenders (including a number of domestic banks and one large foreign bank) have been actively involved in housing finance for high-end property, this has given them an opportunity to become involved in the primary mortgage market alongside two state-owned mortgage banks (Zhu, 2006).

In many Asian cities, *land sharing,* as coordinated by local authorities, has emerged as a successful alternative to compulsory acquisition. Under land sharing partnerships, the landowner (public or private) and the occupiers (squatters) reach an agreement whereby the landowner retains the economically more attractive parts of the land parcel and the dwellers are allowed to build houses on the other part, usually with full tenure rights. This land sharing format is particularly effective where community organization is strong. The benefits for slum-dwellers include security of tenure and proper housing. For private landowners, the attraction is a waiver of development controls, allowing for intensive exploitation of the commercial portion of the land (UN-HABITAT, 2003b).

In Mumbai, land acquisition can take the form of a 'transfer of development rights' (TDR). To the landowner whose land is to be acquired for public purposes, TDR is the alternative to monetary compensation. The scheme offers the benefits of flexibility, giving landowners three options: (i) to use the development rights on the remaining area of land owned (if any), (ii) to use the development rights on any other land owned by them, or (iii) to transfer (sell) the development rights to others who can use it on other land parcels. In Mumbai, TDRs are granted on lands reserved for roads, open spaces and public amenities; they can originate from anywhere in Greater Mumbai, but can be used only within designated zones, which exclude sensitive and congested areas. The uses of the land from which the TDR originated and of the land on which it can be implemented are specified in Mumbai's development control regulations (PADECO, 2007).

As far as housing is concerned, public-private partnerships can also involve various forms of land re-allocation, such as pooling, readjustment or consolidation. These formats enable public authorities to amalgamate individually owned land parcels into a single one for more efficient subdivision and development. Once the land parcels are consolidated, the area is partitioned into serviced sites or plots. Servicing is funded by the sale of some plots. Some are earmarked for public purposes, including low-income housing, and the remainder is distributed among the original landowners. In India's Gujarat state, these land pooling arrangements are known as the Town Planning Scheme and have enabled municipal authorities to develop peri-urban areas, with up to 10 per cent of the land reserved for low-income housing. Various types of land readjustment schemes have been implemented in Indonesia, Japan, the Republic of Korea and Thailand (UN-HABITAT, 2003b; PADECO, 2007).

Private sector housing delivery

The Global Shelter Strategy led by UN-HABITAT in the 1980s advocated an "enabling" role for governments, in order to put the private sector in a better position to deliver low-income housing (Pugh, 1994, 2001). Many Asian governments have done so. Although Asian cities are hosts to more poor (insolvent) than rich households, formal private sector housing follows the reverse pattern, favouring the rich and disregarding the poor. Since supply of urban serviced land is relatively finite and therefore 'inelastic', real-estate developers find themselves hard put to meet the demand, causing an overall rise in property prices. Still, in Mumbai the Maharashtra state government is looking to involve the private sector in housing provision for slum-dwellers (Patel and Arputham, 2008).

One problem in Asia is that housing markets are beset with high transaction costs. In many countries, more than 10 per cent of the property value is spent on such costs; as a result, many transactions take place informally and often in cash, in the process depriving government of revenue. Countries with less transparent markets and more registration procedures also feature higher estate agent fees, particularly the Philippines and Indonesia. Many countries (such as Thailand) are trying to streamline the property transaction process or to reduce transaction costs (for example, stamp duty reform under the national urban renewal programme in India) (Cruz, 2008).

On the whole, and to the exception of a few countries, Asia has no well-developed housing market. While everyone aspires to own a house, the housing tenure pattern in Asian cities is varied – from 30 per cent home ownership in Dhaka to over 85 per cent in Phnom Penh. Although most national governments in Asia promote home ownership and have mechanisms in place for mortgage finance, ownership is not available for those at the bottom of the income pyramid. As a result, home-ownership in Asian cities is much lower than in Europe or North America. In Asia, many urban residents lack the income, or access to housing finance, required to participate in the formal home-ownership market. De Soto (2001) suggests that the poor do not really "own" the property they reside in, because they are not granted any legal title. As a result, the urban poor cannot turn this property into capital, which impairs the wealth accumulation that could help take them out of their state of economic deprivation.

Rental housing

Although significant proportions of urban dwellers are tenants, the number of governments giving effective support to rental housing development is small. The bulk of this housing, when privately-owned, accommodates low-income families through informal arrangements, and is located near city centres and, more recently, industrial estates. Increasingly, rental housing is also available in slums and informal settlements. As for public-sector rental housing, its defining feature is that supply never manages to keep up with demand. Frequently, the poor are excluded because even though public agencies usually provide generous subsidies, the poor are typically not one of the targeted groups. Even where rents were heavily subsidized, governments have often found ways to exclude the neediest (UN-HABITAT, 2003c).

In Asia, some 20 per cent of urban dwellers live in rental accommodation, of which 45 per cent or so benefit from some form of tenure. This proportion remains imprecise as it is difficult to keep count of renters in slum settlements. To Kumar (2001), the rental share in Asian cities represents about 30 per cent of the housing market. City-level data on tenure status suggests that the share of rental housing varies from a high of 65 per cent in Dhaka, Melbourne and Ulaanbaatar, to a low of 30 per cent in Seoul and even 20 per cent in Hanoi (Asian Development Bank, 2001).

Informal rental housing entails lower rents and more flexible lease arrangements, the drawbacks being weaker security of tenure and probably lower-quality public amenities in the immediate surroundings. Squatter housing involves illegal occupation of land, which to law-enforcers seems to be a more serious offence than tax evasion or regulatory noncompliance. Moreover, in many developing countries, the bulk of households cannot afford formal housing. To a large extent, informal housing is housing for the poor, in the same way that informal employment is employment for the poor. This is why issues related to poverty loom larger in policy debates over informal housing than they do in debates over informal labour and product markets. The overregulation of formal housing makes it unaffordable not just for the poor but for much of the middle class as well (Arnott, 2008).

Faced with this problem, some Asian countries have been imposing rent controls since the 1950s in a bid to keep local rental costs from rising to prohibitive levels. In many developing countries, this has increased demand on the back of rapid urbanization, declining real incomes and the general inelasticity (i.e., limited amount) of housing supplies. Some authors contend that rent controls discourage new construction, cause abandonment, delay maintenance and reduce mobility (Alston *et al.*, 1992). Many Asian countries have either repealed rent controls or amended them to keep new housing out of their scope as well as to maintain rents above certain prescribed values in a bid to promote a proper rental housing market.

Bangkok has seen some innovative rental housing, as low-income communities have evolved a practical arrangement with landowners to enable them to live in areas with access to livelihood opportunities. Under this scheme, the poor look out for owners who keep land plots vacant as they wait for these further to gain in value before developing them. The poor offer to rent the land on a short- to medium-term lease, paying what they can. Landowners, find that this arrangement works very well for them as a defence against third-party invasion of their property. In recent years, communities and the authorities have been exploring the provision of basic urban services to temporary settlements. Long-term leases pave the way for higher service standards, but residents must be willing to vacate the area when required. This arrangement has enabled large numbers of poor households to live in areas

▲
In Chengdu (Sichuan, central China), comprehensive revitalization of the rivers Fu and Nan has entailed the removal and subsequent on-the-spot relocation of those living in the riverside slums. ©Fenghui/Shutterstock

that would otherwise have been beyond their (economic) reach. As urban expansion takes livelihood opportunities to other locations, the poor can move with the flow and negotiate similar arrangements with other landowners (Global Land Tool Network, 2008).

4.4.7 The 'People's Process' of housing and slum improvement

Asia can provide many good examples of participatory slum improvement or upgrading. Governments tend to adopt a facilitating role in projects while maintaining financial accountability and adherence to quality norms. In Asian cities, participatory slum improvement is becoming an important indigenous development method (UN-HABITAT, 2007b).

Asia has pioneered the people-led process of housing and slum upgrading - commonly known as the people's process - as spearheaded by dedicated civil society groups. These are strong in the region and have gained ground in many cities as a result of efforts by organisations like Slum Dwellers International or the Asian Coalition for Human Rights, among others. They, promote community-led housing development in Cambodia, India, Indonesia, Mongolia, Nepal, Pakistan, the Philippines, Sri Lanka and Thailand.

Asia also is testament to the fact that while the private sector is able to meet the housing requirements of the rich, the 'people sector' has been able to cater to the poor. Meeting the needs of the poor through social policies is crucial, as the more developed countries in Asia – Malaysia, the Republic of Korea and Singapore – have demonstrated. When government and civil society come together, as in Thailand, large numbers of people can improve their own living conditions. As more cities in Asia adapt these methods and improve the housing conditions of the larger segment of their populations, they stand a good chance of becoming more productive and inclusive at the same time. The Kirtipur Housing Project in Kathmandu (see Box 4.6), the resettlements of slum-dwellers in Mumbai (see Box 4.7), the Baan Mankong Programme in Thailand (see Box 4.12) and Sri Lanka's community contracts (see Box 4.10) all stand out as examples of effective community participation in slum improvement (see Box 4.8).

These various schemes suggest that a citywide slum upgrading approach is more effective than piecemeal, project-based improvement of a few slums. In India, Ahmedabad's Slum Networking programme was designed to take in all the slums in the city. It was conceived as a pilot project, with four main stakeholders joining as partners – the slum community, a private and a non-government organization, together with the Ahmedabad Municipal Corporation. Civil society took care of community mobilization and development while municipal authorities acted as facilitators. In Thailand, the Baan Mankong scheme is now a nation-wide programme.

Programmes that involve integrated upgrading of the entire city take advantage of slums not as urban "islands", but quite the reverse – as together combining into some sort of an urban grid. The spatial spread of slums across a city, together with the contiguity between slum settlements, gives an opportunity to strengthen infrastructure networks. The projects outlined above show that the slum fabric can be used effectively to extend projects from community to citywide scale. They also demonstrate that complex, large-scale urban renewal programmes can be sensitively executed. The key to success is none other than the slum dwelling communities, who show that they are willing to mobilize resources despite their poverty. They have gone into partnerships with government agencies, local authorities, civil society (including women's groups) and local professionals. Slum networking is a bottom-up approach primarily under community control (UN-HABITAT, 2003b).

▲
The settlement of Bosevana in Colombo is where Sevanatha undertook a very successful upgrading project with the Women's Bank in 1993 - one of the first times the resident community was involved in all aspects of settlement upgrading. **©Homeless International**

Community contracts were introduced by the National Housing Development Authority (NHDA) of Sri Lanka in 1987 to the satisfaction of slum communities. The new system came in response to the failure of the conventional competitive tender-contract system to provide infrastructure and services. It was one of the best community-based slum upgrading methods the government has used as part of its so-called One Million Houses Programme (1984-1994). Over the past two decades or so, community contracts have become a popular way of facilitating community participation in infrastructure provision. The system is used by many agencies in Sri Lanka as well as by government entities elsewhere in Asia, and in Africa.

A community contract is a procurement system that involves residents in the planning and implementation of infrastructure in their own living environment. In this partnership arrangement, communities play the three roles – promoter, engineer and contractor – involved in the conventional tender system, and on top of their role as end-users of the service provided. Beyond a procurement mechanism for the provision of infrastructure to slums, community

contracting empowers people as it gives them control over the local development process.

Before the approach was introduced, the government would often provide facilities (such as public toilet blocks) to shanty areas without community involvement. As a result, the facilities were in the wrong location, were not maintained by the community and quickly fell in disrepair. Moreover, the community felt that private contractors tended to do poor-quality work. The frustration was such that an urban poor community told the agency that they could do a better design and construction job with NHDA funding. To demonstrate its capacity, the community designed and built a well with financial and technical support from NHDA.

Based on this experience, municipal councils and non-governmental organisations (particularly *Sevanatha,* which is involved in urban low-income shelter and environmental issues) used the Community Construction Contracts to extend infrastructure to slums. The format provides for a variety of issues such as form of contract, legal status, sharing costs and responsibilities, any risks involved, penalties for non-fulfilment and performance monitoring. In early 2010, the Colombo Municipal Council was

in the process of incorporating the procedures into the municipal procurement system. UN-HABITAT Regional Office for Asia and the Pacific has actively promoted Community Contracts as part of the People's Process of housing and slum improvement in countries including Afghanistan, Bangladesh, Cambodia, Indonesia, Maldives, Mongolia, Sri Lanka and Timor-Leste (UN-HABITAT, 2007b). The International Labour Organization (ILO) has introduced the format in Africa (Tanzania).

Community contracting entails lower overheads than work by private construction firms and is therefore cheaper. Community construction contracts are also easier and faster to process. The savings a community reaps from this type of contract are deposited in a community fund, which makes local people less financially dependent on public authorities. Moreover, transparent procedures and transactions make the system more accountable. Most of all, the format empowers communities as far as their own development and the management of those facilities are concerned. They gain a sense of ownership and attachment to the facility, which automatically ensures long-term maintenance and sustainability.

Source: http://www.unescap.org/pdd/prs/ProjectActivities/Ongoing/Best%20practice/Contracts%20System.pdf

4.4.8 Housing finance for the poor

Housing finance is a key to economic growth as it has linkages to many sectors in the economy – including land, construction and labour markets (Tibaijuka, 2009). The underdevelopment of this sector in Asia reflects structural weakness in domestic capital markets, distortions in the legal and regulatory frameworks, and poor familiarity with housing finance and mortgage lending (Bestani & Klein, 2005).

To this day, Asia's mortgage sector remains the least developed in the world. In many Asian countries, mortgage financing amounts to less than 2 per cent of annual gross domestic product, compared with as much as 88 per cent in the United Kingdom. However, major changes have taken place in recent years. For instance, in the formal housing market, the Republic of Korea is leading in new housing and related finance; China is the largest mortgage market in Asia; and mortgage markets in Singapore and Hong Kong, China, are well developed (Ong, 2005). In recent years in India, housing mortgage finance grew an annual 45 per cent on average, with commercial banks taking the lead. Housing finance has also experienced buoyant growth in Indonesia, Pakistan and Sri Lanka (Cruz, 2007).

For all these favourable recent developments, growth in formal housing finance, largely fails to extend to low-income households. These are effectively left out because residing in informal settlements does not provide any of the comforts or securities typically required by mortgage lenders. As De Soto (2001) argues, this situation can change if the informal property arrangements of low-income households can be incorporated into a formal body of law that is enforceable. De Soto shows that this is possible because existing informal arrangements are based on some quasi-legal precedents that could be mainstreamed into law. Poor urban households in Asia lack the regular incomes that many mortgage lenders demand. Housing finance agencies are also unwilling to seek out clients for small loans because of the operational costs involved. At the same time, it must be recognized that many formal housing finance institutions have sought to "down-market" through mediation by micro-finance agencies or non-governmental organisations. However, the reach of such programmes is limited, again due to high operational costs. For example, in Mongolia, much-needed reforms have been made, but the existing housing finance options remain inadequate. The country's housing markets are constrained by lack of familiarity with mortgage lending, an underdeveloped banking system, and murky land ownership laws (Bestani & Klein, 2005).

Cooperative movements are typically strong in Asia, as is the savings culture. Many self-help and savings groups have been formed among the poor with the help of non-governmental organisations. Micro-finance institutions have also managed to meet the credit needs of the poor, though only to some extent as their reach in urban areas is limited. Many national governments in Asia have supported community savings schemes and housing cooperatives. Cambodia, India, Indonesia, the Philippines, Sri Lanka and Thailand have all established the institutional and financial frameworks enabling self-help groups and other organizations to promote pro-poor development. This is a vital asset for many Asian countries, as demonstrated by Cambodia's Urban Poor Development Fund and Thailand's Baan Mankong Programme (see Boxes 4.11 and 4.12).

Asia's commendable achievement is that if anything, formal market failure to cater to the poor has spawned many innovative alternatives for housing, infrastructure and community development finance for low-income groups. Moreover, with their combinations of savings loans and subsidies, these innovations have had broad-ranging benefits, including negotiated land tenure security, housing construction and improvements, as well as water and sanitation. As part of the "enabling" role of the public sector, and as advocated by international agencies with regard to housing, many public agencies have shifted operations from housing to finance (see Box 4.9 on Singapore). As a result, housing has become a significant part of the microfinance portfolio of many agencies, although borrowings are for house improvements and extension rather than new buildings.

With financial deregulation, more institutions in Asia have taken an interest in mortgage finance, making this type of loan available to a broader range of income categories. The rapid expansion of self-help groups has also had a demonstrated effect on the development of housing finance innovations. These include using savings and loans to transform low-income neighbourhoods (Mitlin, 2008). As is well known, Grameen Bank in Bangladesh has taken the lead in new financial products for the poor over the last three decades, and this experience has been replicated in other Asian countries.

In the Philippines, the Community Mortgage Programme gives access to affordable housing for squatters living on public or private land without security of tenure. The scheme grants subsidised loans to community groups facing eviction for both land purchasing and housing development. As far as housing is concerned, non-governmental organisations and other professional groups, including local government, are given distinct roles and are entitled to act as "originators", i.e., to provide technical support to the communities benefiting from the scheme. The Community Mortgage Programme has enabled 140,000 households to secure tenure through land purchases or housing development loans (UN-HABITAT & Cities Alliance, 2006).

BOX 4.11: GOOD PRACTICE FROM CAMBODIA: THE URBAN POOR DEVELOPMENT FUND

Since Cambodia's first democratic election in 1993, Phnom Penh has experienced extensive development, but commercial and public interests have remained on a collision course with the specific needs of the urban poor. As a result, the poor have been left worse off and struggling to secure a place in the aggressive commercialization of land markets.

In 1998, the Squatter and Urban Poor Federation together with other non-governmental organisations and the Phnom Penh municipality established the Urban Poor Development Fund to provide shelter loans to a specific community to support their relocation from a forthcoming inner-city development project. Since then, the Fund has diversified its activities in response to other community needs.

In particular, the Fund has supported the development of a new City Development Strategy, the basic principle of which was the vital need for a vision of the city's development that was shared between various stakeholders. Preparatory work led to a consensus that options should include *in situ* upgrading, which the Fund duly promoted at its fifth anniversary event (May 2003). The next (2004) national election came as an added incentive for the government to launch this pro-poor upgrading initiative.

The Urban Poor Development Fund provides low-interest loans for housing, improved settlements and income generation for the benefit of those urban poor communities that are actively involved in a community savings process. Loans are made only to communities, not to individuals, through their savings and other communal groups. Besides providing a much-needed source of affordable credit, the Fund supports the poor in several ways: adding capital to community savings to help people overcome financial constraints, supporting community innovations in housing, settlement improvements as well as negotiated tenure formats that demonstrate fresh solutions and test new kinds of institutional set-ups.

Source: ACHR (2005)

BOX 4.12: GOOD PRACTICE FROM THAILAND: THE *BAAN MANKONG* FINANCING PROGRAMME

The *Baan Mankong* Programme ('secure housing' in Thai) was launched by the Thai government in January 2003 as part of efforts to address the housing problems of the country's poorest urban citizens. The programme channels government funds in the form of infrastructure subsidies and 'soft' (i.e., on concessional terms) housing loans directly to poor communities. Beneficiary communities plan and carry out improvements to housing, the environment and basic urban services, and manage the budgets themselves. Those communities under serious threat of eviction are given priority. Instead of delivering housing units to individual poor families, the Baan Mankong Programme puts Thailand's existing slum communities – and their networks – at the centre of a process of developing long-term, comprehensive solutions to land and housing problems. The programme is implemented by the Community Organizations Development Institute (CODI, a public organization under the Ministry of Social Development and Human Security), and is unconventional insofar as it enables poor communities to work in close collaboration with local government, professionals, universities and non-governmental organisations. The programme starts with a survey identifying the needs for upgraded housing among the more deprived urban communities. Based on survey findings, citywide upgrading plans are developed, and once a number of these are selected for implementation the Development Institute channels the infrastructure subsidies and housing loans directly to the communities.

The Thai Government has approved a four-year budget to support the Baan Mankong community upgrading programme, to be implemented in 200 cities across the country between 2005 and 2008. The objective is to upgrade the housing and living environments of 300,000 families in 2,000 poor communities. The government will provide the Development Institute with a total budget of about US $470 million for the subsidies related to infrastructure and housing loan interests. It is then for the Development Institute to grant housing and land-purchase loans to communities from its own revolving fund, and to link with commercial banks to negotiate more community housing loans at a later stage. The government's total subsidy works out to about US $1,650 per household, which covers infrastructure, social and economic facilities, local management and administrative costs, along with a 2 per cent interest rate subsidy on housing loans, and all the expenses involved in capacity-building, learning, meetings, seminars and exposure trips. This subsidy represents about 25 per cent of total upgrading expenditures, with communities contributing 65 per cent (mostly in the form of housing loans and labour), and local authorities provide the remaining 10 per cent.

Since the first 10 pilot upgrading projects were approved in 2003, the Baan Mankong Programme has grown to involve 226 cities and districts in 69 provinces (out of a total 76 in the country). So far, 512 projects have been approved, benefiting 53,976 families in 1,010 distinct areas.

Source: Community Organization Development Institute (CODI), prepared from material on website:
http://www.codi.or.th/downloads/english/Paper/CODI%20Update%205%20High%20Res.pdf

4.5
Access to basic urban services

Kabul city, Afghanistan. ©**UN-HABITAT/Wataru Kawasaki**

A key feature of inclusive and harmonious cities is access to basic urban services (UN-HABITAT, 2008a; 2010). With high urban densities, access to safe and reliable water supply and sanitation services is critical for health, business, social status and dignity, as well as basic security for women and children. If these benefits are to be sustainable, effective and financially viable, utilities are essential. Special measures are also needed if these benefits are to accrue to the urban poor, who often lack access to these services. In this respect, UN-HABITAT and the United Nations Institute for Training and Research (UNITAR) have elaborated a set of 'International Guidelines on Access to Basic Services for All', which were approved by the UN-HABITAT Governing Council in April 2009 (UN-HABITAT Governing Council, 2009). This signals a clear commitment on the part of governments around the world in favour of improved provision of basic services.

4.5.1 Water supply[8]

Sustainable access to drinking water is one of the Millennium Development Goals (MDGs). Asian subregions seem to have done better for water supply than sub-Saharan Africa, but have fallen behind Latin America and Northern Africa (see Chart 4.11) (World Health Organization &

UNICEF, 2010). Eastern Asia has forged ahead to achieve 98 per cent coverage, largely due to China's determined efforts as shown in Table 4.9.

In South-East Asia, Malaysia and Singapore have achieved universal water coverage between 1990 and 2008. Services in Thailand and Viet Nam have expanded significantly over recent years. Indonesia, Cambodia, Myanmar and the Lao People's Democratic Republic still have a long way to go. It must be noted that in South-East Asia, water utilities have made significant contributions to improved access. Still, Chart 4.12 suggests a persistent, though small, shortfall in universal basic water coverage.

In South Asia, Bhutan, Iran, Maldives and Sri Lanka have achieved close to universal coverage of urban water supply services between the years 1990 and 2008 (see Table 4.9). In India, the last steps towards universal service are slow, whereas Pakistan seems to have stalled very close to the target. Bangladesh and Nepal are lagging behind, with 15 and 7 per cent of the urban population still left without any basic water service, respectively.

Between 1990 and 2008, the shares of urban populations with access to safe drinking water have declined by between 3 and 12 per cent in Bangladesh, Indonesia, Myanmar and Nepal (see Table 4.9). Against this worrying background,

CHART 4.11: **STATUS OF URBAN WATER SUPPLY BY MDG REGION, 2008**

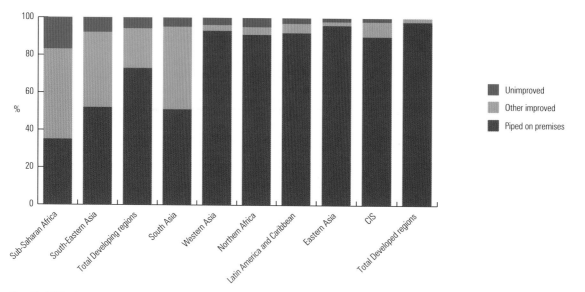

Legend:
- Unimproved
- Other improved
- Piped on premises

Note: The MDG regions are as defined by the United Nations.
Source: World Health Organization & UNICEF (2010:52)

a number of initiatives in Asian cities may show the way forward (see Box 4.13). More attention from policymakers is needed if universal access to basic supply of drinking water is to become effective.

A closer look at Asia's urban realities highlights two major patterns at work in the area of water distribution. In this respect, South Asia stands in sharp contrast to other subregions. Whereas in most of urban Asia, improved water distribution has been achieved through increases in individual piped connections, in South Asia the share of the population with this type of connections has been on the decline (see Chart 4.13).

This decline in the numbers of individual connections to water networks is particularly significant in India, South Asia's largest country. Detailed analysis suggests that while India's basic urban services are now much more widely available, individual piped water connections as a share of the total urban population have actually declined. This is probably linked both to poverty and to the high share of the population living in informal settlements (see Chart 4.13) where lack of legal tenure often bars access to piped water at home.

Though most subregions (and countries) in Asia are likely to achieve the Millennium Development Goal for water supply, most are left to grapple with the fact that 4 to 8 per cent of

TABLE 4.9: **URBAN POPULATIONS: ACCESS TO WATER SUPPLY, 1990-2008**

Country	1990	2000	2008	Country	1990	2000	2008
Eastern Asia				**Eastern Asia**			
Republic of Korea	97	98	100	Democratic People's Republic of Korea	100	100	100
China	97	98	98	Mongolia	81	88	97
South Asia				**South-East Asia**			
Bhutan	N/A	99	99	Malaysia	94	99	100
Maldives	100	100	99	Singapore	100	100	100
Iran	98	98	98	Thailand	97	98	99
Sri Lanka	91	95	98	Viet Nam	88	94	99
India	90	93	96	Philippines	93	93	93
Pakistan	96	95	95	Indonesia	92	90	89
Bangladesh	88	86	85	Cambodia	52	64	81
Nepal	96	94	93	Myanmar	87	80	75
Afghanistan	N/A	36	78	Lao PDR	N/A	77	72

More than 98 per cent   More than 95 per cent   Less than 95 per cent

Source: World Health Organization & UNICEF (2010:38-51)

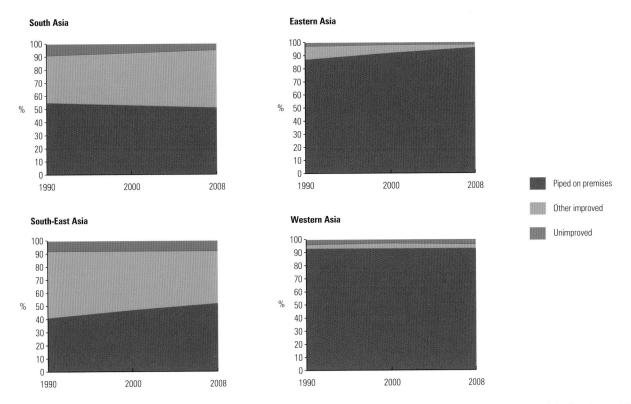

South Asia

Eastern Asia

South-East Asia

Western Asia

Piped on premises

Other improved

Unimproved

Note: Improved drinking water sources include (a) "piped water into dwelling, plot or yard", which include piped household water connection located inside the user's dwelling, plot or yard, (b) "Other improved", which includes public taps or standpipes, tube wells or boreholes, protected dug wells, protected springs or rainwater collection; (ii) Unimproved drinking water sources include unprotected dug well, unprotected spring, cart with small tank/drum, surface water (river, dam, lake, pond, stream, canal, irrigation channels), and bottled water (World Health Organization & UNICEF, 2010:13).
Source: World Health Organization & UNICEF (2010:52)

CHART 4.13: **TRENDS IN NATIONAL LEVEL ACCESS TO WATER, 1990-2008**

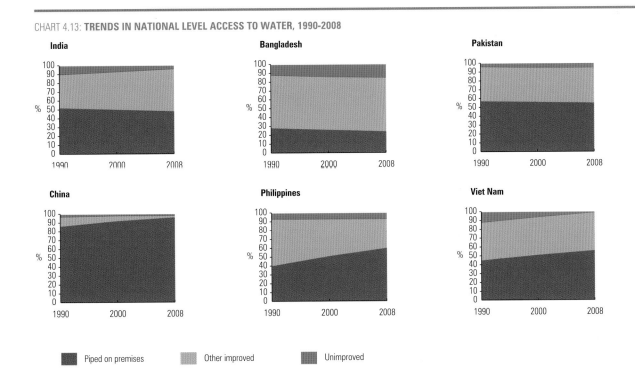

India

Bangladesh

Pakistan

China

Philippines

Viet Nam

Piped on premises   Other improved   Unimproved

Source: World Health Organization & UNICEF (2010:38-51)

POVERTY AND INEQUALITY IN ASIAN CITIES

BOX 4.13: COMMUNITY-MANAGED WATER POINTS IN URBAN SLUMS, BANGLADESH

In Bangladesh since 1996, a non-governmental organisation known as Dushtha Shasthya Kendra (DSK – 'Centre to Help the Helpless through Health' in Bengali) has been working in Dhaka's slums to facilitate access to water and sanitation. DSK acts as an intermediary between the Dhaka Water Supply and Sewerage Authority (DWASA) and poor communities in slum settlements. DSK persuaded the Authority to overcome the obstacle of lack of legal tenure and authorise a number of collective water points[9] in those settlements. DSK helped build slum-dwellers' capacity to manage and maintain the water points; this included user collection of charges on water consumption, which also went towards repaying DSK's initial capital outlays. By 2002, DSK had built nearly 100 water points benefiting about 6,000 slum households. To DWASA, the tangible benefits did not take long to accrue under the form of increased revenues and reduced losses from illegal connections. As a result, the Authority has launched its own "Urban Water and Sanitation Initiative for Dhaka's Urban Poor" with donor funding while reducing the deposit requirements for water points. Under the initiative, replication of the water point scheme to an additional 110 community-managed systems is to improve the living conditions of as many as 60,000 slum-dwellers, not to mention ongoing expansion to other large slums. The success of the scheme is such that DWASA has decided that, subject to local political approval, it will transfer the ownership of the water points to those communities that demonstrate a good track record for maintenance and payment of bills. With the help of WaterAid and other civil society partners, the community-managed water-point model is now replicated in the slums of Chittagong, the country's second largest city.

Sources: Ahmed (2003); Jinnah (2007)

the populations remain persistently deprived of access, except in Eastern Asia (see Chart 4.12). This suggests that even after an overall improvement in service coverage, a 'last mile' effort is necessary to ensure *universal* access to basic urban services.

The 'last-mile' hurdle is proving difficult for many countries to overcome.[10] The reasons may involve combinations of inadequate, poorly targeted public resources, as well as issues related to recognition and/or legal tenure in slum (informal) settlements which in many Asian cities stand in the way of even basic urban services. It is a matter of great concern that some countries in Asia show *declines* in the proportion of urban dwellers with access to basic water supply. This may be a reason for the increase in the numbers of slum-dwellers in some countries (see Table 4.6). These findings would seem to chime in somewhat with a recent finding by UN-HABITAT (2010), whereby a surprisingly large number of informal settlements across the developing world are only one deprivation away from shedding the 'slum' denomination.

All of this suggests that any efforts to improve water distribution in South Asia must address the twin issues of affordability and legal tenure. With regard to affordability,

good practice can be found in South-East Asia where utilities have significantly improved household access to piped water. In Indonesia, Viet Nam and the Philippines, this took a combination of local utilities' own efforts and targeted subsidies (see Box 4.14). In these cases, the subsidies were provided by the Global Partnership for Output-based Aid (GPOBA) instead of more conventional (central or local) government sources. These examples also highlight the need for *well-targeted* subsidies if water distribution is to be effectively improved. More specifically, subsidies must target the appropriate segments of the population while maintaining the utility's performance incentives. As for the other obstacle to improved water distribution (and sanitation) in South Asian cities, it is for urban policies to address land tenure and right-of-way access for networks. A few Indian cities have started to do so. For example, in Ahmedabad, the Municipal Corporation has severed the link between tenure status and service provision. More specifically, the municipal authority issues 'no-objection certificates' which enable those who reside in houses of less than 25 sq. m. to connect to the water network. The certificate is available on payment of a small application fee. In Hyderabad, the Andhra Pradesh state government has granted partial tenure to all slum-dwellers, which gives them the right to continue to reside on their plots of land, but does not grant them the right to sell (Water and Sanitation Programme, 2009). The results of the scheme are quite tangible on a daily basis for those increasing numbers of slum-dwellers who now have access to potable water through taps in their own homes.

On top of government and non-governmental organisations, utilities, too, have developed some innovative methods of sidestepping the land tenure problem and reaching out to the poor in Asian cities. In Colombo, this even took the unexpected shape of privatization, under a project sponsored by the UN Economic and Social Commission for Asia and the Pacific. A small construction company in Sri Lanka's capital overcame the tenure obstacle when it obtained a concession to provide water (purchased in bulk from the utility) through individual connections to 556 slum households that were willing to pay for a better service than the eight stand posts they had so far been sharing between them (i.e., one post for 70 households of about six individuals each). The company laid out the pipes across the slum, installed a meter in each household and took to collecting the bills every month. A partnership between the community, the private company and the water utility has been established to run the system (ESCAP, 2005). This would tend to show that at times, private enterprises are willing to take more risks than government agencies or utilities, although in this instance it was on an admittedly small scale.

This and other experiences amply demonstrate the importance of providing targeted subsidies and/or overcoming lack of tenure if the poor are to benefit from access to basic services in urban slums. Experience also shows that raising water service standards to individual piped connections requires well-functioning and sustainable utilities as well as appropriate incentive structures.

BOX 4.14: **IMPROVING ACCESS TO WATER FOR THE URBAN POOR: A TALE OF THREE CITIES**

Surabaya, Indonesia

In Surabaya, East Java, the second largest city in Indonesia, water and sewerage services are provided by a public utility known as PDAM. The utility has jurisdiction over a population of 2.7 million, of which it is able to serve only 67 per cent through house connections to the water network. Having increased production capacity through optimized water treatment plants, the Surabaya PDAM has started to expand its distribution network and set up new connections in order better to reach out to the urban poor. These find that they can now afford access to piped water through two alternative schemes. For individual connections, households can contract standard two-year loans from Bank Rakyat Indonesia, the country's largest microfinance institution. The second approach involves a subsidised output-based aid scheme which is to extend piped water connections to 15,500 eligible households (or a total 77,500 end-users). The subsidised scheme entails three alternative types of service: (i) infill connections to existing mains; (ii) expansion connections to previously un-served areas; and, (iii) bulk supply or 'master meter' connections for particularly poor, dense, or informal communities not otherwise eligible for individual connections.

Under the master meter approach, no land title is required, which is of special interest to the poorer communities. Thanks to subsidisation, households are to meet only about 40 per cent of the total cost of infill connections (12 per cent for the expansion scheme).

Ho Chi Minh City, Viet Nam

As part of a World Bank project, Ho Chi Minh City's water utility has attempted to improve service quality and reduce water loss. Reducing the volume of unaccounted-for water increases the supply available to customers, cuts operational costs, generates more revenues, and results in greater overall efficiency for capital expenditures. These improvements in turn facilitate service expansion into new (often poor) areas and ultimately help reduce consumer charges through economies of scale. The utility now plans to expand services to the poor with support from the Global Partnership for Output-based Aid. This support entails subsidised rates for new poor-household connections once a reduction in leakages has been demonstrated. Over 150,000 people stand to benefit from nearly 30,000 new connections.

Manila, the Philippines

The Manila Water Company (MWC) has been awarded a 25-year concession to provide services to 5.3 million people in the city's eastern zone. In 1998, the utility launched a flagship programme known as *Tubig Para sa Barangay* ('water for the community') to improve access for the poor. Since then, more than a million poor people have received a regular supply of clean, safe and affordable drinking water. Here again (as in the example of Colombo, Sri Lanka, mentioned earlier, see Box 4.10) the problem of individual connections in the absence of legal land titles (not to mention an often difficult terrain) has been sidestepped through bulk water deliveries, with subsequent distribution among households through pipes and kiosks. In 2007, a grant from the Global Partnership for Output-based Aid supported individual connections for 20,000 homes (or 120,000 end-users). The Filipino government has agreed to subsidise the MWC scheme once it has provided three months' acceptable service. The subsidies will make individual water connections more affordable to households who, for the sake of project sustainability, will still meet part of the connection cost through water bills.

Sources: Viet Nam: GPOBA (2008b); Philippines: IFC Press Note 2007, GPOBA (2008a, 2008c)

BOX 4.15: **COMMUNITY MANAGEMENT OF SHARED SANITATION FACILITIES**

Shared sanitation facilities or community toilet blocks are widespread in many large South Asian cities such as Mumbai, Chennai, Dhaka or Delhi. In the past, poor maintenance would result in low use, but the situation has improved over the past few years thanks to considerable maintenance efforts. Since then, new schemes have involved communities in the design, location and management of facilities.

Over the past decade and a half, efforts have focused on improving the design and management of communal toilet blocks, which were often found to be "the most appropriate sanitation provision in slums where insecure tenure and a shortage of space make household toilets problematic" (Eales, 2008:6). These efforts have been spearheaded by alliances among community organizations (such as the National Slum Dwellers Federation and the *Mahila Milan* women's group)

in partnership with India's Society for the Promotion of Area Resource Centres (see Box 4.7), and carried out in close coordination with local authorities. As might be expected, these alliances and, more generally, civil society have focused on community-led processes; however, links with local authorities have introduced another, useful and complementary dimension, namely, a greater ability to upscale efforts as well as to make bureaucratic processes more responsive to community needs. In Mumbai and Pune, two large metropolitan areas in Western India, over 500 toilet blocks serving thousands of households have been completed and similar initiatives are afoot in nearly 10 other cities all over India. The projects rely on some public funding, but the Society for the Promotion of Area Resource Centres has also mobilised the Community-Led Infrastructure Finance Facility (CLIFF)[11] to smooth

out the construction loan process. As a result in Mumbai, Pune, Kanpur and Bangalore, US $1.5 million worth of bridge loans have benefited 260,000 households. A number of non-governmental organisations have also been involved in similar projects in Dhaka and Chittagong, with funding from UK charity WaterAid. While a number of options were provided to local populations, they have opted for community-managed toilet blocks.

On the whole, the direct benefits of community management stand out quite clearly: improved, well-adapted designs, reduced costs and improved maintenance, all of which combine to enhance sustainability. Indirect benefits are not negligible, either, as communal sanitation facilities typically work better and improve the relationships between utilities and low-income communities.

Sources: Burra et al. (2003); Satterthwaite (2006); Moulik & Sen (2006); Eales (2008)

4.5.2 Sanitation

Sustainable access to basic sanitation is one of the Millennium Development Goals (MDGs). Asian cities have made considerable progress on this score, but many are likely to miss the relevant Millennium target; similarly, Asian subregions as a whole fare better than those in sub-Saharan Africa, but have fallen behind Latin America and Northern Africa. The latest available (2008) data shows the recent status of access to sanitation in Asia (see Chart 4.14). A large share of Asia's urban population lacks access to safe sanitation at home and instead must rely on shared facilities. Open defecation, a source of health hazards and human dignity concerns, is still prevalent in cities of South Asia, Eastern Asia and South-East Asia.

In Asia, the Western subregion is the only one (see Chart 4.15), that has achieved near universal coverage, with only 6 per cent of the urban population using shared sanitation facilities. Despite high rates of urban growth, Eastern Asia has improved coverage through increases in both individual and shared facilities. However, both South and South-Eastern Asia have experienced only slow growth in improved access. South Asia fares the worst: with 24 per cent still lacking access to safe sanitation, and another 19 per cent relying on shared facilities, the subregion seems bound to fall short of the Millennium targets for sanitation in urban areas – unless, of course, public authorities make the efforts required at all levels.

For the time being, and as happens with water in some countries, lack of access to safe sanitation in Asian cities tends to be remedied through increased reliance on shared as opposed to individual household facilities. The practical consequences of this emerging trend are different from those of shared water access, though. Even where they are considered as 'safe sanitation', the inherently limited access to shared facilities may affect regular use by all household members. That is why the Millennium targets do not consider shared facilities as acceptable. Indeed, serious concern has been expressed by the Joint Monitoring Programme for Water Supply and Sanitation[12] (JMP) (UNICEF & World Health Organization, 2008) about two major aspects: actual accessibility throughout the day, and the security of users especially at night.

In most Asian countries, however, the use of shared sanitation facilities seems to be limited to less than five families per unit.[13] This suggests that with proper design and community participation in the management of such shared facilities, safe use can be ensured. While detailed information is not available, experience from South Asia suggests that where communities have been involved in the design and management of shared sanitation facilities, use and maintenance have generally been adequate. For the poor, access to sanitation is generally far worse. For example in 2006, only 47 per cent of the urban poor in India had access to safe sanitation, as compared with 95 per cent of non-poor households.[14] Similar findings are also reported from Viet Nam and Cambodia: "the poor at the bottom three wealth quintiles in Viet Nam have less than 10 per cent access to sanitation, whereas the top two wealth quintiles average 49 per cent access to sanitation, while in Cambodia less than 5 per cent of the poorest quintile had access to improved sanitation in 2004, compared to 63 per cent in the richest quintile" (Robinson, 2007:20).

In India, South Asia's largest country, a specialist non-governmental organisation known as Sulabh International remains an active promoter of shared facilities for improved access to safe sanitation. In 2006 alone, the organisation installed 1.4 million shared household toilets; it also maintains 6,500 public pay-per-use toilets, and an estimated 10 million people used its facilities across the country (UNDP, 2006).

While shared facilities may not be an ideal solution, they may be the only affordable and workable option until housing and, here again, tenure issues in dense slum settlements are resolved. When shared and individual home facilities are combined together, the proportion of urban Asians with access to safe sanitation rises from 68 to 84 per cent.[15] If shared facilities were to be counted in, even South Asia would be more likely to achieve the Millennium targets. If anything, this acts as an incentive to sort out any approaches that can result in proper shared facilities, especially in urban slums. Admittedly, tenure and space constraints may make it difficult to provide individual toilets for slum households. Slum upgrading programmes must be matched by innovative solutions, for which some initiatives are showing the way forward (see Box 4.15).

In this regard, information-sharing has an obvious, crucial role to play, but it cannot be stressed too strongly that so far, it has not been readily available. Sorely lacking is more readily available, detailed data on critical practical issues like connections to sewerage networks or the various methods in use for sewage treatment and disposal. These shortcomings make it difficult to assess the extent of services currently provided by utilities and urban authorities. Household survey-based information is available in a few countries, though.[16] What it shows is that between 1990 and 2004, only China achieved significant increases in household access to sewerage networks, which expanded from 9 per cent in 1990 to 22 per cent in 2004. In India and Pakistan, data shows that increases in the actual numbers of sewerage connections have failed to keep in pace with demographic expansion. Overall and as far as South Asia is concerned, sewer networks remain very limited in scope.

As incomes increase in cities, improved basic services become more important. Better sanitation matters as it results in significant health and economic benefits; and these, difficult as they may be to quantify, are likely far to outweigh the costs of improved sanitation.[17] This is why it is essential to design sanitation and sewerage projects carefully and combine these with innovative financing as well as a focus on information, education and communications efforts.

CHART 4.14: **STATUS OF URBAN SANITATION BY MDG SUBREGION, 2008**

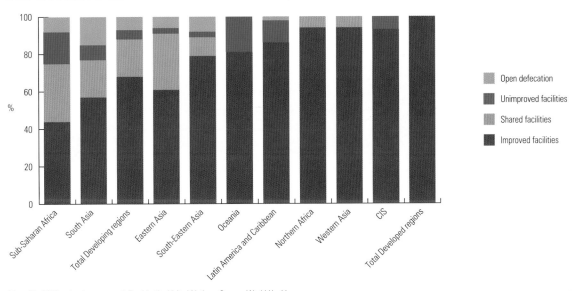

Open defecation

Unimproved facilities

Shared facilities

Improved facilities

Note: The MDG subregions are as defined by the United Nations. Source: World Health Organization & UNICEF (2010:52)

CHART 4.15: **TRENDS IN ACCESS TO URBAN SANITATION BY MDG SUBREGION IN ASIA**

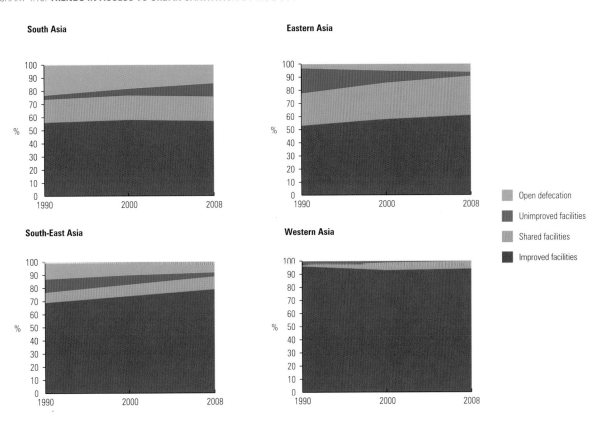

Source: World Health Organization & UNICEF (2010:38-51)

▲
Funafuti, Tuvalu. Solid Waste Management is of growing concern in this atoll nation. ©**Sarah Mecartney**

4.5.3 Solid waste management

Generally speaking and because of different consumption and conditioning/packaging patterns, the urban poor in Asia generate less waste (including solid) than their counterparts in higher income countries. Besides consuming fewer non-food items, they tend to collect, re-use, recover and recycle materials, since 20 to 30 per cent of their waste is recyclable. Municipal refuse collection and disposal systems tend to neglect the poor, a phenomenon for which Laquian (2004) gives the following reasons:

> "First, many urban poor families live in congested slum and squatter areas that are not readily accessible to garbage trucks. Second, it is very hard to organize residents of urban poor communities to collect their garbage, sort it into biodegradable or non-biodegradable categories, and take it to containers located outside their communities where the municipal garbage collectors can pick it up. Third, private business or informal sector garbage recyclers do not find it profitable to sort through the garbage of the urban poor because there is very little of any value they can recover from it. Fourth, the garbage of the urban poor tends to be wet, smelly, and subject to putrefaction such that contractors find it onerous or even hazardous to collect it. As the non-organic part of the waste has already been collected, most of their waste is organic and decomposes rapidly when it is not collected daily. Finally, the urban poor are often reluctant or unable to pay for the garbage collection services. Because of these factors, the garbage

of the urban poor is often uncollected and just dumped in vacant lots, street corners, streams, canals and rivers" (Laquian, 2004:21).

The urban poor play an important role in solid waste management as they routinely sort, recover, re-use and recycle refuse. In many Asian-Pacific cities, large numbers of itinerant, economically poor families with their ubiquitous push carts make a living out of recovering useful items (paper, plastic, aluminium cans, bottles, metals, etc.) from refuse bins. Some rag-picking families reside near urban refuse dumps and recover recyclable items. Some grassroots and civil society groups in Asian cities have launched refuse recovery and recycling programmes that have proved to be beneficial to urban poor families. In Metropolitan Manila, for example, the *Linis Ganda* ('clean and beautiful') project, a privately launched resource recovery and recycling programme, has set up a network of 17 cooperatives and 572 junkshops. In 1999, the project recovered and sold about 95,000 tons of solid waste, providing gainful livelihoods to 1,000 'eco-aides' and their families (Bennagen *et al.*, 2002).

Research has shown that informal sector participation in solid waste collection and disposal saves urban authorities significant amounts of money. About 12 to 15 per cent of the solid waste collected by waste pickers has saved Delhi the equivalent of four to five million US dollars a year (at 2010 exchange rates). In Hanoi, where waste pickers collect and sell 18 to 22 per cent of solid waste, the estimated savings to the city range from US $2.5 to US $3.1 million a year (Maclaren *et al.*, 2007).

A practicable approach to solid waste collection and disposal is the Waste Concern Model introduced by a non-governmental organisation in Dhaka, Bangladesh. The model promotes recycling, treats all urban waste as a resource, involves active, income-generating participation of waste pickers, improves collection services, and reduces transportation costs. In two projects launched under the auspices of the UN Economic and Social Commission for Asia and the Pacific (ESCAP) and other partners, the model was introduced in Matale, a town of 40,000 in Sri Lanka, and Quy Nhon, a city of 200,000 in Viet Nam. In both sites, waste pickers have been properly organised and provided them with pushcarts. Solid waste is brought to a central location to be sorted into useful recoverable materials that are sold to dealers. Organic materials suitable for composting are separated and the remaining waste disposed of in a landfill. In Quy Nhon, the system can treat two to three tons of waste per day. With proper financing, training of more waste pickers, and proper management, an up-scaled version of the model could be designed for larger urban areas (ESCAP, 2007b).

4.5.4 Health

The urban poor who live in deprived urban settings, informal settlements or slums together make up the single largest group of vulnerable populations in Asian cities today. Poor quality of shelter, where any at all, poses a major threat to health in urban slums, i.e., to more than half a billion people in the region. Compelling evidence links various communicable and non-communicable diseases, injuries and psychosocial disorders to the risk factors inherent to unhealthy living conditions, such as faulty buildings, defective water supplies, substandard sanitation, poor fuel quality and ventilation, lack of refuse storage and collection, or improper food and storage preparation, as well as poor/unsafe locations, such as near traffic hubs, dumpsites or polluting industrial sites (Mercado *et al.*, 2007; UN-HABITAT, 2010).

The result is that in Ahmedabad, for instance, infant mortality rates are twice as high in slums as the national rural average. Slum children under five suffer more and die more from diarrhoea or acute respiratory infections than those in rural areas. On average, slum children in Ahmedabad are more undernourished than the average in the whole of Gujarat state. In Metropolitan Manila, the overall picture of child health in the squatter settlements looks alarming, although no research seems to have addressed the issue directly. Infant mortality rates in Manila's slums are triple those in non-slum areas. There is also evidence among slum children of a high incidence of tuberculosis, diarrheal disease, parasitic infections, dengue and severe malnutrition (Fry *et al.*, 2002).

As Islam *et al.* (2006) have found in Manila, the Philippines and Indore, India, urban health services are well aware of the effects of monetization on the health-seeking behaviour of the poor. In particular, they realize that the poor are likely to abandon courses of prescribed medication, or buy less than prescribed, to save on the costs. Health professionals are not surprised when the poor fail to return as requested for follow-ups or progress assessments (Montgomery, 2008). A slightly more paradoxical finding is that since, for the poor, waste of time means earnings shortfalls, some will rather go to a costly private clinic for immediate attention and assistance, rather than to a free public health service where they may have to wait for hours or even days.

Ill health is a factor behind both poverty and unemployment, but this negative linkage can be reversed, as demonstrated in the Philippines. The authorities in Marikina City have launched an innovative volunteer programme that targets health and unemployment issues simultaneously. The scheme recruits local (mainly poor) volunteers and gives them

TABLE 4.10: **TRANSPORTATION IN ASIAN CITIES – MODAL BREAKDOWN**

City	Walking	Cycles	Public Transport	Two-Wheelers	Car	Para-transit	
						Motorized 3-Wheel Taxi	Cycle Rickshaw
Delhi	14	24	33	13	11	1	..
Mumbai	..	..	88	..	7	5 (taxi)	..
Ahmedabad	40	14	16	24	0	5	0
Beijing	14	54	24	3	5	..	..
Shanghai	31	33	25	6	5	..	..
Manila	..	..	29	..	30	41	..
Jakarta	13	..	..	..	..	..	12
Dhaka	62	1	10	4	4	6	13
Bangkok	16	8	30	..	46	..	..

Source: Tiwari (n.d.)

training in primary health care and preventive medicine. The volunteers then work four hours a day for a daily 100 pesos (two US dollars) and a period of three to six months. They do as much as needs to be done, from clerical to health-related work, and this includes teaching families the ways and virtues of basic hygiene. After the volunteers' stints are over, their details and qualifications are added to an employment roster where both private and public entities can look to match their staffing needs with the volunteers' proven individual skills. The scheme has had an immediate impact on the city's health systems and, as had been hoped, the employment opportunities created came as an additional benefit (Mercado *et al.*, 2007).

4.5.5 Energy

Access to modern and sustainable energy resources is critical for the poor if they are to take their fair share of local prosperity and improve living standards. The International Energy Agency estimates that 1.6 billion people across the world still have no access to electricity, including one billion in Asia-Pacific countries. The disparities in access to power grids are wide across the region – from 20 per cent of the population in Cambodia to 56 per cent in India and 99 per cent in China. Faced with this situation, developing countries over the past few decades have launched a wide range of technological schemes and energy sector reforms, ranging from ambitious government-run programmes to small-scale community-led schemes involving the private sector and financial institutions (Asian Development Bank, 2008d).

A variety of reasons – irregular tenure, shared spaces, ill-defined responsibilities for payment, and low consumption – can account for the deficiencies of energy utilities with regard to poor urban communities. These also tend to pay high prices both for relatively poor kerosene-based lighting and for low-quality biomass cooking fuels. Slum-dwellers are frequently ignored or by-passed in favour of rural populations, regardless of their non-negligible contribution to their city's economic expansion (Modi *et al.*, 2006).

As demonstrated in Ahmedabad, power utilities can overcome the issues of affordability and tenure which so far have made it difficult for them to reach out to the urban poor (see Box 4.16). One lesson from the power sector is that regulation of service providers (local utilities or authorities) should focus on servicing all residents and start viewing the urban poor as potential clients.

4.5.6 Urban transport

The poor need easy, affordable access to their places of low-paid work or employment. Since they cannot afford land or housing close to workplaces, they need affordable public transport from home to work. Now, Asia's admittedly overstrained urban transportation systems have not fully integrated the specific needs of the poor, who as a result find it more difficult to participate in the urban economy. Since many of them cannot even afford public transport, they turn to non-motorized modes such as bicycles or walking. In addition, the poor are disproportionately exposed to 'transport externalities': these refer to the risks entailed by inadequate pavements (where any), poor road surfacing or lack of bicycle lanes on trunk roads as well as dangerous crossroads and slack enforcement, for instance. The factors that are specific to public transport in Asian cities include very low user capacity to pay, short commutes and high proportions of pedestrians and non-motorized modes, which reflect specifically urban features such as mixed land use and high population densities (Asian Development Bank, 2006).

In developing countries, the urban poor typically tend to make fewer trips (because most are not regularly employed), but tend to spend more time and a greater share of disposable incomes on transportation. For the working poor, commuting to work and back can cost relatively large amounts of time and money. Those who cannot afford motorized vehicles and face road conditions that make walking or bicycling unsafe spend significant shares of household incomes on bus or minibus fares. The poor do not directly benefit from capital expenditure on urban roads since most are designed for car owners; at the same time, the poor are over-represented among the victims of the frequent adverse effects of such investments in roads (Hook, 2006; WHO, 2009).

Table 4.10 shows that the higher the number of poor residents in a city, the greater the proportion of trips that involve walking, non-motorized vehicles and para-transit modes[18], with Dhaka and Delhi standing out. Para-transit vehicles such as three-wheelers in Delhi and Kolkata and *jeepneys*[19] in Metropolitan Manila are the main transport modes of the urban poor. Interestingly, the proportion of trips in private automobiles is relatively high in cities like Bangkok, Jakarta and Metro Manila, although local incomes are not as high as in Tokyo or Seoul. But then considerable status and prestige are attached to people who drive cars, and gasoline comes relatively cheap in the Filipino, Indonesian and Thai capitals – a phenomenon that may be traced to various policies that favour elites rather than the urban poor, like taxation, import duties, licensing and user-charges for cars.

Non-motorised transport

Walking and non-motorized vehicles have traditionally served as the main modes of transport in Asia. However, both are becoming more difficult and less socially acceptable in many cities. In China and Viet Nam, bicycle lanes built in the 1960s and 1970s are now often taken over by cars or systematically removed. In most Asian cities, walking involves threading one's way along narrow, uneven pavements (where any) past street vendors, urban furniture and parked cars in a noisy, polluted environment where it is difficult to make progress at a steady pace.

Asia's emerging economies currently feature low rates of individual motor ownership. Motorized or not, vehicles are important assets which families use to lift themselves out of poverty. Ownership of a bicycle can do more than reduce daily commuting bus fares and times: it can make it easier to run a small informal business and to by-pass middlemen. In most Asian cities, bicycles are within reach of many poor households and have been widely used for decades. Unlike in most African and Latin American cities, bicycles and the maintenance thereof, are affordable even to those for whom public transport is too expensive. Some bicycle and motorbike owners have become bicycle taxi operators, like *ojeks* in Indonesia. In Bangladesh, India and Indonesia, a cycle rickshaw or *pedicab* is often the first work opportunity fresh migrants can find in urban areas, and owning the vehicle is itself an important first step out of poverty (see Box 4.17) (Hook, 2006). For all these benefits, though, the upfront cost, lack of credit facilities, and fear of theft are significant barriers to bicycle ownership by the very poor, leaving them little alternative other than walking.

Proper walking and cycling facilities enable people to make short trips safely, basically for free. Short of such facilities, the urban poor are forced to resort to more expensive motorized modes, driving up the costs of living for them and of labour

▲
Delhi, India. School-going children often use cycle-rickshaws in South Asian cities. ©**Jakub Cejpek/Shutterstock**

BOX 4.17: CYCLE RICKSHAWS: A POLICY BLIND SPOT

The cycle rickshaw is a sustainable urban transport for short-distance trips (1-5 km). It can also complement and integrate very effectively as a low-cost feeder service to public transport systems, providing point-to-point service (i.e., from home to a bus stop). According to estimates, over seven million passenger/goods cycle rickshaws are in operation in various Indian cities (including some 600,000 in India's National Capital Region) where they hold substantial 'modal share' (i.e., the number of trips or percentage of travellers using a particular type of transport). The cycle rickshaw meets the mobility requirements of low- and middle-income urban dwellers as well as tourists. It is also routinely used to carry household goods as well as business and construction materials. Still, for all its popularity and benefits, this non-polluting type of transport is largely ignored by policymakers and transport planners. Recently in Delhi, a ban on cycle rickshaws resulted in additional traffic problems as people turned to 'auto' (i.e., motorized) rickshaws instead. The ban met with public outcry and opposition from many civil society groups. In a landmark decision in February 2010, the Delhi High Court ruled that the Municipal Corporation's ban on cycle rickshaws was unconstitutional.

Source: Sinha (2008); Delhi High Court (2010)

BOX 4.18: CHINA PROMOTES ELECTRIC BIKES AND SCOOTERS

Electric bikes in China include two-wheel bicycles propelled by pedals and supplemented by electrical power from a storage battery, as well as low-speed electric scooters (with perfunctory pedals to meet legal specifications). These two-wheelers have become popular with the Chinese, providing an inexpensive, effortless alternative to public transport or conventional two-wheelers. Low energy consumption and zero tail-pipe emissions are ideal features for China's congested urban areas, and this is why the national government and many local authorities are promoting electric two-wheelers.

As a result, e-bikes are gaining an increasing share of two-wheeled transportation across the country, and in some cities like Chengdu and Suzhou they have even surpassed conventional bicycles. In fact, the electric bike market has expanded more rapidly than any other mode in China, with production soaring from nearly 40,000 in 1998 to over 10 million in 2005.

Three major reasons have contributed to the expanding market share of e-bikes in China: (i) technical progress (improvements in battery and motor technology), (ii) economic factors, namely, a concomitance of rising incomes, the declining costs attached to mass production, and the rising costs of gasoline, and (iii) policy factors, such as the Road Transportation and Safety Law which classifies e-bikes as non-motorized vehicles.

Source: Weinert et al. (2007)

for employers. Research in Surabaya, Indonesia, showed that as far as trips under three kilometres were concerned (i.e., roughly half of total trips in the city), over 60 per cent were made by motorized vehicles, even among low-income groups. This is due to the fact that 60 per cent of Indonesia's paved roads have no proper, if any, sidewalks and none have cycle paths. If poor Indonesians were able to make the same numbers of short trips using non-motorized vehicles, they would save roughly US $0.30 per day, which to them represents about 20 per cent of total average daily income (Hook, 2006).

Small individual vehicles

Most vehicle fleets in Asian cities comprise large shares of two-wheelers, and as a result the fuel consumption per mile travelled remains relatively low. In China, for instance, the total number of personal vehicles for every 1,000 people remains a modest 45 (of which fewer than 10 are four-wheelers), compared with 530 per 1,000 in Japan (of which 430 are four-wheelers). However, the sheer size of emerging economic giants like China and India would suggest that in a relatively short time, their respective vehicle fleets will become comparable in absolute numbers to that of the United States (Asian Development Bank, 2007b).

About 75 per cent of all two-wheelers in the world are found in Asia, with China and India accounting for 50 and 20 per cent respectively. In India, motorized two-wheelers are cheap and, as incomes rise, a much larger proportion of the population can afford them, which drives the motorization process. Delhi (income per head: US $800) has 120 two-wheelers per 1,000 people, compared with Shanghai's 60 (income per head: US $4,000). A more recent phenomenon in China is the mounting popularity of electric bicycles ('e-bikes') (see Box 4.18).

Public transport systems

Although most Asian cities need public transport more badly than their American or European counterparts, they fare much more poorly when it comes to delivery. Tokyo and Hong Kong, China, can certainly boast excellent public transport with adequate capacities. In contrast, many other cities like Jakarta, Manila and Delhi have fared poorly in terms of capacities relative to European counterparts, although (just like Tokyo and Hong Kong, China) they are much more dependent on public transport. Among other Asian cities, Kuala Lumpur and Bangkok depend heavily on private transport for lack of adequate public networks.

In Asia, a combination of increased incomes and fast urban growth has led to rapid growth in individual motorization in most cities, causing a decline in the relative share of public transport. To the exception of a few prominent instances, most cities in emerging Asia only offer rather low-quality public transport: the systems are not yet adequately developed and capital expenditure has been limited. Bus and para-transit services predominate and are often exclusively operated by the

The Mass Rapid Transit system (MRT) in Taipei, Taiwan, Province of China. ©**Machkazu/Shutterstock**

private sector (as in Colombo, Dhaka and Kathmandu). Poor regulation (where any) of private buses, particularly with regard to routes and schedules, spawns excessive competition; the negative repercussions on financial performance and quality of service negate the very benefits that could be expected from public spending on road construction. Moreover, security and safety issues remain significant – not to mention the high levels of polluting emissions (Asian Development Bank, 2006; Lohani, 2007).

As far as the lower-income segments of Asia's urban populations are concerned, the situation can be summarised as follows: the urban poor cannot afford the transport modes favoured by urban authorities (road-based systems for cars and other vehicles, as well as underground and other rail-based rapid transit systems but those they use instead (walking, bicycles, para-transit systems) are often ignored, or not favoured, by urban authorities or transport planners. Lack of attention to safe pavements, an absence of well-marked and controlled pedestrian lanes, and the location of homes far from work places, all combine to work against the poor (Peñalosa, 2010).

Urban economic growth is contingent upon adequate transport infrastructures. Many Asian cities have invested in underground rail and bus rapid transit systems (BRT), expressways, grade-separated intersections as well as elaborate traffic control mechanisms. These policies have resulted in faster movement of people in cities and have certainly helped the real estate sector. However, in urban transport, "supply creates its own demand" and wider roads and expressways have resulted in nothing but more traffic, in the process shifting congestion to intersections, flyovers, smaller streets and by-lanes. Use of transport facilities is also linked to poverty and inequality in cities. Automobile-based urban transit does not help the poor (Peñalosa, 2010) since roads

are inaccessible and unsafe to pedestrians and non-motorized modes of transport. As for the expensive mass transit systems now introduced in some Asian cities, including underground railways, they remain unaffordable for the poor.

The urban poor are the main victims of transport modes

The urban poor tend to suffer a disproportionate share of the negative consequences ("external costs") of transport modes, including (i) air, water, soil and noise pollution, (ii) traffic accidents and fatalities, (iii) delays caused by traffic jams, (iv) the higher costs of goods and services due to transport difficulties, and (v) high transit fares. In the case of air pollution, for example, the poor, i.e., the bulk of the urban population, often suffer the highest degrees of exposure, since they (including infants, the elderly and the handicapped) often reside and work by the roadside where air pollution is typically higher than farther away. The poor are all the more vulnerable due to the lack of adequate nutrition and health care. As private motor vehicles increase in numbers, they crowd out non-motorized transport and reduce the variety of public transport available to the poor.

In Asian cities, accident rates show that the poor tend to be disproportionately affected (WHO, 2010). In the case of road accidents, the majority of the fatalities are pedestrians and cyclists. In Delhi, car and taxi passengers accounted for only 2 per cent of road accident fatalities in the year 2000, but the proportions for pedestrians, cyclists and motorized two-wheel vehicle users were 42, 14 and 27 per cent respectively (Badami *et al.*, 2004). It is ironical that the poor are the main victims of the travel modes they least use. Moreover, road accidents can be particularly devastating for the poor – apart from the physical and emotional effects, the economic costs of accidents can bring ruin to whole families.

4.6
Diagnosis and future challenges

Shenzhen, China. ©**Mark Henley/Panos Pictures**

The unprecedented pace of economic growth in the Asia-Pacific has led to rapid urbanization. This has posed serious challenges to local authorities and national governments in the face of ever-increasing demand for secure tenure, proper housing and services in urban areas. There is no doubting that economic growth in Asia and the Pacific has pulled millions out of extreme poverty; still, the numbers of those in moderate poverty remain high. The simple truth is that in Asia, and as UN-HABITAT has been warning for years, rapid urbanization has gone hand in hand with the urbanization of poverty. In this as in other developing regions, UN-HABITAT's major concern is that urban economic growth has not benefited all residents equally, with the poor left to bear most of the drawbacks and shortcomings in terms of tenure, shelter, jobs, health, education and the environment. In other words, the distribution of the benefits of urban economic growth in Asia does not match demographic expansion. In this sense, Asia epitomizes the "urban divide" recently highlighted by UN-HABITAT (2010) and the attendant four, inter-related dimensions of exclusion – economic, social, political and cultural.

In the cities of Asia-Pacific and elsewhere in the developing world, slums are the cruellest form of poverty and exclusion. Improving the conditions of 505.5 million slum-dwellers is a major challenge for Asian cities.

A prevalent view is that governments lack the resources required to provide proper housing to all slum-dwellers, and therefore they should play an enabling role, encouraging the private sector to "down-market" housing production and cater to the poor. However, in many poor developing countries, market mechanisms in the housing sector are in no position to solve the problem. More and more poor people dreaming of better living conditions in urban areas become the victims of market forces because of their inability to generate effective demand in housing markets. Market-orientated policies have failed to solve the housing problems for the poor. Instead they have led to a situation where the housing needs of the majority of Asia's urban populations are not catered for either by the market or by government (UN-HABITAT, 2008b).

An author like Arnott (2008) argues that in developing countries, the large size of the informal sector relative to the economy combines with the high proportions of informal housing to stymie the types of demand-side intervention that have been the mainstay of housing policies in more developed countries. Since governments are reluctant to subsidize unauthorized housing, their housing programmes (except for public housing and slum upgrading projects) are biased towards formal (authorized) housing and, therefore, against the neediest households. Furthermore, the inability to measure household incomes with proper accuracy precludes broad housing assistance programmes that are geared to income.

The lessons from Asian cities suggest that small-scale programmes are more conducive to participation by the poor in design and implementation, thereby increasing ownership and enhancing sustainability. Public housing is the solution tried out by many governments. This is apposite when public authorities have enough resources and political commitment. For low-income countries in Asia, the public option, by itself, is inadequate as the resources required for the huge demand are not available. Greater success is achieved in those Asian cities where the urban poor have deployed their own housing and slum upgrading initiatives. These people-led initiatives are small in scale, but often prove to be the more effective when it comes to improving the living conditions of the poor. Indeed, the specific lesson from any programmes designed and implemented at national level is that as far as slum upgrading and low-cost housing are concerned, "one size does *not* fit all". Any projects must be adjusted to local conditions and requirements. Another lesson is that local stakeholder participation in planning, design and implementation of housing programmes has worked well in Asian-Pacific cities (ESCAP, 2005; UN-HABITAT, 2007b).

While falling well short of needs, Asian cities have shown their commitment to improved living conditions for the poor. The 2008 economic recession and subsequent contraction in real estate markets offers opportunities for radical policy reform in the urban housing sector. Such policy reforms should be based on the lessons from those few Asian countries that have managed to make their cities slum-free. On top of UN-HABITAT's more general recommendations (2010), some of these lessons highlight the need for: (i) a leading role for government through proper institutional strengthening at all levels; (ii) empowering the poor through secure tenure; and (iii) developing housing finance mechanisms that cater to the poor, and through which housing savings can be mobilised and subsidies can be targeted. Linking housing loans to savings, providing targeted incentives to households and developers, encouraging both rental housing and home ownership, and investing in all types of environmental infrastructure, could be the basic features of an ambitious revival strategy, modelled on the success of Western Europe in the 1950s and 1960s and, more recently, China (Biau, 2009).

As regards access to basic urban services, Asian cities have fared fairly well on drinking-water. However, on sanitation, performance is poor. A large segment of urban residents depend on shared facilities or simply have no access to any sanitation. The situation is particularly bad for South Asia's urban poor. This subregion is unlikely to meet the Millennium targets for water and sanitation in urban areas unless specific programmes are deployed soon.

On top of water and sanitation, Asia's urban poor face multiple barriers to health and education, the major one being inability to pay for services. This includes not just nominal costs, but also the time lost in gaining access and the income foregone in the process. Some among the urban poor face legal barriers to basic urban services for lack of birth certificates, household registration or residence permits – not to mention, of course, security of tenure. People who live and work in the informal sector are often excluded from all sorts of entitlements, including access.

The ability of the poor to participate in income- and employment-generating activities is contingent upon access to basic services, such as education, health and clean living environments. Lack of such services severely constrains access to education and jobs (especially for young females – UN-HABITAT, 2010) but also for those in gainful employment. Since national governments, local authorities, public or private service providers and civil society organizations share responsibility for the delivery of basic urban services to all, they must negotiate and formalize partnerships among them, taking into account their respective responsibilities and interests. Such partnerships should be encouraged and facilitated through appropriate legal and regulatory frameworks, including clear, results-orientated contracts and monitoring mechanisms (UN-HABITAT Governing Council, 2009).

Asian cities have begun to realise the importance of mass transit and are now making it a policy focus instead of improving vehicle flows. Several cities have deployed bus, skytrain and underground networks to cater to the needs of a larger public, but a good many of those on low incomes cannot even afford public transport. This points out to an urgent need to promote sustainable transport schemes based on affordable, environmentally-friendly, motorized and non-motorized transport.

Reduction of poverty and inequality in cities – the 'urban divide' – is a major challenge in the Asia-Pacific region. Only a few countries have so far been able to promote a develop-ment path that has tackled urban poverty in any effective way. This is no easy task for Asian cities as poverty comes on top of new, major challenges like immigration, ageing, climate change, housing and basic services at a time when the world-wide economic crisis is not over. Asian cities are expected to rebound from the 2008 global credit crunch just as they did from the regional 1997-98 financial crisis, again growing at a much faster pace than those in other regions. The key to revival will be to ensure that this urban economic growth is sustainable, and therefore inclusive. The crisis is an opportu-nity to correct the structural imbalance in urban economies, and to reduce urban poverty and deprivation.

ENDNOTES

1   By adjusting Purchasing Power Parity to 2005 values, the international poverty line is estimated at US $1.25, resulting in an increase of nearly 400 million poor globally (Chen and Ravallion, 2008).

2   As urban rural breakup of poverty for the revised poverty line of $ 1.25 is not available, the analysis of urban poverty is based on 'dollar a day' benchmark.

3   The poverty gap ratio is defined under MDG Target 2 as the mean distance separating the population from the poverty line (with the non-poor being given a distance of zero), expressed as a percentage of the poverty line. It measures the depth of poverty. ESCAP (2008b), Statistical Yearbook for Asia and the Pacific 2008, section 17, Poverty and inequality.

4   In its recent study on implications of the new US $1.25 international poverty benchmark, the Asian Development Bank states, "(this) does not properly reflect the living situations of the majority of Asian's poor. In addition to using the US $2.00 poverty line, the Bank may come up with a set of key indicators for social and environmental poverty that secure a decent living for all. If it were to include such indicators in its reporting system, the Bank would go beyond the narrow, food-focused definition of income poverty (equivalent to 2,000–2400 kcal per person per day – plus basic expenditures for housing and clothing) (Bauer et. al., 2008).

5   The UN-HABITAT estimates given in Table 4.6 are different from national estimates of slums in many Asian countries. For example, the slum population of India was estimated to be 62 million in the year 2001 during its population census, whereas UN-HABITAT estimated that there were 120 million slum-dwellers in India in the year 2000.

6   Chronic lack of reliable data or up-to-date information on the Pacific Islands makes it difficult to assess slum prevalence in this least populated and most remote subregion (UN-HABITAT, 2003b).

7   Data availability for slum populations runs into various problems. Even in UN publications, figures in the main text do not necessary match those in statistical tables.

For this analysis, figures have been taken from the statistical annexes of the mentioned sources.

8   As definitions of "access" can vary widely within and among countries and regions, and as the WHO/UNICEF Joint Monitoring Programme for Water Supply and Sanitation is mandated to report at global level and across time, it has created a set of categories for "improved" and "unimproved" facilities that are used to analyze the national data on which its trends and estimates are based. An improved drinking-water source is defined as one that, by nature of its construction or through active intervention, is protected from outside contamination, in particular from contamination with faecal matter. To make estimates comparable across countries, the Programme uses the following classification to differentiate between "improved" and "unimproved" drinking-water sources: (i) Improved drinking water sources include (a) "piped water into dwelling, plot or yard", which include piped household water connection located inside the user's dwelling, plot or yard, (b) "Other improved", which includes public taps or standpipes, tube wells or boreholes, protected dug wells, protected springs or rainwater collection; (ii) Unimproved drinking water sources include unprotected dug well, unprotected spring, cart with small tank/drum, surface water (river, dam, lake, pond, stream, canal, irrigation channels), and bottled water (World Health Organization and UNICEF, 2010:13).

9   A water point involves a hand pump head on top of an under/overground reservoir connected to the mains, with a platform above or around for water collection, washing and bathing. With a water stand post, a tap or hand pump is directly connected to the mains. Both techniques are applicable in urban areas with centrally managed water supply systems, like Dhaka, Chittagong and Khulna in Bangladesh.

10 This may be even more pronounced as a recent countrywide Health Survey in India suggested that 95 per cent had access to basic services, as compared with the 96 per cent projection from the Joint Monitoring Programme. The 2005-06 National Family Health Survey (NFHS) provided country and state-wide estimates for urban areas.

11 The Community-Led Infrastructure Finance Facility (CLIFF) provides venture capital and other financial support directly to urban poor groups, rather than to government, to support community-led slum upgrading schemes designed in partnership with city authorities.

12 The Joint Monitoring Programme (JMP) is the official United Nations mechanism monitoring progress towards the Millennium Development Goal (MDG) relating to drinking-water and sanitation (MDG 7, Target 7c: "Halve, by 2015, the proportion of people without sustainable access to safe drinking-water and basic sanitation").

13 As reported in Joint Monitoring Programme 2008 (UNICEF & World Health Organization, 2008) based on Multiple Indicators Cluster Surveys (MICS) in several countries.

14 Based on analysis from the 2006 National Family and Health Survey (NFHS) as reported in Urban Health Resource Centre (2008).

15 The definition used by the Joint Monitoring Programme currently excludes shared sanitation facilities as 'safe sanitation' for the purposes of MDG targets.

16 The information displayed on Joint Monitoring Programme 2004 Website pages provides details of household sewerage connections for 1990 and 2004 in several countries. However, this information is not available in more recent Joint Monitoring Programme reports.

17 See for example Water and Sanitation Programme (2008)

18 Paratransit (also known as 'dial-a-ride') is an alternative mode of flexible passenger transportation that does not follow fixed routes or schedules. It includes mini-buses, shared taxis, cabs, vans, rickshaws, tongas, etc.

19 Jeepneys are the most popular public transport in the Philippines and were originally made from US military jeeps left over from World War II.

ACHR. "Cambodia." *Asian Coalition for Human Rights.* December 2005. http://www.achr.net/supf_update. htm (accessed 8 January 2009)

Advanced Engineering Associates International. *Innovative Approaches to Slum Electrification.* Washington DC: Bureau for Economic Growth, USAID, 2004

Ahmed, Rokeya. DSK: *A Model for securing access to water for the urban poor.* Kyoto: Water poverty dialogue initiative, World Water Forum, 2003

Alston, R., J. Kearl & M. Vaughan. "Is there a consensus among economists in the 1990s?" *American Economic Review* 82 May 1992:203-209

Apte, Prakash M. "Dharavi: India's Model Slum" www.planetizen.com/ node/35269 (accessed 6 June 2010)

Arnott, Richard. "Housing Policy in Developing Countries: The Importance of the Informal Economy." In *Working Paper No 13,* by Commission on Growth and Development. Washington DC: World Bank, 2008

ASCI (Administrative Staff College of India) - Centre for Good Governance. *JNNURM Rapid Training Programme-Governance and Reforms.* Hyderabad: Administrative Staff College of India, 2006

Asian Development Bank. "Special chapter: Comparing Poverty across countries: The role of Purchasing Power Parities." In *Key Indicators 2008.* Manila: Asian Development Bank, 2008a

—. "Pakistan - Poverty Assessment Update." December 2008b http://www.adb.org/Documents/ Assessments/Gender/PAK/Poverty-Assessment-Update.pdf (accessed 16 June 2009)

—. *Managing Asian cities.* Manila: Asian Development Bank, 2008c

—. *Energy for all Initiative-ADB Technical Assistance Report.* Manila: Asian Development Bank, 2008d

—. "Special chapter: Inequality." In *Key Indicators 2007.* Manila: Asian Development Bank, 2007a

—. *Energy efficiency and climate change: considerations for on-road transport in Asia.* Manila: ADB and DFID, 2007b

—. ADB *Technical Assistance Report-Sustainable Urban Transport.* Manila: Asian Development Bank, 2006

—. "Special Chapter: Poverty in Asia: Measurements, Estimates and Prospects." In *Key Indicators 2004.* Manila: Asian Development Bank, 2004a

—. Urban Indicators for Managing Cities: Cities Data Book. Manila: Asian Development Bank, 2001

Badami, Madhav.G., Geetam Tiwari, & Dinesh Mohan. "Access and Mobility for the Urban Poor in India: Bridging the gap between policy and needs." *Paper presented at the Forum on Urban Infrastructure and Public Service Delivery for the Urban Poor.* New Delhi: Organized by the Woodrow Wilson International Centre for Scholars, Washington DC and the National Institute of Urban Affairs, New Delhi, June 24-25 2004

Bauer, Armin, Rana Hasan, Rhoda Magsombol, & Guanghua Wan. "The World Bank's New Poverty Data: Implications for the Asian Development Bank." In *ADB Sustainable Development Working Paper Series-No 2,* by Asian Development Bank. Manila: Asian Development Bank, 2008

Bennagen, Ma. Eugenia C, Georgina Nepomuceno, & Ramil Covar. "Solid Waste Segregation and Recycling in Metro Manila: Household Attitudes and Behaviour." Quezon City: Resources, Environment and Economics Center for Studies, Inc. (REECS), 2002

Bestani, Robert, & Johanna Klein. *Housing Finance in Asia.* Mania: Asian Development Bank, 2005

Biau, Daniel. "Where will the money come from now?" *Urban World,* Vol 1-No 2: March 2009 36-39

Bourguignon, François. *The Poverty-Growth-Inequality Triangle.* New Delhi: Indian Council for Research on International Economic Relations, 2004

Burra, S., S. Patel, & T. Kerr. "Community-designed, built and managed toilet blocks in Indian cities." *Environment and Urbanization,* February 15, 2003 11-32

Chen, Shaohua, & Martin Ravallion. "The Developing World Is Poorer Than We Thought, But No Less Successful in the Fight against Poverty." *Policy Research Working Paper No. 4703,* Washington DC: World Bank, 2008

Choe, K. & Laquian, A. *City Cluster Development: Toward and urban led development strategy for Asia.* Manila: Asian Development Bank, 2008

Centre on Housing Rights and Evictions (COHRE), "What are Housing Rights", definition given on the web page http://www.cohre. org/view_page.php?page_id=2 (accessed on 15 July 2010)

Cornia, Giovanni Andrea & Julius Court, "Inequality, Growth and Poverty in the Era of Liberalization and Globalization," *UNU/WIDER Policy Brief No. 4.* Helsinki: UNU/WIDER, 2001. http:// www.wider.unu.edu/publications/ policy-briefs/en_GB/pb4/ files/78807311723331954/default/ pb4.pdf (accessed 15 July 2010)

Crosby, David. *Understanding Asian Cities* - Phnom Penh, Cambodia. Bangkok: Asian Coalition for Housing Rights, 2004

Cruz, Prince Christian. *Housing Sales and Rental Markets in Asia.* January 3, 2007. http:// www.globalpropertyguide.com/ investment-analysis/Housing-Sales-and-Rental-Markets-in-Asia (accessed 17 October 2008)

Dahiya, Bharat & Enkhtsetseg Shagdarsuren. *Mongolia: Improving Lives, Upgrading Ger Areas.* Mongolia Project Note No. 1. Fukuoka: UN-HABITAT Regional Office for Asia and the Pacific. 2007

De Soto, Hernando. *The Mystery of Capital. Why Capitalism Triumphs in the West and Fails Everywhere Else.* New York: Basic Books, 2001

Delhi High Court 2010; available at http://delhicourts.nic.in/Feb10/ Manushi%20Sangthan%20Vs..pdf

Dong, Suocheng, Xue Li, & Xiaojun Zhang. *Policy Responses to Slum Improvement in China.* Beijing: Institute of Geographical Sciences and Natural Resources Research, 2009

Eales, K. "Partnerships for sanitation of the urban poor: Is it time to shift paradigm?" *Sanitation for the Urban Poor: Partnerships and Governance.* IRC Symposium, 2008

ESCAP. *Statistical Yearbook for Asia and the Pacific 2009.* Bangkok: ESCAP, United Nations, 2010

—. *Economic and Social Survey of Asia* and the Pacific 2008: Sustaining Growth and Sharing Prosperity, ST/ESCAP/2476. New York: United Nations, 2008a

—. *Statistical Yearbook for Asia and the Pacific 2008.* Bangkok: United Nations, 2008b

—. *Facing the challenges of urbanization and urban poverty in Asia and the Pacific* - A note by the Secretariat. Bangkok: ESCAP, 2007a

—. "An Innovative Approach to Municipal Solid Waste Management in Least Developed and Low-income Developing Countries." *Regional Seminar and Study Visit on Community-based Solid Waste Management.* Quy Nhon City, December 15-16 2007b

—. "Improving the lives of the urban poor - Case studies on the provision of basic services through partnerships." United Nations, 2005 http://www.unescap.org/pdd/prs/ ProjectActivities/Ongoing/Best%20 practice/Improving%20ubp%20lives. pdf (accessed 9 July 2009)

ESCAP & UN-HABITAT. "Land: A Crucial Element in Housing the Urban Poor." In *Housing the poor in Asian cities: Quick Guides for Policymakers,* by ESCAP & UN-HABITAT. Bangkok: ESCAP; Nairobi: UN-HABITAT, 2008a

—. "Low-income Housing: Approaches to help the urban poor find adequate accommodation." In *Housing the poor in Asian cities: Quick Guides for Policy Makers,* by ESCAP & UN-HABITAT. Bangkok: ESCAP; Nairobi: UN-HABITAT, 2008b

—. "Eviction: Alternatives to the whole-scale destruction of urban poor communities." In *Housing the poor in Asian cities: Quick Guides for Policymakers,* by ESCAP & UN-HABITAT. Bangkok: ESCAP; Nairobi: UN-HABITAT, 2008c

Fry, Sarah, Bill Cousins, & Ken Olivola. *Health of Children Living in Urban Slums in Asia and the Near East: Review of Existing Literature and Data.* Washington DC: Environmental Health Project, 2002

GHK & IIED. *China Urban Poverty Study.* Hong Kong, China: GHK, 2004

Global Land Tool Network. *Secure Land Rights for All.* Nairobi: UN-HABITAT, 2008

Government of India *Poverty Estimates for 2004-05.* New Delhi: Government of India, Press Information Bureau, 2007

GPOBA. *Expanding Piped Water Supply to Surabaya's Urban Poor: Activity profile.* 2008a. http://www.gpoba.org/gpoba/ (accessed 15 July 2010)

—. *Viet Nam Service Expansion and Water Loss Reduction: Activity profile.* 2008b. http://www.gpoba.org/gpoba/ (accessed 15 July 2010)

—. *Manila Water Company: Activity profile.* 2008c. http://www.gpoba.org/gpoba/ (accessed 15 July 2010)

Grant, Ursula. "Urban Economic Growth and Chronic Poverty." *Background Paper for the Chronic Poverty Report 2008-09.* Manchester: Chronic Poverty Research Centre, 2006

—."Economic Growth, Urban Poverty and City Governance", chapter 3 in Nick Devas (ed.) *Urban Governance, Voice and Poverty in the Developing World.* London: Earthscan, 2004 37-52

Hasan, Arif. "The New Urban Development Paradigm and the Changing Landscape of Asian Cities." *International Society of City and Regional Planners (ISoCaRP) Review* 3, June 2007: 28-41

Hashim. S. R. "Economic development and urban poverty." In *India Urban Poverty Report 2009,* by Ministry of Housing and Urban Poverty Alleviation and Government of India. New Delhi: Oxford University Press, 2009

Hook, Walter. "Urban Transportation and the Millennium Development Goals." *Global Urban Development,* 2 2006 http://www.globalurban.org/GUDMag06Vol2Iss1/Hook%20PDF.pdf (accessed 15 July 2010)

Housing and Development Board. *HDB Annual Report.* Singapore: Housing and Development Board, 1962.

—. *HDB Annual Report.* Singapore: Housing and Development Board, 1964

Huong, Pham Lan. *Income Distribution in Viet Nam.* March 2004. http://www.eadn.org/

reports/iwebfiles/i10.pdf (accessed 15 July 2010)

Islam, Iyanatul. "Poverty, Employment and Wages: An Indonesian Perspective." *International Labour Organization.* 2002. http://www.ilo.org/public/english/employment/recon/poverty/download/indonesia.pdf (accessed 17 June 2009)

Islam, M. Mazharul, & Kazi Md Abul Kalam Azad. "Rural–urban migration and child survival in urban Bangladesh: are the urban migrants and poor disadvantaged?" *Journal of Biosocial Science,* 40 2008 83-96

Islam, Mursaleena, Mark R. Montgomery, & Shivani Taneja. *Urban Health and Care-Seeking Behaviour: A Case Study of Slums in India and the Philippines.* Bethesda, MD: PHRPlus Program, Abt Associates, 2006

Jinnah, S. *Rights of Water Connections for Urban Slum-Dwellers in Bangladesh: A study on DSK's experience in three slums of Mirpur.* Dhaka: WaterAid, Bangladesh, 2007

Kothari, Miloon & Shivani Chaudhry. "Unequal Cities: The need for a Human Rights Approach." *Urban World,* No. 5, 2010:12-17. Nairobi: UN-HABITAT

Kumar, S. *Social relations, rental housing markets and the poor in urban India - Final Report.* London: DFID, 2001

Lam, Nguyen Tung. "Reform of Urban Housing Policy and Low-income groups in Hanoi city, Viet Nam." *8th International Conference of the Asian Planning Schools Association.* Penang, 2005

Laquian, Aprodicio A. "Who are the Poor and How Are They Being Served in Asian Cities." *PublicTransport in Asia,* 2004: 14-22

Lohani, Bindu N. Clouds over Asia's future. March 2007. http://www.inwent.org/E+Z/content/archive-eng/03-2007/foc_art3.html (accessed 15 July 2010)

Maclaren, Virginia, Nazrul Islam & Salma A. Shafi. "Solid Waste Management in Asian Cities: Implications for the Urban Poor." In *The Inclusive City: Infrastructure and Public Services for the Urban Poor in Asia,* by A. Laquian, V. Tewari & L. Hanley, pp197-223. Washington, DC and Baltimore, MD: Woodrow Wil-

son Center Press & Johns Hopkins University Press, 2007

Mehta, S.S. *Poverty in Urban Slums of Gujarat.* Working Paper prepared for CEPT University, Ahmedabad: 2007

Mercado, Susan, Kirsten Havemann, Keiko Nakamura, Andrew Kiyu, Moigan Sami, Roby Alampay, Ira Pedrasa, Divine Salvador, Jeerawat Na Thalang, & Tran Le Thuv. "Responding to the Health Vulnerabilities of the Urban Poor in the "New Urban Settings" of Asia." *Improving Urban Population Health Systems-Center for Sustainable Urban Development,* July 15-20, 2007. http://csud.ei.columbia.edu/sitefiles/file/Final%20Papers/Week%203/Week3_Health_Asia_Mercado.pdf (accessed 9 July 2009)

Mitlin, Diana. "Finance for low-income housing and community development." *Environment and Urbanization, Brief no. 16,* 2008: 1-5 http://www.iied.org/pubs/pdfs/10557IIED.pdf (accessed 9 January 2010)

Modi, V., S. McDade, D. Lallement, & J. Saghir. *Energy Services for the Millennium Development Goals.* New York: Energy Sector Management Assistance Programme, United Nations Development Programme, UN Millennium Project & World Bank, 2006

Montgomery, Mark R. *The Health of Urban Populations in Developing Countries.* New York: United Nations, 2008

Moulik, S, & S.Sen. "The Mumbai Slum Improvement programme." *Waterlines,* 25-2: October 2006:19-21

Noda, Toshiyasu. "A study on relationship between inequality and economic growth in Asian cities" (Original in Japanese). In *Annual Report of the Economic Association (Japan).* Tokyo: Economic Association, Vol. 47 2009 141-146

Ong, Eng Seow. *Mortgage Markets in Asia.* Singapore: Department of Real Estate, National University of Singapore, 2005

PADECO. *The Evolving Role of World Bank Urban Shelter Projects: Addressing Land Market and Economy-Wide Constraints.* Tokyo: The World Bank, 2007

Pakistan Ministry of Finance. "Yearbook for financial year 2005-06" *Ministry of Finance, Government of Pakistan.* 2006. http://www.finance.gov.pk/publications/YearBook2005_06.pdf (accessed 15 July 2010)

Patel, Sheela & Arputham, Jockin. "Plans for Dharavi: negotiating a reconciliation between a state-driven market redevelopment and residents' aspirations." *Environment and Urbanization* 20 2008:243-253

Patel, Sheela, Celine d'Cruz, & Sundar Burra. "Beyond evictions in a global city: people-managed resettlement in Mumbai." *Environment and Urbanization* 14 2002:159-172

Peñalosa, Enrique. 2010. "Why cities must build equality", *Urban World,* No. 5, 2010:8-11. Nairobi: UN-HABITAT.

Pugh, Cedric. "The idea of enablement in housing sector development: The political economy of housing for developing countries." *Cities* 11-6 1994:357-371

—. "The theory and practice of housing sector development for developing countries, 1950-99." *Housing Studies* 16-4 2001:399-423

Ravallion, Martin, & Shaohua Chen. "China's (Uneven) Progress Against Poverty." *World Bank Policy Research Working Paper 3408,* by Development Research Group. Washington DC: World Bank, September 2004

Ravallion, Martin, Shaohua Chen, & Prem Sangraula. "New Evidence on the Urbanization of Global Poverty." *World Bank Policy Research Working Paper 4199,* by Development Research Group. Washington DC: World Bank, 2007

RICS. The RICS *Asian Housing Review* 2008. August 2008. http://www.rics.org/NR/rdonlyres/4CF4D6D8-914A-472A-B000-3D484759A304/0/AsianHousingReviewSouthKorea.pdf (accessed 30 June 2009)

Robinson, Andy. *Universal Sanitation in East Asia: Mission Possible?* Water and Sanitation Programme (WHO and UNICEF), in preparation of the EASAN Conference. Beppu City, 2007 http://www.unicef.org/eapro/

EASAN_Joint_Publication_low_res. pdf (accessed 9 January 2010)

Rustagi, Preet, Sandip Sarkar, & Pinaki Joddar. "Gender Dimensions of Urban Poverty." In *India Urban Poverty Report 2009,* by Ministry of Housing and Urban Poverty Alleviation. New Delhi: Oxford University Press, 2009 pp28-49

Satterthwaite, David. "Appropriate Sanitation Technologies for Addressing Deficiencies in Provision in Low- and Middle-Income Nations." In *Human Development Report Office Occasional Paper.* UNDP, 2006 http://hdr.undp.org/en/reports/global/hdr2006/papers/Satterthwaite%20David.pdf (accessed 9 January 2010)

—. *Understanding Asian Cities: A synthesis of the findings from the city case studies.* Bangkok: Asian Coalition for Housing Rights, October, 2005

—. "The under-estimation of urban poverty in low and middle-income nations." In *Working Paper on Poverty Reduction in Urban Areas No.14.* London: International Institute of Environment and Development, 2004

—. "Reducing Urban Poverty; Some Lessons from Experience." In *Working Paper on Poverty Reduction in Urban Areas No. 2.* London: International Institute of Environment and Development, 2002

Sen, Amartya. *Development as Freedom.* New York: Oxford University Press

Sinha, Nalin. "Cycle rickshaw and cycling advocacy in Delhi". *ITDP Strategic Planning Meeting.* Mexico: ITDP India, October, 2008. http://www.itdp.org/documents/Cycle%20Rickshaw%20and%20Cycling%20Advocacy%20in%20Delhi.pdf (accessed 15 July 2010)

Tibaijuka, Anna Kajumolo. *Building Prosperity – Housing and Economic Development.* London: Earthscan 2009.

Tiwari, Geetam. "Towards a Sustainable Urban Transport System: Planning for Non-Motorized Vehicles in Cities." *ESCAP- Transport and Communications Bulletin for Asia and the Pacific - No. 68-Urban Transport in the Asia and Pacific*

Region. New York: United Nations, 1999: 49-66

—."Urban Mobility and Informal Transport", n.d. http://www.downtoearth.org.in/aagc/Urban_Mobility_and_Informal_Transport.doc (accessed 10 January 2010)

Townsend, Peter. *Poverty in the United Kingdom.* London: Penguin, 1979

UNDP. *Case Study: India-Sulabh International: A movement to liberate scavengers by a low-cost safe sanitation system.* 2006. http://www.sulabhinternational.org/downloads/Summary_Case_Study_Sulabh_by_UNDP.pdf (accessed 15 July 2010)

UN Human Rights Council. *Special Rapporteur on adequate housing as a component of the right to an adequate standard of living, and on the right to non-discrimination in this context.* 2007. http://www2.ohchr.org/english/issues/housing/index.htm (accessed 15 July 2010)

UN-HABITAT & Cities Alliance. *Analytical Perspective of Pro-poor Slum Upgrading Frameworks.* Nairobi: United Nations Human Settlements Programme, 2006

UN-HABITAT. *State of the World's Cities 2010/2011* – Bridging the Urban Divide. Nairobi: UN-HABITAT, 2010; London: Earthscan

—. *State of the World's Cities 2008/2009* – Harmonious Cities. Nairobi: UN-HABITAT, 2008a: London: Earthscan

—. *The Role of Government in the Housing Market:* The Experiences from Asia. Nairobi: UN-HABITAT, 2008b

— "Forced Evictions - Towards Solutions?" Nairobi: Second Report of the Advisory Group on Forced Evictions to the Executive Director of UN-HABITAT, 2007a

—. *Accommodating People in the Asia-Pacific Region.* Fukuoka: UN-HABITAT Regional Office for Asia and the Pacific. 2007b

—. *State of the World's Cities 2006/07* – The Millennium Development Goals and Urban Sustainability: 30 Years of Shaping the Habitat Agenda. Nairobi: UN-HABITAT, 2006

—. *Financing Urban Shelter-Global Report on Human Settlements 2005.*

Nairobi: United Nations Human Settlement Programme, 2005; London: Earthscan

—. *Urban Land for All.* Nairobi: UN-HABITAT, 2004a

—. *Pro Poor Land Management-Integrating Slums into City Planning Approaches.* Nairobi: United Nations Human Settlement Programme, 2004b

—. "The Habitat Agenda Goals and Principles, Commitments and the Global Plan of Action." UN-HABITAT. November 13, 2003a. http://www.unhabitat.org/downloads/docs/1176_6455_The_Habitat_Agenda.pdf (accessed 15 July 2010).

—. *Handbook on best practices, security of tenure and access to land.* Nairobi: UN-HABITAT, 2003b

—. *Rental Housing: An essential option for the urban poor in developing countries.* Nairobi: UN-HABITAT, 2003c

UN-HABITAT Governing Council. *International Guidelines on Access to Basic Services for all.* 22nd session of the Governing Council of the Human Settlements Programme (2009), Agenda item 6, HSP/GC/22/2/Add.6/Corr.1/Rev.1

UNICEF & World Health Organization. *Progress on Drinking Water and Sanitation: Special Focus on Sanitation.* WHO/UNICEF Joint Monitoring Programme for Water Supply and Sanitation. New York and Geneva: UNICEF & World Health Organization, 2008

United Nations. *World Urbanization Prospects - The 2009 Revision.* New York: Department of Economic and Social Affairs, United Nations. 2010

—. *World Urbanization Prospects - The 2007 Revision.* New York: Department of Economic and Social Affairs, United Nations, 2007. http://esa.un.org/unup (accessed 16 June 2009)

—. "The Universal Declaration of Human Rights" *United Nations.* n.d http://www.un.org/en/documents/udhr/ (accessed 28 June 2009)

Urban Health Resource Centre (UHRC). *Key Indicators for Urban poor in India from NFHS-3 and NFHS-2.* 2008 http://uhrc.in/downloads/Factsheet-India.pdf (accessed 16 June 2009)

Wang Shaoxiong (2001), "Comprehensive Urban Environmental Renovation--The Fu & Nan Rivers Project", report to the thematic committee of Istanbul+5 by Vice-Mayor of Chengdu (available at http://ww2.unhabitat.org/Istanbul+5/8-China.PDF (accessed on 3 May 2010)

Water and Sanitation Programme. *Global experience on expanding services to the poor.* New Delhi: Water and Sanitation Programme, South Asia, 2009

—. *"Economic Impacts of Sanitation in Southeast Asia: A four country study conducted in Cambodia, Indonesia, the Philippines and Viet Nam",* under the Economics of Sanitation Initiative, Research report, WSP-East Asia Pacific, 2008

Weinert, Jonathan, Ma, Chaktan & Cherry, Christopher. "The transition to electric bikes in China: history and key reasons for rapid growth." *Springer Transportation* 34-3 May 2007:301-318

World Bank. "Viet Nam - Country Overview." June 2008. http://siteresources.worldbank.org/INTVIETNAM/Resources/VietNamCountryOverview.pdf (accessed 16 June 2009)

World Health Organisation. *Global Status Report on Road Safety – Time for Action.* Geneva: WHO, 2009

World Health Organization & UNICEF. Progress on Sanitation and Drinking-Water: 2010 Update. WHO/UNICEF Joint Monitoring Programme for Water Supply and Sanitation. Geneva and New York: World Health Organization & UNICEF. 2010

Yari, Marin. *Beyond "Subsistence Affluence": Poverty in Pacific Island Countries.* 2004. http://www.unescap.org/pdd/publications/bulletin03-04/bulletin03-04_ch3.pdf (accessed 21 June 2009)

Yu, Shi-Ming. "Housing Market in Singapore under Changing Economic Conditions." *International Housing Conference.* Hong Kong, China: Hong Kong Housing Authority, 2004

Zhu, Haibin. "The structure of housing finance markets and house prices in Asia." *BIS Quarterly Review,* December 2006:55-69

PART
05

The Urban Environment
and Climate Change

Quick Facts

1. In their quest for economic growth, Asian cities have not paid sufficient attention to urban environment and climate change issues.

2. In most Asian cities today, the average ecological footprint is in excess of five hectares per head, which is lower than in some other regions but suggests that current consumption patterns are unsustainable.

3. Urban growth in Asia is not environmentally sustainable. Existing infrastructure development and growth patterns may lock Asian cities into unsustainable consumption and production models for years to come.

4. Air pollution in Asia causes as many as 519,000 premature deaths every year.

5. Water supplies and food security are becoming a critical challenge in many urban areas.

6. The Asia-Pacific region stands to be the most affected by climate change, calling for changes to energy use and costs, transportation systems and building designs.

7. Asian cities are among the most vulnerable in the world to natural disasters, with many informal settlements located in fragile environmental areas on shorelines and major river basins.

8. Climate change will have a significant impact on the future development of Asia's coastal cities.

9. Adapting to climate change is a vital challenge for poorer Asian countries such as Bangladesh, as well as the smaller Pacific and Indian Ocean island states, due to very limited resources and options.

10. Due to the effects of climate change, urban and rural areas alike will face the challenges of water supplies, food security and eco-refugees.

11. Among urban areas, the poor are most vulnerable to climate change.

Policy Points

1. Massive investment in basic services is needed to improve the sustainability of Asian cities.

2. Asian cities must improve their air quality to reduce premature deaths caused by air pollution and to maintain their competiveness.

3. As most of Asia's future demographic growth is to occur in cities, these are where the problem of climate change must be addressed most urgently.

4. The energy efficiency of transport systems should be assessed and monitored with a view to reducing fossil energy inputs while facilitating mobility. Energy-efficient building designs should be promoted to reduce greenhouse gas emissions.

5. Solid waste can be used as a resource, as demonstrated in several Asian cities.

6. Asian cities have just started to take adaptation measures in response to climate change. Most countries need more capital spending on urban infrastructure. Managing massive relocation of climate-change refugees requires careful planning which should begin now, rather than later when disasters become more intense.

7. If Asia's urban development is to become more sustainable, governments and communities must give priority to better urban planning and management of urban development, improvements to environmental management, pand better environmental governance on a region wide scale.

5.1
Introduction

▲
Solid waste dumped on a road in Kathmandu, Nepal. ©**Bharat Dahiya**

"In Asia and the Pacific, overall, there has been a coincidence of rapidly expanding economies, poverty and substantial future consumption pressures, as well as a natural resource base that is more limited than any other in per capita terms. Thus, a focus on meeting human needs and improving well-being with the lowest possible ecological cost is more relevant in Asia and the Pacific than in any other global region" (ESCAP, 2008a:8). In their quest for economic growth, Asian cities have not paid sufficient attention to environmental and climate change issues.

The state of the urban environment in the Asia-Pacific region is very much a tale of two types of city. Conurbations in the more developed countries – Australia, Brunei Darussalam, Japan, New Zealand, the Republic of Korea and Singapore – are clean, well-managed, prosperous and safe places to live. In contrast, expanding cities in newly industrialized and rapidly developing countries, which together concentrate large proportions of Asia's urban populations, experience serious environmental, urban management, poverty and development problems. Therefore, to a majority of urban Asians,

daily routines are a struggle: earning a living is fraught with risks, and the quality of life is poor.

From a topographical point of view, many Asian cities – in both developed and developing countries – are located along coastal zones and river floodplains. This makes them particularly vulnerable to the threatening effects of climate change and other natural disasters. From this perspective, urban centres in the Pacific islands are even more at risk than those in Asia.

With modernization, cities are becoming wealthier, as incomes and consumption rise and poverty tends to recede. However, this has often come at a significant cost: unmanaged urban development and poor environmental governance have resulted in mounting pollution, traffic congestion, income disparities and social inequity. Most Asian cities are poorly equipped to manage the effects of natural disasters, climate change, contaminated or unstable land and health pandemics. Many will need massive investments in infrastructure, public services, institutional capacity and environmental programmes if basic security, health, safety and overall conditions are to improve for the majority of urban residents.

Sydney, Australia. ©**Walter Quirtmair/Shutterstock**

Faced with poverty and unemployment, Asian governments have given high priority to economic growth and development through industrialization. Many have accepted that environmental issues are associated with this approach, but consider that these can be addressed once the nation reaches a certain level of development, by which time it is believed that nations can allocate more public funds to environmental management and improvements.

This approach to development was first modelled by Kuznets (1955) as an "inverted-U" function that combines environmental degradation and wealth. According to the Russian-born Nobel laureate, economic inequality increases over time while a country is developing, and begins to decrease once average income has reached a certain point. Applying this notion to environmental conditions suggests that, in countries aiming to reduce poverty and raise living standards, development initially occurs at the expense of the environment. Once a nation achieves a certain level of income per head, the environment tends to improve. Admittedly, many of the problems with Asian urban development bear similarities to those experienced in now-developed economies as they underwent rapid urbanization more than a century ago. Nevertheless, in modern Asian cities the scale, background and pace of urban change are unprecedented in human history. Moreover, climate change could have far-reaching effects on Asia's cities, and greatly compound existing problems. The

implication is that the Kuznets paradigm is unviable, and that fresh, innovative approaches to urban development and environmental management are required.

Although the state of the environment in Asian cities inspires widespread pessimism, the situation is not entirely devoid of promising signs. Governments and expanding urban middle classes are increasingly aware that environmental degradation results from an unsustainable approach to urban and economic development. The challenge is to maintain economic development while substantially reducing environmental damage (see Box 5.1), and it is particularly acute for governments, civil society and the business sector in Asia. Few solutions have been found so far, but many promising initiatives offer opportunities for replication across the region.

This chapter draws on information from a range of reports and data sources to provide a summary perspective on the current state of the environment in Asian cities, outlining some possible pathways to improved urban development and environmental management.

Issues related to climate change will require fresh approaches to mitigation and adaptation, and more specifically with regard to urban development, logistics management, energy sourcing new technologies and 'cleaner' production systems. This chapter presents examples and case studies that demonstrate good practice and show how some Asian cities have solved some complex environmental problems.

5.2
The defining features of Asia's urban environmental challenges

Informal settlements on the bank of a canal in Manila, Philippines. ©**Shadow216/Shutterstock**

The environmental challenges cities are facing in developing Asia come on a scale never seen before in the history of human development. Urban environmental issues are commonly known as the 'brown agenda' (i.e., environmental health issues, as opposed to the 'green' agenda, i.e., ecological sustainability). Bartone *et al.* (1994), describe the 'brown agenda' as a set of problems closely linked to poverty, such as those relating to inadequate water, sanitation, drainage and solid waste services, poor urban and industrial waste management, and air pollution. In view of the increasingly significant challenges of natural disasters and the impacts of climate change on cities, Bigio & Dahiya (2004:xiv) have developed an "*expanded brown agenda,*" which includes four environmental goals for urban areas:

- Goal 1: Protect and enhance environmental health.
- Goal 2: Protect water, soil, and air quality from contamination and pollution.
- Goal 3: Reduce the impact of urban areas on natural resources on a regional and a global scale.
- Goal 4: Prevent and mitigate the impacts of natural disasters and climate change on urban areas.

The need to address brown agenda issues in Asian cities has been emphasised by many authors (Bartone *et al.*, 1994; Bigio & Dahiya, 2004; Roberts & Kanaley, 2006).

5.2.1 The dynamics of economic development and urban environmental issues

The environmental risks facing Asian cities are related to three major issues: (i) poverty (see Chapter 4); (ii) industrial production modes (air and water pollution); and (iii) increasing consumption (higher carbon dioxide emissions, water pollution and land degradation). Bai & Imura (2000) have put these risks in perspective under the form of a model of urban environmental evolution. They propose a four-stage process in the development of urban environmental issues in relation to economic growth (Figure 5.1).

Stage I of the development cycle is characterized by *poverty*: it involves issues like demographic growth and migration to cities, high informal-sector employment, lack of safe drinking water, and inadequate sanitation. In Stage II, *industrial* pollution-related issues arise as a result of the urban concentration of particulate matter and/or sulphur dioxide. Stage III is dominated by *consumption*-related issues, such as urban waste and increasing carbon dioxide emissions per head. Based on China's and Japan's experiences, Bai & Imura (2000) can suggest a time-span for each stage. Stage IV involves a shift towards what has become known as an 'eco-city'[1] (Roseland, 1997) with a focus on sustainability; in other words, in this final stage cities reduce the use of non-renewable resources and adapt to climate change (the 'positive economic outcomes' in Figure 5.1).

FIGURE 5.1: **URBAN ENVIRONMENTAL PROBLEMS AND POSITIVE ECONOMIC OUTCOMES**

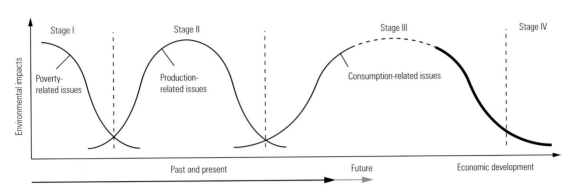

Source: Bai & Imura (2000)

A major difference between previous patterns of urbani-zation and what is happening in Asian cities today is the time-span of each phase, and the complexity of the issue (Bai, 2003). The development stages of Asian cities are the shortest in history and come squeezed together in relatively tight succession, especially in countries like India and China. In Japan's Kitakyushu, for example, Stage 1 lasted about 15 years and Stage II spanned 10 to 12 years – from poverty to fully-fledged industrial development over a single generation or so. Moreover, the environmental issues associated with the expansion of Asian cities are arising much faster than experi-enced by the now-developed world (Marcotullio *et al.*, 2005). In addition, many Asian cities are facing all three types of issues concurrently (Marcotullio, 2008): for instance, Hong Kong, China, today is still facing poverty, industrial devel-opment and waste issues. Virtually none of Asia's cities have effectively overcome Stage III issues; none have reached the 'eco-city' stage and embarked on truly sustainable pathways (Ooi, 2007), even though some early signs of such progress are emerging in Singapore, Hong Kong, China, and some Japanese cities. This is a most welcome development, since it is essential for the sustainability of Asian cities.

5.2.2 Globalization drives urban development

Globalization has played a significant role in the expansion of Asian cities (see Chapter 3). Much of their growth has been driven by direct investment from foreign and multinational corporations, as these took to relocating labour-intensive, less-technology-dependent and environmentally hazardous industries to Asia's developing cities where labour costs are lower, working conditions poorer, and environmental stand-ards less stringently defined or enforced. More recently, large national corporations in countries like China and India have expanded and diversified and now lead the industrialization process in many cities.

Together with economic progress for Asia, foreign direct in-vestment (FDI) has enabled developed countries to externalize environmental costs while improving the quality of their own urban environments, in the process lowering the costs of many goods and services. In many cases, national governments and urban authorities in Asia have provided very attractive tax and other incentives to secure foreign direct investment projects, with the jobs, exports and build-up in foreign exchange re-serves that come with them. For many Asian countries, this has brought greater economic prosperity and development, but often at a heavy cost to the environment (see Box 5.1).

Another undesirable outcome of globalization in Asia has been the prevalence of lax labour and environmental laws, and particularly poor enforcement of those relating to the dis-charge of factory emissions and the treatment of waste. Health and safety standards in factories are low, leading to significant environmental health problems among workers, especially in the textile-apparel, chemical and metal-processing industries (Locke, 2003). While low labour costs are a significant factor in export competitiveness (for instance, apparel production in Delhi and Dhaka), productivity remains low and employ-ees are unlikely to challenge objectionable workplace routines and procedures for fear of losing their jobs.

5.2.3 Mega-demand for land and natural resources

The rapid expansion of Asian cities creates enormous de-mand for natural resources and land for industrial, commer-cial and residential purposes as well as for energy-production infrastructure. On average, Asia's combined urban population grows by over 45 million a year, resulting every day in the conversion of more than 10 sq km of (mainly productive) ru-ral land to urban uses. More than 20,000 new housing units are needed every day to meet basic needs for shelter, creating a huge demand for construction materials and an additional six million ('mega') litres of potable water (Roberts & Kanaley, 2006). Much of this water draws down on existing aquifers, many of which are becoming depleted or contaminated.

Asian cities are among the most densely populated in the world. These very high densities have been there for a long time and today arise from the failure of governments and

BOX 5.1: THE SHENZHEN ENVIRONMENT OUTLOOK: BALANCING ENVIRONMENT AND DEVELOPMENT CHALLENGES

In recent years, Shenzhen has grown from a small border town with a population in the thousands and an area of a few square kilometres into one of the largest cities in China, with an area of 7 million square kilometres and over 10 million residents. This makes the city a typical example of the rapid industrialization and urbanization that has taken place in China, including the challenges municipalities face when trying to balance the competing demands of socio-economic development and environmental protection.

The challenge called for a wide-ranging assessment of existing conditions and future needs and constraints. This is where the UN Environment Programme (UNEP) stepped in with its capacity building scheme in 'Integrated Environmental Assessment'. The venture involved a variety of stakeholders, including scientists, academics, government officials and civil society representatives. The *Shenzhen Environment Outlook 2007* report was the outcome of this joint effort.

The report assessed the city's rapid development over a period of two decades and identified the major environmental challenges (first and fore-most air quality, land and water resources) as well as socio-economic driving forces. Based on four distinct scenarios for the future and a system dynamics model, participants identified a number of policy options to enhance environmental quality and sustainability.

Participants concurred that if sustainable economic growth was to be maintained in Shenzhen, the current model was to be changed. The options were as follows:

- A *business-as-usual* approach may maintain relatively brisk growth rates in the short term, but in the long run, the city would face increasing constraints because of high energy consumption and associated heavy pollution.
- An *environment-friendly* scenario would impose constraints on economic development under the form of stringent environmental standards.
- Those scenarios promoting development based on *resource security* and *high-end industries* were found to strike an acceptable balance between economic growth and environmental preservation.

An imbalance between the supply of and demand for water is one of the major challenges confronting Shenzhen. Although all four scenarios gave some consideration to water saving and use of reclaimed water and sewage, only the 'Resource Security' scenario made this a top priority, as it envisaged the use of all forms of water resources (including sea and rain water) in order to match supply and demand in a consistent sort of way.

The policy options took the form of comprehensive strategies focussing on various areas. Since publication in 2007, these have fed into policies and programmes dealing with industrial restructuring and transformation, efficient use and reuse of natural resources, deployment of an inter-city environmental protection system in the Pearl River Delta, and development of monitoring framework for sustainable urban development.

The *Shenzhen Environment Outlook 2007* has proved so useful that a second report is currently under development. The participatory process behind it brought environmental issues to the attention of various stakeholders and the general public in order to catalyse broad-based responses and action.

Source: Peking University & UNEP (2007)

---

markets to provide land, infrastructure and housing to accommodate the massive inflows of people migrating to cities in the hope of employment and better services. The resultant serious overcrowding and environmental problems affect public health and living conditions. On the one hand, higher densities can result in higher concentrations of environmental pollution and related problems; on the other hand, they have the benefit of lower consumption of land and other natural resources per head, together with economies of scale in the provision of public transport and other urban services. As a result and for all their shortcomings, Asian cities tend to feature much smaller ecological footprints[2] (see next section) compared with cities in other parts of the world, but this comes with a lower quality of life.

Though still relatively high, Asia's urban demographic densities have been on the decline since the 1990s. Based on a selection of cities across the region, Angel *et al.* (2005) estimated the annual demographic growth rate at 2.6 per cent per year on average, compared with 5.5 per cent for urban surface areas, the net effect being an overall decline in urban density of 3.4 per cent on an annual average basis. The reverse side of declining urban densities is a sharp rise in operational and maintenance costs, especially those of energy and utili-ties. If demand for land continues at the current pace until 2030, more than 73,000 sq km of (mostly valuable) agricultural land will be lost to urban development, which may seriously affect food security in countries like Bangladesh and the Philippines.

The decline in population densities is partly associated with a new phenomenon in which manufacturing relocates to the edges of large cities in huge industrial estates, some in excess of 3,000ha; these combine the benefits of better access to transportation and services and cheaper land prices compared with more central urban areas, and provide room for expansion. However, lack of adequate waste treatment facilities turns these sites into major sources of pollution. At the same time, industrial relocation exercises a 'pull' effect on low-income workers, who leave more central areas to settle in housing or fringe villages and towns on the periphery of metropolitan centres (Tacoli, 1998). Expanding middle classes, too, are looking for more spacious living environments and moving to lower-density suburban developments and new master-planned towns. This emerging development pattern is a significant factor behind an insatiable demand for energy, for domestic appliances (e.g., air-conditioning) as well as transportation and construction materials (Ziegler, 2006).

5.2.4 The ecological footprints of Asian cities

The 'ecological footprint' is an average measure of the amount of land required to sustain one individual (Rees & Wackernagel, 1994). Planet Earth can offer a nominal 1.7 global hectares per head (ghph) of habitable land to support the needs of the human race. Now in most Asian cities, the average ecological footprint is in excess of five hectares per head, indicating that current consumption patterns are unsustainable. Although the footprints of Asian cities tend to be smaller than those in developed countries, they are on an upward trend, a phenomenon that is not without consequences for the global environment.

Differences in ecological footprint assessment methods make values difficult to compare. Still, the footprint provides a useful measure of current and evolving urban or nationwide consumption patterns and is becoming a popular measure of urban sustainability. Governments in many developed countries use it to guide development, monitoring and evaluation of resource-saving policies on a national, city and even household scale.

Anecdotal evidence suggests that ecological footprints are expanding much faster in more developed North Asian countries such as the Republic of Korea, Japan and China than in South-East and South Asia. An author like Cole (1999) estimated that the average ecological footprint in India expanded from 0.97ha per head in 1971 to 1.3ha in 1995, a 34 per cent increase over a 24-year period. By comparison, Singapore's ecological footprint stands at 7.1, compared with Hong Kong, China's 6.08, Taipei's 4.75, Tokyo's 4.25 and Seoul's 4.20 (Ng, 2008). Research on eight Chinese cities (Xiao-dong *et al.*, 2005) found that their ecological footprints ranged from 3.4 ghph in Shanghai to 1.31 in Chongqing, with Beijing's estimated at 3.06 ghph.

5.2.5 High vulnerability to climate-change factors

Asian cities are seriously exposed to the factors behind climate change. From a topographical point of view, most of the larger cities in the tropical and subtropical climate zones are low-lying and prone to severe flooding and storm damage. Climate itself is another factor: under the tropics, sanitary and organic wastes decompose quickly, accelerating the concentration of contaminants and the spread of disease in urban areas. Seasonal wind patterns and the geography of many cities often give rise to what is known to experts as 'inversion traps' where little air movement combines with high concentrations of particulates. High humidity rates provide a favourable climate for the breeding of harmful bacteria and disease, at the same time reducing the shelf life of fresh food and other organic products. With their lack of planning and high demographic densities, cities in tropical and subtropical coastal zones or flood plains (such as are often found in Asia) are much more vulnerable to natural disasters and potential pandemics than those in other regions of the world.

Climate factors exacerbate urban poverty in cities, affecting water supply and sewerage systems, with direct effects on the low-income households in environmentally fragile areas. The increasing impact of climate-change factors on cities compounds the vulnerability of people in need of sustainable access to safe drinking water and adequate sanitation, and can also cause displacement of people. The factors behind climate change add to cities' vulnerabilities to disease: beyond air pollution, these factors also threaten failures in food and water security, loss of livelihoods, more natural disasters and more degradation of ecosystems. Some of these factors are discussed under "The challenge of climate change in Asian cities" in Section 5.4.

▲
Peri-urban expansion of Shimla, India. ©**Jason Gutierrez/IRIN**

5.3
Environmental conditions in Asian cities

▲
Ho Chi Minh City, Viet Nam. Collectively, motor vehicles are one of the main sources of urban air pollution in Asian cities. ©**Alvin Ganesh/Shutterstock**

Environmental problems vary significantly across countries and cities depending on respective degrees of economic development, urban form³, geographic location, climate, and population density. Generally speaking, the problems in Asia's more developed economies are less severe, although their consumption patterns are unsustainable, too. The true environmental costs associated with consumer product imports from lesser-developed countries in the region are externalized. The effect is that both developed and developing cities in Asia (as in the rest of the world) are continuing to defer the full environmental costs associated with economic development and production.

This section addresses some of the more significant environmental problems arising from the rapid expansion of Asian cities. Also included are case studies of good practice.

5.3.1 Air quality

Air pollution in Asia is generated from two primary sources (World Bank, 2009):

- *Stationary sources*: These include power plants and industrial outputs as well as residential and commercial buildings, and waste incineration. Coal- and oil-fired power plants are usually the largest urban sources of sulphur dioxide emissions because of the large amounts of fuel they consume (World Bank, 2009). The open burning of rubbish (Mahar *et al.*, 2007), and emissions from small-scale industries, are also significant contributors. The smoke and fumes from cooking and heating can generate considerable indoor air pollution.

- *Mobile sources*: Collectively, motor vehicles are one of the main sources of urban air pollution in Asian cities (Schwela *et al.*, 2006), although their contribution varies

CHART 5.1: **MICRO-PARTICULATE MATTER IN SELECTED ASIAN CITIES (MICROGRAMS PER CUBIC METRE)**

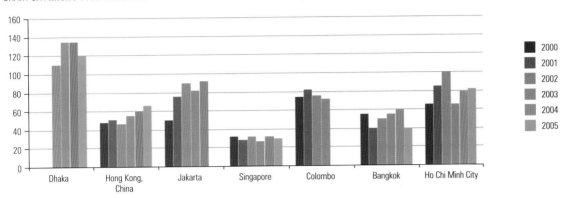

Source: Asian Development Bank (2006b)

CHART 5.2: **NITROUS DIOXIDE IN SELECTED ASIAN CITIES (MICROGRAMS PER CUBIC METRE)**

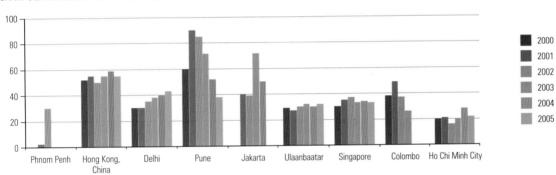

Source: Asian Development Bank (2006b)

CHART 5.3: **SULPHUR DIOXIDE IN SELECTED ASIAN CITIES (MICROGRAMS PER CUBIC METRE)**

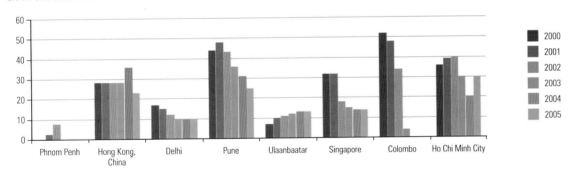

Source: Asian Development Bank (2006b)

significantly across countries and cities. Relatively large amounts of vehicle emissions can be attributed mainly to poorly maintained vehicles, poor fuel quality and inadequate traffic management (World Bank, 2009). The problem has been exacerbated by rapid and unplanned expansion, leading to large increases in vehicle numbers and the many air-quality and health-related problems that come with it.

The World Health Organization (WHO) ranks urban outdoor air pollution as the 13th greatest contributor to disease and death worldwide (Potera, 2004). Another report from the same source estimated that air pollution in Asia caused as many as 519,000 premature deaths every year, mostly in cities, and contributed significantly to the mounting numbers of cardiopulmonary and other respiratory illnesses (HEI, 2004:41; WHO, 2005).

Many urban dwellers in Asia suffer from extremely high exposure to inhalation of micro-particles (i.e., particles of 10 micrometres or less – 'PM$_{10}$') as well as to sulphur and nitrous dioxide emissions (Schwela *et al.*, 2006; WHO, 2005). However, information on air quality is of variable quality, or altogether missing for many cities. No comprehensive survey can be found that provides a comprehensive picture of the current status of, and changes in, urban air quality across Asia. At best, a range of studies provides measures of change in air quality in specific cities.

Charts 5.1 to 5.3 depict the atmospheric concentration of two components of air pollution (PM_{10} and nitrous dioxide) in a sample of Asian cities. In Bangkok, Dhaka and Ho Chi Minh City, air quality is poor though slightly improving (ADB, 2006b; Schwela *et al.*, 2006). In Colombo and Pune, air quality is improving, too. In contrast, it is declining in Jakarta, Phnom Penh and Ulaanbaatar due to increasing rates of vehicle ownership, high manufacturing concentrations in inner city areas, poor vehicle engine maintenance, and burning of low-quality coal and wood in cooking-cum-heating stoves (as is the case in Ulaanbaatar, for instance).

Despite major efforts by many countries to reduce vehicle air pollution, success has been limited, mainly because of ineffective controls (World Bank, 2009). In some cities, air quality has declined because of the rapidly increasing numbers of new vehicles and the large numbers of old, poorly maintained vehicles (especially buses) (Baldasano *et al.*, 2003). In many cities, two-stroke motor (tri)cycles are a major source of urban pollution. Potera (2004) estimates that nearly 100 million two-stroke vehicles are in operation in South-East Asia,

each producing approximately 50 times the pollution of an ordinary four-stroke automobile. Some cities, such as Delhi (see Box 5.7 below) and Dhaka, have taken steps to phase out two-stroke engines and introduce cleaner fuels and other emission reduction measures to improve air quality. In Ho Chi Minh City, Jakarta and Pune, these efforts involve improvements in traffic management, public transport and policing.

Coal is still used in heavy industries and for electricity production in large cities like Beijing, Delhi, Seoul and Shanghai (Mage *et al.*, 1996) and is a major factor in air pollution. Many cities in Asia are moving to substitute natural gas or electricity for coal for domestic uses (heating and cooking). The proportions of diesel-fuelled vehicles remain significant and, collectively, are further major contributors to emissions in Bangkok and Seoul, for instance (Panther *et al.*, 1999). In Manila, poor management of emission controls for diesel buses adds significantly to pollution. Open burning of domestic and industrial waste is still common practice in some cities, including Jakarta, again making significant contributions to air pollution.

In South-East Asia, forest fires are yet another significant source of air pollution in a number of cities. Not only does resulting pollution cause public health hazards, it also affects the performance of local economies. According to the UN

CHART 5.4: **AVERAGE DRY- AND WET-SEASON PARTICULATE CONCENTRATIONS: PM$_{2.5}$ (A) AND PM$_{10}$ (B) IN SIX ASIAN CITIES**

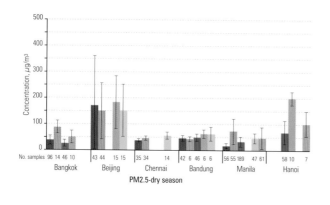

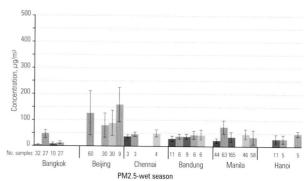

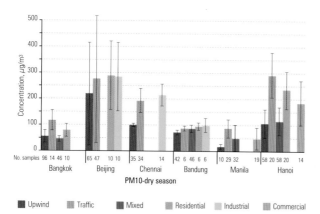

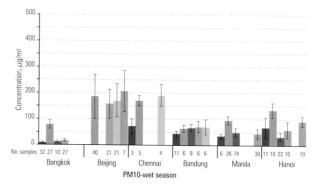

Source: Kim Oanh et al. (2006:3372)

Environment Programme and other sources (Cotton, 1999; UNDP, 2007; UNEP, 2007), in 1997 the haze from forest fires in Indonesia cost the whole South-East Asian population the equivalent of US $1.4 billion, mostly under the form of short-term medical costs in cities. Forest fires have also had a major impact on quality of life and the tourism industry in the region's cities (Hall, 2000).

Air pollution contributes significantly to the increased acidity of rain falling in Asian cities, especially in China (Foell et al., 1995; Schwela et al., 2006). It often happens that air pollution in one area causes acid rain in others: for instance, the World Bank (2007a) found that six provinces in China (Shanxi, Henan, Anhui, Hubei, Hunan and Jiangxi) caused 50 per cent of the acid rain in the whole country. Still in China, over half the estimated acid rain-related damage to buildings occurs in three provinces: Guangdong (24 per cent), Jiangsu (16 per cent), and Zhejiang (16 per cent). Cross-border pollution has become an issue in southern China's Pearl River Delta (Lee, 2002), partly due to relocation of polluting industries further inland and away from more developed coastal cities (Bai, 2002).

Emissions by source

The factors contributing to air pollution vary significantly across the region. Research on particulate emissions in six Asian cities (Kim Oanh et al., 2006) found that the concentrations (PM_{10} and $PM_{2.5}$ (i.e., particles less than 2.5 micrometres in diameter)) in Bandung, Bangkok, Beijing, Chennai, Hanoi and Manila were markedly higher in the dry than in the wet season. The authors found substantial increases in local particulate emissions during the dry season (see Chart 5.4) and suggested that burning of coal for heating (in China), open biomass burning, road dust/soil suspension and stagnant meteorological conditions all contributed to the increases.

Of the six cities in the survey, Beijing featured the highest volume of particle emissions, especially during the dry season, with dust, traffic, residential and industrial sources all contributing to atmospheric pollution. Combined particle emissions (PM_{10}) from all of these sources exceeded 140 mg/m³, which is well above World Health Organisation standards. In Hanoi, the primary contributors to pollution are traffic and residential burning of fossil fuels for cooking and heating. In the other four conurbations in the survey (Bandung, Bangkok, Chennai and Manila), pollution rates of around 100 mg/m³ have been recorded during the dry season, mainly due to traffic and industrial emissions. In those cities, emissions in the residential sector tend to decline in the wet season. With the exception of Beijing, the cities surveyed were in coastal locations, where temperature inversion effects are scarce. Pollution is often much worse in inland conurbations, especially in China and India and during the dry season. It is incumbent on these cities to introduce much stricter conditions on transport and industrial emissions if air quality is to improve in the future.

5.3.2 Water management

Asia is host to some of the world's most arid and water-rich biomes. Drylands are characterised by low soil moisture, low rainfall and high evaporation rates. They are further divided into hyper-arid and arid (deserts), semi-arid (grasslands) and dry sub-humid (forest) areas. Drylands are found in East Asia (China and Mongolia), Central Asia (Kazakhstan) and South Asia (India and Pakistan) (Safriel et al., 2005). Indeed, 11 major deserts can be found in Asia including the Gobi (straddling Mongolia and China), Betpak-Dala (Kazakhstan) and the Cholitan and Thar deserts (India, Pakistan). In Asia's dry land areas, 38 per cent of the population resides in cities.

In contrast, South-East Asia receives abundant rainfall and has ample water resources. Annual renewable water resources per unit of land area range from 2,200 to 14,000 m³/ha across most of the subregion. South-East Asia is also host to several major river systems including 200 in Indonesia and 20 in Thailand. The cross-border Mekong River is 4,600 km in length and drains 800,000 sq km of land. Among the largest lakes in the region are Tonle Sap (Cambodia), Lake Toba (Indonesia), Laguna de Bay (Philippines) and Lake Songkhla (Thailand) (ESCAP, 2005).

Even in water-rich areas, however, concerns over the sustainability and continuing quality of supplies have become prominent urban issues (UNEP, 2002; Marcotullio, 2007). The major river systems in China (Yellow River and Yangtze) and South Asia (Ganges, Brahmaputra) are drawing excessive water and are heavily polluted. Both these systems have their origins in the Asian high plateau region, where ice caps and glaciers are receding due to climate change. As a result, urban and agricultural water use will be affected by reduced or uneven flows in these river systems in the future. This will call for greatly improved water conservation involving complex negotiations between many countries.

Threats to water resources result from many factors, including inadequate fresh water and sanitation infrastructures, river pollution, groundwater overuse, flooding and drought. This section reviews some of the constraints these factors entail for Asian cities, focusing on their effects on human health and environmental quality, and highlighting some of the more relevant good practices in the region.

Water supply

In most Asian cities, supplies of safe drinking water have generally improved since 1990, enabling access by more than 90 per cent of the population. Between 1990 and 2008, the proportion of urban populations with access to improved water supply declined in countries such as Bangladesh, Indonesia, Lao PDR, Myanmar, Nepal and Pakistan, while remaining constant at 93 per cent in the Philippines. Overall, although water supply has made significant progress in Asian cities, safety and reliability remain major challenges, especially where climate change reduces the availability of potable water sources (Chilton & Kinniburgh, 2003).

Today in most Asian cities the problem has less to do with *access* than with the *quality* of potable-water services. In Chennai and Mumbai, for instance, authors like Dasgupta (2000) and Guttikunda *et al.*, (2003) found that coverage was 100 per cent and 97 per cent respectively, but then water was available for only four or five hours a day (Imura *et al.*, 2005b). These findings point to a serious concern, namely, water resources currently available to Asian cities are becoming severely depleted.

According to one United Nations indicator, a country can be considered to be 'water-scarce' if total withdrawals are greater than 40 per cent of annual water resources (UNESCO, 2003b). An Asian Development Bank survey of 18 cities indicates that most were drawing down more than 60 per cent of annual replenishment volumes, and in Chengdu and Shanghai (China) the rate was greater than 80 per cent (ADB, 2004, 2005). Therefore, the challenge for local authorities is to identify the most appropriate means of capturing and treating 'grey' (sullage or wash water) and 'black' (sewage) water at local level.

Another future challenge for many urban authorities in Asia is the maintenance and/or replacement of the older segments of water-supply systems, many of which are plagued by serious amounts of leakage. In Kathmandu, for example, the distribution system loses 35-40 per cent of clean water through leakage; in Karachi, the proportion is 30 per cent and in Chennai, 25 to 30 per cent. The Delhi Water Board has admitted that although the city needs 3.6 billion litres of water per day, available supplies are restricted to 2.9 billion litres because of leakage and other inefficiencies (Chatterjee, 2002). Water leakage leads to subsurface logging which can cause major health hazards; this is because when mains' water pressure drops, contaminated groundwater is siphoned back into the system. Leakages also reduce revenues for water utilities and, more significantly, raise the costs of water for the poor (Agrawal, 2008:2). The relationship between water losses, costs and poor environmental conditions for the lower-income segments of the population has been known for a long time (Muiga & Reid, 1979).

All Asian cities will need to make greater efforts to improve water management if they are to avoid further contamination of supplies and meet increasing demand, including for improved sanitation. Enhanced public awareness of water conservation is also essential if the costs of treatment and the incidence of water-related and sanitation-related diseases and infection are to be reduced. Governments must play a more direct role in raising public awareness about the benefits of sanitation and safe drinking water. This will require effective communication with all segments of the urban population in order to produce the desired behavioural outcomes. Greater equity in the pricing of water is also required to avoid a situation where the poor are paying many times more for water than those better off (purchasing from street vendors, for instance).

Sanitation and wastewater

Since 1990, a majority of countries in Asia have managed to enhance the access of urban populations to improved sanitation, to the exception of a few where this proportion has marginally declined. The issue of access to sanitation is discussed in Chapter 4.

Few Asian cities have the capacity or resources to deploy large-scale wastewater treatment facilities. This is because dense housing and narrow roads combine with land ownership and compensation issues to act as major constraints on any deployment of large-scale treatment systems. Consequently, communal septic tanks, small-bore sewerage and local treatment facilities, appear as the most viable and cost-effective alternative ways of improving urban sanitation and reducing industrial water pollution in Asia's newly developed urban and peri-urban areas. Urban planners must keep in mind that these alternatives require a medium- to long-term vision, as municipal authorities must in the first place purchase or otherwise secure appropriate land plots for these facilities ahead of construction; otherwise, they will likely be faced with the difficult task of acquiring suitable land at some later point in time, when prices are likely to be higher and compensation might be required. Protracted compensation settlement procedures and disputes are major causes of delays for many large-scale environmental improvement projects involving water supply and sanitation.

Urban populations must also be assured that governments will take action on issues related to safe drinking water and sanitation on an equitable basis. Affordability of services is crucial to improving the overall environmental condition of cities in the region. Research in Myanmar (Bajracharya, 2003:148) and the Lao People's Democratic Republic (Lahiri & Chanthaphone, 2003) found that earning income to survive was already such a struggle that most households could not afford latrines.

These findings suggest that (as happened in Europe over a century ago) subsidies can have a major role to play if access to water and sanitation is to improve for poorer households. Therefore, responsibilities for these two basic services in urban centres must be better defined and more clearly allocated. This issue requires increased engagement from public-sector utilities, which are generally the largest providers of water and sanitation services (UN-HABITAT, 2006). On the other hand, the current and future roles of a range of private and community-based service-providers in improved and extended drinking water and sanitation services should be promoted. In short, effective and participatory water and sanitation systems must be well adapted to specific local conditions.

Drought

Parts of Asia have experienced significant periods of drought, including those tropical areas (Java and Sumatra) where abundant rainfall is more typical. Droughts are classified into four interrelated categories which Liu (2007:3) defines as follows:

"Meteorological drought, being climatic variables (precipitation, humidity) and the duration of the dry period; Hydrological drought is associated with effects on surface or subsurface water supplies (i.e., stream flow, reservoir, lake levels, and ground water); Agricultural drought links impacts of meteorological drought to agriculture, focusing on precipitation shortages, differences between actual and potential evapotranspiration, soil water deficits, crop failure; and Socio-economic drought occurs when the demand for an economic good exceeds supply as a result of a weather-related shortfall in water supply."

With rapid demographic growth, all four types of drought have become serious problems for Asia, especially China and the southern subregion, with many cities struggling to keep up with the demand for water. Drought caused by the El Niño effect in the Pacific is also leading to excessive urban drawdowns on groundwater supplies (Carter *et al.*, 2001), as is particularly the case in Pakistan and India.

Droughts can have significant effects on food supplies to cities, as happened in 2006 in Chongqing (Western China) where the overall cost was estimated at US $1.04 billion (Liu, 2007). Earlier, in 2004 and on the back of a short wet season, drought conditions developed rapidly across a vast area from Central China to Southern Thailand to Luzon in the Philippines. This led to significant food shortages and concomitant price increases, especially in smaller cities and towns.

Flooding and catchment management

Flooding is an increasing problem in Asian cities. As urban areas reduce impermeable surfaces, sub-soil drainage is reduced and the likelihood of flooding becomes higher. In many parts of the region, flooding is also exacerbated by higher rainfall intensities. An estimated 46 million people living in Asian cities are threatened by storm-related flooding every year (World Bank, 2008). This number can only increase as populations grow and the risk of flooding rises (as a consequence of climate change, for instance – see section 5.4). Nicholls *et al.* (2007) found that of the 136 port cities worldwide that are exposed to once-in-a-century coastal flooding, 38 per cent are in Asia. Six of the 10 major port cities most at risk (in terms of exposed population) of flooding and inundation are Ho Chi Minh City, Guangzhou, Kolkata, Mumbai, Osaka-Kobe and Shanghai.

It is not just the coastal cities of Asia that are increasingly vulnerable to flooding. Inland cities such as Dhaka, Hanoi, Phnom Penh and Wuhan are also experiencing increasingly severe seasonal flooding (World Bank, 2007b), and poor catchment management is a significant factor. Jakarta, a city criss-crossed by 13 rivers and many Dutch-built canals, has been seriously damaged almost every year by massive flooding triggered by tropical rains. The 2009 floods were particularly severe. When floodwaters reach the city's concrete drainage channels, hydrological efficiency increases, and the resulting acceleration of volumetric flow causes severe damage to low-lying, low-income settlement areas where streams meet the

BOX 5.2: WATER STREAM REGENERATION: GOOD PRACTICE FROM SEOUL

Environmental awareness and economic productivity went hand-in-hand when authorities in Seoul rehabilitated a water stream running in the middle of one of the city's most active business areas. In the mid-1950s, the Cheonggyecheon Stream stood as a symbol of the poverty inherited from colonialism and World War II. Having turned into an open sewer in the very heart of the capital, the stream was simply 'covered up' by a busy motorway. Half a century later, this was the noisiest and most congested area in the city. The only way of resolving the problem was to do something radical with the motorway.

In June 2001, newly elected mayor Lee Myung-bak fulfilled an electoral promise and demolished the motorway to kick off a regeneration process that garnered strong support from the population. The objective was two-fold: making the area attractive to business, foreign financial institutions and tourism, for the sake of economic revitalization; and recovering national pride and the values of traditional culture with the rehabilitation of historical landmarks such as the Gwangtonggyo Bridge (1545). Rehabilitation of the stream was completed in 2005.

▲
Cheonggyecheon Stream, Seoul. ©**Ken McCown**

As the picture shows, the rehabilitation demonstrates a sense of environmental awareness in the middle of a major business centre, with nature and modern life coexisting in harmony. This success could lead to some more 'green' projects in Seoul, mixing preservation of historical features with proper traffic management, exclusive pedestrian areas, eco-friendly zones and competitive business districts. The project could also inspire other Asian cities – in China, for example – looking to highlight a rich cultural heritage as they build prosperous economies.

Source: Referenced from Rinaldi (2007)

coastline. Some cities, like Seoul, have embarked upon major projects to improve catchment management (see Box 5.2).

In many Asian cities, flood mitigation is impeded by poor catchment management in peri-urban areas as well as rubbish accumulation and dumping in the drainage system. A related problem is that vegetation loss continues unchecked in most peri-urban areas and the urban hinterlands of most Asian cities, causing increased erosion and siltation of storm water drainage systems. As rains and run-off become more intense, the size of gullies increases, undermining buildings along urban streams and storm water channel systems, especially in hill cities like Kathmandu and Shimla.

Land disputes and the anticipated increases in the value of land when converted from rural to urban uses make reforestation difficult in urban areas (Long & Nair, 1999). Nevertheless, progress has been made in some cities. Hong Kong, China, Singapore and Kuala Lumpur have each launched urban forestry projects in water catchment areas for the sake of conservation and environmental management in a bid to improve water quality and reduce flooding (Corlett, 1999; Kuchelmeister, 1998; Webb, 1999).

Ground subsidence is another factor behind increased flooding in cities like Dhaka, Jakarta, Shanghai and Tianjin. For instance, a Chinese geological survey found that 46 cities in the country were subsiding due to excessive pumping of groundwater and the weight of high-rise buildings (*China Daily*, 2003). In Indonesia, a report from the Bandung Institute of Technology estimated the subsidence rate in Jakarta's low-lying coastal areas at 8.7 mm a year (Suciu, 2008). A related World Bank-funded study predicted that by 2025, Indonesia's capital could be between 40 cm and 60 cm lower than it is now if nothing is done to check the pumping out of the city's artesian aquifers (Colbran, 2009). The implications for Jakarta and other coastal cities in Asia facing similar problems are potentially significant. Millions would need to be relocated, or expensive dyke systems constructed, to prevent inundation of low-lying coastal settlements. For many cities, it may already be too late to prevent further ground subsidence. In these cities, flooding and inundation can be expected to become a more frequent problem.

5.3.3 Solid waste management

Many cities face serious solid waste management problems, despite significant government efforts to improve services and facilities. In the world as a whole, solid-waste dumping contributes 3 per cent of greenhouse gas emissions (Stern, 2007); on the other hand, more than 72 per cent of total greenhouse gas emissions occurring under anaerobic conditions could be avoided by altering the ambient aerobic/oxidizing conditions (Ritzkowski & Stegmann, 2007). In many developing countries, solid waste management is often inadequate, as is sanitary and industrial waste disposal due to technical and financial constraints. All countries in the region have environmental legislation and policies in place to manage solid waste collection and disposal, but in the lesser-developed countries enforcement is often poor, or local

communities are unaware or dismissive of the regulations. In many cities, polluters go unpunished. It is not uncommon for people to discard or burn waste openly on vacant land, while factories dispose of toxic and other solid wastes in unmanaged and informal dumps (Visvanathan & Norbu, 2006).

The amounts and nature of urban solid waste differ greatly from one Asian city to another (Idris *et al.*, 2004), although in most, the mixed waste stream features large proportions of biodegradable matter (Chiemchaiisri *et al.*, 2007), which reduces opportunities for recycling. Even in more developed countries, where the proportions of non-biodegradable waste are the highest, recycling rates are low compared with those in Europe, for instance. Tokyo recycles more than 50 per cent of its solid waste, Singapore 44 per cent and Hong Kong 35 per cent (Visvanathan & Norbu, 2006). By comparison, in the Netherlands and Denmark recycling rates are in excess of 90 per cent (EEA, 2007). Informal recycling provides a significant source of income for the poor in many Asian cities as they recover various materials and products. For instance in Manila, the Payatas waste management site provides employment for over 4,000 households and recycles 6 per cent of the total waste disposed of at the dump site (Vincentian Missionaries, 1998).

Table 5.1 details estimations of the volumes of solid waste generated in urban areas in Asian countries in 1995 together with projections for 2025. The volumes and nature of solid waste depends mainly on population size, degree of affluence, and the efficiency of the reducing, reusing and recycling processes. For example, Ho Chi Minh City's population of 5.3 million is growing at 2.5 per cent per year, or almost twice as fast as Viet Nam as a whole (1.3 per cent) (World Bank, 2002). The solid waste generation rate in Ho Chi Minh City is 1.3 kg/person/day compared with the nationwide urban rate of 0.7 kilo and 0.3 kilo in rural areas (Klundert, 1995). In Beijing, the nature and calorific value of solid waste has changed dramatically over recent years: total carbon dioxide emitted from solid waste treatment, for example, increased by a factor of 2.8 between 1990 and 2003 (Xiao *et al.*, 2007). However, in many Asian cities, waste management is characterized by inefficient collection and unsanitary disposal conditions (Imura *et al.*, 2005a; Inanc *et al.*, 2004).

Waste collection services are very deficient in many Asian cities, but are improving. In China, 60 per cent of urban solid waste is collected, compared with 70 per cent in the Philippines (Idris *et al.*, 2004). Those communities without municipal waste collection services routinely dump wastes into water bodies, on open land, or at sea (Inanc *et al.*, 2004).

In India, Exnora International, a non-governmental organisation established in Chennai in 1989, has developed the eponymous concept along these lines: to "formulate and practice EXcellent, NOvel and RAdical ideas in solving problems of society involving the same people who are the sources or originators of the problems" (Exnora International, 2010). With regard to solid waste management, the Exnora concept has given rise to community-based organizations called Civic Exnoras, which focus on self-help solid waste management by local communities. Since 1989, about 5,000

TABLE 5.1: **URBAN SOLID WASTE – GENERATION RATE (SELECTED ASIAN COUNTRIES)**

Country	1995		2025*	
	Urban Population (1,000s)	Urban Generation Rate (Kg/Per Head/Day)	Urban Population (1,000s)	Urban Generation Rate (Kg/Per Head/Day)
Bangladesh	27 786	0.49	72 844	0.60
China	374 257	0.79	851 430	0.90
India	253 473	0.46	523 202	0.70
Japan	81 079	1.47	85 877	1.30
Republic of Korea	34 935	1.59	42 910	1.40
Lao People's Democratic Republic	836	0.69	4 050	0.80
Malaysia	11 468	0.81	27 188	1.40
Mongolia	1 289	0.60	2 172	0.90
Myanmar	11 372	0.45	25 539	0.60
Nepal	2 356	0.50	10 717	0.60
Philippines	33 786	0.52	64 951	0.80
Singapore	3 480	1.10	5 362	1.10
Sri Lanka	3 131	0.89	3 788	1.00
Thailand	18 208	1.10	30 679	1.50
Viet Nam	16 202	0.55	41 371	0.70

*Projections
Source: World Bank (1999); United Nations (2010)

such groups have been established in India (see Box 5.3).

Open dumping is the dominant solid waste disposal method in most Asian cities. This is the case with more than 60 per cent of the waste in Bangkok, for instance (Chiemchaiisri *et al.*, 2007). Inadequate collection and disposal of solid waste in urban Asia is a source of health hazards and environmental degradation (UN-HABITAT, 2010b). Therefore, combined management of public awareness, political will and public participation is essential if many of the municipal solid waste issues facing Asian cities are to be addressed.

One of the more significant issues is the degradation of organic waste. This not only creates unpleasant odours but also contaminates local surface and groundwater. Decomposition can lead to eutrophication[4] and putrefaction of streams and ponds, resulting in localized outbreaks of water- and vector-borne diseases. Problems with putrescible waste are most acute in tropical cities. Failure of urban planning and law enforcement to ensure proper disposal of putrescibles is increasing exposure to disease, especially in peri-urban areas.

5.3.4 The urban biosphere

The urban biosphere comprises the natural physical features, soil, hydrology, vegetation, flora and wildlife that can be found in cities. UNESCO (2003a) promotes the creation or preservation of urban biosphere reserves. Many such reserves include peri-urban and urban hinterland areas. Designation of urban biosphere reserves is part of the 1995 Seville Strategy (UNESCO, 2006). Cities that have adopted, or are considering, urban biosphere schemes include: Brighton and Hove, UK; Canberra; the Mornington Peninsula, Melbourne; (ACT, 2006); Cape Town; New York City; São Paulo; and

Seoul. In Sri Lanka, a proposal to turn Kandy, a major religious and ecological landmark, into an urban biosphere is under consideration.

Current changes to urban biospheres – i.e., the clearing of natural vegetation for urban development – have direct, significant effects on micro-climates, vegetation regimes, soils, run-off and the biodiversity of Asia's urban habitats (Dick & Rimmer, 1998; Hara *et al.*, 2008; McGee, 2008); however, more research on the benefits of urban biospheres is needed. Detailed research on urban land conversions is constrained by the poor quality or volume of bio-data, especially in smaller cities. Conversion of agricultural to urban land has been most widespread in China and India (Fazal, 2000; Zhao *et al.*, 2006a, 2006b) to the extent that it is now a cause of concern for future food security.

The description and measurement of the urban areas that might be included in biospheres give rise to definitional and methodological issues across countries. One thing is clear, though: conversion of natural, agricultural and coastal foreshore areas in Asia is occurring at a very brisk pace as the combined population of cities grows by 45 million every year (Roberts & Kanaley, 2006). Against this background, urban biospheres offer the potential for Asian cities to devise policies and development practices that recognise and manage environmental and cultural heritage and values in a more sustainable way.

Loss of biodiversity

Urbanization has a devastating effect on vegetation and wildlife, leading to the loss of biodiversity. In Shanghai, for instance, the number of native plant species in the Sheshan area and on Dajinshan Island has decreased by almost half

BOX 5.3: THE CIVIC EXNORA MOVEMENT IN INDIA

The Civic EXNORA concept was first introduced in the Adyar area of Chennai, India in 1988. The residents who generated garbage regrouped to solve the problem of solid waste accumulation and organise removal and disposal at a specific dumping place. A "street beautifier" was hired to collect waste door-to-door on a tricycle, and the scheme was funded from small subscriptions from community members.

Since then, 5,000 such Civic Exnoras have sprung up in Chennai and elsewhere in Tamil Nadu, Andhra Pradesh, Karnataka, Kerala and a few other states, servicing about 30,000 streets and settlements.

Each Civic Exnora operates on a budget of around 1,500 rupees (or US $30) per month, inclusive of wages to street beautifier and main-tenance charges related to self-help solid waste collection. Since as many as 2,000 Civic Exnoras are now operating in Chennai City alone, the combined turnover amounts to 3 million rupees (US $64,000) per month, or 36 million rupees (or US $770,000) per annum.

Since the start, the concept and practice of Civic Exnora have been replicated and implemented in many places. Three main factors can account for this ease of replication and subsequent sustainability, as follows:

1. Communities were already motivated, and therefore it was easy to mobilize them and push them to higher levels of self-involvement.

2. Since the financial contribution of communities could be kept minimal, and waste management was turned into another kind of resource management, a number of households have generated incomes through recycling and re-using.

3. As the concept was further developed, it became more publicised; as a result, communities found it easier to introduce major Zero Waste Management Concepts like solid waste management at source, decentralized solid waste management or innovative composting processes.

Source: http://www.exnora.org/about_exnora.shtml

Urban soils

Urban soils in Asian cities are altered structurally and functionally by human activity. They are becoming increasingly contaminated by the heavy metals and chemicals contained in industrial wastes.

The full extent of urban soil degradation in Asia is unknown, but in many older cities large areas of land where the topsoil is contaminated can be found. Significant increases in the contamination of soils, especially by cadmium, copper, lead and zinc, have been reported in parts of Bangkok (Wilcke *et al.*, 1998), Danang-Hoian, Viet Nam (Thuy *et al.*, 2000) and Mumbai (Krishna & Govil, 2005). Urban soils in Manila and Hong Kong, China are also increasingly contaminated by some heavy metals (Xue Song Wang *et al.*, 2005). Contamination of urban soils by toxins and heavy metals increases the risk of groundwater contamination, which can have a direct effect on human health, especially in low-income communities that largely or exclusively rely on this type of water. Groundwater supplies in many of Asia's larger developing cities, such as Delhi, Dhaka, Jakarta and Ho Chi Minh City, are facing severe toxicity (Chilton & Kinniburgh, 2003; Mukherjee *et al.*, 2006).

These examples go to show that soil contamination raises a specific and dangerous environmental problem. Moreover, developers may be cautious about engaging in redevelopment projects on former industrial sites, which typically feature high concentrations of heavy metals; this is because of potential future litigation issues, on top of the unknown costs associated with cleaning up contaminated soil and the removal of dangerous chemicals such as dioxins.

Authorised and unauthorised urban waste disposal sites are another source of contamination. Increased degrees of soil toxicity and contamination from such sources have been reported around industrial sites in Dhaka, Hanoi and Ho Chi Minh City (Chilton & Kinniburgh, 2003), and along urban roads in Shanghai (Shi *et al.*, 2008).

5.3.5 Poor urban environment and health

Large numbers of people are in poor health in Asian cities, due mainly to malnutrition, poverty, cramped living conditions, polluted air and contaminated water. Many lack access to adequate medical facilities and other health services. Poor workplace and safety conditions also contribute to ill health and are responsible for high numbers of accidents, especially on construction sites and in factories.

Even in more developed cities, where many of these issues have been addressed, other environmental health problems are emerging, including increased incidence of mesothelioma related to the use of asbestos (Takahashi *et al.*, 1999), pulmonary disease and bronchial asthma, and regardless of declining air pollution (Guo *et al.*, 2008). Obesity is also emerging as a significant health problem in Asian cities as a result of both changes in diet and a reduction in physical exercise as populations make greater use of motorized transport (Tee, 2002).

over the last two decades, contrasting with large increases in the number of non-native species (Zhao *et al.*, 2006b). If they are to preserve or restore biodiversity, it is important for Asian cities to focus on native species in dedicated, well-managed urban and peri-urban habitats (McKinney, 2002). In a bid to restore biodiversity and mitigate the 'heat island' effect[5], cities like Seoul use urban biospheres to make urban areas 'greener', i.e., planting trees and gardens on rooftops, and revegetating degraded urban open spaces (Kwi-Gon Kim, 2004). Other cities such as Putrajaya, south of Kuala Lumpur, are deploying artificial wetlands and lakes along urban drainage systems (Yuen *et al.*, 2006). One of the best examples of urban biosphere restoration is the Can Gio mangrove forest east of Ho Chi Minh City, an area that was almost destroyed by defoliant spray and clearing during the unification war. High degrees of biodiversity have been restored to the mangrove forest, which today is host to more than 200 species of fauna and another 52 of native flora.

The emergence of viral diseases such as severe acute respiratory syndrome (SARS) and avian flu in the past decade posed serious threats to Asian urban populations and economies. The risk of a major pandemic in Asia remains very high (Bloom *et al.*, 2005): the frequent combination of high population densities and unsanitary conditions is particularly conducive to the breeding, mutation and spread of disease. A recent World Economic Forum report on global risks pointed to the increasing threat of pandemic disease arising out of the conditions prevailing in many Asian cities (WEF, 2006).

Although it is difficult to isolate the adverse human health effects of air pollution from those of other lifestyle factors such as smoking, many authors have pointed to a relationship between exposure to air pollution and health effects in Asia (Baldasano *et al.*, 2003; Parekh *et al.*, 2001; Resosudarmo & Napitupulu, 2004; Wong *et al.*, 2001), with significant medical and economic costs. The World-Bank (2007a), for example, found that the health costs of air and water pollution in China amounted to 4.3 per cent of gross domestic product. When the non-health effects of pollution such as loss of productivity are added, the total cost of air and water pollution in China was estimated at 5.8 per cent of total output.

In most Asian cities, rapid demographic growth has been accompanied by increasing contamination of aquifers by industrial, agricultural and urban pollution (Bai & Shi, 2006; Karn & Harada, 2001) and, in coastal cities, by seawater seepage into water supplies (Marcotullio, 2001). The use of contaminated water from lakes, rivers and shallow wells causes diseases such as diarrhoea, intestinal worms, viral hepatitis, typhoid and other infections across Asia, and tropical countries in particular (WHO, 2003). Children and women, especially among the urban poor, usually bear the burden of fetching water, often from contaminated sources. If public health is to improve in Asian cities, situations must be prevented where poor sanitation and drainage continue to pollute (ground) water supplies.

5.3.6 Urban liveability

'Liveability' indicators can provide useful measures of the quality of life in urban environments. The notion refers not only to economic and social well-being, but also to the quality of the environment and, especially, environmental services. For instance, Fukuoka is considered as one of the most liveable cities in Asian and Pacific region as well as the world (see Box 5.4). Well-devised liveability indicators have been compiled for cities around the world, including Asia. The Economist Intelligence Unit (EIU) runs an annual survey of 215 cities worldwide that provides a global ranking of the 'most liveable' based on 39 criteria, ranging from personal safety to the quality of public transportation.

Table 5.2 shows the liveability index and rankings for a selection of Asian cities. Singapore, nine cities in Japan, Kuala Lumpur, Taipei, Shanghai and Hong Kong, China come top in the region, although none features in the top 30 worldwide. All offer good living standards. Chinese cities have become

more 'liveable' in recent years due to massive capital expenditure on public amenities and increased availability of consumer goods subsequent to the country's admission to the World Trade Organization. Emerging business centres such as Bangkok, Taipei and Kuala Lumpur have also become more 'liveable' since the 1997-8 Asian financial crisis. Less-developed cities, especially those where the threat of unrest or terrorism is an issue, fare much worse, with Vientiane, Karachi and Dhaka ranking in the lowest liveability categories (Mercer, 2007).

TABLE 5.2: **LIVEABILITY INDEX FOR 37 ASIAN CITIES (2007)**

Rank	City	Country	Index
34	Singapore	Singapore	102.5
35	Tokyo	Japan	102.3
38	Yokohama	Japan	101.7
40	Kobe	Japan	101.0
42	Osaka	Japan	100.5
54	Nagoya	Japan	99.5
55	Tsukuba	Japan	98.3
63	Yokkaichi	Japan	96.2
69	Omuta	Japan	94.9
70	Hong Kong	China	94.3
73	Katsuyama	Japan	91.4
75	Kuala Lumpur	Malaysia	88.9
83	Taipei	Taiwan, Province of China	86.5
100	Shanghai	China	81.6
101	Johor Baharu	Malaysia	81.2
103	Kaohsiung	Taiwan, Province of China	80.7
109	Bangkok	Thailand	76.8
110	Yeochun (Yosu)	Republic of Korea	76.3
113	Ulsan	Republic of Korea	75.0
131	Guangzhou	China	70.3
132	Rayong	Thailand	69.3
136	Colombo	Sri Lanka	66.3
142	Jakarta	Indonesia	63.7
145	Shenyang	China	63.0
148	New Delhi	India	62.4
150	Ho Chi Minh City	Viet Nam	62.0
161	Mumbai	India	61.7
153	Bangalore	India	61.3
157	Hanoi	Viet Nam	60.1
158	Islamabad	Pakistan	59.8
159	Chennai	India	59.3
161	Jilin	China	57.9
163	Lahore	Pakistan	56.5
169	Vientiane	Lao PDR	55.0
175	Karachi	Pakistan	52.9
184	Almaty	Kazakhstan	49.4
185	Yangon	Myanmar	49.3

Source: EIU (2007)
NB: International 'liveability' surveys do not necessarily include the same sets of cities.

▲
Fukuoka City. ©**Fumio Hashimoto/Fukuoka City**

Fukuoka is located on the southern island of Kyushu in Japan, roughly 1,000 kilometres from Tokyo. Japan's eighth largest city with a population of 1.5 million, Fukuoka enjoys a unique geography, surrounded by the ocean to the north and spacious green suburbs and gentle mountains towards its southern outskirts. It has all the features of a modern urban centre, but none of the rush of a congested mega-city. The interplay of geography and people shapes its character, which is best described as open and friendly. Fukuoka is considered as *'Japan's most liveable city'* by a number of foreign publications. The *New York Times* once saw the city as "a time capsule of modern design' and as 'one of the best places in the world to see the works of world-class contemporary architects side by side."[1]

Even among local business people and their families, Fukuoka is regarded as the most liveable city[2] when they compare living conditions with others in Japan. In a recent survey, over 90 per cent of respondents said they were satisfied with and proud of their city.[3]

Fukuoka offers a high quality of life, enabling a good balance between development and the environment, city and suburbs, modernity and tradition. Commuting is almost stress-free. An efficient public transportation network linking overground and underground railways with bus routes has reduced commuting times to less than half an hour for nearly 50 per cent of the population. Both the airport and the beach are 15-minutes' underground rides from city centre. As most of the populated areas in the city are flat, an estimated 250,000 have been cycling to work or school as a matter of routine long before the environment became a mainstream issue.

Another factor behind Fukuoka's recognised quality of life is the combination of well-managed, in-novative infrastructure and basic services. The city is home to the 'Fukuoka Method', a semi-aerobic landfill waste management process that has been replicated in a number of developing countries. Having experienced several severe water shortages these past few decades, Fukuoka is the only city in Japan with its own large-scale seawater desalination plant, which can produce up to 50,000m[3] (or the volume consumed by roughly 250,000 people) of high quality water every day. The facility supplements river/dam water sources, about which information is publicised daily to raise public awareness on water conservation. Fukuoka is also testing hydrogen as a new source of 'clean', sustainable energy.[4] So far, a pilot scheme (the largest of its kind in the world) has nearly 150 households running entirely on hydrogen power.

The city sits next to, and benefits largely from, the rich natural, agricultural and industrial resources of the surrounding areas of the Fukuoka Prefecture. Over the past several years, the London-based lifestyle magazine *Monocle* has consistently ranked Fukuoka as Japan's second 'most liveable city' (after Tokyo), and 14th among 25 in the world[5]. Prior to that, Fukuoka had been designated 'Best City in Asia' on three occasions by a Hong Kong-based magazine[6]. It is also noteworthy that Fukuoka has been home to UN-HABITAT's Regional Office for Asia and the Pacific since 1997.

Fukuoka is also considered as the 'gateway city to Asia' in Japan, with a number of direct flights to major destinations in the region. The city has historically developed through business, trade and cultural exchange with the region, and this tradition, combined with two-way Asian influences is still very visible today. Fukuoka houses Japan's only museum of modern Asian art. The city's annual film festival is unique in Japan as it features films from the various countries in the region. With its multicultural urban fabric and cosmopolitan outlook, the city has absorbed new and diverse ideas which people bring from Asia and beyond. Fukuoka is host to twelve universities and the workforce is relatively young; moreover, creative industries such as computer games, animation, fashion, design, and leading-edge technologies such as hydrogen energy, robotics and nanotechnologies are proving very attractive for young professionals from outside.

Based on this experience, a "Fukuoka Model" might be a city where the authorities and the population cooperate to create a well-organized transportation system as well as innovative and sustainable basic services; where careful attention is paid to architecture, tradition, the arts and culture; where planning efforts are made to sustain local or nearby agriculture and sources of fresh food, and where advantage is taken of location – in Fukuoka's case, its proximity to the ocean and other major Asian cities.

[1] *The New York Times,* September 24, 2006
[2] Government of Japan, 2003 *Housing and Land Survey*
[3] 2006 Fukuoka Citizen Attitude Survey (over 90% of respondents said Fukuoka was either 'liveable' (60.8%) or 'somewhat liveable' (33.2%)
[4] 'Fukuoka Strategy Conference for Hydrogen Energy', a joint research and practice initiative by Kyushu University, Fukuoka Prefecture, Fukuoka City, other public and private partners, and 600 private companies participating. Also: John Arlidge, 'Hy-life: Welcome to the world's first hydrogen town'. London: *Sunday Times,* 4 July 2010.
[5] *Monocle* magazine No. 35, vol. 04 July/August 2010:37: 'Fukuoka: Japan's 8th largest city punches above its weight in every way'. The city ranked 16th in 2009 and 17th in 2008 in the *Monocle* survey.
[6] *Asiaweek,* 'Asia's Best Cities' survey. Fukuoka ranked first in 1997, 1999, 2000, and second in 1998

Source: Sachiyo Hoshino, UN-HABITAT

5.4
The challenge of climate change in Asian cities

▲
Dhaka, Bangladesh. Rising sea levels have led many 'eco-refugees' to live on boats. ©**Manoocher Deghati/IRIN**

5.4.1 Why are Asian cities vulnerable to climate change?

The Asia-Pacific region's exposure and sensitivity to climate change is bound to have significantly adverse physical, economic and social consequences. Cities in Asia are likely to be among those most affected by climate change: due to size, geographic location and elevation, they are especially vulnerable to frequent extreme weather events such as droughts, floods, cyclones and heat waves (McGranahan et al., 2007). Many are located along coastlines and Lebel (2002) points out for example, that a one-metre rise in sea levels could lead to losses of 34,000 sq km of land in Indonesia and 7,000 sq km in Malaysia; in Viet Nam, the areas at risk include 5,000 sq. km in the North (the Red River Delta), and 15,000–20,000 sq km in the South (the Mekong Delta). Moreover, it is clear that the energy demands of urban areas – including Asia's rapidly growing cities – are a major contributing factor to the production of greenhouse gases (Grimm et al., 2008; Stern, 2007; World Bank, 2008). For example, Dhakal & Imura (2004) report that in 1998, while Tokyo's carbon dioxide emission volume per head was 4.84 tons, Beijing's was 6.9 tons and Shanghai's reached 8.12 tons.

Estimates vary as to the total contribution of the world's cities to greenhouse gas emissions. According to Satterthwaite (2008), this could be as low as 40 percent. Others suggest that as much as 78 per cent of worldwide greenhouse gas emissions from fossil fuels can be attributed to urban areas (Grimm et al., 2008). Asia-Pacific regional estimates have yet to be calculated. More accurate estimates have been made for energy use, of which a combined 66 per cent can be ascribed to the cities of the world (IEA, 2008).

Energy, transportation and the environment

In Asia and the Pacific, energy consumption has expanded rapidly along with economic growth, especially over the past two decades. Moreover, despite volatile oil prices, total consumption of primary energy keeps growing in most countries. In 2006, over 80 per cent of the region's total primary energy supply was made of fossil fuels, including coal, with the remainder split between nuclear power, hydropower and traditional fuels (biomass) such as wood and animal dung. Less than 0.25 per cent came from geothermal or other new and renewable energy sources. As one might expect, fossil and traditional fuels dominated where access to electricity was poor. Since 1990, the region's total energy consumption has increased significantly on the back of substantial increases in electric generation capacity in order to support rapid economic development (ESCAP, 2008b).

High energy consumption has placed a tremendous burden on the region's fragile natural environment. In many Asian countries coal remains the main source of energy for the business sector, accounting for 44 per cent of total primary and 57 per cent of total commercial energy consumption in 2004, compared with world averages of 25 per cent and 28 per cent, respectively. Projections show that rapidly growing China and India will together account for 79 per cent of the expected increase in world coal consumption between 2005 and 2030 (Raufer, 2009).

The immediate fallout of urbanization and economic growth in Asia is increased energy demand for transportation. In urban metropolitan areas, transportation is estimated to account for one-third or more of total emissions of the main greenhouse gases contributing to climate change: carbon dioxide, methane and nitrous oxide (World Bank, 2006). Although technological change and the implementation of tighter emission norms have produced a decline in greenhouse gas emissions per car, these have kept growing overall on the back of increasing urban car numbers across Asian and Pacific region.

It is estimated that the number of vehicles in Asia will increase by more than four times in the next 20 years. Asia's share of global energy consumption is expected to multiply by nearly three from the current 6.5 per cent to 19 per cent by 2030 (see Table 5.3).

Buildings and climate change

Buildings can be resource-intensive; they contribute 8 per cent of greenhouse gas emissions around the world (Stern, 2007). Most of these emanate from building use and maintenance, and the rest from construction materials, the production of which involves significant amounts of energy. However, according to the International Energy Agency, buildings account for as much as 40 per cent of total end-use of energy and about 24 per cent of greenhouse gas emissions in the world (Laustsen, 2008). Accounting for the difference between these two figures is the way end-user demand is calculated or apportioned. In countries like China, the Republic of Korea and Japan, buildings – especially high-rise – tend to be made of materials with high embodied energy (i.e., the materials were energy-intensive to manufacture). On top of this, building design has little regard for the local environment (ESCAP, 2009). For instance, in those regions with high temperatures, buildings with large numbers of windows facing the sun during the hottest part of the day substantially increase air-conditioning requirements and, therefore, energy consumption and operating costs. Many urban planners now recognize the importance of passive energy-efficient design in buildings – all the more so as the payback period for energy-efficient improvements in buildings can be relatively short.

Although the specific contribution of urban Asia to climate change is difficult to evaluate at this point, the more

TABLE 5.3: **PROJECTED CHANGES IN ENERGY USE FOR TRANSPORTATION, 2006-2030**

Country	Vehicle Population (Million)		Energy Use (Mtoe)*	
	2006	2030**	2006	2030**
Australia	14	18	38	49
New Zealand	2	4	6	11
Japan	78	87	213	239
Republic of Korea	16	31	43	85
Malaysia	7	24	20	66
Thailand	10	45	28	123
Indonesia	8	46	22	126
India	23	156	64	428
China	32	390	88	1 069
Pakistan	2	8	7	22
Total	**192**	**809**	**527**	**2 218**
World Total	**928**	**2 080**	**8 084**	**11 664**
Share			6.5 %	19 %

Million tons of oil equivalent ('megatoe')
** Projections*
Source: International Energy Agency, Energy Outlook 2007

general trends that underpin rising greenhouse gas emissions in Asian cities have been extensively documented (Chilton & Kinniburgh, 2003; DFID, 2004; Parry et al., 2007; Preston & Suppiah, 2006; Rockefeller Foundation, 2004; UNCCD, 2009). These trends include the following: rapid population growth, rising personal wealth and consumption, increased vehicle ownership, higher demand for energy, and a lack of taxes or controls on greenhouse gas emissions that might encourage the development of more energy efficient technologies. According to the United Nations Population Fund, demographic expansion is one of the primary drivers of climate change, and one that might be among the more difficult to tackle (UNFPA, 2009). Available data makes it difficult to ascertain the extent to which climate change in Asia is driven by human or natural phenomena, and the only sure thing is that man's role in the more dangerous aspects is significant (Schneider & Lane, 2006).

5.4.2 The effects of climate change on Asian cities

The impacts of climate change on Asian cities will be significant. They will affect not only the human, but also the physical, economic and social environments. A World Wildlife Fund report (World Wildlife Fund, 2009) focuses on 11 major Asian cities most likely to be affected significantly by climate change: Dhaka, Jakarta, Manila, Kolkata, Phnom Penh, Ho Chi Minh City, Shanghai, Bangkok, Kuala Lumpur, Singapore and Hong Kong, China. The report lists Dhaka as the most vulnerable and in Bangladesh a roundtable on climate change estimated that in the next few decades over 20 million of the country's coastal area residents would have to seek refuge from rising sea levels (Muniruzzaman, 2010). Many people who are living in these and thousands of other cities and towns across the region face increasing uncertainty about their future, with millions potentially exposed to upheaval and relocation as 'eco-refugees'. Managing massive relocation will be challenging, and requires careful planning which should begin *now*, rather than later when natural disasters brought on by climate change become more intense.

Production, profitability and consumption

From an economic point of view, Asian cities find themselves exposed to a double threat from climate change and its effects. One is very direct: beyond the prospects of mass relocation away from rising sea levels (Satterthwaite *et al.*, 2007), climate change also stands to reduce clean water supplies and productive (agricultural) soil areas, on top of exposing cities to higher risks of storm damage and flooding. Altered rainfall patterns will affect the ability of rural areas to supply food to cities. The implications for food security will be significant, especially as desertification makes further progress in countries such as China and India (Douglas, 2009).

On top of this, many manufacturing centres are located along coasts or other flood-prone areas, and as part of Asia's 20 per cent share in world output some cities and countries have become dominant in a number of sectors, threatening regional and worldwide economic disruption.

The other threat from climate change on Asian economies is of a more indirect nature. Despite the failure of nations to reach an agreement on global emissions reductions at the Copenhagen Climate Change conference in December 2009, developed countries are likely to introduce emission trading schemes or carbon taxes in the future. This will probably increase production costs, dampening demand for manufactured and assembled goods and eroding the profitability of this sector in the region. A new international arrangement on climate change might impose similar demands on other nations, especially Asian industrializing countries. Emission trading schemes or carbon taxes may lead to a reduction in consumption and slow down urban economic growth in Asia. However, according to the Stern Report (2007), these effects will be relatively small *if* countries in the region act upon climate change *now*, rather than procrastinate for a decade or more.

More natural disasters

Climate change will increase the risk of storm and flood damage in many cities in the region. Nicholls *et al.* (2007) found that Bangkok, Dhaka, Guangzhou, Hai Phong, Ho Chi Minh City, Jakarta, Kolkata, Mumbai, Shanghai and Yangon – all located under the tropics – are the world's most exposed cities to increased flooding due to climate change. Many Asian cities lie on coastal plains, which are bound to suffer more frequent flooding from tidal surges and storm damage (Kreimer *et al.*, 2003).

CHART 5.5: **THE CUMULATIVE IMPACT OF NATURAL DISASTERS BY ASIAN SUBREGION, 1991-2009**

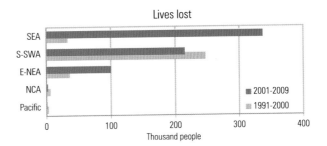

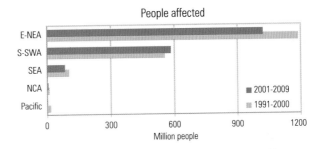

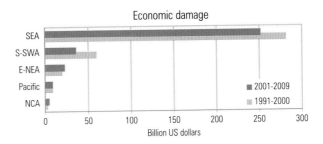

Key: SEA: South-East Asia; S-SWA: South and South-West Asia; E-NEA: East and North-East Asia; NCA: North and Central Asa.
Source: ESCAP (2010:220)

Exposure to extreme weather events – heat waves, tropical cyclones, prolonged dry spells, intense rainfall, tornadoes, thunderstorms, landslides or avalanches – is already high in the Asia-Pacific region. The problems caused by drought will likely increase with climate change and desertification in western China and South Asia, with devastating effects on both water and food supplies as well and urban economies. Coming on top of those resulting from urban expansion, losses of agricultural land due to inundation and other climate-related events can only affect food security in cities. Relocation of eco-refugees will pose a significant challenge, requiring new urban settlements which will further reduce the amounts of land available for food production. In some Pacific Island countries, entire populations – rural and urban alike – will need to be relocated and resettled hundreds or thousands of miles from their home countries.

Over the course of the 20th century, Asia accounted for 91 per cent of all deaths and 49 per cent of all damage due to natural disasters (UNCCD, 2009). More than half a million lives have been lost as a direct result of major climatic events since the 1970s (DFID, 2004). Many of these catastrophes

▲
Floods in Northwestern Pakistan, August 2010. ©**Abdul Majeed Goraya/IRIN**

have affected the region's cities. This situation points to a clear need to address climate change, especially through adaptation.

ESCAP has summarised the region's recent experience as follows: "In Asia and the Pacific the greatest damage is caused by storms and earthquakes – and 2009 was another disastrous year. From January to September 2009, there were 42 disasters, of which 16 were floods, following tropical storms (...). By November 2009, these disasters had affected more than 6.8 million people, left 155,850 homeless, and caused more than US $227 million in economic damage. The death toll is, however, much smaller than [the previous] last year, when two major disasters, the Sichuan earthquake and cyclone Nargis, struck the region killing 232,255 people" (ESCAP, 2010:219).

Rising sea levels

Climate change is expected to bring about a significant rise in sea levels (see Figure 5.2). An estimated 54 per cent of Asia's urban population lives in low-lying coastal zones (UN-HABITAT, 2008). Particularly vulnerable are those conurbations spreading across deltas and low coastal plains such as, again, Ho Chi Minh City, Dhaka, Bangkok, Jakarta, Kolkata and Manila; much of which would be inundated by even small rises in sea

levels (Woodroffe, 2005). Island-states, such as Maldives and Tuvalu, are particularly exposed (Farbotko, 2005).

McGranahan *et al.* (2007) estimated that in the year 2000, a total 238 million people lived in cities located in Asia's Low Elevation Coastal Zone (i.e., less than 10 metres above sea level) which as a result of climate change is exposed to rising sea levels and storm surges (the total, i.e., including rural, population at risk was 466 million). The authors added that 75 per cent of all people living in areas vulnerable to sea level rises are in Asia, with the poorer nations most at risk. As for individual cities, Dhaka, Jakarta, Mumbai and Shanghai – all with populations exceeding 10 million – are seen as particularly exposed. Bangladesh is projected to lose 17.5 per cent of its land area if the sea level rises by one metre (IPCC, 2008). Millions of people would have to be displaced away from Dhaka, the national capital, and most of the country's agricultural and transportation network would be lost. In Shanghai, a similar one-metre rise in sea levels would flood one third of the city, displacing as many as six million people (Hinrichsen, 2000).

Although climate change can affect different places in different ways, urban areas will be especially vulnerable

FIGURE 5.2: **LAND AREA LESS THAN 20M ABOVE SEA LEVEL IN ASIA**

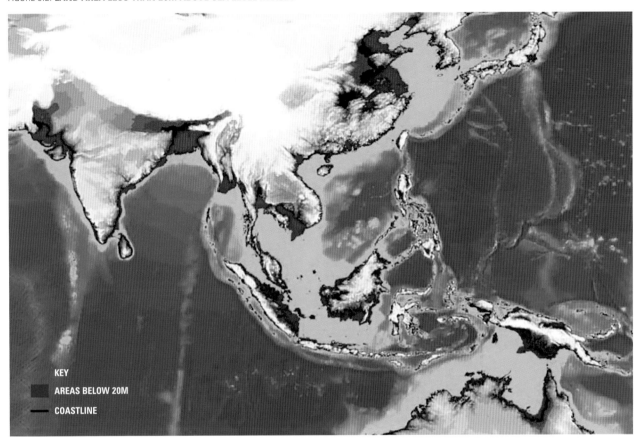

KEY

AREAS BELOW 20M

COASTLINE

Source: Brooks et al. (2006:11)

(Kelkar & Bhadwal, 2007; Lindley *et al.*, 2006) because of high demographic densities, high thermal mass (i.e., capacity to store heat and therefore to smooth out daily fluctuations in external temperature) of buildings, and relatively low vegetation cover (Whitford *et al.*, 2001). On top of this, the Maldives and Sri Lanka, both small island nations, face energy shortages and have unique adaptation needs (Halsnaes & Shukla, 2008). Other large cities away from coastal zones will be vulnerable to more frequent and severe droughts, which will induce shortages in clean drinking water, along with sanitation risks, high temperatures and serious air pollution.

Heat islands

One of the most significant factors associated with climate change will be an increase in the urban 'heat island' effect. Depending on the intensity of global warming, temperatures are projected to rise between one and six degrees Celsius over the course of the 21st century, but in cities the increase is likely to be more pronounced as a result of heat entrapment from temperature inversion and the absorption of solar radiation by paved or other covered land surfaces (Shimoda, 2003). In Hong Kong, China, air-conditioning already accounts for about one-third of total residential electricity consumption (Lam, 2000), and with higher temperatures this proportion

can only increase. According to Wang *et al.* (2008), annual production of room air-conditioning units in China stood at 31.35 million in 2003 and has been growing every year by an average 25 per cent or so. In China's urban areas, most housing units have their own air-conditioner. No wonder that across South-East China, where Hong Kong, Guangzhu and the Pearl River delta are located, mean surface temperature has increased 0.05 degree Celsius per decade under the impacts of urbanization (Zhou *et al.*, 2004). Therefore, it is essential to improve residential and commercial air-conditioning to offset the expected increases in electricity demand, especially where power is from non-renewable sources. Moreover, population sizes in East Asia's eight mega-cities (Bangkok, Beijing, Ho Chi Minh City, Manila, Pyongyang, Shanghai, Seoul and To-kyo) are associated with significant increases in the magnitude and extent of urban 'heat island' effects (Hung *et al.*, 2006). On top of increasing ambient air and surface temperatures in and around cities, heat islands stimulate ozone formation and urban pollution, and excessive heat reduces human productivity. In short, urbanization places a heavy burden on the urban physical environment in Asia.

Climate change will also affect health as well as building designs and energy costs. As most of Asia's future demographic growth is to occur in cities, these are where the problem of climate change must be addressed most urgently.

THE URBAN ENVIRONMENT AND CLIMATE CHANGE

BOX 5.5: ASIA SPEARHEADS UN-HABITAT'S NEW CLIMATE CHANGE INITIATIVE

"Cities have no control over the local impacts that result from a global change in climate. They can only anticipate what the effect might be, calculate the risks and decide the level of response" (UN-HABITAT, n.d.a). This unprecedented, complex challenge is the rationale behind the *Cities and Climate Change Initiative (CCCI)*, which is part of UN-HABITAT's Global Sustainable Urban Development Network (SUD-Net) (see Box 5.8). Given its particular exposure to climate change and its effects, the Asia-Pacific region comes under special focus in this broad-ranging endeavour, which builds cities' capacities in many areas, from vulnerability assessment to governance to policy development and implementation.

Climate change and its effects pose a major threat to cities in the developing world, including their increasing role as 'economic engines' for whole countries and the associated capacity to reduce poverty. Against this background, the UN-HABITAT Initiative pursues the following four objectives:

- to promote active climate change collaboration between local governments and their associations;
- to enhance policy dialogue so that climate change is firmly established on the agenda;
- to support local governments in developing climate change action plans;
- to foster awareness, education, and capacity-building strategies that support the implementation of climate change strategies.

As far as Asia and the Pacific are concerned, climate change and its effects threaten to amplify the vulnerability of a region that is the most populated, most exposed (flooding, drought), most disaster-prone (cyclones, earthquakes, tsunamis) and second poorest in the world.

Even before its formal launch in March 2009, a pilot scheme had been introduced in Sorsogon, the Philippines, a city under the double threat of cyclones and rising sea levels. Since then, the Initiative has also been deployed in South America and Africa, but the Asia-Pacific region dominates the list of participating cities (nine, of which four in Pacific island countries) and the scheme is under serious consideration in China and Viet Nam (see Table 5.4).

As part of the specific CCCI Asia-Pacific strategy, it is expected that by 2015, 300 cities in the region will have enhanced their climate change resilience and have started reducing greenhouse gas emissions. This double objective is to be achieved in partnership with the Asian Development Bank, the World Bank, the Rockefeller Foundation, bilateral development partners, other UN agencies, non-governmental organisations s and academic institutions. The Asia-Pacific strategy takes a three-pronged approach:

(i) Support city-level climate change adaptation and mitigation, including revised urban plans.
(ii) Support national climate change and urban policy review in order to strengthen the national response to the urban dimension of climate change.
(iii) Support Asia-Pacific-wide advocacy and knowledge management, and build capacities for widespread up-scaling

By the time eight Asia-Pacific cities joined the Initiative in March 2010, the pilot scheme in Sorsogon (population: 151,000) demonstrated how it could be deployed for best effect, including nationwide (UN-HABITAT, 2009; n.d.b). A comprehensive participatory vulnerability and adaptation assessment identified vulnerable locations, populations and sectors. In a series of participatory meetings, including several city-wide consultations, climate change adaptation and mitigation options were agreed and prioritized based on broader needs. A shelter plan is under development while land-use and sector development plans come under revision. The livelihoods of the more vulnerable groups are strengthened as part of an ongoing strategy which also includes improved shelter. On top of all this, Sorsogon has introduced a "win-win" energy saving scheme and strengthened disaster preparedness plans. As far as upscaling is concerned, the lessons learned in Sorsogon have been mainstreamed into the Climate Change Act of the Philippines (2009). This statute is exemplary as it attempts to bring clarity to the institutional approach to climate change, stressing the multi-sector dimension and emphasising the role of local authorities in implementation. Another upshot of the pilot scheme took the form of a 'vulnerability assessment tool' which enables the sharing of the lessons learned in Sorsogon across the whole Filipino archipelago. for the whole of has been developed to share the lessons learned in the Philippines. The tool has by now been included in the curriculum of the country's Local Government Academy.

TABLE 5.4: **THE CITIES AND CLIMATE CHANGE INITIATIVE (CCCI) ASIAN-PACIFIC STRATEGY**

Cities/Countries	Achievements
Sorsogon, the Philippines	Comprehensive Vulnerability Assessment and Greenhouse Gas Audit. Identification of key adaptation actions and implementation. Revision of Land-Use Plan and Development plan. Strong engagement with national stakeholders. Replication in other cities.
Batticaloa and Negombo, Sri Lanka	Vulnerability and Greenhouse Gas Assessments in both cities. National Study on Cities and Climate Change. National Climate Change Policy to include urban issues.
Port Moresby, Papua New Guinea	Vulnerability Assessment ongoing, Greenhouse Gas Assessment and National Study on Cities and Climate Change.
Port Vila, Vanuatu	Vulnerability and Greenhouse Gas Assessments and National Study on Cities and Climate Change.
Apia, Western Samoa	Vulnerability and Greenhouse Gas Assessments and National Study on Cities and Climate Change.
Lami, Fiji	Vulnerability and Greenhouse Gas Assessments and National Study on Cities and Climate Change.
Pekalongan, Indonesia	Vulnerability Assessment completed, Action Planning.
Ulaanbaatar, Mongolia	Vulnerability and Greenhouse Gas Assessments and National Study on Cities and Climate Change.
China	Translation of the Vulnerability and Greenhouse Gas Assessment tools and roll-out through select cities.
Viet Nam	National Study on Cities and Climate Change, supported by a comparative analysis of city-level Vulnerability Assessments to strengthen the Sorsogon-developed tool.

Source: UN-HABITAT Regional Office for Asia and the Pacific

BOX 5.6: CLIMATE CHANGE ADAPTATION: A 'FLUID' ALTERNATIVE FOR BANGKOK

▲
'Solid' vs. 'fluid' construction*. ©**Danai Thaitakoo**

Of all major cities in Asia, Bangkok stands among those most at risk from climate change and its by-effects. With modern techniques and impressive infrastructure, prevention and mitigation could cost billions – unless, that is, Thai authorities instead opt for a mix of secular local wisdom and state-of-the-art research, as advocated by some scientists.

The Thai capital is located in the middle of a low-lying flat area dominated by orchards to the west, rice fields to the east, shrimp farms along the coast and fish farms in the lowlands. The settlements over the length and breadth of the Chao Phraya River delta used to support an elaborate network of market towns interconnected by natural and constructed waterways, which helped turn the city into a major trading centre. Indeed, today's much sought-out combination of climate change adaptation and economic development has been a fact of life for centuries in that part of central Thailand.

The liquid element is so ubiquitous that Bangkok is known as 'the city of three waters'. These include the tides of the Gulf of Siam, the river, and tropical monsoons. Across the delta, heavy rainfalls compound the perennial conflict between high tides and the river, causing seasonal flooding in some parts of the city despite the presence of floodwalls and pumping stations. The problem is that in the future, climate change (including rising sea levels) may tamper with long-standing hydrological patterns in a much more destructive way. Since the area is totally controlled by hydrological and climatic factors, the temptation is to keep these under check with rigid flood protection structures. Now these would inhibit the natural flow of water; natural life behind them would become static and slowly die as the dynamics and nutrient flow of water are stymied. Since they resist any changes in water levels or volumes across the area, barriers would destroy the age-old consistency between land and the liquid element. In this perspective, water no longer is seen as the lifeline it has been for centuries in this area; instead, it appears as a hazard that must be tackled head-on or altogether eliminated. The resulting disjunction between land, water and population would cause much more damage to land use and hydrological patterns than did the post-World War II rapid increase in built-up areas.

Resilience does not mean rigidity. Instead of a 'solid', centralised system, it is better to adjust local practices to the levels of water. This 'fluid' perspective does not represent a return to any pre-modern, locally controlled, human ecosystem watershed model. What is needed is a restoration of the canal network and hydrological matrix based on scientific monitoring and networked technologies. This alternative is characterized by dynamic flow management systems which interact locally through locks and adjustable check dams, weirs and water gates. Sub-catchment watershed management is based on a system of small polders which, together with canal networks, can accommodate local water surpluses or droughts depending on the season. The rationale behind this 'fluid' alternative is that flexible and open traditional structures allow for the natural flow of water. This is all the more important as the Bangkok area's cultural, social and economic life is tied to the dynamics of water, with resilience and adaptation evolving over time with seasonal flows. In this way, the consistency between land, water and local populations is restored: water is one aspect of vulnerability, but it remains manageable.

In terms of governance, the 'fluid' alternative calls for a bottom-up approach for the sake of participatory, sustainable development. In this patchwork of urban and agricultural areas, localized air, water and food quality management could be made visible and publicly accessible along canals and orchards. These physical connections could act as 'feedback loops' between farmers, consumers and policymakers, opening up a fresh eco-cultural landscape.

This comprehensive approach to the role of ecosystems in urban design (including housing, see below) combines the notion of fluidity with indigenous practices in the Chao Phraya Delta and state-of-the-art urban ecosystem research.

*'Solid' vs. 'fluid' construction - The house on the left exemplifies the 'solid' approach to climate change. Sitting on rubble and soil, the property hinders the natural flow of water and restricts the accommodation and retention of higher volumes. The house on the right espouses the traditional, 'fluid' approach: standing on stilts above the water, it does not disturb the natural flow and allows for higher volumes. The 'solid' approach braces for the excess water which the 'fluid' alternative stands ready to accommodate.

Source: Thaitakoo & McGrath (2010)

5.4.3 Responding to climate change: Adaptation and mitigation

Faced with climate change, cities must improve planning and building capacities for adaptation (responding to effects) and/or mitigation (reducing the causes). The larger greenhouse gas-producing nations and cities must give greater priority to *mitigation*, and for that matter reduced individual demand for energy. Poorer, lower emitting nations must concentrate on *adaptation*. Failure in Copenhagen in late 2009 to agree on a detailed successor agreement to the Kyoto Protocol should not preclude developed countries from agreeing on a new scheme that can offset the costs of mitigation and adaptation in developing countries.

Adaptation

Since Asian cities are particularly vulnerable to climate change, they need substantial strengthening of adaptive capacities (Adger *et al.*, 2003). Many Asian cities also find themselves grappling with the issue of 'readiness': this refers to the argument that more urgent and pressing environmental issues are requiring all their attention, and that they are not prepared today to tackle climate-change adaptation given their specific economic stages of development or financial and human capacities, or degrees of citizen awareness (Bai, 2007b). This is where UN-HABITAT's new Cities and Climate Change Initiative (CCCI) can help, with a regional strategy that is well adapted to the special threats and needs associated with Asia and the Pacific (see Box 5.5).

Asian cities should also look to improve adaptive capacities among all stakeholders, such as urban poor communities, local and national governments, and non-governmental organisations (Rockefeller Foundation, 2009). Adaptation to climate change also calls for reduced future vulnerability and risks for residents. For example, improved methods and materials for low-income housing can significantly reduce the consequences of catastrophic storms on poorer communities.

Regarding climate change adaptation, the role of traditional knowledge and location-specific approaches cannot be underestimated. Over time, local communities in various cities and countries have made efforts at climate change adaptation. These location-specific amendments to human settlements have typically built on traditional knowledge and local practice. In Bangkok, local communities have adapted to rising water levels with a 'fluid' concept of human settlements, which has served them well (see Box 5.6).

Mitigation

Asian countries can already begin mitigating the longer-term impacts of climate change in a variety of ways. This is of particular importance for the larger polluting countries like China, India, Japan and the Republic of Korea. These and others are beginning to reduce greenhouse gas emissions by switching to cleaner fuels and alternative sources as far as electric power generation is concerned; they have also taken to reduce industrial, domestic and public transport demand for fossil fuels, but the pace of change is not fast enough.

In the transportation sector, the conversion of private (cars, motorized tricycles) and public vehicles to natural gas in several Asian cities has brought significant reductions in greenhouse gas emissions (see Box 5.7). Other measures are in the course of investigation or introduction in many Asian cities, including solar panels, improved housing and building insulation, bio-gas, industrial ecology and methane capture from solid waste dumping sites.

Research has shown that large reductions in greenhouse gases would be achieved by a shift from large numbers of small, private vehicles for personal transportation to fewer, larger-capacity vehicles (World Bank, 2006). Table 5.5 displays greenhouse gas emissions for various transportation modes. It would seem that diesel-powered articulated buses (i.e., double-length, with a walk-through trailer) produce the least greenhouse gas emissions per passenger-kilometre (due to exceptional capacity) on top of being cost-effective public transport options.[6]

With regard to buildings, according to the above-mentioned International Energy Agency report (Laustsen, 2008, also cited in ESCAP, 2009), energy-efficiency standards in buildings across the world would reduce energy use by about 11 per cent by 2030 compared with a business-as-usual scenario. In China, the city of Rizhao (see Box 5.8) has demonstrated that overall energy demand and greenhouse gas emissions can be reduced through sustainable building design and energy use.

Sustainable construction can be supported in a variety of ways in Asia, especially through improved and well-enforced building codes and planning regulations. Voluntary methods such as energy-rating schemes and standards and labelling can also be effective (ESCAP, 2009). However, these must be supplemented for best effect, such as through innovative construction methods (to lengthen the life and reduce the energy requirements of buildings), which can reduce the use of natural resources and therefore the ecological footprint of buildings, in the process supplementing broader climate-change mitigation efforts.

Linkages between environmental problems and climate change are increasingly apparent in Asia, but mitigation or adaptation strategies can be found in only a small number of cities (World Bank, 2008). Integrating climate change into urban management remains a major challenge in the region (Bai, 2007b). Asian countries together stretch over a vast area and are highly diverse in respect of population, size, altitude, climate and economic development. Consequently, the effects of and responses to climate change – both in cities and in countries at large – will vary widely. Mitigating, and adapting to, climate change will require greater collaboration and cooperation among communities, businesses and governments. To date, most Asian countries have focused on the process of ratifying the United Nations Framework Convention on Climate Change (UNFCCC). Now is the time to take practical steps.

However, it must be recognised, that existing models are not accurate enough to predict the precise effects of climate change on any particular conurbation. In this situation and

▲
Compressed Natural Gas-powered auto-rickshaw in Delhi, India.
©Paul Prescott/Shutterstock

India's capital once ranked among the 10 most polluted cities in the world, with measured amounts five times as high as international benchmarks. Public transport contributed 70 per cent of the pollution, and buses were identified as one of the major culprits.

This situation brought the non-governmental Centre for Science and Environment to launch a protracted campaign in favour of controls on bus emissions, which culminated in much-publicized public interest proceedings before the Supreme Court of India. In 1998, the Supreme Court directed the Delhi Government to convert all public transport and para-transit vehicles from diesel or petrol engines to compressed natural gas (CNG). In the process, the Court also paved the way for stricter environmental norms and ordered the phasing out of old, highly polluting commercial vehicles.

Subsequent conversion to gas and introduction of low-sulphur fuel demonstrated that major change could occur on a large scale, as long as appropriate policies were deployed and enforced (although, in the case of Delhi, the judiciary had to step in and tell public authorities what to do).

Natural gas has made Delhi cleaner and more environment-friendly (Narain & Krupnick, 2007). The use of low-sulphur diesel has also led to significant reductions in sulphur dioxide and suspended particulate matter. However, the benefits arising from the introduction of compressed natural gas are diminishing due to the rapidly increasing numbers of private vehicles that run on petrol. More recently (October 2008), 'eco-friendly' hybrid rickshaws have been introduced in the Indian capital. Known as 'solekshaws', these vehicles are fuelled by solar-generated electric power which is produced and distributed by a dedicated facility located in central Delhi (GoI, 2008).

Sources: CNG Busses in Delhi http://www.cleanairnet.org/infopool/1411/ propertyvalue-19513.html

for the time being, the best that developing countries can do is to address a number of factors which currently put their respective environments under stress. These factors include urban poverty (food security, water availability), combating land degradation and reducing the potential loss of biological diversity and 'ecosystem services'[7]. A major concern of many urban authorities in Asia is global warming, arising from the increase in greenhouse gas emissions due to urban services and amenities such as transportation, electricity generation, solid waste disposal and food production, among others. Some urban authorities have found that the most effective way to mitigate global warming is to launch integrated, multi-pronged strategies involving infrastructures and services (see Box 5.10).

When it comes to climate change mitigation, authors like Bai (2007b) and Bulkely (2003) find significant capacities and potential in Asian cities, with reductions in energy use (including both supply and demand) standing out as an apt starting point. Urban energy consumption can be reduced through the transformation of infrastructure, particularly transportation and energy production systems, as well as changes to the population's behaviour and consumption patterns. Some of the larger economies such as China and India will likely find themselves in better positions to adapt to climate change thanks to recent economic, managerial, technological and infrastructure improvements. It is the poorer countries, such as Bangladesh, and the smaller Pacific and Indian Ocean island states, which will struggle to adapt due to very limited resources and options.

It is important to understand that mitigation of greenhouse gas emissions in Asian cities must be addressed across all segments of society, from the large-size polluters to individuals. Just as important is sharing lessons learnt from effective strategies to address both the mitigation of, and adaptation to, climate change impacts between cities, which requires networks and partnerships between countries and cities in the region (see Boxes 5.8 and 5.11).

Whereas UN-HABITAT takes a worldwide perspective on information-sharing, the Asian Cities Climate Change Resilience Network (Rockefeller Foundation, 2009) focuses on a specific region. In this effectively complementary role, the Asian Network, too, acts as a catalyst for information-sharing, funding, action and other partnerships between cities, institutions, financiers and consultants in a joint effort to enhance the resilience to climate change of economically deprived and vulnerable people. The purpose is to devise models and methodologies for assessing and addressing risk through the active engagement of various cities. Institutions in four countries – India, Indonesia, Thailand and Viet Nam – act as major resource centres for network development. Three cities in India and another three in Viet Nam are currently developing city-level climate change adaptation strategies with assistance from the network (Rockefeller Foundation, 2009). The new model is based on the concept of "mass collaboration" (Tapscott & Williams, 2006), which resorts to holistic and collaborative approaches to address complex business, social and environmental problems.

TABLE 5.5: **GREENHOUSE GAS EMISSIONS, SELECTED TRANSPORT SYSTEMS**

Mode of Transport	Maximum Capacity (Passengers/Vehicle)	Average Capacity (Passengers/Vehicle)	GHG Emissions (Grams) Per Vehicle-Kilometre	GHG Emissions (Grams) Per Average Passenger-Kilometre
Gasoline scooter (two-stroke)	2	1.2	118	98
Gasoline scooter (four stroke)	2	1.2	70	64
Gasoline car	5	1.2	293	244
Diesel car	5	1.5	172	143
Diesel minibus	20	15	750	50
Diesel bus	80	65	963	15
Compressed Natural Gas bus	80	65	1 000	16
Diesel articulated bus	80	65	1 000	7

Source: Hook & Lloyd (2002); World-Bank (2006:5)

Admittedly, integrating global issues such as climate change into urban management remains a challenge for most developing cities in the region (Bai, 2007a; World Bank, 2008). In many cases, required action will be expensive – relocating millions of people, or deploying protective structures to prevent or reduce inundation (McGranahan *et al.*, 2007).

5.4.4 Financing climate change policies

Although difficult to predict, the economic costs of unmitigated climate change in Asia are likely to be very high. According to research by Oxfam (2008), climate change was to reduce India's gross domestic product by 9 to 13 per cent in 2010. According to an OECD report (2008), however, the costs of limiting climate change are manageable (although higher in China and India than in OECD countries).

In a speech to the United Nations Climate Change Conference in Bali, Indonesia in 2007, OECD Secretary-General Angel Gurría said that if greenhouse gas emissions were to be cut to reach the more ambitious 2050 international targets under discussion at the time, this would shave 0.1 per cent off the world's combined production of goods and services every year until mid-century. As far as OECD countries were concerned, he added, a harmonized worldwide carbon tax would reduce the world's output by only 0.2 per cent in 2030 and 1.1 per cent in 2050. However, outside the OECD, gross domestic product would experience more pronounced declines in China and India: 5.5 per cent of total output in 2030 and 1.4 per cent in 2050 (Gurría, 2007).

In Asia as elsewhere in the world, a major question when addressing the issue of climate change is, who will bear the costs? Adaptation will be expensive and will require significant national and international borrowing and the raising of revenue through a variety of user-pay means. Most costs will have to be borne by urban dwellers, since cities contribute most to greenhouse gas emissions. Reducing these will call

for a variety of strategies. Some – such as the introduction of cleaner fuels and engine conversions for public transport, which is already occurring in many South Asian cities – will become widespread across the region. Because of the diversity in climatic, geographic and economic conditions, however, individual cities will also need specific strategies to suit their own circumstances.

As far as the financial dimension of climate change adaptation/mitigation is concerned, some Asian countries have adopted, or are considering schemes based on, emissions trading, carbon taxes and the Clean Development Mechanism

BOX 5.8: **UN-HABITAT'S INNOVATIVE URBAN NETWORK**

Climate change is a vast and complex phenomenon and if cities are to become more sustainable all tiers of government must benefit from a wide range of knowledge and experience. This is the rationale behind the Sustainable Urban Development Network ('SUD-Net'), a worldwide interdisciplinary link supported by UN-HABITAT.

SUD-Net assists cities in a variety of ways: mobilizing partners and networks, building partnerships, implementing innovative, pro-poor projects, stimulating the acquisition and sharing of knowledge, and disseminating good practice. The network provides access to up-to-date information (tools and guidelines, resource packages, documents) as well as feedback on ongoing debates, initiatives and activities at the global, regional, national and local levels. SUD-Net also supports institutional capacity-building through improved governance and leadership against a background of decentralized public authorities. Over the past year or so, links have been established with local urban knowledge networks, city councils and universities, as well as the World Bank.

Source: UN-HABITAT (2010a:14)

(CDM), a legacy of the Kyoto Protocol that is particularly favoured by developing countries. The UNFCCC-run mechanism provides a basis for developed-country investors to launch energy-efficient projects in developing countries, in the process earning pollution credits in the form of 'certified emission reductions' (CERs). Three types of 'Clean Development' projects[8] are available: stand-alone, bundled, and programmatic (Hinostroza *et al.*, 2007).

The Clean Development Mechanism is particularly efficient because reductions take place where they can be made most cheaply, and it also offers developing countries an incentive to address their own environmental problems. Asian countries currently account for more that 75 per cent of the total certified emission reduction credits issued by the UNFCCC through the mechanism, with China and India among the more extensive issuers, accounting for more than 70 per cent together with the Republic of Korea.

Under the mechanism, a large majority (over 90 per cent) of the formal credits have been issued to supply-side energy reduction projects involving cleaner, large-scale power generation, a sector responsible for over 35 per cent of total fossil energy use. Demand-side reduction projects could include improved efficiency of public transport systems

as well as manufacturing and agriculture, together with domestic heating and cooking. Since most of non-renewable energy consumption in cities is demand-driven, significant additional opportunities are available to use the Clean Development Mechanism to reduce greenhouse gas emissions in Asian cities.

Several papers from the OECD (Ellis, 2006; Ellis & Kamel, 2007; Ellis & Levina, 2005) suggest that the current interpretation and focus of 'programmatic' clean development mechanism projects may be constraining the potential of the initiative. Ellis (2006) suggests that consideration should be given to broadening the interpretation and scope of 'Clean Development' projects to include funding of public transport systems, as well as urban development and infrastructure projects which focus on reducing both the demand-side requirement for energy and greenhouse gas emissions. Such broadening could provide significant opportunities for Asian cities. Evidence shows that improvements to building and urban form, density and infrastructure, transport and urban logistics systems can lower greenhouse gas emissions (Droege, 2008). Authors like Hinostroza *et al.* (2007) suggest that it should be possible to expand the scope of 'programmatic' projects into this area.

BOX 5.10: THE CLIMATE CHANGE MITIGATION INITIATIVE IN BANGKOK

▲
'BTS SkyTrain' has transformed public transportation in Bangkok, Thailand. ©**1000 Words/Shutterstock**

With its Action Plan on Global Warming Mitigation, the Bangkok Metropolitan Administration seeks to reduce greenhouse gas emissions by 15 per cent between 2007 and 2012. As shown in Table 5.6, the Action Plan has identified the urban functions that contribute most to global warming, and taken a number of steps to curb greenhouse gas emissions.

In the transportation sector, the Metropolitan Administration proposed expanding Bangkok's rapid transit system with additional bus routes to outlying areas, a more affordable option rail-based transit. The Metropolitan Administration also encourages walking and non-motorized transport modes, while at the same time planning to increase the number of buses that will act as feeders to the rapid transit systems. The Metropolitan Administration has also launched a campaign urging people to turn off vehicles while parked.

Electricity generation in Bangkok produces just under 15 million tons of greenhouse gases per year. In a bid to reduce these, the Metropolitan Administration has launched a campaign to encourage people to shift from ordinary to compact fluorescent electric bulbs. In May 2007, the city also asked all residents to turn off all electric lights for 15 minutes every day to help reduce greenhouse gas emissions. On top of this and as an integral part of the Action Plan, the BMA urged the Bangkok population to adopt 'recover, re-use and recycle' routines in order to reduce solid waste, and to favour reusable cloth bags over plastic bags. Instead of relying mainly on landfills and open dumps, the Metropolitan Administration proposed capturing methane gas from waste and to use it as an energy source. Finally, the Administration has also promoted the planting of three million trees and the expansion of parks and open spaces in the whole Bangkok metropolis.

In 2009, the UN Environment Programme (UNEP) provided technical support to the Bangkok Metropolitan Administration to assess the impacts of climate change and vulnerability of Bangkok and area. The Bangkok Assessment Report on Climate Change (BARCC) identified "energy efficiency and emissions reduction" as one of its long term initiatives to mitigate climate change impacts. The assessment identified two priority mitigation responses: (i) adopt and encourage energy efficiency and conservation among the population; and (ii) increase the use of renewable energy, both in terms of passive design and power generation, in individual homes, other buildings and the local grid (Bangkok Metropolitan Administration et al., 2009).

For implementation, the Metropolitan Administration is collaborating with the Ministry of Energy and various non-governmental organisations to support local business, using audits to establish energy efficiency standards and building codes and encouraging stakeholder involvement in the Action Plan in order to build strong community support.

TABLE 5.6: **GHG EMISSIONS IN BANGKOK METROPOLITAN AREA (2007 - 2012*)**

Sector	CO_2 Equivalent, Million Tons		
	GHG Emissions 2007	**GHG Emissions 2012*, Business as Usual**	**GHG Emissions 2012*, Under BMA Action Plan**
Transportation	21.18	25.30	19.77
Electricity generation	14.86	16.00	13.75
Waste production	1.13	1.13	0.95
Others, methane from rice production, etc.	5.58	6.36	6.36
Reduction of GHG emissions from bio-fuel energy			(0.61)
Reduction of GHG emissions from improved waste disposal			(0.28)
Reduction of GHG emissions from expanded parks and green areas			(1.00)
TOTAL	**42.65**	**48.69**	**38.94**

* Projections
Source: Bangkok Metropolitan Administration (2008)

Source: Bangkok Metropolitan Administration et al. (2009); Bangkok Metropolitan Administration (2008)

5.5

Towards improved environmental planning and management in Asian cities

▲
Phnom Penh, Cambodia. ©**Wdeon/Shutterstock**

Asian cities are facing serious environmental problems which, if not addressed, will have serious local, regional and worldwide consequences. Clearly, if urban development in the Asia-Pacific region is to become more sustainable, governments and communities must give priority to actions in three major areas: (i) better urban planning and management of development, (ii) improved environmental management, and (iii) better environmental governance and compliance. These points are detailed below.

5.5.1 Better urban planning and management of development

Sustainable urban development in Asian cities will make more efficient use of urban resources through better spatial planning of development and improved logistics systems, and by paying greater attention to the mitigation of, and adaptation to, the effects of climate change.

Improved urban planning and development practices

Urban development in Asian cities is increasingly driven by consumption, which in turn is highly dependent on the use of non-renewable resources. This pattern is unsustainable, as supplies of non-renewable resources are bound to dwindle in the future. In peri-urban areas, relatively low-density residential development is accompanied by broad-acre industrial estates (ADB, 2008). In city centres, high-rise commercial, retail and residential structures are replacing old urban fabrics, with the loss of heritage buildings and marginalization of lower-income families and communities. The poor are forced to the edges of cities by a combination of rising rents and decentralization of employment. This pattern of urban development will increase the unit/per head costs of transportation, infrastructure and communal and other public services, resulting in increased demand for energy.

To address such problems, local and national governments should give more attention to stabilizing urban demographic densities, ensuring mixed-use development with balanced localized employment, developing integrated transportation systems, and enforcing those environmental and planning regulations and laws that support sustainable development.

Institutional capacity for urban environmental planning and management

Better planning and capacity-building for the purposes of improved urban environments and climate change mitigation and adaptation will be essential in all cities across Asia and the Pacific. Making developing-country cities more sustainable is a daunting technical, economic and political challenge at all levels of government and decision-making. Local authorities and the various stakeholders need improved institutional capacities for urban environment planning and management if the goal of sustainable urban development is to be reached. Under the joint UN-HABITAT – UNEP Sustainable Cities Programme, technical support has been provided to more than 60 cities in the Asia-Pacific region (see Box 5.11). With effective technology transfers, developing countries can take advantage of the scientific advances achieved by those more developed. Prosperity puts Asian cities collectively in a better position to fund sustainable development once donor support is terminated (Staniskis, 2005). Apart from technology and funding, a vital component in this effort is none other than political will, in order to mobilise the public as well as all tiers of government. In short, the transition to sustainability demands technical, economic and political commitment from all stakeholders.

Decentralized urbanization

Unless better managed, high urban growth rates will continue to damage the environment in Asia's mega-cities. Therefore, decentralized urban expansion through development of secondary and tertiary cities is a major task for governments. Such a strategy will not solve the environmental problems associated with urbanization; rather, it will draw activities away from mega-cities, alleviating the pressure those cities are under, and provide them with 'breathing space' to improve planning processes and urban services. Gurgaon in the Delhi National Capital Region, and Cyber Jaya to the south of Kuala Lumpur, are examples of successful decentralization within a large metropolitan region. Sprawling, poorly planned cities come with large ecological footprints, generate large quantities of waste and pollution, and have a significant impact on rural hinterlands and coastlines. Decentralization will require improved urban management, especially with regard to spatial planning.

Congestion and logistics management

Asian cities are among the most congested in the world, undermining business competitiveness and making major contributions to environmental problems, including greenhouse gas emissions.

Adequate public transport is critical to the operational efficiency of Asian cities. Most of these need mass-transit systems but rising personal wealth and lack of efficient urban transportation have combined to increase the proportion of the population now using private cars. Nevertheless, cities

▲
Beijing, China . The China International Energy Saving and Environmental Protection Exhibition (EnerChina 2010). ©**Testing/Shutterstock**

BOX 5.11: THE 'SUSTAINABLE CITIES PROGRAMME', 20-PLUS YEARS ON

Chennai, India. ©Jaimaa/Shutterstock

Even before the landmark 1992 'Earth Summit' in Rio de Janeiro, UN-HABITAT (UNCHS) and the UN Environment Programme (UNEP) had undertaken to help urban authorities across the world to reconcile economic development and environmental preservation as advocated by the UN-sponsored World Commission on Environment and Development. The joint effort launched in 1988 took the form of the Sustainable Cities Programme (SCP), now in its fourth stage in 66 Asian cities.

The basic rationale was that sustainable cities are more productive engines of growth, and therefore degradation of the urban environment must be tackled through a proactive approach that addresses the complex interactions between development and the environment (UNCHS & UNEP, 1998a). More specifically, cities (including the public, private and community sectors) must build the capacities and strengthen the institutions needed to deploy the well-balanced environmental planning and management approaches that can meet local development challenges while implementing global environmental agreements and conventions. Chennai, India, was the designated pilot city in the Asia-Pacific region.

The Programme helps stakeholders to place environmental concerns at the forefront of urban development decision-making through a gradual, cross-sector, participatory Environmental Planning and Management (EPM) process. Stakeholders are brought together in order better to understand the complex urban development and environmental interactions, discuss strategies and seek solutions to priority issues of common concern, in the process improving urban management methods, partnerships and capacities. To support these efforts, the Programme looks to build a stakeholders' coalition at national level in order to

mainstream environmental concerns into urban development policies and relevant legislation. Further support is provided by region-wide sharing of information and technical cooperation between cities through networks and regional conferences. The Programme benefits from the worldwide expertise of the two UN agencies with regard to best practice, awareness-raising, capacity-building, policy development and local-national-regional replication.

The end result is a well-proven cross-sector and participatory Environmental Planning and Management process that addresses priority environmental issues in a city with a focus on "action" and results. Capacity-building aims at strengthening four core areas: (i) environmental information and technical expertise, (ii) broad-based stakeholder participation, (iii) environmental planning and decision making, and (iv) cross-sector and inter-institutional coordination (UNCHS & UNEP, 1998b).

The initial phase (1988-1995) of the Programme focused on integrating environmental concerns into urban decision making. Participating cities learned how to prepare their own environmental profiles, and to elicit broad-based stakeholder participation through consultations and issue-specific working groups in order to develop strategies and test them through demonstration projects to be documented with the aim of influencing national policies.

Having identified local needs and implemented pilot projects, participating cities (by then more than 15 in the Asia-Pacific region) deployed 'sustainability' strategies on a broader, "citywide" scale between 1995 and the year

2000 (2nd phase). For instance, cities in India, the Philippines and Sri Lanka introduced household composting and neighbourhood recycling centres as well as biogas for market waste in a bid to reduce costs and pollution. In China, Shenyang and Wuhan addressed pressing environmental concerns such us air pollution, river water quality and solid waste management.

This citywide upscaling was supported by Programme staff with the development of three new 'global' instruments: one on air quality management, an "Environmental Management Information System" and another one aimed at "integrating gender responsiveness in environmental planning and management."

By the year 2000, the Programme had matured and it was time to establish a sustained response structure, especially as by then the Millennium Development Goals were coming on top of Agenda 21 and Habitat Agenda principles and objectives. The regional arm of SCP became the Asian-Pacific Regional Environmental Support Programme, with UN-HABITAT, through its regional office in Fukuoka, Japan providing capacity-building and institutional strengthening support to some 66 demonstration cities and their national partners in 10 countries. This 3rd phase was characterized by extensive efforts to build a region-wide capacity-building support structure through partnerships with regional and national universities and local government training institutions, making use of their specialised expertise and mainstreaming SCP lessons learned into curricula. Further efforts focused on improved national-regional up-scaling and replication capacities through professional networking, expert group meetings, websites and publications.

Since 2008, the Sustainable Cities Programme has been supporting participants' efforts to 'localize the global agenda', i.e., to implement a number of international agreements and conventions on the environment (global warming, land-based pollution, urban biodiversity and ecological management) This makes it easier for urban authorities to asses and prioritize local environmental concerns and to have a voice in national and global environmental negotiations.

The Asian-Pacific arm of the Programme has reviewed its own country-support operations, listing the 'Factors of Success' from more than 10 years' experience. The objective is to put cities in the region in a better position to address climate change, with support from UN-HABITAT's global Sustainable Urban Development Network (SUD-Net) and its "Cities in Climate Change Initiative" (see Boxes 5.5 and 5.8).

Source: Chris Radford and Angela Pinzon, UN-HABITAT

such as Beijing, Shanghai, Singapore, Tokyo and Hong Kong, China, have begun to develop public transportation and logistics systems that will serve them well in the future. Many Asian countries are trying to discourage the public from using private vehicles and instead to develop public-private partnerships for mass transit. Many successful examples can be found across the region, including Jakarta's mass rapid bus project and the Singapore congestion charge.

Improvements to environmental health

Asian-Pacific cities must combine technical, political and economic initiatives in order to control air pollution and manage hazards and vulnerabilities. Air pollution is one of the easiest types of pollution for cities to address, because the costs can be distributed across the population and businesses through carbon and other taxes on fossil fuels at source. This is not the case with water or solid waste pollution, where taxing and policing become more difficult. Technology can certainly help control motor vehicle carbon dioxide emissions, but this must be supplemented with government action in favour of better public transportation and incentive policies, for instance. Detailed assessment of public policies is essential to ensure that the urban poor are not unduly affected. Urban managers and planners must be fully informed about local air quality and engage actively with local populations to address the problems. Effective air monitoring and modelling systems should be put in place. Problem-solving calls for coordination between all tiers of government and communities.

In view of the above-mentioned lack of accurate figures regarding individual cities, more information on and research into the health effects of indoor and outdoor air pollution in Asian-Pacific cities is badly needed. Ambient concentrations of pollutants could be assessed, as well as the characteristics and main sources of urban air pollution, and the size and distribution of particulate emissions.

Securing the funds needed for air pollution control schemes (for instance, eradication of two-stroke engines, introducing cleaner fuels for domestic cooking and heating and for public and goods transport as well as industry) remains a major challenge for cities in the region. It is important for Asian-Pacific cities to take advantage of economic growth to provide the resources required for urban air pollution control.

Eco-efficient infrastructure and industrial production

Eco-efficiency is the major prerequisite for more sustainable urban development and improved quality of life in Asian-Pacific cities, and therefore must be brought to bear on buildings, infrastructure and industrial production systems. Few cities or industries in the Asia-Pacific region actively recycle water or waste materials, or work in favour of more efficient power generation, distribution and use. The case studies of Rizhao (Box 5.8) and Kitakyushu (Box 5.12) show how two Asian cities are adopting more eco-efficient infrastructure and industrial production systems. Industrial

ecology offers a way of turning wastes and energy losses into commercial use, or, in other words, great opportunities to make industrial production systems more sustainable in Asia (Chiu & Yong, 2004).

5.5.2 Improvements to environmental management

Environmental management is concerned with more efficient use of natural resources and handling of any related waste.

Adopting an integrated '3R' approach to waste management

As its name suggests, the 'reduce, re-use and recycle' (3R) approach handles urban solid waste in an integrated way. Solid waste can be considered as a resource – what is waste to some people is a valuable resource to others, and a considerable proportion of the waste generated in cities can be used for other purposes. The 3R approach provides economic and environmental benefits as it reduces (i) the amounts of waste dumped in landfills, (ii) reliance on virgin materials, and (iii) pollution, while also saving energy (Visvanathan & Norbu, 2006). Prompted by its own solid waste management problems, the Government of Japan is spearheading the implementation of 3R in Asia (GoJ, 2005). The Government of China has adopted the concept of a 'circular economy' and sees the 3R approach as one of its essential components (Guomei, 2006).

The 3R approach in general features a number of issues that must be overcome. First, recycling in practice is market-driven and underestimates environmental externalities. For instance, plastic shopping bags are generally not recycled because they are so cheap to produce from virgin material – but then their environmental costs are often much higher than their market prices (they are not bio-degradable).

The 3R approach involves other practical issues. On the one hand, environmental externalities should be internalized, where possible, into market prices to reduce consumption and encourage substitute products. On the other hand, 3R implementation sometimes relies on strong government intervention. For example, in 2008, the Government of China banned the provision by vendors of free plastic shopping bags to customers in an effort to reduce 'white pollution' (*China Daily*, 2008; *National Geographic*, 2008). In support of 3R policies, environment-friendly products should be promoted through subsidies or awards.

Second, public awareness of local recycling schemes and waste issues is, in general, still low (Scott, 1999). Environmental education is needed if this is to change. Enforcement of and compliance with recycling obligations should be strengthened.

Third, lack of financial resources is another obvious constraint on the 3R approach. Unlike developed countries, most 3R activities in the Asia-Pacific region involve a more or less informal sector of waste-pickers – either employees or scavengers – whose work methods are labour-intensive and unsafe. This informal workforce plays a significant role in the recycling of up to 30 per cent of the waste generated in Asian-Pacific cities (Visvanathan & Norbu, 2006).

Water management

Water faces Asian-Pacific cities with three major challenges: (i) halting the depletion of available water resources; (ii) reversing the degradation of water quality; and (iii) the reticulation and treatment of wastewater. Cities in the region are rapidly running out of potable water to service expanding populations. For the many cities located along rivers, one's wastewater becomes another's water supply problem. Heavy metals and other industrial pollution, together with water-borne diseases from urban wastewater discharge, remain major health problems. Increasing contamination of surface and groundwater systems is leading Asian-Pacific cities towards mounting water crises. Moreover, disputes over access to water are festering within and among countries. Improving water management, and especially recycling, must become a high priority for Asian-Pacific urban authorities.

Improving air quality

Air pollution, primarily from fossil fuel combustion, is having a major impact on the health of Asia-Pacific's urban populations. This not only affects public health and well-being, but also reduces productivity and performance through sickness and infirmity, not to mention the social problems deriving from cancer and respiratory diseases. Reducing the demand for fossil fuel-based energy is a challenge for all Asian-Pacific cities. Dhaka and Delhi (see Box 5.7) have demonstrated how cities can develop non-polluting, efficient public transport systems and introduce cleaner vehicle fuels (Singh & Pannu, 2005; Narain & Krupnick, 2007).

Solid waste management

Most waterways and river systems in the Asia-Pacific region are heavily polluted by the dumping of urban domestic and industrial solid waste. Groundwater aquifers in low-lying cities are also becoming increasingly contaminated with domestic and industrial waste, heavy metals and other industrial pollutants.

Most solid waste in Asian-Pacific cities is disposed of locally, leading to soil contamination and the spread of disease in overcrowded urban areas. One of the challenges for governments is to improve solid and hazardous waste management and to promote opportunities for recycling and the reprocessing of waste into commercial and other usable products.

5.5.3 Better environmental governance and compliance

Good governance

Continued urban governance reforms are in order if Asian cities are to address the mounting environmental problems facing them. Local authorities lack some of the resources and powers required for environmental management plans and law enforcement. Legislation on decentralized environmental management has failed clearly to apportion distinct powers and responsibilities to national and sub-national tiers of government, leading to ineffective environmental governance.

In many Asian-Pacific cities, one of the most challenging dimensions of urban governance is industry compliance with standards and policy guidelines. To many governments, economic growth for the sake of development and poverty alleviation must be the first priority. Compliance with environmental regulations and norms is often overlooked or open to corrupt practices.

A conference on environmental law in Asia (Bangkok, January 2008) found that only a few countries and cities were enforcing national environmental laws (Casey, 2008). As a result, widespread passive corporate attitudes to pollution have little incentives to change. One of the most effective ways of enforcing environmental regulations is to delegate responsibilities and power to local governments and in particular to their environmental protection agencies. Environmental compliance strategies must be considered in their specific circumstances and take into account governments' enforcement capacities.

Environmental education

Short of improved environmental stewardship, the quality of life of many urban residents can only decline (Richman, 1994). Building environmental awareness is a priority for any urban climate change mitigation strategy (Gokhale, 2001).

Awareness of the local environment and its problems must feature as one of the main planks of environmental and development agendas. The rationale is a triple one: (i) increasing knowledge about the biophysical environment and its problems; (ii) enhancing awareness of any strategies dealing with those problems; and (iii) securing practical engagement in favour of a resolution of those problems (Stapp et al., 1969), cited in (Fisman, 2005:39).

In the Asia-Pacific region, environmental education is embedded in all forms of tuition (including social and physical sciences at higher education level) and many examples of environmental innovation and eco-businesses can be found (Bhandari & Abe, 2000). Nevertheless, such efforts do not seem to have led to significant society-wide changes in environmental behaviour. In this respect, four major issues must be addressed, as follows:

1. Environmental education should be recognized as a policy priority for the sake of more effective sustainability. In coordination with non-governmental organisations, government agencies should promote environmental education, with relevant issues and solutions added to formal and non-formal curriculums and programmes.

2. Poverty and demographic factors shape the outcome of environmental education programmes, if in an underhand sort of way. Therefore, any educational programmes should acknowledge the interests and incentives of the various socio-economic segments of society.

3. Greater gender equity is important to the management of environmental assets. Women play the main role in shaping household behaviour related to hygiene, energy consumption and waste disposal (Schaefer-Preuss, 2008). The need for greater gender equity relates especially to land rights and ownership, which are often denied to women under traditional (including inheritance) systems. Consequently, any environmental education programmes should be accessible to women.

4. Being aimed at an audience with a variety of perspectives, backgrounds, politics and cultures, environmental education programmes should be participatory, practical, and capable of dealing with complexity. If it is to be successful, "environmental education needs to vary from region to region and be realized in different ways" (Barraza et al., 2003:349).

5.5.4 Environmental issues call for more regional responses

By their very nature and scope, environmental issues, including climate change, are complex and varied, involving multiple spatial scales from local to global (UN-HABITAT, 2010b). This is why the measures described above cannot be met by national governments or urban authorities acting independently. Cities can certainly begin to improve their own environments; however, issues such as climate change, cross-border pollution (air, waterways, and relocation of industries) and the containment of disease and epidemics call for new, broader forms of governance, management mechanisms and technical and financial responses among many stakeholders.

Clearly, environmental improvements in Asian-Pacific cities will require greatly increased regional cooperation, collaboration and commitment. This calls for close coordination of environmental policies, standards and practices to a degree that is unprecedented in the region. Changes to customs, traditions and governance practices that date back hundreds of years are also in order. Changing attitudes and practices to improve the environment in Asian-Pacific cities may prove to be the greatest challenge of all for governments and populations alike. Environmental education, greater openness and trust-building are the foundations of success in this regard.

5.6
Urban Asia and the environment: Diagnosis and policies

As far as Asia is concerned, the prognosis for many cities is that environmental conditions are to worsen for some time to come. However, improvements can be expected once better urban environmental planning and management practices are adopted and the economic benefits of growth become more widespread.

Cities have the potential to influence both the causes and consequences of climate change. They can also contribute to national and international strategies to prevent unacceptable climate change impacts. It is for cities to provide leadership and direction and implement practical initiatives for the benefit of their and national populations (UN-HABITAT, n.d.a).

A particularly difficult issue will be dealing with climate change-refugees inside and across borders. This will be a very significant problem in Bangladesh, China, India and the Pacific island-states. At the same time, governments must also address poverty and the issues of food and water security, and create sustainable economic development opportunities. Most Asian cities and governments face a difficult balancing act in this regard.

The age-old, inefficient physical and economic infrastructure that is underpinning the rapid expansion of Asian-Pacific cities is likely to remain in place for the next 50 to 100 years. Instead of overturning it overnight, the priority is to adjust it in order to make transport, industrial and energy production systems more sustainable. This is likely to be an incremental process, although rapid change will be necessary in some cases to address more serious environmental problems. The sheer number and sizes of Asian-Pacific cities and the resources needed to service them pose great challenges to sustainable-minded governments and urban managers. Few cities in Asia have the massive resources required to reinvent themselves. They lack the capacity to inject the vast amounts of capital that could radically transform development, production and consumption practices.

However, the business-as-usual approach to development and environmental management is no longer an option. The way Asian-Pacific countries handle urban development and management in the future must change if further environmental deterioration is to be avoided. In order to remain competitive, viable, healthy and liveable places, Asian-Pacific cities must embark upon more sustainable development pathways. Working towards 'green growth', Asian-Pacific economies should make efforts to improve eco-efficiency of their economic growth, which will help in meeting "the most important challenge to sustainable development in this region reducing the pressure on the natural resource base while continuing to meet human needs" (ESCAP, 2008a:8).

We should not, however, be apocalyptic or overly pessimistic about the future of Asian-Pacific cities. Undoubtedly, they face massive problems of congestion, pollution, inadequate infrastructure, weak governance and poverty. But they are also very dynamic and vibrant places that have demonstrated remarkable resilience and the capacity to recover from past catastrophes. As noted in Chapter 3, this was especially the case in the aftermath of the 1997-98 Asian financial crisis.

Nevertheless, given the unprecedented scale and pace of urbanization, it is clear that fresh approaches must shape the way Asian-Pacific cities are planned, managed and governed. Urgent action is required from all tiers of government to address pressing matters related to climate change – both mitigation and adaptation, and with a special focus on water security, wastewater and solid waste. These requirements are such that cooperation among countries, public authorities, business and communities will be required on a scale never seen before in the region. Admittedly, differences in language, politics, culture, history and the extent of economic development will stand in the way of such cooperation, but they must be overcome if Asian-Pacific cities are to become more sustainable and better places to live.

ENDNOTES

[1] The prefix 'eco' designates a fully sustainable town or city, i.e., one that can feed itself with minimal reliance on the surrounding countryside, and power itself with renewable sources of energy. An eco-city/town has the smallest possible ecological footprint and produces the lowest possible amounts of pollution, thanks to efficient land use, composting/recycling/conversion of used materials, etc.

[2] The ecological footprint is a measure of human demand on the Earth's ecosystems. It compares human demand with planet Earth's ecological capacity to regenerate. The 'footprint' represents the amount of biologically productive land and sea area that are needed (i) to regenerate the resources a human population consumes and (ii) to absorb and render harmless the corresponding waste. This measurement

makes it possible to estimate how much of the Earth (or how many planets Earth) it would take to support humankind if everyone lived the same lifestyle.

[3] Urban form or 'morphology' refers to the physical fabric and street-patterns of a city, and the people and processes that shape these patterns.

[4] Eutrophication is a process where water bodies receive overabundant amounts of nutrients (e.g., phosphorus, nitrogen) that stimulate excessive plant growth and cause water degradation.

[5] An urban heat island is a conurbation with significantly higher temperatures than surrounding rural areas. The phenomenon is caused by the changes brought to the land surface by urban development which uses materials that effectively retain heat. Spatial urban expansion increases the effect.

[6] Articulated buses have been operating in some major Western cities for some time. Recent experience led London's mayor in late 2008 to pronounce the phasing-out of 'bendy' buses after only five years. According to figures from *Transport for London*, articulated buses (18m in length) cause 5.6 pedestrian injuries per million miles operated, compared with 0.97 per million for all other buses, are involved in 2.62 collisions with cyclists per million miles, compared with 0.97 for other buses, and have 153 accidents per million miles, compared with 87 per million on routes operated by standard buses. 'Bendy' buses are also more prone to fare evasion. (Source: 'Johnson ditches London's bendy buses', *The Independent*, London, 6 December 2008). http://www.independent.co.uk/news/uk/home-news/johnson-ditches-londons-bendy-buses-1054433.html (accessed 22 August 2010)

[7] 'Ecosystem' is a term formalised and popularised by the United Nations 2004 Millennium Ecosystem Assessment, which refers to the wide variety of resources and processes that are supplied by natural ecosystems and notionally benefit all humankind (e.g., clean drinking water or waste decomposition). According to the UN, ecosystems fall into four broad categories: *provisioning*, such as the production of food and water; *regulating*, such as the control of climate and disease; *supporting*, such as nutrient cycles and crop pollination; and *cultural*, such as spiritual and recreational benefits.

[8] See *Glossary of CDM Terms*, UNFCCC website: http://cdm.unfccc.int/Reference/Guidclarif/glos_CDM.pdf

REFERENCES

ACT. Issues Paper - Biosphere Reserve. Canberra: Australian Capital Territory Government. 2006

Asian Development Bank. *Managing Asian Cities*. 2 vols. Manila: Asian Development Bank, 2008

—. "Asia Water Watch 2015: Are countries in Asia on Track to meet Target 10 of the Millennium Development Goals?" Asian Development Bank, United Nations Development Programme, United Nations Economic and Social Commission for Asia and the Pacific and World Health Organization. Manila: Asian Development Bank, 2006a

—. Urban Air Quality Management: Summary of Country/City Synthesis Reports across Asia. In *Asian Development Bank Clean Air Initiative for Asian Cities Centre*, Manila: Asian Development Bank, 2006b

—. Asia Water Watch 2015: Are countries in Asia on Track to meet Target 10 of the Millennium Development Goals? Manila: Asian Development Bank, 2005

—. Water in Asian cities: Utilities' performance and civil society views, Manila: Asian Development Bank, 2004

Adger, W. Neil, Saleemul Huq, Katrina Brown, Declan Conway, & Mike Hulme. "Adaptation to climate change in the developing world", *Progress in Development Studies* 3 3 2003:179-195.

Agrawal, Pronita Chakrabarti. "Designing an Effective Leakage Reduction and Management Programme" in A. S. Gupta (ed.) *Water and Sanitation Programme - South Asia*. New Delhi: World Bank, 2008.

Angel, S., S. C. Shepherd, & D. L. Civco. The Dynamics of Global Urban Expansion, Washington, DC: World Bank, 2005.

Bai, Xuemei M, & P Shi. "Pollution Control: In China's Huai River Basin: What Lessons for Sustainability? Environment: Science and Policy for Sustainable Development", *Environment Science and Innovation for Sustainable Development* 48 7 2006:22-38

Bai, Xuemei M. "Industrial Relocation in Asia: A Sound Environmental Management Strategy?" *Environment* 44 2002:8-12

—. "Integrating Global Concerns into Urban Management: The Scale Argument and Readiness Arguments", *Journal of Industrial Ecology* 11 2007a:15-29

—. "Rizhao, China: Solar-Powered City" in *State of the World 2007: Our Urban Future*, Washington D.C: World Watch Institute, 2007b:198

—. Integrating Global Environmental Concerns into Urban Management: The Scale and the readiness Arguments. Journal of Industrial Ecology 11(2):15. 2007c

—. "The process and mechanism of urban environmental change: an evolutionary view", *International Journal of Environment and Pollution* 19 2003:528-541

Bai, Xuemei M., & Hidefumi Imura. "A Comparative Study of Urban Environment in East Asia: Stage Model of Urban Environmental Evolution", *International Review for Environmental Strategies* 1 1 2000:135–158

Bajracharya, D. "Myanmar experiences in sanitation and hygiene promotion: lessons learned and future direction", *International Journal of Environmental Health Research* 13 1 2003:S141 - S152

Baldasano, J, E. Valera, & P. Jimenez. "Air quality data from large cities", *The Science of the Total Environment* 307, 2003:141-165

Bangkok Metropolitan Administration, Green Leaf Foundation and United Nations Environment Programme. *Bangkok Assessment Report on Climate Change*. 2009. Bangkok: BMA, GLF and UNEP. Available at: http://www.roap.unep.org/pub/BKK_assessment_report_CC_2009.pdf

Bangkok Metropolitan Administration. *Action Plan on Global Warming Mitigation 2007-2012*, Bangkok: BMA, 2008

Barraza, Laura, Ana M. Duque-Aristizabal, & Geisha Rebolledo.

"**Environmental education: from policy to** practice", *Environmental Education Research* 9 2003:347-357

Bartone, C, J. Bernstein, J. Leitmann & J. Eigen. 1994. Towards environmental strategies for cities, Washington, D.C: World Bank, 1994

Bhandari, Bishnu B., & Osamu Abe. "Environmental education in the Asia-pacific region: Some problems and prospects", *International Review for Environmental Strategies* 1 2000:57-77

Bigio, Anthony, & Bharat Dahiya. Urban Environment and Infrastructure: Toward Liveable Cities, Washington, D.C.: World Bank, 2004

Bloom, Erik, Vincent de Wit, & Mary Jane Carangal-San Jose. "Potential Economic Impact of an Avian Flu Pandemic on Asia", *ERD Policy Brief No 42*, Manila: Asian Development Bank, 2005

Brooks, N., R. Nicholls, & J. Hall. 'Sea-Level Rise: Coastal Impacts and Responses', Wissenschaftler **Beirat der Bundesregierung 2006.** http://www.wbgu.de/wbgu_sn2006_ex03.pdf (accessed 20 March 2010)

Bulkeley, H., & M. Betsill. *Cities and Climate Change*, London: Routledge, 2003

Carter, Lynne M., Eileen Shea, Mike Hamnett, Cheryl Anderson, Glenn Dolcemascolo, Charles Guard, Melissa Taylor, Tony Barnston, Yuxiang He, Matthew Larsen, Lloyd Loope, LaShaunda Malone & Gerald Meehl. "US-Affiliated Islands of the Pacific and Caribbean", in *US National Assessment of the Potential Consequences of Climate Variability and Change*, Cambridge: Cambridge University Press. 2001:158

Casey, Michael. "Asia's courts failing to enforce environmental laws", *International Herald Tribune*, 14 January, 2008

CEE. *Centre for Environmental Education*, Ahmedabad. http://www.ceeindia.org/cee/index.htm (accessed 11 July 2010)

Chatterjee, Patralekha. "South Asia's thirsty cities search for solutions", *The Lancet* 359 2002: 2010

Chiemchaiisri, C, J P Juanga, & C Visvanathan. "Municipal solid waste management in Thailand and disposal emission inventory", *Environmental Monitoring Assessment* 135 8 2007:13-20

Chilton, J. & Kinniburgh, D. (2003) Soil and Groundwater Protection in the Southeast Asia Region, *ESCAP Water Resources Journal*, 87-94.

China Daily. 'Cities Sinking Due to Excessive Pumping of Groundwater', In *China Daily* HK Edition. Hong Kong. 2003. http://english.people.com.cn/200312/11/eng20031211_130178.shtml (accessed 11 July 2010)

—. China Daily. 'From June, shops can't give free plastic bags'. 2008. http://www.chinadaily.com.cn/china/2008-01/09/content_6379872.htm (accessed 10 March 2010)

Chiu, Anthony S.F, & Geng Yong. "On the industrial ecology potential in Asian Developing Countries", *Journal of Cleaner Production* 12 2004:1037-1045

Colbran, Nicola. "Will Jakarta Be The Next Atlantis? Excessive Groundwater Use Resulting From A Failing Piped Water Network", *Law and Environmental Development Journal* 5 2009:24

Cole, Victoria. *The Growing Ecological Footprint of a Himalayan Tourist Centre,* Winnipeg: Natural Resources Institute University of Manitoba, 1999

Corlett, Richard. T. "Environmental Forestry in Hong Kong: 1871-1997", *Forest Ecology and Management* 116 1999:93-105

Cotton, James. "'Haze' over Southeast Asia: Challenging the ASEAN Mode of Regional Engagement", *Pacific Affairs* 72 1999:331-351

Dasgupta, N. "Environmental enforcement and small industries in India: Reworking the problem in the poverty context", *World Development* 28 2000:945-967

DFID. 'Climate Change in Asia' Key Sheets, http://webarchive.nationalarchives.gov.uk/+/http://www.dfid.gov.uk/documents/publications/climatechange/6disasterproof.pdf (accessed 14 July 2010)

Dhakal, Shobhakar & H. Imura. *Urban Energy Use and Greenhouse Gas Emissions in Asian Mega-Cities, Policies for a Sustainable Future*. Kitakyushu: IGES. 2004

Dick, H. W., & P. J. Rimmer. "Beyond the Third World City: The New Urban Geography of South-East Asia", *Urban Studies* 35 1998:2303-2321

Douglas, Ian. "Climate change, flooding and food security in South Asia", *Food Security* 1 2009:127-136

Droege, Peter (ed.) *Urban Energy Transition*, New York: Elsevier, 2008:665

EEA Use of land filling, incineration and material recovery as treatment options in 2004. Copenhagen: European Environment Agency, 2007

EIU. 'Table of the 50 best cities in the world.' Economist Intelligence Unit, April 2007. http://www.citymayors.com/environment/eiu_bestcities.html (accessed 11 July 2010)

Ellis, Jane. "Issues related to implementing "programmatic CDM", in Expert Group on the UNFCCC. Paris: Organization for Economic Co-operation and Development, 2006

Ellis, Jane & Sami Kamel. *Overcoming Barriers to the Clean development Mechanism*. Paris: Organization for Economic Co-operation and Development, 2007

Ellis, Jane & Ellina Levina. *Developing the CDM Market.* Paris: Organization for Economic Co-operation and Development. 2005:15

ESCAP. *Statistical Yearbook for Asia and the Pacific 2009.* Bangkok: UN Economic and Social Commission for Asia and the Pacific, 2010

—. *Turning Crisis into Opportunity: Greening Economic Recovery Strategies.* Bangkok: UN Economic and Social Commission for Asia and the Pacific, 2009

—. *Greening Growth in Asia and the Pacific – Follow-up to the World Summit on Sustainable Development: Taking Action on the Regional Implementation Plan for Sustainable Development in Asia and the Pacific, 2006-2010.* Bangkok: UN Economic and Social Commission for Asia and the Pacific, 2008a

—. *Statistical Yearbook for Asia and the Pacific 2008.* Bangkok: UN Economic and Social Commission for Asia and the Pacific, 2008b

—. *State of the Environment in Asia and the Pacific 2005.* Bangkok: UN Economic and Social Commission for Asia and the Pacific, 2005

Exnora International. *About Exnora*. 2010. http://www.exnora.org/about_exnora.shtml (accessed 9 August 2010)

Farbotko, Carol. "Tuvalu and Climate Change: Constructions of Environmental Displacement in the *Sydney Morning Herald*", *Geografiska Annaler: Geografiska Series B, Human Geography Geography* 87 2005:279-293

Fazal, Shahab. Urban expansion and loss of agricultural land – a GIS based study of Saharanpur City, India, Environment & Urbanization 12 2000:133-150

Fisman, L. "The effects of local learning on environmental awareness in children: An empirical investigation", *The Journal of Environmental Education* 3 2005:39-43

Foell, W., C. Green, M. Amann, S. Bhattacharya, G. Carmichael, M. Chadwick, S. Cinderby, T. Haugland, J. P. Hettelingh, L. Hordijk, J. Kuylenstierna, J. Shah, R. Shrestha, D. Streets, & D Zhao. "Energy use, emissions, and air pollution reduction strategies in Asia", *Water, Air, & Soil Pollution* 85 1995:2277-2282

Gokhale, A. "Environmental Initiative Prioritization with Delphi approach: A case study", *Environmental Management* 28 2001:187-193

GoI – Government of India, 2008. "Solekshaw' Eco-Friendly Dual-Powered Rickshaw Launched" http://www.dst.gov.in/whats_new/press-release08/solekshwa-launched.htm (accessed 30 June 2010)

GoJ – Government of Japan, Ministry of the Environment (MoE), Japan's Experience in Promotion of 3Rs. Tokyo: MoE, 2005

Grimm, Nancy B., Stanley H. Faeth, Nancy E. Golubiewski, Charles L. Redman, Jianguo Wu, Xuemei Bai & John M. Briggs. "Global Change and the Ecology of Cities", *Science* 319 2008:756-760

Guo, P., Yokoyama, K., Suenaga, M. & Kida, H. (2008) Mortality and life expectancy of Yokkaichi Asthma patients, Japan: Late effects of air pollution in 1960-70s. *Environmental Health,* 7, pp1-8.

Guomei, Z. Promoting 3R strategy: e-wastes management in China. *Asia 3R conference.* Tokyo: Japan State Environmental Protection Administration of China, 2006

Gurría, Angel. "The Economics of Climate Change: The Fierce Urgency of Now" *in* United Nations Climate Conference, Bali: OECD. 2007

Guttikunda, Sarath K., Gregory R. Carmichael, Giuseppe Calori, Christina Eck, & Jung-Hun Woo. "The contribution of mega-cities to regional sulphur pollution in Asia", Atmospheric Environment 37 2003:11-22

Hall, Colin Michael. Tourism and the Environmental Problems, Institutional Arrangements and Approaches in C. M. Hall & S. Page (eds.) *Tourism in South and Southeast Asia: Issues and Cases,* New York: Butterworth-Heinemann Elsevier, 2000:320

Halsnaes, K, & P Shukla. "Sustainable development as a framework for developing country participation in international climate change policies", Mitigation and Adaptation Strategies for Global Change 13 2008:105-130

Hara, Yuji, Danai Thaitakoo, & Kazuhiko Takeuchi. "Landform transformation on the urban fringe of Bangkok: The need to review land-use planning processes with consideration of the flow of fill materials to developing areas", Landscape and Urban Planning 84 2008:74-91

HEI. Health effects of outdoor air pollution in developing countries of Asia: a literature review. Special Report No. 15, Boston, MA: Health Effects Institute, 2004:129

Hinostroza, Miriam, Chia-Chia Cheng, Xainli Zhu, Jorgen Fenham, Christian Figueres & Fransciso Avendano. "Potentials and barriers for end-use energy efficiency under programmatic CDM", in CD4CDM Working Paper Nairobi: Riso Centre, United Nations Environment Programme, 2007

Hinrichsen, D. The Oceans Are Coming Ashore. *World Watch* November/December, 2000:26-35.

Hook, Walter, & Wright Lloyd. 2002. "Reducing GHG Emission by Shifting Passenger Trips to Less Polluting Modes", Background paper for the Brainstorming Session on Non-Technology Options for Stimulating Modal Shifts in City Transport Systems, Nairobi, March 25-26, 2002

Hosaka, Mitsuhiko, & Peter M. Shimokawa. *The State of the Urban Poor in Japan,* Asian Coalition for Housing Rights 1999. http://www.achr.net/sup_japan.htm (accessed 11 July 2010)

Hung, Tran, Daisuke Uchihama, Shiro Ochi, & Yoshifumi Yasuoka. "Assessment with satellite data of the urban heat island effects in Asian mega cities", *International Journal of Applied Earth Observation and Geoinformation* 8 2006:15

Idris, Arzni, Bulent Inanc, & Mohd Nassir Hassan. "Overview of waste disposal and landfills/dumps in Asian countries", *Journal of Materials Cycles Waste Management* 6 2004:104-110

Imura, H., Yedla, S., Shirakawa, H. & Memon, M. A. (2005) Urban Environmental Issues and Trends in Asia—an Overview. International Review for Environmental Strategies, 5, pp357-382.

Inanc, Bulent, Azni Idris, Atsushi Terazono, & Shin-ichi Sakai. "Development of a database of landfills and dump sites in Asian countries", *Journal of Material Cycles and Waste Management* 6 2004:97-103

International Energy Agency (IEA). *World Energy Outlook.* Paris: OECD/IEA 2008

International Energy Agency. *World Energy Outlook 2007.* Paris: IEA, 2007

IPCC. Climate Change and Water. In B. Bates, Z. W. Kundzewicz, S. Wu & J. Palutikof (eds.) *IPCC Technical Paper V*, Nairobi: UNEP & WMO, 2008

Karn, Sunil Kumar, & Hideki Harada. "Surface water pollution in three urban territories of Nepal, India, and Bangladesh", *Environmental Management* 28 2001:483-496

Kelkar, U, & S Bhadwal. "South Asian Regional Study on Climate Change Impacts and Adaptation: Implications for Human Development", *Occasional Paper.* New York: United Nations Development Programme, Human Development Report Office, 2007

Kim Hee-sung. 'President Lee announces establishment of Global Green Growth Institute' 16 June 2010 www.korea.net/news.do?mode=detail&guid=47660 (accessed 7 July 2010)

Kim Oanh, N.T., N. Upadhyay, Y.H. Zhuang, Z.P. Hao, D.V.S. Murthy, P. Lestari, J.T. Villarin, K. Chengchua, H. X. Co, N.T. Dung, & E.S. Lindgren. "Particulate air pollution in six Asian cities: Spatial and temporal distributions, and associated sources", *Atmospheric Environment* 40 2006:3367-3380

Klundert, Arnold van de, & Inge Lardinois. *Community and private (formal and informal) sector involvement in municipal solid waste management in developing countries.* Urban Management Programme, 10-12 April 1995. http://www.gdrc.org/uem/waste/swm-finge1.htm (accessed 10 August 2009)

Kojima, Masami, Carter Brandon, & Jitendra Shah. "Improving Urban Air Quality in South Asia by Reducing Emissions from Two-Stroke Engine Vehicles", Washington DC: World Bank, 2000

Government of Korea (GoK), Ministry of Environment. 'Trilateral action plan for environmental cooperation adopted' press release, 25 May 2010. http://www.korea.net/news.do?mode=detail&guid=46914 (accessed 7 July 2010)

Kreimer, A, M Arnold, & A Carlin. *Building Safer Cities: The Future of Disaster Risk, Series 3*, Washington, D.C.: World Bank, 2003

Krishna, A. K., & P. K. Govil. Heavy metal distribution and contamination in soils of Thane-Belapur industrial development area, Mumbai, Western India. *Environmental Geology* 47 2005:1054-1061

Kuchelmeister, G. "Asia-Pacific Forestry Sector Outlook Study: Urban Forestry in the Asia-Pacific Region - Situation and Prospects" *Outlook Study Working Paper Series.* Rome: FAO, 1998

Kuznets, Simon. "Toward a theory of economic growth", in R. Lekachman (ed.) *National Policy for Economic Welfare at Home and Abroad*, Garden City, New York: Doubleday, 1955, Paperback edition, London: W. W. Norton & Company, 1968:12-85

Kwi-Gon Kim. "The Application of the Biosphere Reserve Concept to Urban Areas: The Case of Green Rooftops for Habitat Network in Seoul" *Annals of the New York Academy of Sciences* 1023 2004:187-214

Lahiri, S, & S Chanthaphone. "Water, sanitation and hygiene: A situation analysis paper for Lao PDR", *International Journal of Environmental Health Research* 13 2003 pp107-114

Lam, Joseph C. "Residential sector air conditioning loads and electricity use in Hong Kong", *Energy Conversion and Management* 41 2000:1757-1768

Laustsen, Jens. *Energy Efficiency Requirements in Building Codes, Energy Efficiency Policies for New Buildings.* Paris: International Energy Agency. 2008

Lebel, Louis. "Global change and development: a synthesis for Southeast Asia", in P. Tyson, R. Fuchs, C. Fu, L. Level, A.P. Mitra, E. Odada, J. Perry, W. Steffen and H. Virji (eds.) G*lobal-regional linkages in the earth system*, Berlin: Springer, 2002:151–184

Lee, Y.F. "Tackling Cross-border Environmental Problems in Hong Kong: Initial Responses and Institutional Constraints", *The China Quarterly* 172 2002:986-1009

Lindley, S, J., Handley, N. Theuray, E. Peet, & D. Mcevoy. "Adaptation strategies for climate change in the urban environment: Assessing climate change related risk in UK urban areas", *Journal of Risk Research* 9 2006:543-568

Liu, Lianyou. *Background Paper on Drought - An Assessment of Asian and Pacific Progress,* Bangkok: UN Economic and Social Commission for Asia and the Pacific, 2007

Locke, Richard M. *The Promise and Perils of Globalization: The Case of Nike,* Cambridge, MA: MIT, 2003

Long, Alan J., & P. K. Ramachandran Nair. "Trees outside forests: agro-, community, and urban forestry", *New Forests* 17 1999:145-174

Mage, D, G Ozonlins, P Peterson, A Webster, R Orthofer, V Vandeweerd, & M Gwynne. "Urban air pollution in mega-cities of the world", *Atmospheric Environment* 31, 1996:681-686

Mahar, Aman, Tahira Ahmed, Zahiruddin Khan, Mauzam, & Ali Khan. "Review and Analysis of Current Solid Waste Management Situation in Urban Areas of Pakistan", in *Proceedings of the International Conference on Sustainable Solid Waste Management.* Chennai, India, 2007

Marcotullio, Peter, J. "Socio-ecological and urban environmental conditions in the Asia Pacific region", in *United Nations Expert Group Meeting on Population Distribution, Urbanization, Internal Migration and Development*, 21-23 January, New York: United Nations, 2008:249-286

—. "Urban water-related environmental transitions in Southeast Asia", Sustainability Science 2 2007:2 7-54

—. "Asian urban sustainability in the era of globalization", Habitat International 25 2001:577-598

Marcotullio, Peter, J. Eric Williams & Julian D. Marshall. "Faster, sooner, and more simultaneously: How recent road and aviation transportation CO_2 emission trends in developing countries differ from historic trends in the United States of America," *Journal of Environment and Development,* 14 2005:125-148

McGee, Terrance. "Managing the rural–urban transformation in East Asia in the 21st century", *Sustainability Science* 3 2008:155-167

McGranahan, Gordon, Deborah Balk, & Bridget Anderson. "The rising tide: assessing the risks of climate change and human settlements in low elevation coastal zones" *Environment & Urbanization* 19 2007-1:7-37

Mckinney, M. L. Urbanisation, Biodiversity and Conservation. *BioScience,* 52, 2002:883-890

Mercer. *Highlights from the 2007 Quality of Living Survey,* Mercer Human Resource Consulting 2007. http://www.mercer.com/summary.jhtml?idContent=1128060 (accessed 2 April 2000)

Muiga, Michael I., & George W. Reid. "Cost analysis of water and waste water treatment processes in developing countries", *Journal of the American Water Resources Association* 15 1979:838-852

Mukherjee, Amitava, Mrinal Kumar Sengupta, M. Amir Hossain, Sad Ahamed, Bhaskar Das, Bishwajit Nayak, Dilip Lodh, Mohammad Mahmudur Rahman & Dipankar Chakraborti. "Arsenic Contamination in Groundwater: A Global Perspective with Emphasis on the Asian Scenario", *Journal of Health population Nutrition* 24 2006:142-163

Narain, U. & Krupnick, A. The impact of Delhi's CNG program on Air Quality *Discussion Papers.* Washington, D.C: Resources for the Future, 2007:1-54

National Geographic. China Bans Free Plastic Bags. 2008. http://news.nationalgeographic.com/news/2008/01/080110-AP-bags.html (accessed 10 March 2010)

Ng, Mee Kam. "Asian World City Contest: Global Competitiveness and Local Sustainability", in *International Symposium on Growth Management of the Metropolitan Region* Seoul: Centre of Urban Planning and Environmental Management, University of Hong Kong, 2008

Nicholls, R.J., S. Hanson, C. Herweijer, N. Patmore, S. Hallegatte, J. Corfee-Morlot, J.Chateau, & R. Muir-Wood. Ranking Port Cities with High Exposure and Vulnerability to Climate Extremes Exposure Estimates. Paris: OECD, 2007

OECD. OECD Environmental Outlook: How much will it cost to address today's key environmental problems? Paris: Organization for Economic Cooperation and Development, 2008

Ooi, G. L. Urbanization in Southeast Asia: Assessing Policy Process and Progress toward Sustainability. *Journal of Industrial Ecology* 11, 2, 2007:31-42

Oxfam. Rethinking Disasters: Why Death and Destruction is Not Nature's Fault but Human Failure New Delhi: Oxfam International, 2008

Panther, B.C., M.A. Hooper, & N.J. Tapper. "A comparison of air particulate matter and associated polycyclic aromatic hydrocarbons in some tropical and temperate urban environments", *Atmospheric Environment* 33 1999:4087-4099

Parekh, P, H Khwaja, A Khan, R Naqvi, A Malik, S Shah, K Khan, & G Hussain. "Ambient air quality of two metropolitan cities of Pakistan and its health implications", *Atmospheric Environment* 35 2001:5971-5978

Parry, M. L., Canziani, O. F., Linden, P. J. V. D. & Hanson, C. E. (Eds.) *Climate Change 2007: Impacts, Adaptation and Vulnerability – Contribution of the Working Group II to the Fourth Assessment Report of the IPCC.* Cambridge: Cambridge University Press, 2007

Peking University & UNEP. SZEO 2007: *Shenzhen Environment Outlook.* Shenzhen: Peking University & UNEP. 2007. Available at: http://www.rrcap.unep.org/pub/EO/SZEO/index.cfm

Potera, C. Air Pollution: Asia's Two-Stroke Engine Dilemma. *Environmental Health Perspectives* 112, 2004:613-614

Preston, Benjamin L., Ramasamy Suppiah, Ian Macadam, and Janice Bathols. Climate Change in the Asia/Pacific Region: A Consultancy Report Prepared for the Climate Change and Development Roundtable. Melbourne: Commonwealth Scientific and Industrial Research Organization, 2006

Rees, William E., & Mathis Wackernagel, *Ecological footprints and appropriated carrying capacity: measuring the natural capital requirements of the human economy.* Edited by A. M. Jansson, M. Hammer, C. Folke & R. Costanza, *Investing in Natural Capital: The Ecological Economics Approach to Sustainability.* Washington, D.C: Island Press, 1994:362-390

Resosudarmo, B, & J Napitupulu. "Health and Economic Impact of Air Pollution in Jakarta", *The Economic Record (special issue)* 80 2004:65-75

Raufer, Roger. *Energy System Integration in Asian Cities-Promoting change for development and sustainability.* Asia-Pacific Forum on Low Carbon Economy – China, 2009: Beijing, June, 2009

Richman, Barbara.T. "Air pollution in the world's mega-cities", *Environment* 36 1994:25-37

Rijsberman, Frank R. "Water scarcity: Fact or fiction?" *Agricultural Water Management* 80 2006:5-22

Ritzkowski, M., & R. Stegmann. "Controlling greenhouse gas emissions through landfill in situ aeration", *International Journal of Greenhouse Gas Control* 1 2007:281-288

Roberts, Brian, & Trevor Kanaley. (eds.) *Overview* in *Urbanization and Sustainability in Asia: Case Studies of Good Practice*, Manila: Asian Development Bank & Cities Alliance 2006:1-11

Rockefeller Foundation. *Asian Cities Climate Change Resilience Network*, Rockefeller Foundation 2009 http://www.rockfound.org/initiatives/climate/acccrn.shtml (accessed 10 August 2009)

Roseland, Mark. "Dimensions of the eco-city", Cities 14 1997:197-202

Safriel, Uriel, Zafar, Adeel, Niemeijer, David, Puigdefabregas, Juan, White, Robin, Lal, Rattan, Winslow, Mark, Ziedler, Juliane, Prince, Stephen, Archer, Emma, King, Caroline "Dryland systems," in Rassan Hassan, Robert Scholes & Neville Ash (eds.) *Ecosystems and Human Well-Being: Current State and Trends, Volume 1,Millennium Ecosystem Assessment*, Washington DC: Island Press, 2005:623-662

Satterthwaite, David. "Cities' contribution to global warming: notes on the allocation of greenhouse gas emissions", *Environment & Urbanization* 20 2008:539-549

Satterthwaite, David, Saleemul Huq, Mark Pelling, Hannah Reid, & Patricia Romero. "Adapting to climate change in urban areas: the possibilities and constraints in low and middle-income nations" *International Institute for Environment Working Paper*. London: International Institute for Environment and Development, 2007

Schaefer-Preuss, Ursula. "Climate Change and Disaster Risk Management: Legislating Gender-Responsive Mitigation, Adaptation, and Women's Participation", in Third Global Congress of Women in Politics and Governance Gender in Climate Change Adaptation and Disaster Risk Reduction. Manila:

The CAPWIP Institute for Gender, Governance and Leadership, 2008

Schneider, Stephen H. & Janica Lane. "An Overview of 'Dangerous' Climate Change", in Hans Joachim Schellnhuber, Wolfgang Cramer, Nebojsa Nakicenovic, Tom Wigley and Gary Yohe (eds.) *Avoiding Dangerous Climate Change,* Cambridge: Cambridge University Press. 2006:7-24

Schwela, Dieter, Gary Haq, Cornie Huizenga, Wha-Jin Han, Herbert Fabian & May Ajero. *Urban Air Pollution in Asia Cities.* Stockholm: Stockholm Environment Institute, the Clean Air Initiative for Asian Cities, the Korean Environment Institute and UNEP, 2006

Schwela, Dieter, Gary Haq, Cornie Huizenga, Wha-Jin Han, Herbert Fabian, & May Ajero. *Urban Air Pollution in Asian Cities Status, Challenges and Management.* London: Earthscan, 2006

Scott, D. "Equal opportunity, unequal results: Determinants of household recycling intensity", *Environment and Behaviour* 31 1999 pp267-290

Shi, Guitao, Zhenlou Chen, Shiyuan Xu, Ju Zhang, Li Wang, Chunjuan Bi, & Jiyan Teng. "Potentially toxic metal contamination of urban soils and roadside dust in Shanghai, China," *Environmental Pollution* 156 2008:251-260

Shimoda, Y. "Adaptation measures for climate change and the urban heat island in Japan's built environment", *Building Research & Information* 31 2003:222-213

Siemens. *NEWater Singapore: A sustainable use of water for the Future,* Siemens 2008 http://wap.my-siemens.de/en/megatrends/water-solutions-newater.html (accessed 2 August 2009)

Singh, J. P. & Pannu, V. Economics of CNG Vehicle Program in Dhaka City. *Research Papers.* New Delhi: VisionRI Research Links, 2005:1-8

Staniskis, Jurgis. "Cleaner production in the developing world", *Clean Technologies and Environ-*

mental Policy 7 2005:145-147

Stapp, W.B *et al.* "The Concept of Environmental Education", *Journal of Environmental Education* 1 1969:30-31

Stern, Nicholas. *The Economics of Climate Change: the Stern Review,* Cambridge: Cambridge University Press. 2007:692

Suciu, Peter. 'Jakarta sinking Jakarta Sinking and We Don't Mean Just Its Stock Market, *AsiaOne News*, Singapore, 7 October edition, 2008, Reuters. http://www.brighthub.com/environment/science-environmental/articles/10180.aspx#ixzz0tcUDsQP4 (accessed 12 July 2010)

Tacoli, Cecilia. "Rural-urban interactions: a guide to the literature", *Environment & Urbanization* 10 1998:147-167

Takahashi, Ken, Matti S Huuskonen, Antti Tossavainen, Toshiaki Higashi, Toshiteru Okubo & Jorma Rantanen. "Ecological Relationship between Mesothelioma Incidence/Mortality and Asbestos Consumption in Ten Western Countries and Japan", *Journal of Occupational Health 41* 1999:8-11

Tapscott, Don, & Anthony D. Williams. *Wikinomics: How Mass Collaboration Changes Everything,* New York: Portfolio, 2006

Tee, E. Siong. "Obesity in Asia: prevalence and issues in assessment methodologies", *Asia Pacific Journal of Clinical Nutrition* 11 2002:S694-S701

Thaitakoo, Danai, & Brian McGrath. Bangkok Liquid Perception: Waterscape Urbanism in the Chao Phraya River Delta and Implications for Climate Change Adaptation, in Shaw, Rajib, and Danai Thaitakoo (eds.), *Water Communities: Community, Environment and Disaster Risk Management*, Vol. 2. Bingley, UK: Emerald Group Publishing, 2010:35-50

Thuy, H.T.T., H.J. Tobschall, & P.V. An. "Distribution of heavy metals in urban soils – a case study of Danang-Hoian Area (Viet-

nam)", *Environmental Geology* 39 2000:603-610

Umali, Claire M. "East Asian trilateral cooperation focuses on green issues" (dated 27 May 2010). http://www.ecoseed.org/en/general-green-news/green-topics/green-policies/climate-change/7265 (accessed 7 July 2010)

UNCCD. Climate Change Impacts in the Asia/Pacific Region. United Nations Convention to Combat Desertification, 2009

UNCHS & UNEP. *SCP Process Activities: A snapshot of what they are and how they are implemented, SCP Sourcebook Series*. Nairobi: UNCHS & UNEP, 1998a

—. *Programme Approach and Implementation, SCP Sourcebook Series*. Nairobi: UNCHS & UNEP, 1998b

UNDP. *Human Development Report 2007/2008: Fighting climate change: Human solidarity in a divided world*, United Nations Development Programme 2007. http://hdr.undp.org/en/reports/global/hdr2007-2008/ (accessed 16 July 2010)

UNEP *Global Environmental Outlook 3, Past, Present and Future Perspectives*. London: Earthscan, London, 2002

UNEP. *Geo4 Report UN*, Nairobi, Kenya: United Nations Environment Programme, 2007

UNESCO. *Urban Biosphere Reserves in the context of the Statutory Framework and the Seville Strategy for the World Network of Biosphere Reserves,* 2003. Geneva: United Nations Education, Scientific and Cultural Organization, 2003a

—. *Water for People: Water for Life*, Paris: United Nations Education, Scientific and Cultural Organization. 2003b

—. *The Seville Strategy for Biosphere Reserves*, Geneva: UNESCO, 2006

UNESCWA. *Population and Development Report Water Scarcity in the Arab World*, New York: UN Economic and Social Commission for Western Asia, 2003

United Nations. *World Urbanization Prospects: the 2007 Revision.* New York: United Nations Department of Economic and Social Affairs, Population Division. 2007

—. *World Urbanization Prospects: the 2005 Revision.* New York: United Nations Department of Economic and Social Affairs, Population Division. 2006

UNFPA. *State of world population 2009 – Facing a changing world: women, population and climate,* New York: United Nations Population Fund. 2009

UN-HABITAT. *Climate Change Strategy 2010-2013.* Nairobi: UN-HABITAT, n.d.a

—. *Cities and Climate Change – Initial Lessons from UN-HABITAT.* Nairobi: UN-HABITAT, n.d.b

—. *Annual Report 2009.* Nairobi: UN HABITAT, 2010a

—. *State of the World's Cities 2010/2011 – Bridging the Urban Divide,* Nairobi: UN HABITAT, 2010b

—. *Cities and Climate Change Initiative: Sorsogon City,* UN-HABITAT 2009. http://www.unhabitat.org/downloads/docs/6007_66066_Sorsogon_Philipines.pdf (accessed 11 July 2010)

—. *State of the World's Cities 2008/09 – Harmonious Cities,* Nairobi: UN-HABITAT. 2008

—. *Meeting development goals in small urban centres: Water and sanitation in the world's cities 2006,* Nairobi: UN-HABITAT; London, Sterling, VA: Earthscan, 2006

Van Berkel, René, Tsuyoshi Fujita, Shizuka Hashimoto & Yong Geng. "Industrial and urban symbiosis in Japan: Analysis of the Eco-Town programme 1997-2006", *Journal of Environmental Management* 90 2009:1544-1556

Vincentian Missionaries, "The Payatas Environmental Development Programme: microenterprise promotion and involvement in solid waste management in Quezon City", *Environment & Urbanization* 10 1998:55-68

Visvanathan, C, & T. Norbu. "Promoting the 3R in South Asia: Issues and possible solutions" Promoting Reduce, reuse and recycle in Southeast Asia, 30 August – 1 September 2006, Kathmandu, Nepal, 2006

Wang, Lin, Aihua Ma, Xiwen Zhou, Yingying Tan, Xiaona Yan, & Yu Wang. Environment and Energy Challenge of Air Conditioner in China. In *Bioinformatics and Biomedical Engineering, 2008 ICBBE. The 2nd International Conference.* Shanghai: Bioinformatics and Biomedical Engineering, 2008

Wang, Xue Song, Yong Qin, & Shu Xun Sang. "Accumulation and sources of heavy metals in urban topsoils: a case study from the city of Xuzhou, China", *Environmental Geology* 48 1 2005:101-107

WCEA. *Popularization of Clean Energy in Rizhao.* World Clean Energy Awards 2007 http://www.cleanenergyawards.com/top-navigation/awards/winners-2007/ (accessed 2 August 2009)

Webb, Richard. Urban and Peri-Urban Forestry: Case Studies in Developing Countries. Rome: Food and Agriculture Organization, 1999

WEF. *Global Risks.* Geneva: World Economic Forum MMC (Marsh & McLennan Companies, Inc.) Merrill Lynch and Swiss Re, 2006

Whitford, V. A. Ennos, & J Handley. "City Form and natural process – indicators for the ecological performance of urban areas and their application to Merseyside, UK", *Landscape and Urban Planning* 57 2001:91-103

World Health Organization (WHO). *Emerging Issues in Water and Infectious Disease,* Geneva: World Health Organization, 2003

—. WHO Air quality guidelines for particulate matter, ozone, nitrogen dioxide and sulphur dioxide. Geneva: World Health Organization, 2005

Wilcke, Wolfgang, Silke Muller, Nualsri Kanchanakool, & Wolfgang Zech. "Urban soil contamination in Bangkok: heavy metal and aluminium partitioning in topsoils", *Geoderma* 86 3-4 1998:211-228

Wong, C., S. Ma, A. Hedley, & T Lam. "Effect of Air Pollution on Daily Mortality in Hong Kong", *Environmental Health Perspectives* 109 2001:335-340

Woodroffe, C. "Southeast Asian Deltas", in A. Gupta (ed.) *The Physical Geography of Southeast Asia.* Oxford: Oxford University Press, 2005:219-36

World Bank. Statistical Yearbook 2002. In *2002:* World Bank General Statistical Office, Viet Nam, 2002 http://econ.worldbank.org/WBSITE/EXTERNAL/EXTDEC/EXTRESEARCH/EXTLSMS/0,,print:Y~isCURL:Y~contentMDK:21709831~menuPK:4196952~pagePK:64168445~piPK:64168309~theSitePK:3358997~isCURL:Y~isCURL:Y,00.html (accessed 16 July 2010)

—. Promoting Global Environmental Priorities in the Urban Transport Sector: Experience from World Bank Group - Global Environment Facility Projects. Washington, D.C: Global Environment Operations Environment Department, World Bank, 2006

—. Climate Resilient Cities. Washington, D.C: World Bank, 2008

—. *Environment in East Asia and the Pacific,* World Bank, 2009 http://web.worldbank.org/WBSITE/EXTERNAL/COUNTRIES/EASTASIAPACIFICEXT/EXTEAPREGTOPENVIRONMENT/0,,contentMDK:20282861~menuPK:502915~pagePK:34004173~piPK:34003707~theSitePK:502886,00.html (accessed 2 August 2009)

—. Cost of Pollution in China: Economic Estimates of Physical Damages. Beijing: World Bank, 2007a

—. "East Asian Environment Monitor: Adapting to Climate Change", *The Environmental Monitor Series.* Washington D.C: World Bank, 2007b

—. What a waste: Solid Waste Management in Asia. Washington, D.C.: World Bank, 1999

World Wildlife Fund. *Mega-Stress for Mega Cities.* Gland, Switzerland: World Wildlife Fund. 2009

Xiao-dong, Kou, Li Guang-jun, Wang Qing, Yang Lin, & Xue Hui-feng. "Application Research of Ecological Footprint: Time Sequence and Comparative Analysis of Selected Chinese Cities", Institute of Resources and Environmental Information Engineering, North-Western Polytechnical University, 2005

Xiao, Yi, Xuemei Bai, Zhiyun Ouyang, Hua Zheng, & Fangfang Xing. "The composition, trend and impact of urban solid waste in Beijing", *Environmental Monitoring and Assessment* 135 2007:21-30

Yuen, Belinda, Supian Ahmad, & Chin Siong Ho. "Urbanization and Sustainability in Asia: Malaysia", in B. Roberts & T. Kanaley (eds.) *Urbanization and Sustainability in Asia: Good Practice Approaches in Urban Region Development.* Manila: Asian Development Bank and Cities Alliance, 2006:223-243

Zhao, Shuqing, Liangjun Da, Zhiyao Tang, Hejun Fang, Kun Song, & Jingyun Fang. "Ecological consequences of rapid urban expansion: Shanghai, China", *Frontiers in Ecology and the Environment* 4 2006a:341-346

Zhao, Shuqing, Changhui Peng, Hong Jiang, Dalun Tian, Xiangdong Lei, & Xiaolu Zhou. "Land use change in Asia and the ecological consequences", *Ecological Research* 21 2006b:890-896

Zhou, Liming, Robert E. Dickinson, Yuhong Tian, Jingyun Fang, Qingxiang Li, Robert K. Kaufmann, Compton J. Tucker, & Ranga B. Myneni. "Evidence for a significant urbanization effect on climate in China", *Proceedings of the National Academy of Sciences of the United States of America* 101 2004:9540-9544

Seoul, South Korea.
©Grafica/Shutterstock

PART
06

Urban governance, management and finance

Quick Facts

1. Experience has shown that, on their own, the technocratic approaches traditionally used by urban authorities in Asia have had limited efficiency.

2. The past two decades have seen a broadening of the scope of governance in Asia from being related to the 'business' of government to that the 'process' of governance which involves various stakeholders.

3. Recent constitutional and statutory changes in a number of Asian countries reflect the recognition of the vital role of civil society participation in urban governance, as non-governmental and grassroots organisations demand greater involvement in local affairs.

4. Participatory budgeting leads to improvements in infrastructure, services and accountability, but various elements in Asian urban governance are standing in the way.

5. Many smaller urban settlements are finding it difficult to achieve development goals, due to inadequate financial, human, institutional and legal resources or frameworks, as well as poor political leadership, but national governments tend to ignore their predicament.

6. The emergence of mega urban regions in Asia has posed serious challenges to both urban planning and governance.

7. Urban authorities in Asia would need to spend close to US $10 trillion over 10 years if they were to meet all their requirements in terms of infrastructures and institutional frameworks.

Policy Points

1. Effective, broad-based governance increases cities' contributions to national economic, social and environmental development.

2. Since the highest rates of urban growth in Asia are found in small cities and towns, these must be empowered to manage their own development. Urban governance initiatives should be directed to smaller urban settlements, in the process stimulating development in adjoining rural areas.

3. Well-formulated, well-executed city cluster development schemes can bring a number of benefits, including much-needed employment and integrated urban infrastructure and services.

4. Mixed systems of government are predominant in Asia and are well-placed to bring about more comprehensive planning, mobilize appropriate financial resources, improve management efficiency, and involve the private sector.

5. Mega urban regions in the Asia-Pacific region need new urban planning and governance structures.

6. If urban governance is to be effective and sustainable, devolution of authority and power to urban local governments is needed, along with adequate financial, revenue-raising and human capacities. Decentralization requires central government support to avoid excessive regional disparities within countries.

7. Local governments associations should promote city-to-city ('C2C') cooperation for to support sharing and exchange of lessons learnt and good practices in order to achieve intra-regional learning on sustainable urban development and good urban governance.

6.1
Introduction

▲
Chongqing, China. ©**JingAiping/Shutterstock**

Urban governance, management and finance had been on the policy agenda in the Asian-Pacific region for two decades or so but with the worldwide economic crisis that began in 2008 these issues have taken on a more visible and acute dimension. As governments turned to fiscal stimulus in a bid to kick-start flagging economies (see Chapter 3), the main beneficiaries were none other than cities in the expectation that they would generate substantial multiplier effects. Clearly, this recognition of the major role of cities in national economic prosperity was not unwelcome *per se;* however, it also highlighted the various institutional deficiencies and shortcomings that leave Asian cities ill-prepared to face present and future challenges.

As the ripple effects of the US financial crisis began to spread across the world, the Asian Development Bank (ADB) and the International Monetary Fund had already measured up the amounts of capital expenditure required if the Asian region as a whole was to upgrade both physical and institutional infrastructures to face up to those challenges: it would take US $4.7 trillion over 10 years to meet urban infrastructure requirements, an additional US $1.6 trillion to replace aging infrastructure and another US $3.1 trillion to strengthen institution-building and management capacity (Asian Development Bank, 2008a; IMF, 2008a, 2008b, 2009), or close to US $10 trillion in total.

In recent years, many Asian cities have sought to improve governance in a bid to achieve sustained economic and social development. However, the recent economic crisis has tended to worsen conditions in some cities already plagued by various governance-related woes such as slum and squatter settlements, traffic gridlock, inadequate water supply, poor sanitation, unreliable energy systems and serious environmental pollution. The gated communities of the rich and the ghettoized enclaves of the poor come as dramatic illustrations of an 'urban divide' (UN-HABITAT, 2010a) often characterized as 'a tale of two cities.' Inner cities deteriorate as development moves to outlying areas and results in automobile-induced urban sprawl. Pervasive graft and corruption mar the implementation of many projects. All these problems dent the capacity of urban areas to act as development hubs and call for a vital need for improved governance.

The general concept of governance has evolved over the years. In 1992, the World Bank defined governance as "the manner in which power is exercised in the management of a country's economic and social resources for development" (World Bank, 1992:3). However, the Bank's emphasis on management has been deemed too government-orientated. A few years later in 1995, the Organization for Economic Co-operation and Development (OECD) defined governance as "the sum of the many ways individuals and institutions, public or private, manage their common affairs" (OECD, 1995).

As noted by Cheema & Rondinelli (2005:1), "The fact that people's lives were also shaped by decisions made by individual entrepreneurs, family enterprises, and private firms; by multinational corporations and international financial institutions; and by a variety of civil society organizations operating both within and outside of national territories became more apparent." With this realization, urban authorities recognized the need for a broader understanding of governance, one that went beyond the formal institutional realm of government action. Consistent with this broader concept, the United Nations Development Programme (UNDP) has defined governance as "the exercise of economic, political and administrative authority to manage a country's affairs at all levels" (UNDP, 2003:170).

BOX 6.1: A DECENTRALISED POLITICAL 'SPACE' FOR SUSTAINABLE URBANISATION

Participatory local governance is one of the tenets of sustainable development and to be effective calls for a political 'space' which only decentralisation can provide. Widely different national institutional systems, as can be found in Asia, have long stood in the way of a universal framework, but the efforts deployed by UN-HABITAT since 1996 have finally delivered a well-recognised set of meaningful guidelines. These together provide for the improved coordination which public authorities need if they are to pave the way for more sustainable, inclusive cities and achieve the Millennium Development Goals (UN-HABITAT, 2010a).

As a follow-up to the 1996 Habitat II Conference in Istanbul, UN-HABITAT produced a draft *World Charter on Local Self-Government* modelled on the European Charter on Local Self-Government. The draft set out the rights and responsibilities of local authorities and gave them the stronger role they needed for a more effective implementation of the Habitat Agenda that had been adopted in Istanbul.

Despite the Habitat II call for more decentralised and participatory governance, the draft was met with dissent rather than consensus. Some countries saw it as too ambitious and too inflexible in view of the diversity of national institutional, socio-economic and historical backgrounds. This is why in 2001 member states requested UN-HABITAT to look for a compromise. Those in favour of the draft Charter felt that an international agreement would facilitate the implementation of the Habitat Agenda but they also found that the draft should better accommodate different types of constitutional settings. Opponents

called instead for a declaration of principles which would not be as binding as the proposed Charter but would still support what was then known as the 'Istanbul+5' process.

In the meantime, many countries around the world continued their search for viable decentralisation options to improve local democracy and delivery of basic urban services. Experience shows that it takes a lot more than just political will for decentralisation to succeed. A range of actions must be taken in a variety of areas; this includes improved public accountability and political management through promotion of democratic and participatory decision-making arrangements, as well as enhancing the legitimacy and effectiveness of sub-national tiers of government through legal and fiscal reforms and capacity development.

A report on emerging decentralisation trends was commissioned by UN-HABITAT and was discussed at the first World Urban Forum in 2002. Whereas Habitat Agenda partners re-affirmed the potential role of decentralisation (including stronger local authorities, anchoring democracy in developing and transition countries, etc.), they also argued that a determining factor for effective decentralisation is the involvement of central government in the process. With local empowerment an essential building block of national and sub-national democracy, decentralisation becomes a major factor of democratic governance, economic growth and sustainable development at the local, national and international levels.

The next step came in 2003 when the UN-HABITAT Governing Council endorsed a proposal

to create an Advisory Group of Experts on Decentralisation (AGRED) with a mandate to (i) examine and review existing policies and decentralisation legislation; (ii) develop principles and recommendations; and (iii) document cases of good practice in support of the international principles and recommendations on decentralisation and strengthening of local authorities.

After a fresh round of discussions at the 2004 World Urban Forum, another dedicated working group was set up the following year. This was when the Governing Council requested UN-HABITAT to identify a number of underlying principles on access to basic services for all which could pave the way for sustainable human settlements as well as enhanced human dignity and quality of life. Now working in parallel, the two groups each developed a set of principles that could be used as common denominators, being derived from existing policies, regulations and frameworks on decentralisation and universal basic services.

UN-HABITAT's efforts culminated when its Governing Council finally endorsed the *International Guidelines on Decentralisation and Strengthening of Local Authorities* in 2007 (see Box 6.8) and the *International Guidelines on Access to Basic Services* in 2009. These two sets of guidelines assist policy and legislative reform at the country level. As such they represent a significant milestone in the agency's efforts to mobilize member states and secure the decentralised political 'space' required for improved delivery of basic urban services and more sustainable settlements.

Source: http://www.unhabitat.org/pmss/pmss/electronic_books/2613_alt.pdf

As for *urban* governance, UN HABITAT sees it as "the sum of the many ways individuals and institutions, public and private, plan and manage the common affairs of the city. It is a continuing process through which conflicting or diverse interests may be accommodated and cooperative action can be taken. It includes formal institutions as well as informal arrangements and the social capital of citizens" (UN-HABITAT, 2005:20).

As globalization pervades urban societies, it has become quite obvious that local self-government plays a vital role in any effective democratic politics. UN-HABITAT's Global Campaign on Urban Governance (launched in 1999) is focused on participatory and inclusive governance. UN-HABITAT's Urban Governance Index provides a methodology to assess urban governance practices. When the UN-

HABITAT Governing Council adopted a set of International Guidelines on Decentralization and Strengthening of Local Authorities (see Boxes 6.1 and 6.8), its members set out the main principles underlying the democratic, constitutional, legal and administrative aspects of local governance (UN-HABITAT Governing Council, 2007). United Cities and Local Government (UCLG) has also highlighted the importance of urban governance in effective democracy. In its 2008 Global Observatory on Local Democracy and Decentralisation ('GOLD') Report, United Cities and Local Government stated: "local self-government denotes the rights and the ability of local authorities within the limit of the law to regulate and manage a substantial share of public affairs under their own responsibility and in the interest of the local population" (UCLG, 2008:19).

6.2
Urban governance and operational structures

Beijing, China. ©**Sunxuejun/Shutterstock**

Ever-improving economic and social conditions combine with internal and international migration and the widespread effects of globalization to change the nature of Asian-Pacific urban settlements. Demographic expansion brings more diversity to urban communities, in the process creating more tension and social fragmentation. At the same time, this expansion enables economies of scale and agglomeration with productive concentrations of capital (human, financial and physical) and larger markets for goods and services –

what is known as the 'productivity of social diversity.' The importance of social diversity and its role in productivity has, in turn, generated ideas and policies designed to enhance 'inclusiveness' in urban governance (Stren, 2001; Stren & Polese, 2000; UN-HABITAT, 2010a).

Urban authorities in the Asian-Pacific region have traditionally relied on operational structures and processes such as city and regional plans, zoning codes, regulations and standards, financing schemes, proper personnel management and the use of performance evaluation and audit methods for

FIGURE 6.1: **BASIC STAKEHOLDERS IN URBAN GOVERNANCE**

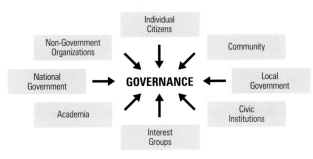

Source: Laquian (2005:109)

the sake of cost-effectiveness and accountability. However, experience has shown that technocratic approaches, by themselves, had limited efficiency in urban areas for two main reasons: (i) the informal sector makes a significant contribution to local economies, and (ii) urban authorities are chronically short of capital and operating funds. In recent years, urban authorities have greatly benefited from the participation of citizens, business, community and other civil society groups that have become actively involved in the governance process (World Bank, 2009; ADB, 2008b).

6.2.1 The stakeholders in urban governance

"Governance of human settlements in Asia today involves multiple actors and stakeholders, interdependent resources and actions, shared purposes and blurred boundaries between the public and the private, formal and informal, and state and civil society sectors. The active involvement of these varied actors in governance indicates a greater need for coordination, negotiation and building consensus." UN-HABITAT (2001)

Consistent with the shift to a broader scope, governance is now recognized as involving much more than the business of *government* which focuses mainly on the way formal institutions operate. The definition of urban governance has more recently been broadened to include "the critical role played by organizations in urban civil society where formal structures are weak and unable to provide basic services" (McCarney *et al.*, 1995; Laquian, 2005). As pointed out by McCarney *et al.*, (1995:95), "urban governance is concerned with the relationship between civil society and the state, between rulers and the ruled, the government and the governed."

Recent constitutional and statutory changes in a number of Asian countries reflect the recognition of the vital role of civil society participation in urban governance. In India, the 73rd and 74th amendments to the Constitution have done more than decentralizing authority and devolving power to local government units: they have also specified the roles to be played in governance by grassroots or community-based organizations, women's groups, the urban poor and

various emanations of civil society. In the Philippines, the 1987 revised Constitution upholds the right of community-based, non-governmental, and sector-based organizations to become directly involved in governance, enabling people, within the extant democratic framework, to pursue and protect their legitimate and collective interests and aspirations through peaceful and lawful means (Art. XIII, Section 15). In Pakistan, the law reorganizing urban authorities grants a formal role to non-elected members of the public: 'Citizen Community Boards' are empowered to spend one fourth of budgets on community needs. In Thailand, the Constitution Act of 1997 prescribes the establishment of local personnel committees with representatives not only from government agencies, but also "qualified persons" from local populations. The Thai Constitution (Art. 286 and 287) also grants citizens the right to recall votes when elected officials are not trustworthy (Amornvivat, 2004). In India, the infrastructure funding programme of the Jawaharlal Nehru Urban Renewal Mission (JNNURM) requires state governments to embed citizen participation in legislation (GoI, 2009).

A diagram used by UN-HABITAT's Urban Management Programme in its training materials lists eight main stakeholders in urban governance (Figure 6.1). Their mutual interactions enable urban societies to evolve consensus, formulate and enforce laws, adopt and enforce regulations, and legitimately manage urban affairs for the sake of justice, welfare and environmental protection.

- *Local Governments,* as part of their legislative, executive and judicial functions, promulgate, execute, finance and evaluate public programmes or policies. At the same time, local authorities rely on the public for inputs in policymaking and feedback on outcomes and performance.
- *Civic Institutions* help secure consistency between particular concerns and the more general, public interests they typically advocate, and also assess and monitor performance. They augment government resources through voluntary efforts and resource mobilization in support of public programmes.
- *Interest Groups,* including the *Business Sector* and *Labour/ Trade Unions* pursue more narrowly focused objectives that also contribute to public welfare. Private sector participation in the financing, operation and management of urban infrastructure and services has become a critical element in urban governance. As for labour unions, they stand for equity and social justice in the allocation of the benefits arising from public policies and programmes.
- The *Academic* community is an excellent source of research-based policy analysis that methodically assesses the effects and impact of specific public actions. Academic research also contributes to good management and governance, including with experimental pilot projects before these are mainstreamed in public programmes.
- *National governments,* on top of maintaining public order and the conduct of foreign affairs, can levy taxes, a prerogative that can be shared with local government units. Effective, strategically sound decentralization and

devolution has a crucial role to play in urban management and governance.

- *Non-governmental organizations* are voluntary groups that represent special interests based on issues, group affiliation, geographic areas and other fields. They act as advocates for specific causes and influence the formulation, adoption or implementation of public policies that help make urban areas more sustainable.

- *Individual citizens* exert their own influence on urban management and governance through participation in elections, plebiscites and referendums. They also evaluate how public programmes positively or negatively affect their lives, and use the media or civic action to make their voices heard and their influence felt. Although citizens may appear powerless as individuals, they can exert direct influence on local government when they are organized and mobilized around specific issues.

- Active participation of individuals organized at *Community* or grassroots level is the basis for peoples' initiatives, especially when regrouped in community-based organizations (CBOs). The community level is where public interests are best formulated, as citizens tend to be more aware of local conditions and local leaders in a better position to heed their demands, with human and material resources mobilized in the pursuit of common goals. Community-level stakeholders can also monitor and evaluate governance, ensuring better efficiency and equity.

The above-listed eight types of stakeholders in urban governance are crucial to economic, social and environmental sustainability in urban areas, to which they contribute in the following ways:

- Individual citizens, interest groups and communities, together with civic institutions, the academic community and non-governmental organisations, make possible the accurate identification of peoples' needs and requirements through interest aggregation and expression which can guide public authorities when devising policies and programmes, facilitate monitoring and evaluation, and promote transparency and accountability. Civil society can act as a two-way channel, including for feedback about the nature and performance of public policies and the need for any changes.

- Local and central governments are guided by grassroots participation in the formulation, implementation and evaluation of those policies and programmes designed to achieve common societal goals.

- Good urban governance enhances direct or indirect involvement of communities and various sectors of society in government affairs, which contributes to democratic decision-making.

- Active involvement of individuals, communities, interest groups, civic institutions and non-governmental organisations in urban governance facilitates the collection and allocation of resources in a fair, equitable and inclusive manner.

- Good urban governance comes hand in hand with agreed, appropriate ethical standards of behaviour and performance for holders of public office.

As sections 6.2.1 to 6.2.4 in this chapter show, many urban authorities in Asia have undertaken to reform local management and governance. For all these efforts, though, these authorities remain confronted with a number of critical problems. Effective governance structures and institutions may well be conducive to participation, but they do not always support the principles of broad-based governance. The management of urban services suffers from lack of coordination, as functionally orientated central government departments compete with geographically truncated local/urban authorities. Formal government programmes come into conflict with the interests of people living in informal settlements because administrative and legal reforms are not effectively adjusted to grassroots realities. Central-local relationships also need reviewing in order to facilitate broader participation in governance.

Another problem with urban governance is that it often fails to take into account informal stakeholders, although these play a significant role in community life. The urban poor living in slum and squatter settlements, and more particularly street vendors, waste pickers and people in other informal sector jobs, have become organized and can wield considerable political influence; to borrow UN-HABITAT's finding in connection with 'the urban divide' (2010), informal business associations can contribute to political inclusion. The reverse side of this welcome phenomenon cannot be ignored, though: organized crime syndicates become a *de facto* government in some low-income settlements, especially when they enjoy the support of corrupt government officials or civil servants (Aliani *et al.*, 1996).

Those intent on reforming municipal governance often overlook the class-based nature of urban society. City dwellers can be broadly divided into a small elite group, the middle classes, and the poor. Often, the ruling classes wield the most power because they are better organized, control greater economic resources and have better access to communication channels than other groups. As noted in UN-HABITAT's report *State of the World Cities – Bridging the Urban Divide* (2010:90), "The markets for land, basic services and labour are skewed in favour of private interests, enabling these to claim more than their fair share [and causing] massive displacement [...] to the detriment of the habitats and livelihoods of the poor." The urban poor hold the least degree of power although in recent years they have become better organized and in some cases, have been able to influence elections and thwart proposed forced eviction by public authorities. The middle classes are best placed to become politically engaged and in some Asian cities have become the moving forces behind the non-governmental and community-based organisations that have spearheaded much-needed governance reforms (ESCAP, 2002).

6.3
The principles of urban governance

▲
Yangon Town Hall, Myanmar. ©**Bumihills/Shutterstock**

The cardinal principles of urban governance include responsiveness to the public's needs and demands, as well as accountability of decision-makers. Responsiveness goes hand in hand with the principles of participation, transparency and the pursuit of consensus, while accountability is linked to the rule of law, effectiveness, efficiency and equity (UNDP-TUGI, 2003). In most Asian-Pacific cities, the population can participate in the performance of public functions such as elections, the budgetary process and reviews of public actions. UN-HABITAT suggests further indicators of participation in urban governance such as: (i) formation of civic associations; (ii) number of people's forums; (iii) voting turnout in local elections; (iv) direct election of mayors; and (v) direct election of city councils. Monitoring of these indicators in a number of Asian countries, including Mongolia and Sri Lanka, measures progress made in urban governance (UN-HABITAT, 2005).

Practice so far shows that the process of urban governance requires more than formal adherence to government procedures. As the agenda of the UN-HABITAT Global Campaign on Urban Governance plainly states, "Governance is not government." Indeed, and as suggested above, governance is a more complex process that calls for active involvement from various stakeholders, including business and the public.

6.3.1 Participation and representation

Historically, central governments in the Asia-Pacific region have dominated local agendas. With ever more complex urban conditions and pervasive globalization, however, grassroots and special-interest groups as well as non-governmental organizations have demanded greater participation in local affairs. They have taken to campaigning in favour of causes like social justice, environmental protection and preservation, equitable gender roles, alleviation of poverty and other social causes. During the 1970s and 1980s, governments in countries like Indonesia, the Philippines, the Republic of Korea and Pakistan sought to restrict civic participation. These regimes have not survived, though, and strong-armed rule by leaders like Suharto in Indonesia and Marcos in the Philippines has collapsed (Douglass, 2005).

A comparative study of 15 countries in the Asia-Pacific region has identified almost a dozen techniques of participatory urban governance (ESCAP, 1999). The most direct form of participation is through local elections, referendums, petitions and attendance at committee meetings. In India, mission-specific non-governmental organizations have concentrated on advocating and fighting for developmental or remedial issues. They also use the mass media to campaign for specific

Elections in the Philippines, May 2010. ©**Tony Magdaraog/Shutterstock**

reforms. Urban residents in Indonesia have become directly involved in the 'bottom up' planning process that brings up local concerns. In China, direct participation has taken the form of community consultation and dialogue with local officials. In the Republic of Korea, urban dwellers have come up with frequent demands for audits of, and investigations in, government programmes. In Thailand, the government has set up a "court of governance" which citizens can turn to in order to resolve conflicts with public authorities.

While local elections generally ensure public participation, the fact that the smallest municipal authorities generally lack resources to pursue public programmes acts as a major hindrance. The reverse can also happen: in China, central government has seemingly devolved authority to urban local governments while at the same time maintaining its grip on real power. Elections have been held in Chinese villages since November 2001 in a bid to eradicate local corruption. The central government decided, however, that no such open elections were to be held at the township, prefecture or higher tiers of government. The officials who framed the decentralization law merely expressed the hope that "as experience is gained with democracy at the bottom, similar elections will be required at the far more significant levels of the township … and gradually move up the ladder to provincial and national levels" (Eckholm, 2001:20).

In some Asian-Pacific cities, mass protests and demonstrations have been used by the population as participatory instruments. The "people power" revolutions in the Philippines have found echoes in similar waves of protest in Indonesia, the Republic of Korea, Thailand and other Asian countries. On top of these, pro-reform movements have exposed cases of graft and corruption in the mass media. Other major causes taken up by the public included affordable housing, employment,

welfare services and greater social justice for the urban poor. Civil society groups have campaigned for gender equality and environmental protection. In almost all Asian cities, thousands of community-based organisations and other civil society groups have taken up causes and exerted political pressures on power holders.

Participatory policymaking has recently been introduced in a number of Asian cities. In India, under the 1992 Constitutional Amendment Act, state governments must make sure that municipal councils are more representative with at least one-third of all seats reserved for women. In Pakistan, recent reorganization efforts have introduced a three-tier metropolitan governance structure in Karachi, including Citizen Community Boards, in order to encourage more participatory governance (see 6.2.1 above and Box 6.2).

Some Asian governments have deployed 'accommodating' policies that include marginalized groups in governance. In Kuala Lumpur and Quezon City, urban authorities have refrained from arresting sidewalk vendors and confiscating their goods, and instead build kiosks for them in legally sited areas, complete with water and sanitation facilities. In Bandung, Bangkok and Manila, community-upgrading programmes now provide housing and basic services *in situ,* rather than evicting squatters and slum-dwellers (except those occupying dangerous and disaster-prone areas). Most low-cost housing programmes for the urban poor in Asian cities now include clear provisions for self-help, mutual aid and co-financing, tapping the resources of the urban poor themselves in a bid to augment limited government resources through so-called 'enabling' strategies. A statute in the Philippines prohibits eviction of squatters or slum-dwellers unless they are relocated to a new site with acceptable housing and urban amenities (see the section on evictions in Chapter 4).

BOX 6.2: PARTICIPATORY URBAN GOVERNANCE: GOOD PRACTICE FROM KARACHI

Being host to a population of 14 million, Karachi is the largest city in Pakistan. The City of Karachi Municipal Act (1933) established the office of the Mayor, a Deputy Mayor and 57 councillors. In the year 2000, a devolution plan abolished second-tier administrative subdivisions and merged Karachi's five districts into a single 'City District'. Over the next few years, a federated governance system was deployed including a city district council, 18 'town' councils and 178 'union' or neighbourhood councils. It is worth noting that this federated three-tier system was specifically designed to encourage greater participation in governance.

Sitting at the top of the Karachi municipal system is the City District Government, followed by Town Municipal Administration units and Union Administration units. The towns are governed by elected municipal administrations responsible for infrastructure and spatial planning, development facilitation and municipal services. The Union Councils are each composed of 13 directly elected members including a 'nazim' (Urdu for mayor) and a 'naib nazim' (deputy mayor). The 'nazim' heads the union administration, links with the City District Government and keeps higher authorities updated on citizen concerns.

The core of the participatory system is the Union Council where all the members are elected from residents in the neighbourhoods. A specified number of seats on the district, town and union councils are reserved for civil society groups such as the urban poor, women and underprivileged groups. These representatives emanate from the Citizen Community Boards (CCBs) which local communities have set up to develop and improve service delivery to the needy through voluntary, proactive and self-help initiatives. The Boards raise funds through voluntary contributions, gifts, donations, grants and endowments, and generally fund their own activities.

Some of the Boards enter into cost-sharing arrangements with urban authorities to pursue development projects. As non-profit organizations, the Boards can use their assets and incomes for designated purposes only. This procedure is specifically required when they receive matching grants from urban authorities (which can be as much as 80 per cent of the budgeted amounts in a project). Those projects involving public funding are subject to government audits. The commitment to transparency and accountability is so firmly held that the Mayor of Karachi has invited non-governmental organisation Transparency International to study what could be done to help the city implement a more transparent and accountable system from the bottom up.

Source: Fahim (2005)

Inevitably, political leaders or activists on occasion have manipulated participatory governance for their own ends. For example, some public authorities have co-opted a number of non-governmental organisations as auxiliaries of political party machines, turning them into 'government-controlled non-governmental organisations' ('GONGOs') when not creating them from scratch. In Kolkata, a political party known as the Left Front has been accused of using its campaign in support of informal street vendors in a so-called "Operation Sunshine" that aimed at evicting homeless people living on the pavements. According to one researcher, the Left Front has actually cleared land to make way for land subdivisions for the middle classes (Roy, 2002).

6.3.2 Participatory budgeting

Participatory budgeting, whereby ordinary residents decide local resource allocations among competing items, has been quite late in coming to the Asia-Pacific region but it is gaining in popularity. The process originated in Porto Alegre, Brazil, in 1989. In a bid to involve low-income people and civil society groups in governance processes, the city empowered neighbourhood, district and city-wide groups and associations to elect budget delegates who identified spending priorities and decided which items should be implemented and funded. A participatory budgeting cycle was instituted whereby specific steps in the process were carried out at designated times over the course of the year. Evaluation found that participatory budgeting increased the numbers of desired outputs, raised the quality of public services and improved both transparency and the accountability of local officials.

In Indian cities, a number of civil society groups have engaged in analyses of state budgets, prepared budget briefs and influenced local legislators to allocate more resources to programmes that benefit poor and underserved communities. In Pune, the municipal authorities enabled both the citizens and city officials to submit requests for projects. In 2006 and 2007, the process was refined and members of self-help groups in low-income communities received specific training. In 2008 and 2009, the participatory budgeting exercise was extended to residents at the ward level. For example, in one ward where the collection, sorting and selling of solid waste was the main source of income, a rag pickers' professional group helped municipal authorities devise a budget that allocated funds for the construction of sorting sheds. In other municipal wards, residents participated in the formulation of budgets for the construction of bus stops and municipal markets, together with the allocation of designated zones for street vendors (Janwani, 2010).

In Indonesia and Pakistan in 2005-06, the Asian Development Bank provided training programmes in participatory budgeting in those locations where community consultation was explicitly required for formulation and voting. Because participatory budgeting was a new concept, the pilot projects involved preparation of training and instruction materials as well as expert technical advice. In the Pakistani pilot scheme, the government required that at least 25 per cent of development funds be set aside for projects proposed by Citizen Community Boards (Ahmad & Weiser, 2006).

In Indonesia, the government has set up an elaborate system of public consultation meetings that starts in villages and continues to the district level. The objective was "enhancing civil society's awareness of resource allocation and the budgeting process and their actual involvement in the budget decision-making process" (Ahmad & Weiser, 2006). Advocates of participatory budgeting anticipated that through informed and constructive engagement, public service delivery would become more responsive to the needs of the poor.

Experience in Latin America shows that participatory budgeting leads to direct improvements in urban infrastructure and services such as water connections, clinics and schools, and therefore improves conditions for poor and marginalized groups. The large numbers of participants involved have a cumulative effect as they encourage even more citizen involvement. In fact, the experience in Pune, where the rag-pickers association were directly involved in budgeting, demonstrates that direct community involvement has the capacity to reverse policies and programmes which otherwise would have adversely affected the lives of the urban poor (UN-HABITAT, 2006).

The Asian Development Bank's pilot projects in Indonesia and Pakistan showed that although participatory budgeting has achieved largely similar results as in Latin America, some elements in Asian governance called for remedial measures. In Indonesia and Pakistan, for instance, municipal technical staff tended to dominate the budgetary process. Although local consultations were nominally open to all citizens, community leaders and local politicians tended to be the main participants. As a result, the tendency was to go for projects that mainly benefited specific groups. The interests of the poor and marginalized groups were upheld only when vocal civil society and other non-governmental organisations championed their own causes (Ahmad & Weiser, 2006).

6.3.3 The mechanisms for accountability and transparency

Two of the most serious governance problems in Asian-Pacific cities are how to enhance the transparency of public decision-making and how government officials can be made more accountable for their actions. Although legislation formally enhances transparency and accountability, corruption remains a serious issue in many Asian countries. As described in the *Urban Governance Toolkit* published by UN-HABITAT in 2004, corruption takes a number of forms, including bribery, embezzlement, theft, fraud, extortion, abuse of discretion, favouritism, nepotism and patronage (UN-HABITAT & Transparency International, 2004). Moreover, corruption is detrimental to the poorer segments of the population (UN-HABITAT, 2010a).

Many reasons can be given for the persistence of corruption in Asian cities. The more widespread are the following: (i) low pay for local officials; (ii) as in some more developed countries, the high costs of elections entice politicians to recoup expenses through corruption; (iii) faulty administrative methods (especially in procurement) can be manipulated for private gain; (iv) strong influence of family and kinship ties and other particular affiliations; and, (v) vague or overly complex rules

or regulations give too much discretionary power to local officials (Kidd & Richter, 2003).

Faced with these problems, central governments and urban authorities in Asia have managed to improve transparency and curtail graft and corruption. Research has shown that in Hong Kong, China, one of the main reasons for corruption was the overly complex and cumbersome public procurement procedure. Each successive step in a tender was perceived as an opportunity for discretionary decisions, and therefore for corruption. Subsequently, streamlined procurement procedures have had a restraining effect on corruption. Hong Kong, China, has also set up an Independent Commission against Corruption with strong powers to punish erring officials (Wong, 2003). In Singapore, the certainty that corrupt acts, once discovered, are promptly and severely punished have also served to rein in corruption (Ali, 2000). In general, experience has shown that the most widespread anti-corruption strategy (and more specifically with regard to bribery, embezzlement, theft, fraud, extortion or abuse of authority) is to turn it into a criminal offence.

On top of combating corruption, some urban authorities in Asia have pursued various approaches to improve transparency and accountability. For example, the 'City Managers' Association Gujarat' has adopted a Code of Ethics to guide members in their daily routines. A major provision in the Code is an affirmation of the importance of keeping the community informed about municipal affairs. Members of the professional group encourage communication between citizens and all municipal officers. Another important item in the code is an assurance that municipal officials will not seek favour, and will not use insider information or other benefits of office to secure personal advancement or profit (UN-HABITAT & Transparency International, 2004).

As part of its Global Campaign on Urban Governance, UN-HABITAT has launched a more wide-ranging initiative in favour of accountability, participation, equity and effectiveness in urban governance, which takes the form of the 'Urban Governance Index' (UGI). Technically, the index can be described as an advocacy and capacity building tool with which citizens can monitor the quality of urban governance. In Asia, the index has been applied in Mongolia and Sri Lanka. The extent to which an urban authority genuinely seeks to enhance accountability can be assessed through specific actions such as: (i) setting up an Anti-Corruption Commission; (ii) establishing facilities that receive complaints from the public; (iii) requiring public officials to disclose incomes and assets; (iv) adoption of a code of conduct for public officials; (v) establishing systems for independent audits of public transactions; and (vi) formal publication of contracts, tenders, budgets and accounts (UN-HABITAT, 2005).

In Pakistan, the Karachi Water and Sewerage Board has adopted an "Integrity Pact for Transparency in Public Procurement Procedures", which includes a formal no-bribery commitment by all bidders for the Board's projects. In case of averred bribery, sanctions are immediately meted out against erring bidders or officials. The Karachi Board blacklists individuals or companies found engaged in bribery.

▲
Leh, India. Information and Communication Technologies have enabled even remote cities to inter-connect. ©**Think4photop/Shutterstock**

Similarly, in Guishan-e-Iqbal Town, Karachi, a system known as 'OPEN' (for 'Online Procedures Enhancement for Civil Applications') has been introduced through a memorandum of understanding between the Mayor and non-governmental organisation Transparency International; the scheme enables the public to monitor the process of applications and public procurement through the Internet. The system requires officials to input the date and time of each application they handle, which can be openly viewed in real time. This transparent method eliminates the need for personal contact with officials and prevents payment of so-called "express fees" to hasten procedures. At the same time, the scheme helps prevent delays in project execution (UN-HABITAT & Transparency International, 2004).

In many Asian countries, a strong and vocal press has not only enhanced transparency but also restrained corruption. However, rent seeking among some media professionals has had the reverse effect on occasion, although others stand out as defenders of the truth. In India, Indonesia and the Philippines, investigative journalists have been instrumental in exposing corruption cases that have resulted in the indictment and imprisonment of some officials.

Civil society activism has also forced local authorities to become more transparent and accountable. The role of civil society in development is now apparent not just at the local but the national levels, too (Sen, 1999). At the 14th summit of the Association of South-East Asian Nations (ASEAN) in Bangkok in March 2009, the heads of 10 member countries signed a regional charter that agreed to establish a rules-based entity largely similar to the European Union by 2015. Three member countries of the Association (Indonesia, the Philippines and Thailand) have fully recognized the role of civil society in governance, especially in the opening up of government processes and the active participation of civil society groups in decision-making (Macan-Markar, 2009).

6.3.4 New technologies and e-governance

Recent advances in information and communication technologies (ICT) in the Asia-Pacific region have had significant effects on urban governance. This is particularly true in India where it has been said that "the ubiquitous computer mouse has become revered as the vehicle of Lord Ganesha – the remover of all obstacles" (Data Quest CIO Handbook 2009, 2009:12). In India during the 1970s, electronic ('e') governance efforts focused on in-house applications of computers by government departments for the purposes of economic and social planning, fiscal monitoring, census, elections and tax administration. In the 1980s, the country's National Informatics Centre undertook to link all district headquarters in an inter-connected national grid. In the early 1990s, the new technologies were used to involve the private sector, non-governmental organizations and civil society groups in governance. India's e-governance efforts have received support from international agencies like the United Nations, the World Bank and private companies specializing in the new technologies.

Many local authorities in India have by now introduced computers and the Internet in governance systems. For example in Delhi, municipal authorities have improved transport management with an automatic electronic vehicle tracking system. In Mumbai, urban authorities run an online complaint management system to elicit immediate feedback from the public. Bangalore has introduced a Fund-Based Accounting System that makes the city's quarterly financial statements available online. This direct monitoring answers taxpayers' queries about the way their monies are spent (Data Quest CIO Handbook 2009, 2009).

Other micro-level applications of computers and the Internet with regard to governance include payment of municipal charges, property assessment, tax collection, police operations, on-line response to public enquiries, electronic libraries, handling complaints and grievances, as well as information collection and dissemination campaigns. The new technologies have also enhanced efficiency with the shift away from manual paperwork, enabling a significant degree of services consolidation. The most visible example of this is the creation of 'single windows' or 'one-stop shops' (such as those advocated by UN-HABITAT (2010b) for urban youth inclusion) (see Chapter 3).

In Malaysia in 2002, the Ministry of Housing and Local Government instructed all local authorities to use computers and the Internet for the purposes of public transactions. That same year, the Government issued the Malaysian Government Multipurpose Card (known as 'Mykad') to facilitate business between citizens and public authorities. The single smart card was introduced initially in the "Multimedia Super Corridor," a 15 by 50 km high-technology incubation centre focused on Cyberjaya, a formal, planned township created in 1997 south of Kuala Lumpur. The town has since then been integrated with Malaysia's forthcoming new national capital, Putrajaya, which is overtly designed as a 'city of the future'. So far in Malaysia, e-governance has been applied to most government functions. For example, public procurement is conducted through *ePerolahan,* an online tender service for suppliers. Taxpayers are also able to file their tax returns online and have all their documents stamped by using a Mykad. Information and communication technologies have even been applied to the operations of the Malaysian judiciary system, with automation of court records, decisions, rules and precedents (Government of Malaysia, 2009).

Although these new technologies are becoming widespread in Asia, their application to e-governance is running against a number of issues. First among these is *equity,* marked by the wide gap among citizens (and geographical areas) in terms of access to modern means of electronic communication (the 'digital divide'). Most low-income urban dwellers do not own, or lack ready access to, computers, let alone telephones, radio sets or other communication equipment. In India, for example, states and cities differ widely for access to telephone services ('teledensity'), with just under 27 telephones per 100 people in Delhi in 2003, compared with1.32 per 100 in Bihar, for instance. As for Internet connectivity, the International Telecommunications Union estimated in 2001 that bandwidth availability in India was at 1,475 megabits per second, as compared with 2,639 in Singapore, 5,432 in Republic of Korea, 6,308 in Hong Kong, China, and 7,598 in mainland China (GoM, 2009).

A second obstacle to effective e-governance is *interoperability* among the vast variety of information and communication systems available. In 2007, the Asia-Pacific Development Information Programme of the UN Development Programme (UNDP) released three publications recommending a roadmap with a Government Interoperability Framework (GIF) based on flexible and universally comparable technologies focusing on good governance. As noted in the report, "All too often, today's e-government deployments can resemble a hand-stitched patchwork of incompatible ICT solutions rather than flexible and reusable assets that provide essential building blocks of services for citizens" (UNDP Asia-Pacific Information Development Programme, 2007:18). Based on the collaborative work of 14 governments that reviewed existing e-government systems, the report recommended the adoption of new guidelines to achieve interoperability based on an International Open Source Network.

A third issue related to e-governance is *security* as applied to dealings with public authorities. As in other parts of the world, people in Asia are often leery of relying on information and communication technologies for confidential business like taxes, bills and other functions. With widespread public concerns about computer hacking, identity theft and the use of the new technologies to carry out various forms of scams, safeguarding the security of relevant systems is a high priority among citizens and urban authorities in Asia.

While a number of Asian countries are still at early stages of e-governance, prospects for the application of information and communication technologies to public processes are quite favourable. This two-way process facilitates public participation in government decision-making as well as public authorities' responsiveness to civil society needs and demands. The ability for people to air grievances online has the potential of curbing petty graft and corruption. The efficiencies achieved via information and communication technologies in tasks such as collecting taxes, paying local bills, purchasing goods and services, and other routine and repetitive business have become widely acknowledged. If the role of new technologies in e-governance is to be further enhanced, however, Asian cities must build adequate capacities through appropriate staff training and well-chosen technical platforms and systems. Advocates of e-governance also stress that, when setting up systems, the emphasis should be on governance applications (software) rather than electronic components (hardware).

6.4
Types of urban governance systems

Makati City, Philippines. ©**Jonas San Luis/Shutterstock**

Some national governments in Asia take a federal form but almost all operate in a highly centralized way. This feature can be traced to imperial history (Japan and Thailand), Western colonial experience (Indonesia, Malaysia, Myanmar, the Philippines), both imperial history and colonization (Bangladesh, India, Pakistan), or socialist ideology (People's Republic of China, Democratic People's Republic of Korea, Lao People's Democratic Republic, Socialist Republic of Viet Nam). In highly centralized Asian states, urban authorities are heavily dependent on national government resources.

Before some Asian countries became independent nation-states, they were ruled by autonomous, indigenous local authorities; after independence, these became subservient to central governments, which grant them only limited powers. Even the election of local officials is dominated by central government parties and figures. In socialist countries, the communist party apparatus strengthens the hold of the national bureaucracy. Residents elect leaders at the lowest tiers of government but central and provincial governments appoint officials at intermediate local levels.

In general, Asian urban governance systems involve autonomous municipal corporations, metropolitan bodies and central government. Also involved are smaller local government units like districts, regencies, prefectures, cantonments and neighbourhood councils, but these are usually in a state of functional and other subordination under constitutional provisions or legislative statutes. Municipal governments are usually governed by charters that specify their objectives, territorial scope, structure and functionalities. Metropolitan entities may be created by municipal bodies in a bid to create region-wide federations, or alternatively they can be imposed by higher tiers of government. Central government is usually in charge of the areas where national capital cities are located (e.g., the Kuala Lumpur federal territory in Malaysia and the Bangkok Municipal Authority in Thailand).

6.4.1 The governance of towns & smaller cities

The emergence of very large cities in Asia, especially national capitals like Bangkok, Dhaka, *Jakarta Raya* (i.e., Greater Jakarta) and Metropolitan Manila has tended to focus the attention of policymakers on mega-city problems (Douglass, 2005). This exclusive preoccupation has been to the detriment of the development problems of smaller cities and towns. This is a serious oversight, because demographers have consistently documented the fact that smaller human settlements in Asia are growing at a much faster rate than mega-cities (United Nations, 2008).

In general, smaller urban settlements in the Asia-Pacific region face many problems such as lack of authority and power to deal with local issues, poor infrastructure and services, inadequately trained staff, a limited tax base, and heavy reliance on higher tiers of government for financial assistance. For all the efforts at decentralization and local autonomy, most municipal officials are vested with only limited authority and power, and any effectiveness they may have is a function of linkages with national legislative or executive bodies, including government departments. In almost all Asian-Pacific cities, governance structures include a policymaking body such as a town or city council and an executive arm like a mayor. However, because of the dominant power and influence of central governments, holders of those policymaking or executive functions are often mere appendages of individuals or groups at the national level.

A critical factor in the governance of towns and smaller cities is the inability of urban authorities to raise financial resources through taxation, borrowing, collecting user charges for urban services, or levying fees and fines. On paper, some decentralization schemes make fund allocations to urban authorities mandatory. In the Philippines, for example, the

Local Government Act of 1991 entitles local authorities to 40 per cent of the internal revenue they generate, and in Thailand, the Decentralization Act of 1999 mandated that by 2006, locally derived revenues should contribute at least 35 per cent of total local authority resources. In practice, however, central government fund transfers are subject to arbitrary decisions by national officials. Local leaders who do not belong to the political party in power or incumbent administration often find it a challenge to have their specified shares of funds released. Central government officials may use lack of funds as an excuse, or raise nit-picking questions about the documentation submitted by local officials to delay release. This makes central government fund releases unpredictable, which, coupled with the lack of local revenue resources, does not put local government officials in a good position to devise realistic fiscal plans.

Another serious problem is the inability of smaller towns and cities to attract and hold on to professional managers and technical personnel, who tend to see local government positions as mere stepping stones on their way to better careers, and pay, in larger cities or central government. The fact that elected local officials often wield more authority or power also serves as an enticement for administrators to run for elective political office.

A variety of elements make it more difficult for many smaller urban settlements to achieve development goals: inadequate financial resources, limited professional and technical staff skills or abilities, traditional political leadership, antiquated institutional governance structures and outdated (often colonial) legal frameworks. National government officials often pay limited attention to the plight of smaller cities. National officials seem to be concerned about smaller urban settlements only at election time when local votes are needed. Even international financial institutions that might be willing to assist smaller urban authorities may be precluded from extending loans in the absence of sovereign guarantees, which central governments are reluctant to provide. For these and many other reasons, most towns and smaller cities in Asia are not able to live up to their developmental potentials. This has serious implications for their capacity to serve as development hubs with positive spillover effects for adjacent rural areas.

6.4.2 City cluster development

"Despite the fact that mega-cities in Asia are getting most of the attention of policymakers and development specialists, the highest rates of urbanization in the region are actually occurring in small and medium-sized cities where problems of planning and governance are more acute. The ADB, therefore, sees city cluster development as an appropriate instrument for enhancing development in smaller urban settlements." Asian Development Bank (2008d).

City cluster development (CCD) promotes the potential of cities and towns within a single urban region through strategic links with a combination of urban infrastructure and services as well as innovative financing schemes. Drawing the

FIGURE 6.2: **THE CLUSTERING OF URBAN NODES IN THE BANGKOK METROPOLITAN REGION**

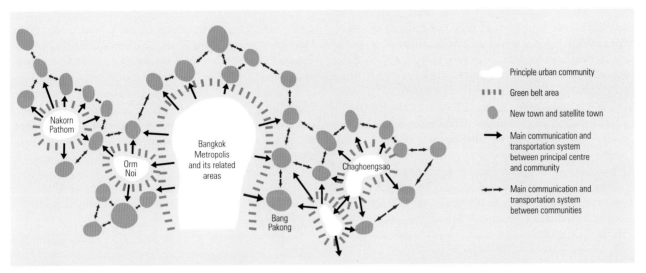

Source: Laquian (2005:171)

▲
Bangkok, Thailand. ©**Vichie81/Shutterstock**

lessons of cluster-based economic and industrial development as a way of enhancing the competitiveness of certain areas where resources are concentrated, the Asian Development Bank has adopted the approach as an integral part of a long-term strategy designed to reduce poverty through "inclusive development and growth promoting activities." The Bank believes that well-formulated and well-executed city cluster development schemes can bring a number of benefits, including the following:

• Deployment of integrated urban infrastructure and services over whole city-regions, rather than confined to individual towns and cities.

• Availability of financial and other resources to develop urban clusters, with common taxation standards and operations, improved credit ratings and more equitable tax burdens among cities and towns in any given cluster.

• Better opportunities for attracting private sector participation in area-wide development projects, especially those focused on urban infrastructure and services.

• Improved capacity to deal with urban problems like environmental pollution, health, flooding and others that ignore political boundaries.

• Inclusive development that integrates both urban and rural areas in a region (ADB, 2008d:15).

The cluster approach is based on the seminal work of Porter (1990:26) who, from a business-orientated perspective, saw clusters as "groups of companies and institutions co-located in a specific geographic region that are linked by interdependencies in providing a related group of products and/or services." Following Porter, a number of development experts have expanded the concept as a form of economic development strategy focused on business clusters.

The methodology can give rise to planned development of clusters of towns and small cities or urban authorities located close to a large city within a metropolitan region. The development of the Bangkok-centred region shows how the cluster process can help plan mega-city expansion. Since 1855, the capital of Thailand has grown rapidly on the back of agri-food and manufacturing industries. In the 1960s, municipal authorities launched the Greater Bangkok Plan 2000, which envisioned a city of 6.5 million spreading over 820 sq km. In 1970, the capital merged with Thonburi to form Greater Bangkok, and two years later parts of the adjoining provinces of Phra Nakorn and Thonburi were in turn merged with Greater Bangkok to create the Bangkok Metropolitan Area. By the 1980s, the continued expansion of Bangkok gave rise to the Bangkok Metropolitan Region, which encompasses parts of the five neighbouring provinces of Pathun Thani, Nontaburi, Samut Prakan, Samut Sakhorn and Nakhon Pathom (see Figure 6.2).

Concerns over the planned development of the Bangkok Metropolitan Region in the late 1980s led Thailand's National Economic and Social Development Board (NESDB) to design a plan involving clustered development in specific areas (NESDB, 1990). More specifically, development nodes in the region were to be closely linked by infrastructure and communication networks. The Development Board noted the emergence of an "extended Bangkok Metropolitan Region" that included areas in an additional five provinces (Ayuthaya, Saraburi, Chachongsao, Chon Buri and Rayong). The total population of this extended metropolitan area was projected to grow to 17 million by 2010. However, the Government of Thailand did not adopt the Development Board plan. This was unfortunate, as the plan highlighted the need for a more comprehensive clustered development approach from the very beginning, which could have avoided the piecemeal approaches since deployed in the Metropolitan Region.

6.4.3 Clustered development and smaller city regions

Smaller city regions generally lack urban infrastructure and services. Because urbanized nodes are usually separated from each other by rural areas, building and managing integrated infrastructure and services is expensive. In these conditions, the clustered development approach can enhance integrated development of urban and rural areas through well-planned, comprehensive provision of urban infrastructure and services. The method can also be used to strengthen economic links among urban clusters. In Europe, for example, mega-region planning has effectively linked development clusters and enhanced complementary development. Japan has resorted to variants of city-cluster development when planning the development of various urban nodes. China, in its efforts to accelerate development in the countryside, has launched a number of city cluster development projects, especially in remote, less developed hinterlands. The Asian Development Bank is currently exploring clustered development in connection with a number of projects in Bangladesh, India and Sri Lanka (ADB, 2008e).

The Government of India has used city clusters as a way of promoting development in about 20 cities, including Ahmedabad, Mirzapur and Tirupur (see Box 6.3). The rationale is that government capital expenditure on infrastructure will generate alternative employment for the tens of thousands of workers laid off by textile mills, brass foundries, jewellery workshops and other small and medium-size enterprises. Other specially targeted areas for cluster-type projects are Behrampore, Coimbatore and Howrah where, again, many workers have been made redundant. As part of the employment schemes, those jobless people would be guaranteed an annual 100 days' paid work in public works projects (Chowdhury, 2009).

Although smaller cities are growing faster than mega-cities, Asian policymakers are likely to focus on the latter in the near future. Four main factors can be found behind this trend:

• Central government officials with the power to control urban development resources are concentrated in capital cities and other large city-regions, and their political power bases are in those areas.

BOX 6.3: CITY CLUSTER DEVELOPMENT: THE POTENTIAL IN INDIA

Research by the Asian Development Bank has identified four city-regions in India where cluster development (through infrastructure and services) would be appropriate, as follows:

- *The Bangalore-Tumkur-Mysore Cluster in Karnataka state (south-central India):* This city-region is one of the fastest growing areas in the state. Bangalore (population: 6.5 million) has become a world-famous centre for information technology. Mysore is an educational and cultural centre as well as a popular tourist destination. The state of Karnataka is well-recognised for administrative reforms and efficient urban management.
- *The Pune-Pimpri-Chinchwad Cluster in Maharashtra state (western India):* The proximity to Mumbai makes it a good site for city cluster development. Pune is a major industrial centre and the home of manufacturers of motor vehicles, Bajaj, Tata Motors, and Daimler Chrysler. The city is also host to many software designers, manufacturing firms and reputed academic institutions.
- *The Coimbatore-Tirupur Cluster in Tamil Nadu (south-central India):* Coimbatore is a major industrial centre that mixes textiles, engineering and automobile parts factories. Tirupur, about 50 km from Coimbatore, is another major textile centre. Tamil Nadu's human development index (HDI) ranks third among Indian states.
- *The Dehradun-Haridwar-Rishikesh Cluster in Uttarakhand (along the borders with China state and Nepal).* This popular religious pilgrimage site is a good candidate for tourism-centred cluster development. Haridwar, according to Hindu mythology, is one of four sites where drops of the elixir of immortality *(Amrita)* were accidentally dropped by the celestial bird, *Garuda.* Rishikesh is often called the Yoga capital of the world and is the starting point for pilgrim routes to the four *'dhams'* (sacred shrines) of Uttarakhand. Because of the religious significance of the cities in this cluster, improving infrastructure and services would most likely accelerate local development.

Source: Asian Development Bank (2008d:79-98)

- A strong desire to achieve "global city status" on the part of central government and mega-city officials focuses attention on larger conurbations.
- It is easier to expand urban infrastructure and services from existing mega-cities out to outlying small settlements and rapidly urbanizing rural areas in order to achieve economies of scale and agglomeration.
- Smaller urban settlements are usually fragmented and it is difficult to organize and mobilize local officials to pursue common objectives.

At the moment, urban decentralization is sought through devolution of central authority and power to the smallest and lowest administrative tiers like urban districts or villages. Unfortunately, such small urban settlements lack the financial resources, professional and managerial skills, technological capabilities or political leadership to bring about comprehensive urban development. The principle of 'subsidiarity', which mandates the assignment "to the lowest level of government possible those local public goods and services which can best be delivered at that level" (UCLG, 2008) is an excellent way of achieving a democratic way of life. However, if central governments fail at the same time to devolve required resources to appropriate levels of governance, then sustainable economic, social and environmental development will be extremely difficult to achieve (see Section 6.6).

6.4.4 The governance of metropolitan and mega urban regions

In recent years, most Asian governments have been focused on mega-cities and mega urban regions. These sprawling city-regions are usually governed by several bodies, and on top of this also suffer from administrative fragmentation among central and provincial/state departments and agencies. Lack of cooperation or coordination among urban authorities and central and provincial/state bodies pose major challenges to metropolitan planning and governance (Bigio & Dahiya, 2004; Dahiya & Pugh, 2000).

In general, Asian governments currently use three types of governance approaches for metropolitan areas and city-regions: (i) autonomous urban authorities; (ii) mixed systems of regional governance; and (iii) combined metropolitan authorities. Historical and cultural factors have influenced the evolution of each type of governance system. Each type also comes with specific benefits and shortcomings.

Autonomous urban authorities

In a system of autonomous urban authorities, cities, towns and municipalities within a city-region are distinctly separate from each other both functionally and territorially. Every local authority is in charge of its own planning, policymaking, legislation and programme/project execution. The city charter or statute creating the city clearly defines the boundaries of the local unit. In some countries, like the Philippines, the *Revised Administrative Code* and other statutes specify the attributes required for city status such as population size and annual income.

The autonomous status of local authorities in a city-region creates many problems. Because such authorities have different revenue-raising capabilities, they cannot provide the same scope or quality of urban services or amenities – especially when the richer urban authorities are reluctant to share resources with poorer ones. Businesses may try to take advantage of urban authorities by making them compete against each other, demanding tax concessions or other favours if they are to locate in a specific area. Further adding to this fragmentation is the fact that cooperation among local officials can be difficult where they belong to different political parties or factions.

Function	Central Government	Metropolitan Government	Shared by Regional & Urban Authorities	Purely Urban Local Government	Private Sector
Electricity supply	Policy setting	Financing & management	Management	Metering, Collecting user charges	Financing, Management
Water & sewerage	Policy & financing	Financing & management	Management	Metering & collection	Financing, Management
Transport & Traffic	Policy & financing	Financing & management	Management	Regulation & control	Financing, Management
Housing & related services	Policy & financing	Financing & management	Management	Maintenance, Housing codes & building standards	Construction Financing Management Popular housing
Solid waste collection	Policy setting		Environmental standards setting	Management Supervision of NGO efforts	Financing Management Civil society efforts
Solid waste disposal	Policy	Financing & management	Financing	Sorting, composting	Financing Management
Education	Policy	Management	Management	Management, Supervision of disposal sites	Financing Management Business ventures
Health	Policy & financing	Metro level hospitals	Management, Financing	Local health clinics	Service provision
Police and security	Policy	Metropolitan police commands	Management & financing	Local police forces	Additional private security
Fire protection	Setting standards	Financing & Management	Management	Local fire Departments, Volunteer brigades	Equipment supply
Environmental protection	Policy & standards	Financing & management	Management	Management	Civil Society efforts

Source: Laquian (2005:121)

In Dhaka and Karachi, attempts have been made to set up metropolitan authorities to coordinate area-wide activities, but local officials have resisted these efforts, fearing a reduction in their powers. Central government departments in charge of public works, transportation and communication, environmental control and other services also object to such metropolitan bodies and refuse to give up their powers and authority. The case of Metropolitan Manila illustrates the problems arising from autonomous urban authorities (see Box 6.4).

Mixed systems of regional governance

In a mixed system of city-region governance, authority and power are vested in formal structures such as central government departments, regional authorities, metropolitan bodies, special-purpose authorities, cities, towns and villages. Each of these governance bodies is responsible for functions such as policy-setting, financing, planning and implementation of programmes and projects. In some cities, a specific governance structure may be responsible for just one function. In others, a number of units may share the responsibility for specific services.

Under a mixed system of regional governance, specific functions may be carried out by separate agencies operating at different levels. These functions may also be shared by a number of government bodies. A survey of 14 metropolitan areas in Asia has focused on the allocation of responsibilities of key urban functions among various bodies in a mixed regional governance system, and the results are shown in Table 6.1.

In some Asian city-regions like Delhi, Dhaka, Jakarta, Karachi and Kuala Lumpur, various entities share responsibility for specific activities. For example, in the case of water supply, a central government department (usually 'environment and natural resources') may be responsible for ensuring availability of raw water by protecting a watershed area. A special authority may be responsible for impounding water and managing a system of reservoirs. A government-owned or controlled corporation or a private concessionaire may look after the purification and distribution of potable water; it may also take care of metering water consumption at the household or plant level. In some cities, water charges are collected at the neighbourhood level. In mixed systems, therefore, specific functions may be allocated to a government body or shared by a number of entities (including private firms).

BOX 6.4: CITY-REGION GOVERNANCE: METROPOLITAN MANILA

In the 1960s, Metropolitan Manila was made up of Manila, Caloocan, Pasay and Quezon City and the towns of Las Pinas, Makati, Malabon and Mandaluyong. Fragmented urban authorities made governance so difficult that in 1975, the Marcos government created the Metropolitan Manila Commission (MMC) to govern the capital area. The Commission established a region-wide land use plan, approved zoning codes and land use regulations, set up a planning, programming and budgeting system, launched slum redevelopment and community upgrading programmes and public housing projects, and built a rapid transit system. What made these achievements possible was the concentration of authority in a Governor (the then-First Lady Imelda Marcos) and the hiring of professional planners and managers to run the Commission.

When the Marcos regime ended, however, President Corazón Aquino restored the authority and power of Metropolitan Manila mayors and councils. A revised Philippine Constitution in 1987 provided that "The Congress may, by law, create special metropolitan subdivisions subject to a plebiscite." As the Constitution set out, "The component cities and municipalities shall retain their basic autonomy and shall be entitled to their own local executives and legislative assemblies. The jurisdiction of the metropolitan authority that will be created shall be limited to the basic services requiring coordination" (Constitution of the Republic of the Philippines, 1987).

In 1990, the Metropolitan Manila Authority (MMA) replaced the Commission. The Authority's policymaking was lodged in a council composed of the mayors of the 17 constituent local authorities. The Authority Chairman was changed every six months, effectively emasculating executive power. By 1995, the ineffective Authority was abolished and the Metropolitan Manila Development Authority (MMDA) was created. The President of the Philippines appoints the Development Authority Chairman. However, all Development Authority decisions are subject to review and approval by the Metro Manila Mayors' Council.

By law, the Development Authority is responsible for traffic management and solid waste disposal. It is supposed to be responsible for metropolitan planning but the authority has not formulated any new plans so far. Instead, local authorities now prepare individual land use plans that are poorly coordinated with each other. The Development Authority lacks the authority required to coordinate the area's autonomous local authorities all of which (except one) have been granted special city charters by Congress. On top of this, the Development Authority is heavily dependent on the financial contributions of each constituent local unit and on budgetary allocations from the central government. Some of the cities in the metropolitan area manage larger budgets and employ better-trained staff than the Development Authority. In sum, the current situation in Metropolitan Manila is essentially that of an autonomous local governance system despite the presence of the Development Authority.

Source: Laquian (2002b)

Mixed regional government systems predominate in Asia. In general, central or senior levels of government serve as the apex body in order to overcome local government fragmentation and lack of coordination. In recent years, the need to provide area-wide services such as regional transport, waterworks, energy and waste management has enhanced the need for mixed systems of governance to bring about more comprehensive planning, mobilize appropriate financial resources and improve management efficiency. A noteworthy feature of mixed regional governance systems is the vigorous participation of private-sector providers of urban services, reflecting their insistence on a more "businesslike" approach to urban affairs. The Kuala Lumpur case study (see Box 6.5) shows how a mixed system of regional governance can operate and involve privatization.

Unified metropolitan government

In those city-regions with unified metropolitan governments, a single governing body plans, manages, finances, supports and maintains services in an area-wide territory. Any local authorities within the city-region are subordinated to the unified government. This approach has been used mainly in national capitals where the central government's authority is dominant (e.g., Seoul). It is also favoured in countries in transition, such as China (e.g., Beijing, Shanghai and Shenzhen (see Box 6.6) and Viet Nam, as well as in cities that have suffered from protracted war conditions such as Kabul.

Supporters of unified metropolitan government argue that it achieves efficiency in the management of area-wide services. Urban problems such as environmental pollution, epidemics, floods and organized crime are impervious to formal political boundaries. Large-scale government systems take advantage of economies of scale, agglomeration and location. Rationalized regional tax structures enable access to more financial resources, as do the higher credit ratings deriving from the pooling of local authority assets. Higher incomes also enable unified metropolitan governments to attract highly qualified urban management professionals.

On the other hand, unified metropolitan government has been criticized as tending to become too large, bureaucratic and inaccessible to citizen demands. Supporters of local autonomy view a regional authority as an unnecessary tier between traditional local authorities and the provincial/state or central government. Some civil society activists abhor the bureaucratic attitudes of region-wide authorities. Because central governments often appoint officials who head unified metropolitan structures, elected local officials also view them as undemocratic and unresponsive to the needs of their constituencies.

BOX 6.5: A MIXED SYSTEM OF REGIONAL GOVERNANCE: KUALA LUMPUR

Kuala Lumpur City Hall.

Kuala Lumpur became the capital of Malaysia in 1963. Having gained 'city' status in 1972, by 1974 it was turned into a federal territory, covering an area of 243 sq km. However, the territory's sphere of influence extends beyond administrative boundaries to include the adjoining satellite towns of Petaling Jaya, Ampang, Selayang and other urban areas in the Klang Valley region. In 2006, the city proper had a population of 1.6 million but the Greater Kuala Lumpur region was host to 7.2 million. In the National Physical Plan of Malaysia, the Kuala Lumpur-Klang Valley-Seremban area is referred to as the Kuala Lumpur City Region, with a potential population of 8.6 million by 2020.

The Kuala Lumpur City Hall is the centre of local government and is responsible for municipal functions such as public health, sanitation, waste management, town planning, environmental protection, building control, social and economic development and maintenance of infrastructure within city boundaries. The city is headed by a Mayor who is appointed by the Federal Territories Minister of Malaysia for a three-year term. Other local authorities in the Greater Kuala Lumpur area are under the control and supervision of Selangor state. Major national government functions are carried out by relevant ministries. Politically, residents in the Greater Kuala Lumpur area are represented by 11 Members of Parliament in the Malaysian House of Representatives.

The establishment of the federal territory of Putrajaya in 2001 and the attendant transfer of executive and administrative offices have focused Kuala Lumpur's development on business, trade and technological innovation. Under the strategy known as "Malaysia Incorporated", the role of urban authorities in the region shifted from simple delivery of urban services to partnerships with private business and the citizenry to achieve sustainable economic, social and environmental development. In 2007, the Prime Minister of Malaysia created a 'Special Task Force to Facilitate Business' in order to coordinate development in an inclusive sort of way. For example, the government has sought to coordinate transport systems in the region through cooperative management. In the same vein, the Malaysian government has instructed local authorities to consult with, and gain feedback from, residents before reporting to the Economic Council, a body chaired by the Prime Minister. The government has also used e-governance to coordinate operations between local authorities and government departments. A single window now enables entrepreneurs and the public at large to deal with public bodies via the 'myGOVernment' portal. Inter-agency dialogue and communication as well as any decisions abide by the government's slogan of "One Service, One Delivery, No Wrong Door".

Sources: Jusoh et al. (2009); Muhamad (1997)

6.5
Mega urban region development

Shenzhen government building, China. ©**Bartlomiej Magierowski/Shutterstock**

The emergence of mega urban regions in Asia has posed serious challenges to both urban planning and governance. Traditional approaches to planning in the region have focused on the physical dimension, i.e., building and maintaining infrastructure and services. However, this focus on "hardware" is sorely inadequate when it comes to managing the growth of mega urban regions whose development is closely linked to the economic and social forces of globalization.

An equally important challenge posed by mega urban regions is the need to manage and govern the multiple political jurisdictions at work in the expanded built-up areas. Governing frameworks in mega urban regions are extremely fragmented: vertical division among various tiers of government (national, regional, metropolitan, city, district and neighbourhood) mixes with the functional fragmentation of government departments (public works, transportation and communications, environmental control) and territorial fragmentation (metropolitan area, chartered cities, municipalities, villages).

The problems created by fragmentation in a mega urban region are readily apparent in China's Pearl River Delta region. Historically, development in the region focused on older cities like Guangzhou (formerly Canton), Macao, China and Hong Kong, China. The latter two, being former Western colonies with 'special administrative region' (SAR) status, are not readily accessible to Chinese citizens. Restrictions also apply to Shenzhen and Zhuhai, both special economic zones. All in all,

the Pearl River Delta region involves three types of urban settlements – the three large cities of Guangzhou, Shenzhen and Hong Kong, China; the eight medium-sized cities of Zhuhai, Foshan, Jiangmen, Zhongshan, Dongguan, Huizhou, Zhaqing and Macao, China; and finally, 22 small county-level cities and about 300 towns. In addition, the region also features a great variety of urban local governments such as prefectures, districts and 'designated' towns and villages.

While all the urban settlements mentioned above are located in China's Pearl River Delta, cooperation among them as well as coordination of government actions are extremely difficult. This situation is reflected in the proliferation of infrastructure and urban services brought about by competition among urban or local authorities. As shown in Figure 6.3, the Pearl River Delta features no fewer than eight international airports. In addition to Hong Kong, China, the region also has three major seaports and 70 smaller ones along its extensive seaboard. On top of the Beijing-Guangzhou-Kowloon railway, expressways and ultra-modern telecommunication networks crisscross the region. To deal with this proliferation of infrastructure projects and achieve better region-wide coordination, planners from both Hong Kong, China and the Chinese mainland have proposed the creation of a "South China Megalopolis" which would be host to a population of 51 million and generate US $1.1 trillion in gross domestic product by 2022. The megalopolis would require an (as yet undefined) efficient governance framework (Yeung *et al.*, 2009; Enright *et al.*, 2003; Wong & Shen, 2002).

FIGURE 6.3: **SOUTH CHINA'S PEARL RIVER DELTA REGION**

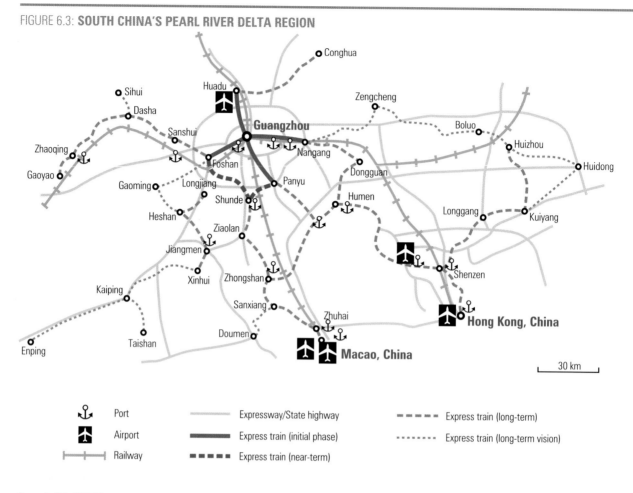

⚓ Port	⎯⎯⎯ Expressway/State highway
✈ Airport	⎯⎯⎯ Express train (initial phase)
⊢⊢⊢ Railway	▬ ▬ ▬ Express train (near-term)
	- - - - Express train (long-term)
	⋯⋯⋯ Express train (long-term vision)

Source: Xu & Xu, 2002:131

BOX 6.6: **UNIFIED METROPOLITAN GOVERNMENT AND GOVERNANCE: SHENZHEN, CHINA**

Shenzhen was the first special economic zone (SEZ) established in China. Before 1979, it had a population of about 30,000, which more than doubled to 70,000 after the change of status. By 1988, Shenzhen was turned into a provincial-level city. China's National People's Congress gave Shenzhen the authority to pass its own laws and enforce its own zoning codes and regulations in 1992. By 2007, when Shenzhen's population had reached 8.6 million, its gross domestic product amounted to an equivalent US $ 90 billion, making it the fourth richest city in China. Shenzhen is under the jurisdiction of the Guangdong Provincial Government. Its 'sub-provincial city' status also places it directly under the authority of China's central government. The Shenzhen Municipal People's Government is the unified authority for the city's seven

districts. Policymaking is lodged in the Shenzhen Municipal People's Congress and the Shenzhen Committee of the Chinese People's Political Consultative Conference, a primarily advisory body. The municipality is headed by a Mayor, who is assisted by a Deputy Mayor and a number of assistant mayors who act as the heads of functional departments or bureaus.

The unified government has greatly facilitated timely decision-making in Shenzhen. In the early years of the city's development, urban infrastructure and services were managed by wholly government-owned enterprises. In order to sustain the massive scale and rapid rate of infrastructure development, however, the municipal government soon ventured into public-private partnerships with foreign companies for the financing and management of such infrastructure.

In a review of the Shenzhen unified metropolitan government system in 2008, an Asian Development Bank group of Indian and Chinese experts mentioned the entrepreneurial spirit of Shenzhen authorities as the key to the city's development. The unified system made the formulation of a region-wide plan possible; it has also effectively dealt with the problems caused by local government fragmentation, clarifying the specific roles of central, provincial, city and other urban or local authorities. As for governance, the Shenzhen municipality has provided effective methods of public participation through consultative committees and groups at various levels. On top of this, efficient information technology systems enable citizens to air complaints and make suggestions to improve the delivery of urban services.

Source: Asian Development Bank (2008c:19-27)

6.6
Decentralization and government functions

▲
Ripon Building, Chennai. Established in 1688 Chennai (Madras) is the oldest municipal government in India.

In the decade after World War II, decentralization in Asia mainly involved *deconcentration* of bureaucratic structures, from central governments to field offices. Later, governments took to *delegation* of authority and power to special purpose-units which, although they enjoyed some form of autonomy, continued to be run by the centre. By the mid-1980s, central governments engaged in *devolution* of authority and power to urban authorities, which involved effective transfers of functions and power.

As observed by Cheema & Rondinelli (2005), devolution was associated with market liberalization and recognition of the complementary role of the private sector in public projects. Since the 1990s, devolution has enhanced local democracy in urban areas, with civil society (including non-governmental and community-based organisations) and business taking on increasingly important roles in local government affairs.

In their decentralising drive, Asian governments have resorted to three types of policies: *deconcentration*, *administrative delegation* and *political devolution* of authority and power.

6.6.1 Deconcentration

Decentralization through *deconcentration* shifts administrative responsibilities for urban affairs from central government ministries and departments to regional and local bodies, establishing field offices and transferring some authority for decision-making to field staff. Under deconcentration and strictly speaking, the authority and power of centrally appointed officials are "localised" only to the extent that they are exercised in a specific geographic region. Although they operate at local level, these "deconcentrated" officials do so as agents of the central government.

In some countries, so-called "decentralization" programmes have been launched to strengthen and autonomise local government. However, so long as the central government machinery remains intact, these programmes do not actually achieve their objectives. In Thailand, for example, a number of "decentralization" programmes have only served to make local elective positions more attractive to national politicians instead of achieving local autonomy, because central government failed to give away any of its functions (see Box 6.7).

6.6.2 Delegation

Delegation involves shifting management authority from the central government to local authorities, semi-autonomous or parastatal bodies, state enterprises, regional planning and area development agencies, as well as multi- or single-purpose public authorities (Wongpreedee, 2007). In practice, though, delegation does not really strengthen local autonomy because the units created and given delegated powers still belong to the central government, and therefore retain an element of primacy over local bodies. The specific authority and power of the units to which authority is delegated are set out in the statutes or executive orders creating them.

In China, the central government has delegated authority to four large cities (Beijing, Chongqing, Shanghai and Tianjin) that remain under its direct control and where it appoints the mayors and other top officials. In practice, municipal officials enjoy some leeway in their managerial functions (mayors, for example, are empowered to approve projects up to a specific budget amount without prior government approval). However, because these officials have only delegated authority, central institutions can discipline or even fire them at will.

Some sub-provincial or prefectural level cities in China can also find themselves under direct central government control. For example, although the Shenzhen Municipality nominally comes under the jurisdiction of the Guangdong Provincial Government, it has been given the status of a prefectural-level city under central government control, with associated financial and other benefits. Top municipal officials exercise an entrepreneurial type of leadership and promote programmes and projects, but they remain central or provincial government officials.

As in the rest of the world, Asian-Pacific countries generally organize central government departments along functional lines like public works, communications and highways, commerce and industry, education and health. The resulting functional fragmentation can stand in the way of coordinated action. This can be overcome with delegated functions and power to special-purpose units with jurisdictions over clearly defined areas. For example, the Port of Singapore Authority was turned into a State-owned commercial company in 1997 in order better to manage the operations of one of Asia's busiest seaports. The body was originally set up in 1964 to take over the functions, assets and liabilities of the Singapore Harbour Board. The Authority's operations expanded with the development of the Jurong Industrial Estate in 1965, the conversion of the former British naval base into the Sembawang

THE STATE OF ASIAN CITIES 2010/11

BOX 6.7: DECONCENTRATION AND DECENTRALIZATION IN THAILAND

As a "unitary and indivisible state" (Sec. 1 of the 2007 Constitution), the Kingdom of Thailand features three functional tiers of government: central, provincial and local ('tambon' or sub-district, and 'mooban' or village). The Ministry of the Interior, through its Department of Local Administration, plays the central role in this framework. The Ministry also has authority over the Bangkok Metropolitan Administration that governs the national capital.

Administration of Thai provinces is the responsibility of governors who coordinate provincial departments, which are field units of the central government. The Provincial Department of Local Administration manages municipalities as well as the City of Pattaya. District Heads appointed by the Department of Local Administration exercise authority over sub-districts ('tambon') and villages.

As part of its decentralizing drive during the 1990s, Thailand moved to reform its deconcentrated local government system with the 1994 *Tambon* Council and Administration Organization Act. The 1997 Constitution and the 1999 Decentralization Act also promised to strengthen local governance. Articles 284 and 285 of the Act granted autonomous powers to local authorities to carry out policy formulation, administration, finance, and personnel management. Articles 289 and 290 enabled urban authorities to carry out additional functions in order to provide suitable living conditions.

However, and despite the supposed decentralization of powers to urban authorities, under a 1997 act it fell to the central government to appoint provincial governors, who also chaired the 'Provincial Administrative Organization' (PAO). This latter position subsequently became elective six years later, and in 2004 the first PAO elections took place in all of Thailand's 75 provinces. However, all the chairs went either to former national government officials or established local politicians, and none to other types of candidates.

An analysis of the results of the Thailand's 2004 PAO polls concluded that granting more powers to local governments through the Decentralization Act had not actually strengthened local autonomy. All it managed to do was to make local office more attractive to traditional centre-orientated politicians. A new (2007) Constitution grants autonomy to local authorities (Section 14), but Thailand has effectively retained a centrally dominated government system.

Source: Wongpreedee (2007:454-470)

Wharves, the opening of the Tanjong Pagar container berth in 1972 and the Pasir Panjang Wharves in 1974. The Authority opened the World Trade Centre in 1972 and the Singapore Cruise Centre in 1991. The 1997 change of status also enabled the port authority to retain its core business (container terminals), and its delegated authority was expanded to allow it to engage in related harbour-front developments, warehousing and logistics, including the management of the Singapore Expo Convention and Exhibition Centre in Changi (National Library of Singapore, 2005).

Vientiane City Hall, Lao PDR. ©**Juha Sompinmäki/Shutterstock**

6.6.3 Devolution

Devolution is a form of decentralization that involves the transfer of authority and power from central to local government units to enable the latter to provide services and infrastructure, raise local revenue, and to formulate, adopt and carry out policies and programmes. Recent decentralization in India and the Philippines is a good example. A crucial element in political devolution is *fiscal decentralization,* where local government units are granted the authority to raise and spend financial resources and are entitled to specific central government fund transfers.

A strong commitment to liberal democracy has been a prime mover behind devolution of powers to urban authorities. In the Philippines, the American colonial government was prompt to introduce municipal corporate bodies and city charters after pacifying the country by military force at the beginning of the 20th century. In the 1960s, the independent Filipino government passed the Barrio Council Law that gave local autonomy to rural villages. The Local Government Code of 1991 devolved authority and responsibility to provinces,

cities, municipalities and villages over functions such as public health, infrastructure development, social welfare and peace and order. The national government officials who used to manage these functions were transferred to local authorities. The law granted broad powers to urban authorities to levy taxes, contract loans, engage in economic enterprises, collect user charges, levy service fees and impose penalties and fines, but many of the local authorities failed to exercise these powers for lack of resources (Laquian, 2002a).

Some evaluations of devolution programmes in Asia have suggested that rapid and large-scale transfer of responsibilities and authority to urban authorities creates a number of problems. In Thailand, for example, the Decentralization Act of 1999 initially had the positive effect of increasing the share of local public expenditures in gross domestic product from 1 per cent in 2001 to 2 per cent in 2002. The share of local authority expenditures in the total public sector budget also increased, from 5 per cent to 7.3 per cent in the same period. However, research found that the bulk of local government expenditures (around 40 per cent) went to pay for administrative costs, mainly due to the reallocation of personnel from central government agencies to local areas. In fact, less than one-third of the expenditures for transferred programmes were paid from local funds and the rest were paid from central government allocations (Amornvivat, 2004).

In Indonesia, the devolution programme mandated by law in 1999 but officially launched in 2001 transferred authority and power to urban authorities at the level of the '*kabupaten*' (regency), '*kota*' (town or city), '*kecamatan*' (sub-district) and '*kampung*' (village). Substantive areas formerly under the responsibility of the central government were transferred to urban authorities. Three years after the launch of the programme, an evaluation found a number of problems. First, the resources allocated to urban authorities do not match the functions assigned to them. Second, reliance on proceeds from natural resources development (oil, mining, forestry) creates a serious imbalance among urban authorities, as regencies and towns in resource-rich areas secure the bulk of funds. Third, the heads of regencies, districts, sub-districts and other lower-tier urban authorities have been made elective, but this democratic enhancement has given rise to "money politics," petty graft and corruption. Finally, the fact that provinces remain formal branches of central government (with governors acting as both heads of autonomous regions and representatives of central government) restricts effective devolution of powers in a significant way, because the bulk of fiscal resources and formal authority remains vested in provincial and central authorities (Decentralization in Indonesia, 2009).

In the Philippines, the Local Government Code of 1991 mandated functional transfers to lower tiers of government. As in Indonesia, the Filipino central government failed to devolve commensurate resources to urban authorities. The devolution programme also failed to recognize that the strengthening of autonomous urban authorities could cause fragmentation. This is a serious problem because metropolitan areas are precisely the units with adequate economic and leadership capabilities to carry out crucial urban functions. Specific provisions in the 1987 Constitution of the Philippines make it extremely difficult to set up metropolitan authorities because they require voluntary agreement among local leaders and residents. Given the severely fragmented nature of urban authorities in the country, it is not surprising that hardly any metropolitan authorities have emerged in the Philippines in recent times (Laquian, 2002b).

A similar policy that devolved authority to the smallest urban authorities and at the same time denied it to higher-level units was carried out in Taiwan, Province of China in the mid-1990s. Constitutional reform devolved authority to village and township authorities. However, the law also provided that provincial governors (until then an elective position) were now to be appointed by the central government, effectively strengthening the latter's hold over local affairs (Cheng & Hsia, 1998).

In China, almost a decade after local elections were first introduced, they do not involve senior officials at higher local government tiers. In late 2008, a draft proposal on "Shenzhen's Reforms for the Future" was posted on the city's official website, including direct elections for deputies to the district's People's Congress as well as mayoral elections. While this announcement was hailed as indicative of Shenzhen's potential leadership in political reforms, the proposals have not been implemented (Yeung *et al.*, 2009; Bergsten *et al.*, 2008).

Decentralization has become a major theme of governance reform throughout the Asia-Pacific region over the past decade. Local democracy has been enhanced as a result, although under a wide variety of forms and patterns, and the outcomes, have reflected the diversity of national backgrounds. Clearly, these arrangements feature many weaknesses and further reforms will undoubtedly be required (UCLG, 2008). UN-HABITAT's recent set of guidlines are designed to assist all government tiers in this admittedly complex endeavour (see Box 6.8).

BOX 6.8: UN-HABITAT'S GUIDELINES ON DECENTRALISATION: AN OVERVIEW

Decentralisation is a major component of the democratic governance required to achieve sustainable development at all levels of government. Strengthening local authorities and other intermediate tiers is important as these are considered as the "closest partners" of national governments for the purposes of the universally recognized 1996 Habitat Agenda.

The 2007 *International Guidelines on Decentralisation and Strengthening of Local Authorities* are split into four main sections: (i) "governance and democracy at the local level", (ii) "the powers and responsibilities of local authorities", (iii) "administrative relations between local authorities and other spheres of government", and (iv) "the financial resources and capacities of local authorities". They set out a number of basic rules, including representative and participatory democracy to empower citizens to take part in decision-making and build the capacity of local government to carry out their tasks. The Guidelines also advise politicians and local authority officials to "discharge their tasks with a sense of responsibility and accountability. At all times, they should maintain a high degree of transparency."

The Guidelines highlight the principle of subsidiarity as the "rationale underlying the process of decentralisation". Subsidiarity promotes separation of powers and is closely related to the principle of 'proportionality'. While decision-making should be as close to the citizen as possible, decisions of public interest should be taken at the level where they can best be carried out; the Guidelines request

increases not just in local authority functions, but also in the capacities needed for the effective exercise thereof. For instance, Indonesia's 2001 "autonomy laws" show how the principle of subsidiarity can be effectively mainstreamed into a country's decentralised framework.

Far from operating in a void, local authorities are engaged in multi-level systems of governance where they need adequate degrees of autonomy while cooperating with other tiers of government. It is imperative for decentralised governance systems to recognise the significant role played by local authorities at the sub-national level. This is why the Guidelines call for formal legislative recognition of local authorities (and where possible in the constitution) as autonomous sub-national entities with the potential to contribute to national planning and development. They further recommend formal, clear and equitable sharing of powers and responsibilities, whereby the powers entrusted to sub-national tiers of government are commensurate with the financial resources made available to facilitate the delivery of expected services. In some cases, it can take an Act of Parliament to reinforce or specify existing constitutional arrangements. For instance in Australia, the Commonwealth (i.e., federal) Constitution makes no reference to local authorities, which on the other hand are recognized in the

constitutions of all individual federated states (and the Northern Territory), where a comprehensive Local Government Act sets out their powers, roles and responsibilities.

The UN-HABITAT Guidelines emphasize the importance of local autonomy, including where decentralised authorities draw most of their financial resources from central government grants and transfers. In Indore, India, municipal authorities have demonstrated that political commitment as manifested in simple but firm measures can mobilize large, untapped tax revenues and meet a significant part of a local authority's services requirements. Such autonomy represents a major boost for local democracy, as it provides an institutional framework conducive to well-balanced national development. In a decentralised governance system, management of public finances must be based on the principles of openness and accountability, including public participation in financial matters as well as equitable distribution of national revenue and tax-raising powers.

The Guidelines having been approved by UN member states, they must now be mainstreamed into, and adapted to, national institutional frameworks in order to improve urban policies and the delivery of basic urban services. To this end, UN-HABITAT focuses on three components to fast-track implementation: (i) advocacy and partnerships at the national level, (ii) capacity development, and (iii) monitoring and reporting on progress.

Sources: Alain Kanyinda, UN-HABITAT.

Jodhpur, 'the Blue City', India. ©**Luisa Puccini/Shutterstock**

6.7
Financing urban development

Guangzhou, China. ©**Hung Chung Chih/Shutterstock**

I n almost all Asian-Pacific cities, the lack of financial, human and technological resources poses a serious challenge to good governance. It has been said that many Asian countries have "rich cities, but [economically] poor city governments." One possible reason for this is that most urban authorities in the region are not using to the full their powers to raise revenue from local sources. As a result, they are heavily dependent on tax revenue allocations, grants-in-aid and other forms of financial assistance from central and provincial/state governments. Furthermore, the power of urban authorities to borrow from domestic and foreign sources to finance infrastructure and other capital-intensive projects is often legally constrained by central governments. Institutional and private sector investors as well as foreign venture capitalists are often reluctant to extend credit for local urban projects without national government ('sovereign') guarantees.

6.7.1 Intergovernmental transfers

Crucial issues in inter-governmental fiscal relations primarily involve the appropriate level for raising revenue and allocating it among different tiers of government. Traditionally, it falls to central governments to collect the revenue required for basic functions as well as for economic and social development across the country. When determining the allocation of authority between central and urban or local authorities, governments face two problems: *vertical imbalance,* where the bulk of resources go to the central government, creating a serious "fiscal gap" at the local level; and *horizontal imbalance,* where inequality occurs among various local government units with different developmental resources and capacities.

Because of the highly centralised nature of the fiscal systems in most Asian countries, urban authorities have traditionally been heavily dependent on central government fund transfers.

In recent years, decentralization laws have given urban governments more authority and power to raise local revenue and decide on expenditures. In Thailand, for example, the 1999 Decentralization Law stipulated that by 2006, locally raised revenue should make up at least 35 per cent of a local authority's total resources. Prior to 1999, more than 80 per cent of local authority financial resources came from central government fund transfers (Amornvivat, 2004).

In Thailand, central government fund transfers take four different forms. First, *general-purpose grants* are made to local authorities based on specific indicators such as population size, amount of locally raised revenue, number of villages in the local unit, numbers of students and elderly people, etc. Second, *specific grants* are earmarked for individual projects such as infrastructures. Third, *subsidies with functional transfers* are allocated to urban authorities to manage the transition from central to local service delivery. Fourth and finally, *sector-specific block subsidies* are earmarked for well-defined purposes (education, health or public works). Thailand introduced these types of subsidies in fiscal year 2003 with the proviso that they would end once the beneficiary local authority had achieved the 35 per cent target set for local revenue share. Under the stage-by-stage process set out in the decentralization law, general- and specific-purpose grants started in the year 2000 and were continued until 2006. Those subsidies involving functional transfers started in 2001 and sector-specific block subsidies in 2003. With this phased implementation, the Government of Thailand hoped to make fund allocation more rational. However, the system does not seem to have put an end to the occasionally arbitrary and politically-influenced process of fund transfer management (Amornvivat, 2004).

Local revenue-raising capabilities vary widely across Asia's urban authorities, with larger and richer bodies often better positioned to meet their own needs. Guided by this consideration and as far as India is concerned, the Jawaharlal Nehru National Urban Renewal Mission (JNNURM) has devised a graduated pattern for fund allocations to urban infrastructure and governance projects. Under the scheme, the percentage of funds allocated by the central government, the states and local, urban or parastatal bodies or local financial institutions was dependent on the population size of cities as well as the nature of projects (Government of India, Ministry of Urban Development, 2009).

6.7.2 Local revenue sources

In Asia, local authorities can generally collect revenue within their jurisdictions, levying taxes on property or real estate, sales and motor vehicles, surcharges on personal income tax, excise, user charges, fines and penalties as well as fees from local amenities such as public markets or abattoirs. In India, Nepal and other South Asian countries, the '*octroi*' (French for 'toll', a tax traditionally levied by municipal authorities on commercial goods that are brought into their territories) used to be a major source of local revenue. However, at present, in India the '*octroi*' is used only in Maharashtra state and even

there, some enterprises are actively campaigning for its abolition (Indiainfo, 2009; Pradhan, 2008). In Nepal, the Local Government Act of 1999 empowered urban authorities to raise property-based taxes, but many did not use these extensively because "political office holders preferred to collect revenue through '*octroi*', which was not directly felt by voters and was easy to collect administratively" (Khadka, 2002:11). However, in the year 2000, the '*octroi*' tax was abolished in Nepal.

In Asia, the bulk of local revenues are collected by central governments in the form of personal or corporate income taxes, import duties, value-added (VAT) and excise taxes, user charges and income from government enterprises. By tradition, central government shares a portion of the revenues from these sources through internal revenue allotments (IRAs), grants and various forms of subsidies to urban and other local authorities. In the Philippines, for example, the Local Government Code specifies that urban authorities are entitled to such revenue allotments based on population, land area and the principle of "equitable sharing" (i.e., proportional sharing of funds where poorer urban authorities are entitled to a larger share). In 2008, it was projected that the total internal revenue allotted to local authorities in the whole of the Philippines amounted to about US $4 billion. Of this amount, 23 per cent was earmarked for provinces, 23 per cent for cities, 34 per cent for municipalities, and 20 per cent for '*barangays*' (villages or urban communities) (Llanto, 2007).

Critics of the internal revenue allotment system have questioned the formula used for calculating the amounts to be transferred. While population is considered a fair criterion, size of land area has been questioned because the boundaries of urban authorities are arbitrarily set. Some officials argue that the individual performance of urban authorities in terms of socioeconomic development should be used as an additional criterion for allocations, which would be larger for the more progressive municipal bodies. Other officials have objected to the efforts of some legislators bent on amending the law that mandates automatic disbursement of internal revenue allotments upon approval of the national budget. They claim that in practice, those urban authorities governed by the same party as the one controlling the central government are promptly provided with their allotments, which is not the case for those controlled by opposition parties.

Although the Philippine Local Government Code of 1991 has been seen as enhancing local autonomy, evaluations have shown that its fiscal provisions do not go far enough to enable urban authorities to raise revenue. Six major factors are at play here. Two have to do with restrictions on the tax powers of lower tiers of government, according to Tapales (1993). First, those items that urban authorities are allowed to tax are listed and specified in the law (real property, and the professions (under the form of licenses and fees). Any items not specified in the law are considered the purview of the central government (like personal income taxes and import duties). Second, some of the items that urban authorities are allowed to tax, or require licenses for, typically do not bring in high revenues (taxes on fighting cocks or dog licenses).

Effective revenue-raising is also restricted at the local level in the Philippines because unduly complex procedures challenge both local officials and tax-payers, which only political connections can bypass. Many urban authorities lack the trained personnel required for proper assessment, collection and audit (after the Local Government Code became law, many Department of Finance officials who had been seconded to local authorities transferred to other jobs because local government pay and benefits were too low). On top of this, administrative revenue-raising methods are often outdated, overly complex and cumbersome (provisions for assessment, collection and reporting of real estate taxes are often so complex that tax payers resort to fixers and bribe tax collectors to "facilitate" transactions). The system is bypassed in another way: national politicians have traditionally used their power to allocate government funds to their constituents as the basis of their local influence through "countryside development funds" and other forms of pork barrel politics. The availability of such central government funds acts as a disincentive for local leaders to raise funds from local sources (Tapales, 1993).

Finally, local authorities in the Philippines find that securing loans for capital expenditure from domestic or foreign market sources is not much of an alternative to revenue-raising through taxation, as foreign bank or financial loans generally require approval by central government authorities.

The case of Makati, the business district of the Filipino capital Manila, shows that local authorities with rich tax bases usually find it easy to raise revenue and do without central government allocations. The Makati municipality holds an estimated US $420 million in assets and ranks third among Filipino cities in terms of income. The population soars from a permanent 0.5 million (2007 estimate) to 3.7 million in daytime as the district is host to many banks, companies, offices and educational institutions. Thanks to this prosperity, Makati is not heavily dependent on national grants or subsidies. In order further to accelerate its own development, the Makati municipality has proposed that the central government give it more authority to borrow funds for infrastructure development and to allow it to engage in higher-yielding types of business (Seva, 2007).

6.7.3 Property-based taxes

In Asia, most municipal revenue bases are weak because the collection of property-based taxes – the traditional source of local authority revenue in technologically advanced countries – is hampered by antiquated assessment techniques, poor record keeping, inadequate land titling systems, non-computerization of tax rolls, and petty graft and corruption. According to research for the Asian Development Bank, most taxable properties in Asian cities are under-assessed and fewer than 5 per cent of real estate taxes are based on real market value (Roberts & Kanaley, 2006).

In theory, property-based taxes are the most appropriate sources of local revenue. They satisfy the criterion of *autonomy*, as urban authorities are empowered to fix tax rates according to local conditions. Property-based taxes also enhance *accountability*, since residents are directly aware of the tax liability and they can complain if tax revenues are mismanaged or do not support their preferred policies. Property-based taxes are also *localized* and their incidence is clearly *observable*. Because of the directly observable relationship between tax revenues and their allocation to specific expenditure items (infrastructure, amenities, security, etc.), they enhance *compliance* on part of taxpayers. Furthermore, property-based taxes are *equitable* because they are based on the value of properties owned by different individuals.

Evidence in Asia has shown that property tax proceeds account for less than 20 per cent of local authority revenues. As some of those authorities have found, streamlining property assessment and collection systems has dramatically increased revenues. In India, cities have moved to the unit-area method of property tax assessment. The use of information technology, and geographic information systems (GIS) in particular, has dramatically improved property tax collection. In Metropolitan Manila, Quezon City has computerized all tax rolls, resulting in significant increases in revenues (by a multiple of three between 2005 and 2008 for real estate taxes, for instance) and eliminating petty graft like the issuance of fake receipts by collection agents (Echeminada, 2008).

In Karnataka state, India, the government set up the Bangalore Agenda Task Force to spearhead reforms. One of these involved the development of a revenue model based on geographic information systems (GIS). To improve real estate tax collection, ward maps were prepared that indicated the location of properties. The features of the properties were then verified by on-the-ground enumeration and physical surveys. Property tax records were integrated into a computerized database directly linked to maps. A pilot test of the geographic information system carried out in Ward 76 of Bangalore City brought some refinements to the GIS application and resulted in a series of various display and reporting options for improved real estate tax collection (Kalra, 2009).

6.7.4 Domestic and foreign borrowings

With their fairly large capital amounts, long durations and revenue-generating capacity, large urban infrastructure projects lend themselves well to domestic or foreign borrowings (including syndicated bank loans and bond issues). Since the year 2000 in China, government-owned or controlled enterprises under the responsibility of local authorities have taken to issuing bonds to finance infrastructure. By 2005, the value of corporate bond issues outstanding in the country had reached US $59.9 billion, made up of (long-term) bonds, (medium-term) notes and (short-term) commercial paper. It falls to China's National Development and Reform Commission to approve all bond-financed fixed-asset construction projects. Bond issuers are required by law to obtain credit ratings from approved specialist agencies, and all bond issues must be underwritten by official financial institutions like the China Construction Bank. Typical bond maturities range between 10 and 20 years with interest rates between 4 and 5.8 per cent (ADB, 2008c).

Muzzaffarabad, Pakistan. ©**UN-HABITAT/ Veronica Wijaya**

In most Asian countries, though, the problem with domestic or foreign market borrowings has to do with lack of access: either because it is formally restricted (especially in the case of foreign borrowings), or because local banking or financial markets are not large enough, or because borrowers are not considered suitable for one reason or another. This is where regional development banks and their financial expertise can play a significant intermediary role.

Before 2003, the Asian Development Bank would grant loans denominated in US dollars, Japanese yen or euros only. In order to respond to the changing needs of Asian member countries, in 2003 the Bank began to grant loans denominated in a number of local currencies. These were initially restricted to private sector borrowers, but were extended to public authorities in 2005. Local currency loans enable cities and other local authorities or bodies avoid foreign exchange risk on interest and principal payments, making project costs more predictable. The Bank offers two formats when lending funds in local currencies: *back-to-back* funding, for specific projects only; and *pool* funding, where the Bank maintains a pool of liquidity in a local currency such as Indian rupees or Chinese '*renminbi*' that can be tapped for various projects (ADB, 2008e). Whatever the format, local currency loans require reasonably well-developed banking and financial markets in the country of the currency, where its top-quality credit-rating enables the Bank to borrow relatively large amounts at the best possible rates; the proceeds are on-lent to local companies which (for a number of reasons, including lack of a formal credit rating) may not have as easy or cheap an access, if any, to financial or bank loan markets.

India was one of the earliest countries to use local currency loans to finance infrastructure projects. In early 2003, the Asian Development Bank granted Powerlinks Transmission Limited a rupee-denominated, fixed-interest rate loan for a 1,150-kilometre power transmission line from Siliguri in West Bengal to Mandaula near Delhi. The power from the Tala Hydro Electric Power Project in Bhutan would support industrial development in northern India's urban areas. The overall objective was to reduce poverty through more robust economic growth, human resource development, narrower gender disparities and stronger urban governance. The ADB provided up to US $70 million in Indian rupees; this reflected the fact that all project revenues were in local currency and that the company needed to match its liabilities with its rupee-denominated assets (ADB, 2003).

In February 2004, the ADB launched its first bond issue denominated in Indian rupees with an aggregate principal amount equivalent to US $100 million, a 10-year maturity and a 5.4 per cent coupon. This issue, priced at 17 basis points over the comparable Indian Government rate, was a 'first' on three other counts: it was the first-ever bond issue by a foreign entity on the Indian capital market, the first by a supranational entity and the first rupee-denominated issue awarded the top 'triple-a' rating by Fitch, Standard and Poors and Moody's Investment Services. The ADB on-lent the proceeds to Powerlinks in the form of a 15-year fixed-rate loan, providing the long-term, fixed-interest rate, local-currency financing the company badly needed for infrastructure projects in urban areas, again in northern India (ADB, 2008e).

In China, Shenzhen's huge port development projects required large amounts of financing, which as it turned out blended a variety of domestic and foreign sources, including: (i) loans from foreign governments; (ii) issuance of shares; and (iii) a bond issue. The construction of the port of Yantian, for example, was financed by a US $116 million loan from the Government of Japan. The Shenzhen Municipality also raised capital by issuing shares in the three companies in charge of port development, which together raised about US $155.6 million in capital when they were first listed on a stock exchange (ADB, 2008c).

As the Indian and Chinese experiences show, domestic and foreign borrowings are good sources of capital or finance for infrastructure development. Other Asian countries have also tried these approaches but have run against a number of constraints. For one, borrowings from foreign banks or markets usually require sovereign guarantees which central governments are reluctant to provide for fear of foreign exchange risk and its potential impact on budget expenditures. Moreover, in some Asian countries, institutional structures such as investment banks, stock markets and bond rating agencies may also be underdeveloped, making borrowings rather difficult.

6.7.5 The private sector and urban infrastructure finance

Private sector participation (PSP) is playing an increasingly significant role in urban Asia as a source of both revenue and management expertise in connection with development projects. 'Private sector participation' refers to all types of cooperative ventures whereby the private and public sectors together carry out government-type functions without any financial risk on the government's side. This latter aspect is what makes private sector participation different from conventional public-private partnerships (PPPs), where the public sector shares in any financial risks. Most urban infrastructure and services projects entail large investments, require advanced technology and take a long time to design, finance, construct, and maintain. This is why most Asian urban authorities have resorted to a variety of private sector participation modalities including 'design-build-operate', 'build-operate-transfer', 'buy-build-operate', or 'build-own-operate-manage' arrangements.

The benefits of private sector participation include access to capital to finance lumpy infrastructure projects, the ability to use the advanced technologies offered by modern firms and to secure funding from regional or global financial institutions that are familiar with the PSP format. China has taken advantage of these features in a large number of projects, so much so that by 2005, it was estimated that more than 40 per cent of the country's total output, 60 per cent of economic growth and 75 per cent of new employment were contributed

by the private sector. Box 6.9 provides a case study of private sector participation in China.

6.7.6 Privatization of urban infrastructure and services

In many Asian cities, the private sector currently carries out the financing, operation and management of urban infrastructures such as transport, electricity, gas supply, telecommunications, and solid waste collection and disposal. All government does is to set policies and procedures for private companies to go by. The main argument in favour of privatization is that private companies tend to be more efficient than public bodies when it comes to managing business-like operations like public utilities. The profit-making rationale is said to result in efficiency gains that make private ownership and management of urban services more cost-effective than public ownership, whereas in developed countries government agencies tend to be prone to political interference, patronage, nepotism, and graft and corruption.

The crucial issue facing urban authorities in Asia is how to determine the benefits and drawbacks of privatization schemes. Important questions raised by privatization include:
a) Are such schemes really more efficient and cost-effective than publicly-run utilities?
b) Do such schemes actually tap into private sector capital and expertise?
c) How does privatization affect the lives of the urban poor?
d) Are privatization schemes conducive to political interference, anomalies, graft or corruption?

A case study of the water provision in Greater Jakarta ('Jakarta Raya') provides some insights into the effects of privatization (see Box 6.10). The switchover resulted in greater efficiency, especially because it cut down overstaffing and patronage in the water agency. The scheme brought in international financing, but the extent of local private investment was unclear because the private partner (the son of President Suharto) relied more on political connections than local capital. A major criticism of the scheme was that it delivered more water services to well-off communities than to low-income areas. In 1999, when President Suharto was overthrown, the political anomalies involved in the scheme were exposed. This would go to show that like other economic arrangements with demonstrated positive potential, privatization is exposed to the risk of corruption and mismanagement.

6.7.7 Land as a resource for development

In Asian cities, a frequently neglected resource is the use of urban land. Tapping land as a resource is a distinct advantage in socialist countries like China and Viet Nam where land is owned by government. In these countries, land is usually not sold outright but leased for periods of 50 to 70 years. In China, Art. 18 of the Administration Law on Real Estate (1994) sets out that all fees paid by developers when granted land use rights are to be turned over to the State Treasury. These funds

▲
Suzhou, China. ©**Mikhail Nekrasov/Shutterstock**

Private sector participation under a variety of forms has enabled the city of Suzhou, founded in 514 BC, to become a powerhouse of China's development. A combination of local resources with foreign and domestic capital was behind the launch of five economic development zones, the largest of which was the Suzhou Industrial Park, a joint venture between China and the Government of Singapore.

The city set up the Suzhou City Construction, Investment and Development Co., Ltd. (SCCIDC) in August 2001 to manage the planning, financing and construction of urban utilities as well as to look after industrial investments and assets. Accordingly, five subsidiaries were created to manage gas supply, port development and other ventures. The company also set up seven holding subsidiaries and 11 shareholding companies. In 2007, the SCCIDC's combined capital assets were worth US $3.37 billion.

In order to finance infrastructure projects, Suzhou relied on a combination of capital allocations from municipal authorities, domestic bank loans and foreign direct investment. By 2007, the Suzhou Municipal Finance Bureau had allocated US $689 million to the SCCIDC for various projects. In addition, urban authorities extended loans amounting to US $551 million to the company's subsidiaries. The company issued shares to finance road construction and gas works. The China Development Bank financed the construction of the Suzhou train station and domestic commercial bank loans supported other projects. The main plank in the project was the city's allocation of more than 170 ha of public land to Suzhou Industry Co, Ltd., in order to strengthen the company's assets.

In order to attract foreign direct investment, Suzhou offered incentives and privileges. Investors in the Suzhou Industrial Park were allowed to lease land for plants and factories, some of which could be available on a turn-key basis. The Park guaranteed investors adequate and reliable sources of energy, potable water, efficient sewerage, solid waste management, telecommunication facilities, a well-trained and disciplined workforce and comfortable housing for expatriate staff. The municipality also extended tax exemptions to foreign investors, waiving the standard 15 per cent corporate tax under certain conditions.

Another factor behind Suzhou's success was that the central government delegated powers to enable the municipality to manage its affairs efficiently. Local authorities guaranteed foreign investors that any projects in line with national policies could be approved within three days. China's Ministry of Foreign Affairs facilitated the issuance of visas to foreign investors. The Suzhou Industrial Park operated its own customs office and bonded logistics centre, greatly reducing delays for goods shipment and delivery. Suzhou owes this success with foreign investors to a combination of efficient management reforms and privileges.

Source: Asian Development Bank (2008c)

BOX 6.10: PRIVATIZATION OF WATER SERVICES: GREATER JAKARTA

In 1997, the Indonesian government privatized the water and sewerage system in Greater Jakarta. Britain's Thames Water Overseas, Ltd. and France's Suez Lyonnaise des Eaux took over the utility in partnership with Indonesia's own PT Kekar Pola Airindo and PT Garuda Depta Semesta. The concessionaires took over *Pam Jaya*, the metropolitan water and sewerage system. The International Finance Corporation, the World Bank and the Asian Development Bank financed most of the privatization scheme.

With the transfer of management from Indonesian to foreign concerns, 2,800 of the 3,000 *Pam Jaya* staff were seconded to the concessionaire. Problems arose because local staff were paid 2.5 to 5 times less than those directly hired by the foreign concessionaire. Moreover, the 1997-98 Asian financial crisis raised the foreign-currency denominated costs of the project. Subsequently, President Suharto fell from power in 1999, creating problems because the main Indonesian partner was headed by his son.

The first two years of the project went quite well. The foreign consortium claimed that water connections increased by 50 per cent. However, a more in-depth evaluation found that although production rose initially, water rates were increased by 40 per cent and then raised again on at least six occasions. Privatization did not benefit low-income residents as the concessionaire extended more lines to well-off areas. Internally, local staff turned against the foreign concessionaire and campaigned to return the water company to municipal management. An almost exclusive focus on potable water supplies was detrimental to sewerage and wastewater disposal operations, with adverse effects in a city where flood damage is a routine by-product of the rainy season. Finally, adverse foreign exchange rates caused a dramatic increase in the indebtedness of the water company (the value of the Indonesian Rupiah fell more than 300 per cent vis-à-vis the US dollar) which the company could not entirely recoup through persistently higher charges.

The main features of the water privatization scheme were as follows:	
1. Total population in service area:	11.0 million
2. Water production per day before project was launched:	1,320,325 cubic metres
3. Number of utility connections:	567,398
4. Population serviced before privatization:	38-42 per cent
5. Expected population to be serviced after privatization:	43-61 per cent
6. Cost of every 10 cubic metres of water (US dollars):	1.00
7. Non-revenue water before privatization:	53-57 per cent
8. Expected non-revenue water after privatization:	47-49 per cent
9. Expected water connections to households in poor areas:	55 per cent

Source: Hasibuan (2007); Argo & Laquian (2007:224-248)

are earmarked solely for financing urban infrastructure and land development schemes. A revision of the law in 2004 allocated 30 per cent of the land fees to the Ministry of Finance and 70 per cent to the relevant local authority. The law provides that all land use fees must be paid in full upon approval of the development of land parcels, which enables urban authorities to budget this resource in a rational way.

Although many urban authorities in China have used land fees to fund infrastructure and services, some have run against a number of problems. Experience has shown that land as a resource for investment tends to encourage short-term developments. This is because the bonanza from the unlocked monetary value of the land is available only for a limited period (usually at the beginning of a project). Unless the urban authority has access to alternative sources of financing, it must rely on other partners (like private investors) to pursue long-term projects.

Elsewhere in Asia, where land is privately owned, using it as a resource to support development is more complicated. In these countries, the government must purchase private land at fair market value if it is used for public purposes. In Bangladesh, India, the Philippines and the Republic of Korea, government can use its right of "eminent domain" (also known as compulsory purchase/acquisition, or expropriation) to gain access to private land for public purposes, but this can entail expensive and long drawn-out litigation. Some forward-looking urban authorities in India and Bangladesh have engaged in "land banks", which involve purchasing land for future public use while it is still relatively cheap. However, in many cases, private landowners increase plot values once they hear of the government's intentions.

Recognizing the importance of land as a resource, the Government of India has suggested the repeal of the Urban Land Ceiling Act and rationalisation of the Stamp Duty Act to enable state governments to make more land available for urban development. Revising the Stamp Duty Act, for example, would involve reducing the rate on land transactions from 13-14 per cent to 5 per cent, which would stimulate land sales. In Indonesia, Thailand and the Philippines, where land speculation is widespread, urban authorities have imposed punitive taxes on idle land with the double aim of discouraging the practice and earning additional revenue. Some urban authorities have exercised their right to clean up idle lands, charging the costs to absentee landowners. In the Republic of Korea, public authorities can develop private land in exchange for ownership of a part of the plot. In Hong Kong, China, and Singapore, land swaps have enabled public authorities to use well-located plots for public infrastructure and other development projects.

6.8
Performance in service delivery management

People's committee building, Ho Chi Minh City, Viet Nam. ©**Magicinfoto/Shutterstock**

In the past, most urban authorities in Asia viewed the availability of urban services as a simple issue of service delivery. With the increasing complexity of urban life, the higher costs and expanding scale and scope of services, it has become clear that fresh steps such as decentralization and local finance reforms were needed. At its 22nd session in April 2009, the Governing Council of UN-HABITAT acknowledged the need for complementarity between the agency's guidelines on access to basic urban services and those on decentralization (UN-HABITAT Governing Council, 2007, 2009). The Council called for the strengthening of local authorities to achieve this objective: UN-HABITAT's governing body also highlighted the need for transparent and accountable management of public services as well as partnership with the private sector and non-government organisations for the delivery of such services.

6.8.1 Water supply and sanitation

Under the Millennium Development Goals (MDGs), the proportion of the population without sustainable access to drinking water and basic sanitation was to be cut by half by 2015. By 2008, Eastern Asian cities, particularly in China, had already achieved 98 per cent coverage, and some countries (Malaysia, Republic of Korea and Singapore) have achieved universal coverage (World Health Organization & UNICEF, 2010). However, in some Asian cities, access to individual piped water connections has not yet achieved the 96 per cent level (Pakistan: 95 per cent; Nepal: 93 per cent; Mongolia: 97 per cent; Indonesia: 89 per cent; and Bangladesh: 85 per cent). More alarming still was the finding by the United Nations Joint Monitoring Programme (JMP) for Water Supply and Sanitation, namely, that the proportion of urban residents with adequate supply of safe water actually *declined* between 1990 and 2008, from 96 to 95 per cent in Pakistan, 96 to 93 per cent in Nepal, 92 to 89 per cent in Indonesia, and 88 to 85 per cent in Bangladesh (World Health Organization & UNICEF, 2010) (see Chapter 4).

If the decline in safe water supply to urban residents is worrying, lack of official attention to water and sanitation is even more so. An Asian Development Bank impact evaluation of water and sanitation projects in China, India, Malaysia, the Philippines and Sri Lanka found that where local authorities paid inadequate attention to sanitation, results were mixed and limited (ADB, 2010). The Bank concluded that, in contrast to government-sponsored projects, those run by non-governmental organizations (NGOs) that provided sanitation services through community mobilization proved more successful. As stated by the Bank, "It is not enough to simply provide adequate quantities of good quality water. India's model, where sanitation subprojects were implemented by NGOs, shows that sanitation, hygiene, and health promotion are needed and complementary, and these represent a distinct factor for success." (ADB, 2010:2).

The role of community residents as organized by non-governmental organizations can be illustrated by the Orangi Pilot Project model launched in the 1980s in Karachi. The scheme involved two levels of sanitation: the basic level was made up of the latrine in a house and the underground lane and sewerage collector; and the second level included the connection to the trunk sewer, the natural drainage channel and the treatment plant, which are under public authority control. Proper integration of these two parts of the system was crucial to the success of the Orangi scheme. This led to replication in 338 settlements in 18 cities all over Pakistan, as well as in 47 villages in Sind and Punjab provinces (Anzorena, 2009).

In a number of Asian cities, water providers, private or public, have used positive management approaches to extend safe supplies to the urban poor. In Indonesia, India, Viet Nam and the Philippines, subsidies from the Global Partnership for Output-based Aid (GPOBA) have enabled water companies to serve low-income communities. Some urban authorities have reviewed policies related to land tenure and agreed to extend water to squatter areas regardless of legal issues. As already mentioned in Chapter 4 (see Box 4.15), in some slums in Dhaka a non-governmental organisation known as *Dushtha Shasthya Kendra* (DSK) has acted as an intermediary with the public utility to facilitate access to water and sanitation. In Metropolitan Manila and with support from the above-mentioned Global Partnership, the privatized water company set up a "flagship programme" that extended connections to more than 20,000 homes, benefiting 120,000 people. Maynilad, another consortium providing water to the western sector of Metropolitan Manila, entered into private agreements with leaders in low-income areas whereby residents could have access to water if they managed the collection of individual charges based on consumption measured by one water meter for the whole community.

Traditionally in urban Asia, water providers tended to be more interested in *expanding networks* than in proper management. In recent years, good water managers have stressed demand regulation and management as a solution to water problems. *Demand regulation and management* includes rational allocation of water among competing users based on a system of priorities, using quotas as a method of water allocation, and appropriate pricing. Water systems have also adjusted their operations to city-region scale, including public spaces for effective control of watershed areas: they allocate water supplies to agricultural producers, domestic households, commercial units, production enterprises, government agencies and various institutions. In many Chinese city-regions, systems have been able to save significant volumes of water through improved use and conservation methods in agricultural production (lining irrigation canals, shifting to sprinkler methods, etc.).

Appropriate pricing of water has proven to be one of the most effective approaches to limit waste. In Metropolitan Manila, the Maynilad concessionaire found that a consumption-based, graduated charge scheme was an effective way of tackling wastage. The gradual pricing method enabled Maynilad to lower household charges (especially in low-income urban areas), with cross-subsidisation by commercial and industrial users (Singson, 2008). Phnom Penh provides another good instance of effective water management (see Box 6.11).

Over the past few years in Asia, comparative performance data on urban water utilities has been collected by the Asian Development Bank in its Utility Data Book. Similar documents have been developed for one subregion (the Southeast Asian Water Utilities Network) and two major countries (India and the Philippines). Comparative performance information is also available for Indonesia and Viet Nam thanks to respective national water utility associations and the World Bank's International Benchmarking Network for Water and Sanitation Utilities (IBNET) platform. These efforts need considerable strengthening and support if reliable information is to be available on a regular basis.

In South Asia, utilities find themselves in a low-level 'equilibrium trap' where poor services result in low water charge recovery, and the concomitant lack of economic viability makes it difficult to improve service standards. Equally or even more importantly, institutional structures in the urban water sector do not provide adequate degrees of autonomy in service operations, as in most cases water and sanitation remain as departmental functions within urban authorities. Even where separate water utilities have been set up in some South Asian cities, adequate degrees of operational autonomy remain out of reach, particularly with regard to staff recruitment and remuneration policies.

Still, a number of good performers have emerged among water utilities in various subregions. Some utilities have proved particularly successful against various socio-economic and political backgrounds. Table 6.2 summarises good practice from a few top performers. Their experience can provide a basis for performance improvement by others.

- *Autonomy of the utility in day-to-day operations* is critical and essentially stems from its *legal status*. Most well-performing utilities are autonomous by law, either as a statutory entity or as set up under company law. South Asia's relatively poorer performance may have to do with lack of autonomy as most utilities operate as municipal departments and have no autonomous status.
- *Utility governance* seems to be a crucial determinant both in terms of *Board composition and autonomy* (including external experts), and *autonomy in recruitment policies,* particularly including market-based wages (as in Singapore, Ho Chi Minh City, for instance). Ability to provide market-based wages to recruit and retain good staff appears to be a critical factor in utility success.
- *Appropriate incentives* include performance-linked wages as well as access to government grants or donor concessionary

BOX 6.11: EFFECTIVE WATER MANAGEMENT: PHNOM PENH

Phnom Penh. 13.8 million residents now have access to safe water, including those living in slum and squatter areas ©Komar/Shutterstock

One of the physical casualties of the 1975-93 war in Cambodia was the almost total collapse of the water supply system in the capital, Phnom Penh. By 1993, barely 20 per cent of the city's population had access to water and low-income residents suffered from shortages. The system was able to deliver only 10 hours per day. Non-revenue water (i.e., leakage, illicit connections and other losses) represented as much as 72 per cent of production. The system's earnings barely covered 50 per cent of operating costs. In 1994, the Cambodian government changed the management structure of the Phnom Penh Water Supply Authority (PPWSA). The utility was provided with external assistance amounting to US $130 million from the Asian Development Bank, the World Bank, the United Nations Development Programme and the Governments of Japan and France.

The Water Authority management immediately launched a programme that increased water production; reduced the proportion of non-revenue water; maximized water bill collection; and revised charge schemes to reflect the true cost of water delivered. To reduce non-revenue water, the utility replaced old pipes with new ones, installed accurate water meters, set up an emergency leak repair team on duty 24/7; divided the distribution network into zones and identified problem areas, and cancelled contracts with water wholesalers. The bill collection system was computerized, meter readers were trained, incentives were given to customers who paid regularly and on time and penalties were imposed on those who did not. Water rates were rationalized, with customers using less water charged less than those using more.

The staffing of the authority was streamlined, with the number of personnel reduced from 20 per 1,000 water connections to only four. Most importantly, the Water Authority deployed an efficient customer service programme, made bill payment more convenient, and acted quickly to deal with customer complaints.

By 2009, the Authority was listed by the Asian Development Bank and the World Bank among the most efficient water utilities in Asia. About 90 per cent of Phnom Penh's 1.5 million residents now have access to safe water, including those living in slum and squatter areas. 'Non-revenue' water has been reduced to 6.1 per cent in 2009. Finally, the proportion of customers who pay bills on a regular basis has more than doubled from 45 per cent in 1994 to 99 per cent in 2009.

Source: Chan (2009)

loans. To make such performance-linked incentives effective, information systems back stringent reporting requirements. Most well-performing utilities have clear operational goals and performance-linked improvement plans. These are monitored throughout implementation.

• *Strong customer orientation* has acted as another major success factor; this involves understanding, and responding to, customer needs, as well as an ability to terminate service delivery for defaulters. Empowerment of local staff (e.g.,

the Manila Water Company) also supports this strong customer orientation. Customer awareness campaigns and use of various communication channels are widespread.

• *Internal innovation in operations management* seems to be critical to ensure viability and financial sustainability over time. Such innovations are made possible by operational autonomy and triggered by performance-linked incentives. Almost all utilities listed in Table 6.2 use innovative methods to improve operational efficiency through reduction in

	Phnom Penh Water Supply Authority, Cambodia	Public Utilities Board (PUB), Singapore	Jamshedpur Utilities and Services Company, India	Manila Water Company, the Philippines	Hai Phong Water Supply Company, Viet Nam
Autonomy and governance					
Legal Structure	Municipal-owned	Statutory body under the Public Utilities Act	Private company, owned by Tata Steel	Private company with 25-year concession	Statutory body owned by Provincial People's Committee
Board composition	Includes the General Director (GD), and local and national government representatives	Includes broad spectrum of stakeholders appointed by the relevant Minister	Includes owners and relevant experts	Includes private shareholders, with stakeholder involvement for transparency	Under Hai Phong People's Committee and managed by Transport, Urban and Public Works Dept.
Staff recruitment and wages	GD hires and fires staff; training and higher wages as key incentives; focus on teamwork and training	Decisions on hiring and promotions lie with PUB, market-based wages	Full control of the management, market-based wages	Managing Director (MD) in control; 80% are agency employees; market-based wages; employee stock option plan; 'best employee' awards	Autonomy as per State-Operated Enterprises law, but external pressures on high staffing levels. Pay scales determined by HPWSC and backed by trainin
Rate setting and approval, regulation	Proposed a 3-step increase in rates over 7 years; 3rd step redundant as revenues covered the costs by then	PUB suggests rates; final approval by Cabinet on recommendations from Ministry of Finance	Full control of rates, with owners (Tata Steel) meeting operating losses	Progressive regulatory framework by Metropolitan Waterworks and Sewerage System (MWSS)	HPWSC suggests rates; final approval by Haiphong People's Central Committee (HPCC) after checking by TUPWS and the Finance Department
Incentives and monitoring					
Performance contract/ targets	Performance evaluation of staff based on measurable results	Must meet performance targets set by owners	Performance targets reviewed every 6 months	21 key performance / business efficiency indicators	Yes, but targets set at low levels
Business plan and funding	-	Funding approved on the basis of a business plan prepared by PUB	Capital provided by owners, backed by rigorous financial viability assessment	BP updated every 5 years; funding from MFIs* and private equity; Initial public offering in 2005	Required by lenders with financial covenants (where any)
Operations and innovations					
Customer Orientation	Developed a utility-customer relationship based on long-term community building; Awareness campaigns to generate broad support for tariff increases	Innovations in bill payments; customer feedback regularly sought; good complaint response record	24/24 customer complaint centre with service standard guarantees	Strong focus under sustainable development framework; decentralization and empowerment of local staff; significant improvement in customer service	Regular reporting by public media; customer surveys; focus on one phuong** at a time for better service
Benchmarking	Participates in regional benchmarking	Internal benchmarking done	Extensively used for internal processes	Extensively used internally to set targets	Participates in national benchmarking
NRW / UFW management***	Dramatic improvement over 12 years: NRW reduced from 72% to 6%, staff per 1,000 connections ratio down from 22 to 4	High performance with UFW down to 4.8% in 2002	NRW reduced to 11.5%; focus on total productive maintenance and setting up of district metering areas	Reduction in NRW from 63% in 1997 to 25% in 2007	-
Cost recovery	Collection ratio improved from 48% in 1993 to 99.9% by 2006	Very good with operating ratio at 0.58 in 2002	Very good with operating ratio at 0.62	Very good with full cost recovery, and generating market-type returns for MWC	-
Serving the poor	Overall coverage increased to 90%. families in poor communities with subsidized/and instalment-based connection fees; use of a revolving fund to reach the poor	100% access; targeted subsidies for lower-income users	Improved access for the poor through corporate social responsibility	Reduced rates for the poor; special grants in recent years (subsidised rates for new connections and basic sanitation)	-

* MFIs: Multilateral financial institutions
** A phuong is an administrative subdivision
*** NRW: Non-revenue water; UFW: Unaccounted-for water
Sources: Asian Development Bank (2004); Baietti et al. (2006); Southeast Asian Water Utilities Network and Asian Development Bank (2007);
http://www.adb.org/water/actions/CAM/Internal-Reforms-Fuel-Performance.asp, http://www.adb.org/Water/Champions/chan.asp, and http://www.adb.org/water/actions/CAM/PPWSA.asp

▲
Dhaka, Bangladesh. Cycle rickshaws carry passengers in all seasons including monsoon. **©Manoocher Deghati/IRIN**

non-revenue water and improved cost recovery, including billing and collection systems.

- *Upfront rate increases have not been needed, and public procurement rules are generally enforced.* Among high-performing utilities, water rate endorsement by politicians is widespread, restricting the scope for increases. As a result, initial emphasis has generally been on cost reduction through efficiency improvements rather than rate increases. Rates are politically endorsed at the local level and often ratified by the state or national government; however, this process by itself does not seem to act as a major hindrance to utility performance. This makes high performance on billing and collection efficiency an essential requirement for success. Public sector procurement rules are generally adhered to, which, again, does not seem to have hindered performance.

6.8.2 Urban transport, energy and air pollution

In 2001, about a third of residents in Jakarta, Manila, Seoul and Singapore and 50 per cent of those in Hong Kong, China, used public transport. The proportions of those going on foot were 40 per cent in Dhaka, 31 per cent in Shanghai, 24 per cent in Osaka, 23 per cent in Jakarta and 20 per cent in Delhi. Despite these patterns, however, use of private automobiles in Asian countries has been increasing in recent years, accounting for 34 per cent of trips in Jakarta, 32 per cent in Bangkok, and 30 per cent in Metropolitan Manila. This pattern is consistent with global trends, which see rapid increases in car ownership as average urban income per head ranges between US $3,000 and US $10,000 (in purchasing power parity terms) (Veolia Environmental Services, 2009).

Another trend in Asian cities is the introduction of rail-based transport systems, including high-tech magnetic levitation trains in Shanghai. While these state-of-the-art transport modes have enhanced the status and prestige of some cities, the bulk of the populations have found transit fares too expensive. In general, Asian urban authorities have paid scant attention to the mobility needs of the urban poor. For example, although many low-income people commute by foot, they find that sidewalks are hardly practicable as street vendors often clog already limited space. Bicycle lanes are provided in only a few cities. The urban poor are crammed in slow-moving buses, while better-off car-drivers create traffic jams. The majority of traffic accidents involve pedestrians and cyclists. Most serious of all, the health of urban pedestrians is adversely affected by the air pollution generated by the transport modes they cannot afford to use, rather than by those they use. Unequal access to urban transportation and energy is reviewed in Chapter 4.

In Asian metropolitan areas, transportation is estimated to account for at least a third of total greenhouse gas (GHG) emissions. Research has shown that a shift from small private cars to energy-efficient public transport (like diesel-powered articulated buses) can dramatically reduce greenhouse gas emissions (Veolia Environment Services, 2009). Bus rapid transit systems (BRTs) can be built (and operated) much more cheaply and rapidly, than rail-based equivalents. In those cities relying heavily on smaller vehicles, a shift from diesel to compressed natural gas (CNG) can further curb emissions, as in New Delhi (see Box 5.7 in Chapter 5).

However, despite the averred benefits of such alternatives, the transport policies favoured by Asian urban authorities instead promote privately- owned vehicles and expensive rail-based rapid transit systems.

6.8.3 Solid waste collection and disposal

One of the major challenges faced by Asian cities is the collection and disposal of solid waste. Most urban authorities have set up specialist departments to deal with this issue, but their efforts are often complemented by community-based alternatives where voluntary grassroots groups fill the gap in waste collection. This type of scheme is found in Bangalore (garbage collection and composting), Dhaka (marketing of compost produced by backyard composting), Chennai (collection, sorting, recycling and composting), and Delhi and Hanoi (garbage collection and recycling).

On the outskirts of the southern Indian City of Chennai, a women-led grassroots organization has demonstrated that civil society can play an important role in improving the quality of life and local governance (see Box 6.12).

Many such projects have been supported by organizations committed to environmental sustainability and have achieved significant results. However, in many instances, private solid waste collection and disposal companies and local government units have not been supportive, often viewing civil society groups as overly critical and, at times, confrontational competitors. As a result, these environmentally-concerned efforts have rarely been integrated into municipal solid waste management systems (Laquian, 2004).

BOX 6.12: A WOMEN'S GROUP REVOLUTIONISES WASTE MANAGEMENT IN SOUTH INDIA

Pammal, a small town on the periphery of Chennai, generates 17 tonnes of solid waste daily, 10 of which are collected by the municipal sanitation service. Like any other town *panchayat* (local governing bodies) across India, the Pammal municipal council lacks adequate (including financial) capacities and is prevented from employing new staff by a cumbersome approval procedure with the state government. For lack of a solid waste disposal facility, the *panchayat* dumps waste on a dried-up lake bed within the town's boundaries.

In Shri Shankara Nagar, a middle-income neighbourhood of Pammal, residents used to dispose of waste on vacant lots as the *panchayat* failed to collect waste left at official collection points. In 1994, a group of 10 women bent on cleaner streets founded a *'Mahalir Manram'* ('women's association' in Tamil). It took time to sensitise neighbours to the need to pay for the house-to-house collection service they set up. When in 1996 an unsupportive councillor caused

the *panchayat* to discontinue waste collection, *Mahalir Manram* organised door-to-door solid waste collection service using tricycles and collection points, causing anger among those residing next to the mounting piles of waste. In response, the women's group resolved to turn waste into manure and travelled widely to learn more about vermicomposting. Having reassured sceptical residents that the technique would not create any nuisance (odour, insects) they were given land where they built a sustainable facility. Since then, the scheme has achieved the following:

- led to the composting of over four fifths of all solid waste generated in Shri Shankara Nagar.
- generated income by the sale of compost and recycled paper, plastic, metal, glass and rubber.
- reduced the quantity of neighbourhood waste dumped at the town's disposal site to 10% of total waste.

- created a cleaner environment, persuading people of the benefits and sustainability of community-managed waste.

News of the composting success story in Shri Shankara Nagar has spread far and wide. The Chennai mayor has become a vermicomposting enthusiast and relations between the *panchayat* and *Mahalir Manram* have greatly improved as solid waste is now taken seriously by local politicians and officials.

In the process, the women of Shri Shankara Nagar have demonstrated the following:

- local-level civil society innovation can have dramatic ripple effects, improving not just the environment but also urban governance.
- strategic networking with higher-level political figures is vital to building consensus for public action.
- the emergence of civil society organisations, harnessing a 'can do' determination and a spirit of self-help, is sure to create antagonism in some quarters.

Based on: Dahiya (2003)
Source: http://www.eldis.org/assets/Docs/45646.html

6.9
Cooperation networks

Ulaanbaatar, Mongolia. ©Sang H. Park/Shutterstock

With good governance now recognized as a vital development instrument, national, regional and global cooperative networks have grown that enable interested individuals to exchange ideas, best practice and lessons learned, sharing them with municipal officials, administrators and researchers. They operate at the individual and institutional levels. For example, as early as 1913, the International Union of Local Authorities (IULA) began to support information exchanges among members with regard to governance and urban management.

In the field of urban planning and management, the East Asia Organization for Planning and Housing (EAROPH) has been conducting conferences, seminars and workshops since foundation in 1956. The organisation also publishes technical papers and monographs on urban planning, management and finance that are destined for urban and regional planners as well as housing specialists. The Eastern Regional Organization for Public Administration (EROPA) has also served as a support mechanism for good governance through regional conferences, technical seminars and workshops, training programmes, observation-study tours and publications.

In 2004, the International Union of Local Authorities merged with the World Federation of United Cities-United Towns and Metropolis (an organization of metropolitan areas) and the consolidated organisation became known as United Cities and Local Government. The UCLG Asia-Pacific Regional Section supports "strong and effective democratic local self-government throughout the region/world through promotion of unity and cooperation among members" and facilitates information exchange among local authorities in the region. CITYNET, a regional network of local authorities, supports the strengthening of institutional planning and management capabilities at the local and grassroots levels through technical cooperation among local authorities as well as governmental and non-governmental bodies. The network supports capacity-building through training, exchange of experts and sharing of experience and know-how (Tjandradewi & Marcotullio, 2008).

With the rapid increase in city-to-city ('C2C') relationships in Asia in recent decades, CITYNET has sought to assess their efficiency. In 2005-2008, the network carried out a survey of more than 70 urban authorities in over 20 Asian countries. Respondents were asked to rate (on a scale of one to four) which specific elements were considered important or

▲
Huahine island, French Polynesia. ©**Xavier MARCHANT/Shutterstock**

not for the success of city-to-city cooperation. Interestingly, the survey found that respondents' rankings clustered around three levels. The environment, health and education and the social-cultural dimensions were found to be the areas where city-to-city links made the most significant contribution. Security/disaster management, employment/economic development, and housing/shelter ranked second. Urban infrastructure, municipal finance and gender/poverty were where city-to-city cooperation found to contribute the least (Tjandradewi & Marcotullio, 2008).

The CITYNET survey highlights the shortcomings of current approaches to urban development in Asia. More specifically, the findings suggest that most Asian local authority officials still hold on to a traditional approach, one that focuses on technical aspects related to urban management rather than governance (let alone finance). Lack of emphasis on gender empowerment and poverty reduction further emphasises this restrictive notion of urban management. These blind spots point to the need for an urban vision that places the highest priority on democratic decision-making, community participation, inclusiveness, equity, empowerment and people-centred development, as recently highlighted by UN-HABITAT (2010a).

In almost all Asian countries, there are associations of local governments and local government officials that support good governance. For instance, the All-India Council of Mayors, a non-statutory body made up of elected representatives of municipal corporations, has raised concerns about issues related to decentralization and lobbies for legislation and administrative measures that strengthen local governance. Also in India, the City Managers Association acts as a cooperation network in support of urban reform. Across the northern border, development issues are advocated by the Municipal Association of Nepal. The Association of the Cities of Viet Nam promotes cooperative links among cities in areas like construction, management and development. The Mongolian Association of Urban Centres promotes good governance and exchange of urban planning experiences amongst cities and towns in the country.

In the Philippines, good governance is strongly supported by a number of local associations such as the League of Provinces of the Philippines, the League of Cities, the League of Municipalities, the Vice Governors League, the Vice Mayors League, the Provincial Board Members League and the Philippine Councillors League. Similar organizations exist in most Asian-Pacific countries, where they lobby national governments on urban development and governance issues.

Although most local authority associations work hard to achieve good governance, four main factors tend to dampen their effectiveness, as follows:
- Most local officials belong to political parties and partisan groups and this tends to make sustained and truly collaborative actions difficult.
- Elective local officials may be in office only for short periods, which stands in the way of continuity in policies and programmes.
- Many of the associations lack the financial and technical capacities required for effective good governance programmes.
- Given the wide variety of local governance systems in Asia, lessons learned in one jurisdiction might not be replicable in others.

6.10
Diagnosis and future challenges

▲
Tokyo, Japan. Urban management remains a day-to-day challenge even in well-managed cities. ©**Aaleksander/Shutterstock**

I n the Asian-Pacific region as in other parts of the world, cities have become the engines of economic growth and social change, but their sustainable development is largely dependent on effective and efficient management and governance. Unfortunately, over the past few years, the global economic crisis has had a detrimental effect. The additional financial resources provided by fiscal stimulus (in China, Japan, Republic of Korea, Singapore and Taiwan, Province of China) have concentrated on infrastructure and social investments in large conurbations, overlooking small and medium-sized urban areas. This is unfortunate because if urbanization is to accelerate the development of rural areas, policies and projects should focus on smaller urban

settlements, where demographic growth is stronger. City cluster development may encourage this approach and it will be interesting to see whether countries other than Bangladesh, China, India and Sri Lanka adopt it in the very near future.

A notable trend in Asia is the fact that a number of countries have made significant strides in the transition to more participatory and democratic forms of governance. This is particularly apparent in Bangladesh, Indonesia, Malaysia, the Republic of Korea and Taiwan, Province of China. Other countries – India, Pakistan, the Philippines and Thailand – have embarked on decentralization (in the form of deconcentration, delegation and devolution of powers to local/urban authorities); although any tangible benefits remain to be fully realized. In a number of countries, a significant proportion of urban dwellers now enjoy the benefits of liberal democracy, such as grassroots participation and engagement of civil society groups in public affairs. However, financial empowerment largely remains a challenge for Asia's urban authorities, and many are still found struggling to provide basic infrastructure and services.

Delegation of power to those urban authorities encompassing metropolitan areas arguably has prevented these from fragmenting into autonomous units. This urban management approach has had positive effects in countries in transition like China and Viet Nam, where mixed or unified metropolitan governance has delivered urban services in an efficient sort of way. As might have been hoped, water and sewerage, public transport, energy generation and distribution, and solid waste management are the services most favoured by coordinated management under area-wide authorities. At the same time, smaller local authorities have improved capacities in areas like water and electricity charge collection or even solid waste management thanks to community engagement.

Some urban authorities in Asia have financed development projects through public-private partnerships, foreign direct investment and more innovative schemes. Some have resorted to information technologies and e-governance to improve revenue-raising, keep the populations informed and involved, and take advantage of global development opportunities. Welcome as they are, these innovations must not obfuscate the need for a wholesale overhaul of Asian cities' basic legal and institutional frameworks and structures, some of which are still rooted in traditional practices. In this regard, the collection, analysis and dissemination of accurate and reliable information about urban trends has a crucial role to play if urban authorities are to be in a position to formulate and implement well-adapted, forward-looking reforms in the face of current and forthcoming challenges.

Raising the financial resources required to face those challenges remains a serious issue for most urban authorities in the Asian-Pacific region. Most are still financially dependent on higher tiers (central and/or state/provincial) of government which control the bulk of tax revenues and are often reluctant to share with urban authorities. In some Asian countries, however, urban authorities have been able to tap dormant or fresh financial resources. In India, Malaysia and the Philippines, computerization of tax rolls has significantly increased revenues from property taxes. China, India, Indonesia and Viet Nam have harnessed private sector participation in large-scale urban infrastructure. On top of this, the Asian Development Bank has also developed innovative techniques (like loans denominated in local currencies) to finance urban infrastructure and services.

In Asia as in other developing regions, environmental problems are increasingly being felt in cities and city-regions. However, most local officials are only beginning to understand how carbon taxes can raise the resources needed to mitigate or tackle climate change. More extensive sharing of information about carbon taxes and other innovative revenue generation methods is needed if local officials are to manage urban settlements and improve urban living conditions in a forward-looking way.

As highlighted in Chapter 5, the by-effects of global warming stand out as the most serious threat confronting settlements in the Asia-Pacific region. Some of the largest urban settlements in the region are located in coastal areas where rising sea levels may seriously disrupt urban life and livelihoods. While some urban authorities have instituted emergency preparedness procedures to cope with extreme weather conditions, many lack the financial and managerial resources effectively to deal with serious calamities.

In view of the environmental problems they are to face in the future, a rapid assessment of 10 Asian cities by the Institute of Development Studies has focused on their capacity to plan and implement integrated climate change resilience programmes, based on a number of relevant 'good governance' components (Tanner et al., 2009). The results highlight the need for integrated urban management systems, including comprehensive planning, provision of infrastructure and services, adequate financing and improved management capacities.

Although environmental issues represent an important future challenge for urban governance, current, basic issues remain, such as poverty eradication, sustainable development (economic, social and environmental), social equity and the security of individuals and their living environment, which together only strengthen the case for integrated approaches. In its Global Campaign on Urban Governance, UN-HABITAT mentioned a growing international consensus that "the quality of urban governance is the single most important factor for the eradication of poverty and the emergence of prosperous cities." Good urban governance, according to UN-HABITAT, is inextricably linked to the welfare of the populations. It enables women and men to access the benefits of urban citizenship including adequate shelter, security of tenure, safe water, sanitation, a clean environment, health, education and nutrition, employment, and public safety and mobility. Most importantly, good urban governance provides urban citizens with the platform that allows them to use their talents to the full to improve their social and economic conditions (UN-HABITAT, 2005).

Over the past decade, the UN-HABITAT Global Campaign on Urban Governance has significantly raised the awareness of the importance of good governance among urban authorities in the Asia-Pacific region. In this regard, continued monitoring and evaluation is crucial for sustainable urban development in the region. Cities can use the Urban Governance Index to improve the way they fulfil their mandates. In the past few years, much of the discussions on urban governance have moved beyond conceptual, definitional and normative issues. More and more cities in Asia are formulating, implementing and evaluating reforms aimed at improved governance. Their experiences and the lessons learned from them have a crucial role to play in any future progress.

Ahmad, Raza, & Erin Thebault Weiser. *Fostering Public Participation in Budget-making.* Manila: Asian Development Bank, 2006

Ali, Muhammed, "Eradicating Corruption – the Singapore Experience," Paper presented at the International Seminar on International Experience on Good Governance and Fighting Corruption," Bangkok, Thailand, 17 February 2000

Aliani, Adnan, Hasan, Arif, Shah, Kirtee & Wakely, Patrick. "Living in Asian Cities, The Impending Crisis - Causes, Consequences and Alternatives for the Future". *Report of the Second Asia-Pacific Urban Forum.* ESCAP, 1996

Amornvivat, Sutapa. *Fiscal Decentralization - the Case of Thailand.* Bangkok: Ministry of Finance, 2004

Andrade, Jeanette. "Quezon City Village Execs to Help Collect Real Estate Tax." *Philippine Daily Inquirer.* November 7, 2007, p7.

Anzorena, Jorge. "Muawin and Lodhiran Pilot Sanitation Projects," In *Anzorena's Selavip Newsletter,* April 2009. http://www.anzorenaselavip.org/article.php?id=11 (accessed 15 August 2010)

Argo, Teti & A. Laquian. "The Privatization of Water Services: Effects on the Urban Poor in Jakarta and Metro Manila," In *The Inclusive City: Infrastructure and Public Services for the Urban Poor in Asia,* by A. Laquian, V. Tewari and L. Hanley, eds., pp224-248. Washington DC and Baltimore, MD: Woodrow Wilson Center Press and Johns Hopkins University Press, 2007

Asian Development Bank. *Impact Evaluation Study on Water Supply and Sanitation Projects in Selected Developing Member Countries,* Manila: ADB Independent Evaluation, 2010. http://www.adb.org/Documents/IES/Water/Water-Supply-Sanitation-Projects (accessed 15 August 2010)

—. *Strategy 2020: The Long Term Strategic Framework of the Asian Development Bank 2008-2020.* Manila: Asian Development Bank, 2008a

—. *Managing Asian Cities.* Manila: ADB, 2008b

—. *Urban Development Experience and Vision-India and the People's Republic of China.* Manila: ADB Urban Development Series, 2008c

—. *City Cluster Development, Toward an Urban-Led Development Strategy for Asia.* Manila: ADB Urban Development Series, 2008d

____. Clustered Cities Development Project in South Asia, Second Roundtable (India), New Delhi: ADB 15 October, 2008e

—. *Water in Asian Cities: Utilities' Performance and Civil Society Views.* Manila: Asian Development Bank, 2004

____. "IND: Tala-Delhi Power Transmission," Project No. 36915-01, Approved by ADB Board, 16 January 2003

Baietti, Aldo, W. Kingdom, & M. Ginneken. "Characteristics of Well Performing Public Water Utilities." In *Water Supply and Sanitation Working Note No. 9.* Washington, DC: World Bank, 2006

Bergsten, C. Fred, Charles Freeman, Nicholas Lardy, & Derek Mitchell. "Democracy with Chinese Characteristics? Political Reform and the Future of the Chinese Communist Party." In *China's Rise: Challenges and Opportunities,* pp. 55-74. Washington, DC: Peterson Institute for International Economics, 2008

Bigio, Anthony, & Bharat Dahiya. *Urban Environment and Infrastructure: Toward Livable Cities.* Washington, D.C.: World Bank, 2004

Chan, Ek Sonn. "Phnom Penh Water Supply Authority (PPSWA): City Water Rebuilt from Ruins." Paper presented to the Mission of the High Powered Expert Committee on Investment Requirements for Urban Infrastructure in India. Manila: Asian Development Bank, April 28-29, 2009

Cheema, G. Shabbir, & Dennis A. Rondinelli. *From Government Decentralization to Decentralized Governance.* 2005. http://www.

brookings.edu/~/media/Files/Press/Books (accessed May 4, 2009)

Cheng, Lucie, & Chu-Joe Hsia. "Exploring Territorial Governance and Transterritorial Society: Alternative Visions of 21st Century Taiwan." In *Urban and Regional Governance in the Asia Pacific*, by John Friedmann, pp101-14. Vancouver: Institute of Asian Research, University of British Columbia, 1998

Chowdhury, Jayanta Roy. "Urban Job Plan on Government Table." *The Telegraph.* New Delhi, February 14, 2009 (accessed 14 March 2009)

Constitution of the Republic of the Philippines. Section 11, Article 10. 1987

Dahiya, Bharat. Hard struggle and soft gains: environmental management, civil society and governance in Pammal, South India, *Environment & Urbanization.* 15 1 2003:91-100

Dahiya, Bharat, & Cedric Pugh. "The Localization of Agenda 21 and the Sustainable Cities Programme." In Cedric Pugh, ed. *Sustainable Cities in Developing Countries: Theory and Practice at the Millennium.* London: Earthscan. 2000 pp152-184

Data Quest CIO Handbook 2009. *E-Governance: 20 Hot eGov Projects in India.* 2009. http://www.dqindia.ciol.com/content/top_stories/103101501.asp (accessed 26 March 2009)

Decentralization in Indonesia, An Overview. March 22, 2009. http://www.Indonesia-ottawa.org (accessed 24 April 2009)

Douglass, Mike. "Local City, Capital City or World City? Civil Society, the (Post-) Developmental State and the Globalization of Urban Space in Pacific Asia." *Pacific Affairs,* 78 Winter 2005 pp543-558

Echeminada, Perseus. "Quezon City Tax Collection Target Totals P9.4 Billion." *Philippine Star.* December 6, 2008, p1

Eckholm, Erik. "China's Villagers Vote, But Its Party Rules." *The New York Times.* November 4, 2001, p1A20

Economic Commission for Asia and the Pacific (ESCAP). "An Innovative Approach to Municipal Solid Waste Management in Least Developed and Low-income Developing Countries." *Regional Seminar and Study Visit on Community-based Solid Waste Management.* Quy Nhon City, December 15-16 2007

—. "Training Module on Understanding and Operationalizing Good Governance," ESCAP/LOGOTRI/LDTA National Workshop on the Concept and Characteristics of Good Urban Governance, 24-28 June 2002, Pokhara, Nepal

—. *Local Government in Asia and the Pacific: a Comparative Analysis of Fifteen Countries.* 1999. www.unescap.org/huset/lgstudy/comparison1.htm (accessed 14 February 2009)

Enright, Michael, Ka-mun Chang, Edith Scott, & Wen-hui Zhu. *Hong Kong and the Pearl River Delta, the Economic Interaction.* Hong Kong: Hong Kong 202 Foundation, 2003

Fahim, Mayraj. "Karachi's Federated Structure has Led to More Responsive City Government." *City Mayor Monitor.* July 12, 2005. http://www.citymayors.com/government/karachi_government.html (accessed 6 February 2009)

Government of India, Ministry of Urban Development. The Jawaharlal Nehru National Urban Renewal Mission (JNNURM). 2009. http://jnnurm.nic.in (accessed 2 April 2009)

Government of Malaysia. *MyKad, the Malaysian Government Multipurpose Card.* 2009. http://www.egov.vic.gov.au/index.php (accessed 23 March 2009)

Hasibuan, Dameria. "Jakarta Water Privatization: Workers Campaign to Bring Back Water in Public Hands." *ADB Forum on Water Privatization.* Kyoto, April 2007

Indiainfo. *Is Octroi Constitutional?* March 28, 2009. http://www.indiainfo.com/reviews/octroi.html (accessed 14 April 2009)

International Monetary Fund (IMF). *World Economic Outlook.* Washington DC: IMF, October 2008a

___. *World Economic Outlook.* Washington DC: IMF, November 2008b

—. *World Economic Outlook.* Washington DC: IMF, January 2009

Janwani. "Participatory Budgeting," Pune, 2010. http://www.janwani.org/index.php?option=com_contents&task=viewed&id=19&Itemid=28 (accessed 13 August 2010)

Jusoh, Hamzah, Jalaluddin Abdul Malek & Azmizam Abdul Rashid. "The Role of Efficient Urban Governance in Managing Kuala Lumpur City-Region Development," *Asian Social Science,* 5 August 2009 14-28. www.ccsenet.org/journal.html (accessed 23 March 2009)

Kalra, Harmit. *Property Enumeration and Mapping System for Bangalore.* March 24, 2009. http://www.gisdevelopment.net/application/urban/overview/urbano0027pf.htm (accessed 14 November 2009)

Khadka, Rup. "Municipal property taxes: theoretically sound but ineffective." *The Kathmandu Post.* March 28, 2002, p3

Kidd, John & Frank-Jurgen Richter, eds. *Fighting Corruption in Asia, Causes, Effects and Remedies.* Singapore: World Scientific Publishing Co. Pte. Ltd, 2003

Laquian, Aprodicio. *Beyond Metropolis, the Planning and Governance of Asia's Mega urban regions.* Washington, DC and Baltimore, MD: Woodrow Wilson Center Press & Johns Hopkins University Press, 2005

—. "Who are the Poor and How Are They Being Served in Asian Cities." *Public Transport in Asia,* 2004: 14-22

—. "Urban Governance, Some Lessons Learned." In *Democratic Governance and Urban Sustainability,* by Joseph S. Tulchin, Diana H. Varat & Blair A. Ruble, pp97-125.

Washington, DC: Woodrow Wilson International Center for Scholars, 2002a

—. "Metro Manila: People's Participation and Social Inclusion in a City of Villages." In *Urban Governance Around the World,* by Blair A. Ruble, Richard E. Stren, Joseph S. Tulchin & Diana H. Varat, pp. 74-110. Washington, DC: Woodrow Wilson International Center for Scholars, 2002b

Llanto, Jesus. "IRA Formula Makes Local Governments Complacent." *Newsbreak.* September 27, 2007, p2

Macan-Markar, Marwaan. "South-East Asia: Civil Society Sees Influential Ally in Thai Government." *Interpress News Agency,* March 6, 2009, p1

McCarney, Patricia, Mohamed Alfani & Alfredo Rodriguez. "Toward an Understanding of Governance: The Emergence of an Idea and its Implications for Urban Research in Developing Countries." In *Urban Research in the Developing World, Perspectives on the City, Vol. 4,* by Richard Stren & Judith K. Bell. Toronto: Centre for Urban and Community Studies, University of Toronto, 1995, pp14-24

Muhamad, Jamilah. "An LRT-Bus Strategy for Greater Kuala Lumpur: What Future Integration?" *Sarjana, Malaysian Journal of Arts and Social Sciences,* 14, 1997 pp57-75

National Library of Singapore, "Port of Singapore Authority (PSA)," *Singapore Infopedia,* http://infopedia.nl.sg/artcles/SIP_577_2005-01-27-html (accessed 27 January 2005)

NESDB. *National Urban Development Policy Framework-Final Report, Vol. 1.* Bangkok: National Economic and Social Development Board, 1990

Organization for Economic Cooperation and Development (OECD). "Participatory Development and Good Governance," *OECD Development Cooperation Guidelines Series,* Paris: OECD, 1995.

Porter, Michael. *The Competitive Advantage of Nations.* New York: Macmillan, 1990

Pradhan, Prachi Karnak. "Octroi, tax reforms by BMC to mop up revenue." *The Financial Express.* February 11, 2008 p1

Roberts, Brian & Kanaley, Trevor (eds.). *Urbanization and Sustainability in Asia: Case Studies of Good Practices,* Manila: Asian Development Bank & Cities Alliance, 2006

Roy, Ananya. "Marketized? Feminized? Medieval? Urban Governance in an Era of Liberalization." In *Democratic Governance and Urban Sustainability,* by Joseph Tulchin, Diana Varat & Blair Ruble, 29-44. Washington, DC: Woodrow Wilson International Center for Scholars, 2002

Sen, Amartya. *Development as Freedom.* Oxford: Oxford University Press, 1999.

Seva, Violeta Somera. "Challenges in Financing Local Infrastructure in Makati City, Philippines." Paper delivered at the Committee of Local Finance Development Meeting. Barcelona: United Cities and Governments (UCLG), January 1-12, 2007

Singson, Rogelio, "Maynilad Water Services, a Re-privatization Case," Presentation made at the Fourth World Urban Forum, Nanjing, China, 3-6 November 2008. Accessed at: http://www.adb.org/Documents/Events/2008/Fourth-Urban-Forum/Rogelio-Singson.pdf (accessed 25 May 2010)

Southeast Asian Water Utilities Network and Asian Development Bank. *Data Book of Southeast Asian Water Utilities 2005.* ADB, 2007

Stren, Richard. "Thinking about Urban Inclusiveness." Paper presented at the Woodrow Wilson International Center for Scholars, Washington, D.C, USA, 6 August 2001

Stren, Richard & Mario Polese. *The Social Sustainability of Cities: Diversity and the Management*

of Change. Toronto: University of Toronto Press, 2000

Tanner, Thomas, Tom Mitchell, Emily Polack & Bruce Guenther. "Urban Governance for Adaptation: Assessing Climate Change Resilience in Ten Asian Cities." In *IDS Working Paper 315.* Brighton: Institute of Development Studies at the University of Sussex, 2009

Tapales, Proserpina. *Devolution and Empowerment: the Local Government Code of 1991 and Local Autonomy in the Philippines,* Diliman, Quezon City: Center for Integrative and Development Studies & University of the Philippines Press, 1993

The Sustainability Fund, *Smart Energy Zones: Case Study, Dongtan, China,* 2005. http://www.resourcesmart.vic.gov.au/documents/SEZ_Case_Study_Dongtan.pdf (accessed 30 April 2009)

Tjandradewi, Bernadia, I., & Peter Marcotullio. *City-to-city networks: Asian perspectives on key elements and areas for success.* Habitat International, 33 (2009), pp. 165-172

The United Cities & Local Governments. *Decentralization and Local Democracy in the World.* First Global Report (The UCLG Gold Report). Barcelona: UCLG; Washington DC: The World Bank, 2008

UNDP. "The Urban Governance Initiative (UNDP-TUGI)," *Environment and Urbanization,* 15 April 2003, pp159-170

—. Asia-Pacific Information Development Programme. *New Guidelines on e-Government Interoperability Developed by Governments for Governments.* Bangkok: UNDP Regional Centre, 2007

UN-HABITAT. *State of the World Cities 2010-2011 – Bridging the urban divide.* Nairobi: UN-HABITAT; London: Earthscan, 2010a

—. *State of the Urban Youth 2010-2011 – Levelling the Playing Field.* Nairobi: UN-HABITAT; London: Earthscan, 2010b

—. World Training Event, "Inclusive Urban Governance: How to Walk the Talk," Vancouver, 20 June 2006, www.unhabitat.org/downloads/docs/wuf3/PB.ppt#257.2,Contents (accessed 19 July 2009)

—. *Urban Governance Index*, Nairobi: Global Campaign on Urban Governance, 2005. http:www.unhabitat.org/content.p?typeid=19&catid=25&cid=2167 (accessed 25 May 2009)

—. *Cities in a Globalizing World, Global Report on Human Settlements*. Nairobi: UN-HABITAT, and London: Earthscan, 2001

UN-HABITAT Governing Council. *International Guidelines on Access to Basic Services for all*. 22nd session of the Governing Council of the Human Settlements Programme (2009), Agenda item 6, HSP/GC/22/2/Add.6/Corr.1/Rev.1

—. *International Guidelines on Decentralization and Strengthening of Local Authorities*. 21st Governing Council Decisions, Resolution 21/3. Nairobi: UN-HABITAT, April 16-20, 2007

UN-HABITAT & Transparency International. *Tools to Support Transparency in Local Governance-Local Governance Toolkit Series.* Nairobi: UN-HABITAT & Transparency International, 2004

United Nations. *World Urbanization Prospects - The 2007 Revision.* New York: Department of Economic and Social Affairs, Population Division, February 2008

Veolia Environmental Services. *Reducing Greenhouse Gas Emissions,* 2009, http://veoliaes.com/Environmental%Data?id=1839&lid=1 (accessed 11 January 2010)

Wong, Kwan-jiu, & Jianfa Shen (eds.). *Resource Management, Urbanization and Governance in Hong Kong and the Zhujiang Delta.* Hong Kong: Chinese University of Hong Kong Press, 2002

Wong, H.Y., "Anti-corruption Strategy of the Hong Kong Special Administrative Region of the People's Republic of China," Presentation at the 4th Regional Anti-corruption Conference, Kuala Lumpur, Malaysia, 3-5 December 2005.

Wongpreedee, Achakorn. "Decentralization and its Effects on Provincial Political Power in Thailand." Asian and African Area Studies, 6 2007 pp454-470

World Bank. "Concentration without Congestion, Policies for Inclusive Urbanization." *World Development Report,* Chapter 7. Washington, DC: World Bank, 2009

—. Governance and Development, Washington, DC: 1992

World Health Organization & UNICEF. *Progress on Sanitation and Drinking-Water: 2010 Update.* WHO/UNICEF Joint Monitoring Programme for Water Supply and Sanitation. Geneva and New York: World Health Organization & UNICEF. 2010

Xu Xueqiang & Xu Yongjian, "A Study on an Integrated Cross-Border Transport Network for the Pearl River Delta." In *Building a Competitive Pearl River Delta Region, Cooperation, Coordination and Planning,* edited by Anthony Gar-On Yeh, Yok-shiu F. Lee, Tunney Lee & Nien Dak Sze, Hong Kong: Centre of Urban Planning and Environmental Management, University of Hong Kong, 2002 pp127-142

Yeung, Yue-man, Joanna Lee & Gordon Kee. *China's Special Economic Zones at 30.* Hong Kong: Chinese University of Hong Kong Press, 2009

Urban and rural population in the Asia-Pacific region

Major area, region, country or area	Total Population (1,000s)								Urban Population (1,000s)			
	1990	1995	2000	2005	2010*	2015*	2020*	2025*	1990	1995	2000	2005
World	5,290,452	5,713,073	6,115,367	6,512,276	6,908,688	7,302,186	7,674,833	8,011,533	2,254,592	2,539,470	2,837,431	3,166,711
Asia	3,178,810	3,448,034	3,698,296	3,936,536	4,166,741	4,390,603	4,596,256	4,772,523	1,002,731	1,175,181	1,360,900	1,567,983
East and North-East Asia									430,533	511,002	594,676	703,603
China (1)	1,142,090	1,210,969	1,266,954	1,312,253	1,354,146	1,395,998	1,431,155	1,453,140	301,995	374,257	453,029	557,884
China, Hong Kong SAR (2)	5,704	6,214	6,667	6,883	7,069	7,398	7,701	7,969	5,677	6,214	6,667	6,883
China, Macao SAR (3)	372	412	441	488	548	568	588	603	371	411	441	488
Dem. People's Republic of Korea	20,143	21,717	22,859	23,529	23,991	24,399	24,802	25,128	11,760	12,817	13,581	14,072
Japan	123,191	125,442	126,706	127,449	126,995	125,791	123,664	120,793	77,726	81,079	82,633	84,068
Mongolia	2,216	2,270	2,389	2,550	2,701	2,855	3,002	3,134	1,264	1,289	1,358	1,516
Republic of Korea	42,983	44,651	46,429	47,566	48,501	49,153	49,475	49,484	31,740	34,935	36,967	38,693
South-East Asia												
Brunei Darussalam	257	295	333	370	407	443	478	513	169	202	237	272
Cambodia	9,690	11,380	12,760	13,866	15,053	16,357	17,707	18,973	1,221	1,611	2,157	2,601
Indonesia	177,385	191,501	205,280	219,210	232,517	244,191	254,218	263,287	54,252	68,087	86,219	94,369
Lao People's Democratic Republic	4,207	4,809	5,403	5,880	6,436	7,028	7,651	8,273	649	836	1,187	1,610
Malaysia	18,103	20,594	23,274	25,633	27,914	30,041	32,017	33,770	9,014	11,468	14,424	17,332
Myanmar	40,844	43,864	46,610	48,345	50,496	53,087	55,497	57,585	10,092	11,372	12,956	14,695
Philippines	62,427	69,965	77,689	85,496	93,617	101,734	109,683	117,270	30,333	33,786	37,283	41,126
Singapore	3,016	3,480	4,018	4,267	4,837	5,059	5,219	5,362	3,016	3,480	4,018	4,267
Thailand	56,673	60,140	62,347	65,946	68,139	69,939	71,443	72,628	16,675	18,208	19,417	21,302
Timor-Leste	740	849	815	992	1,171	1,385	1,618	1,869	154	191	198	259
Viet Nam	66,247	72,957	78,663	84,074	89,029	93,647	98,011	102,054	13,418	16,202	19,263	22,981
South and South-West Asia												
Afghanistan	12,580	18,084	20,536	24,507	29,117	34,246	39,585	44,970	2,277	3,459	4,148	5,223
Bangladesh	115,632	128,086	140,767	153,122	164,425	175,217	185,552	195,012	22,908	27,786	33,208	39,310
Bhutan	549	509	561	650	708	770	820	865	90	104	143	201
India	862,162	953,148	1,042,590	1,130,618	1,214,464	1,294,192	1,367,225	1,431,272	220,260	253,473	288,430	324,671
Iran (Islamic Republic of)	56,733	62,205	66,903	70,765	75,078	79,454	83,740	87,134	31,958	37,470	42,952	47,829
Maldives	216	248	272	292	314	338	362	384	56	64	75	99
Nepal	19,105	21,624	24,432	27,222	29,853	32,503	35,269	38,031	1,692	2,356	3,281	4,333
Pakistan	115,776	130,397	148,132	165,816	184,753	205,504	226,187	246,286	35,400	41,514	49,088	57,175
Sri Lanka	17,290	18,233	18,767	19,531	20,410	21,167	21,713	22,033	3,217	3,131	2,971	2,877
Turkey	56,086	61,206	66,460	71,169	75,705	79,966	83,873	87,364	33,204	38,023	43,027	47,886
North and Central Asia												
Armenia	3,545	3,223	3,076	3,065	3,090	3,139	3,175	3,181	2,390	2,129	1,989	1,965
Azerbaijan	7,212	7,784	8,121	8,453	8,934	9,426	9,838	10,128	3,876	4,064	4,158	4,356
Georgia	5,460	5,069	4,745	4,465	4,219	4,084	3,982	3,888	3,005	2,729	2,498	2,343
Kazakhstan	16,530	15,926	14,957	15,194	15,753	16,289	16,726	17,025	9,301	8,906	8,417	8,676
Kyrgyzstan	4,395	4,592	4,955	5,221	5,550	5,877	6,159	6,378	1,660	1,669	1,744	1,832
Russian Federation	148,065	148,497	146,670	143,170	140,367	137,983	135,406	132,345	108,670	108,955	107,582	104,414
Tajikistan	5,303	5,775	6,173	6,536	7,075	7,761	8,446	9,075	1,679	1,668	1,635	1,722
Turkmenistan	3,668	4,187	4,502	4,843	5,177	5,509	5,816	6,072	1,653	1,875	2,062	2,291
Uzbekistan	20,515	22,919	24,776	26,320	27,794	29,456	31,185	32,715	8,241	8,810	9,273	9,653
Pacific												
Australia (4)	17,091	18,118	19,171	20,395	21,512	22,607	23,675	24,703	14,596	15,601	16,710	17,987
New Zealand	3,386	3,685	3,868	4,111	4,303	4,492	4,669	4,831	2,869	3,145	3,314	3,537
Fiji	724	768	802	828	854	874	888	905	301	349	384	413
New Caledonia	171	193	215	235	254	271	288	304	102	116	127	136
Papua New Guinea	4,131	4,709	5,388	6,118	6,888	7,678	8,468	9,265	619	663	711	770
Solomon Islands	314	362	416	474	536	599	662	725	43	53	65	80
Vanuatu	149	172	190	216	246	276	307	338	28	35	41	51
Guam	134	146	155	169	180	191	201	211	122	134	144	157
Kiribati	72	77	84	92	100	107	115	123	25	28	36	40
Marshall Islands	47	51	52	57	63	70	75	79	31	34	36	40
Micronesia (Fed. States of)	96	107	107	109	111	114	118	122	25	27	24	24
Nauru	9	10	10	10	10	11	11	11	9	10	10	10
Northern Mariana Islands	44	58	69	80	88	96	104	111	39	52	62	73
Palau	15	17	19	20	21	21	22	23	10	12	13	16
American Samoa	47	53	58	63	69	74	80	86	38	45	51	57
Cook Islands	18	19	18	19	20	20	21	21	10	11	11	14
French Polynesia	195	216	236	255	272	289	304	318	109	116	124	132
Niue	2	2	2	2	1	1	1	1	1	1	1	1
Pitcairn	0	0	0	0	0	0	0	0	—	—	—	—
Samoa	161	168	177	179	179	181	184	188	34	36	39	38
Tokelau	2	1	2	1	1	1	1	1	—	—	—	—
Tonga	95	97	99	102	104	105	108	112	21	22	23	24
Tuvalu	9	9	10	10	10	10	10	11	4	4	4	5
Wallis and Futuna Islands	14	14	15	15	15	16	17	17	—	—	—	—

*Projections

Notes:
(1) For statistical purposes, the data for China do not include Hong Kong and Macao, Special Administrative Regions (SAR) of China.
(2) As of 1 July 1997, Hong Kong became a Special Administrative Region (SAR) of China.
(3) As of 20 December 1999, Macao became a Special Administrative Region (SAR) of China.
(4) Including Christmas Island, Cocos (Keeling) Islands, and Norfolk Island.

Major area, region, country or area	Urban Population (1,000s)				Rural Population (1,000s)							
	2010*	2015*	2020*	2025*	1990	1995	2000	2005	2010*	2015*	2020*	2025*
World	3,486,326	3,824,073	4,176,234	4,535,925	3,035,859	3,173,603	3,277,937	3,345,565	3,422,362	3,478,113	3,498,599	3,475,608
Asia	1,757,314	1,958,246	2,168,798	2,383,268	2,176,079	2,272,854	2,337,395	2,368,553	2,409,427	2,432,357	2,427,458	2,389,255
East and North-East Asia												
China (1)	635,839	713,091	786,761	851,430	840,095	836,712	813,925	754,369	718,307	682,907	644,394	601,710
China, Hong Kong SAR (2)	7,069	7,398	7,701	7,969	28	—	—	—	—	—	—	—
China, Macao SAR (3)	548	568	588	603	1	0	—	—	—	—	—	—
Dem. People's Republic of Korea	14,446	14,874	15,413	16,018	8,383	8,900	9,278	9,457	9,545	9,525	9,389	9,110
Japan	84,875	85,527	85,848	85,877	45,466	44,363	44,073	43,381	42,120	40,264	37,817	34,917
Mongolia	1,675	1,842	2,010	2,172	952	980	1,031	1,034	1,026	1,013	992	962
Republic of Korea	40,235	41,474	42,362	42,910	11,243	9,716	9,462	8,873	8,265	7,679	7,113	6,574
South-East Asia												
Brunei Darussalam	308	344	379	415	88	93	96	98	99	99	99	98
Cambodia	3,027	3,560	4,214	4,982	8,469	9,769	10,603	11,265	12,026	12,798	13,493	13,991
Indonesia	102,960	112,229	122,257	133,419	123,133	123,414	119,061	124,841	129,557	131,962	131,961	129,868
Lao People's Democratic Republic	2,136	2,732	3,381	4,050	3,557	3,973	4,216	4,270	4,300	4,296	4,269	4,223
Malaysia	20,146	22,755	25,128	27,188	9,089	9,126	8,849	8,301	7,768	7,285	6,889	6,582
Myanmar	16,990	19,690	22,570	25,539	30,752	32,491	33,654	33,650	33,505	33,397	32,927	32,046
Philippines	45,781	51,265	57,657	64,951	32,094	36,179	40,406	44,370	47,836	50,469	52,026	52,319
Singapore	4,837	5,059	5,219	5,362	—	—	—	—	—	—	—	—
Thailand	23,142	25,286	27,800	30,679	39,998	41,932	42,930	44,643	44,997	44,653	43,643	41,949
Timor-Leste	329	422	538	680	586	657	617	733	842	963	1,080	1,189
Viet Nam	27,046	31,474	36,269	41,371	52,829	56,755	59,400	61,093	61,983	62,173	61,743	60,682
South and South-West Asia												
Afghanistan	6,581	8,315	10,450	13,047	10,304	14,625	16,388	19,284	22,537	25,931	29,134	31,923
Bangladesh	46,114	53,966	62,886	72,844	92,724	100,300	107,559	113,812	118,276	121,251	122,667	122,169
Bhutan	246	297	348	400	459	404	419	449	463	473	472	465
India	364,459	410,490	463,328	523,202	641,901	699,675	754,160	805,946	850,005	883,702	903,896	908,070
Iran (Islamic Republic of)	53,120	58,424	63,596	67,983	24,775	24,735	23,951	22,935	21,958	21,030	20,145	19,151
Maldives	126	156	186	216	160	184	197	194	188	182	175	168
Nepal	5,559	7,015	8,739	10,717	17,413	19,268	21,150	22,888	24,294	25,488	26,529	27,314
Pakistan	66,318	77,420	90,199	104,735	80,376	88,884	99,045	108,641	118,435	128,083	135,987	141,551
Sri Lanka	2,921	3,080	3,360	3,788	14,073	15,102	15,796	16,654	17,489	18,087	18,353	18,245
Turkey	52,728	57,475	62,033	66,316	22,882	23,183	23,433	23,283	22,977	22,491	21,840	21,048
North and Central Asia												
Armenia	1,984	2,032	2,087	2,136	1,155	1,094	1,087	1,100	1,107	1,107	1,088	1,045
Azerbaijan	4,639	4,977	5,332	5,684	3,335	3,720	3,964	4,097	4,294	4,449	4,506	4,444
Georgia	2,225	2,182	2,177	2,194	2,455	2,340	2,247	2,122	1,994	1,902	1,806	1,694
Kazakhstan	9,217	9,820	10,417	10,977	7,229	7,020	6,539	6,518	6,537	6,469	6,309	6,049
Kyrgyzstan	1,918	2,043	2,202	2,393	2,734	2,923	3,211	3,389	3,633	3,834	3,957	3,985
Russian Federation	102,702	101,683	100,892	100,058	39,395	39,542	39,088	38,756	37,665	36,300	34,513	32,287
Tajikistan	1,862	2,082	2,364	2,708	3,624	4,108	4,538	4,813	5,213	5,679	6,083	6,367
Turkmenistan	2,562	2,861	3,175	3,487	2,015	2,312	2,440	2,552	2,614	2,648	2,642	2,584
Uzbekistan	10,075	10,787	11,789	13,030	12,274	14,109	15,502	16,667	17,720	18,669	19,396	19,685
Pacific												
Australia (4)	19,169	20,328	21,459	22,548	2,495	2,517	2,461	2,408	2,343	2,279	2,216	2,154
New Zealand	3,710	3,885	4,058	4,225	517	541	554	573	594	607	611	606
Fiji	443	472	501	534	422	419	418	415	411	402	387	372
New Caledonia	146	156	169	183	69	77	88	99	108	115	120	121
Papua New Guinea	863	999	1,194	1,473	3,512	4,046	4,676	5,348	6,026	6,679	7,275	7,792
Solomon Islands	99	123	152	188	271	309	350	393	436	476	510	537
Vanuatu	67	78	95	116	121	137	149	166	183	199	212	222
Guam	168	178	188	198	12	12	11	12	12	13	13	12
Kiribati	44	48	54	60	47	49	48	52	56	59	62	63
Marshall Islands	45	51	56	61	17	17	16	17	18	18	18	18
Micronesia (Fed. States of)	25	27	29	33	71	80	83	85	86	87	88	89
Nauru	10	11	11	11	—	—	—	—	—	—	—	—
Northern Mariana Islands	81	88	96	103	4	6	7	7	8	8	8	8
Palau	17	18	20	21	5	5	6	4	3	3	2	2
American Samoa	64	70	76	82	9	8	6	5	5	4	4	4
Cook Islands	15	16	17	18	8	8	6	6	5	4	4	4
French Polynesia	140	150	160	172	86	100	112	123	132	140	144	145
Niue	1	1	1	0	2	1	1	1	1	1	1	1
Pitcairn	—	—	—	—	0	0	0	0	0	0	0	0
Samoa	36	36	38	41	127	132	138	141	143	145	146	147
Tokelau	—	—	—	—	2	1	2	1	1	1	1	1
Tonga	24	25	28	31	73	75	76	78	80	79	81	81
Tuvalu	5	5	6	6	5	5	5	5	5	5	5	4
Wallis and Futuna Islands	—	—	—	—	14	14	15	15	15	16	17	17

Notes:
0 and/or 0.0 indicates that the magnitude is zero or less than half of the unit employed.
A minus sign (-) before a figure indicates a decrease.
Years given refer to 1 July.
Use of hyphen (-) between years, for example, 1995-2000, signifies the full period involved, from 1 July of the beginning year to 1 July of the end year.

Source: United Nations, Department of Economic and Social Affairs, Population Division (2010). World Urbanization Prospects : The 2009 Revision. CD-ROM Edition - Data in digital form (POP/ DB/WUP/Rev.2009).

STATISTICAL ANNEX

253

Percentage of population residing in urban and rural areas in the Asia-Pacific region

Major area, region, country or area	Percentage of Population Residing in Urban Areas (%)								Percentage of Population Residing in Rural Areas (%)							
	1990	1995	2000	2005	2010*	2015*	2020*	2025*	1990	1995	2000	2005	2010*	2015*	2020*	2025*
World	42.6	44.5	46.4	48.6	50.5	52.4	54.4	56.6	57.4	55.5	53.6	51.4	49.5	47.6	45.6	43.4
Asia	31.5	34.1	36.8	39.8	42.2	44.6	47.2	49.9	68.5	65.9	63.2	60.2	57.8	55.4	52.8	50.1
East and North-East Asia																
China (1)	26.4	30.9	35.8	42.5	47.0	51.1	55.0	58.6	73.6	69.1	64.2	57.5	53.0	48.9	45.0	41.4
China, Hong Kong SAR (2)	99.5	100.0	100.0	100.0	100.0	100.0	100.0	100.0	0.5	—	—	—	—	—	—	—
China, Macao SAR (3)	99.8	99.9	100.0	100.0	100.0	100.0	100.0	100.0	0.2	0.1	—	—	—	—	—	—
Dem. People's Republic of Korea	58.4	59.0	59.4	59.8	60.2	61.0	62.1	63.7	41.6	41.0	40.6	40.2	39.8	39.0	37.9	36.3
Japan	63.1	64.6	65.2	65.6	66.8	68.0	69.4	71.1	36.9	35.4	34.8	34.0	33.2	32.0	30.6	28.9
Mongolia	57.0	56.8	56.9	59.5	62.0	64.5	67.0	69.3	43.0	43.2	43.1	40.5	38.0	35.5	33.0	30.7
Republic of Korea	73.8	78.2	79.6	81.3	83.0	84.4	85.6	86.7	26.2	21.8	20.4	18.7	17.0	15.6	14.4	13.3
South-East Asia																
Brunei Darussalam	65.8	68.6	71.1	73.5	75.7	77.6	79.3	80.9	34.2	31.4	28.9	26.5	24.3	22.4	20.7	19.1
Cambodia	12.6	14.2	16.9	18.8	20.1	21.8	23.8	26.3	87.4	85.8	83.1	81.2	79.9	78.2	76.2	73.7
Indonesia	30.6	35.6	42.0	43.0	44.3	46.0	48.1	50.7	69.4	64.4	58.0	57.0	55.7	54.0	51.9	49.3
Lao People's Democratic Republic	15.4	17.4	22.0	27.4	33.2	38.9	44.2	48.9	84.6	82.6	78.0	72.6	66.8	61.1	55.8	51.0
Malaysia	49.8	55.7	62.0	67.6	72.2	75.7	78.5	80.5	50.2	44.3	38.0	32.4	27.8	24.3	21.5	19.5
Myanmar	24.7	25.9	27.8	30.3	33.6	37.1	40.7	44.3	75.3	74.1	72.2	69.6	66.4	62.9	59.3	55.7
Philippines	48.6	48.3	48.0	48.1	48.9	50.4	52.6	55.4	51.4	51.7	52.0	51.9	51.1	49.6	47.4	44.6
Singapore	100.0	100.0	100.0	100.0	100.0	100.0	100.0	100.0	—	—	—	—	—	—	—	—
Thailand	29.4	30.3	31.1	32.3	34.0	36.2	38.9	42.2	70.6	69.7	68.9	67.7	66.0	63.8	61.1	57.8
Timor-Leste	20.8	22.5	24.3	26.1	28.1	30.5	33.2	36.4	79.2	77.5	75.7	73.9	71.9	69.5	66.8	63.6
Viet Nam	20.3	22.2	24.5	27.3	30.4	33.6	37.0	40.5	79.7	77.8	75.5	72.7	69.6	66.4	63.0	59.5
South and South-West Asia																
Afghanistan	18.1	19.1	20.2	21.3	22.6	24.3	26.4	29.0	81.9	80.9	79.8	78.7	77.4	75.7	73.6	71.0
Bangladesh	19.8	21.7	23.6	25.7	28.1	30.8	33.9	37.4	80.2	78.3	76.4	74.3	71.9	69.2	66.1	62.6
Bhutan	16.4	20.5	25.4	31.0	34.7	38.5	42.4	46.2	83.6	79.5	74.6	69.0	65.3	61.5	57.6	53.8
India	25.5	26.6	27.7	28.7	30.0	31.7	33.9	36.6	74.5	73.4	72.3	71.3	70.0	68.3	66.1	63.4
Iran (Islamic Republic of)	56.3	60.2	64.2	67.6	70.8	73.5	75.9	78.0	43.7	39.8	35.8	32.4	29.2	26.5	24.1	22.0
Maldives	25.8	25.6	27.7	33.7	40.1	46.1	51.5	56.2	74.2	74.4	72.3	66.3	59.9	53.9	48.5	43.8
Nepal	8.9	10.9	13.4	15.9	18.6	21.6	24.8	28.2	91.1	89.1	86.6	84.1	81.4	78.4	75.2	71.8
Pakistan	30.6	31.8	33.1	34.5	35.9	37.7	39.9	42.5	69.4	68.2	66.9	65.5	64.1	62.3	60.1	57.5
Sri Lanka	18.6	17.2	15.8	14.7	14.3	14.6	15.5	17.2	81.4	82.8	84.2	85.3	85.7	85.4	84.5	82.8
Turkey	59.2	62.1	64.7	67.3	69.6	71.9	74.0	75.9	40.8	37.9	35.3	32.7	30.4	28.1	26.0	24.1
North and Central Asia																
Armenia	67.4	66.1	64.7	64.1	64.2	64.7	65.7	67.1	32.6	33.9	35.3	35.9	35.8	35.3	34.3	32.9
Azerbaijan	53.7	52.2	51.2	51.5	51.9	52.8	54.2	56.1	46.3	47.8	48.8	48.5	48.1	47.2	45.8	43.9
Georgia	55.0	53.8	52.6	52.5	52.7	53.4	54.7	56.4	45.0	46.2	47.4	47.5	47.3	46.6	45.3	43.6
Kazakhstan	56.3	55.9	56.3	57.1	58.5	60.3	62.3	64.5	43.7	44.1	43.7	42.9	41.5	39.7	37.7	35.5
Kyrgyzstan	37.8	36.3	35.2	35.1	34.5	34.8	35.7	37.5	62.2	63.7	64.8	64.9	65.5	65.2	64.3	62.5
Russian Federation	73.4	73.4	73.3	72.9	73.2	73.7	74.5	75.6	26.6	26.6	26.7	27.1	26.8	26.3	25.5	24.4
Tajikistan	31.7	28.9	26.5	26.4	26.3	26.8	28.0	29.8	68.3	71.1	73.5	73.6	73.7	73.2	72.0	70.2
Turkmenistan	45.1	44.8	45.8	47.3	49.5	51.9	54.5	57.4	54.9	55.2	54.2	52.7	50.5	48.1	45.4	42.6
Uzbekistan	40.2	38.4	37.4	36.7	36.2	36.6	37.8	39.8	59.8	61.6	62.6	63.3	63.8	63.4	62.2	60.2
Pacific																
Australia (4)	85.4	86.1	87.2	88.2	89.1	89.9	90.6	91.3	14.6	13.9	12.8	11.8	10.9	10.1	9.4	8.7
New Zealand	84.7	85.3	85.7	86.1	86.2	86.5	86.9	87.5	15.3	14.7	14.3	13.9	13.8	13.5	13.1	12.5
Fiji	41.6	45.5	47.9	49.9	51.9	54.0	56.4	59.0	58.4	54.5	52.1	50.1	48.1	46.0	43.6	41.0
New Caledonia	59.5	60.1	59.2	58.0	57.4	57.5	58.5	60.3	40.5	39.9	40.8	42.0	42.6	42.5	41.5	39.7
Papua New Guinea	15.0	14.1	13.2	12.6	12.5	13.0	14.1	15.9	85.0	85.9	86.8	87.4	87.5	87.0	85.9	84.1
Solomon Islands	13.7	14.7	15.7	17.0	18.6	20.5	23.0	25.9	86.3	85.3	84.3	83.0	81.4	79.5	77.0	74.1
Vanuatu	18.7	20.2	21.7	23.5	25.6	28.1	31.0	34.4	81.3	79.8	78.3	76.5	74.4	71.9	69.0	65.6
Guam	90.8	92.1	93.1	93.1	93.2	93.3	93.5	93.8	9.2	7.9	6.9	6.9	6.8	6.7	6.5	6.2
Kiribati	35.0	36.4	43.0	43.6	43.9	44.9	46.5	48.8	65.0	63.6	57.0	56.4	56.1	55.1	53.5	51.2
Marshall Islands	65.1	66.7	68.4	70.0	71.8	73.5	75.3	77.1	34.9	33.3	31.6	30.0	28.2	26.5	24.7	22.9
Micronesia (Fed. States of)	25.8	25.1	22.3	22.3	22.7	23.6	25.1	27.3	74.2	74.9	77.7	77.7	77.3	76.4	74.9	72.7
Nauru	100.0	100.0	100.0	100.0	100.0	100.0	100.0	100.0	—	—	—	—	—	—	—	—
Northern Mariana Islands	89.7	89.6	90.2	90.8	91.3	91.9	92.4	92.9	10.3	10.4	9.8	9.2	8.7	8.1	7.6	7.1
Palau	69.6	71.4	70.0	77.7	83.4	87.2	89.6	91.1	30.4	28.6	30.0	22.3	16.6	12.8	10.4	8.9
American Samoa	80.9	85.3	88.8	91.3	93.0	94.1	94.8	95.3	19.1	14.7	11.2	8.7	7.0	5.9	5.2	4.7
Cook Islands	57.7	58.7	65.2	71.0	75.3	78.7	81.4	83.4	42.3	41.3	34.8	29.0	24.7	21.3	18.6	16.6
French Polynesia	55.9	55.5	52.4	51.8	51.4	51.7	52.7	54.3	44.1	46.5	47.6	48.2	48.6	48.3	47.3	45.7
Niue	30.9	31.5	33.1	35.2	37.5	40.1	43.0	46.1	69.1	68.5	66.9	64.8	62.5	59.9	57.0	53.9
Pitcairn	—	—	—	—	—	—	—	—	100.0	100.0	100.0	100.0	100.0	100.0	100.0	100.0
Samoa	21.2	21.5	22.0	21.2	20.2	20.0	20.5	21.8	78.8	78.5	78.0	78.8	79.8	80.0	79.5	78.2
Tokelau	—	—	—	—	—	—	—	—	100.0	100.0	100.0	100.0	100.0	100.0	100.0	100.0
Tonga	22.7	22.9	23.0	23.2	23.4	24.2	25.6	27.6	77.3	77.1	77.0	76.8	76.6	75.8	74.4	72.4
Tuvalu	40.7	44.0	46.0	48.1	50.4	52.9	55.6	58.5	59.3	56.0	54.0	51.9	49.6	47.1	44.4	41.5
Wallis and Futuna Islands	—	—	—	—	—	—	—	—	100.0	100.0	100.0	100.0	100.0	100.0	100.0	100.0

*Projections

Notes:
(1) For statistical purposes, the data for China do not include Hong Kong and Macao, Special Administrative Regions (SAR) of China.
(2) As of 1 July 1997, Hong Kong became a Special Administrative Region (SAR) of China.
(3) As of 20 December 1999, Macao became a Special Administrative Region (SAR) of China.
(4) Including Christmas Island, Cocos (Keeling) Islands, and Norfolk Island.

Average annual rate of change of urban and rural population in the Asia-Pacific region

Major area, region, country or area	Average Annual Rate of Change of the Urban Population (%)								Average Annual Rate of Change of the Rural Population (%)							
	1985-1990	1990-1995	1995-2000	2000-2005	2005-2010*	2010-2015*	2015-2020*	2020-2025*	1985-1990	1990-1995	1995-2000	2000-2005	2005-2010*	2010-2015*	2015-2020*	2020-2025*
World	2.63	2.38	2.22	2.20	1.92	1.85	1.76	1.65	1.12	0.89	0.65	0.41	0.45	0.32	0.12	-0.13
Asia	3.63	3.17	2.93	2.83	2.28	2.17	2.04	1.89	1.16	0.87	0.56	0.26	0.34	0.19	-0.04	-0.32
East and North-East Asia																
China (1)	4.52	4.29	3.82	4.16	2.62	2.29	1.97	1.58	0.67	-0.08	-0.55	-1.52	-0.98	-1.01	-1.16	-1.37
China, Hong Kong SAR (2)	2.26	1.81	1.41	0.64	0.54	0.91	0.80	0.68	-52.80	—	—	—	—	—	—	—
China, Macao SAR (3)	3.98	2.05	1.39	2.01	2.32	0.75	0.67	0.50	-15.42	-17.34	—	—	—	—	—	—
Dem. People's Republic of Korea	1.72	1.72	1.16	0.71	0.53	0.58	0.71	0.77	1.11	1.20	0.83	0.38	0.18	-0.04	-0.29	-0.60
Japan	1.20	0.84	0.38	0.34	0.19	0.15	0.07	0.01	-0.96	-0.49	-0.13	-0.32	-0.59	-0.90	-1.25	-1.60
Mongolia	3.69	0.40	1.04	2.20	2.00	1.90	1.75	1.55	2.08	0.58	1.00	0.05	-0.15	-0.26	-0.41	-0.62
Republic of Korea	3.78	1.92	1.13	0.91	0.78	0.61	0.42	0.26	-4.71	-2.92	-0.53	-1.28	-1.42	-1.47	-1.53	-1.58
South-East Asia																
Brunei Darussalam	3.96	3.59	3.17	2.74	2.48	2.20	1.97	1.80	0.84	1.04	0.79	0.38	0.21	0.04	-0.09	-0.16
Cambodia	3.59	5.55	5.84	3.74	3.03	3.24	3.37	3.35	3.59	2.86	1.64	1.21	1.31	1.24	1.06	0.72
Indonesia	4.95	4.54	4.72	1.81	1.74	1.72	1.71	1.75	0.52	0.05	-0.72	0.95	0.74	0.37	-0.00	-0.32
Lao People's Democratic Republic	5.04	5.04	7.03	6.09	5.65	4.92	4.27	3.61	2.43	2.21	1.19	0.25	0.14	-0.02	-0.12	-0.22
Malaysia	4.51	4.82	4.59	3.67	3.01	2.44	1.98	1.58	1.38	0.08	-0.61	-1.28	-1.33	-1.28	-1.12	-0.91
Myanmar	2.25	2.39	2.61	2.52	2.90	2.95	2.73	2.47	1.58	1.10	0.70	-0.00	-0.09	-0.06	-0.28	-0.54
Philippines	4.94	2.16	1.97	1.96	2.14	2.26	2.35	2.38	0.47	2.40	2.21	1.87	1.50	1.07	0.61	0.11
Singapore	2.15	2.86	2.88	1.20	2.51	0.90	0.63	0.54	—	—	—	—	—	—	—	—
Thailand	2.44	1.76	1.29	1.85	1.66	1.77	1.90	1.97	1.14	0.94	0.47	0.78	0.16	-0.15	-0.46	-0.79
Timor-Leste	4.65	4.29	0.68	5.36	4.84	4.98	4.83	4.69	1.76	2.30	-1.25	3.43	2.77	2.68	2.30	1.93
Viet Nam	2.75	3.77	3.46	3.53	3.26	3.03	2.84	2.63	1.88	1.43	0.91	0.56	0.29	0.06	-0.14	-0.35
South and South-West Asia																
Afghanistan	1.81	8.36	3.63	4.61	4.62	4.68	4.57	4.44	0.18	7.01	2.28	3.25	3.12	2.81	2.33	1.83
Bangladesh	4.80	3.86	3.56	3.37	3.21	3.13	3.06	2.94	1.75	1.57	1.40	1.13	0.77	0.50	0.23	-0.08
Bhutan	7.37	3.00	6.23	6.88	4.01	3.75	3.17	2.80	1.84	-2.53	0.70	1.39	0.61	0.44	-0.03	-0.31
India	3.10	2.81	2.58	2.37	2.31	2.38	2.42	2.43	1.82	1.72	1.50	1.33	1.06	0.78	0.45	0.09
Iran (Islamic Republic of)	4.24	3.18	2.73	2.15	2.10	1.90	1.70	1.33	1.87	-0.03	-0.64	-0.87	-0.87	-0.86	-0.86	-1.01
Maldives	3.48	2.64	3.43	5.38	4.87	4.24	3.60	2.93	3.11	2.85	1.31	-0.32	-0.60	-0.66	-0.73	-0.83
Nepal	6.01	6.63	6.63	5.56	4.98	4.65	4.40	4.08	2.06	2.02	1.86	1.58	1.19	0.96	0.80	0.58
Pakistan	4.09	3.19	3.35	3.05	2.97	3.10	3.06	2.99	2.92	2.01	2.16	1.85	1.73	1.57	1.20	0.80
Sri Lanka	-0.23	-0.54	-1.05	-0.64	0.30	1.06	1.74	2.40	1.72	1.41	0.90	1.06	0.98	0.67	0.29	-0.12
Turkey	4.21	2.71	2.47	2.14	1.93	1.72	1.53	1.34	-1.28	0.26	0.21	-0.13	-0.26	-0.43	-0.59	-0.74
North and Central Asia																
Armenia	1.29	-2.31	-1.36	-0.25	0.19	0.48	0.53	0.47	0.99	-1.08	-0.13	0.25	0.11	0.01	-0.34	-0.81
Azerbaijan	1.65	0.94	0.46	0.93	1.26	1.40	1.38	1.28	1.45	2.18	1.27	0.66	0.94	0.71	0.25	-0.28
Georgia	0.95	-1.93	-1.77	-1.28	-1.03	-0.39	-0.05	0.15	0.27	-0.96	-0.81	-1.15	-1.25	-0.95	-1.04	-1.27
Kazakhstan	1.02	-0.87	-1.13	0.60	1.21	1.27	1.18	1.05	0.81	-0.59	-1.42	-0.07	0.06	-0.21	-0.50	-0.84
Kyrgyzstan	1.50	0.11	0.87	0.99	0.91	1.27	1.49	1.67	2.01	1.33	1.88	1.08	1.39	1.08	0.63	0.14
Russian Federation	1.03	0.05	-0.25	-0.60	-0.33	-0.20	-0.16	-0.17	-0.46	0.07	-0.23	-0.17	-0.57	-0.74	-1.01	-1.33
Tajikistan	2.02	-0.13	-0.40	1.04	1.56	2.24	2.54	2.72	3.46	2.50	1.99	1.18	1.60	1.71	1.37	0.91
Turkmenistan	2.15	2.52	1.90	2.11	2.24	2.20	2.08	1.88	2.88	2.75	1.08	0.90	0.48	0.26	-0.05	-0.44
Uzbekistan	2.15	1.33	1.02	0.80	0.86	1.37	1.78	2.00	2.61	2.79	1.88	1.45	1.23	1.04	0.76	0.30
Pacific																
Australia (4)	1.56	1.33	1.37	1.47	1.27	1.17	1.08	0.99	1.65	0.18	-0.46	-0.43	-0.55	-0.56	-0.56	-0.56
New Zealand	0.92	1.84	1.05	1.30	0.95	0.92	0.87	0.81	-0.68	0.91	0.49	0.68	0.70	0.44	0.13	-0.19
Fiji	1.96	2.98	1.89	1.45	1.40	1.28	1.17	1.28	-0.62	-0.19	-0.05	-0.12	-0.19	-0.46	-0.75	-0.81
New Caledonia	2.17	2.61	1.87	1.33	1.33	1.41	1.55	1.65	1.58	2.15	2.61	2.34	1.84	1.26	0.74	0.20
Papua New Guinea	3.92	1.36	1.41	1.59	2.27	2.93	3.56	4.21	2.32	2.83	2.89	2.68	2.39	2.06	1.71	1.37
Solomon Islands	4.77	4.25	4.15	4.15	4.25	4.25	4.25	4.25	2.58	2.63	2.52	2.32	2.07	1.73	1.38	1.05
Vanuatu	4.73	4.33	3.40	4.19	4.27	4.22	4.12	3.99	1.99	2.48	1.55	2.18	1.98	1.67	1.29	0.92
Guam	1.95	1.94	1.50	1.66	1.31	1.21	1.13	1.03	5.95	-1.27	-1.55	1.66	1.11	0.74	0.39	0.02
Kiribati	3.59	2.25	4.99	2.09	1.74	1.93	2.14	2.28	2.31	1.01	0.60	1.61	1.45	1.14	0.83	0.46
Marshall Islands	5.18	2.02	0.92	2.17	2.71	2.35	1.94	1.55	2.50	0.53	-0.57	0.60	1.04	0.58	0.07	-0.41
Micronesia (Fed. States of)	2.08	1.56	-2.34	0.43	0.60	1.26	1.90	2.41	2.43	2.35	0.69	0.43	0.22	0.25	0.24	0.12
Nauru	2.27	1.71	0.15	0.14	0.28	0.61	0.45	0.31	—	—	—	—	—	—	—	—
Northern Mariana Islands	7.85	5.48	3.71	3.14	2.07	1.75	1.64	1.54	5.07	5.86	2.38	1.74	0.67	0.34	0.23	0.12
Palau	2.47	3.18	2.03	2.96	1.81	1.38	1.62	1.41	0.41	1.42	3.45	-5.09	-5.49	-4.65	-3.16	-2.10
American Samoa	4.35	3.27	2.63	2.24	2.11	1.81	1.63	1.56	0.45	-2.94	-3.57	-3.39	-2.57	-1.92	-1.14	-0.31
Cook Islands	0.76	1.14	1.06	3.37	2.04	1.42	1.18	0.91	-1.28	0.35	-4.48	-2.01	-2.33	-2.44	-2.16	-1.90
French Polynesia	1.81	1.14	1.35	1.35	1.17	1.30	1.40	1.46	2.97	3.01	2.28	1.83	1.43	1.08	0.63	0.14
Niue	-3.45	-1.31	-1.30	-1.50	-1.39	-1.26	-0.16	-0.28	-3.32	-1.80	-2.80	-3.39	-3.41	-3.44	-2.48	-2.83
Pitcairn	—	—	—	—	—	—	—	—	0.95	-1.27	-1.01	-2.97	0.00	0.40	1.51	-0.37
Samoa	0.55	1.15	1.37	-0.43	-0.96	-0.00	0.80	1.63	0.55	0.76	0.84	0.46	0.25	0.31	0.18	0.08
Tokelau	—	—	—	—	—	—	—	—	0.19	-1.40	0.45	-4.68	-0.12	-0.23	0.17	0.15
Tonga	0.80	0.73	0.38	0.78	0.70	0.79	1.76	2.15	0.30	0.54	0.21	0.62	0.39	-0.09	0.28	0.07
Tuvalu	3.99	2.28	1.59	1.35	1.35	1.39	1.49	1.49	-1.49	-0.44	-0.06	-0.33	-0.48	-0.62	-0.70	-0.86
Wallis and Futuna Islands	—	—	—	—	—	—	—	—	0.04	0.67	0.49	0.32	0.70	0.71	0.63	0.43

Notes:
0 and/or 0.0 indicates that the magnitude is zero or less than half of the unit employed.
A minus sign (-) before a figure indicates a decrease.
Years given refer to 1 July.
Use of hyphen (-) between years, for example, 1995-2000, signifies the full period involved, from 1 July of the beginning year to 1 July of the end year

Source: United Nations, Department of Economic and Social Affairs, Population Division (2010). World Urbanization Prospects : The 2009 Revision.
CD-ROM Edition - Data in digital form (POP/ DB/WUP/Rev.2009)..

100 largest cities in the Asia-Pacific region

Population of Urban Agglomeration, 1990-2025* (1,000s)

	Urban Agglomeration	Country	1990	1995	2000	2005	2010*	2015*	2020*	2025*
1	Tokyo	Japan	32,530	33,587	34,450	35,622	36,669	37,049	37,088	37,088
2	Delhi	India	9,726	12,407	15,730	19,493	22,157	24,160	26,272	28,568
3	Mumbai (Bombay)	India	12,308	14,111	16,086	18,205	20,041	21,797	23,719	25,810
4	Shanghai	China	7,823	10,171	13,224	15,184	16,575	17,840	19,094	20,017
5	Kolkata (Calcutta)	India	10,890	11,924	13,058	14,284	15,552	16,924	18,449	20,112
6	Dhaka	Bangladesh	6,621	8,332	10,285	12,555	14,648	16,623	18,721	20,936
7	Karachi	Pakistan	7,147	8,467	10,021	11,618	13,125	14,818	16,693	18,725
8	Beijing	China	6,788	8,138	9,757	11,455	12,385	13,335	14,296	15,018
9	Manila	Philippines	7,973	9,401	9,958	10,761	11,628	12,587	13,687	14,916
10	Osaka-Kobe	Japan	11,035	11,052	11,165	11,258	11,337	11,365	11,368	11,368
11	Moskva (Moscow)	Russian Federation	8,987	9,201	10,005	10,418	10,550	10,641	10,662	10,663
12	Istanbul	Turkey	6,552	7,665	8,744	9,710	10,525	11,164	11,689	12,108
13	Seoul	Republic of Korea	10,544	10,256	9,917	9,825	9,773	9,767	9,767	9,767
14	Chongqing	China	3,123	4,342	6,039	7,266	9,401	9,850	10,514	11,065
15	Jakarta	Indonesia	8,175	8,322	8,390	8,795	9,210	9,709	10,256	10,850
16	Shenzhen	China	875	2,304	6,069	7,931	9,005	9,827	10,585	11,146
17	Guangzhou, Guangdong	China	3,072	4,745	7,330	8,165	8,884	9,669	10,409	10,961
18	Tianjin	China	4,558	5,513	6,670	7,278	7,884	8,559	9,216	9,713
19	Wuhan	China	3,417	4,763	6,638	7,204	7,681	8,253	8,868	9,347
20	Chennai (Madras)	India	5,338	5,836	6,353	6,919	7,547	8,253	9,043	9,909
21	Tehran	Iran (Islamic Republic of)	6,365	6,687	6,880	7,044	7,241	7,614	8,059	8,387
22	Bangalore	India	4,036	4,744	5,567	6,465	7,218	7,913	8,674	9,507
23	Lahore	Pakistan	3,970	4,653	5,449	6,294	7,132	8,087	9,150	10,308
24	Hong Kong	China, Hong Kong SAR	5,677	6,214	6,667	6,883	7,069	7,398	7,701	7,969
25	Krung Thep (Bangkok)	Thailand	5,888	6,106	6,332	6,614	6,976	7,399	7,902	8,470
26	Hyderabad	India	4,193	4,825	5,445	6,117	6,751	7,396	8,110	8,894
27	Thành Pho Ho Chí Minh (Ho Chi Minh City)	Viet Nam	3,411	3,802	4,336	5,264	6,167	7,140	8,067	8,957
28	Ahmadabad	India	3,255	3,790	4,427	5,122	5,717	6,277	6,892	7,567
29	Dongguan, Guangdong	China	553	1,416	3,631	4,692	5,347	5,971	6,483	6,852
30	Shenyang	China	3,651	4,081	4,562	4,788	5,166	5,650	6,108	6,457
31	Pune (Poona)	India	2,430	2,978	3,655	4,412	5,002	5,505	6,050	6,649
32	Foshan	China	429	569	754	4,033	4,969	5,455	5,903	6,242
33	Chittagong	Bangladesh	2,023	2,578	3,308	4,180	4,962	5,680	6,447	7,265
34	Chengdu	China	2,955	3,403	3,919	4,467	4,961	5,441	5,886	6,224
35	Singapore	Singapore	3,016	3,480	4,018	4,267	4,837	5,059	5,219	5,362
36	Xi'an, Shaanxi	China	2,157	2,821	3,690	4,382	4,747	5,038	5,414	5,726
37	Sankt Peterburg (Saint Petersburg)	Russian Federation	4,989	4,836	4,719	4,598	4,575	4,561	4,557	4,557
38	Nanjing, Jiangsu	China	2,497	2,944	3,472	3,966	4,519	5,076	5,524	5,845
39	Sydney	Australia	3,632	3,839	4,078	4,260	4,429	4,592	4,733	4,852
40	Yangon	Myanmar	2,907	3,213	3,553	3,928	4,350	4,873	5,456	6,022
41	Haerbin	China	2,392	2,860	3,419	3,789	4,251	4,473	4,800	5,080
42	Surat	India	1,468	1,984	2,699	3,558	4,168	4,607	5,071	5,579
43	Ankara	Turkey	2,561	2,842	3,179	3,572	3,906	4,174	4,401	4,591
44	Hangzhou	China	1,476	1,887	2,411	3,516	3,860	4,145	4,470	4,735
45	Melbourne	Australia	3,117	3,257	3,433	3,641	3,853	4,022	4,152	4,261
46	Kabul	Afghanistan	1,282	1,616	1,963	2,994	3,731	4,616	5,665	6,888
47	Shantou	China	724	950	1,247	3,375	3,502	3,704	3,983	4,222
48	Kanpur	India	2,001	2,294	2,641	3,020	3,364	3,706	4,084	4,501
49	Busan	Republic of Korea	3,778	3,813	3,673	3,533	3,425	3,407	3,409	3,409
50	Qingdao	China	1,332	1,882	2,659	3,029	3,323	3,622	3,923	4,159

Population of Urban Agglomeration, 1990-2025* (1,000s)

	Urban Agglomeration	Country	1990	1995	2000	2005	2010*	2015*	2020*	2025*
51	Dalian	China	1,884	2,311	2,833	3,060	3,306	3,599	3,896	4,132
52	Nagoya	Japan	2,947	3,055	3,122	3,199	3,267	3,292	3,295	3,295
53	Jinan, Shandong	China	1,923	2,134	2,592	2,951	3,237	3,522	3,813	4,044
54	Taiyuan, Shanxi	China	1,637	2,024	2,503	2,819	3,154	3,504	3,812	4,043
55	Jaipur	India	1,478	1,826	2,259	2,748	3,131	3,458	3,813	4,205
56	Kunming	China	1,100	1,679	2,561	2,857	3,116	3,405	3,691	3,915
57	Zhengzhou	China	1,134	1,663	2,438	2,715	2,966	3,245	3,519	3,734
58	Lucknow	India	1,614	1,906	2,221	2,567	2,873	3,169	3,497	3,858
57	Faisalabad	Pakistan	1,520	1,804	2,140	2,496	2,849	3,252	3,704	4,200
60	P'yongyang	Dem. People's Republic of Korea	2,526	2,749	2,777	2,805	2,833	2,859	2,894	2,941
61	Fukuoka-Kitakyushu	Japan	2,487	2,619	2,716	2,771	2,816	2,833	2,834	2,834
62	Hà Noi	Viet Nam	1,136	1,344	1,631	2,144	2,814	3,516	4,056	4,530
63	Fuzhou, Fujian	China	875	1,316	1,978	2,368	2,787	3,201	3,509	3,727
64	Izmir	Turkey	1,741	1,966	2,216	2,487	2,723	2,917	3,083	3,224
65	Nanchang	China	912	1,226	1,648	2,380	2,701	2,978	3,236	3,436
66	Sapporo	Japan	2,319	2,476	2,508	2,601	2,687	2,718	2,721	2,721
67	Wuxi, Jiangsu	China	992	1,182	1,409	2,435	2,682	2,951	3,206	3,405
68	Wenzhou	China	1,111	1,318	1,565	2,187	2,659	3,119	3,436	3,650
69	Mashhad	Iran (Islamic Republic of)	1,680	1,854	2,073	2,348	2,652	2,919	3,128	3,277
70	Taipei	China	2,737	2,698	2,630	2,627	2,633	2,725	2,921	3,102
71	Nagpur	India	1,637	1,849	2,089	2,351	2,607	2,875	3,175	3,505
72	Incheon	Republic of Korea	1,785	2,271	2,464	2,527	2,583	2,621	2,630	2,631
73	Surabaya	Indonesia	2,467	2,544	2,611	2,623	2,509	2,576	2,738	2,923
74	Shijiazhuang	China	1,372	1,621	1,914	2,192	2,487	2,789	3,044	3,235
75	Daegu	Republic of Korea	2,215	2,434	2,478	2,466	2,458	2,474	2,481	2,481
76	Zibo	China	777	1,207	1,874	2,168	2,456	2,752	3,004	3,192
77	Changsha, Hunan	China	1,089	1,504	2,077	2,197	2,415	2,655	2,885	3,066
78	Bandung	Indonesia	2,035	2,097	2,138	2,280	2,412	2,568	2,739	2,925
79	Hefei	China	1,100	1,298	1,532	2,065	2,404	2,626	2,850	3,029
80	Ürümqi (Wulumqi)	China	1,149	1,399	1,705	2,025	2,398	2,767	3,040	3,231
81	Suzhou, Jiangsu	China	689	952	1,316	1,992	2,398	2,619	2,842	3,021
82	Sendai	Japan	2,021	2,135	2,184	2,284	2,376	2,410	2,413	2,413
83	Patna	India	1,087	1,331	1,658	2,030	2,321	2,569	2,839	3,137
84	Lanzhou	China	1,290	1,561	1,890	2,085	2,285	2,507	2,724	2,896
85	Ningbo	China	634	909	1,303	1,897	2,217	2,536	2,782	2,959
86	Zhongshan	China	393	736	1,376	1,768	2,211	2,643	2,927	3,114
87	Tashkent	Uzbekistan	2,100	2,116	2,135	2,169	2,210	2,279	2,420	2,616
88	Xiamen	China	639	952	1,416	1,765	2,207	2,641	2,926	3,112
89	Indore	India	1,088	1,314	1,597	1,914	2,173	2,405	2,659	2,939
90	Guiyang	China	1,080	1,417	1,860	2,015	2,154	2,325	2,519	2,679
91	Xuzhou	China	781	1,033	1,367	1,715	2,142	2,559	2,833	3,015
92	Medan	Indonesia	1,718	1,816	1,912	2,023	2,131	2,266	2,419	2,586
93	Nanning	China	759	1,118	1,445	1,826	2,096	2,306	2,508	2,669
94	Hiroshima	Japan	1,986	2,040	2,044	2,063	2,081	2,088	2,088	2,088
95	Changzhou, Jiangsu	China	730	883	1,068	1,876	2,062	2,267	2,466	2,624
96	Rawalpindi	Pakistan	1,007	1,206	1,520	1,772	2,026	2,318	2,646	3,008
97	Baku	Azerbaijan	1,733	1,766	1,806	1,867	1,972	2,082	2,190	2,291
98	Hai Phòng	Viet Nam	1,474	1,585	1,704	1,831	1,970	2,164	2,432	2,722
99	Brisbane	Australia	1,329	1,471	1,603	1,780	1,970	2,096	2,178	2,245
100	Baotou	China	1,044	1,212	1,406	1,826	1,932	2,072	2,243	2,388

*Projections
Note: Cities are ranked based on the estimated population for the year 2010.
Source: United Nations, Department of Economic and Social Affairs, Population Division (2010). World
Urbanization Prospects : The 2009 Revision. CD-ROM Edition - Data in digital form (POP/ DB/WUP/Rev.2009).

Urban population, proportion of urban population living in slum area and urban slum population

Country	Urban Population at Mid-Year by Country (1,000s)[a]					Proportion of Urban Population Living in Slum Area[b]					Urban Slum Population at Mid-Year by Country (1,000s)				
	1990	1995	2000	2005	2007	1990	1995	2000	2005	2007	1990	1995	2000	2005	2007
China	314,845	380,553	454,362	530,659	561,251	43.6	40.5	37.3	32.9	31.0	137,272	153,985	169,600	174,587	173,988
Mongolia	1,264	1,357	1,397	1,464	1,497	68.5	66.7	64.9	57.9	57.9	865.8	905.3	906.8	847.5	866.7
Bangladesh	22,396	27,398	32,893	39,351	42,191	87.3	84.7	77.8	70.8	70.8	19,552	23,206	25,574	27,860	29,871
India	219,758	253,774	289,438	325,563	341,247	54.9	48.2	41.5	34.8	32.1	120,746	122,376	120,117	113,223	109,501
Nepal	1,692	2,361	3,280	4,269	4,712	70.6	67.3	64.0	60.7	59.4	1,194	1,589	2,099	2,591	2,798
Pakistan	34,548	40,676	47,884	55,135	58,487	51.0	49.8	48.7	47.5	47.0	17,620	20,271	23,304	26,189	27,508
Cambodia	1,222	1,613	2,161	2,753	3,022				78.9		964	1,273	1,705	2,172	2,385
Indonesia	55,922	70,188	88,918	108,828	116,832	50.8	42.6	34.4	26.3	23.0	28,407	29,912	30,620	28,574	26,852
Lao People's Democratic Republic	629	815	1,148	1,551	1,740				79.3					1230	
Myanmar	9,986	11,270	12,860	14,700	15,575				45.6					6703	
Philippines	29,863	37,053	44,621	53,032	56,503	54.3	50.8	47.2	43.7	42.3	16,224	18,817	21,080	23,175	23,891
Thailand	15,974	17,416	18,893	20,352	21,021				26.0					5,291	
Viet Nam	13,403	16,284	19,204	22,454	23,888	60.5	54.6	48.8	41.3	38.3	8,109	8,897	9,366	9,274	9,137
Turkey	33,949	38,974	44,126	49,097	51,101	23.4	20.7	17.9	15.5	14.1	7,947	8,055	7,911	7,610	7,202

Source:
a. World Urbanization Prospects: The 2007 Revision
b. Computed from country household data using the four components of slum (improved water, improved sanitation, durable housing and sufficient living area

Proportion of urban population living in slums 1990-2010

Major region or area	Urban Population at Mid-Year by Region (1,000s)[a]						Urban Slum Population at Mid-Year by Region (1,000s)[b]					
	1990	1995	2000	2005	2007	2010	1990	1995	2000	2005	2007	2010
Developing Regions	1,424,631	1,676,635	1,949,244	2,231,883	2,350,358	2,534,978	656,739	718,114	766,762	795,739	806,910	827,690
Northern Africa	57,402	65,141	72,397.5	80,145.8	83,435	88,666	19,731	18,417	14,729	10,708	11,142	11,836
Sub-Saharan Africa	146,564	182,383	222,733	269,246	289,938	323,525	102,588	123,210	144,683	169,515	181,030	199,540
Latin America and the Caribbean	313,852	353,457	394,099	432,554	448,006	471,177	105,740	111,246	115,192	110,105	110,554	110,763
Eastern Asia	365,574	436,582	513,919	592,873	624,430	671,795	159,754	177,063	192,265	195,463	194,020	189,621
Southern	315,726	368,423	423,518.3	479,718.3	504,697	545,766	180,449	190,276	194,009	192,041	191,735	190,748
South-eastern Asia	139,355	169,980	206,682.6	245,895.5	262,101	286,579	69,029	76,079	81,942	84,013	83,726	88,912
Western Asia	84,584	98,922	113,979.9	129,355.1	135,576	145,164	19,068	21,402	23,481	33,388	34,179	35,713
Oceania	1,572	1,748	1,914.8	2,095.6	2,176	2,306	379	421	462	505	524	556

Major region or area	Proportion of Urban Population						Proportion of Urban Population Living in Slum Areas					
	1990	1995	2000	2005	2007	2010	1990	1995	2000	2005	2007	2010
Developing Regions	34.9	37.5	40.1	42.7	43.7	45.3	46.1	42.8	39.3	35.7	34.3	32.7
Northern Africa	48.6	50.1	51.3	52.5	53.0	53.7	34.4	28.3	20.3	13.4	13.4	13.3
Sub-Saharan Africa	28.2	30.6	32.8	35.0	35.9	37.3	70.0	67.6	65.0	63.0	62.4	61.7
Latin America and the Caribbean	70.6	73.0	75.3	77.5	78.3	79.4	33.7	31.5	29.2	25.5	24.7	23.5
Eastern Asia	30.0	33.9	38.1	42.5	44.3	46.8	43.7	40.6	37.4	33.0	31.1	28.2
Southern	26.5	27.7	29.0	30.2	30.8	31.8	57.2	51.6	45.8	40.0	38.0	35.0
South-eastern Asia	31.6	35.3	39.7	44.1	45.8	48.2	49.5	44.8	39.6	34.2	31.9	31.0
Western Asia	61.5	63.1	64.6	65.9	66.4	67.1	22.5	21.6	20.6	25.8	25.2	24.6
Oceania[c]	24.4	24.1	23.6	23.3	23.3	23.4	24.1	24.1	24.1	24.1	24.1	24.1

a. United Nations Population Division, World Urbanization Prospects: The 2007 Revision
b. Population living in household that lack either improved water, improved sanitation, sufficient living area (more than three persons per room), or durable housing
c. Trends data are not available for Oceania. A constant figure does not mean there is no change

Distribution of households by shelter deprivation, country 2005

Country	All Types of Slums	One Shelter Deprivation	Two Shelter Deprivations	Three Shelter Deprivations	Four Shelter Deprivations
Bangladesh	70.8	27.5	29.7	13.4	0.2
Cambodia	78.9				
China	32.9				
India	34.8	27.8	6.9	0.0	N/A
Indonesia	26.3	22.4	3.1	0.8	N/A
Iran (Islamic Republic of)	30.3				
Lao People's Democratic Republic	79.3	30.9	35.2	13.2	N/A
Mongolia	57.9	36.1	18.8	2.9	0.0
Myanmar	45.6	36.6	7.9	1.0	0.0
Nepal	60.7	34.4	12.3	14.0	0.0
Pakistan	47.5				
Philippines	43.7	30.1	10.4	3.3	0.0
Thailand	26.0				
Turkey	15.5	13.5	2.0	0.0	0.0
Viet Nam	40.5	28.0	9.8	2.6	0.9

Distribution of households by type of residence, country 2000-2005

Country	Type of Household	Distribution of Urban Households by Type of Residence			
		Area with 25% or Less Slum Households	Area with 26-50% Slum Households	Area with 51-75% Slum Households	Area with 75+% of Slum Households
Bangladesh	Non-slum household	31.5	23.8	28.2	16.4
Bangladesh	Slum household	0.7	2.8	7.3	89.2
India	Non-slum household	14.9	54.4	28.1	2.6
India	Slum household	3.3	36.8	43.3	16.5
Indonesia	Non-slum household	38.6	36.0	19.7	5.6
Indonesia	Slum household	6.3	19.7	33.1	40.8
Nepal	Non-slum household	62.0	14.6	14.2	9.2
Nepal	Slum household	7.0	8.9	17.5	66.7
Pakistan	Non-slum household	15.3	19.5	46.7	18.5
Pakistan	Slum household	5.1	5.8	36.7	52.4
Philippines	Non-slum household	63.1	30.5	5.6	0.7
Philippines	Slum household	24.9	40.7	22.0	12.4
Viet Nam	Non-slum household	52.2	35.5	9.3	3.0
Viet Nam	Slum household	17.0	23.9	18.9	40.1
Armenia	Non-slum household	73.5	11.7	9.1	5.7
Armenia	Slum household	9.8	11.4	25.6	53.3
Turkey	Non-slum household	49.1	34.1	14.8	2.0
Turkey	Slum household	11.9	31.2	36.8	20.1
Kazakhstan	Non-slum household	43.9	30.3	18.4	7.4
Kazakhstan	Slum household	5.0	14.5	24.4	56.1
Kyrgyzstan	Non-slum household	68.9	14.0	10.5	6.7
Kyrgyzstan	Slum household	4.6	2.9	7.4	85.1
Uzbekistan	Non-slum household	42.8	23.7	19.8	13.8
Uzbekistan	Slum household	1.5	2.8	6.2	89.5

Type of fuel for cooking type of household

Country	Year	Type of Cooking Oil	Urban	Non Slum Household	Slum Household	One Shelter Deprivation	Two Shelter Deprivations
Bangladesh	2006	Electricity	0.5	1.0	0.1	0.3	0.1
Bangladesh	2006	Liquid propane gas (LPG)	3.8	7.2	0.2	0.7	0.0
Bangladesh	2006	Natural gas	15.5	37.6	4.2	10.3	2.1
Bangladesh	2006	Biogas	0.1	0.3			
Bangladesh	2006	Kerosene	0.6	1.0	0.1	0.3	0.1
Bangladesh	2006	Wood	55.0	42.9	49.3	56.2	46.9
Bangladesh	2006	Straw/shrubs/grass	2.4	1.9	1.5	1.8	1.4
Bangladesh	2006	Animal dung	6.0	2.4	9.2	7.0	10.0
Bangladesh	2006	Agricultural crop residue	14.6	4.8	33.4	21.8	37.3
Bangladesh	2006	Other	1.6	0.8	1.9	1.6	2.0
Bangladesh	2006	Missing	0.0	0.1			
Bangladesh	2006	**Solid fuel**	**77.9**	**52.0**	**93.4**	**86.8**	**95.7**
India	2006	Electricity	0.9	1.0	0.9	1.0	0.6
India	2006	LPG/Natural gas	58.7	78.0	43.7	56.7	23.2
India	2006	Biogas	0.5	0.6	0.4	0.5	0.2
India	2006	Kerosene	8.2	6.3	9.7	11.2	7.4
India	2006	Coal, lignite	4.3	3.0	5.3	4.8	6.1
India	2006	Charcoal	0.5	0.4	0.6	0.6	0.6
India	2006	Wood	22.0	8.1	32.8	21.1	51.4
India	2006	Straw/shrubs/grass	0.5	0.1	0.9	0.3	1.8
India	2006	Agricultural crop	0.8	0.6	0.9	0.7	1.3
India	2006	Animal dung	2.8	0.8	4.3	2.5	7.1
India	2006	Other	0.8	1.1	0.5	0.6	0.3
India	2006	**Solid fuel**	**30.9**	**13.0**	**44.8**	**30.0**	**68.3**
Indonesia	2002	Electricity	0.7	0.8	0.6	0.8	0.1
Indonesia	2002	LPG, natural gas	18.6	25.6	7.6	9.5	1.9
Indonesia	2002	Kerosene	63.9	65.3	61.6	65.8	49.1
Indonesia	2002	Coal, lignite	0.1	0.1			
Indonesia	2002	Charcoal	0.1	0.1	0.1	0.1	0.1
Indonesia	2002	Firewood, straw	15.9	7.1	29.8	23.5	48.6
Indonesia	2002	Other	0.8	1.0	0.3	0.4	0.2
Indonesia	2002	**Solid fuel**	**16.0**	**7.2**	**29.9**	**23.6**	**48.7**
Kazakhstan	2006	Electricity	20.5	21.1	9.7	10.5	4.5
Kazakhstan	2006	Liquid propane gas (LPG)	36.5	31.2	45.8	45.8	45.9
Kazakhstan	2006	Natural gas	36.1	41.4	17.8	18.5	13.9
Kazakhstan	2006	Kerosene			0.1	0.1	0.0
Kazakhstan	2006	Coal/lignite	6.2	5.6	20.0	19.4	23.9
Kazakhstan	2006	Charcoal	0.1	0.0	0.3	0.3	0.7
Kazakhstan	2006	Wood	0.6	0.4	4.3	4.0	6.5
Kazakhstan	2006	Animal dung	0.0	0.2	1.9	1.5	4.6
Kazakhstan	2006	Other					0.1
Kazakhstan	2006	**Solid fuel**	**6.8**	**6.3**	**26.6**	**25.2**	**35.6**
Kyrgyzstan	2006	Electricity	28.7	29.5	32.1	33.3	27.4
Kyrgyzstan	2006	Liquid Propane Gas (LPG)	9.3	12.1	4.2	4.6	2.8
Kyrgyzstan	2006	Natural gas	49.2	28.4	14.4	17.6	2.1
Kyrgyzstan	2006	Coal/Lignite	6.2	12.7	16.3	17.1	12.8
Kyrgyzstan	2006	Charcoal	2.4	3.2	4.9	3.0	12.2
Kyrgyzstan	2006	Wood	2.7	10.7	17.9	16.3	24.3
Kyrgyzstan	2006	Straw/shrubs/grass			0.1	0.1	
Kyrgyzstan	2006	Animal dung/pressed dung	0.4	2.4	6.7	6.2	8.8
Kyrgyzstan	2006	Agricultural crop residue	0.6	0.6	3.1	1.7	8.6
Kyrgyzstan	2006	Other (specify)	0.2	0.1	0.3	0.1	1.0
Kyrgyzstan	2006	Missing	0.3	0.2	0.1	0.1	0.0
Kyrgyzstan	2006	**Solid fuel**	**6.2**	**16.9**	**32.6**	**27.2**	**53.9**

Country	Year	Type of Cooking Oil	Urban	Non Slum Household	Slum Household	One Shelter Deprivation	Two Shelter Deprivations
Mongolia	2006	Electricity	38.5	80.0	18.3	28.2	11.5
Mongolia	2006	Liquid propane gas (LPG)	0.6	0.9	0.3	0.4	0.2
Mongolia	2006	Coal/lignite	31.0	5.3	20.5	27.8	15.5
Mongolia	2006	Briquette	0.2		0.2	0.1	0.3
Mongolia	2006	Wood	24.8	8.4	34.0	27.0	38.7
Mongolia	2006	Straw/shrubs/grass	0.2	0.2	1.1	0.5	1.5
Mongolia	2006	Animal dung	3.9	5.0	24.8	15.0	31.4
Mongolia	2006	Agricultural crop residue		0.2			
Mongolia	2006	Sawdust	0.7		0.5	0.8	0.3
Mongolia	2006	Other	0.1		0.3	0.1	0.4
Mongolia	2006	**Solid fuel**	**60.9**	**19.1**	**81.1**	**71.3**	**87.9**
Nepal	2006	Electricity	0.4	0.8			
Nepal	2006	LPG	40.2	59.9	20.9	35.2	6.2
Nepal	2006	Natural gas	0.2		0.3	0.6	
Nepal	2006	Biogas	3.3	3.2	3.4	4.6	2.1
Nepal	2006	Kerosene	15.8	16.0	15.6	20.2	10.7
Nepal	2006	Charcoal	0.1	0.2	0.1	0.2	
Nepal	2006	Wood	35.6	18.2	52.4	35.5	69.9
Nepal	2006	Straw/shrubs/grass	0.6		1.2	0.2	2.2
Nepal	2006	Agricultural crop	0.2		0.4	0.8	
Nepal	2006	Animal dung	2.5	0.3	4.7	1.4	8.1
Nepal	2006	No food cooked in HH	0.5	1.0	0.1		0.1
Nepal	2006	Other	0.6	0.3	0.9	1.3	0.5
Nepal	2006	**Solid fuel**	**39.1**	**18.7**	**58.9**	**38.1**	**80.3**
Tajikistan	2006	Electricity	52.0	47.8	46.4	46.1	46.7
Tajikistan	2006	Liquid propane gas (LPG)	10.5	13.4	3.6	5.0	2.3
Tajikistan	2006	Natural gas	29.8	34.2	11.5	15.7	7.7
Tajikistan	2006	Kerosene	0.0			0.1	
Tajikistan	2006	Coal/lignite	0.4	0.5	0.8	0.6	1.0
Tajikistan	2006	Wood	6.5	2.6	29.1	28.4	29.8
Tajikistan	2006	Straw/shrubs/grass	0.1	0.2	2.3	0.8	3.8
Tajikistan	2006	Animal dung	0.5	0.8	3.4	2.2	4.5
Tajikistan	2006	Agricultural crop residue		0.2	2.8	1.2	4.3
Tajikistan	2006	Other	0.1	0.3			
Tajikistan	2006	**Solid fuel**	**7.5**	**4.3**	**38.4**	**33.1**	**43.2**
Thailand	2006	Electricity	6.0	3.8	2.3	2.4	2.0
Thailand	2006	Liquid propane gas (LPG)	69.3	62.5	45.9	46.8	42.0
Thailand	2006	Biogas	0.2	0.3	0.3	0.3	0.3
Thailand	2006	Kerosene					0.1
Thailand	2006	Coal/lignite		0.1			
Thailand	2006	Charcoal	5.3	12.2	24.5	24.0	26.7
Thailand	2006	Wood	4.3	11.4	23.8	22.9	27.8
Thailand	2006	Straw/shrubs/grass					
Thailand	2006	Animal dung					
Thailand	2006	Agricultural crop residue			0.2	0.2	0.1
Thailand	2006	Other					
Thailand	2006	No Cooking	14.8	9.7	3.0	3.5	1.1
Thailand	2006	**Solid fuel**	**9.6**	**23.6**	**48.5**	**47.0**	**54.6**
Uzbekistan	2006	Electricity	2.0	1.2	1.1	1.0	1.4
Uzbekistan	2006	Liquid propane gas (LPG)	3.0	2.5	2.8	2.6	3.8
Uzbekistan	2006	Natural gas	94.4	81.7	79.8	82.5	67.5
Uzbekistan	2006	Kerosene					0.1
Uzbekistan	2006	Coal/lignite					0.1
Uzbekistan	2006	Charcoal		0.1	0.1	0.1	0.2
Uzbekistan	2006	Wood	0.6	14.4	15.1	13.2	23.9
Uzbekistan	2006	Agricultural crop residue			0.9	0.5	2.9
Uzbekistan	2006	Other			0.1		0.2
Uzbekistan	2006	**Solid fuel**	**0.7**	**14.5**	**16.1**	**13.8**	**27.0**

Progress on sanitation and drinking-water: Country estimates for 1990, 2000 and 2008

| Subregion / Country | Year | Use of Sanitation Facilities (Percentage of Population) | | | | Use of Drinking-Water Sources (Percentage of Population) | | | |
| | | Improved | Unimproved | | | Improved | | | Unimproved |
			Shared	Unimproved Facilities	Open Defecation	Total Improved	Piped on Premises	Other Improved	
East and North-East Asia									
China	1990	48	25	24	3	97	86	11	3
	2000	55	28	12	5	98	92	6	2
	2008	58	30	6	6	98	96	2	2
Democratic People's Republic of Korea	1990	--	--	--	--	100	--	--	0
	2000	58	--	42	--	100	81	19	0
	2008	--	--	--	--	100	--	--	0
Japan	1990	100	--	0	0	100	97	3	0
	2000	100	--	0	0	100	98	2	0
	2008	100	--	0	0	100	99	1	0
Mongolia	1990	--	--	--	--	81	52	29	19
	2000	66	32	2	0	88	42	46	12
	2008	64	31	2	3	97	32	65	3
Republic of Korea	1990	100	--	0	0	97	96	1	3
	2000	100	--	0	0	98	97	1	2
	2008	100	--	0	0	100	99	1	0
South-East Asia									
Brunei Darussalam	1990	--	--	--	--	--	--	--	--
	2000	--	--	--	--	--	--	--	--
	2008	--	--	--	--	--	--	--	--
Cambodia	1990	38	5	9	48	52	17	35	48
	2000	50	7	6	37	64	33	31	36
	2008	67	9	2	22	81	55	26	19
Indonesia	1990	58	8	16	18	92	24	68	8
	2000	63	8	12	17	90	31	59	10
	2008	67	9	8	16	89	27	52	11
Lao PDR	1990	--	--	--	--	--	--	--	--
	2000	62	4	8	26	77	35	42	23
	2008	86	5	3	6	72	55	17	28
Malaysia	1990	88	4	7	1	94	86	8	6
	2000	94	4	1	1	99	95	4	1
	2008	96	4	0	0	100	99	1	0
Myanmar	1990	--	--	--	--	87	19	68	13
	2000	81	10	8	1	80	17	63	20
	2008	86	10	4	0	75	15	60	25
Philippines	1990	70	14	8	8	93	40	53	7
	2000	76	15	3	6	93	51	42	7
	2008	80	16	0	4	93	60	33	7
Singapore	1990	99	--	1	--	100	100	0	0
	2000	100	--	0	0	100	100	0	0
	2008	100	--	0	0	100	100	0	0
Thailand	1990	93	5	0	2	97	78	19	3
	2000	94	5	0	1	98	82	16	2
	2008	95	5	0	0	99	85	14	1
Timor-Leste	1990	--	--	--	--	--	--	--	--
	2000	55	4	20	21	69	28	41	31
	2008	76	5	0	19	86	28	58	14
Viet Nam	1990	61	3	10	26	88	45	43	12
	2000	79	4	7	10	94	51	43	6
	2008	94	5	1	0	99	56	43	1

Subregion / Country	Year	Use of Sanitation Facilities (Percentage of Population)				Use of Drinking-Water Sources (Percentage of Population)			
		Improved	Unimproved			Improved			Unimproved
			Shared	Unimproved Facilities	Open Defecation	Total Improved	Piped on Premises	Other Improved	
South and South-West Asia									
Afghanistan	1990	--	--	--	--	--	--	--	--
	2000	46	--	43	11	36	10	26	64
	2008	60	--	38	2	78	16	62	22
Bangladesh	1990	59	27	7	7	88	28	60	12
	2000	57	26	12	5	86	26	60	14
	2008	56	26	15	3	85	24	61	15
Bhutan	1990	--	--	--	--	--	--	--	--
	2000	87	--	9	4	99	81	18	1
	2008	87	--	9	4	99	81	18	1
India	1990	49	19	4	28	90	52	38	70
	2000	52	20	6	22	93	50	43	7
	2008	54	21	7	18	96	48	48	4
Islamic Republic of Iran	1990	86	--	14	--	98	96	2	2
	2000	86	--	14	--	98	96	2	2
	2008	--	--	--	--	98	96	2	2
Maldives	1990	100	--	0	0	100	47	53	0
	2000	100	--	0	0	100	68	32	0
	2008	100	--	0	0	99	95	4	1
Nepal	1990	41	24	5	30	96	43	53	4
	2000	47	27	4	22	94	48	46	6
	2008	51	30	4	15	93	52	41	7
Pakistan	1990	73	6	14	7	96	57	39	4
	2000	72	6	16	6	95	56	39	5
	2008	72	6	17	5	95	55	40	5
Sri Lanka	1990	85	7	4	4	91	37	54	9
	2000	87	7	3	3	95	53	42	5
	2008	88	7	3	2	98	65	33	2
Turkey	1990	96	1	3	0	94	91	3	6
	2000	96	2	2	0	97	95	2	3
	2008	97	2	1	0	100	98	2	0
North and Central Asia									
Afghanistan	1990	95	4	1	0	99	96	3	1
	2000	95	4	1	0	99	96	3	1
	2008	95	4	1	0	98	97	1	2
Bangladesh	1990	--	--	--	--	88	67	21	12
	2000	63	8	29	0	88	72	16	12
	2008	51	6	41	2	88	78	10	12
Bhutan	1990	97	3	0	0	94	81	13	6
	2000	96	3	1	0	97	86	11	3
	2008	96	3	1	0	100	92	8	0
India	1990	96	3	1	0	99	91	8	1
	2000	97	3	0	0	99	87	12	1
	2008	97	3	0	0	99	82	17	1
Islamic Republic of Iran	1990	94	5	1	0	98	75	23	2
	2000	94	5	1	0	98	82	16	2
	2008	94	5	1	0	99	89	10	1
Maldives	1990	93	--	7	--	98	87	11	2
	2000	93	--	7	--	98	90	8	2
	2008	93	--	7	--	98	92	6	2
Nepal	1990	93	4	3	0	--	--	--	--
	2000	94	4	2	0	92	78	14	8
	2008	95	4	1	0	94	83	11	6
Pakistan	1990	99	--	1	--	97	--	--	3
	2000	99	--	1	--	97	81	16	3
	2008	99	--	1	--	97	--	--	3
Sri Lanka	1990	95	--	5	0	97	86	11	3
	2000	97	--	3	0	98	86	12	2
	2008	100	--	0	0	98	85	13	2

Subregion / Country	Year	Use of Sanitation Facilities (Percentage of Population)				Use of Drinking-Water Sources (Percentage of Population)			
		Improved	Unimproved			Improved			Unimproved
			Shared	Unimproved Facilities	Open Defecation	Total Improved	Piped on Premises	Other Improved	
The Pacific Region									
Australia	1990	48	25	24	3	97	86	11	3
	2000	55	28	12	5	98	92	6	2
	2008	58	30	6	6	98	96	2	2
New Zealand	1990	--	--	--	--	100	--	--	0
	2000	58	--	42	--	100	81	19	0
	2008	--	--	--	--	100	--	--	0
Melanesia									
Fiji	1990	--	--	--	--	--	--	--	--
	2000	--	--	--	--	--	--	--	--
	2008	--	--	--	--	--	--	--	--
Papua New Guinea	1990	38	5	9	48	52	17	35	48
	2000	50	7	6	37	64	33	31	36
	2008	67	9	2	22	81	55	26	19
Solomon Islands	1990	58	8	16	18	92	24	68	8
	2000	63	8	12	17	90	31	59	10
	2008	67	9	8	16	89	27	52	11
Vanuatu	1990	--	--	--	--	--	--	--	--
	2000	62	4	8	26	77	35	42	23
	2008	86	5	3	6	72	55	17	28
Micronesia									
Guam	1990	99	--	1	--	100	--	--	0
	2000	99	--	1	--	100	--	--	0
	2008	99	--	1	--	100	--	--	0
Kiribati	1990	36	7	16	41	76	46	30	24
	2000	47	9	3	41	77	48	29	23
	2008	--	--	--	--	--	--	--	--
Marshall Islands	1990	77	11	--	--	94	--	--	6
	2000	80	12	--	--	93	--	--	7
	2008	83	12	1	4	92	1	91	8
Micronesia (Federated States of)	1990	55	--	45	--	93	--	--	7
	2000	59	--	41	--	94	--	--	6
	2008	--	--	--	--	95	--	--	5
Nauru	1990	--	--	--	--	--	--	--	--
	2000	--	--	--	--	--	--	--	--
	2008	50	23	26	1	90	--	--	10
Northern Mariana Islands	1990	85	--	15	--	98	--	--	2
	2000	92	--	8	--	98	--	--	2
	2008	--	--	--	--	98	--	--	2
Palau	1990	76	--	24	--	73	--	--	27
	2000	92	--	8	--	78	--	--	22
	2008	96	--	4	--	--	--	--	--
Polynesia									
Cook Islands	1990	100	--	0	0	99	--	--	1
	2000	100	--	0	0	99	--	--	1
	2008	100	--	0	0	98	--	--	2
French Polynesia	1990	99	--	1	--	100	99	1	0
	2000	99	--	1	--	100	99	1	0
	2008	99	--	1	--	100	99	1	0
Niue	1990	100	--	0	0	100	--	--	0
	2000	100	--	0	0	100	--	--	0
	2008	100	--	0	0	100	--	--	0
Samoa	1990	100	--	0	0	99	--	--	1
	2000	100	--	0	0	92	74	18	8
	2008	100	--	0	0	--	--	--	--
Tonga	1990	98	--	2	--	--	--	--	--
	2000	98	--	2	--	100	72	28	0
	2008	98	--	2	--	100	--	--	0
Tuvalu	1990	86	--	14	--	92	--	--	8
	2000	87	--	13	--	95	--	--	5
	2008	88	--	10	2	98	97	1	2

Source: World Health Organization & UNICEF. Progress on Sanitation and Drinking-Water: 2010 Update. WHO/UNICEF Joint Monitoring Programme for Water Supply and Sanitation. Geneva and New York: World Health Organization & UNICEF. 2010:38-51

""""NA"" represents data not applicable, and ""--"" represents data not available at the time of publication."

* Shown as NA because of negative gain in access as a result of negative population growth.

Gini coefficients for selected cities and provinces

Country	City	Year	Gini
Armenia	Yerevan	2001[i]	0.31
Azerbaijan	Baku	2001[i]	0.38
Bangladesh	Chittagong	2000[c]	0.29
Bangladesh	Dhaka	2000[c]	0.31
Bangladesh	Khulna	2000[c]	0.35
Cambodia	Phnom Penh	2004[c]	0.37
China	Beijing	2003[i]	0.22
China	Hong Kong	2001[i]	0.53
China	Shanghai	2004-05[i]	0.32
China	Wuhan	2004-05[i]	0.37
China	Shengyan	2004-05[i]	0.37
China	Fuzhou	2004-05[i]	0.34
China	Xian	2004-05[i]	0.35
China	Wuxi	2004-05[i]	0.39
China	Yichan	2004-05[i]	0.42
China	Benxi	2004-05[i]	0.29
China	Zhuhai	2004-05[i]	0.45
China	Baoji	2004-05[i]	0.34
China	Daqing	2004-05[i]	0.41
China	Shenzhen	2004-05[i]	0.49
Georgia	Tbilisi	2001[i]	0.37
India	Andhra Pradesh[p]	2004[c]	0.37
India	Assam[p]	2004[c]	0.31
India	Bihar[p]	2004[c]	0.33
India	Gujarat[p]	2004[c]	0.30
India	Haryana[p]	2004[c]	0.36
India	Karnataka[p]	2004[c]	0.37
India	Kerala[p]	2004[c]	0.40
India	Madhya Pradesh[p]	2004[c]	0.39
India	Maharashtra[p]	2004[c]	0.37
India	Orissa[p]	2004[c]	0.35
India	Punjab[p]	2004[c]	0.39
India	Rajasthan[p]	2004[c]	0.37
India	Tamil Nadu[p]	2004[c]	0.36
India	Uttar Pradesh[p]	2004[c]	0.37
India	West Bengal[p]	2004[c]	0.38
Indonesia	Jakarta	2005[c]	0.27
Jordan	Amman	1997[i]	0.39
Jordan	Irbid	1997[i]	0.31
Jordan	Zarqa & Mafrq	1997[i]	0.33
Jordan	Balqa & Madaba	1997[i]	0.35
Jordan	Jerash & Ajloun	1997[i]	0.31
Kazakhstan	Astana	2001[i]	0.26
Kyrgyzstan	Bishkek	2001[i]	0.27
Malaysia	Kuala Lumpur	1999[i]	0.41
Malaysia	Johor Bahru	1999[i]	0.37
Malaysia	Kuching	1999[i]	0.38
Malaysia	Ipoh	1999[i]	0.37
Mongolia	Ulaanbaatar	2006[c]	0.37
Philippines	Manila	2006[i]	0.40
Philippines	Cebu City	2003[i]	0.38
Philippines	Davao City	2003[i]	0.44
Philippines	Zamboanga	2003[i]	0.42
Russia	Moscow	2001[i]	0.47
Sri Lanka	Colombo City	2002[i]	0.46
Tajikistan	Dushanbe	1999[i]	0.36
Thailand	Bangkok	2006	0.48
Thailand	Nonthaburi[p]	2006	0.43
Thailand	Samutprakan[p]	2006	0.34
Thailand	Nakhon Ratchasima[p]	2006	0.49
Thailand	Songkhla[p]	2006	0.49
Thailand	Chonburi[p]	2006	0.36
Thailand	Udonthani[p]	2006	0.56
Thailand	Chiangmai[p]	2006	0.58
Turkmenistan	Ashgabat	1998[i]	0.29
Uzbekistan	Tashkent	2000[i]	0.28
Viet Nam	Ha Noi (Red Delta region)	2002[i]	0.39
Viet Nam	Ho Chi Minh City	2002[i]	0.53

i. Refers to Gini coefficients based on Income
c. Refers to Gini Coefficients based on consumption
p. Province (urban)

Gini coefficients for urban at national level, selected countries

Country	Year	Gini
Armenia	2001[i]	0.28
Azerbaijan	2001[i]	0.40
Bangladesh	2000[c]	0.37
Cambodia	2004[c]	0.43
China	2002[i]	0.32
Georgia	2001[i]	0.36
India	2004[c]	0.37
Indonesia	1999[c]	0.33
Kazakhstan	2001[i]	0.29
Kyrgyzstan	2001[i]	0.28
Malaysia	1999[i]	0.42
Mongolia	2006[c]	0.39
Nepal	1996[i]	0.43
Pakistan	2004[c]	0.34
Philippines	2003[i]	0.45
Russia	2001[i]	0.44
Sri Lanka	2006-07[c]	0.43
Sri Lanka	2006-07[i]	0.55
Tajikistan	1999[i]	0.36
Turkmenistan	1998[i]	0.40
Uzbekistan	2000[i]	0.29
Viet Nam	2002[i]	0.41

Percentage of female and male aged 15-24 years non-employed by shelter deprivation

Country	Year	FEMALE							MALE						
		Urban	Rural	Non Slum	One Shelter Deprivation	Two Shelter Deprivations	Three Shelter Deprivations	All Slum	Urban	Rural	Non Slum	One Shelter Deprivation	Two Shelter Deprivations	Three Shelter Deprivations	All Slum
Armenia	2005	13.9	7.9	14.5	9.9	9.1	22.1								
Bangladesh	1996	69.4	66.4	67.8	81.6	57.3	100.0	70.7	7.2	2.6			20.9		13.9
Bangladesh	1999	72.8	80.0	66.8	79.2	78.1	75.0	78.3							
Bangladesh	2004	68.7	76.1	64.6	70.4	70.2	69.7	73.5							
India	1999	84.5	64.4	88.0	80.4	79.0		80.3							
Kazakhstan	1999	27.7	38.9	19.6	31.6	30.3	39.2	32.5	19.7	37.4	15.5	12.1	31.0	43.7	22.7
Kyrgyzstan	1997	26.1	47.2	16.2	14.0	32.8	54.8	29.4							
Nepal	1996	52.7	19.4	84.8	71.3	38.0	6.1	47.8							
Nepal	2002	45.2	22.7	61.0	45.3	34.7	0.0	35.1							
Pakistan	1990	84.2	82.6	82.7	88.9	85.7	84.2	88.5							
Philippines	1998	15.3	30.6	12.6	19.8	28.6	33.3	22.2							
Philippines	2003	17.6	31.5	23.5	14.3	23.3	34.0	25.9							
Turkey	1993	84.5	53.3	85.6	82.5	89.7	33.3	81.4							
Turkey	1998	49.5	41.8	51.3	47.3	32.4	33.3	45.5	1.2	15.5	2.2				
Uzbekistan	1996	42.7	46.8	29.5	40.4	47.2	45.7	45.2							
Viet Nam	2002	16.7	10.4	18.8	12.5	16.7		12.5							

Percentage of female and male aged 15-24 years in the informal employment by shelter deprivation

Country	Year	FEMALE							MALE						
		Urban	Rural	Non Slum	All Slum	One Shelter Deprivation	Two Shelter Deprivations	Three Shelter Deprivations	Urban	Rural	Non Slum	All Slum	One Shelter Deprivation	Two Shelter Deprivations	Three Shelter Deprivations
Armenia	2000	10.8	18.9	14.0	1.9	2.4									
Armenia	2005	9.5	19.9	8.3	21.3	26.0	5.7		70.7	89.3	81.2	68.6		68.6	
Bangladesh	1996	61.7	82.6	57.7	62.9	60.0	64.0		31.3	28.0	12.5	30.1	29.2	30.2	33.3
Bangladesh	1999	19.0	33.6	17.9	21.3	25.7	15.4		21.7	29.9	18.2	29.5	12.5	35.4	
Bangladesh	2004	27.6	46.8	25.1	28.7	27.8	33.8	9.0	37.6	58.0	25.0	53.1	49.1	51.5	55.3
India	1998	56.9	57.5	57.8	56.1	54.2	68.3								
Indonesia	1994	88.1	92.0		88.1	86.3	95.3	100.0							
Indonesia	1997	88.6	96.7		88.6	88.4	86.5								
Indonesia	2002	41.1	59.9	39.3	45.1	44.6	41.0								
Kazakhstan	1999	11.1	19.1	12.3	10.4	10.0	12.9	13.3	4.2	14.3	11.1	5.9	2.6	7.7	12.5
Kyrgyzstan	1997	19.2	31.3	11.8	21.2	17.9	23.5	16.7							
Nepal	1996	72.7	84.3	100.0	70.0	66.7	76.9	80.0							
Nepal	2001	65.4	69.7	69.0	65.2	85.7	63.6	40.0	26.7	38.9	7.1	40.9	11.1	40.8	55.0
Pakistan	1990	84.2	79.3	81.5	90.0	88.9	100.0								
Philippines	1998	74.7	73.6	74.0	77.0	76.0	80.8	83.3							
Philippines	2003	51.3	68.6	50.5	57.6	53.3	67.7	100.0	7.3	18.9	10.0	15.3	11.7	25.9	27.3
Turkey	1993	75.3	94.4	71.2	90.5	88.9	100.0	100.0							
Turkey	1998	17.5	54.7	17.0	18.7	20.1	5.6		15.3	38.1	21.4	21.1	24.1		66.7
Uzbekistan	1996	14.1	8.7	19.4	13.0	18.0	11.1	7.1							
Viet Nam	2002	64.9	62.5	64.9	63.2	69.2	40.0	100.0							

Enrolment in primary education in urban and rural areas (female and male)

Country	Year	ENROLMENT MALE								ENROLMENT FEMALE							
		Urban	Rural	Total	Non Slum Household	Slum Household	One Shelter Deprivation	Two Shelter Deprivations	Three Shelter Deprivations	Urban	Rural	Total	Non Slum Household	Slum Household	One Shelter Deprivation	Two Shelter Deprivations	Three Shelter Deprivations
Armenia	2000	55.7	58.7	57.1	55.5	57.9	56.6	100.0		57.0	58.5	57.7	56.7	60.1	59.8	63.3	
Armenia	2005	65.2	69.9	67.4	65.8	64.1	64.3	58.9	100.0	64.7	67.3	65.8	68.1	59.3	58.1	71.5	.
Azerbaijan	2000	89.4	87.2	88.3	88.2	89.6	90.6	88.2	89.4	90.5	86.2	88.4	93.0	90.0	89.2	91.0	93.3
Azerbaijan	2006	72.8	71.4	72.1	80.4	71.7	73.2	73.7	61.4	69.9	69.6	69.8	51.6	72.1	74.8	67.1	74.3
Bangladesh	1996	77.7	77.7	74.4	87.0	66.2	69.3	59.0	.	74.9	74.9	78.6	75.8	73.7	70.4	81.0	100.0
Bangladesh	1999	78.2	76.1	76.4	84.8	74.3	73.9	75.2	57.1	75.8	78.4	78.0	77.3	74.6	76.2	72.5	69.8
Bangladesh	2004	79.0	81.5	81.0	92.5	77.7	88.1	81.4	74.4	80.9	85.3	84.4	78.4	81.1	83.9	86.7	78.8
Cambodia	2000	73.8	64.6	65.9	85.8	71.4	88.3	71.4	62.2	70.0	62.5	63.5	82.7	67.2	74.8	69.7	61.2
Cambodia	2005	76.1	75.2	75.3	79.8	75.7	82.9	79.9	69.4	79.0	76.7	77.0	81.3	78.7	87.2	84.8	72.9
India	1993	73.2	57.4	61.1						71.3	43.5	50.1					
India	1998	91.0	82.6	84.5	96.6	86.8	90.0	81.0	79.2	88.2	74.7	77.8	95.2	83.2	87.5	74.6	77.3
India	2005	80.1	75.3	76.5	86.5	77.7	81.8	74.0	61.2	80.5	71.5	73.8	86.5	78.4	83.8	72.1	62.5
Indonesia	1991	77.1	70.5	72.4	80.9	75.0	76.3	74.0	71.6	76.8	71.0	72.7	78.7	75.8	76.6	77.5	68.1
Indonesia	1994	78.2	75.5	76.2	77.1	78.8	78.0	82.5	70.0	76.8	74.7	75.3	73.1	79.1	81.1	77.2	73.5
Indonesia	1997	77.0	78.1	77.8	76.2	78.2	77.9	79.6	77.4	77.0	77.1	77.1	76.8	77.4	76.3	82.3	74.2
Indonesia	2002	76.6	76.1	76.3	76.3	77.2	78.2	72.5	82.0	73.5	76.2	75.0	73.7	73.1	73.0	74.9	68.0
Indonesia	2007	75.9	76.5	76.3	74.1	79.4	78.4	82.0	82.7	72.7	74.8	74.0	71.7	74.6	74.7	76.0	68.7
Kazakhstan	1995	90.6	89.3	89.8	92.9	89.5	87.2	93.8	100.0	86.6	93.3	90.5	81.7	89.3	88.7	92.0	83.4
Kazakhstan	1999	86.5	87.3	86.9	89.6	84.7	84.2	85.4	87.8	85.4	90.1	88.3	88.9	82.7	83.3	86.5	68.2
Kazakhstan	1997	77.0	78.6	78.1	77.4	76.4	76.1	78.8		76.1	75.0	75.3	81.5	69.9	69.7	71.5	
Mongolia	2000	65.2	57.8	61.0	67.1	64.9	70.2	63.4	61.2	63.7	59.3	61.1	68.7	62.6	66.2	61.7	57.1
Myanmar	2000	84.8	75.9	77.9	87.5	84.3	85.3	83.2	73.7	84.7	75.7	77.5	84.0	84.9	86.5	83.0	72.6
Nepal	1996	83.8	72.6	73.5	93.5	80.7	93.9	83.0	69.8	85.5	54.2	56.3	97.4	81.5	92.9	79.9	69.2
Nepal	2001	92.3	78.8	80.0	97.6	87.4	88.5	88.8	71.2	87.5	64.7	66.6	94.6	81.0	90.6	71.8	83.1
Nepal	2006	93.5	89.1	89.7	98.5	91.6	94.3	92.8	84.8	89.4	83.3	84.0	97.7	85.8	94.4	81.3	72.6
Pakistan	1990	75.0	55.2	60.6	83.0	73.7	78.5	64.9	46.2	69.9	32.8	43.8	83.5	67.7	75.2	51.7	25.1
Pakistan	2006	78.1	66.4	69.7	83.4	76.9	82.6	73.1	54.8	76.4	56.2	62.2	87.1	73.7	81.5	65.9	51.0
Philippines	1993	66.2	62.1	64.0	74.5	64.6	71.0	63.9	60.6	67.9	65.5	66.6	72.1	67.1	72.8	68.2	59.3
Philippines	1998	86.5	76.3	80.8	91.9	82.9	86.2	80.0	72.5	89.9	80.3	84.5	95.6	86.3	90.3	83.6	77.6
Philippines	2003	88.7	84.0	86.2	89.9	86.4	87.9	83.6	68.1	89.3	85.6	87.3	90.6	86.7	89.1	82.9	49.2
Tajikistan	2000	71.1	74.7	73.9	88.5	69.9	70.7	71.0	65.0	73.9	76.8	76.2	75.0	73.8	81.1	73.5	59.0
Turkey	1993	75.1	71.3	73.5	80.9	65.5	67.4	64.8	53.0	72.2	67.7	70.2	75.8	65.5	67.6	66.1	41.3
Turkey	1998	77.0	67.5	73.4	81.3	68.0	70.4	54.9	70.4	73.3	64.3	69.9	83.1	67.6	57.0	59.4	64.2
Turkey	2004	69.2	65.9	68.1	72.7	61.4	60.6	69.0	70.7	69.3	63.3	67.3	73.3	60.4	61.1	51.2	71.6
Uzbekistan	1996	56.1	60.1	58.7	55.8	56.6	57.6	48.1	70.8	55.9	54.1	54.7	59.1	51.8	48.5	63.9	100.0
Uzbekistan	2000	78.9	75.0	76.1	78.8	79.0	81.7	76.2	78.9	73.8	75.1	74.7	74.7	73.7	75.9	72.2	68.3
Viet Nam	1997	86.6	83.1	83.5	91.8	84.5	89.8	86.2	62.0	90.0	85.0	85.6	93.0	88.4	90.9	96.0	76.1
Viet Nam	2002	96.8	96.4	96.4	98.2	95.4	98.1	90.6	96.4	96.7	95.4	95.5	98.1	95.5	98.0	88.3	100.0
Viet Nam	1991	61.3	51.8	53.3	70.1	59.5	62.7	62.5	45.3	58.5	20.4	26.8	65.8	56.6	59.6	57.7	46.9

Proportion of malnourished (underweight) children (under five)

Country	Year	Urban	Rural	Total	Non Slum	Slum	One Shelter Depv	Two Shelter Depv	Three Shelter Depv	Four Shelter Depv
Armenia	2000	10.1	16.0	13.0	11.1	8.5	7.4	16.5		
Armenia	2005	14.0	11.5	13.0	15.2	12.3	13.4	7.7	20.9	
Bangladesh	1996	39.4	56.2	54.6	28.5	51.1	49.3	55.9		
Bangladesh	1999	35.0	46.6	44.6	22.7	44.0	41.8	49.8	38.6	
Bangladesh	2004	37.7	44.3	43.0	23.7	47.6	44.8	51.4	66.5	
Bangladesh	2007	30.6	37.4	36.0	11.2	37.2	29.0	40.6	45.8	
India	1992	44.5	54.0	51.8	39.0	52.6	51.1	58.6		
India	1998	35.2	47.9	44.9	29.5	46.0	46.1	44.7		
India	2005	34.3	45.2	42.5	21.0	39.5	33.9	42.3	53.7	48.8
Kazakhstan	1995	7.5	21.8	15.8	1.7	9.9	6.0	19.1	24.3	
Kazakhstan	1999	5.8	12.3	9.7	5.3	6.1	6.4	7.4		
Kyrgyzstan	1997	14.8	27.7	24.8	10.1	16.5	13.3	19.2	47.1	
Nepal	1996	35.4	49.3	48.4	15.7	38.1	29.0	42.0	54.6	
Nepal	2001	36.3	51.5	50.5	30.1	40.7	32.5	46.3	52.2	
Nepal	2006	29.0	44.6	42.7	15.6	34.8	30.7	30.5	46.5	55.5
Pakistan	1990	40.4	54.5	49.6	37.2	50.7	51.1	45.6		

Source: Global Urban Indicators Database, 2010